W9-DGJ-304

THE COLUMBIA GUIDE TO

America in the 1960s

The Columbia Guides to American History and Cultures

THE COLUMBIA GUIDES TO AMERICAN HISTORY AND CULTURES

Michael Kort, *The Columbia Guide to the Cold War*

Catherine Clinton and Christine Lunardini, *The Columbia Guide to American Women in the Nineteenth Century*

THE COLUMBIA GUIDE TO

America in the 1960s

David Farber and Beth Bailey
with contributors

COLUMBIA UNIVERSITY PRESS

NEW YORK

Columbia University Press
Publishers Since 1893
New York   Chichester, West Sussex
Copyright © 2001 Columbia University Press
All rights reserved
Library of Congress Cataloging-in-Publication Data

The Columbia guide to America in the 1960s / David Farber and Beth Bailey.
p. cm. — (Columbia guides to American history and cultures)
Includes bibliographical references (p.) and index.
ISBN 0-231-11372-2 (cloth : alk. paper)
1. United States—History—1961–1969. 2. United States—Social conditions—1960–1980.
I. Farber, David R. II. Bailey, Beth L., 1957– III. Series.

E841 .C575 2001
973.923—dc21

00-065577

Casebound editions of Columbia University Press books are printed on permanent and durable
acid-free paper.
Printed in the United States of America
c 10 9 8 7 6 5 4 3 2

CONTENTS

ACKNOWLEDGMENTS

We were lucky to have excellent research assistance in preparing this book. Jeff Roche played a critical role in the basic research design of the book and in researching "The Sixties A to Z," with assistance from Jeff Sanders and Catherine Kleiner. Amy Scott's meticulous research was invaluable in creating the annotated bibliography. And Wesley Chenault, with great good humor, found things no one else believed existed for the "Portrait" section. Thanks to the History and American Studies departments at the University of New Mexico for helping to fund their work. Thanks also to James Warren at Columbia University Press for his support and encouragement, to Jeremey Hockett for solving computer crises, and, as always, to our friends and family.

INTRODUCTION

The Sixties era was among the most colorful, complex, and eventful periods in American history. More than any other decade of the twentieth century, the 1960s continue to be the subject of passionate debate and political controversy in the United States, a touchstone in struggles over the meaning of the American past and the direction of the nation's future. Amid all the polemics and the myths, making sense of the 1960s and its legacies is a real challenge. This book is for all those who want to try.

Because there are so many "Sixties," this volume offers multiple approaches to the era and different perspectives on it. We hope that readers will treat *The Columbia Guide to the 1960s* as a kind of toolkit. Each section of the book provides a different tool for understanding the decade, and readers can use various combinations of these tools to construct histories of the Sixties that are most suited to their interests, needs, and levels of knowledge.

This book is divided into six sections. The first offers a narrative overview of the era. It serves as a clear and accessible introduction to the 1960s for those who know little about them and provides a historical perspective for those who lived through the tumultuous events of the decade.

In the second section, "Debating the Sixties," ten essays by prominent historians discuss some of the most significant issues of the era—ranging from the Vietnam War to race relations to the sexual revolution—and their legacies. Each essay provides an overview of current historiographical debates for students and scholars, as well as for readers interested in how the Sixties have been interpreted by scholars and other writers. These essays also take a stand: each of the authors ends by explaining his or her position in the debate.

The third section, "The Sixties A to Z," contains alphabetically organized entries on some of the most interesting and significant people of the era, as well as on its major events and movements. This section supplements the narrative section, offering biographical information and more detailed discussion of specific events. It also serves as a stand-alone reference. Eight brief topical essays follow it. These present overviews of important topics that are not covered in detail in the book's narrative section.

The fourth section focuses on the Sixties as most Americans lived them. What were the most popular songs in 1962? How many young men received student deferments from the draft and how many served in Vietnam? What was the average age at marriage in 1965? Who won the World Series in 1967? How many pounds of beef did the average American eat each year? What was Richard Nixon's campaign slogan? Clearly organized by topic, this section offers the sort of information that is often dismissed, ignored, or forgotten in traditional histories. The facts and figures and opinions contained here make it possible for readers to create their own histories of daily life in 1960s America.

The fifth section is a brief chronology, useful as a quick orientation to the decade or as a supplement to the narrative.

The sixth and final section of this work is an extensive annotated bibliography, organized by topic. The bibliography gives a sense of the enormous range and depth of writing on the 1960s, and readers who are interested in exploring specific subjects in more depth will find ample resources here.

THE COLUMBIA GUIDE TO

America in the 1960s

PART I

The American Sixties: A Brief History

CHAPTER ONE

John Kennedy and the Promise of Leadership

This chapter provides an overview of Cold War liberalism. Most major Republican and Democratic politicians shared a vision of domestic harmony based on economic growth and of world leadership based on anticommunist interventionism. President Kennedy is profiled and the nation's prosperity is highlighted.

THE POSTWAR ERA: COLD WAR PROSPERITY

In the presidential election year of 1960, the United States was the richest and most powerful nation on earth. A country of some 180 million people, the United States had undergone immense changes in the 15 years since the end of World War II. Few would have guessed, in 1960, that even greater challenges still lay ahead for the American people.

World War II had been a transition between two completely different eras in American life. Before the wartime mobilization, unemployment and poverty had torn at the fabric of tens of millions of American families. Up until December 7, 1941, the day of the Japanese attack on Pearl Harbor, a large majority of Americans had demanded that the United States remain isolated from the complicated affairs of Europe and Asia. World War II changed these facts of American life as it brought an end both to the economic downturn of the 1930s and to American isolationism.

In the postwar years the sustained growth of the economy surprised economists and corporate leaders at the same time as it encouraged the growth of families across the nation. Less well-received but generally accepted by the American people were the United States' new military and economic commitments to nations throughout the world. By 1960 these unexpected results of World War II—domestic prosperity and global responsibility—had become fundamental aspects of American life. Post–World War II American internationalism was forged in the horrors of the global conflagration and hardened during the nearly worldwide chaos and conflict that followed. For reasons of both national security and international economic development, President Harry Truman and most leading members of Congress had decided that the United States must do what it could to shape the postwar world order. The internationalist resolve of American policymakers was greatly fortified by their fear of Soviet expansionism.

After World War II the Soviets, in the words of Winston Churchill, Great Britain's wartime leader, had drawn an "Iron Curtain" over most of Eastern and Central Europe. The Soviets had suffered 20 million dead in the war, and Soviet leader Josef Stalin had insisted that, for his country's own security, the nations of Poland, East Germany, Czechoslovakia, Hungary, Romania, Bulgaria, and Albania must be kept under the control of the Soviet Union.

The Soviet takeover, the economic and political instability in most of the rest of Europe, which had been devastated by war, and then the successful communist takeover of China in 1949 greatly strengthened the commitment of American political leaders to an unprecedented international role. Based on a policy of "containment," or the freezing of Soviet aggression and influence in the world, the United States, between 1948 and 1951, gave $13 billion in foreign aid through the Marshall Plan to rebuild Western European countries, especially France, Great Britain, and West Germany. In 1949, the United States established the North Atlantic Treaty Organization with Canada and ten noncommunist European nations. This mutual defense pact was founded on the premise that any attack on a member state would be considered an attack against them all. A system of military trip wires was eventually set up around the world to convey the message that attacking an American ally meant going to war with the United States.

The reach of that military commitment became clear both to the American people and the rest of the world on June 25, 1950, when communist North Korean forces attempted to impose their political system and create one nation on the Korean peninsula. Although at that time Korea was of no direct economic or security interest to the United States, President Truman, under the impression that Soviet Premier Stalin was behind the North Korean offensive, vowed: "We've got to stop the sons of bitches right here and right now."[1]

Under the aegis of the newly organized United Nations, the United States led the way in protecting noncommunist South Korea against the attack. The United States military, which formed the preponderance of the UN's international forces, fought in Korea from the summer of 1950 until the summer of 1953. Some 33,642 Americans lost their lives beating back North Korean and Communist Chinese troops and restoring the South Korean government.

By 1960, the United States, a nation that before World War II had refused to maintain a strong military force and had stationed no troops outside its own territories, was assuming military responsibilities around the world. Hundreds of thousands of American fighting men were stationed throughout Europe and Asia, and aboard ships that patrolled the oceans of the world. Approximately 20,000 nuclear warheads stood at the ready to annihilate America's enemies. The cold war standoff against the Soviet Union, the second strongest military power in the world, was at the heart of the United States' immense military commitment. And in 1960, the cold war was heating up. Even as the cold war, with its threats of nuclear devastation, darkened many Americans' outlook, tens of millions of American families enjoyed material abundance. New technologies—most importantly television and a host of electric appliances—had created new ways of life for Americans. Between 1929 and 1960, the gross national product had exploded from $181.8 billion to $439.9 billion, and personal consumption over the same period had grown from $128.1 billion to $298.1 billion. As the world's leading producer of autos, steel, electric appliances, and textiles, the United States easily dominated the world economy, much of which was still recovering from wartime devastation.

In the summer of 1959, Vice President Richard Nixon had made the case for American-style free-market economics in the heart of the enemy's camp. At a trade fair in Moscow, Nixon and Soviet Premier Nikita Khrushchev toured the exhibits, each boasting of his nation's greatness. Khrushchev seemed to get the better of Nixon when he proclaimed Soviet superiority in missile technology. Only two years earlier the Soviets had been the first nation to deploy successfully an intercontinental ballistic missile, and shortly thereafter, on October 4, 1957, the Soviets had been the first to orbit a satellite around the Earth: the world-famed *Sputnik*, weighing just 184 pounds.

Nixon knew that the Soviets led the Americans in the space race, but he believed the United States was ahead in matters of far greater importance to most people, Soviet, American, or otherwise. Nixon brought the Soviet premier over to the centerpiece of the American trade-fair exhibit. It was a full-scale model of a typical suburban tract home. Nixon pointed out the "push-button" kitchen with its gleaming counters, hot and cold running water, and electric appliances. With a wave at those affordable pleasures, Nixon concluded: "To us, diversity, the right to choose . . . is the most important thing. . . . We have many manufacturers and many different kinds of washing machines so that housewives have a choice. . . . Would it not be better to compete in the relative merits of washing machines than in the strength of rockets?"[2]

Prosperity and the cold war were wrapped up together in Nixon's pithy explanation of the American way of life. In 1960 those two central themes—fighting communism abroad and maintaining prosperity at home—dominated the presidential election campaign and the politics of most, if by no means all, Americans.

The Election

The two candidates for president of the United States in 1960 shared many characteristics. Both were men born in the twentieth century—a presidential-election first. Both had been junior officers in the navy during World War II. And both, upon their discharge, had almost immediately gone into politics and enjoyed meteoric careers. On critical policy matters little divided them.

Richard Nixon had grown up in a middle-class family in Whittier, California. Extremely ambitious, intellectually incisive, and an immensely diligent worker, he won a scholarship to Duke Law School and, soon after graduating, went to war. In 1946 he was one of many veterans elected to Congress.

In Washington, Nixon recognized that anticommunism was the "hot button" issue of the day and became one the fiercest anticommunists in Congress. He gained a national reputation by proving that a high-ranking official in the State Department, Alger Hiss, had associated with a known Communist and then lied about his relationship. In 1950, Nixon was elected to the United States Senate and, just two years later, became Dwight D. Eisenhower's vice president.

John Kennedy, too, had been elected to the United States House of Representatives in 1946. In 1952 he was elected senator from Massachusetts. Whereas Nixon was a self-made man, Kennedy was the son of Joseph P. Kennedy, a former diplomat and one of the richest men in the nation. Family wealth and connections helped place Kennedy on the political fast track. His own intelligence, discipline, charm, and good looks moved him quickly along that track. Kennedy's marriage to the chic and beautiful Jacqueline Bouvier in 1953 added another valuable element to his charismatic public image.

The 1960 election was dominated by the twin themes of cold war internationalism and national prosperity. Both candidates promised to make the United States even stronger and more prosperous. Nixon, the two-term vice president, ran on the favorable record of President Eisenhower. His theme song was "Merrily We Roll Along," and his platform echoed the Cold War internationalism of both Truman and Eisenhower. In his acceptance speech for the Republican Party nomination, he blasted Soviet communism, warning of "the mortal danger it presents," and insisted that the American people must be ready to defend themselves against not only overt military threats but also "the even more deadly danger of the [communist] propaganda that warps the mind."[3]

John Kennedy accepted the Democratic Party presidential nomination with a not dissimilar speech. He, too, spoke of standing up to communism at home and around the world. He added, however, a more stirring call: "We are not here to curse the darkness, but to light the candle that can guide us through that darkness to a safe and sane future. . . . We stand today on the edge of a New Frontier."[4] While their core policies did not appear to differ in significant ways, John Kennedy more successfully presented himself to the American people as a leader capable of moving the nation forward into a new era.

Winning with the narrowest of margins—just 112,881 votes out of over 68 million votes cast—John Kennedy became the next president. Some attributed his victory to his dashing appearance in a televised debate with Richard Nixon, whose sallow complexion, sweaty brow, and five-o'clock shadow did not serve him well on the era's black-and-white television screens. Others pointed, more pragmatically, to Kennedy's success in winning large majorities among African Americans, many of whom hoped that the young Democrat would follow the lead of President Harry Truman and work for racial justice in the United States.

Critically, Kennedy's religion—he was only the second Catholic to run for the presidency—had not hurt him at the polls. Unlike Al Smith in the election of 1928, when the Irish-Catholic politician had faced a sizeable anti-Catholic vote, Kennedy experienced little religiously inspired backlash. In one of the many hopeful signs of a changing America, Kennedy's election signaled that at least some of the old, traditional prejudices that divided Americans were fading from the scene.

THE KENNEDY PRESIDENCY

John Kennedy had promised the American people even greater prosperity and more energetic leadership in the fight against world communism. For most of his presidency, these two issues would dominate his agenda.

President Kennedy believed that the federal government could and should play a vital role in both stabilizing the economy and in fueling economic growth. Here, he differed from Nixon and Eisenhower. Kennedy was following the conventional wisdom of political liberals dating from the late years of the New Deal. President Truman and congressional liberals had institutionalized this belief through the Employment Act of 1946, which created the Council of Economic Advisors (CEA). Through the CEA, leading economists advised the president on creating federal government policies aimed at maximizing jobs, production, and consumer purchasing power. President Eisenhower had rejected the pro-growth, government-intervention policies of liberal economists. John Kennedy put those economic policies at the front and center of his administration.

Pointing at the economic slowdown or "Eisenhower Recession" of 1959–1960, Kennedy, during his campaign, had promised that, as president, he would insure that the American economy grew by five per cent a year. Once elected, Kennedy immediately began to forge an economic policy dedicated to what some have called "growth liberalism."[5] To stimulate the economy, Kennedy offered a large income-tax cut and special tax breaks for businesses that invested in new machinery and equipment. Second, to help more Americans become productive and capable workers, Kennedy moved a series of education, training, and manpower-development bills through Congress.

While these initiatives made few headlines or excited many people, overall they worked. Between 1961 and 1965, Kennedy's economic promise to the American people was made good with an average yearly economic growth of more than five per cent. At the beginning of 1966, with Kennedy's policies fully in place, the unemployment rate (which in the nightmare year of 1933 had reached some 25 per cent) had dropped to less than four per cent. The number of Americans living in poverty fell from more than one out of five in 1960 to about one in seven by 1966.

Prosperity in the United States in the early and mid-1960s reached unprecedented levels. The journalist Theodore White argued that this economic boom produced "a new generation of Americans who saw the world differently from their fathers. [They believed] . . . that whatever Americans wished to make happen, would happen."[6] Americans, in the words of writer Tom Wolfe, were living in the midst of a "happiness explosion."[7]

While the United States economy hummed along, stimulated by liberal government policies, the Kennedy administration faced a series of cold war crises. These global events tested the courage and capacity of both President Kennedy and the entire nation. In his eloquent inaugural address, Kennedy had staked out a militant cold war position: "Let every nation know, whether it wishes us well or ill, that we shall pay any price, bear any burden, meet any hardship, support any friend, oppose any foe to assure the survival and the success of liberty. This much we pledge—and more."[8]

Kennedy was to act almost immediately on his pledge. His first opportunity to prove his mettle involved Cuba, just 90 miles off the shores of Florida. In 1959, after Fidel Castro and his guerrilla army had overthrown a corrupt dictator, Cuba became the first Latin American nation to embrace Soviet-style Communism. Just days after Kennedy became president, representatives from the Central Intelligence Agency (CIA) explained to him that they had trained over 1,400 anti-Castro Cubans to invade Cuba and ignite a popular revolt against the Communist government. Without consulting Congress or the American people, Kennedy approved the operation.

On April 17, 1961, the CIA-supported force landed at the Bay of Pigs on the southern tip of Cuba. They were met by the Cuban army, which remained loyal to Castro. The outgunned invaders were trapped. While the CIA urged Kennedy to send in American air support, Soviet Premier Nikita Khrushchev warned, "Cuba is not alone."[9]

Faced with an escalating military situation, as well as the anger of other Latin American nations fearing American intervention in their own domestic affairs, Kennedy chose to do nothing. Trained and assisted by Americans, the invasion force, after suffering heavy casualties, surrendered to its Communist foes. Kennedy had begun his presidency with a resounding foreign-policy failure.

Nonetheless, Kennedy continued to try to bring down the Castro government. The CIA plotted to assassinate the Communist leader and, under the code name Operation Mongoose, sponsored guerrilla attacks on Cuba. As hostilities between the two nations increased, Castro in September 1962 arranged with Khrushchev to base in Cuba ballistic missiles armed with nuclear warheads. Only weeks earlier, President Kennedy had explicitly warned Khrushchev not to use Cuba as a site from which to threaten the United States. Thinking Kennedy was weak, Khrushchev ignored the warning.

On October 16, President Kennedy learned from his national-security advisors what the Soviets had done. Over the next seven days, Kennedy and his most trusted men, including his brother, Attorney General Robert Kennedy, debated the options. After seriously considering an immediate air attack on the missile sites, Kennedy chose instead a less belligerent plan. He went before the American people, told them what had happened, and said what he felt he must do: "We will not prematurely or unnecessarily risk the costs of worldwide nuclear war, in which even the fruits of victory would be ashes in our mouth—but neither will we shrink from that risk at any time it must be faced."[10] Kennedy demanded that the Soviets remove the missiles and stated that, starting immediately, the United States would begin a total naval blockade of Cuba.

As Soviet ships sped toward Cuba and the American blockade, all the world watched with horror. For the first time ever, America's Strategic Air Command, whose primary mission was the nuclear destruction of the Soviet Union, went to *DEFCON* 2, in full pre-attack readiness. American troops streamed southward, prepared to invade Cuba. World War III seemed imminent. Americans who had prepared atomic-air-raid shelters took cover.

Two days after Kennedy issued his nonnegotiable demands, the Soviet Union backed down. The Soviets agreed to withdraw the missiles. Kennedy had won. The world has never come so close, before or after this crisis, to nuclear war.

Such dramatic—and dangerous—moments characterized John Kennedy's presidency. As he himself understood, cold war duties gave him the opportunity to demonstrate his resolve and his courage under fire. Kennedy believed that the presidency was above all a leadership position, a means to amplify and to act on, both at home and throughout the world, core American beliefs. In June 1963, in the divided city of Berlin, he gave testimony to that conviction in a speech that captured the imagination of people around the globe.

Almost two years earlier, on August 13, 1961, the Communist government of East Germany, aided by the Soviet Union, had built a 110-mile concrete and barbed-wire wall to stop East Berliners from fleeing into democratic and more prosperous West Berlin. (Berlin had been split in two by the victorious Allied nations after World War II; both East and West Berlin lay well within East Germany.) The cold war had long gripped the divided city, and the Wall had brought that dangerous tension to a near breaking point.

After many months of heightened danger and uncertainty over the status of Berlin, and of Germany in general, President Kennedy chose to go to West Berlin. He wanted the people of Berlin to know that he and the United States stood by them during their time of grave risk. In words that resonated with people around the world who were living under threat of dictatorship, he told cheering crowds: "All free men, wherever they may live, are citizens of Berlin, and therefore, as a free man, I take pride in the words *Ich bin ein Berliner* [I am a Berliner]."[11]

While defending Europe remained the primary concern of American policymakers in the early 1960s, President Kennedy understood that it was in

Latin America, Africa, and much of Asia that the contest between capitalism and communism would be most aggressively played out. In the aftermath of World War II, Europe's imperialist control of its vast colonial regions was ended, either through wars of liberation or through the voluntary withdrawal of the colonizers. One new nation after another was choosing its own path. Because many of them associated Western Europe and its allied imperialist power, the United States, not with ideals of freedom and democracy but with decades of economic exploitation and political repression, these new nations often looked for inspiration to the Soviet and Chinese communist models of political and economic development. The Soviet Union encouraged these suspicions of the West by supporting the attempts of formerly colonized peoples to end all vestiges of Western imperialism and forge their "national liberation."

In an effort to combat Soviet influence and bring the new nations into the American-dominated alliance, Kennedy forged a policy based on a mixture of idealism, financial incentives, and military solutions. The prime example of the idealistic component of this policy was the Peace Corps, through which the Kennedy administration offered aid and assistance to economically developing nations around the world. This program sent American volunteers, most of them in their twenties, to live among the poorest people in the world, where they would fight illiteracy and disease, and work to improve economic opportunity and agricultural productivity.

To bolster this person-to-person form of international aid, the Kennedy administration also worked through programs like the Latin America–associated Alliance for Progress. The Alliance, like most American foreign-aid programs, was divided between promoting economic development and building up strong, anticommunist military forces.

Finally, the Kennedy Administration helped to develop a new elite fighting force, the U.S. Army's Green Berets, trained to counter communist guerrilla forces in Third World countries. President Kennedy, along with most Americans, believed it was up to the United States to create the post–World War II international order. If the United States did not maintain constant vigilance and aggressive action, then the Soviet Union would spread its influence around the world.

President Kennedy had run for office pledging to keep the United States strong and prosperous. Those were his priorities, and they were the issues that drove him and captured his creative energies. But during the early 1960s, even as the president and his key advisors sought to implement policies of economic growth and international anticommunism, an unexpected crisis had developed at home. While the president wanted to dedicate himself to containing the wars of "national liberation" that were erupting around the world, he was forced, more and more, to address an unexpected revolution within the borders of the United States. African Americans, long denied many of the most basic rights and opportunities their nation promised its citizens, had launched their own liberation struggle.

NOTES

1. Alonzo Hamby, *Liberalism and Its Challengers: F.D.R. to Reagan* (New York: Oxford, 1985), 84.

2. Elaine Tyler May, *Homeward Bound: American Families in the Cold War Era* (New York: Basic, 1988), 17.

3. Theodore White, *The Making of the President 1960* (New York: Atheneum, 1961), 207–208.

4. White, *The Making of the President 1960*, 177.

5. Robert Collins, "Growth Liberalism in the Sixties," *The Sixties: From Memory to History*, ed. David Farber (Chapel Hill: University of North Carolina Press, 1994), 11.

6. Collins, "Growth Liberalism in the Sixties," 19.

7. David Farber, *The Age of Great Dreams* (New York: Hill and Wang, 1994), 64.

8. *Inaugural Addresses of the Presidents of the United States* (Washington, D.C.: United States Government Printing Office, 1969), 268.

9. David Burner, *John F. Kennedy and a New Generation* (Boston: Little. Brown, 1988), 67.

10. "President Kennedy Addresses the Nation on the Missile Crisis, 1962," *Major Problems in American History Since 1945*, ed. Robert Griffith (Lexington, Mass.: D. C. Heath, 1992), 262.

11. John F. Kennedy, in Burner, *John F. Kennedy*, 79.

CHAPTER TWO

The Civil Rights Revolution

This chapter describes the struggle over racial equality in the early 1960s, highlighting both the grassroots nature of the civil-rights movement and the leadership of Martin Luther King Jr.

THE CIVIL RIGHTS MOVEMENT: ORIGINS

While most white Americans in 1960 probably thought the presidential election was the year's most important political event, many black Americans expressed a very different kind of political perspective. Beginning on February 1, 1960, a sustained mass movement was started among young black men and women in the South when four students initiated a "sit-in" at a Woolworth lunch counter to protest racial discrimination. Over the next five years, civil-rights activists organized marches, demonstrations, boycotts, and rallies aimed at empowering black Americans, while converting or enlisting white supporters, and ending racially discriminatory laws and practices within the United States.

The civil rights movement did not start in the 1960s. African Americans had been working ceaselessly for equal rights and opportunities from the time of their origins in America as slaves. In the 1960s, however, for the first time, black Americans in large numbers, in churches and on the streets, through nonviolent protests and dramatic confrontations in every part of the nation, demanded their rights as citizens under the United States Constitution.

Like so many other aspects of the 1960s, the civil rights movement was shaped by World War II and its aftermath. During the war, African Americans had asked for a "double victory" over the fascist enemies abroad as well as racism at home. White Americans had to confront the hypocrisy of fighting the German Nazis, Italian Fascists, and Japanese militarists with segregated armed forces, and of claiming to be champions of freedom and equality while enforcing a domestic racial caste system.

The cold war intensified that internal contradiction as Americans insisted to the people of Latin America, Asia, and Africa that the United States stood as a model of democracy and individual rights, knowing full well that the overwhelming majority of black Americans did not receive equal protection under the law and black Southerners were not even allowed to vote. Such concerns about America's image in the world contributed to President Harry Truman's decisions in 1948 to end segregation in the armed forces and in the federal civil service. Truman's executive orders gave African Americans some hope that, more than 80 years after the Civil War had ended, racial justice in the United States might be a possibility.

Building on these first steps, lawyers for the National Association for the Advancement of Colored People Legal Defense Fund brought legal challenges against racially segregated schools in the South. They won a series of major Supreme Court cases, culminating in the *Brown v. Board of Education* ruling in 1954. In that decision, the Court ended states' legal right to segregate students by race. Chief Justice Earl Warren wrote the unanimous opinion: "To separate them [black students] from others of similar age and qualifications solely because of their race generates a feeling of inferiority as to their status in the community that may affect their hearts and minds in a way unlikely ever to be undone. . . . We conclude that in the field of education . . . separate educational facilities are inherently unequal."[1] With reference to the Fourteenth Amendment of the Constitution, which states that all citizens of the United States are entitled to equal protection under the law, school segregation had been outlawed.

Throughout the South, whites angrily denounced the Supreme Court ruling. Ninety-six southern congressmen, representing almost every southern congressional district, signed the "Southern Declaration on Integration." The federal court, they asserted, ". . . is destroying the amicable relations between the white and Negro races. . . . It has planted hatred and suspicion where there has been heretofore friendship and understanding. We pledge ourselves to use all lawful means to bring about a reversal of this decision. . . ."[2]

These white leaders argued that black Americans did not want to vote, did not want to serve on juries, and preferred attending segregated schools. They claimed that blacks did not want to enroll in state universities, enjoyed sitting in the back of buses and trains, liked being refused entrance to theaters and restaurants, did not care to serve as police officers or other public officials, and had no interest in decent, well-paying jobs. To make sure that black Americans were able to continue enjoying a life of segregation and discrimination, hundreds of thousands of southern whites in the late 1950s and early 1960s promised a campaign of "massive resistance" and joined organizations like the Citizens Councils and the Ku Klux Klan.

African Americans, too, were energized by the Brown decision. On December 1, 1955, the first major post–World War II nonviolent protest by African Americans against racial segregation began. On that day, in Montgomery, Alabama, Rosa Parks, a middle-aged seamstress and stalwart member of the local chapter of the NAACP, was riding home from work on the local bus. She was ordered by the bus driver to give up her seat so that a white person could sit down. She refused, and the bus driver had her arrested.

A remarkable group of veteran African-American activists in Montgomery, including Jo Anne Robinson of the Women's Political Caucus and E. D. Nixon of the NAACP and the Brotherhood of Sleeping Car Porters, as well as Parks herself, used this incident to launch an attack on bus segregation in their city. They and others organized a bus boycott by Montgomery's entire African-American population.

A new minister in town, Martin Luther King Jr., became the leader of the protest. Just 26 years old, King preached with an eloquence of astonishing power. His rhetoric, which combined a secular understanding of political protest and a Christian message of redemption through the power of love, inspired his listeners to maintain the hard path of nonviolent resistance to injustice to which they had committed themselves.

Montgomery's black citizens stayed the course until, once again, the NAACP's lawyers convinced the Supreme Court to come down on their side and order the end of such demeaning racial segregation. In the aftermath of the Montgomery victory, King joined with other African-American ministers in forming the Southern Christian Leadership Conference (SCLC), in order to carry the civil rights movement forward.

The Montgomery achievement, however, was a relatively isolated victory. White resistance to integration and the end of racial discrimination was fierce. For the next few years, no sure means of confronting the centuries-old traditions of racial injustice emerged. While sporadic protests and some legal and political victories were achieved between 1956 and 1960, the promise of a mass struggle remained undeveloped.

MASS PROTEST

On February 1, 1960, a breakthrough occurred. This time it was not the courts or veteran civil-rights organizers who led the way. Four young college students at an all-black school in North Carolina decided to take a personal stand against racial segregation and discrimination. At a whites-only lunch counter in Greensboro, the young men politely asked to be served. When refused, they "sat in," refusing to leave until they were allowed to buy a cup of coffee like any other customer.

Over the next few months, this sit-in tactic spread like wildfire throughout the South, with some 70,000 people in 150 towns and cities joining the movement. While the sit-in protesters were sometimes beaten, abused, and arrested, they maintained at all times their polite, nonviolent decorum. With dignity, they were putting their own bodies on the line in a mass struggle to end Jim Crow racism in the South.

Many of these young sit-in protesters, counseled by one of the civil rights movement's wisest and most dedicated veterans, Ella Baker, joined together to form the Student Nonviolent Coordinating Committee (SNCC). At their founding conference in April 1960, in Raleigh, North Carolina, the students committed themselves to nonviolent protest: ". . . Nonviolence is the foundation of our purpose, the presupposition of our faith, and the manner of our action. . . . Love is the central motif of nonviolence. Love is the force by which God binds man to himself and man to man."[3]

This philosophy of nonviolent protest, whose adherent "remains loving and forgiving even in the midst of hostility," would be sorely tested by waves of brutal violence and repression unleashed by white supremacists upon civil-rights activists over the next several years.[4] Some movement activists, like Martin Luther King, Jr., and SNCC leader John Lewis, would remain nonviolent. Other activists would turn, in time, to more confrontational tactics and more radical solutions.

Between 1960 and 1963, a growing number of African Americans and white supporters organized protests throughout the South. Stores that refused to hire African Americans were picketed, voter-registration campaigns were organized, theaters that forced black ticket holders to sit in the balcony were boycotted, and restaurants that refused service to African Americans faced sit-ins. Most of these protests garnered little or no mass-media attention. They were local affairs in which white town residents were forced to see that their black neighbors did not accept second-class citizenship and could not be terrorized into submission by Ku Klux Klan violence and acts of economic terrorism.

Some protests, often because of the extraordinary violence meted out against the demonstrators, did reach beyond the local and became national news. In 1961, James Farmer, the leader of the Committee on Racial Equality

(CORE), called for "freedom rides" throughout the South to protest white Southerners' refusal to comply with a Supreme Court order ending segregated interstate transportation and bus and train waiting rooms. In May 1961, an integrated group of 13 men and women attempted to travel by bus from Washington, D.C., to Alabama and Mississippi. In most cities along the route they were met by violent mobs. The worst violence came in Birmingham, Alabama, where police chief Bull Connor made a secret agreement with the Ku Klux Klan to allow a white mob to attack the "freedom riders." The freedom rides made national and international headlines. Still, political leaders, like President Kennedy, tried to keep the civil rights agenda off the political front burner.

President Kennedy's efforts to keep his distance from the civil rights issue became more difficult in the fall of 1962. On September 20, a young black man, James Meredith, attempted to register at the all-white University of Mississippi. Despite a federal court order stating that Meredith must be enrolled, Governor Ross Barnett personally blocked his entrance to the university. At that point, Attorney General Robert Kennedy, the president's younger brother, sent 500 federal marshals to insure Meredith's enrollment and safety. In response, at a pro-segregation rally in which hundreds of Confederate flags were waved, Governor Barnett defended white supremacy to rapturous approval: "I love our people, I love our ways, I love our traditions."[5]

A riot broke out in which several thousand whites, very few of whom were university students, attacked the federal marshals that were protecting James Meredith. After some 160 of the 500 marshals were wounded, 26 of them by gunfire, President Kennedy ordered in 5,000 army troops to quell the violence. Attorney General Robert Kennedy, stunned by the racism and violence, said that he now understood how Adolf Hitler had come to power in Germany. Achieving racial justice in the United States would take more than simple acts of courage; it would take the concerted effort of millions of Americans backed up, however grudgingly, by the full force of the federal government.

To produce a national commitment to the civil-rights struggle, Martin Luther King and other key civil rights activists planned a major series of protests in Birmingham, Alabama, a city famous among African Americans for the ferocity of its racial oppression. King hoped that a major confrontation between peaceful African-American activists and violent defenders of white supremacy would force a majority of white Americans throughout the nation to recognize the just and necessary nature of the civil rights movement. In particular, King wanted President Kennedy and other leading politicians to get off the fence and work with the movement to end legal segregation and discrimination in the United States.

After several days of peaceful protest in April 1963, King himself was jailed in Birmingham. From his cell, he smuggled out an impassioned letter, addressed specifically to his fellow clergymen, defending the civil rights movement and asking them to help him confront the manifest evil of racism: "Like a boil that can never be cured so long as it is covered up but must be opened with all its ugliness to the natural medicines of air and light, injustice must be exposed, with all the tension its exposure creates, to the light of human conscience and the air of national opinion before it can be cured."[6]

Soon after King's release from jail, the confrontation he had predicted arrived. In full view of the nation's mass media, Birmingham's all-white police force, under the direction of Bull Connor, attacked peaceful protesters, many of whom were just children. Police used clubs and fists on the protesters and turned loose their police dogs on them. Firemen knocked the demonstrators off their feet and smashed them into the sides of buildings with high-pressure water hoses—while television cameras flashed these brutal images across the country.

In the weeks that followed, over 700 more civil rights protests occurred in the United States. In response to this massive campaign against racial injustice and in the face of the fierce white resistance it provoked in much of the South, President Kennedy decided to act. In the immediate aftermath of another academic standoff—this time it was Alabama Governor George Wallace who "stood in the schoolhouse door" and refused admission to a black student—Kennedy gave a nationally televised speech: "We are confronted primarily with a moral issue. It is as old as the Scriptures and is as clear as the American Constitution. The heart of the question is whether all Americans can be afforded equal rights and equal opportunities, whether we are going to treat our fellow Americans as we want to be treated. . . ."[7]

That night President Kennedy promised to send Congress a comprehensive civil rights bill that would make the promise of freedom and equality a reality for all Americans regardless of the color of their skins.

Most civil rights activists were thrilled by Kennedy's June 11 speech. To assure that Congress recognized the moral strength and power of the movement, a broad coalition of civil rights groups decided to hold a massive demonstration for jobs and freedom on the National Mall in Washington, D.C.

On August 28, 1963, some 250,000 Americans rallied. A. Phillip Randolph, whose struggles for racial justice began in the early years of the twentieth century and who had first conceived the idea of marching on Washington, led the rally. Speakers representing SNCC, CORE, NAACP, and the SCLC called for freedom. Martin Luther King electrified the crowd, crying out: "*I have a dream* that my four little children will one day live in a nation where they will not be judged by the color of their skin but by the content of their character. *I have a dream today. . . .*"[8]

FEDERAL CIVIL RIGHTS LEGISLATION

John Kennedy would not live to see that dream tested by reality. On November 22, 1963, he was assassinated in Dallas, Texas. Lee Harvey Oswald, a social misfit who had lived for a time in the Soviet Union, was arrested for the shooting within hours.

Just a day later, a Dallas nightclub owner, Jack Ruby, killed Oswald in full view of live television cameras as he was being moved from city to county jail.

An official government report, the Warren Report, stated that Oswald alone was responsible for Kennedy's death. Most scholars agree with this conclusion. However, because of Oswald's own murder and a series of irregularities surrounding the investigation of the assassination, others claim, without sufficient proof, that circumstantial evidence indicates a conspiracy lay behind President Kennedy's death.

In the days that followed the assassination, Americans mourned the loss of their youthful president. Jacqueline Kennedy had the president buried at Arlington National Cemetery on a hillside overlooking the capital. The funeral ceremony was televised, and most Americans watched with a mixture of pride and sadness at the dignity with which the First Family coped with their loss. Throughout the world, people grieved for the American president whose words and ideals had moved them.

With Kennedy's death, Vice President Lyndon Baines Johnson became president. In style and background, Johnson and Kennedy were near opposites. Johnson was tall and powerful, a raw-boned Texan who favored a cowboy hat. Born in 1908, he had grown up in Texas hill country, in and around the tiny town of Johnson City, whose population at that time was 323. His family never had much money and, at times, lived in poverty. Lyndon Johnson had begun his life with none of the advantages of a Kennedy.

His first real job was as a schoolteacher in an all–Mexican-American school in Cotulla, Texas. The experience solidified Johnson's commitment to helping the underdog and rejecting the racism that whites in his part of the United States then took for granted. He later said, "You never forget what poverty and hatred can do when you see its scars on the face of a young child."[9]

Those memories, and his own ambitions to build on the Kennedy legacy and create his own monumental presidency, inspired President Johnson to throw all his power and energy behind the civil rights bill Kennedy had introduced to Congress before his assassination. In his first speech as president, before a joint session of Congress, Johnson consoled the nation and then declared: "First, no memorial oration or eulogy could more eloquently honor President Kennedy's memory than the earliest possible passage of the civil-rights bill for which he fought so long. We have talked long enough in this country about equal rights. We have talked for one hundred years or more. It's time now to write the next chapter, and to write it in the books of law."[10]

Over the next few months, Johnson moved the civil rights bill through Congress. In the Senate, southern Democrats did everything they could to stop the bill, just as they had stopped so many other equal-rights measures in the past. For 81 days they filibustered, refusing to yield the floor of the Senate unless the civil-rights bill was withdrawn. Johnson teamed up with Minnesota Democratic Senator Hubert Humphrey and the Republican Minority leader, Illinois Senator Everett Dirksen, to convince enough Democratic and Republican senators to vote cloture (the ending of debate). With the southern filibuster defeated, and the House already having voted in the affirmative, the Senate quickly went on to pass the historic 1964 Civil Rights Act.

The 1964 Civil Rights Act changed the United States in fundamental ways. Not only did it attack racial discrimination, but as a result of unexpected, last-minute maneuvering in Congress, the new law also attacked America's long-standing tradition of second-class citizenship for women. The act outlawed job discrimination based on race or gender. It outlawed discrimination in all public accommodations, including restaurants, hotels, waiting rooms, and theaters. It prohibited the federal government from funding any program at the national, state or local level that discriminated. The Justice Department was given greater powers to fight against school discrimination, and a new federal agency, the Equal Employment Opportunity Commission, was created to fight employers who practiced discrimination.

The civil rights movement, almost a century after the end of the Civil War, had succeeded in enlisting the federal government in the fight against racial injustice. Essentially on their own, a bloc of moderate and liberal Republican and Democratic congressmen had extended that fight to include justice for women as well.

Of course, the war was not over. Several other fronts remained. And on some, the alliance between the Johnson administration and the civil-rights movement would not hold.

On one of those fronts, voting rights, the alliance did hold.

Despite the civil rights victory, many southern states still found ways to keep African Americans from voting. Using literacy tests, constitutional-interpretation tests, and a variety of other means, almost all of which were applied in a racially discriminatory fashion by white voter-registration officials, many southern states made it almost impossible for black southerners to register to vote.

In the early months of 1965, civil rights activists began a series of protests against the discriminatory practices of Alabama state officials. On March 7, 1965, Martin Luther King led thousands of protesters in a 50-mile march from Selma, Alabama, to Montgomery, the state capital. Once again, before the network television cameras, Alabama state troopers and local policemen violently attacked the marchers. During the weeks of the voting-rights protests, three civil rights marchers were killed.

In response to the violence, President Johnson sent army troops to protect the marchers. Then, taking a cue from his predecessor, John Kennedy, he spoke to the nation: "What happened in Selma is part of the far larger movement which reaches into every section and state of America. It is the effort of American Negroes to secure for themselves the full blessings of American life. Their cause must be our cause, too. . . . It is all of us who must overcome the crippling legacy of bigotry and injustice. *And we shall overcome.*"

A few months later, in early August, Congress passed the comprehensive 1965 Voting Rights Act.

On August 6, in the same White House room where Abraham Lincoln, exactly 104 years earlier, had signed a law freeing slaves forced to serve in the Confederate army, President Johnson signed the bill into law. This measure largely ended the disenfranchisement of African Americans in the South.

Two of the main goals of the civil rights movement had been achieved. The power of the federal government had been enlisted in stamping out racial discrimination in schools, jobs, and public accommodations. Legal segregation had been outlawed. In addition, the exclusion of black voters, which had destroyed African Americans' access to the democratic political system, had been overcome.

Many Americans hoped that those measures were sufficient to remove the stains of racism. Few, however, in the civil rights movement believed that the need for struggle was over. President Lyndon Johnson agreed with those activists. But these uncertain allies would discover that on many critical issues they would find little common ground.

NOTES

1. Chief Justice Earl Warren, "Opinion of the Court in Brown v. Board of Education," May 17, 1954, "Brown v. Board of Education": A Brief History with Documents, ed. Waldo Martin (Boston: Bedford, 1998), 173–174.

2. "The Southern Manifesto," March 12, 1956, Brown v. Board of Education, 221.

3. Clayborne Carson, In Struggle: SNCC and the Black Awakening of the 1960s (Cambridge: Harvard University Press, 1981), 23–24.

4. Carson, In Struggle, 24.

5. David Farber, "Democratic Subjects in the American Sixties," Mid-America 81:3 (Fall 1999), 327.

6. Robert Weisbrot, Freedom Bound: A History of America's Civil Rights Struggle (New York: Norton, 1990), 70.

7. Farber, The Age of Great Dreams, 88.

8. Weisbrot, Freedom Bound, 82.

9. Bruce J. Schulman, Lyndon B. Johnson and American Liberalism: A Brief Biography with Documents (Boston: Bedford, 1995), 9.

10. Lyndon B. Johnson, "Address before a Joint Session of the Congress," November 27, 1963, in Schulman, Lyndon B. Johnson, 171.

11. Lyndon B. Johnson, "The American Promise: Special Message to the Congress," March 15, 1965, in Schulman, Lyndon B. Johnson, 196.

CHAPTER THREE

The Great Society

This chapter details the fight to create a strong federal presence in Americans' lives, ranging from social-provision legislation to environmental regulation to the implementation of civil rights laws. The chapter is structured by a debate among liberals, radicals, and conservatives over the role of government in the United States.

DEBATING RACIAL JUSTICE

During the mid-1960s, liberals, conservatives, and radicals offered competing visions for solving the nation's basic domestic problems. Liberals, led by President Lyndon Johnson, called for an activist federal government that would right racial injustice and wage a "War on Poverty." Conservatives, with Arizonan Barry Goldwater as their standardbearer in 1964, insisted that the federal government had no right to intervene in racial matters and little role to play in American domestic life. The only real problem Americans faced at home, said Goldwater, was an overreaching federal government that threatened core American values.

Leftist radicals, both white and black, rejected the answers of both liberals and conservatives. Many argued for a more participatory democracy, in which communities would be better able to determine their own fates. They also sought far greater economic equality than either mainstream Democrats or Republicans advocated. By the mid-Sixties, amid an increasingly rancorous public life, the American people had clear political choices.

The first major collision among these competing national visions was between an increasingly radical element of the civil rights movement and the liberal Johnson administration. It occurred most publicly in August, 1964, in Atlantic City, New Jersey, the site of the 1964 Democratic Party Presidential Nominating Convention. There, 68 Mississippians—men and women, black and white—representing the Mississippi Freedom Democratic Party (MFDP) appeared before the Democratic Party convention rules committee. They wanted the committee to bar the all-white Mississippi Democratic Party delegation, which had been selected without the participation of even a single African American and to seat their integrated delegation in its place.

This demand, that the Democratic Party do more than just promise equal opportunity but also do the hard work of assuring that equality was actually achieved, had become an ever more urgent force within a powerful faction of the civil rights movement.

The increasingly radical position of some civil rights activists had become clear to movement insiders by August 1963, during the March on Washington. SNCC activists, whose origins lay in the Sit-In movement, had become frustrated with what appeared to them to be the slow pace of reform and the failure of the federal government to stop the murderous violence white supremacists were unleashing upon them and other activists.

At the March on Washington, John Lewis, the SNCC speaker, was prepared to deliver a fiery speech condemning the Kennedy administration for its lack of political courage. He also wanted to blast Southern whites by promising to "march through the heart of Dixie, the way Sherman did."[1] To white Southerners, even some sympathetic to the movement, conjuring up Civil War General William Tecumseh Sherman's campaign of violent destruction through the South would undoubtedly be heard as a violent threat. Lewis was talked out of using the more incendiary aspects of his speech by Martin Luther King and other movement elders. However, the anger and the concerns underlying Lewis's original speech were not quelled.

Black activists' experiences in the Deep South throughout 1963 and much of 1964 only intensified their suspicion of white-led reform. Many of the younger activists in the movement, by then, had undertaken grassroots voter-registration work in the Deep South. With their energies focused in Mississippi, these organizers witnessed crushing poverty and brutal oppression. The activists themselves faced unrelenting white hostility, which took the form of beatings, shootings, and constant harassment from and arrests by local law enforcement. The starkness of the poverty and the brazenness of the white supremacists forced many civil rights workers to ponder the nature of the society they hoped to change.

In 1964, the Mississippi movement, led by Robert Moses, organized Freedom Summer, a campaign in which white and black volunteers attempted to register African Americans to vote. Just after the summer campaign began, three of the volunteers—James Chaney, Andrew Goodman, and Michael

Schwerner—were murdered. By the time the campaign ended in August, over 1.000 volunteers had been arrested, 80 had been beaten, 35 bombings had taken place, and three more activists had been killed.

Freedom Summer had, however, helped to launch the Mississippi Freedom Democratic Party (MFDP).

When the MFDP challenged the all-white Mississippi delegation at the 1964 Democratic Convention, the delegates believed they had the moral right on their side. They were fighting for a new South and a new America in which racial justice prevailed. MFDP delegate Fannie Lou Hamer put the matter plainly: "If the Freedom Democratic Party is not seated now, I question America."[2]

The MFDP delegation was not seated. President Johnson had been told by Texas Governor John Connally that if the MFDP was seated instead of the all-white Mississippi delegation, which had been selected by state and party rules and regulations, all the Southern delegates at the convention would walk out in full view of the television cameras. President Johnson, using intermediaries, tried to forge a compromise, offering the MFDP two at-large seats and a promise that the next party convention would exclude delegates selected through discriminatory practices. The MFDP, however, rejected the compromise.

Many left Atlantic City convinced that white liberals, when pressured, could not be counted on to pursue racial justice. Stokely Carmichael, perhaps the most incisive leader of the radicals, argued: "The national conscience was generally unreliable. . . . black people in Mississippi and throughout this country could not rely on their so-called allies."[3] Carmichael and others began to look for new answers to remedy the subordinate position African Americans had been forced into by white Americans.

THE 1964 PRESIDENTIAL ELECTION

While most radical civil rights activists would not have acknowledged it, President Johnson also believed that the United States needed to find new solutions to vexing American problems of poverty and racial inequality. Johnson wanted to build on John Kennedy's domestic policies and greatly expand them—although not as far or as fast as his radical critics demanded.

Johnson laid out his vision of what he called "the Great Society" at the University of Michigan on May 22, 1964:

The Great Society rests in abundance and liberty for all. It demands an end to poverty and racial injustice, to which we are totally committed in our time. . . . For better or for worse, your generation has been appointed by history to deal with those problems and to lead America to a new age. . . . You can help build a society where the demands of morality, and the needs of the spirit, can be realized in the life of the Nation. So will you join in the battle to give every citizen the full equality which God enjoins and the law requires, whatever his belief or race, or the color of his skin? Will you join in the battle to give every citizen an escape from the crushing weight of poverty?[4]

To realize this vision, Johnson would have to greatly expand the power and reach of the federal government. And in order to do that, first of all, he would have to win the 1964 presidential election.

Barry Goldwater was the Republican nominee for president. He stood diametrically opposed to Johnson's domestic policies. Goldwater believed that the federal government had no right to interfere in American lives except in the narrowest of cases. In his view, each American had to make the best life he or she could, based on his or her own individual efforts. Collective grievances, whether elicited by racism or sexism or poverty, made no sense to Goldwater. He asserted a complete trust in individualism. Most explosively, in 1964, this limited view of government meant that Goldwater opposed every single civil-rights measure. Race relations, Goldwater believed, must be solved at the local level.

In part, this anti–civil rights stance was based on Goldwater's core principles. It was also good politics. In order to become president, Goldwater needed to win the South. In 1964, most black southerners were prevented from voting one way or another; only white votes mattered in the South. A large majority of southern whites in 1964 remained resolutely opposed to civil rights legislation. As Goldwater told a meeting of Republicans in Atlanta, Georgia, describing his campaign strategy, "We ought to go hunting where the ducks are."[5] Opposing civil rights at that time was a winning move in the South.

At the July Republican Convention, Goldwater outlined his vision of America. Liberals and civil rights activists were increasingly focused on equality; Goldwater made plain his rejection of that priority and put in its place another. The Republican Party, Goldwater shouted, "with its every action, every word, every breath, and every heartbeat, has but a single resolve and that is Freedom! . . . . I would remind you that extremism in the defense of liberty is no vice. And let me remind you that moderation in the pursuit of justice is no virtue."[6]

Goldwater and his fellow conservatives had declared their independence from the relatively pragmatic, problem-solving mentality that had characterized both President John Kennedy and his 1960 Republican opponent Richard Nixon. Goldwater hoped to lead the nation away from the direction it had taken since the New Deal of the 1930s. He wanted less government, less regulation, less of a mandatory social-safety net, and less control by nationally oriented technocratic elites. Goldwater believed in an older America in which local businessmen and clergymen maintained community standards — even if those standards were racist — and in which America's world affairs were determined by drawing lines in the sand.

Scorning almost all domestic policies created by the national government, Goldwater did fervently advocate a bigger, better funded, and far more aggressive campaign against communism both at home and abroad. Certain that the Soviet Union planned worldwide domination, Goldwater wanted to spend tens of billions more on the American military, accelerate America's nuclear-weapons buildup, and launch aggressive efforts to roll back communism throughout the world. Goldwater, as he himself put it, represented "a choice, not an echo."[7]

Lyndon Johnson could not have been happier with his political opponent. Goldwater's embrace of extremism allowed Johnson to run as a moderate. Johnson supporters cheerfully mocked Goldwater's campaign slogan, "In Your Heart, You Know He's Right," by adding "Extremely Right!" (They also rhymed, "In your guts, you know he's nuts.")[8] Goldwater's casual campaign remark advocating the use of atomic bombs in the fight against communism gave the Johnson campaign a powerful symbolic weapon. The resulting television commercial pictured a little girl pulling the petals off a daisy, one by one. As she plucks off the petals, a man's voice urgently begins a countdown. When he reaches zero, the girl's image dissolves into an atomic-bomb mushroom cloud. Over that image, President Johnson intones: "These are the stakes — to make a world in which all of God's children can live, or go into the dark. We must either love each other, or we must die."[9]

President Johnson won the 1964 election in a landslide, gaining 61.1 percent of the popular vote. On his coattails, he carried into office the most liberal Congress since the zenith of President Franklin Roosevelt's New Deal in the 1930s.

Johnson's victory was far from complete. Goldwater had succeeded in "hunting where the ducks are." For the first time, because of Johnson's embrace of the civil rights movement, most white voters in the deep South turned their backs on the Democratic Party and voted for what was, ironically, the party of Abraham Lincoln. In Mississippi, where black citizens were still fighting for the simple right to vote, over 90 percent of whites had voted for the Republican presidential candidate. Like Senator Goldwater, these voters did not believe that the federal government had any right to legislate equal-employment opportunities, integrated schools, or equal voting rights. On that basis, they switched traditional political-party allegiance.

Only a few months earlier, on a national television program, Martin Luther King had warned that he foresaw the Republican Party turning into a "white man's party," which would be "tragic for the Republican Party as well as tragic for the nation."[10]

LBJ AND THE GREAT SOCIETY

President Johnson was alarmed by the desertion of white voters in the South. But his great victory and the new Democratic Congress he had carried into office gave him much to celebrate. He had the support, he knew, to take the "Great Society" from campaign slogan to enacted legislation. Under Johnson's leadership, the Eighty-ninth Congress would be one of the busiest in the nation's history, churning out one pathbreaking law after another.

Johnson and his liberal supporters worked on many fronts. The Johnson Administration wanted to improve the quality of American life and create economic opportunity for all Americans. They addressed, often for the first time, air pollution, water quality, and highway beautification. They passed legislation that improved tire safety, mine safety, highway safety, child safety, and that funded child health medical assistance and medical research. In addition to the monumental 1964 Civil Rights Act and the 1965 Voting Rights Act was the equally momentous 1965 Immigration Act, which ended decades-old discriminatory restrictions on immigration from Asia and Latin America. The Johnson Administration also created the National Endowment for the Humanities and the National Endowment for the Arts.

At the heart of Johnson's Great Society was the War on Poverty. Johnson pinned his hopes for presidential greatness on ending both racial discrimination and poverty in the United States. The federal government, President Johnson believed, could and should provide poor Americans the resources they needed to get decent educations and job skills, as well as an economic safety net that would keep them healthy, housed, and fed. Johnson's liberal vision of government took shape in the War on Poverty.

The War on Poverty programs, most of which were administered by the new Office of Economic Opportunity, were intended to improve opportunities for poor Americans throughout their lives. For pre-school children, the Headstart program provided early enrichment and "school-readiness" skills. The Elementary and Secondary Education Act of 1965 provided a billion dollars to improve poor children's schooling. The Job Corps attempted to take wayward young adults and turn them into wage earners. The Community Action Program set out to help all residents of impoverished neighborhoods escape from a "culture of poverty" by enlisting the "maximum feasible participation" of the poor themselves in solving their community problems.

Other programs worked to create an economic safety net for the poor. For the working poor, the minimum wage was raised. For all Americans who lived below the poverty level, the Medicaid program provided free medical care. The Food Stamp program and the Aid to Families with Dependent Children program (often called "welfare") were liberalized so that more people were eligible for them. More public housing was supplied for low-income people. For all elderly Americans, poor or not, the Medicare program provided guaranteed medical benefits. These programs, and more, represented a massive increase in the federal government's role in protecting Americans from economic hardship. They also represented a massive increase in federal spending.

The Great Society and the War on Poverty were immensely controversial throughout America. Many employers were displeased with the numerous new safety and environmental regulations they had to comply with in running their businesses. A majority of white Americans believed that too much money was being spent on minorities, and some still firmly believed that the government had no right to make equal opportunity and equal access the law of the land.

At the same time, many minority Americans believed that Great Society programs were underfunded and failed to deliver benefits and services sufficient to meet the needs of minority communities. State and local government officials across the nation argued that the federal government was usurping their power at the same time that it was mandating new regulations for which local communities had to pay. Conservatives argued that the War on Poverty was a losing battle, for it created dependency on government handouts instead of fostering individual responsibility.

Champions of the Great Society insisted that significant aspects of government policy worked. They pointed to the new environmental regulations and work-safety laws as critical successes. They heralded Project Headstart and other federally funded education measures as opportunity enhancers for the whole country. Medicare and Medicaid, though expensive, were helping Americans live healthier and longer lives. These programs and others, they said, proved that, on balance, the liberal Great Society programs made America a more just and equitable nation.

By the end of his presidential term, Lyndon Johnson had mixed feelings about his Great Society programs. To pass critical pieces of legislation, Johnson had made some tough compromises. Deals with Congress had meant that federal education money could be spent somewhat haphazardly at the local school-district level, minimizing its effectiveness in helping disadvantaged and under-performing students. Powerful lobbying by the American Hospital Association and the American Medical Association had turned Medicare and Medicaid into hugely profitable windfall programs for medical professionals and immensely expensive programs for the government.

Johnson also realized that the Great Society was turning out to be a political problem. Despite the numerous Great Society federal programs like Medicare that were helpful to the middle class, the War on Poverty was perceived by too many Americans, for reasons of racial prejudice and for just plain financial reasons, as a waste of their tax dollars. White, middle-class voters were turning away from the Big Government policies of liberals like Johnson.

That disillusionment, Johnson knew, could spell disaster both for his Democratic Party and for his own presidential dreams of greatness. On top of everything else, by 1967, America's burgeoning commitments to Vietnam were becoming ever more expensive, draining American resources away from domestic programs. As Johnson memorably stated, "That bitch of a war [destroyed] the woman I really loved—the Great Society."[11]

THE NEW LEFT

The war in Vietnam did more than take money away from domestic reform. It also polarized the nation. However, well before the war split the country apart in the late 1960s, a radical movement had begun questioning the basic political and economic organization of the United States. A "New Left" political movement, based on American university campuses, challenged conservatives and liberals, Republicans and Democrats alike. This student-organized New Left called for a more participatory democracy, new relations with the revolutionary governments of the "Third World," and a completely different standard of economic justice in the United States. Strongly influenced by the civil rights movement, the New Left looked at the United States "from the bottom up" and judged the nation's success by how well it served the needs of the minorities and the poor, and by how successfully it created not just material abundance but spiritual growth.

Like the civil rights movement, the student New Left had roots in previous decades. Multiple influences fed its rise. Cultural rebels of the 1950s as diverse as Beat writers Jack Kerouac and AllenGinsberg, comedian Lenny Bruce, and movie stars James Dean and Marlon Brando helped to foster an outsider sensibility even among white middle-class kids growing up in suburbia. Older, often tiny, radical or oppositional groups like the Catholic Worker, the War Resisters League, the Committee for a Sane Nuclear Policy, and the Committee for Nonviolent Action kept alive a dissident tradition in the United States. Most importantly, the civil rights movement sparked an understanding among some white students that they, too, could make a difference in America's political life.

The New Left emerged in 1960 when a group of young people based at the University of Michigan in Ann Arbor formed the Students for a Democratic Society (SDS). Unlike many earlier leftist groups, SDS had no ties to or interest in the communism espoused by the Soviet Union—the Old Left. Their New Left orientation pointed them toward a traditional American belief in democracy, though reclaimed for "the people," and toward greater economic equality as well.

The Port Huron Statement, the formal declaration of principles that the young people of SDS wrote in June 1962, expresses their hope for a more democratic, egalitarian, and communitarian America:

> As a social system we seek the establishment of a democracy of individual participation. . . . That the individual share in those social decisions determining the quality and direction of his life. . . .That the economy itself is of such social importance that its major resources and means of production should be open to democratic participation and subject to democratic social regulation.[12]

SDS members were not alone among students in the early to mid-1960s seeking out more direct democratic participation in American life and a means to creating a more equitable society. While SDS spread outward from Ann Arbor, more than 2,000 miles away, at the University of California, Berkeley, other young people also had begun to organize.

At Berkeley, student protest had deep roots. By the early 1960s, small groups of students had protested against vestiges of McCarthyite anticommunism, the death penalty, and racial discrimination. Several dozen white students had gone south as volunteers in the civil rights movement, and approximately ten per cent of all students had participated in a civil rights protest. In October 1964, this inchoate student movement exploded onto the public scene.

On October 1, university officials decided to stop people from handing out political pamphlets on campus. In response, students massed on the campus's main public area, Sproul Plaza, and demanded the right to free speech. In the weeks that followed, the student members of the Free Speech Movement, as it was soon named, began to protest what they called the "dehumanizing" system of education they faced at the University of California. Protest leader Mario Savio memorably summed up their discontent:

> There comes a time when the operation of the machine becomes so odious, makes you so sick at heart that you can't take part; you can't even tacitly take part, and you've got to put your bodies upon the levers, upon all the apparatus and you've got to make it stop. And you've got to indicate to the people who run it, to the people who own it, that unless you're free, the machine will be prevented from working at all.[13]

This spirit of resistance typified the New Left. Short on specifics and unclear about exact alternatives, the New Left protesters, to paraphrase the Port Huron Statement, rejected "the modest comfort" offered by the American Dream and looked "uncomfortably to the world we inherit."[14] Inspired by the civil rights movement, they wished, somehow, to create "the beloved community" Martin Luther King advocated. Idealistically, they thought they could make the United States a more generous, peaceful, and just society.

In the mid-1960s, when America's involvement in the Vietnam War began to escalate dramatically, this relatively small student movement would explode. Its critique of the United States, which had seemed quite radical even to most young people in the early 1960s, suddenly began to make sense to hundreds of thousands of students. The Vietnam War would make many Americans begin to doubt that either Republicans or Democrats, conservative or liberal political leaders, understood how to create a morally just society.

NOTES

1. Weisbrot, *Freedom Bound*, 81.
2. Farber, *The Age of Great Dreams*, 99.
3. Farber, *The Age of Great Dreams*, 100.

4. Lyndon B. Johnson, "Remarks at the University of Michigan," May 22, 1964, in Schulman, *Lyndon B. Johnson*, 174, 176–177.

5. Farber, *The Age of Great Dreams*, 99.

6. Theodore White, *The Making of the President 1964* (New York: Atheneum, 1965), 216–217.

7. White, *The Making of the President 1964*, 218.

8. Kathleen Hall Jamieson, *Packaging the Presidency: A History and Criticism of Presidential Campaign Advertising* (New York: Oxford, 1996), 220.

9. Jon Margolis, *The Last Innocent Year: America in 1964* (New York: Morrow, 1999), 327.

10. Margolis, *The Last Innocent Year*, 208.

11. Schulman, *Lyndon B. Johnson*, 127.

12. "The Port Huron Statement," in James Miller, *"Democracy Is in the Streets": From Port Huron to the Siege of Chicago* (New York: Simon and Schuster, 1988), 333.

13. Wini Breines and Alexander Bloom, eds., *"Takin' It to the Streets": A Sixties Reader* (New York: Oxford, 1995), 111–112.

14. "The Port Huron Statement," in Miller, *Democracy*, 329.

CHAPTER FOUR

The Vietnam War

This chapter provides a brief history of the Vietnam War. It explains how and why the United States became involved in the war and the controversies that surrounded that involvement. The focus is on the decision-making processes of those who managed the war and those who protested against it.

BACKGROUND TO DIRECT AMERICAN INVOLVEMENT

The United States government became involved in Vietnam slowly. Each step of the way, for more than 20 years, policy-makers debated options, considered alternatives, and ultimately chose deeper involvement. By mid-1965, a series of incremental steps resulted in American ground troops facing combat in Vietnam. By 1968, the war had become a quagmire with no clear road to victory. Only in 1973, after suffering massive casualties and laying waste to much of Vietnam, would the United States ingloriously pull out the last of its troops. America's longest war tore the nation apart.

Before World War II, dating back to the mid-nineteenth century, Vietnam had been a French colony. In 1940 the Japanese invaded Vietnam, drove out the French, and made it their colonial possession. During World War II, the Vietnamese nationalist leader Ho Chi Minh waged a guerrilla war against the Japanese, in part with American-supplied weapons. In 1945, when Japan was defeated, Ho declared the end of Vietnam's colonial status. To mark the occasion he quoted from the American Declaration of Independence. This declaration of independence started the Vietnam War. For the Vietnamese, the war would last nearly 30 years.

The French did not accept Vietnamese independence. For economic as well as internal political reasons, French leaders wanted their colony back. Already by the end of 1945, French troops, supplied with American military equipment, returned to Vietnam bent on restoring French imperial control. Until 1954, the French and the Vietnamese fought. Outgunned, the Vietnamese fought a guerrilla war. They sought simply to wear down the French by making the price of empire—in French blood and money—too high a cost to bear.

The United States played only a limited role in this war, giving France financial support and then direct military aid. The United States aided France for two reasons. First, France was a critical European ally in the cold war struggle against the Soviet Union. Second, and directly related, Vietnam's independence movement was communist-led—Ho Chi Minh having long-standing ties to the Soviet Union.

Both President Truman and President Eisenhower feared that a victorious, communist-led independence movement in Vietnam could tip all of Southeast Asia into the "Red" camp. This "Red" tide might then force Japan and the Philippines—for economic and geopolitical reasons—to accommodate themselves to the Soviet Union as well. Because of cold war pressures, the United States found itself helping French imperialists wage war against independence-seeking Vietnamese. It was an awkward policy for Americans who believed in national self-determination. Nonetheless, by 1954 United States military aid to France totaled over a billion dollars.

It wasn't enough. In 1954, France's key military base at Dien Bien Phu was overrun by the Vietnamese, led by General Vo Nguyen Giap. The French decided that they had had enough. Some 95,000 French Union troops had been killed trying to prevent Vietnam's attainment of independence. The Vietnamese had lost over 300,000 soldiers, and approximately 1,000,000 civilians had died during the fighting. Despite the lopsided casualty figures, when the first Indochina War was over, Vietnam had won.

NATION-BUILDING

As an independent nation, Vietnam seemed once again to have fallen under the control of foreign leaders. Under the Geneva Accords peace agreement, signed by the French and the Vietnamese, Vietnam was to be temporarily divided into two regions. Ho's forces would immediately take over the northern region. The southern region, where the French had been strongest, would be ruled by Vietnamese who had been loyal to the French. In 1956, North and South together would elect a new democratic government to lead the reunified nation.

During this period, the Eisenhower Administration struggled to find a winning Vietnam policy. As the Dien Bien Phu debacle was unfolding, President

Eisenhower had considered a military intervention on the side of France. After both the British and Ike's main military advisor, General Matthew Ridgway, strongly argued against the move, Eisenhower backed off.

However, with the French defeat and the subsequent "temporary" division of Vietnam, Eisenhower and his main foreign policy advisor, Secretary of State John Foster Dulles, saw an opportunity. What if the United States offered massive assistance to the government set up in the South? What if the United States could build a viable, successful nation in the South? Such an experiment in nation-building, Eisenhower and Dulles hoped, would prove not just to the Vietnamese but to newly independent, decolonizing nations around the globe that the United States, not the Soviet Union, made the best ally.

Between 1954 and 1960, the Eisenhower administration poured money into the Republic of Vietnam (South Vietnam), spending over $1.65 billion. Americans tried to create a free-market economic system, improve South Vietnam's infrastructure, and train the police and military.

In 1956, with the support of the United States, the South Vietnamese government refused to participate in the national election called for by the Geneva peace treaty. The aristocratic leader of South Vietnam, Ngo Dinh Diem, knew that Ho Chi Minh would win an open election. Instead, Diem attempted to consolidate his control of the South.

Unfortunately for the United States, Diem was extremely unpopular with the Vietnamese people. They resented his attempt to spread his Roman Catholic religion by repressing Buddhism, the faith of 90 percent of the Vietnamese. Most Vietnamese correctly believed the Diem regime to be corrupt and uninterested in bettering the lives of the rural peasants who made up the majority of the Vietnamese population. Diem's lack of legitimacy in the eyes of the people of South Vietnam created grave difficulties for the U.S. government's commitment to nation-building.

In the North, Ho Chi Minh and his communist government were having problems of their own. Failed land-reform policies and the general difficulty of creating an independent society after decades of French oppression meant that Ho had to concentrate, at first, on simply consolidating his own power in the North. Plans for reunifying Vietnam had to be delayed.

INCREASING INVOLVEMENT

By the time John F. Kennedy became president in 1960, the situation in Vietnam was grave. By the late 1950s, pro-unification Vietnamese who lived in the

South—known as the Viet Cong—had begun a guerrilla war against the Diem government. They followed two main tactics. First, they took land from rich landowners and redistributed it to poor peasants (a policy which, ironically, the United States had tried to get Diem to follow). Second, the Viet Cong began to murder government officials who worked throughout the South in villages and small towns.

Diem fought back, using the South Vietnamese Army (the Army of the Republic of Vietnam or ARVN) to hunt down Viet Cong and kill them, in turn. In 1959, to aid the Viet Cong, Ho began sending North Vietnamese soldiers south to help fight the South Vietnamese military.

In late 1963, President Kennedy's advisors believed the situation in Vietnam was rapidly deteriorating, and most of them strongly urged him to take action. Diem's attempts to crush the Viet Cong had largely backfired. The brutal tactics used by the South Vietnamese Army had turned millions of peasants against the government. Diem's continued, malicious anti-Buddhist campaign had further undermined his support.

Viet Cong forces grew both in numbers and in their ability to control more and more territory within South Vietnam. To counter the Viet Cong, President Kennedy had increased the number of American military advisors in Vietnam from around 900 to more than 16,000, and had spent another billion dollars during his presidency. By late 1963, 108 Americans had lost their lives while advising the South Vietnamese military.

In an attempt to turn the situation around, Kennedy signed on to a CIA-supported Vietnamese military coup against Diem. On November 2, 1963, Diem and two other high government officials were assassinated, and a new military government took control of South Vietnam. Kennedy was horrified that the coup had resulted in the murder of Diem. He also realized that despite all the American aid and military advisement, the Vietnam situation was a mess. On November 21, 1963, he asked a trusted aide, National Security Council staff member Michael Forrestal, to prepare to review American policy in Vietnam and assess "whether or not we should be there."[1] President Kennedy was himself assassinated before that report could be prepared.

When Lyndon Johnson took over the presidency, Vietnam was far from his mind. He wanted to fight a domestic war on poverty, not a war in Southeast Asia. When his advisors briefed him on the deteriorating situation, Johnson complained that he felt like a fish that had "grabbed a big juicy worm with a right sharp hook in the middle of it."[2] Defense experts told the president that he had to increase pressure on the communists or South Vietnam would fall.

Johnson was loath to commit the United States to a land war in Southeast Asia, for Vietnam was no security threat to the United States and represented no direct American interests. On the other hand, he feared that if he allowed America to fail in Vietnam, the Soviet Union and China might perceive America as weak and begin to contemplate attacks on American allies in the region. Johnson, like his predecessors, feared that Vietnam might be the first Southeast Asian "domino" to fall to communism, bringing down other nations with it. Seeing no good options, Johnson let policy drift for the next several months, acting only to increase the number of American military advisors in Vietnam to around 20,000 by the summer of 1964.

Then, in August 1964, Johnson acted. The presidential election campaign was heating up, and Republican Barry Goldwater had made Vietnam an issue, declaring that Johnson was about to lose Vietnam to the communists. Goldwater called for air attacks and even floated the idea of using atomic bombs on the Vietnamese enemy. In response to Goldwater, and in an attempt to slow down the Viet Cong and the North Vietnamese, Johnson used an incident in the Gulf of Tonkin, off the coast of North Vietnam, as a reason to launch a military offensive.

Officers aboard two American destroyers on a reconnaissance mission off the Vietnamese coast reported that they believed North Vietnamese ships had fired torpedoes at them. While no damage had occurred—indeed it was not clear that torpedoes actually had been fired—Johnson ordered a retaliatory air attack on North Vietnam. He appeared on national television and informed the American people that "aggression by terror against peaceful villages of South Vietnam has now been joined by open aggression on the high seas against the United States of America."[3] Further, he asked for and received from Congress—in what was called the Gulf of Tonkin Resolution—the power "to take all necessary measures to repel any armed attack against the armed forces of the United States and to prevent further aggression."[4] Although it was not yet clear to the American people or even to President Johnson, the die had been cast: the United States had moved from an advisory role in Vietnam to that of an active belligerent in the war.

THE ESCALATING WAR

Between 1965 and 1968, the Johnson administration greatly increased American military involvement in Vietnam. In 1965, 184,300 American troops were sent there to fight. By 1968, 550,000 American fighting men were "in country." Without that escalation, the American-allied South Vietnamese government would have been defeated by the Viet Cong and North Vietnamese military.

The war was fought not in North Vietnam but in the South, against the Viet Cong and North Vietnamese soldiers who had gained control of large areas of the South Vietnamese countryside. American policy-makers hoped that if enough enemy soldiers were killed, the North Vietnamese government would decide to stop its bloody effort to reunify the country. No policy-maker believed that the United States should try to conquer North Vietnam—such an effort would have caused international opprobrium; it would have demanded total war mobilization by the American people; and it would have produced an immense number of American casualties over a period of many years.

As a result, American success was measured not by taking territory or by winning key battles but by the "body count," the number of enemy dead. The problem with this strategy was that no one could say how many enemy dead it would take to end the war. The Viet Cong and the North Vietnamese were clearly willing to make extraordinary sacrifices to win the civil war.

This "war of attrition," fought in South Vietnam, was catastrophic for both the Vietnamese and America's fighting men. Huge areas of South Vietnam were laid to waste. Herbicides—including the infamous defoliant known as Agent Orange—ravaged the countryside as the United States military attempted to deprive the enemy of cover. Massive air bombardments rained death and destruction down upon not only the enemy but often upon civilian populations as well.

American soldiers and marines often had a difficult time differentiating enemy guerrilla soldiers from "friendly" South Vietnamese villagers. This common problem in guerrilla warfare led some American soldiers to mistreat the civilian population brutally. As a result, one of the war's major objectives, "winning the hearts and minds" of the Vietnamese people away from the communists and to the American side, was tragically undermined.

From the perspective of America's men in the field, Vietnam was often maddening. Marine platoon commander Philip Caputo wrote, "Without a front, flanks, or rear, we fought a formless war against a formless enemy who evaporated like the jungle mists, only to materialize in some unexpected places."[5]

When American troops were able to confront large numbers of Viet Cong or North Vietnamese soldiers in battle, they almost always crushed them. Too often, however, American troops walked through the jungles and rice paddies of Vietnam without ever seeing the enemy. Soldiers were shot by snipers and blown up by booby traps. Helicopter gunships took enemy fire from supposedly "friendly" villages, and the troops learned that even some of the Vietnamese who worked on American military bases were loyal Viet Cong guerrillas. In a war of attrition, in which the enemy could be anyone, in which days went by without a single enemy sighting, and in which no clear territorial lines separated the enemy from the ally, America's fighting men faced an extraordinarily challenging mission.

THE WAR AT HOME

Until the 1964 Gulf of Tonkin incident, few Americans had paid much attention to the situation in Vietnam. In 1965, when American troops begin to play a major role in the fighting, the American public overwhelmingly supported the war effort. However, by 1967 an increasing number of Americans had begun to question and even actively oppose the war. In 1968, after the Viet Cong launched a major military offensive during *Tet* (the Vietnamese holiday associated with the lunar New Year), tens of millions of Americans lost their confidence in the government's Vietnam policy.

Among the first to speak out against the war were members of groups most Americans would have considered fringe elements: left-wing radicals, pacifists, and civil-rights militants. Few of the millions of Americans who would eventually protest against the war became members of these groups. However, because radicals were among the first to oppose the war, they gained both visibility and credibility for their critiques of American society. They argued that American policy in Vietnam was not just a mistake. It was, they said, indicative of how the American government worked on behalf of the rich and powerful to exploit poor people both at home and internationally.

The first major anti-war protest was held in Washington, D.C., in April 1965. It was sponsored by the New Left organization Students for a Democratic Society (SDS). Paul Potter, president of SDS, declared that the Vietnam War revealed that America was run "by faceless and terrible bureaucracies . . . that consistently put material values before human values."[6] Potter argued that the American government was no longer ruled by the democratic wishes of the people but by "the system," which made policies in secret and then manipulated the American people into following them.[7] Protesting the war, SDS activists believed, was one small step in challenging the Washington policy-makers by restoring the citizens' right to be heard on matters of vital concern to the nation.

University campuses became centers for the growing antiwar movement. Student protesters espoused the basic democratic belief that it was the duty of American citizens not to leave policy-making to government officials but to speak out and be heard. By 1968, as the war showed little sign of ending, campus-based protests took place at almost every university in the nation. At Columbia University, for example, several hundred students attempted to close down the school by sitting in at several campus buildings, protesting both against the war and against alleged racism by university administrators. At other schools, students as well as faculty held "teach-ins" to discuss the war, protested against campus-based war research, marched, picketed and rallied.

Antiwar activism was restricted neither to small organized groups nor to university campuses. Several nationally organized protests took place. In April 1967, a coalition of antiwar activists held simultaneous marches in San Francisco and New York. These marches, which attracted some 250,000 Americans, were dominated by nonradical, nonmilitant protesters, most of whom wanted President Johnson to negotiate a peaceful withdrawal of American troops from Vietnam. Unlike SDS members, the great majority of whom believed that the war indicated the moral illegitimacy of the American government, most of these protesters felt that the Vietnam War was just a tragic mistake.

A few months later, another national protest took place, this time in Washington, D.C., when approximately 50,000 of the more militant protesters marched on the Pentagon. In symbolic protest against the war and the secretive nature of its military escalation, demonstrators deliberately trespassed on government property. More than 600 were arrested and some 50 others were hospitalized after being teargassed or beaten. While still avowedly nonviolent, these more militant protesters sought more confrontational tactics that would "disrupt and block the war machine."[8]

By 1968, a great many voices had been raised against the war. Martin Luther King spoke for many Americans when he declared: "I oppose the war in Vietnam because I love America. I speak out against it not in anger but with anxiety and sorrow in my heart."[9] Hundreds of other clergymen joined him in speaking out against the war, as did business executives, housewives, doctors, scientists, union members, and many others, as hundreds of grassroots antiwar organizations sprang up in every part of the country.

Most Americans, however, disapproved of the antiwar protesters, even as many began to worry that something was wrong with American policy in Vietnam. At the beginning of 1968, about 56 percent of Americans polled said they were "hawks," who believed that America should increase or maintain its involvement in Vietnam. Only 28 percent advocated troop withdrawal. President Johnson did his best to keep alive Americans' faith in his war policies by emphasizing that the war was going well and that there was "light at the end of the tunnel," meaning that victory was in sight. This faith, however, was badly shaken in early February 1968.

Beginning on January 31—*Tet*, the Lunar New Year—the Viet Cong launched a massive offensive, targeting almost every major city and town in South Vietnam. They attacked at a time when the American people had been led to believe that the enemy was on its last legs, incapable of major aggression. Although American and South Vietnamese troops successfully stopped the offensive and dealt the Viet Cong a crushing blow, many Americans understood that the war was far from over. As CBS news anchor Walter Cronkite editorialized: "To say that we are mired in stalemate seems the only realistic, yet unsatisfactory conclusion."[10]

After Tet, Americans were about equally divided between those who believed the war could and should still be fought to victory and those who believed some kind of American withdrawal was the only solution.

Still, despite the increasing number of Americans weary of or downright opposed to the war, a majority of people in mid-1968 disapproved of the antiwar movement in all its forms, making little distinction between militant and more moderate protesters. They felt that public protest against the war while American soldiers were risking their lives in combat was unpatriotic or even traitorous. A popular bumper sticker at the time pictured an American flag and read, "Love it or leave it." Antiwar protests tested Americans' conception of the nature, purpose, and limits of free speech and free assembly.

By mid-1968, no key American policy-makers believed the war could be won. Despite this growing conviction, no consensus had emerged either among elite Washington insiders or among the American people on how to end American involvement. Over the next several years, as the war went on and on, Americans became ever more bitterly divided about the causes, the course, and the consequences of the Vietnam War.

NOTES

1. John Newman, "Kennedy's Plan for American Withdrawal," *Major Problems in the History of the Vietnam War*, Robert J. McMahon, ed. (Lexington, Mass.: D. C. Heath, 1995), 198.

2. Michael H. Hunt, *Lyndon Johnson's War* (New York: Hill and Wang, 1996), 79.

3. Farber, *The Age of Great Dreams*, 136.

4. "The Tonkin Gulf Resolution, 1964," McMahon, *Major Problems*, 210.

5. Philip Caputo, *Rumor of War* (New York: Ballantine, 1977), 89.

6. Paul Potter, "The Incredible War," in Breines and Bloom, *Takin' it to the Streets*, 218.

7. Potter, "The Incredible War," 218.

8. David Farber, *Chicago '68* (Chicago: University of Chicago Press, 1988), 69.

9. Farber, *The Age of Great Dreams*, 162.

10. "'Mired in Stalemate' 1968," McMahon, *Major Problems*, 529.

CHAPTER FIVE

Polarization

The year 1968 marked a turning point in American politics. Over 120 urban up-risings starkly dramatized the continuing discontent of African Americans, even as they embittered millions of whites, who demanded an end to unrest. Conservative politicians gained favor as they called for a restoration of law and order. The Vietnam War and the antiwar movement continued to polarize the nation and played a critical role in the nation's politics. The 1968 presidential victory of Richard Nixon marked an end to the liberalism of Kennedy and Johnson. During Nixon's first term, he brought the Vietnam War to a close, though he took four more years to do so. During those years, the American people became increasingly bitter and fragmented.

1968

By 1968, President Johnson felt besieged. Everywhere he went in public, protesters shouted, "Hey, hey, LBJ! How many kids did you kill today?" Johnson's increasingly unpopular Vietnam policies were also tearing apart his own Democratic Party. The Democrats' antiwar wing not only demanded a change in policy but also refused to support Johnson's bid for a second term in office.

Minnesota Senator Eugene McCarthy was the first challenger. Given little notice by national pundits, McCarthy shocked both Johnson and the political establishment by almost winning the first presidential primary in New Hampshire. His campaign attracted thousands of antiwar student volunteers, who went door to door to convince voters that McCarthy would "bring the boys home."

McCarthy's surprising success convinced New York Senator Robert Kennedy to run against Johnson on an antiwar platform as well. Between March and June 1968, either McCarthy or Kennedy won every presidential primary.

In response to the successful challenges of McCarthy and Kennedy—and even more so to his own declining health and the stress of leading the nation in an ever less popular war—Johnson chose not to run for re-election. On March 31, he announced that, instead of running again for the presidency, he would devote himself to negotiating a peace settlement in Vietnam.

Johnson threw his support not to Kennedy or McCarthy but to his vice president, Hubert Humphrey. Because in 1968 only a minority of convention delegates were selected through presidential primaries, while the majority of delegates were appointed by party leaders, Johnson's support meant that Humphrey would almost surely win the Democratic nomination.

During the presidential race, the country went through a series of horrifying shocks. In early April, Martin Luther King Jr. was in Memphis, Tennessee, to support a strike by poorly paid sanitation workers. While continuing to work for African-American civil rights, he was planning a major new organizing effort: a Poor People's Campaign, aimed at bringing economic justice to all impoverished Americans. His leadership in this nascent movement was, however, cut short. On April 3, he told a hushed audience, "Longevity has its place. But I'm not concerned about that now. I just want to do God's will. And He's allowed me to go up to the mountain! And I've looked over and I've seen the promised land! I may not get there with you, but I want you to know tonight that we as a people will get to the promised land."[1] The next day, he was assassinated by James Earl Ray, a white Southerner.

Even as much of the nation mourned the tragedy, riots broke out in the African-American sections of some 130 towns and cities. In Washington, D.C., enraged black arsonists torched dozens of buildings just blocks from the U.S. Capitol and Supreme Court. In Chicago, looters and arsonists destroyed the West Side commercial district of their own ghetto neighborhood. Nationally, some 46 people were killed, 41 of them African-American. Over 20,000, nearly all African-American, were arrested. To restore order, 130,000 fully armed soldiers and national guardsmen were deployed in American cities.

Senator Robert Kennedy was campaigning in Indianapolis when King was assassinated. Rejecting officials' advice that he cancel his scheduled speech to local African-American residents, Kennedy reached out across the racial divide. He drew on his own memories of grievous loss as he mourned King's martyrdom, quoting Aeschylus, the ancient Greek playwright: "Even in our sleep, pain which cannot forget falls drop by drop upon the heart, until in our own despair, against our will, comes wisdom through the awful grace of God."[2]

Two months later, moments after giving a victory speech celebrating his victory in the California primary, Kennedy was slain by a lone assassin. The nation, again, was stunned.

Then in August, Americans watched aghast as law and order broke down in Chicago at the Democratic National Convention. About 10,000 antiwar protesters had come to march and rally against Johnson's war policies. Refused permits to march on the convention site, the protesters were ordered by the Chicago police department to disperse. As order broke down, the police attacked the demonstrators. Horrified, they chanted, *"The whole world is watching!"* as police beat and clubbed hundreds of protesters, reporters and bystanders.

Television cameras broadcast the events across the nation. Despite the nearly one-sided violence, a majority of Americans believed that the police were right to attack the demonstrators. They believed that the riots, assassinations, and demonstrations all added up to an unacceptable and frightening level of disorder that must come to an end.

Two presidential candidates pledged to end that disorder. The first was Alabama Governor George Wallace, who ran for president as a right-wing independent. The second was former vice president Richard M. Nixon, the Republican nominee, who campaigned as a moderate conservative.

Wallace ran a fierce campaign. His national reputation was based on his pro-segregation, anti–civil rights record. While his somewhat veiled white-supremacy rhetoric was most successful in the Deep South, he also gained support among northern working-class whites, who feared that civil rights legislation might force them to compete for jobs with African Americans, while losing the power to keep them from moving into their own neighborhoods. Wallace also gained national support by ridiculing and attacking antiwar protesters and student radicals, as well as "pointy-headed" intellectuals and the mass media.

Nixon, too, tried to assuage the fears of the majority of Americans, who felt that forces of rebellion and chaos were tearing at the national fabric. While eschewing the racial rhetoric of Wallace, he had little good to say about the civil-rights struggle, as he promised to bring law and order to America. He vowed that his presidency would support "the nonshouters and the nondemonstrators, the millions who ask principally to go their own way in decency and dignity and to have their own rights accorded the same respect they accord the rights of others."[3] Seeking a middle ground on Vietnam, Nixon stated simply, if ambiguously, that he would end the war.

Democratic Party nominee Humphrey ran as a liberal. He insisted that Americans must embrace principles of "human equality and human opportunity."[4] He pledged to support the labor-union movement and to use government power to fight poverty and inequity. He tried to persuade Americans that he would not continue President Johnson's failed Vietnam policy. Humphrey, through a vigorous campaign, managed to make the election a close race.

Richard Nixon won the presidency by a narrow margin of just half a million votes. That number, however, belied the sea change that had happened in American politics. Nixon probably would have won by a substantial majority if not for George Wallace's electoral success. Wallace won five Southern states—Alabama, Arkansas, Georgia, Louisiana, and Mississippi—and 13.5 percent of the total popular vote. The two conservative candidates combined won almost 57 percent of the vote, while the liberal Humphrey received just under 43 percent, or almost 12,000,000 fewer votes than the liberal Johnson had won against the conservative Goldwater in 1964. The civil rights protests and subsequent equal-rights and antipoverty legislation, along with antiwar protests, urban riots, and a gut-level sense that the country's moral compass was spinning too fast and too far in a new direction, had moved substantial numbers of voters to the right.

RACIAL MILITANCY

The urban uprisings that followed the assassination of Martin Luther King were far from the first race riots in the 1960s. Every summer from 1965 through 1968 had seen acts of violent, collective unrest in America's segregated African-American ghettoes. These domestic "rebellions," combined with the increasing popularity of "Black Power" politics among young African Americans, contributed to an increasingly angry debate about the future of race relations in the United States.

The 1968 urban riots were the most violent and widespread of the 1960s. However, the first major Sixties-era riot occurred in 1965, in the Watts section of Los Angeles. Most Americans were shocked by the event, which occurred just days after President Johnson had signed the 1965 Voting Rights Act. This first Sixties-era violent uprising occurred in response to a case of perceived police brutality against a young black man. Police brutality, however, was by no means the only cause of the urban riots.

In July 1967, President Johnson created the National Advisory Commission on Civil Disorders, chaired by Illinois Governor Otto Kerner, to explain why African-American communities in Detroit, Newark, and several other cities had exploded that summer into violence. In early 1968, the blue-ribbon panel

issued a stark statement: "What white Americans have never fully understood—but what the Negro can never forget—is that white society is deeply
implicated in the ghetto. White institutions created it, white institutions
maintain it, and white society condones it."[5] While many whites were infuriated by the claim that white society bore responsibility for the violence that
had erupted in America's black ghetto neighborhoods, many African Americans felt that the report, if anything, softpedaled the harsh truths of racism.

Many northern African Americans felt that the civil rights legislation of the
mid-1960s did not address the racist practices that affected their lives. They argued that rigid housing segregation, underfunded inner-city schools, rampant
job discrimination, poor transportation, discriminatory banking, credit, and
mortgage practices, and unequal protection before the law locked millions of
African Americans into lives of poverty and despair. These, they felt, were the
causes of the frustration that had resulted in the riots.

While the civil rights movement nonviolently and patiently worked to end
what the Kerner Commission had described as "two societies, one black, one
white—separate and unequal,"[6] some African Americans had begun to turn
in another direction.

Malcolm X, in the early 1960s, had been among the first African-American
leaders to reject the nonviolent, integrationist approach of the civil rights
movement. While he was a member of the Nation of Islam, an African-
American religious denomination created during the 1930s by Elijah Muhammad, Malcolm insisted that white racism was intractable, and that whites
were "devils" who would never allow blacks equal rights. "Our enemy is the
white man," he argued. Blacks should instead create a separate nation, "a land
of our own, where we can reform ourselves, lift up our moral standards, and
try to be godly."[7]

Malcolm's black nationalism begun to gain favor with many African-
American activists in the latter half of the 1960s. In the Deep South, white violence and extreme black poverty caused some of the civil rights movement's
most stalwart organizers to reconsider their integrationist, nonviolent approach. And in the North, ghetto riots and the slow pace of reform led many
other black activists to consider the more confrontational, black-nationalist
approach advocated by Malcolm X.

In 1966, SNCC leader Stokely Carmichael repudiated nonviolence. Before a large crowd in Greenwood, Mississippi, he proclaimed: "The only way
we gonna stop them white men from whuppin' us is to take over. We've been
saying *freedom* for six years—and we ain't got nothin'. What we gonna start
saying now is 'Black Power!'"[8]

The next year, in Cambridge, Maryland, SNCC chairman H. Rap Brown proclaimed: "I mean don't be trying to love that honkey to death. Shoot him to death. Shoot him to death, brother, cause that's what he's out to do to you."[9]

Martin Luther King and the leadership of the NAACP passionately opposed this violent turn. They argued that the "Black Power" slogan and the turn to violence was morally wrong, drove away white support, and led to no practical gains. Many of the younger organizers and hundreds of thousands of African Americans, however, thrilled to the angry antiwhite rhetoric of Black Power and to the more confrontational style of politics it spawned.

Some black militants by 1968 insisted that only an armed revolution would bring social justice to African Americans. The Black Panther Party for Self-Defense, led by Huey Newton, was the best known of the late-1960s revolutionary organizations. The Black Panthers took special aim at the largely white police forces that patrolled African-American urban neighborhoods. They called for armed resistance to police brutality, often chanting: "Off the Pigs!" Between 1967 and 1969, nine policemen were killed and 56 were wounded in shoot-outs with the Panthers. The police, in turn, killed ten Panthers and wounded dozens more, sometimes in execution-style hits.

Most Black Power advocates, while insisting on the need for radical change, pursued less incendiary goals. Black college students demanded Black Studies programs, the teaching of African-American history and literature, higher quotas of black faculty and students, and black housing or student centers. More moderate black activists adapted calls for Black Power to more traditional political goals, urging black voters in inner-city neighborhoods to register to vote and to support black candidates.

This kind of moderate Black Power activism resulted in the election of African American mayors in Cleveland, Ohio; Newark, New Jersey; and Gary, Indiana. In addition, activists reinvigorated a black cultural nationalism by urging African Americans to celebrate their African heritage—to take pride in themselves by not imitating white hair styles but instead growing "Afros," and proclaiming: "Black is beautiful."

A majority of whites failed to take into account the multiple meanings and actions that fit uneasily under the rubric of "Black Power." As moderate civil rights activists feared, most whites were infuriated by Black Power advocates, lumping all African-American activists together and tending to tar much of the African-American movement for social justice with the brush of the most incendiary and violent factions. Furthermore, most Americans in the late 1960s did not view the militant turn by some African-American activists as an isolated event. Rather, they perceived the Black Power movement—and the uprisings in America's black ghettoes—as part of a major ongoing rupture in American politics and culture.

GROWING POLARIZATION AND RADICALIZATION

Overlapping radical movements were also gaining strength among young, primarily middle-class white Americans. By the late 1960s, a small faction of the antiwar movement, composed largely of New Left student radicals, had become increasingly confrontational and sometimes violent in its protests against American involvement in Vietnam. Some of the most radical antiwar militants began to openly support the North Vietnamese and Viet Cong. Like the Black Power militants, some of these white radicals advocated a "revolution" and praised the communist regimes in Cuba, China, and North Korea.

The best known of these radical groups was the Weathermen, which emerged in 1969 out of the original New Left organization Students for a Democratic Society, or SDS. The Weathermen called themselves revolutionary communists and hoped, somehow, to launch a guerrilla war against the American government. On October 8, 1969, they acted out "The Days of Rage" in Chicago, fighting the police as they broke windows, smashed cars, and spray-painted radical slogans. On March 6, 1970, three Weathermen were killed when a primitive antipersonnel bomb they were making blew up in a New York City townhouse. The Weathermen, the self-proclaimed "vanguard of the revolution," had moved far away from their roots in a movement dedicated to creating "participatory democracy."

Other members of the antiwar movement also felt themselves pushed to more extreme measures by the continuing war in Vietnam. After President Richard Nixon admitted to the American people on April 30, 1970 that he had expanded the war into Cambodia, militant demonstrations broke out on university campuses around the country. While most of the 100 or so student strikes on university campuses remained relatively peaceful, some did not. At the University of Kansas the student union was burned down. At Kent State, in Ohio, the ROTC building was set afire. In response to that blaze the Ohio governor sent in the National Guard. When students taunted the guardsmen and threw rocks at them, the young soldiers opened fire, killing four people and wounding nine others.

In reaction against the Kent State shootings, on top of the expanding war in Cambodia, over 1,200 colleges and universities erupted into protest, some

30 ROTC buildings were burned or bombed, and National Guard troops were called onto university campuses in 16 states.

Three-quarters of Americans surveyed shortly after the Kent State shootings and subsequent protests said that it was wrong to protest against the government. To put a stop to antiwar protests, a majority of Americans believed, basic freedoms guaranteed by the Bill of Rights should be restricted. In late May, 60,000 New Yorkers, most of them members of building and trade unions, waving hardhats and American flags, rallied at City Hall in support of Nixon's policy in Vietnam. Around the country, war supporters sported American-flag lapel pins and plastered "America—love it or leave it!" bumper stickers on their cars. The war continued to rend the country.

RICHARD NIXON'S WAR IN VIETNAM

During these years of turmoil, President Nixon slowly withdrew American troops from Vietnam. In his inaugural address, Nixon had told the American people, "We are caught in war, wanting peace."[10] Although American involvement in Vietnam would continue throughout Nixon's first term, the president was able to report, just prior to the 1972 election, that "peace is at hand." Nixon's war in Vietnam, however, took an immense toll on the American people, most especially those Americans engaged in fighting it.

Nixon's core strategy was the "Vietnamization" of the war. Soon after taking office in 1969, the president began steadily to reduce the numbers of American ground troops fighting in Vietnam. By the end of 1971 Nixon had reduced troop strength from over half a million to just 139,000. At the same time, Nixon escalated the air war and began turning over billions of dollars in military equipment to the South Vietnamese.

Nixon's first major move, taken in March 1969, was to begin bombing Vietnamese-communist strongholds in neighboring Cambodia—a tactic kept secret from the American people. In 1970, American planes began bombing North Vietnam. And in 1972, after the North Vietnamese began a large-scale invasion of the South, Nixon ordered a series of bombing runs which culminated in raids in which 36,000 tons of bombs falling on Hanoi and the port city of Haiphong. Overall, the United States military would drop about three times the tonnage of bombs during the Vietnam War as it had during all of World War II.

Nixon's war had little strategic success. His bombing campaign in Cambodia, which was followed up in April 1970 by a full-scale invasion by American and South Vietnamese troops, did badly hurt the opposing forces, depriving them of a sanctuary critical to their attacks on the South. But the political cost of expanding the war to another country was a massive increase in militant numbers to the antiwar movement, increased Congressional opposition to the war, and even the resignation of several key Nixon officials. And, while the bombing campaigns inflicted hundreds of thousands of casualties on the Viet Cong and North Vietnamese, it did not break their will to fight on.

AMERICA'S FIGHTING MEN

While the North Vietnamese and Viet Cong soldiered on, American fighting men increasingly lost confidence in the rationale for the war. As increasing numbers of American ground troops were withdrawn, many of those who remained "in country" grew embittered. They knew better than anyone that the war was not being won. Nobody wanted to be the last soldier to die fighting a losing battle for what many GIs saw as the cynical goal of "peace with honor."

As a result, many soldiers turned against the war. Desertion rates soared, as did "combat refusals." Officers who were seen as too "gung-ho" were threatened by their own men and, in several hundred cases, "fragged" (deliberately killed or wounded). By 1972, over 200 antiwar newspapers were being published by GIs. About 30,000 men who were back from the fighting and out of the service joined the Vietnam Veterans Against the War. On April 23, 1971, the war still raging, some 800 of these antiwar vets gathered in Washington, D.C., outside the Capitol. And then one by one, some on crutches, some in wheelchairs, they took off their medals and threw them away. Jack Smith, the first man in the long line of veterans, stated: "We now strip ourselves of the medals of courage and heroism. . . . We cast them away as symbols of shame, dishonor, and inhumanity."[11]

Many of the men and women who served in Vietnam were saddened and angered by how they were treated when they came home. Some were scorned by antiwar activists. But far more felt betrayed by those who simply ignored them. Army nurse Jacqueline Rhoades recollects: "There was no welcome home, not even from the army people who processed your papers. . . . My parents were proud of me, of course. But other civilians? 'Oh, you were in Vietnam? . . . . That's nice.' And then they'd go on talking about something else."[12]

In the early 1970s, a large majority of Americans just wanted the war to go away. Few Americans were prepared to deal with the men and women who had sacrificed so much in a losing effort. Caught in a brutal war that was not of their own making, Americans who served in Vietnam paid dearly for their nation's longest war.

ENDING THE WAR

The Vietnam War officially ended on January 27, 1973. In return for an exchange of all prisoners of war, a cease-fire, and vague language stating that elections would determine the fate of South Vietnam, the United States agreed to withdraw all troops within 60 days. While the American armed forces had not been beaten on the field of battle, Nixon and the American people had had enough of the war. The president claimed he had attained "peace with honor," but the treaty he signed contained almost no provision that could not have been produced four years earlier when he first took office. On April 30, 1975, the South Vietnamese government was defeated, and Vietnam was unified under communist rule.

All told, over 58,000 Americans died in Vietnam. At least 1.5 million Vietnamese were killed in fighting the French, the Americans, and each other.

NOTES

1. Harvard Sitkoff, *The Struggle for Black Equality 1954–1980* (New York: Hill and Wang, 1981), 220–221.

2. Lewis Chester, Godfrey Hodgson, and Bruce Page, *An American Melodrama: The Presidential Campaign of 1968* (New York: Viking, 1969), 18.

3. Farber, *The Age of Great Dreams*, 225.

4. Farber, *The Age of Great Dreams*, 226.

5. *Report of the National Advisory Commission on Civil Disorders* (New York: Ballantine, 1968), 2.

6. *Report*, 1

7. Weisbrot, *Freedom Bound*, 173.

8. William L. Van Deburg, *New Day in Babylon: The Black Power Movement and American Culture, 1965–1975* (Chicago: University of Chicago Press, 1992), 32.

9. Sitkoff, *The Struggle for Black Equality*, 217.

10. Richard Nixon, Inaugural Address, January 20, 1969, *Inaugural Addresses of the Presidents of the United States*, 276.

11. Andrew E. Hunt, *The Turning: A History of the Vietnam Veterans Against the War* (New York: New York University Press, 1999), 113.

12. James W. Mooney and Thomas R. West, eds., *Vietnam: A History and Anthology* (St. James, N.Y.: Brandywine Press, 1994), 230.

CHAPTER SIX

Sixties Culture

In the Sixties era, Americans challenged cultural boundaries as they sought to build better lives amid general economic prosperity. Young people reaped the whirlwind of material affluence and led society into new consumer fads and a more forthrightly hedonistic lifestyle. Others found America's material rewards spiritually insubstantial and sought to build a counterculture based on alternative values. Black Power advocates looked on mainstream culture with disdain. They worked to sustain and to foster their own cultural heritage.

THE GOOD LIFE

During the Sixties era, racial justice and the Vietnam War were not the only sources of conflict in American society. People from all walks of life often heatedly debated how to lead a good life amid national prosperity. While the majority celebrated the material abundance that prosperity made possible, some young people scorned what they regarded as the soulless materialism of America's consumer society. As one cultural radical commented: "Why should we work 12 or 16 hours a day now when we don't have to? For a color TV? For wall-to-wall carpeting? An automatic ice-cube maker?"[1]

It was not just the young rebels who questioned the value of rampant materialism. In a speech given in May 1964 at the University of Michigan, President Lyndon Johnson, too, asked "whether we have the wisdom to use . . . [our] wealth to enrich and elevate our national life, and to advance the equality of our American civilization." Americans, he insisted, must "prove that our material progress is only the foundation on which we will build a richer life in mind and spirit."[2]

While politicians, cultural rebels, and many others questioned the societal meaning of material abundance, most middle-class people simply reveled in the opportunities consumer capitalism provided them. Every single month between 1961 and 1969, the United States economy continued to grow. It was the longest period of continuous economic growth in American history, only exceeded by the expansion that began later in 1991.

Unemployment hovered around 4 percent for much of the decade. Per capita income soared while the official poverty rate dropped from more than 22 percent of Americans in 1960 to just 12 percent by 1969. Millions more had extra money in their pockets, and tens of millions had disposable incomes that were unimaginable during the catastrophic Great Depression of the 1930s.

As a result of this increasingly widespread affluence, people found new opportunities to have more fun. Traditional activities like bowling, hunting, fishing, and boating experienced boom times as millions more people had both the money and time enough away from work to enjoy leisure activities. More people than ever bought tickets to professional sporting events; baseball, football and basketball teams expanded throughout the nation, moving south and west, with new franchises and new stadiums. Between 1960 and 1970, attendance at major-league baseball games alone grew by over ten million people.

Foreign travel, once the nearly exclusive preserve of the wealthy, became a normal rite of passage for middle-class Americans. Passport applications rose from a mere 300,000 in 1950 to 2,219,000 in 1970. Domestically, too, Americans were vacationing as never before, flying in new jet-propelled passenger liners like the Boeing 747 (introduced in 1969), which could seat 374 passengers; or they were driving their new cars on the recently built interstate highway system.

American prosperity seemed to be symbolized by Americans' love affair with the automobile. Whereas in the late 1940s a majority of working-class Americans did not own one car, 29.3 percent of American families had two or more cars by the end of the 1960s—an increase of more than 50 percent in a single decade.

Emblematic of Sixties-era vehicles were a series of so-called "muscle cars," which were sold overwhelmingly to young men: the Pontiac GTO, the Plymouth Road Runner, the Mercury Cougar Eliminator, and most successful of all, the Ford Mustang. These vehicles could be bought with huge engines (the Road Runner could handle a 426-cubic-inch engine) that would allow their drivers to hurtle down American highways with rocket-like speed. Even as some people, most famously consumer advocate Ralph Nader in 1965, began to voice doubts about the safety, reliability, and social costs (such as pollution) of American automobiles, throughout the 1960s a majority of Americans took special pride in their stylish and powerful automobiles.

Just as auto ownership had become an American birthright in the 1960s, television had become Americans' favorite form of entertainment. Commercial television broadcasting had begun only in 1947; by 1970, though, 96 percent of American families had at least one TV set in their homes. For most of the 1960s, the most popular TV shows revealed a nostalgia for a simpler, rural or small-town way of life. Favorites like *The Andy Griffith Show*, *Gomer Pyle*, and *The Beverly Hillbillies* showed good-hearted country folk upholding traditional values like neighborliness and love of family, even as they were sometimes gently made objects of fun for their slow-mindedness and lack of familiarity with the rapidly changing world around them.

Even if most popular TV shows eschewed the political controversies of the 1960s, throughout the era America's most popular mass medium increasingly began to reflect the nation's concerns. In 1965, television history was made when white actor Robert Culp and black actor Bill Cosby costarred as American intelligence agents in the hit action series *I Spy*. Never before had television portrayed a white man and a black man as friends and as equals. That Cosby played the smart partner and Culp the brawnier partner—going against contemporary stereotypes—made the show seem even more daring.

By the late 1960s a few popular TV shows began to grapple with the nation's cultural and political divisions. In February 1967 *The Smothers Brothers Comedy Hour* premiered on CBS. It regularly featured humorous but pointed political commentary, and it contested network censorship rules. The Smothers Brothers invited folksinger Pete Seeger to appear on their show, ignoring the TV taboo against blacklisted performers accused in the 1950s of being communists. At first, CBS censored Seeger, refusing to broadcast his performance of the anti–Vietnam War song "Waist Deep in the Big Muddy." Under pressure from the Smothers Brothers and their fans, CBS relented, and the performance was aired amid great controversy.

In 1969, however, CBS executives decided the Smothers Brothers' political brand of humor was too controversial and canceled the show.

A lighter take on the nation's controversies, *Rowan and Martin's Laugh-In*, first aired in January 1968. Marijuana jokes, comedy sketches about the sexual revolution ("Sock it to me!"), and a general spirit of irreverence about society's sacred cows animated the show, which had a huge appeal for youthful audiences.

YOUTH CULTURE

The combined social forces of economic prosperity and political controversy were most visibly reflected by the fads, consumer choices, and serious commitments of America's burgeoning population of young people. The "Baby Boomers," defined by demographers as those born between 1946 and 1964, and numbering some 76 million people, rolled through America with the force of a cultural tidal wave, leaving a changed society in their wake.

By the late 1950s, the buying power of America's post–World War II baby boom was already being reckoned with by the business community. *Life* magazine quantified the matter in a sensational feature story titled, "A Young $10 Billion Power: The US Teen-Age Consumer Has Become a Major Factor in the Nation's Economy."[3] As this huge generation of young people, born amid prosperity and a general optimism about the nation's future, moved through American society, their desires shaped both the marketplace of goods and services and their own new lifestyles.

In the 1960s, young people made popular music—above all rock 'n' roll— the center of their cultural universe. Already by the Fifties (and some historians would point back to the "bobby soxer" music crazes of the Forties, which included Frank Sinatra) young people had enough buying power to make their favorite music stars into national celebrities.

Most famously, Elvis Presley, with his gyrating hips, sneering lips, and pounding vocals had became a teen idol in the 1950s. Blending African-American rhythm 'n' blues, white-Southern country and western, gospel music, and his own unique style, Presley helped to create the rock 'n' roll sound. Savaged by most older listeners as a "sexhibitionist" and hated by many racists for his "mongrel" music, Presley's record sales demonstrated that young people had the money to make their tastes count at the cash register.

By the early 1960s, white teenagers had fallen into a decade-long love affair with a very different kind of rock music. In February 1964 the number-one hit song in the United States was "I Want to Hold Your Hand," by a British group called the Beatles. Until they announced their break-up in 1970, the Beatles were the most popular music group in the United States, selling records almost exclusively to young people. Each of the record albums they released over the course of the Sixties managed simultaneously to mirror and to shape the cutting edge of youth culture, from the sunny, rebellious antics of *Meet the Beatles* in 1964 to the drug-influenced, mystical, and antiestablishment *Sergeant Pepper's Lonely Hearts Club Band* in 1967 to the elegiac uncertainties of *Let It Be* in 1970.

Young people cherished the Beatles not only because they were brilliant pop musicians but because their confident, rebellious, adventurous style perfectly expressed the spirit of their times. Almost completely apolitical (though at the end of the decade John Lennon did speak out against the Vietnam

War), the Beatles offered a youthful insouciance that entertained and inspired their fans. When John Lennon announced in 1966 that the Beatles were more popular than Jesus, he appalled most adults, but Beatles fans heard in his words an acknowledgment of their own power to bend American culture to their desires and aspirations.

By the early 1970s, rock music accounted for about 80 percent of all record sales. Youths in the Sixties—at a time when society was wracked by conflict over civil rights and, increasingly, the Vietnam War—used rock music as a proud emblem of their rebellion against the more staid and conservative aspects of the society they were poised to inherit. For most of these young people, that rebellion was little more than a demand that their consumer-lifestyle choices—"mod," and then later "hippie"-style clothes, scruffier hairdos, and loud, pulsating music—be accorded respect from their elders. They wanted to be able "to do their own thing." For some young people, however, cultural rebellion became a more overtly political and radical challenge to societal norms.

COUNTERCULTURE

For most Americans in the Sixties, the term "counterculture" referred to the lifestyle of those whom they generally called "hippies." At least some of these hippies, also known as "freaks" and "longhairs," sought to create an alternative way of life that overlapped with the more general youth culture but which went much further in its alienation from middle-class consumer society. These young men and women struggled to set up their own economic, cultural, and even political structures. Many hoped to become relatively independent from mainstream America.

The most visible manifestations of the counterculture took shape by the mid-1960s in numerous cities and towns around the country. Hippie districts—like the Haight-Ashbury in San Francisco, Old Town in Chicago, the Lower East Side in New York City, and Dinkytown in Minneapolis—began to flower. In these places young people ranging in age from their late teens to their late twenties—many of them runaways—began to congregate. They set up "crash pads," "communal" houses, food co-ops, and an array of restaurants, rock clubs, bookstores, and "head shops." The most successful among them built semi-separate urban enclaves in which they could pursue an alternative way of life.

These lifestyle experiments challenged most Americans' values. In San

Francisco, the Diggers, an edgy, loosely affiliated group of men and women, scorned consumer society and attempted to create a subculture independent of the monetary economy. They believed that everything should be "free," with goods and services bartered, exchanged, or simply given away. In 1967 and 1968, they and their allies set up a free-food giveaway in Golden Gate Park, and also established a free store, a free transportation network, free medical care, and free concerts featuring rock groups like the Grateful Dead. They, and many others like them around the country, set up rural communes and a variety of co-ops that fostered a collective, nonmaterialistic way of life.

Rejecting traditional standards of behavior and seeking new experiences, the young people of the counterculture openly embraced drug use and often practiced a far more open and "liberated" sexuality than the norm. They used marijuana and hallucinogenics such as LSD and peyote. Cheered on by visionaries as diverse as ex-Harvard professor and "acid guru" Timothy Leary, the acclaimed writer Ken Kesey, and the Beat poet Allen Ginsberg, members of the counterculture sought to establish new lifestyles in which cooperation replaced competition and in which Eastern spiritual practices often replaced traditional Christianity.

Most older Americans, and many young people as well, looked with horror at the drug-using, anti-materialist, sexually promiscuous counterculture that was so visibly springing up across the country by the late 1960s. Some young women involved in the counterculture also began to find fault with this alternative way of life. Too often they found themselves being sexually exploited, finding they were expected by their male counterparts to do all the traditional "women's work" such as housekeeping, cooking, and child care.

By 1970, almost all of the countercultural urban enclaves had fallen apart. Too many criminals (most famously, the vicious Charles Manson, who would later be jailed as the ringleader of a mass-murder crime spree) and too many emotionally disturbed young people had been drawn to hippie communities by the promise of sex, drugs, and an "anything goes" atmosphere.

The counterculture did not completely disappear, however, as many seekers of an alternative way of life moved into rural parts of America in a "back-to-the-land movement."

Even as the counterculture retreated, much of its energy and style was repackaged by clothing manufacturers and the entertainment industry. Young people who had little interest in directly challenging social norms but who wished to partake of the rebellious and hedonistic impulses of the counterculture eagerly consumed the countercultural lifestyle, buying psychedelic rock albums and "groovy" clothes.

BLACK CULTURE

The hippies were not the only alternative cultural movement in the United States in the 1960s. While their actions were less publicized, many African Americans also deliberately turned away from so-called mainstream culture. They rejected "white" society and built on generations of ancestral struggle to create a black cultural-nationalism.

Evoking an African-American worldview, this cultural struggle was a key component of the Black Power movement. While aspects of this movement, like that of the primarily white counterculture, would be co-opted by mainstream America, the black nationalists of the 1960s offered African Americans a distinctly alternative set of cultural expressions and practices.

The purpose and power of the African-American cultural movement was best articulated and promoted by Malcolm X, who was, until shortly before his assassination in 1965, a leader of the Nation of Islam (popularly known as the Black Muslims). Speaking before a large crowd in Harlem in 1964, he explained: "We must recapture our heritage and our identity if we are ever to liberate ourselves from the bonds of white supremacy. We must launch a cultural revolution to *unbrainwash* an entire people."[4]

Malcolm X and other black nationalists believed that African Americans needed to take pride in their African heritage, hold up their own standards of beauty and culture, and create black-controlled and community-based institutions. Through these actions, African Americans could gain greater control over their individual lives and their communities. Black cultural nationalism was a pointedly political ideology.

In practice, black cultural nationalism took multiple forms. Most visibly, African Americans in the 1960s began to reject white standards of appearance. Prior to the mid-1960s, many black men and women used harsh chemicals to straighten their hair so that it would look like white people's hair. And many within the African-American community placed a premium on having light skin and Euro-American features. In 1966, Black Power leader Stokely Carmichael expressed the changing attitude held by an increasing number of young African Americans: "We have to stop being ashamed of being black. A broad nose, a thick lip and nappy hair is us, and we are going to call that beautiful whether they like it or not. We are not going to fry our hair anymore."[5]

By the late 1960s, as black men and women let their hair grow naturally into "Afros" and donned dashikis and other African-inspired clothing, the phrase "Black is Beautiful" reverberated throughout the United States.

Black cultural nationalists tried, too, to build alternative institutions and cultural practices that would promote what they called an African-American worldview. As one radical activist stated: "To leave the education of black children in the hands of the people who are white and who are racists is tantamount to suicide."[6]

Some cultural nationalists believed that it was necessary to create an entirely new school curriculum that featured black achievements and prepared African-American young people to challenge the political and economic system that had made them second-class citizens from birth. Maulana Ron Karenga, a Los Angles–based activist, invented a new African-inspired set of beliefs, the *Nguzu Saba*, and a new holiday, *Kwanzaa*, to help African Americans create a cultural alternative to mainstream white society.

Insistently political, black cultural nationalism was popular among African Americans of all ages, particularly the young. By the early 1970s, most young African Americans had let their hair grow naturally, spoke proudly of black "Soul," and demanded more respect for their culture in the wider society.

This movement directly affected white Americans as well. African Americans, with support from some whites, successfully pressed for the inclusion of black history and African-American literature into school curriculums, at all levels and in all districts. Over time, many Americans would come to accept the idea of multiculturalism, in which it is assumed that the heritages and traditions of all racial and ethnic groups in the United States should be shown equal respect. While some of the political rage that animated Black Power leaders like Malcolm X and Stokely Carmichael in the mid-1960s was dissipated by the mid-1970s, the black cultural-nationalist movement did not end with the Sixties.

CONCLUSION

Sixties culture took many forms. Much divided the countercultural hippies, black cultural nationalists, and the exuberant consumers of Detroit's muscle cars. Yet, in some ways, these very different cultural expressions were linked. All expressed a growing acceptance of cultural pluralism in the United States. To some extent, this cultural pluralism was a natural outgrowth of America's expanding consumer marketplace, in which people—at least those with disposable income—were free to purchase an extraordinary array of goods and services that were expressive of whatever lifestyle they wished to pursue.

In addition, Americans' turn toward greater cultural diversity and social experimentation was a part of a larger societal trend. More and more Americans accepted the idea that personal expression and individual freedom were a critical aspect of the American way of life. While this notion sounds like it could be a "hippie" credo, it was very much at the core of mainstream culture as well.

The Supreme Court, in a series of rulings in the late 1960s and early 1970s, gave Constitutional protection to a far more open society. In a 1971 ruling, *Cohen v. California*, the Court struck down most government obscenity laws, ruling: "One man's vulgarity is another's lyric," and that since the government "cannot make principled decisions in this area," state authorities should leave "matters of taste and style largely to the individual."[7]

The Sixties were a time of tremendous consumer power, racial unrest, civil disorder, and cultural rebellion. All these forces combined to create a far more open, pluralistic, individualistic, and chaotic culture, the effects of which Americans are still confronting.

NOTES

1. Terry Anderson, *The Sixties* (New York: Longman, 1999), 140.

2. Lyndon Johnson, "Remarks at the University of Michigan," May 22, 1964, in Schulman, *Lyndon B. Johnson and American Liberalism*, 174, 177.

3. The article is reprinted, under the title "*Life* Magazine Identifies the New Teen-Age Market, 1959," in Griffith, *Major Problems in American History Since 1945*, 203.

4. Van Deburg, *New Day in Babylon*, 5.

5. Van Deburg, *New Day in Babylon*, 201.

6. Van Deburg, *New Day in Babylon*, 124.

7. Ken Cmiel, "The Politics of Civility," in David Farber, ed., *The Sixties* (Chapel Hill: University of North Carolina Press, 1994), 279.

CHAPTER SEVEN

New Directions

This chapter summarizes the last years of the Nixon presidency, including the end of the Vietnam War and the Watergate debacle. It also explores the rise of new social-change movements at the end of the Sixties era.

THE NIXON RECORD

Despite the cultural and political turmoil at home, President Richard Nixon put his greatest energies into American foreign relations. For most of his first term, the focus was on Vietnam. Even before the war ended, however, the president and his national security advisor, Henry Kissinger, a crafty practitioner of *realpolitik*, had begun working on a fundamental reshaping of international relations.

By July 1971, Nixon surprised much of the world by announcing that the United States was opening up diplomatic relations with the People's Republic of China. (The United States had refused to recognize the Chinese government since the 1949 communist takeover). Pragmatically, Nixon believed that better relations with China would enable the United States to pressure its primary cold-war communist enemy, the Soviet Union, and help to stabilize Asia in the wake of the Vietnam debacle.

As planned, Nixon used his opening to China to pressure the Soviet Union. In a superpower summit meeting in Moscow, he told the stolid Soviet Premier Leonid Brezhnev, "I have the reputation of being a hard-line, anti-Communist."[1] But, he continued, the time had come for cooperation. Nixon preached a doctrine of détente: "an easing of strained relations."

Nixon proceeded to work out new trade arrangements, a commitment to a joint space mission, and the Strategic Arms Limitations Talks (leading to agreements known as *SALT-I*), which slowed the nuclear arms race and limited the deployment of antiballistic missiles (ABMs). Nixon had succeeded in reducing the level of hostility between the world's two military superpowers.

Nixon's domestic record offered few such successes. Uninterested in most domestic policy, Nixon worked the "hot button" issues for political advantage. Nixon's political priority was to convert white southerners, in general, as well as white northern working-class voters to the Republican Party. To win their support, Nixon launched a highly vocal attack on school busing as a means of integrating public schools, and promised to reign in the Supreme Court's aggressive efforts to desegregate the nation. While never pandering to outright racists, Nixon hoped to use racially divisive issues to win millions of white voters over to the Republican ranks in the 1972 election.

Nixon's vice president, Spiro T. Agnew, launched even more incendiary attacks. At President Nixon's behest, Agnew lashed out at the mass media, dismissing them as "nattering nabobs of negativism."[2] He lambasted antiwar protesters as traitorous dupes led by "avowed anarchists and communists who detest everything about this country."[3] In 1968, Nixon had run for the presidency promising to bring the nation together. Two years later, his vice president raged: "If in challenging, we polarize the American people, I say it is time for a positive polarization. . . . It is time to rip away the rhetoric and to divide on authentic lines."[4]

Nixon understood that the turmoil of the 1960s and early 1970s had shattered old political loyalties, and he meant to recast the identity of the Republican Party. The Republican Party, he believed, should be perceived not just as the champion of businessmen and farmers but also the voice of what he dubbed "the silent majority." Nixon declared: "All over this country today, we see a rising tide of terrorism, of crime, and on the campuses . . . we have seen those who . . . engage in violence. . . . It's time to draw the line and say we're not going to stand for that! . . . It's time for the great silent majority of Americans to stand up and be counted."[5]

The Democratic Party in 1972 was moving in a very different direction. Dozens of leading Democratic senators and congressman had embraced the antiwar movement, and thousands of antiwar activists had made common cause with the Democrats in hopes of nominating a strong antiwar presidential candidate. South Dakota Senator George McGovern, with activists' strong support, succeeded in winning the Democratic Party's presidential nomination.

On the campaign trail, McGovern attacked Nixon's Vietnam policy. He also argued for a renewed government effort to fight poverty and racism. Nixon, in turn, argued that in Vietnam he was producing "peace with honor, not peace with surrender." He promised to strengthen the American military and suggested that his opponent would leave America weak. While McGovern embraced the social-change movements of the 1960s, Nixon denounced protesters of all kinds and insisted that he would bring law and order to America's streets.

On election day, Americans voted overwhelmingly for Nixon. He won 60.7 percent of the popular vote and carried every state except Massachusetts. Most Americans had had enough of protest, criticism, and social change. They wanted what Nixon promised: domestic tranquility.

WATERGATE

Despite his popular support, throughout his presidency Nixon believed himself to be surrounded by enemies. He felt besieged by the antiwar movement, by a Democratic Congress, a liberal federal bureaucracy, and a hostile mass media. To counter these "enemies," Nixon created his own secret team of loyalists. The activities of these underlings, when discovered, led Nixon to a series of illegal acts that culminated with his resignation from the presidency.

The first major episode in what came to be called the Watergate scandals occurred in July 1971. At Nixon's orders, White House aides had formed a secret group, called the Plumbers, to plug all leaks of secret information from the executive branch.

The Plumbers' first target was Daniel Ellsberg. A former Pentagon consultant, Ellsberg had inspired Nixon's wrath by leaking a secret government history of the Vietnam War, dubbed "The Pentagon Papers," to the *New York Times*. These documents revealed that the U.S. government had continuously misled Congress and the American people about the course of the war. Nixon had tried to stop the Pentagon Papers from being published, but the Supreme Court had ruled in favor of the *Times*. In September 1971, in hopes of destroying Ellsberg's credibility, the Plumbers broke into his psychiatrist's office, looking for embarrassing personal records.

While little came of this break-in, the Plumbers and other covert operatives were off and running. Phones were bugged throughout the White House, and government resources were used to investigate members of the press and other White House "enemies." During the 1972 election campaign, they branched out and began a series of "dirty tricks" against the Democrats. On June 17, 1972 the Plumbers, now working directly with Nixon's Committee to Re-Elect the President (CREEP), sent a team to the Watergate apartment and office complex to "bug" the Democratic National Committee offices. They got caught by the Washington, D.C., police.

At this point, Nixon made a fateful decision. He chose to conceal his re-election team's connection to the break-ins. He ordered the CIA to inform the FBI that the Watergate break-in was done for national security purposes, and on those grounds to stop their investigation. Nixon also approved "hush money" for the Watergate burglars to stop them from informing on their CREEP connections. Nixon had committed a felony: he had obstructed justice.

With the FBI stopped in its tracks, at first the only serious investigation of the break-in was done by two young, then relatively unknown reporters for the *Washington Post*, Carl Bernstein and Bob Woodward. Their history-making series of stories became a model for a generation of journalists and greatly contributed to the rise of a far more skeptical and hard-hitting style of investigative reporting.

The Watergate cover-up further unraveled under the scrutiny of both the courts and Congress. The federal judge in charge of the Watergate burglars' trial, John Sirica, informed the defendants that he would give them long prison terms unless they cooperated with the authorities. Just before sentencing was to take place, the head of the burglary team confessed that perjury had been committed at the trial and that a cover-up was in effect.

From May to August 1973, a special Senate Watergate Committee held televised hearings. On July 13, a former White House aide told the committee that Richard Nixon had secretly tape-recorded all conversations held in the Oval Office.

At first, Nixon refused to turn over the tapes but the Supreme Court ruled in July, 1974, that all the tapes had to be released. The White House tapes provided powerful evidence of Nixon's direct involvement in the Watergate cover-up: "I don't give a shit what happens," Nixon told his aides. "I want you all to stonewall it. . . . cover up or anything else, if it'll save the plan. That's the whole point."[6]

On August 9, 1974, facing certain Congressional impeachment and conviction, Richard Nixon resigned the presidency. Fifty-six men, many of them key White House officials, were convicted of Watergate-related crimes. Nixon's 1972 running mate Spiro Agnew had been forced to resign from the vice presidency in October 1973 for crimes he had committed while governor of Maryland. As a result, the scandal-ridden presidency fell to the unelected, recently appointed vice president, Gerald R. Ford.

By the time Nixon quit, Americans' trust in government had plummeted. In 1958, according to public opinion polls, only 24 percent of all Americans distrusted their government. By late 1973, more than 57 percent chose that response. An era of distrust and cynicism, fueled by the failed war in Vietnam and greatly exacerbated by the Watergate debacle, had taken root in the United States.

WOMEN'S LIBERATION MOVEMENT

As the federal government faced growing public cynicism in the late 1960s and early 1970s, new grassroots social-change movements exploded throughout the nation. The most successful of these new mass movements was the women's liberation movement. Feminist activists fought to end the historical subordination of women by men. They demanded full equality, including an end to economic discrimination.

Many factors contributed to the rise and success of the women's movement. One key factor was the increasing number of women working outside the home. Between 1945 and 1970, the proportion of women who were in the work force rose from around 17 percent to over 35 percent. These working women faced an openly discriminatory job market in which women were confined to the poorer paying sectors of the economy, were rarely promoted, and faced dead-end careers.

As a partial response to working women's concerns, the liberal Democratic administrations of Presidents Kennedy and Johnson began to offer some legal redress. The Kennedy administration passed the Equal Pay Act of 1963, which assured that men and women doing the same job with the same job title would be paid equally. Far more significantly, the 1964 Civil Rights Act had, through a last-minute amendment, offered women the same federal protection against job discrimination as was guaranteed to racial minorities. However, to make employers comply and to ensure that the government would enforce the law required political pressure. Fighting job discrimination drove some women, then, to begin organizing.

Other women—especially college-educated, middle-class, young married women— were motivated by other concerns. By the early 1960s, many women worried about the limits on life that they had voluntarily chosen with marriage. In 1963, Betty Friedan published *The Feminine Mystique*, which described how many young, well-educated married women felt frustrated as they watched life go by from the suburban sidelines. Friedan's book became a Sixties best-seller. It gave voice to many housewives' desire for a richer life that encompassed both the home and the larger, male-dominated public world.

A third group of women would provide the most visible activists and theorists of the women's movement. These were women who had become politically active in the civil rights, antiwar, and student movements. For years, they had fought against oppression and for a more just world. But as one of these activists, Robin Morgan, wrote: "It was a slowly dawning and depressing realization that we were doing the same work and playing the same roles in the Movement as out if it: typing the speeches men delivered, making coffee but not policy, being accessories to the men whose politics would supposedly replace the Old Order."[7]

Already experienced political organizers, these "movement" women were primed to turn from fighting against the oppression of others to fighting for their own rights and freedoms as women.

The new feminists of the late 1960s and 1970s worked at two parallel and then increasingly interconnected lines of political activity. A group of relatively moderate women, led by Betty Friedan, organized the National Organization for Women (NOW) in 1966 to lobby the federal government and to work through the courts to end discrimination against women. More radical women, most of them in their twenties or early thirties, fought a more public battle to change the ways in which Americans thought about gender roles, and to expand women's fundamental rights. Their goal was to "raise women's consciousness," so that millions of women would become activists, both in their communities and in their personal lives, against the myriad ways in which they were subordinated to men in American society.

The first nationally visible women's liberation protest took place at the 1968 Miss America pageant in Atlantic City. Protresters nominated a sheep for Miss America and filled a trash can with bras, girdles, hair curlers, and high heels. They argued that, through events like the Miss America pageant, women were turned into sex objects and judged narrowly on their looks and "feminine" attributes, like "charm" and demure behavior. In this protest and others, feminists demanded that women should have the same right as men to shape the political, economic, and cultural spheres of American life.

In the early 1970s, feminists published a series of searing attacks on the "politics of gender" in America: *Sisterhood Is Powerful* (1970), *Sexual Politics* (1970), *The Dialectic of Sex* (1970), *Our Bodies, Ourselves* (1971), *The Female Eunuch* (1972), and *Against Our Will: Men, Women and Rape* (1975). In 1972 an overtly feminist women's magazine, *Ms.* (a coined term, equivalent to "Mr.," which avoided making marital status a key identifier of a woman), hit the newsstands and sold out 250,000 copies in eight days.

As the mass media profiled the explosive movement, new words and phrases entered the American vernacular: "sexism" and "sexist"; "macho" and "bimbo"; "male supremacy" and "male chauvinist pig," and "the personal is political." Across the country, in suburban kitchens, church basements, and college dorm rooms, women met in "consciousness-raising groups" (promoted in *Ms.* magazine and by other feminist organizations), to discuss how in their everyday lives women were subordinated by men treated like second-class citizens by society, and what they could do to change their situation.

Throughout the early 1970s, the women's movement recorded major successes. On March 22, 1972, after massive lobbying by women's organizations including NOW, the YWCA, the League of Women's Voters, and the American Association of University Women, Congress approved the Equal Rights Amendment (ERA). The ERA simply stated that "men and women shall have equal rights throughout the United States." For many years thereafter, state legislatures would heatedly debate ratification of this constitutional amendment.

Also in 1972, Congress passed Title IX of the Higher Education Act. Title IX cut off federal funds to any college or university that discriminated against women. One result of this act was a tremendous financial boost to women's and girl's athletics in schools. Previously, men's school athletics had received almost all such funding.

In 1973, the women's movement convinced the federal government to pressure the nation's largest private employer, AT&T, to stop discriminating against women and to award back pay to some 13,000 women employees. Before the government acted, 98.6 percent of AT&T's well-paid craft workers were men, and 96.6 percent of the lower-paid office and clerical workers were women.

In January 1973, the Supreme Court decided *Roe v. Wade*, ruling that a woman's "right to choose" an abortion was protected by the constitutional "right of personal privacy."

Because of the women's movement, more and more Americans began to act on the premise that men and women deserved equal rights and equal opportunities. But by no means did all Americans believe that feminism and the women's liberation movement were good for the United States.

Opposition to the movement came from all parts of the nation. Self-described conservative women, often religiously motivated, as well as conservative male religious leaders, became the most ardent opponents of the women's movement. Fundamentalist Christians pointed to the writings of St. Paul: "Wives, be subject to your husbands, as to the Lord. For the husband is the head of the wife, as Christ is head of the church"; and "As the church is subject to Christ, so let wives be subject in everything to their husbands."[8]

In the 1970s, anti-feminism became a powerful ideological component of a burgeoning New Right political coalition.

LIBERATION, POWER, AND PRIDE

The women's movement was the most powerful *new* political force in America at the end of the 1960s, but other downtrodden Americans also mobilized for social justice. Influenced by the civil-rights movement, antiwar activism, the Black Power movement, and their own historical dynamics, minority groups around the country sought political power and cultural recognition.

Among the most significant of these revitalized struggles for social justice was the Chicano movement. In 1970, Mexican-Americans numbered over nine million of America's 203 million people. Often treated as second-class citizens, they faced job, housing, and school discrimination.

César Chávez led the most visible Chicano struggle for economic justice. Chávez, who had left school after the seventh grade to work full-time as a farm laborer, helped to organize the United Farm Workers (UFW) in California. Between 1965 and 1970, Chávez used nonviolent tactics to lead a strike against growers who refused, Chávez argued, to provide livable wages and decent working conditions for farm laborers, most of whom were of Mexican ancestry. With the backing of the United Auto Workers and the support of leading Democratic politicians, Chávez promoted a nationwide boycott of grapes (and later lettuce) as a means of bringing the growers to the bargaining table. In 1970, Chávez and the UFW won their fight with the growers and signed a historic agreement.

More radical struggles were launched by other Mexican-Americans throughout the Southwest. On September 16, 1969, hundreds of thousands of Mexican-American students boycotted their schools, demanding that teachers and administrators show respect for them and the Chicano culture. On college campuses, Mexican-American students, inspired by their African-American peers, demonstrated for greater representation of Mexican-Americans in the student body, on the faculty, and in the college curriculum.

Chicano activists in the early 1970s brought Mexican-American history and culture into the school curriculum and increased the pressure on local public officials to reckon with discriminatory practices. Activists in the Southwest formed a third party called *La Raza Unida* (RUP). While short-lived, the RUP registered tens of thousands of Chicano voters and won several local elections.

American Indians also became increasingly politicized in the late 1960s. The poorest, least healthy, and worst educated minority group in the nation, American Indians had suffered from decades of national indifference. But between 1968 and 1975, Native American activists—ranging from moderates working closely with government officials to militant radicals who advocated armed revolt—forced Americans to hear their demands and to seek reform of federal policies.

On November 28, 1969, a small group of activists, who were members of the newly formed American Indian Movement (AIM), captured national public attention by occupying Alcatraz Island in San Francisco Bay. They had taken the island, they said, to protest both the many treaties that the whites had broken with the Indian peoples and the millions of acres of land that had been stolen from them.

In 1972, AIM members similarly occupied a Bureau of Indian Affairs office in Washington, D.C., and then in 1973 a trading post at Wounded Knee, South Dakota, where army troops had massacred American Indians in 1890. Tens of thousands of Indians in cities, towns, and on reservations were inspired by these actions and others to demand changes in government policy.

At the same time, more moderate activists, working through pan-tribal organizations like the National Congress of American Indians, the Native American Rights Fund, and the National Indian Youth Council, lobbied Congress and the executive branch for new laws and regulations. Like Black Power activists—albeit with a very different historical context—American Indians asked for greater rights and resources to govern themselves and to strengthen their traditional cultures.

In 1975, the Indian Self-Determination and Educational Assistance Act was made law, guaranteeing American Indians far more power and additional federal funds to govern their own reservations and to control their children's education. In addition, federal courts and Congress responded to Indian claims by turning millions of acres of land back to tribal ownership. While economic and social problems continued to plague American Indians, activists had won major victories in their fight for cultural survival.

Among minority groups in the United States at the cusp of the Sixties and Seventies, homosexuals faced the most overt legal and social discrimination. They were barred from serving in the armed forces, were not hired as teachers in many communities, were prohibited from serving in many government offices, and were commonly not hired for many types of jobs. In almost every state, homosexual practices were illegal, and people suspected of being homosexual were hounded and harassed. Homosexuality was seen as a perversion by a majority of Americans, and officially labeled a mental disorder by the American Psychiatric Association.

Because of this economic, legal, social, and medical onslaught, lesbians and gay men overwhelmingly chose to hide their sexual preference. They stayed "in the closet." As a result, while many gays protected themselves from job discrimination, prosecution, and public harassment they remained politically unorganized. This relative political invisibility changed, quite dramatically, in the summer of 1969.

While small gay-rights organizations such as the Mattachine Society and the Daughters of Bilitis had begun years earlier, and while a lesbian and gay-bar culture had existed for decades, many gay activists date the origin of the gay movement to the events that occurred on June 28, 1969. On that date, the New York City police came to Greenwich Village to shut down a gay bar, the Stonewall Inn.

Typically, when a gay bar was raided, the patrons fled from police. Many of them were not openly gay and meant to keep their homosexuality secret from families, friends and employers. But at the Stonewall, that night, the patrons fought back. As word spread through New York City's gay community, hundreds more joined in the confrontation. When daylight broke in Greenwich Village, New Yorkers found a new slogan spray-painted on the walls: *Gay Power.*

Inspired by the Stonewall "riot," many gay men and women decided the time had come to work openly and militantly for gay rights. Deeply affected by the women's movement and the Black Power movement, gay activists focused on a dual agenda: legal equality and consciousness-raising. Gay Power would be accompanied by Gay Pride.

By 1973, some 800 gay organizations existed. Mostly based in big cities and on university campuses, many of the groups aimed to create a supportive environment in which gay men and lesbians could "come out of the closet." Once "out," gay men and lesbians could use their numbers—"We are everywhere" was a popular slogan—to apply pressure for political reform. The gay rights struggle would continue to gain strength throughout the 1970s.

Despite the gay movement's success in creating both "Gay Pride" and a gay political lobby, most Americans in the 1970s remained opposed to the legitimization of homosexuality. The majority of heterosexual Americans did not believe that homosexuality was an acceptable lifestyle, and they did not approve of gay marriage, gay adoption, gays in the military, or laws specifically protecting homosexuals from discrimination. By the late 1970s, fighting gay rights would become another powerful cause for an increasingly well-organized, New Right political movement.

NOTES

1. William Safire, *Before the Fall: An Inside View of the Pre-Watergate White House* (New York: Ballantine, 1977), 573.

2. Safire, *Before the Fall*, 417.

3. William Chafe, *The Unfinished Journey: America Since 1945* (New York: Oxford, 1995), 387.

4. Chafe, *The Unfinished Journey*, 387.

5. John Morton Blum, *Years of Discord: American Politics and Society 1961–1974* (New York: Norton, 1991), 372.

6. Stanley I. Kutler, *The Wars of Watergate* (New York: Norton, 1990), 287.

7. Robin Morgan, *Sisterhood Is Powerful* (New York: Vintage, 1970), xxiii.

8. Eph. 5.22–23; as cited in Jane J. Mansbridge, *Why We Lost the ERA* (Chicago: University of Chicago Press, 1986), 302.

CHAPTER EIGHT

Conclusion

The Sixties era was marked by a failed war abroad and turmoil at home. At the same time, it was a period of nearly unequaled economic prosperity and global leadership. The apparent contradictions—national affluence and massive discontent, global leadership and military defeat—explains much about American society in the 1960s.

America's very successes—international leadership and unprecedented national affluence—helped to make the changes and challenges of the era possible. The post–World War II prosperity helped to produce the Baby Boom, which in turn led to record numbers of college students in the 1960s.

Many of these students were born and raised amid plenty. They grew up in the glow of America's glorious defeat of fascist militarism and, like President John Kennedy, the figurehead of their generation, they believed in American greatness. When they discovered governmental failures and other national shortcomings, they did not take them in cynical stride but instead felt betrayed. And some of them—a minority, often short on practical answers but long on idealistic hopes—demanded better from their society.

African Americans, in particular, felt the tension and possibilities of that historic moment. The United States claimed to be the leader of the Free World and yet had denied a whole class of its citizens their basic equal rights. At a time when television linked the nation together as never before, the paradox of poverty amid plenty and the irony of racial discrimination were impossible to hide and difficult to dismiss as the "peculiar" problem of one region of the country. Fueled by the same hopes and possibilities that fired so many Americans in the post-war economic boom, African Americans across the nation fought for the good life that the United States claimed to hold out for all its citizens. Other minorities and exploited citizens would follow their lead.

If historical circumstances enabled individuals to form successful mass movements, they also helped pull the federal government into wars both at home and abroad. What would have been unthinkable only a generation earlier—that the United States would become involved in a land war in Asia for no concrete and immediate national interest—by 1965 seemed a reasonable extension of America's cold-war commitments. Similarly, President Johnson's War on Poverty could only have been undertaken in a nation flush with wealth, confident that even the poor could be elevated to the middle class if only the economic playing field were leveled.

Both wars, at least partially, were justified by the assumption that a kind of American middle-class way of life could be bestowed by our government on one and all. That both failed—and in Vietnam the failure cost more than a million lives—forced Americans to reckon with their national limitations. The tempering of national pride, dramatically exacerbated by the economic failures of the 1970s, marked the end of the post–World War II optimism that made so much of the Sixties era possible.

Failure, however, was not the main characteristic of the Sixties era. The equal-rights revolution that ended legally sanctioned racism and sexism stands out as an extraordinary effort of that time toward bringing the United States closer to its core ideals. Similarly, after the scarring experiences of the Great Depression, the rigors of World War, and the politically repressive years of the early cold war, Americans in the Sixties once again laid claim to their democracy by challenging their leaders through massive protests, rallies, and organized opposition. That chaotic, unruly use of the people's power, as codified in the Constitution's Bill of Rights, was harrowing for the nation but uplifting for those who believed in the ideals of democracy and the sovereignty of the people.

No simple balance sheet can express the reality of the Sixties in America. A confluence of historical circumstances and remarkable men and women created a time of national passion and collective social examination the likes of which have rarely been seen in history.

PART II

Debating the Sixties

The Upheaval of Jim Crow: African Americans and the Struggle for Civil Rights in the 1960s

Beth Tompkins Bates

Several decades after the civil rights movement, debates over affirmative action, de facto residential segregation, and economic disparities between white Americans and African Americans have raised the question: Just what was achieved, and for whom, during one of the most important social movements in American history? These concerns, and others, have caused scholars to ask: What, if anything, was "overcome" during the heady days of sit-ins, nonviolent demonstrations, rallies, protest marches, and speeches that galvanized the nation? Different perspectives on the history of the civil rights movement reflect the various ways scholars have understood the purpose of the movement, and these perspectives shape the ongoing debate over the movement's successes and failures.

Some scholars and policy makers argue that American society is now color blind, thanks largely to the movement's success, which can be measured by the large numbers of African Americans who have realized dreams and opportunities not possible in the late forties.[1]

Others do not think the movement was quite so successful and suggest that much remains to be done to complete the civil rights movement's unfinished agenda.[2] Still others argue that until the full history is recovered, we cannot locate the fault lines created by the social and political upheaval of the civil rights movement nor comprehend its impact on the lives of black and white Americans.[3]

The history of the civil rights movement, when it was first written in the late Sixties and early Seventies, was bracketed by the Supreme Court's decision for desegregation of public schools in *Brown v. Board of Education* in 1954 and the passage of the Voting Rights Act in 1965. Scholars focused on leaders, events, and organizations that had national significance. The outpouring of memoirs and biographies conveyed the idea that protest succeeded in overcoming the oppression that had held African Americans in second-class status for decades. Southern white racists yielded when confronted by the overwhelming power of black Americans, their white allies, and the federal government.

This interpretation emphasized figures of national prominence, leading many to equate the movement with the Reverend Martin Luther King Jr. The national perspective also emphasized the political impact of events in Washington. Thus voting and civil rights were considered part of a national campaign for civil rights reform, which was shepherded along by President Kennedy and President Johnson. This struggle for civil rights was incorporated into a progressive account of American life. In this version Americans in the 1960s finally overcame what the Swedish author Gunnar Myrdal called the "American dilemma": racial oppression in a nation built on the ideals of democracy, equality, and individual freedom.

Although this perspective was embraced by a national coalition of liberals, it was not shared by all white Americans, nor did division occur along a north-south axis. Votes for George Wallace, governor of Alabama, in 1964 and 1968 testify to the reservoir of white resentment that began to swell after 1965 with each wave of rioting in America's inner cities. As Robert J. Norrell notes, although white supremacy lost its legitimacy in the law and in national public discourse, "it still lived in the hearts and minds of many Americans," in Boston as well as in Birmingham, in Detroit as well as in the Delta.[4] A significant white minority found its voice and cried out against further changes in the racial status quo. For those who subscribed to this perspective, too many racial barriers had been overcome.

Yet another perspective came from television, which reduced centuries of contradictions embedded in American history to symbols projected on a screen. When Eugene ("Bull") Connor "beat" well-scrubbed black citizen protesters with powerful water hoses or Alabama state troopers slugged marchers on the Pettus Bridge in Selma, the pulse of America quickened. Such acts were not just wrong, they were un-American, for they made a mockery of democracy. Martin Luther King understood well the role that television played in legitimating the protest for black civil rights in the eyes of white Americans at the March on Washington in 1963.[5]

But the value added to the movement when television recognized and validated civil rights as a national issue came at a cost, in terms of clarity. As television cameras beamed on the 250,000 civil rights marchers at the Lincoln Memorial in August 1963, King's dream for a color-blind society projected images of freedom on citizens' minds across the land. But as those images were refracted through the individual experiences of the viewers, they acquired multiple meanings. Could a color-blind society be constructed without recognizing economic rights of citizenship? Might some individual rights be sacrificed in the process of ushering in a color-blind society? A fundamental antagonism between ideals associated with freedom and those associated with democracy emerged, not for the first time in American history, as demands for racial and economic equality threatened structural change. As William Chafe notes, when the movement "entered areas that would require a redistribution of political and economic power, resistance set in."[6]

At the same time, television conducted a national civics lesson as the civil rights battles of the early Sixties marched through living rooms across the nation, redeeming American democratic institutions in the process. By early 1965 the convergence between television and public policy seemed close when President Johnson, drawing from the language of activists after the Pettus Bridge beatings, declared "we shall overcome."[7] Shortly thereafter America erased a stain on its principles when Congress passed the Voting Rights Act. But how inclusive was the president's "we," and were expectations for social justice harbored by African Americans realized by 1965 as well? Whose past had been overcome—America's sin of racism or black America's diminished sense of belonging?

Black Americans mobilized around their ongoing search for freedom and citizenship, which they had exercised for a brief moment in the first decade after emancipation. Efforts to secure the fruits of emancipation during Reconstruction, Patricia Sullivan argues, nurtured an "expansive vision of democracy," which sustained black communities in the decades ahead.[8] In terms of the larger goal—attaining first-class citizenship—there is no question that a fundamental obstacle had been overcome by 1965 with civil rights legislation designed to end de jure segregation. The decade between *Brown v. Board of Education* and the Voting Rights Act produced more civil rights legislation than any other decade in American history, delivering part of the promise of equal citizenship. But were the contradictions of American democracy and the inequality in race relations that those contradictions engendered also resolved in the span of ten years? If so, why did the Los Angeles neighborhood of Watts erupt into flames on August 11, 1965, just five days after the signing of the Voting Rights Act? C. Vann Woodward pointed out that a historic movement reached a peak of achievement and optimism and "immediately confronted the beginning of a period of challenge and reaction that called into question some of its greatest hopes and most important assumptions."[9] Other episodes of violence followed, as the movement shifted from what is usually called the "nonviolent, direct-action" phase to the Black Power phase that followed. Was this a paradox, or did these controversial events merely reflect a larger impulse within the black community, which flowed from aspects of the struggle for citizenship unleashed in an earlier period?

When Stokely Carmichael of the Student Nonviolent Coordinating Committee (SNCC) raised the Black Power fist, perplexed white Americans could not understand SNCC's turn to black self-determination, its interpretation of Black Power, nor the violence that erupted increasingly from 1965 onward as the movement's center shifted north.[10] A significant obstacle was the myth, perpetuated by the 1963 March on Washington, identifying the civil rights movement with "a band of integrated marchers proceeding to the Lincoln Memorial."[11] As many histories have now shown, the movement was rooted in black activism for freedom and citizenship that grew out of a decades-long struggle within segregated black communities, north and south. Not only did the civil rights movement not fall out of the sky with the Greensboro, North Carolina, sit-in in 1960, but its past was the prologue that served to animate and mobilize thousands into a social movement for civil rights.[12] Without the prologue for context, the perplexity felt by liberal whites in 1965 is understandable.

Scholars of the movement, writing in the late 1970s and early 1980s, brought the prologue into sharper focus by examining local communities and grassroots organizations.[13] These studies revealed further complexities, as activists often embodied both militant and moderate political tendencies and participants shared a broad-based interpretation of the meaning of citizenship, touching on political as well as economic concerns. Throwing the spotlight on black communities uncovered protest networks steeped in a tradition of civil rights activism reaching back into the 1920s. Recent research has led scholars to pay attention, as Steven F. Lawson has, to the "ways in which efforts in the national arena intersected with those at the grassroots level."[14] Finally, as Timothy B. Tyson's work documents, we now know that the Black Power movement and the civil rights movement "grew out of the same soil . . . and reflected the same quest for black freedom."[15]

To place the prologue of the civil rights movement in the larger context of African-American history, it is important to keep the major goal of the civil rights movement, from the perspective of black Americans, in the foreground. The movement's initial goal was to destroy Jim Crow, a system of institutionalized racial segregation designed to keep black Americans in "their place." Destroying the legal framework that supported Jim Crow institutions was a major victory, as anyone who remembers what life was like in segregated America will acknowledge. On the other hand, the elimination of Jim Crow through legislation did not get at the heart of what Richard Wright once called "the ethics of living Jim Crow," the assumption that black Americans adopt a second-class demeanor in the company of whites. The issue of exercising full human rights continues to fuel the debate over whether the movement was successful or not.

Wright recalled that he was taught to calculate and "exercise a great deal of ingenuity to keep out of trouble" by pretending to know his "place."[16] The white South, he said, claimed that "I had a 'place' in life. Well, I had never felt my 'place;' or, rather, my deepest instincts had always made me reject the 'place' to which the white South had assigned me."

> Not only had the southern whites not known me, but, more important still, as I had lived in the South I had not had the chance to learn who I was. The pressure of southern living kept me from being the kind of person that I might have been. I had been what my surroundings had demanded, . . . and what whites had said that I must be. Never being fully able to be myself, I had slowly learned that the South could recognize but a part of a man, could accept but a fragment of his personality, and all the rest—the best and deepest things of heart and mind—were tossed away in blind ignorance and hate.[17]

At its most basic level, Jim Crow sought to blot out black humanity through a politics of exclusion. When black Americans migrated north, they learned from bitter experience of the ubiquitous nature of the politics of exclusion and the relationship between de jure and de facto segregation. Richard Wright spoke of the color line in black Chicago, which "placed the life of blacks below that of whites."[18] Although Chicago was not Natchez, Mississippi, the politics of exclusion continued to mobilize African Americans to overcome the racial status quo and claim full citizenship rights by asserting their right to self-determination. Viewed from the perspective of African-American history, legally resolving the American dilemma was a necessary but not sufficient condition for reclaiming humanity. To both northern and southern black Americans, the struggle for freedom and citizenship meant much more than political rights. It also meant claiming economic rights, an issue that came to the fore during the first wave of the Great Migration to the Promised Land. But connecting citizenship with the right to organize in the workplace and the right to equal opportunities in the labor market can be traced as far back as Reconstruction. Although largely a civic ideology "grounded in a definition of American citizenship," Reconstruction radicalism, as Eric Foner explains, possessed an economic agenda derived from the free-labor ideology that "insisted the freedmen were entitled to the same economic opportunities enjoyed by white laborers."[19]

Black Americans raised this issue of entitlement again when President

Franklin D. Roosevelt mobilized defense industries to supply the war in Europe during the Second World War. To abolish discrimination against African Americans by industrialists, A. Philip Randolph, head of the Brotherhood of Sleeping Car Porters, demanded a special order by the President banning racial discrimination in government employment, defense industries, and training programs. Roosevelt reluctantly issued Executive Order #8802, but only after 100,000 black Americans threatened to march on segregated Washington if the order was not signed. Randolph gained a measure of economic citizenship when he extracted the order from President Roosevelt by utilizing the power of mass, direct-action tactics to claim equal rights. But just as important, he departed from the political etiquette that normally framed the negotiation process and broke a tradition whereby black leaders beseeched white leaders for the opportunity to participate fully in society as American citizens. When Randolph refused to play by the "ground rules," as William Chafe has described the process in another context, he substituted a language of protest designed to "shake up white America." Randolph's 1941 March on Washington Movement foreshadowed the Black Power phase of civil rights, with its all-black membership and challenge to the politics of civility that lent support to the racial status quo.[20]

Heightened expectations that emerged from World War II were reinforced by two demographic shifts, which by 1960 had contributed to changing the economic and social position of African Americans. One was movement out of the South, and the other was the shift from rural to urban America. By the 1960s, for the first time in American history, almost as many black Americans lived outside the Old South as in it, and blacks residing in northern and western cities outnumbered the remaining rural southern black population. Of those staying in the South, nearly 60 percent resided in cities.[21] In the process of moving from one place to another, more questions were raised about the terms of the social contract and the place to which black Americans were relegated. Increasingly, black Americans answered by asserting their right, as they understood it, to self-determine their place in post–World War II America.

But, at the same time, pressure from external forces created conflicting goals within black America, which fractured the movement after political rights were attained and fueled debate over the movement's agenda and tactics. Since 1951 the gap between incomes of northern black and white workers had been widening. The economic experience of blacks in cities during the 1950s was one of severe underemployment and outright unemployment.[22] Thus many African Americans living in northern areas decided that the acute problems they faced were not addressed through the Voting Rights Act of

1965. The slow retreat of *de jure* segregation in the South was paralleled by a rapid advance of *de facto* discrimination and segregation in the northern job market. As Malcolm X explained, "I'm not going to sit at your table and watch you eat, with nothing on my plate, and call myself a diner. Sitting at the table doesn't make you a diner. . . . Being here in America doesn't make you an American."[23]

Civil rights workers discovered that poverty as well as racism was a source of oppression and that the two could not be separated. Experience with economic oppression, disease, poor housing, and malnutrition caused activists to question the American system and the perfidy of many democratic institutions. Many who had believed in the initial goodness of America felt betrayed by promises made by white liberals.[24] The ensuing distrust of government led grassroots activists to rely on their own resources, which sometimes included armed self-defense. James Baldwin captured these sentiments when he asked: "Do I really *want* to be integrated into a burning house?"[25] When the scales fell from the eyes of young, black activists, many turned to alternative community-based institution building and began to raise the issue of self-reliance to a higher level. In the process, the desire to find a place in America was overwhelmed by the determination to change America. By the mid-Sixties, the experience of struggling for civil rights, which had once galvanized the community, split the movement, and the loose parts broke off in many new directions.

When movement activist Ella Baker told the first SNCC Conference in 1960 that they "are concerned with something much bigger than a hamburger or even a giant-sized coke," she tapped into the movement's vision of full citizenship in terms of its larger social and economic agenda.[26] But as early as 1965 the larger vision—with its economic agenda—would prove to be the movement's Achilles heel. By then the upheaval that successfully challenged Jim Crow had given birth to a more radical challenge to the structure of the American economic system. The "beloved community" that SNCC believed could be built through the power of organized, disciplined, confrontational nonviolent struggle appeared to require fundamental restructuring of society; the civil rights movement was overcome by the movement for human rights.

In trying to come to terms with Watts, Martin Luther King Jr. noted the importance of economic enfranchisement and moved closer to the philosophy more often linked to Malcolm X and Stokely Carmichael. Between 1965 and 1968 King continued to espouse nonviolent tactics, but he expanded the reach of the movement's goals to include all of the nation's dispossessed—poor black, white, and brown Americans. The struggle for freedom and citizenship had been transformed into a crusade for systemic changes to over-come inequality and injustice.[27] When King expanded his efforts to connect political rights with the need for jobs and equal economic opportunity, the national coalition that he had helped forge during the legislative period began to fragment. The very success of the political phase paved the way for questioning contradictions in the economic arena and revealed the striking incongruities between the needs of the black inner city and the goals and strategies of the southern phase of the movement. Class division and dissent over tactics further complicated the situation. Many urban black Americans thought middle-class leaders of the southern movement knew very little about the poverty of the urban poor. While that may have been an accurate observation, King and his coalition were learning on the streets of Cicero, Illinois, in 1966, and Memphis, Tennessee, in 1968—lessons King would pay for with his life. During the Memphis sanitation workers' strike the movement was revitalized as economic and civil rights issues were fused. The signs carried by the garbage strikers expressed the spirit of the struggle with the words, "I AM a man." They marched to claim dignity and self-respect as human beings, which was, as A. Philip Randolph had declared some forty years before, the "unfinished task of emancipation."[28]

The civil rights movement took blacks from the back of the bus to the front of the bus, from accommodating whites by moving aside to let them pass, to sitting-in at what larger society considered "white" lunch counters. In the process of initiating and carrying out challenges to the racial status quo, the politics of these experiences transformed black and white Americans. Overcoming political disenfranchisement not only reformed the American creed, it breathed new life into that creed. But when the dialectic sparked by the challenge to Jim Crow unleashed a second movement to transform society, raised the question of economic rights of citizenship to the top of the agenda, and opened up the vision of a restructured America, the economic system was challenged. While renewal of the creed created the conditions for imagining a new future constructed around the human needs of all citizens, to reach the goals of the second movement required overcoming obstacles greater than those that confronted the first.

Finally, in addition to the movement's success in reforming the political status quo, the movement provided a model for other groups during the 1960s organizing to change their place in society and gain more power. Thus the citizens cordoned off from mainstream America as, at best, "second-class," showed citizens with more power—especially middle-class white women— how to ferment change. Through their own efforts black Americans triumphed over legal segregation, and in the process American politics was reformed. But these successes must be weighed against the failure to get America to confront and deal with the many levels of inequality generated by its political and economic systems. Through the experience of challenging Jim Crow, African Americans raised their expectations of American democracy. Many black children grow up today assuming the American Dream includes people of color. They are told they can thank their foremothers and forefathers for their assumed rightful place in America. But when they find that the natural order of things in a democratic society—the right to live wherever they desire, the right to equal schooling, the right to equal access to job opportunities—does not always include them, these children learn why the agenda spawned by the civil rights movement remains unfinished.

NOTES

1. The most successful proponents of this view are Abigail and Stephen Thernstrom, *America in Black and White: One Nation, Indivisible* (New York: Simon and Schuster, 1997).

2. Julian Bond, "The Politics of Civil Rights History," in *New Directions in Civil Rights Studies*, ed. Armstead L. Robinson and Patricia Sullivan (Charlottesville: University of Virginia Press, 1991), 8–16.

3. See, for example, Claybourne Carson, "Civil Rights Reform and the Black Freedom Struggle," in *The Civil Rights Movement in America*, ed. Charles W. Eagles (Jackson: University of Mississippi Press, 1986), 19–32.

4. Robert J. Norrell, "One Thing We Did Right: Reflections on the Movement," in *New Directions in Civil Rights Studies*, ed. Armstead L. Robinson and Patricia Sullivan (Charlottesville: University Press of Virginia, 1991), 75.

5. For further discussion of the role of the media in the civil rights movement, from which this essay draws, see Norrell, "One Thing We Did Right," 72–77, and Armstead L. Robinson and Patricia Sullivan, *New Directions in Civil Rights Studies* (Charlottesville: University Press of Virginia, 1991), 3–5.

6. William H. Chafe, "One Struggle Ends, Another Begins," in *The Civil Rights Movement in America*, ed. Charles W. Eagles (Jackson: University Press of Mississippi, 1986), 147. For further discussion of these issues, see J. Mills Thornton III, "Commentary," in *The Civil Rights Movement in America*, ed. Eagles (Jackson: University Press of Mississippi, 1986), 148–155.

7. Norrell, "One Thing We Did Right," in *New Directions in Civil Rights Studies*, ed. Robinson and Sullivan, 73–74.

8. Patricia Sullivan, *Days of Hope: Race and Democracy in the New Deal Era* (Chapel Hill: The University of North Carolina Press, 1996), 14.

9. C. Vann Woodward, *The Strange Career of Jim Crow*, 3d ed. (New York: Oxford University Press, 1974), v.

10. Norrell, "One Thing We Did Right," in *New Directions in Civil Rights Studies*, ed. Robinson and Sullivan, 76.

11. William H. Chafe, "One Struggle Ends, Another Begins," in *The Civil Rights Movement in America*, ed. Eagles, 130.

12. For example, see William H. Chafe, *Civilities and Civil Rights: Greensboro, North Carolina, and the Black Struggle for Freedom* (New York: Oxford University Press, 1980); Adam Fairclough, *Race and Democracy: The Civil Rights Struggle in Louisiana, 1915–1972* (Athens: University of Georgia Press, 1995); John Dittmer, *Local People: The Struggle for Civil Rigts in Mississippi* (Urbana: University of Illinois Press, 1994); Charles M. Payne, *I've Got the Light of Freedom: The Organizing Tradition and the Mississippi Freedom Struggle* (Berkeley: University of California Press, 1995); Mark V. Tushnet, *The NAACP's Legal Strategy against Segregated Education, 1925–1950* (Chapel Hill: University of North Carolina Press, 1987).

13. Steven F. Lawson, "Freedom Then, Freedom Now: The Historiography of the Civil Rights Movement," *American Historical Review* 96:2 (April 1991): 456–71, especially 457.

14. Steven F. Lawson, "Commentary," in *The Civil Rights Movement in America*, ed. Eagles, 34.

15. Timothy B. Tyson, "Robert F. Williams, 'Black Power,' and the Roots of the African American Freedom Struggle," *Journal of American History* 85(2) (September 1998): 541.

16. Richard Wright, *Uncle Tom's Children* (New York: Harper and Row, 1965), 10–15.

17. Richard Wright, *Black Boy* (New York: Harper and Row, 1966), 283–84.

18. Richard Wright, *Black Boy (American Hunger): A Record of Childhood and Youth* (New York: Harper and Brothers, 1945; reprint [restored-text edition], New York: HarperCollins, 1993), 312.

19. Eric Foner, *Reconstruction: America's Unfinished Revolution* (New York: Harper & Row, 1988), 233, 235.

20. For more on the etiquette of civility, see Chafe, *Civilities and Civil Rights*, 8. For more on the background of the 1941 March on Washington, see Beth Tompkins Bates, *Pullman Porters and the Rise of Protest Politics in Black America, 1925–1945* (Chapel Hill: The University of North Carolina Press, 2001), and "Call to Negro America," an editorial in *Black Worker*, May 4, 1941.

21. Daniel R. Fusfeld and Timothy M. Bates, *The Political Economy of the Urban Ghetto* (Carbondale: Southern Illinois University Press, 1984), 52.

22. Fusfeld and Bates, *The Political Economy of the Urban Ghetto*, 115–117.

23. George Breitman, ed., *Malcolm X Speaks: Selected Speeches and Statements* (New York: Grove Press, 1965), 26.

24. Chafe, "One Struggle Ends, Another Begins," 134.

25. James Baldwin, *The Fire Next Time* (New York: Dell, 1962), 127.

26. For Baker quote, see Chafe, "One Struggle Ends, Another Begins," 131; for more on Baker's "More Than a Hamburger" speech, see Payne, *I've Got the Light of Freedom*, 96; James Forman, *The Making of Black Revolutionaries* (New York: Macmillan, 1972; and Claybourne Carson, *In Struggle: SNCC and the Black Awakening of the 1960s* (Cambridge: Harvard University Press, 1981).

27. For a compelling analysis of the civil rights movement between 1955 and 1968, see Vincent Harding, "So Much History, So Much Future: Martin Luther King Jr., and the Second Coming of America," in *A History of Our Time: Readings on Postwar America*, 2d ed., ed. William H. Chafe and Harvard Sitkoff (New York: Oxford University Press, 1987), 161–77.

28. *The Messenger* 8(4) (April 1926): 114.

SOURCES

Baldwin, James. *The Fire Next Time*. New York: Dell, 1962.

Bates, Beth Tompkins. *Pullman Porters and the Rise of Protest Politics in Black America, 1925–1945*. Chapel Hill: University of North Carolina Press, 2001.

Black Worker. "Call to Negro America," editorial (May 4, 1941).

Bond, Julian. "The Politics of Civil Rights History." In *New Directions in Civil Rights Studies*, edited by Armstead L. Robinson and Patricia Sullivan. Charlottesville: University of Virginia Press, 1991.

Carson, Claybourne. *In Struggle: SNCC and the Black Awakening of the 1960s*. Cambridge: Harvard University Press, 1981.

———. "Civil Rights Reform and the Black Freedom Struggle." In *The Civil Rights Movement in America*, edited by Charles W. Eagles. Jackson: University of Mississippi Press, 1986.

Chafe, William H. *Civilities and Civil Rights: Greensboro, North Carolina, and the Black Struggle for Freedom*. New York: Oxford University Press, 1980.

———. "One Struggle Ends, Another Begins." In *The Civil Rights Movement in America*, edited by Charles W. Eagles. Jackson: University Press of Mississippi, 1986.

Dittmer, John. *Local People: The Struggle for Civil Rights in Mississippi*. Urbana: University of Illinois Press, 1994.

Eagles, Charles W., ed. *The Civil Rights Movement in America*. Jackson: University of Mississippi Press, 1986.

Fairclough, Adam. *Race and Democracy: The Civil Rights Struggle in Louisiana, 1915–1972*. Athens: University of Georgia Press, 1995.

Foner, Eric. *Reconstruction: America's Unfinished Revolution*. New York: Harper and Row, 1988.

Forman, James. *The Making of Black Revolutionaries*. New York: MacMillan, 1972.

Fusfeld, Daniel R, and Timothy M. Bates. *The Political Economy of the Urban Ghetto*. Carbondale: Southern Illinois University Press, 1984.

Harding, Vincent. "So Much History, So Much Future: Martin Luther King Jr. and the Second Coming of America." In *A History of Our Time: Readings on Postwar America*, edited by William H. Chafe and Harvard Sitkoff. New York: Oxford University Press, 1987.

Lawson, Steven F. "Commentary." In *The Civil Rights Movement in America*, edited by Charles W. Eagles. Jackson: University Press of Mississippi, 1986.

———. "Freedom Then, Freedom Now: The Historiography of the Civil Rights Movement." *American Historical Review* 96(2) (April 1991): 456–71.

Malcolm X. "The Ballot or the Bullet." In *Malcolm X Speaks: Selected Speeches and Statements*, edited by George Breitman. New York: Grove Press, 1965.

Norell, Robert J. "One Thing We Did Right: Reflections on the Movement." In *New Directions in Civil Rights Studies*, edited by Armstead L. Robinson and Patricia Sullivan. Charlottesville: University Press of Virginia, 1991.

Payne, Charles M. *I've Got the Light of Freedom: The Organizing Tradition and the Mississippi Freedom Struggle*. Berkeley: University of California Press, 1995.

Robinson, Armstead L., and Patricia Sullivan, eds. *New Directions in Civil Rights Studies*. Charlottesville: University of Virginia Press, 1991.

Sullivan, Patricia. *Days of Hope: Race and Democracy in the New Deal Era*. Chapel Hill: The University of North Carolina Press, 1996.

Thernstrom, Abigail and Stephen. *America in Black and White: One Nation, Indivisible*. New York: Simon and Schuster, 1997.

Thornton, J. Mills, III. "Commentary." In *The Civil Rights Movement in America*, edited by Charles W. Eagles. Jackson: University Press of Mississippi, 1986.

Tushnet, Mark V. *The NAACP's Legal Strategy against Segregated Education, 1925–1950*. Chapel Hill: The University of North Carolina Press, 1987.

Tyson, Timothy B. "Robert F. Williams, 'Black Power,' and the Roots of the African American Freedom Struggle." *Journal of American History* 85:2 (September 1998).

Woodward, C. Vann. *The Strange Career of Jim Crow*, 3d ed. New York: Oxford University Press, 1974.

Wright, Richard. *Black Boy (American Hunger): A Record of Childhood and Youth*. New York: Harper and Brothers, 1945; reprint (restored-text edition), New York: HarperCollins, 1993.

———. *Uncle Tom's Children*. New York: Harper and Row, 1965.

———. *Black Boy*. New York: Harper and Row, 1966.

The New Left: Democratic Reformers or Left-Wing Revolutionaries?

Doug Rossinow

RADICALISM, AT HOME AND ABROAD

The organized "new left" of the 1960s was primarily a movement of young, white, college-educated Americans committed to redressing social and political inequalities of power. Its main nationwide organization was the Students for a Democratic Society, or *SDS*, which grew during the decade from a small political-education group into a militant association that commanded the allegiance of hundreds of thousands of young Americans.

SDS members emphasized two basic issues. First, they called for what they termed "participatory democracy" in the United States. Second, they opposed the cold war between the United States and the forces of communism around the world.

Democracy means, literally, "rule by the people." New left radicals felt that true democracy had not been achieved in the United States, where periodic elections offered sharply limited choices. As one key example of the limits to American democracy, they pointed to the power in Congress of Southern white segregationists, who were able to keep black Southerners from gaining the right to vote.

In general, members of the new left wished to see citizens involved more actively and directly in public life. They believed that, if Americans were organized into mass movements, they could force their elected officials to tend to the needs of all the people, not just special interests.

Taking the civil rights movement as their model, SDS members encouraged the political organization of African Americans, university students, and the poor, on the assumption that the unification of these groups would push American politics to the left. The most committed activists in SDS devoted their energies to organizing efforts, mainly in urban ghettos and on university campuses.

The young radicals believed, moreover, that this kind of activism would have an immediate beneficial effect for those who practiced it, countering the "alienation" from which they claimed that many Americans suffered. As they said in the *Port Huron Statement*,[1] the influential SDS document of 1962, through political involvement, Americans might hope to find "a meaning in life that is personally authentic."

In an authentic, nonalienated society, presumably, people would feel connected to one another in deeply felt ways, and would be able to develop their own "real" and best selves. Participatory democracy would help to bring about this authenticity.

The new left's second core concern, its dissent from the cold war, proved to be more controversial. The young radicals thought it reasonable that third world nationalists should look to socialism as a way of reversing the effects of their countries' historical exploitation. They also feared that cold-war brinkmanship would lead to nuclear war. Moreover, they had experienced firsthand the social havoc that the obsession with fighting communism had wreaked in domestic politics.

The new leftists had little admiration for the Soviet Union. Yet, by taking a "plague upon both your houses" attitude toward the cold war, they separated themselves from their early liberal mentors, who, like President John Kennedy, thought it morally justifiable for the United States to combat revolutionary socialism wherever in the world it broke out. Liberals, at least until 1965, tended to view protesters against the cold war, whatever their motives, as dupes of Moscow, while many conservative Americans considered any attempt to make a separate peace, whether in a hot war or a cold one, to be virtually treasonous.

The escalation of the Vietnam War in the second half of the 1960s was the factor most responsible for both the rapid expansion of the new left and its radicalization. Young radicals, deeply embittered by their own government's actions, concluded that the United States was the leading enemy of peace and justice on the planet.

If this was so, then making a separate peace was not enough. The movement became fully committed to mass insurgencies—primarily those of students and racial minorities—whose goal was to destroy the existing political and social system, rather than promote change within that system. The new leftists declared their solidarity with Vietnamese revolutionaries as they organized disruptive antiwar protests.

In the movement's last years, new left radicals sought to lay the foundations of a healthier society by establishing a wide range of cooperative institutions, from women's centers to organic food stores. But such activities grabbed few headlines. Groups such as "the Weathermen," who planted bombs and engaged in shoot-outs with the police, produced the most widespread and long-lived images of the 1960s-era radical left.

Thus began the polemics over the question of the new left's intentions and loyalties. Was it an "anti-American" movement, as conservatives charged? Or, as liberals contended, were the young radicals simply idealists gone bad, foolishly drawn to violent revolution and undemocratic political methods?

DEBATING THE NEW LEFT

Some cultural critics like Peter Collier and David Horowitz (who in the 1960s were left-wing journalists) excoriate the moral failings of the new left. Many others retain sympathy for the movement, and defend it as having the wholesome intentions of applying the principles of traditional American democracy in the creation of a more just society. This kind of argument revives the familiar controversy of whether leftist radicalism is truly "American."

To some extent, the differing answers to these questions reflect the choice of focus between international or domestic affairs. Collier and Horowitz stress foreign relations, and they depict the new left, in cold-war fashion, as a band of communist stooges who were disloyal to their country. They see the new left as having been a dangerous and destructive enemy of the state, in much the same way as did J. Edgar Hoover.

On the other hand, today's backers of the new left emphasize the movement's domestic vision of participatory democracy. In perhaps the most influential book written on the new left, James Miller goes furthest in arguing that it was "in the American grain." He places the SDS within the history of American debates over democracy, enlisting its youngsters in the cause of John Dewey's "civil republicanism" and pitting them against Walter Lippmann's 1922 brief for elite authority, Public Opinion.

A second debate over the new left—one conducted mainly among sociologists—asks how much of this movement's radical dissent stemmed from personal and psychological factors, and how much from a simple recognition of social injustice. Severe critics dismiss the "manifest" politics of the young radicals, asserting that they were "acting out" anger against their parents. This charge echoes the complaint, voiced widely during the 1960s by various conservative commentators, that dissenting youth were simply spoiled brats who had not been properly disciplined by their parents.

Sympathetic analysts like Richard Flacks and Kenneth Keniston link such personal factors both to overarching social trends (such as the growth of society's "knowledge sector") and to political conflicts (for example, over the uses of the university) that were the objects of explicit radical attention. These scholars tend to blur the distinction between personal and political interpretations of the new left. This tendency would have been congenial to new left radicals themselves, who continually stated that their political outlook was, and that everyone's ought to be, rooted in their personal strivings toward authenticity.

Whatever the ultimate sources of their radicalism, by the watershed year of 1968, new left radicals had declared themselves ready for revolution, inspiring some liberals as well as conservatives to condemn them as "totalitarian" for allegedly plotting to seize power, and for not believing sufficiently in the power of reason or in the need for tolerance of differing opinions. They questioned the radicals' commitment to the fundamental principles of democracy. Since then, while right-wing scourges of the new left have expressed confidence that the movement was bent on revolution, more sympathetic historians have been divided about whether it was seeking revolution or reform.

Early historians of the new left emphasize the movement's revolutionary aspect. James O'Brien, its first historian, analyzes the movement primarily as a phase in the history of revolutionary socialist politics. John P. Diggins concerns himself with new left ambitions to replace the existing social system with a new one based on "postscarcity" values. Among later historians, Van Gosse, whose viewpoint is similar to that of new left activists, comes closest to confirming the movement as "revolutionary," stressing the new left's solidarity with Cuban socialism. He returns us to the international emphasis of Collier and Horowitz, but offers a very different viewpoint.

One way for sympathetic historians to defend the new left during the conservative 1980s and 1990s has been to argue that the members of this movement simply wanted to improve American society, not destroy it. New left radicals called themselves revolutionaries, but as time has passed it has become easier for historians to downplay these repeated statements of intent.

Historian Terry Anderson views SDS activists as part of a much larger reformist wave that included civil rights activists and supporters of George McGovern, Ralph Nader, and Abbie Hoffman. Todd Gitlin and Wini Breines are ambivalent. While proud of the militant and radical dissenting edge of the new left, they are eager to link this movement to widely accepted changes in society such as multiculturalism, feminism, and the relaxation of 1950s-era sexual mores. They also give the new left credit for helping to end the Vietnam War. For the most part, these writings present the new left as a movement whose main purpose was to correct imperfections in American society.

One more disagreement among historians of the new left—one that has begun to emerge only recently—is worth noting. This involves the question of who exactly comprised it, and specifically the movement's racial composition.

Historians of the movements of the Sixties naturally seek to relate them all to the most successful (and now hallowed) mobilization of the era: the civil rights movement. Some black liberation activists, notably members of the Student Nonviolent Coordinating Committee and the Black Panther Party, did articulate a leftist agenda, and members of other movements of color did the same. Some historians therefore include such activists in the category of "new left," evoking a kind of rainbow radicalism. Others insist that the "new left" of the 1960s included only the white left, as the almost entirely white membership of SDS might suggest.

White and black radicals of the 1960s, especially after 1965, generally agreed that they occupied separate, if friendly, movements. African-American and other nonwhite leftists typically made it clear that their first priority was "national liberation," and they identified themselves clearly with racially defined aspirations. To some, however, the aura of moral seriousness surrounding the civil rights struggle, as well as its uncontestable "Americanness," are so attractive that they seek to blur the lines that separated it from true "new left" radicalism.

INTENTION AND RESULT

The new left was both a movement in love with democracy and a movement that desired wholesale social transformation. It was, of course, an American movement, but the rise of similar movements in most other industrialized countries during the 1960s indicated the broad nature of the new left's concerns. New left members cherished a dream of making their country over—if not the world—and to rid it of both injustice and alienation. While some of them cherished the idea that a vanguard revolution might topple "the system" with a few dramatic strokes, most hoped that grassroots activism would bring about this change.

New left radicals recognized two means of effecting peaceful revolution. The first was the technique of mass mobilization that the civil rights movement and the antiwar movement brought to new heights in the 1960s. The second lay in cultural change, in which the new left increasingly placed its hopes and aspirations in its later years. New-left radicals would develop an alternative way of life, built upon values opposed to the familiar world of competition and materialism—values like love, peace, equality, and cooperation. Dissident youth would then demonstrate a superior alternative to the social mainstream, and gradually convert that mainstream to its values.

This emphasis on values and lifestyle indicates the importance of the relationship between the new left and the hippie counterculture. New-left radicals were far more committed than the advocates of "peace and love" to a direct struggle against dominant political forces. Yet both movements were convinced that dissident youth were the advance guard of a social revolution, and both sought to grow a new society within the old through a libertarian, neoanarchist method. In the late 1960s, despite the prominent discussions about violence and nonviolence, national loyalties, and "totalitarianism," this was the deepest and broadest reality of new-left activism.

Ironically, the new left's impact on American society was largely reformist. Sixties radicals did rejuvenate American democracy through their activism, and they infused the social mainstream with the values they celebrated, yet without altering the basic outlines of the American social, economic, or political systems. The radicals were wrong to think that American society could not tolerate their dissent and their militance without collapsing. They managed to improve certain parts of society, even if they had meant, instead, to overturn the whole thing. We can make sense of this discrepancy between intention and result, and take account of differing estimations of new-left politics, simply by understanding that with all political movements, rhetoric, intentions, and results frequently diverge, and must be analyzed separately.

Finally, new-left radicals, in the late 1960s, did express a degree of hostility to American society, but theirs was nevertheless a characteristically American movement, and a democratic one. The antagonism was mainly a reaction to the brutality of the Vietnam War. For most of its history and for most of its members, the new left political movement was an expression of faith that American society could find sufficient internal resources to renew its best features and become a qualitatively more humane and just society.

New-left radicals were democrats, but some of the earliest criticisms directed against them indicate that there is more than one kind of democrat. The liberal complaint that these revolutionaries were not democrats because they seemed intolerant and unreasonable, indicates that the authors of such criticism upheld a specifically liberal concept of democracy, one that was very influential during the early years of the cold war. This liberal concept depicted democracy as a stable arena for competing interests making specific, incremental demands in an orderly fashion.

The new-left concept of democracy was a different, messier one. New-left radicals believed in free speech, but as a means to "authentic" self-expression and to the spread of radical dissent. The essence of the liberal criticism was that the radicals were not real liberals, an idea with which the radicals happily agreed. The new left's abiding vision was one of Americans in perpetual motion, disrupting and challenging inequalities, changing society, and above all exercising power—in a living demonstration of democracy. It was a vision that both conservatives and liberals had reason in the 1960s, as they do today, to find disturbing.

NOTE

1. See James Miller, *"Democracy Is in the Streets": From Port Huron to the Siege of Chicago* (New York: Simon and Schuster, 1987), p. 332. Miller's book includes the full text of the *Port Huron Statement* as an appendix (pp. 329–374).

SOURCES

Anderson, Terry H. *The Movement and the Sixties: Protest in America from Greensboro to Wounded Knee.* New York: Oxford University Press, 1995.

Breines, Wini. "Whose New Left?" *Journal of American History* 75 (Sept. 1988).

Collier, Peter, and David Horowitz. *Destructive Generation: Second Thoughts about the 60's.* New York: Summit Books, 1989.

Diggins, John P. *The Rise and Fall of the American Left.* New York: Norton, 1992. Orig. published in 1973 as *The American Left in the Twentieth Century.*

Flacks, Richard. *Making History: The American Left and the American Mind.* New York: Columbia University Press, 1988.

Gitlin, Todd. *The Sixties: Years of Hope, Days of Rage.* New York: Bantam: 1987.

Gosse, Van. *Where the Boys Are: Cuba, Cold War America, and the Making of a New Left.* New York: Verso, 1993.

Keniston, Kenneth. *Youth and Dissent: The Rise of a New Opposition.* New York: Harcourt Brace Jovanovich, 1971.

Miller, James. *"Democracy Is in the Streets": From Port Huron to the Siege of Chicago.* New York: Simon and Schuster, 1987.

O'Brien, James. "Beyond Reminiscence: The New Left as History." *Radical America* 6 (July–Aug. 1972).

Losing Ground? The Great Society in Historical Perspective

Edward Berkowitz

Ronald Reagan, one of the country's most canny politicians, once explained that a key to his success was attacking the Great Society and defending the New Deal. When the press criticized him for dismantling many New Deal programs during the first years of his presidency, Reagan reminded reporters that he had voted for President Roosevelt four times. "I'm trying to undo the Great Society," he said. "It was LBJ's war on poverty that led us to our present mess."[1]

In making this accusation, Reagan fed on a conservative critique of the Great Society that culminated in the publication of Charles Murray's *Losing Ground* in 1984. The book's title expressed its thesis. Murray argued that America had been making progress in its efforts to reduce the poverty rate until the arrival of the Great Society in 1964. These social programs had the effect of making people dependent on the government, undermining their initiative, and leaving them poorer than they would have been without those programs. The poverty rate fell from 15.6 percent in 1965 to 11.4 percent in 1978 (from 12.1 percent to 6.1 percent when "in-kind" transfers, such as subsidized housing and money to buy food, are included). According to Murray, this drop reflected the fact that the government propped up the economy through such strategies as welfare. He argued that the "latent" poverty rate, which reflected people's "true" incomes rather than their welfare receipts, had actually risen during these years. In other words, the Great Society program, far from improving the situation, actually made it worse, and the country would have been better off trusting in the workings of the private economy. As Ronald Reagan put it, "the big taxers and spenders in the Congress had started a binge that would slowly change the character of our society and, even worse, it threatened the character of our people." As a result, "economic progress for America's poor had come to a tragic halt."[2]

As the success of Murray's book indicated, Reagan had touched a raw nerve. His victories in the 1980 and 1984 elections indicated, if only indirectly, that a majority of the nation's voters shared his views. He succeeded in making the Great Society a metaphor for the federal government's inability to manage social problems and its inferiority to the private market. Liberal politicians, such as 1984 Democratic presidential candidate Walter Mondale, sought, without much success, to promote a different metaphor that equated government intervention with progress. Mondale argued that the Great Society should be praised and preserved for its pathbreaking environmental legislation, its achievement of greater racial and gender equality and justice, its creation of educational opportunities and, in general, for its promotion of a more inclusive, equitable society.

As academic commentators usually do, those who framed the debate over the Great Society tended to see the issue in more complex terms than did the politicians. In academia, the relative strength of liberals and conservatives was reversed, with those on the left far outnumbering those on the right. Among followers of the debate on the Great Society, a minority of conservative economists, such as the Hoover Institution's Martin Anderson, and political scientists, such as New York University's Lawrence Mead, tended to share Reagan's and Murray's view that the Great Society had increased the effective poverty rate and made solving contemporary social problems more difficult. A majority of historians and historically minded social scientists, such as Jill Quadagno, disputed Murray's findings, although they were not uncritical of the Great Society. Liberal writers, such as Allen Matusow and Irving Bernstein, found fault with the design and implementation of its War on Poverty programs, even if they praised its civil rights and environmental programs. More radical leftist academics, such as Michael Brown, criticized the Great Society for substituting programs designed to provide work opportunities, such as the Job Corps, for more fundamental income redistribution. If those on the right believed the Great Society went too far in preferential treatment of African Americans and increased government spending, those on the left felt it had not gone far enough.

A great deal of misunderstanding on the part of nearly all of the participants pervades this debate. President Reagan emphasized the differences between the Great Society and the New Deal but tended to mix up the details of the two. Politicians and academic critics often had one program, such as the Community Action Program, in mind and equated it with the entire Great Society. They often failed to appreciate the wide range of Great Society programs, never considering, for example, the reforms that Lyndon Johnson's administration made in the field of immigration. These misunderstandings underscore the need for a brief overview of the Great Society.

Although one might contend, as historian Paul Conkin has, that the Great

Society was not particularly ideological in orientation, there are some unifying themes. First and foremost, the Great Society was about giving people an opportunity to participate in America's abundance. As President Johnson stated in the May 1964 speech that marked the project's formal unveiling, "the Great Society rests on abundance."[3] In making this statement, the president hoped to turn the Democratic Party away from the depression-oriented programs of the New Deal to a new set of initiatives that gave people the chance to join America's affluent society. Johnson and other liberal politicians believed that there were three key components to this process: education, civil rights, and urban redevelopment.

Under the Great Society, the federal government would support education by giving money to local school districts, providing scholarships to college students, and supplying funds for vocational training. The idea was to use federal revenues to invest in people, make them more productive, and ultimately reduce poverty and increase the nation's wealth. The strategy depended on removing significant barriers to participation in the labor markets. As these barriers were understood in 1964, that meant ending racial discrimination. Hence, civil rights became an important and enduring part of the Great Society, with major laws passed in 1964, 1965, and 1968.

The Great Society also sought to improve the areas where the poor lived. In addition to aid aimed at people, therefore, the Great Society initiated a series of programs aimed at places. In the past such aid had slanted toward rural areas to enable them to catch up with the progress assumed to be characteristic of cities. Hence, beginning in 1946, the federal government supplied money for hospital construction so that people living in rural areas could receive the same quality of medical care as those living in urban areas. The Great Society programs were aimed much more at cities; they included the Community Action Program that was part of the War on Poverty and the Model Cities Program. These programs attempted to increase what sociologists at the time called "community competence" and ensure that being from a bad neighborhood did not trap someone in "a culture of poverty."

Not only individual neighborhoods but also entire cities were beneficiaries of Great Society programs, as the federal government invested in rejuvenating downtown business areas and improving the transportation systems that connected various parts of metropolitan areas. "In the next forty years," President Johnson announced in his May 1964 speech, "we must rebuild the entire urban United States. . . . Our society will never be great until our cities are great."[4]

As the ambitious nature of the urban redevelopment program implied, the goals of the Great Society extended beyond providing opportunity to embrace a more fundamental aspiration: to improve the quality of life for all Americans. Central to this endeavor was using the power of the federal government to redress the imbalance between what economist John Kenneth Galbraith called "private affluence and public squalor."[5] Hence, President Lyndon Johnson and Lady Bird Johnson launched a campaign to beautify America by, among other things, removing garish billboards from the sides of highways and creating the National Endowment for the Arts. Reaching back to concerns that dated from the Progressive era, the Great Society included efforts to increase the size of national forests and parks, purify the air, and clean the water.

What distinguished the agenda of the Great Society from previous postwar reform efforts and made it such a tempting target for Ronald Reagan and left-wing critics was that President Johnson's proposals actually became law. Ronald Reagan could use these laws to illustrate the evils of government intervention in the private economy. Left-wing critics could lament the way in which these same laws perpetuated the status quo and blocked more fundamental reform.

Medicare is a representative example of the Great Society's impressive political triumphs and perplexing policy dilemmas. Like other Great Society programs, Medicare, passed in 1965, meant the achievement of a goal that, in one form or another, had been part of the Progressive era, New Deal, and postwar liberal reform agendas. Although this goal had often been expressed as achieving national health insurance, Medicare emerged in the late 1950s and early 1960s as a proposal to pay the hospital bills of elderly Americans. In this form it became one of the items on which John F. Kennedy campaigned in 1960. Although Kennedy pushed the idea when he became president, he was unable to get the proposal past Southern and conservative congressmen. As a consequence, Medicare was part of the unfinished business of the Kennedy administration that automatically got transferred to the Great Society. In this case, as in many others, President Johnson succeeded where Kennedy had failed.

Though the idea of Medicare originated in the 1950s, the completed version bore many of the earmarks of Great Society legislation. Like civil rights legislation, it guaranteed a previously excluded group—in this case, elderly Americans— access to a system that could improve their quality of life. It also represented an investment in the nation's future, since it would presumably make the elderly healthier and hence more productive and less of a burden on working Americans. Because the law was passed in 1965, it benefited from the previous passage of the 1964 civil rights law, of which Title VI mandated that institutions that received federal funds be racially integrated. Hospitals were among the most segregated institutions in the nation. If they intended to avail themselves of the Medicare law, they would need to integrate their facilities, and federal authorities made inspections throughout the South to make sure this was done. Passage of Medicare, therefore, was a primary force in the integration of the nation's hospitals.

Indeed, the implementation of Medicare showed that, contrary to later conservative laments, the federal government was capable of undertaking complex tasks. The head of the responsible agency later noted that in preparation for Medicare his employees inspected nearly all of the nation's hospitals to make sure they met the criteria for participation in the program, opened 100 new district offices, and issued 19 million Medicare cards. "As I look back on it . . . I don't know how the hell we did it, to tell you the truth," the agency chief said.[6] President Johnson, with typical hyperbole, compared beginning Medicare on July 1, 1966 with planning the invasion of Normandy. In many ways a great success, Medicare also revealed some of the Great Society's flaws. One problem was cost. The price of congressional passage was the accommodation of professional interests representing the doctors and the hospitals. Allen Matusow thus described the program as a "ruinous accommodation between reformers and vested interests" that produced runaway inflation in health care costs because the federal government agreed to reimburse hospitals their "reasonable costs" and doctors their "reasonable charges" for the care of the elderly.[7] The result was something like cost-plus contracts, in which neither the hospitals nor the doctors had any reason to hold down costs. Not surprisingly, then, Medicare became a very expensive endeavor, very quickly. The price of hospital care, for example, went from $1 billion in 1966 to $4.3 billion in 1968. By fiscal year 1993, Medicare and Medicaid (which paid the medical bills of people on welfare) would together account for 14 percent of the total federal budget, making these health programs the third largest item after Social Security and defense. By that same year Medicare and Medicaid would represent 44 cents of every dollar received by U.S. hospitals.

Another problem with Medicare was that it could not easily be adapted to the economic conditions of the 1970s. In that and subsequent decades, the program faced criticism from liberals and conservatives alike. Stripped to its essentials, Medicare, despite its social insurance trappings, functioned as a grant of money from the federal government to the nation's hospitals and doctors. Despite periodic efforts to monitor the quality of care, the federal government demanded little in return except that these hospitals and doctors serve the elderly. In other words, Medicare allowed access to the existing medical system. When in the depression decade between 1973 and 1983 the issues shifted to health care cost containment and the fundamental reform of the system to accommodate groups other than the elderly, Medicare became perceived as part of the problem rather than the solution. Conservative critics, such as the Heritage Foundation's Stuart Butler, questioned the ability of the federal government to run an effective program. Liberal critics, such as Paul Starr, realized that the constant fiscal pressure on Medicare made it more difficult to achieve the liberal goal of national health insurance. Nearly everyone conceded by the 1990s that changes were needed.

If Medicare engendered a backlash against government intervention in the medical field, the Elementary and Secondary Education Act (ESEA), another signature piece of Great Society legislation, produced similarly unintended effects in the field of education. Begun in 1965 with the great hope of transforming local school systems and making them conduits to economic opportunity, the act evolved into a means of increasing the budgets of local school systems. In Baltimore, for example, federal funds from ESEA and other Great Society programs accounted for 11 percent of the school budget by academic year 1971–1972. Few believed, however, that the Baltimore schools had improved between 1965 and 1972. To be sure, many variables intervened in the relationship between the level of federal funds and the performance of the city's schools, yet the fact remained that the ESEA had failed to transform those schools for the better. By the 1990s even liberal historians, such as Michael Katz, reported, "Massive flow of funds to schools that served poor children made no dramatic impact on the quality of urban education, which, as report after report has documented . . . remains a scandal."[8] Conservatives pushed for public money to be spent on private schools in the form of vouchers. Few liberals, other than bureaucrats with an obvious self-interest, rushed to defend the public schools.

Thus, in the fields of health and education, two of the vital centers of the Great Society, the crucial 1965 laws failed to live up to the hopes stirred by their passage. Instead, they simply perpetuated the status quo by providing more people with access to the basic systems. In the absence of sustained prosperity, continuation of what had come before meant a deterioration in the quality of services and fed the charge that, because of the Great Society, the nation was losing ground.

The backlash extended beyond the Great Society programs to their beneficiaries. Civil rights was the obvious example, but the notion applied to social welfare programs, such as Medicare, as well. Civil rights programs, sold in the 1960s as a means of making the economy function more efficiently by ending costly forms of segregation and discrimination, were perceived in the 1970s as another kind of special privilege. Policies such as affirmative action, hinted at by President Johnson in a famous speech at Howard University in 1965 and expanded upon by President Nixon, had the ironic effect of turning a vehicle for integration into what critics such as Herman Belz perceived as a costly and inefficient form of segregation. The Great Society was viewed as a breeding ground for programs that gave special advantages to a few at the expense of the many.

To use the language of historian James Patterson, the Great Society began by offering racial minorities and other groups overrepresented among the poor a "hand up" and ended by giving them a "hand-out."[9] The War on Poverty, a complex array of programs with an emphasis on manpower and training, started as part of a campaign to substitute jobs for welfare. Instead, it had the effect of greatly expanding the welfare rolls. Between 1965 and 1970, for example, the number of people on Aid to Families with Dependent Children increased in a given month from 4.3 million to 8.5 million. The increase tended to stigmatize the recipients, who were disproportionately African American and were unable to hold jobs at a time when America had never been more prosperous.

The reaction against the beneficiaries of Great Society programs involved more than race. By the Reagan era, because of programs like Medicare and Social Security, a New Deal program that was greatly expanded in the Johnson and Nixon eras, a backlash against the elderly had begun to develop. By 1982, the poverty rate among the elderly was slightly lower than for other age groups. Senior citizens enjoyed subsidized medical care through Medicare and income benefits that were indexed to the rate of inflation, an idea discussed during the Great Society and implemented by President Nixon. The working population, by contrast, struggled with rising medical care costs, relatively high levels of unemployment, and an inflation rate that was only just beginning to come under control. The elderly, it seemed, had life easy, due to government programs paid for by people who could barely afford to do so. This form of special privilege sparked intergenerational conflict.

As these examples make clear, the scope of government expanded considerably as a result of the Great Society. The combination of presidential exuberance and congressional politics in the form of interest group liberalism produced a large and often unwieldy set of grant-in-aid programs designed, it seemed to critics such as George Gilder, to accommodate every conceivable interest except that of the general public. The number of federal grant programs increased from 132 in 1960 to 379 by 1967. Outlays for these grants grew from $8.6 billion in 1963 to $20.3 billion in 1969. Before the Great Society, federal grants had gone for such basic governmental functions as highways and public assistance; they now were spent for a bewildering number of purposes, from family planning to school breakfasts, from mass transit aid to alcohol and drug abuse treatment. Even liberal economist Robert Reischauer believed that although such grants helped to expand the scope of domestic services, they left state and local governments badly overextended.

From Ronald Reagan's point of view, such grants represented a dangerous form of social engineering in which remote Washington experts presumed to know more than local experts. Furthermore, as the economy weakened, each grant in aid to the poor lessened the distance between the dependent and the working poor. The closing gap between what one could make on welfare and what one could get from a minimum-wage job created resentment among some working Americans. All too often the resulting conflicts had racial overtones and worsened the tensions between whites and blacks in urban settings.

Because of all of these factors, Ronald Reagan was able to peel away the Democrats' core constituencies who had supported the New Deal. In 1984 he argued that he, rather than liberal Democrat Walter Mondale, was being true to Franklin Roosevelt's memory. In the South, the once solid Democratic Party began to splinter as the Jim Crow system ended and African Americans began to vote in large numbers (thanks in large part to the Great Society's voting rights act of 1965). As early as 1964, southern states started to support the Republican Party. Working-class white ethnics, also strong supporters of the Democratic Party, found Ronald Reagan's critique of the Great Society attractive and voted for him in large numbers. By 1984, according to the conventional wisdom that could be found in any history textbook, "Reagan's triumph had reduced Roosevelt's coalition to rubble."[10]

One could, therefore, claim that the ultimate legacy of the Great Society was a bridge between the Eisenhower and Reagan eras. One might argue that it represented a temporary aberration, occasioned by the death of President Kennedy and fueled by a serendipitous prosperity, in which Americans momentarily laid aside their antistatist tendencies only to wake up in the next decade and realize they had done serious damage to the fabric of their society.

To be sure, the Great Society was an aberration. Seldom in this century has an ambitious president with a strong interest in domestic policy met a compliant Congress. Even in Johnson's case, the window of congressional tolerance closed quickly. In 1967, for example, it was much harder to gain congressional approval for domestic initiatives than it had been in 1965. But Johnson took full advantage of the available opportunities in 1964, 1965, and 1966. Some of the resulting programs were ephemeral, such as the Community Action Program, and some, such as the Elementary and Secondary Education Act of 1965, failed to meet their proponents' expectations. But others, such as the Civil Rights Act of 1964 and the Medicare program of 1965, proved to be lasting programs that permanently improved the conditions of American life. And if they had not passed during the era of the Great Society, they might never have passed. If, for example, the electoral dynamics had been slightly different and Richard Nixon had won the election of 1960, then there would not have been a Great Society. Although conceivably Nixon might have endorsed a sweeping civil rights law, we know that he would not have backed Medicare.

So, in the end, the Great Society must be seen as the entirety of Lyndon Johnson's domestic program and not just as one part of the War on Poverty legislation. Taking this perspective, one cannot come to all-encompassing judgment except to say that some of the programs worked and some did not. Charles Murray's and Ronald Reagan's evaluations are too sweeping, too glib. A more tempered conclusion seems in order: the Great Society changed America, particularly in such fields as social welfare and civil rights, and set it on a course that even Ronald Reagan found difficult to alter.

NOTES

1. Ronald Reagan, diary entry for 28 January 1982.

2. Quoted in Bruce J. Schulman, *Lyndon B. Johnson and the American Dream* (New York: Bedford, 1995), 100.

3. Quoted ibid., 174.

4. Quoted ibid., 175.

5. John Kenneth Galbraith, *The Affluent Society* (New York: New American Library, 1976), 187.

6. Robert Ball quoted in Edward Berkowitz, *Mr. Social Security: The Life of Wilbur J. Cohen* (Lawrence: University Press of Kansas, 1995), 243.

7. Allen Matusow, *The Unraveling of America* (New York: Harper and Row, 1984), 228.

8. Michael B. Katz, *In the Shadow of the Poorhouse* (New York: Basic, 1986), 258.

9. James T. Patterson, *America's Struggle Against Poverty* (Cambridge: Harvard University Press, 1986), 142.

10. Mary Beth Norton et al., *A People and a Nation* (Boston: Houghton Mifflin), 1016.

SOURCES

Anderson, Martin. *Welfare: The Political Economy of Welfare Reform in the United States*. Palo Alto: Hoover Institution, 1978.

Belz, Herman. *Equality Transformed: A Quarter Century of Affirmative Action*. New Brunswick, N.J.: Transactions, 1991.

Berkowitz, Edward. *Mr. Social Security: The Life of Wilbur J. Cohen*. Lawrence: University Press of Kansas, 1995.

Bernstein, Irving. *Guns or Butter: The Presidency of Lyndon Johnson*. New York: Oxford University Press, 1996.

Brown, Michael K. *Race, Money and the American Welfare State*. Ithaca, N.Y.: Cornell University Press, 1999.

Butler, Stuart and Anna Kondratas. *Out of the Poverty Trap*. New York: Free Press, 1987.

Conkin, Paul. *Big Daddy of the Pedernales*. Boston: Twayne, 1987.

Farber, David. *The Age of Great Dreams: America in the 1960s*. New York: Hill and Wang, 1994.

Galbraith, John Kenneth. *The Affluent Society*. 3rd ed., rev. New York: New American Library, 1976.

Gilder, George. *Wealth and Poverty*. New York: Basic, 1981.

Kaplan, Marshall and Peggy L. Cuciti, eds. *The Great Society and Its Legacy*. Durham, N.C.: Duke University Press, 1986.

Katz, Michael B. *In the Shadow of the Poorhouse*. New York: Basic, 1986.

——. *Improving Poor People: The Welfare State, the "Underclass," and Urban Schools as History*. Princeton, N.J.: Princeton University Press, 1995.

Matusow, Allen J. *The Unraveling of America: A History of Liberalism in the 1960s*. New York: Harper and Row, 1984.

Mead, Lawrence. *The New Politics of Poverty*. New York: Basic, 1992.

Murray, Charles. *Losing Ground: American Social Policy 1950–1980*. New York: Basic, 1984.

Norton, Mary Beth. *A People and a Nation: A History of the United States*. Boston: Houghton Mifflin, 1986.

Patterson, James T. *America's Struggle Against Poverty*. Cambridge, Mass.: Harvard University Press, 1986.

Pemberton, William E. *Exit with Honor: The Life and Presidency of Ronald Reagan*. Armonk, N.Y.: M. E. Sharpe, 1998.

Quadagno, Jill. *The Color of Welfare: How Racism Undermined the War on Poverty.* New York: Oxford University Press, 1994.

Schulman, Bruce J. *Lyndon Johnson and American Liberalism: A Brief Biography with Documents.* Boston: Bedford, 1995.

Starr, Paul. *The Social Transformation of American Medicine.* New York: Basic, 1982.

Urban Uprisings: Riots or Rebellions?

Heather Ann Thompson

In Detroit this week, America lost what was left of her innocence. During four terrible days and nights of burning, looting, and killing, civil society fell apart.

—*Washington Post*, July 30, 1967[1]

Between 1965 and 1970 Americans were shocked to see social unrest surface repeatedly in inner cities across the United States. During this tumultuous period poor urbanites rocked major American cities to their foundation by taking to the streets and engaging in bitter clashes with law enforcement, both local and federal. It was the violence that gripped Los Angeles during the summer of 1965 that first called national attention to the severe conflicts tearing America's urban centers asunder. On August 11 of that year, a relatively routine incident occurred, in which Los Angeles police officers stopped a black motorist for questioning. Quite unexpectedly, however, the poor residents of Watts responded to this particular event by taking to the streets, damaging cars, looting and burning stores, and fighting with the police. Then, only one year after the fires had been extinguished in Watts, the streets of Chicago witnessed similarly vicious clashes between poor blacks and local police. Peace did not return to that city until the mayor called in over 4,000 National Guardsmen.

The year 1967 witnessed an additional 164 eruptions in 128 cities across the United States. Of those, the upheavals in Newark and Detroit garnered the most national attention. Paralleling what had happened in Watts, violence descended upon Newark after rumors spread that an African American cab driver had been injured by the police during his arrest for a traffic violation. In the Motor City, urban residents burned their neighborhoods after a police raid during the wee hours of July 23, 1967. Before long, the mayor and governor decided to call in Army paratroopers, in addition to scores of National Guardsmen, to manage the deteriorating situation. As reporters from the *Washington Post* put it days later,

A metropolis of nearly two million people stood paralyzed for 72 hours. Its vital functions as a city were suspended. Detroit was ruled by the law of the tank, the .50 caliber machine gun, and the fire bomb. And the people of Detroit during the upheaval were ruled by fear. Picture, if you can, a major American city in which everything is closed—stores, offices, factories, banks, restaurants, theaters, and bars. Garbage and trash collection has stopped. The mails are halted. Telegrams are undelivered. Many phones are dead.[2]

By the time the military had restored order in the Motor City, 43 people had already been killed, and the damage done to both commercial and residential property totaled over 40 million dollars. If the Detroit upheaval of 1967 did not convince Americans that something deeply ominous was taking place in their nation's urban centers, the 130 uprisings that took place across the country only one year later, following the assassination of the Reverend Martin Luther King Jr., surely did.

But while most Americans became all too familiar with the days of violence that plagued inner cities across the United States during the 1960s, few seemed really to grasp why so much chaos was taking place. And, in the many years since those conflict-ridden times have passed, even fewer have been able to agree about what legacy, if any, this tumultuous decade has left. A critical debate has also raged in scholarly circles regarding how we should assess the historical impact of Sixties urban upheaval. Did the urban violence of the 1960s stem merely from reckless "riots," which served primarily to undermine postwar political stability and erode the existing possibilities for inner-city vitality? Or were they reasonable "rebellions" intended to call attention to the continuing inequality in these same urban centers?

Ironically, this scholarly debate is itself rooted in the tumultuous 1960s. Urban uprisings had become such a common occurrence by the close of that decade that President Lyndon Johnson appointed a special commission to determine why such conflict was erupting at the very height of his ambitious plans to improve life for America's poor. Personally, Johnson suspected that militant, black nationalist troublemakers had sparked the nation's urban uprisings and that those with a natural propensity for disorder and lawlessness had fueled them recklessly. The experts that Johnson appointed to the Kerner Commission, however, disagreed with his view and argued that these uprisings were, in fact, the expression of pent-up (and largely legitimate) frustration with the persistence of de facto segregation, the ever-present reality of racial discrimination, and the numerous incidents of police brutality in African American areas of the nation's cities.

The scholarship of academics writing about urban uprisings as they were happening reflected the same polarization as that between Johnson and his appointed conflict analysts. For example, writing only a few years after Detroit burned, historian Robert Fogelson weighed into the riot/rebellion debate with his contention that urban upheaval was, in fact, a legitimate protest of real grievances that African Americans held with conviction. Two years later scholars David O. Sears and John McConahay furthered Fogelson's position by arguing that by the mid-1960s there were African Americans living in inner cities who had grown justifiably impatient with the substandard social and economic opportunities offered them, and thus they protested in the streets. These "new urban blacks," as Sears and McConahay termed them, were better educated than their southern counterparts, and their civic rebellion was motivated by concrete and politically sophisticated goals. The "rebellion" thesis of Fogelson, Sears, and McConahay did not go unchallenged, however. It was scholar Edward Banfield who best articulated the competing "riot" interpretation after examining Harlem in 1964, Los Angeles in 1965, and Detroit in 1967. In short, Banfield argued for the wholly apolitical and destructive nature of urban uprisings. To Banfield, young urban blacks rioted because they lacked direction and were undisciplined, and because they were seeking the thrill and excitement occasioned by looting and burning.

However pitched the riot/rebellion debate was during the late 1960s, it was perhaps more so thirty years later. By the 1980s America's inner cities had declined dramatically. American whites had abandoned urban centers in droves, and the nation as a whole had largely repudiated the politics of Sixties-style liberalism. The fact that such dramatic transformations took place within such a relatively short period of time quickly piqued scholarly interest in a reexamination of both American cities and politics. In seeking the origins of urban crisis and conservative ascendancy, scholars found themselves reassessing the character and effect of Sixties urban uprisings once more. But while all seemed to agree that the civic upheaval of the 1960s had shaped America's future, the consensus ended there. Virtually overnight the riot versus rebellion debate of yesteryear began again.

Although many engaged in analysis of urban America's past and present during the 1980s, the works of scholars Jonathan Rieder, Jim Sleeper, and Fred Siegel argued most vociferously for understanding the tragic transformation of inner cities and the rise of conservatism as clear cut products of the havoc wrecked by sixties "riots." In contrast, it was historians Arnold Hirsch, Thomas Sugrue, and James Ralph who most successfully refuted this view, armed as they each were with detailed analyses of the very urban centers where those Sixties uprisings had taken place. While none of these authors explicitly set out to enter the riot/rebellion debate, their works fueled it dramatically. And notably, whether these recent scholars based their analyses of America's cities and politics on either the riot or the rebellion interpretation of civic upheaval during the Sixties, they all tended to judge the politics of the Great Society quite harshly. To the riot theorists, Great Society liberals did too little to rein in the excesses of the black militants and to address the fears and needs of urban whites. To those suggesting a more rebellion-based interpretation of the past, Sixties liberals did too little to rectify the severe imbalance of power and opportunity between the black and white communities of the nation's urban centers—allowing racism too often to thrive unchecked.

It was in 1985 that Jonathan Rieder wrote his pioneering history of the Canarsie section of Brooklyn, New York, which sought to make sense of what had happened during the tumultuous 1960s and 1970s to generate the racial polarization, white flight, and white disaffection with liberalism that so characterized New York by the mid-1980s. According to Rieder, throughout the 1950s Canarsie's primarily Jewish and Polish whites not only were committed to the politics of postwar liberalism, they specifically supported liberal strategies for attaining greater civil rights for urban blacks. Significantly, however, "when there were riots in the ghetto, whites tended to fuse the political violence of black protest with the ordinary criminality of the underclass . . . [and] by the middle of the 1960s the image of violence had tarnished the positive reputation earned by black protesters earlier."[3] Gradually, white residents of Brooklyn turned away from the inner city and the politics of liberalism itself because, as Rieder put it, they "tended to view rioting not as an outcry against grievous wrong but as a manifestation of the ghettos dwellers' tendency to scream for benefits, to wallow in self-pity about exploitation long past, and to use lofty ideals to mask thuggery."[4]

Five years later journalist Jim Sleeper published another study that connected the collapse of liberalism and the escalating urban decay of New York City to the misguided "riots" of the 1960s even more explicitly than did Rieder. Like Rieder, Sleeper saw the 1950s as years of racial coexistence and hope, which were severely tested only when black militants came along in the 1960s and engaged in the "politics of spite."[5] Even worse, Sleeper maintained, liberal politicians responded positively to the threat of rioting and, thus, in the minds of urban whites, they only encouraged blacks' commitment to the offputting "politics of resentment."[6] Indeed, because liberal leaders were blackmailed into catering to black militant excess (fearful as they were of more rioting or being labeled racist), they contributed directly to "the specter of rapid-fire neighborhood decay."[7] It was not that urban whites grew unsympathetic to civil rights goals per se, they simply grew disgusted with the liberal pay-outs to black extortionists unwilling to take any responsibility themselves for the plight of inner-city African Americans.

In 1997 writer Fred Siegel extended Rieder and Sleeper's analysis of New York to the cities of Los Angeles and Washington, DC. Siegel parroted Rieder and Sleeper's overall contentions by arguing that urban whites had supported liberalism and civil rights until it became clear to them that riots had become "a racial version of collective bargaining," where blacks threatened more violence if liberals did not give them more hand-outs.[8] According to Siegel, because Sixties liberals embraced "a political agenda based on threat and intimidation"[9] and because distinct urban riots evolved into a "'rolling riot,' an explosion of crime," after the 1960s had passed,[10] urban whites fled the inner city and the Democratic Party for reasons regrettable but logical.

Clearly, Rieder, Sleeper, and Siegel saw urban uprisings as riots primarily because they first assumed that the decades leading into the 1960s were ones of liberal "consensus" in which urban blacks and whites not only participated equally, but both benefited from as well. According to this perspective, all was on the right track in the cities of the late 1950s and early 1960s—racism was on its way out and the future looked bright—until impatient and largely self-interested black militants fractured the liberal coalition. The tragic outcome of this was that whites who had long been sympathetic to civil rights became alienated and thus felt compelled to turn forever away from progressive possibilities for America's inner cities. Secondly, and as important, these authors' analysis of both the present and the past was dependent upon the idea that the programs of the Great Society were doing too much, not too little, to help the ghetto poor, particularly since urban blacks refused to pay any dividends on the liberal, and the tax payers', investment in them.

But during the 1980s and 1990s historians Hirsch, Sugrue and Ralph each published books that challenged many of the key premises underlying these conclusions about Sixties liberalism and upheaval. Specifically, by taking a much more critical look at the evolution of northern urban centers after the Second World War, and by digging far deeper into the complexity of the post-war city itself, these historians discovered urban centers quite unlike those written about by Rieder, et al. To Hirsch, Sugrue, and Ralph all was not fine in America's cities prior to the tumultuous 1960s, and thus their understanding of both Sixties unrest and the crisis that befell urban centers and liberalism existed as a thorough refutation of the now repopularized "riot" interpretation.

Hirsch's book, *The Making of a Second Ghetto*, came out two years before Rieder published his study of Canarsie. Notably, Hirsch's portrait of the city during the Fifties undergoing racial recomposition as a result of the Second Great Migration was far less romantic than Rieder's. Hirsch made it clear that urban blacks who dreamed of decent housing and an equal voice in coalition politics upon their sojourn to the "promised land" of Chicago were shocked and disappointed to discover how determined urban whites were to keep them in the worst neighborhoods and to relegate them to second-class status in the political realm. Indeed, Hirsch argued, the barriers to black social and economic equality manifested themselves not only in the violent attacks launched by working-class whites against blacks seeking housing in better neighborhoods but also in the more subtle, but equally effective, discriminatory tactics of realtors, white-owned businesses, and the Chicago elite, which actively created the black ghetto as a permanent feature of postwar Chicago. Hirsch's examination of Chicago ended in 1960, before urban centers burned across the United States, but his detailed documentation of the rigid social and economic segregation that flourished during the 1950s, as well as the active white participation to maintain it, made clear that the civic upheavals of the 1960s did not jeopardize viable liberal solutions to racial discrimination. Rather they were trying to call attention to the movement's shortcomings.

Sugrue's path-breaking 1998 book, *The Origins of Urban Crisis*, made explicit the connections between the persistence of inequality throughout the 1950s and the explosion of urban unrest during the 1960s, which were only hinted at by Hirsch. In this study Sugrue examined the city of Detroit, which was known nationally as both a beacon of economic prosperity during the 1940s and 1950s and a "model city" of racial progressivism in the early to mid-1960s. Not only did the meticulous research in Sugrue's book indicate that Detroit's black community was effectively shut out of the city's living-wage jobs throughout the 1940s and 1950s (as a result both of overt employment discrimination and because unskilled jobs were becoming less plentiful since a process of deindustrialization already had begun), it also illustrated that urban working-class whites went to extraordinary lengths to ensure that blacks would be relegated to ghetto neighborhoods and substandard housing. Importantly, Sugrue pointed out that even when the Motor City became designated a "model city" of Great Society liberalism and began to wage an all-out War on Poverty, brutal discrimination in housing and employment continued to flourish. When urban blacks took to the streets in July 1967, they were not creating racial hostility—they were reacting to it. As important, Sugrue pointed out that the whites who fled the Motor City after 1967 had clearly decided that liberal strategies for integration and racial economic parity were not for them decades before Detroit burned.

Whereas both Hirsch and Sugrue focused on the social and economic fabric of the Fifties city, which urban unrest tore asunder in the 1960s, Ralph dissected the Sixties city itself. Ralph's book, aptly titled *Northern Protests*, picked up on Hirsch's urban blacks of the 1950s, who were still trying to move into better neighborhoods well into the 1960s. Specifically, Ralph examined the Open Housing Movement launched by Chicago's civil rights leaders, and led by none other than Martin Luther King Jr. Ralph's discoveries were quite illuminating—in part because of King's leadership, and perhaps more because Chicago's black community still desired to challenge segregation through the established mechanisms for doing so. The Open Housing Movement initially chose the strategy of marching, picketing, and petitioning to fully integrate the city's neighborhoods. As Ralph made clear, however, the reaction of white working-class Chicagoans to these efforts was brutally violent. As peaceful efforts to desegregate Chicago continued to be met with violence by whites in neighborhoods and the empty promises of city officials as well as real estate agencies, urban blacks in Chicago became angrier and increasingly determined to take what would not be given willingly. Ultimately, Ralph's study made it clear that the blacks who took to the streets shouting "Black Power" by the mid-1960s had watched their parents' strategies for equality come up short and were seeking a different way.

While Hirsch, Sugrue, and Ralph did not refer to the urban uprisings of the 1960s specifically as "rebellions," the preponderant evidence in their works suggests that rebellions is exactly what they were. Clearly, the white working-class uprisings in the streets of Chicago during the mid-1950s, or those during the Open Housing movement of the 1960s, were rebellions against liberally-sanctioned strategies for integration long before whites chose to vote for Reagan. As clearly, the African Americans who set cities aflame in the latter half of the 1960s were rebelling not only against white violence toward them but also against what they believed to be the empty promises of true equality and opportunity proffered by liberal leaders of the Sixties.

In the end it is not only the more probing and complex historical works of scholars such as Hirsch, Sugrue, and Ralph that suggest adoption of the "rebellion" interpretation of Sixties urban upheaval. The economic evisceration of America's inner–cities, which took place during the Reagan Eighties itself, as well as the infamous uprising which paralyzed Los Angeles in 1992, offers more concrete evidence of the intimate connections between economic deprivation, social exclusion, and the explosion of urban unrest as an expression of dissent. With eerie familiarity, the majority of those who analyzed the causes of the Los Angeles uprising have found that when a poor urban population is consistently shut out of economic opportunity, educational advancement, and equal treatment under the law, frustration mounts and urban insurrection becomes virtually inevitable.[11] And, for those who still wonder if the excesses of the Great Society might have caused the urban upheaval of the 1960s, it is instructive to note that when such a liberal experiment was abandoned in cities like Miami and Los Angeles after 1980, and the conservative politics of exclusion flourished unchecked, urban rebellions not only continued to plague America's cities—they were as desperate and dramatic as they had ever been.

NOTES

1. As quoted in Ann K. Johnson, *Urban Ghetto Riots, 1965–1968: A Comparison of Soviet and American Press Coverage* (Boulder, Colo.: East European Monographs, 1996), 78.

2. Ibid.

3. Jonathan Rieder, *Canarsie: The Jews and Italians of Brooklyn Against Liberalism* (Cambridge, Mass.: Harvard University Press, 1985), 70.

4. Ibid., 108.

5. Jim Sleeper, *The Closest of Strangers: Liberalism and the Politics of Race in New York* (New York: Norton, 1990), 90.

6. Ibid., 195.

7. Ibid., 33.

8. Frederick Siegel, *The Future Once Happened Here* (New York: Free Press, 1997), 17.

9. Ibid., 10.

10. Ibid., 9.

11. See collected essays in *Reading Rodney King, Reading Urban Uprising*, ed. Robert Gooding-Williams (New York: Routledge, 1993).

SOURCES

Banfield, Edward C. *The Unheavenly City: The Nature and Future of Our Urban Crisis*. Boston: Little, Brown, 1970; rev. ed., 1974.

Fogelson, Robert. *Violence as Protest: A Study of Riots and Ghettos*. Westport, Conn.: Greenwood Press, 1980.

Gooding-Williams, Robert, ed. *Reading Rodney King, Reading Urban Uprising*. New York: Routledge, 1993.

Hirsch, Arnold R. *Making the Second Ghetto: Race and Housing in Chicago, 1940–1960*. Cambridge: Harvard University Press, 1983.

Johnson, Ann K. *Urban Ghetto Riots, 1965–1968: A Comparison of Soviet and American Press Coverage*. Boulder, Colo.: East European Monographs, 1996.

Ralph, James. *Northern Protests: Martin Luther King Jr., Chicago, and the Civil Rights Movement*. Cambridge: Harvard University Press, 1993.

Rieder, Jonathan. *Canarsie: The Jews and Italians of Brooklyn Against Liberalism*. Cambridge: Harvard University Press, 1985.

Sears, David O., and John B. McConahay. *The Politics of Violence: The New Urban Blacks and the Watts Riot*. Boston: Houghton Mifflin, 1973.

Siegel, Frederick. *The Future Once Happened Here*. New York: Free Press, 1997.

Sleeper, Jim. *The Closest of Strangers: Liberalism and the Politics of Race in New York*. New York: Norton, 1990.

Sugrue, Thomas J. *The Origins of Urban Crisis: Race and Inequality in Postwar Detroit*. Princeton, N.J.: Princeton University Press, 1996.

Explaining the Tragedy of Vietnam

Richard H. Immerman

There may be no historical debate more contentious than the one that continues to rage over why the United States lost the war in Vietnam. In part this is because the question cannot be divorced from questions about the origins and character of the war and the causes for U.S. intervention. But in larger part, what drives the debate are the war's consequences and legacy. The Vietnam War cost America more than more than 58,000 of its young (and additional thousands who were physically or psychologically maimed), its economic vitality, its domestic consensus, even its faith in its government leaders and institutions. At least as important, America lost its innocence and ethos of exceptionalism as well as its confidence in its invincibility, all fundamental aspects of its self-image. George Bush announced that the victory in the Gulf War cured Americans of the "Vietnam Syndrome." The experiences of Bush's successor, Bill Clinton, demonstrate that Bush's proclamation was wildly premature.

The Vietnam Syndrome is so intractable because an explanation for the U.S. failure in Vietnam is so elusive and divisive. The world's wealthiest and most powerful nation committed millions of its men, billions of its dollars (from 1961 to 1975, military expenditures are estimated at $150 billion), and the minds and energies of its best and brightest for the purpose of defeating a poor, preindustrial adversary. On a country about the size of the British Isles, the United States rained down three times the tonnage of bombs the combined Allied forces dropped in all theaters during World War II. The United States lost nary a battle in the conventional sense. In the end, nevertheless, communists ruled over not only a unified Vietnam but also neighboring Laos and Cambodia. How could this happen?

The riddle is so perplexing that some people refuse to concede that America in fact lost the Vietnam War. They maintain that Vietnam was important only as a domino whose fall could trigger the toppling of more vital noncommunist states from Japan to the Middle East. That this did not happen, that even neighboring Thailand and Indonesia remained outside the communist orbit, demonstrates that the United States achieved its fundamental goal. Rather than premise their interpretation on the discredited domino theory, others, best represented by Richard Nixon, insist that the United States won the war in 1973 only to have Congress throw away the victory.

Nixon's argument is self-serving. The overwhelming consensus is that the United States did indeed fail in Vietnam. There is no agreement, however, as to why. On one side of a profound divide are those scholars and journalists who evaluate the U.S. effort as untenable from the start. They attribute the Communist victory to conditions indigenous to Vietnam: the enemy, the ally/client, and history and culture. Those on the other side, among whom America's military community and to a lesser extent its political community are disproportionately represented, believe that the war was winnable. They ascribe America's defeat to either insufficient or ineffective application of power. America came to grief in Vietnam because of the conditions here at home, not over there.

The earliest students of the Vietnam War almost universally stressed the daunting challenge confronting America from the beginning of its military engagement. George C. Herring and George McT. Kahin are the exemplars of this school of thought, an amalgam of "liberalism" and "realism." The foundation for their argument is the policy of containment, the basis for which was George Kennan and other Atlanticists' assessment of the situation in post–World War II Europe. The objective was to safeguard the nations of Western Europe from Soviet designs by bolstering their recovering economies, political stability, and military capabilities.

Conditions in Vietnam, however, were entirely different. The conflict was essentially internal in origin, a civil war not caused by external intervention. What is more, South Vietnam (the Republic of Vietnam [RVN]) was illegitimate, inherently unstable, and wholly dependent on the United States for its survival. Its governments in Saigon, from Ngo Dinh Diem to Nguyen van Thieu, garnered more contempt than support from its population. Indeed, whereas in principle the intention of containment was to promote self-determination, as applied to Vietnam containment promoted secession.

U.S. policy makers nonetheless applied containment, as both a policy and a strategy, to Vietnam. To Herring, Kahin, and like-minded scholars, the results were largely predictable. Rejecting the so-called quagmire theory associated with Arthur Schlesinger Jr., these authors present compelling evidence that the United States did not, step by misinformed step, stumble into a war much larger than it was ever prepared to take on. Policy makers were acutely aware of the likely magnitude of the military venture, and they did not expect

a qualitative improvement in the performance of either the South Vietnamese leadership or its army (ARVN) (although they misled the U.S. public
and Congress about both and underestimated the enemy's pain threshold).
They plunged ahead on the bases of their can-do spirit and arrogance of power, faith in their managerial skills and America's technological wizardry, belief
that luck was their ally, and fear of the domestic consequences if they did not.
They justifiably refused seriously to consider committing the resources, or accepting the risks, that would make victory possible.

These historians of U.S. foreign policy receive support from a number of
military historians who concur that the prospects for victory in Vietnam were
always extremely remote. In a very important book, Andrew Krepinevich argues that the United States was ill prepared effectively to wage war on Vietnam's terrain and in Vietnam's political environment. Success in a war without fronts required the skillful use of counterinsurgency and pacification
tactics. Formulated with Europe in mind, however, U.S. military doctrine was
rigidly conventional, calling for large combat units buttressed by massive fire-
power. Those in charge were never able to develop a strategic antidote for
their doctrinal shortcomings. In brief, the American way of war was inappropriate for Vietnam. Recent scholarship underscores that few U.S. military
leaders predicted a positive result from intervening. Yet for political and institutional reasons, they muted their reservations.

A more radical interpretive school, whose foremost proponent is Gabriel
Kolko but whose most renowned advocate is Noam Chomsky, agrees that the
U.S. defeat in Vietnam was a foregone conclusion. Yet the explanation for the
outcome, and for that matter American intervention, has little to do with politics, geopolitics, or culture and lots to do with economics. The United States'
attitude toward Vietnam was that of a traditional imperial power: ravenous, intolerant of any challenge to its hegemony, and loath to grant the challenger
legitimacy. Consistent with this mindset, it sought to eradicate the challenger,
but without burdening its own economy. Hence, America relied heavily on
"cheap labor" within Vietnam (the Saigon regime and its ARVN forces) and
an air war that was advertised as providing more bang for the buck.

North Vietnamese Communists and the National Liberation Front (NLF),
however, had only their strategy and ideology to rely on. Ascribing more
agency to the indigenous Vietnamese than practically any other U.S. scholar,
Kolko stresses how effectively Hanoi's People's Army of Vietnam (PAVN) exploited its assets (flexibility, mobility, experience, dedication, courage) to retain the initiative. More important, in contrast to such counterproductive
schemes as the strategic hamlet program and corrupt agrarian reforms identi-

fied with the RVN and its American patron, the Democratic Republic of Vietnam (DRV) in the north, true to its revolutionary promises, pursued enlightened and popular social programs that produced widespread fealty and cooperation.

Against this formidable opponent, the U.S. attempt to win on the cheap became prohibitively expensive. The Gold Crisis signaled that by 1968 the effort had become unsustainable. For this reason the Johnson administration began the process of disengagement that the Nixon administration could only complete. Neither North Vietnamese guns nor triple-canopied forests nor a misguided strategy defeated the United States. The war in Vietnam was primarily a competition between social systems, and that promoted from Hanoi proved vastly superior.

Ronald Reagan's description of the Vietnam War as a "noble cause" generated momentum for a revisionist interpretation that holds that America's objectives were achievable as well as honorable. Stalwarts in the military, represented prominently by Generals William Westmoreland and Curtis LeMay, had consistently maintained that had the civilians in Washington not proscribed an unrestricted bombing campaign and otherwise refused to allocate sufficient resources to win, the United States could not have been denied victory. In the event, Washington's obsession with the concept of limited war fitted the American soldier with a straightjacket while allowing the enemy the sanctuary his survival required.

The conservative political climate of the 1980s united this "forced to fight with one hand tied behind the back" lament with a "stab in the back" conspiracy theory according to which the U.S. effort was sabotaged by "long-haired peaceniks" abetted by Congress and the press. This combination proved particularly pernicious when, with the broadcast media in the vanguard, the failure of the Tet offensive in early 1968 was portrayed publicly as an American defeat. The results of this distortion: Johnson denied Westmoreland's request for additional troops, approved a partial halt to the U.S. bombing, and agreed to negotiate with Hanoi (and, of course, decided not to seek reelection). In short, the enemy was on the ropes, but the United States retreated. Nixon's effective combination of force and diplomacy still produced an honorable peace, but Congress allowed the Communists to violate it and overrun the South with impunity.

The most trenchant conservative voices are those of General Bruce Palmer and Colonel Harry Summers. Unlike most revisionists, both Vietnam veterans repudiate the "stab in the back" thesis. They concur that the war was winnable. The villains in their story, however, are not America's domestic dissenters but its political leaders and military strategists. By not seeking a declaration of war, President Johnson never insisted that the American public take its proper share of responsibility for prosecuting the war. Only this degree of commitment would have allowed for the appropriate deployment of forces, mobilization of the economy, international sanctions, and other prerequisites for victory.

Palmer and Summers target the military brain trust for even greater criticism. Westmoreland personally and the Joint Chiefs of Staff collectively disregarded virtually every Clauswitzian axiom of warfare and consequently failed to develop a viable strategy. In the view of Palmer and Summers, Vietnam was a conventional war of aggression by the North. Hence, instead of focusing on the southern insurgency by pursuing counterinsurgency tactics and, worse, a strategy of "search and destroy" that ceded the initiative to Hanoi, America should have adhered to Clauswitz's principles of offensive, mass, economy of force, and maneuver.

Summers's preference would have been to define the objective as the destruction of the enemy and to launch an offensive north of the 17th parallel. He settles for Palmer's recommendations because containment remained the policy. The United States should have cut off the infiltration of troops and supplies from the north and isolated the battlefield in the south by concentrating its forces along the Demilitarized Zone (DMZ) and extending west through Laos to Thailand. Bombing the DRV and blockading its ports would have further crippled Hanoi even as the ARVN cleared the enemy out of the South. The Vietnam War then would have ended like the Korean War. Instead, the United States fought defensively in an effort to wear down the enemy. America wore down first.

The interpretation of the conservative revisionists does not persuade. The most powerful of their arguments, those of Summers and Palmer, are fatally flawed. Aside from violating international law, the deployment of sufficient forces to form a impermeable line from Thailand through Vietnam would have far exceeded U.S. capabilities and been logistically impossible. Even if constructing such a barrier were feasible, moreover, the fundamental problem of the impotence, incompetence, and unpopularity of the U.S. client in the South would not have been mitigated. Liberals may have painted an overly benign portrait of the DRV's leadership or exaggerated the autonomy of the NLF. Their characterization of the conflict in Vietnam as an indigenous struggle, nevertheless, is on the mark. For more than two decades the United States sought to create and defend a nation in South Vietnam. But one can't make something out of nothing. One can't fight something with nothing, either.

Victory over an extraordinarily experienced, disciplined, and mobilized enemy in the inhospitable environment of Vietnam without local or foreign allies would have required a commitment of forces and sacrifice of resources that few Americans were willing to make. Fewer still were willing to accept a war of annihilation, the only real alternative to a war of attrition under the circumstances. Even those who believed Vietnam important to U.S. interests did not think it *that* important.

In response to the U.S. defeat in Vietnam, the so-called Weinberger Doctrine warns against military intervention without clearly defined purposes and objectives, a realistic strategy to both achieve these ends and then get out, an understanding of what commitments and sacrifices are necessary, and a willingness to make them. However prudent, these strictures ignore the seminal cause for America's failure: its ignorance of Vietnam's internal dynamics.

SOURCES

Baritz, Loren. *Backfire: A History of How American Culture Led Us Into Vietnam and Made Us Fight the Way We Did.* New York: Morrow, 1985.

Berman, Larry. *Planning a Tragedy: The Americanization of the War in Vietnam.* New York: Norton, 1982.

Braestrup, Peter. *Big Story: How the American Press and Television Reported and Interpreted the Crisis of Tet 1968 in Vietnam and Washington.* 2 vols. Boulder, Colo.: Westview, 1976.

Buzzanco, Robert. *Masters of War: Military Dissent and Politics in the Vietnam Era.* New York: Cambridge University Press, 1996.

Chomsky, Noam. *Rethinking Camelot: JFK, the Vietnam War, and U.S. Political Culture.* Boston: South End Press, 1993.

Gelb, Leslie with Richard Betts. *The Irony of Vietnam: The System Worked.* Washington, D.C.: Brookings Institution, 1979.

Halberstam, David. *The Best and the Brightest.* New York: Random House, 1972.

Herring, George C. *America's Longest War: The United States and Vietnam, 1950–1975.* 3rd ed. New York: McGraw-Hill, 1996.

Kahin, George McT. *Intervention: How America Became Involved in Vietnam.* New York: Knopf, 1986.

Kissinger, Henry. *Years of Renewal.* New York: Simon and Schuster, 1999.

Kolko, Gabriel. *Anatomy of a War: Vietnam, the United States, and the Modern Historical Experience.* New York: Pantheon, 1985.

Krepinevich, Andrew F. *The Army and Vietnam*. Baltimore: Johns Hopkins University Press, 1986.

LeMay, Curtis E. with MacKinlay Kantor. *Mission with LeMay: My Story*. Garden City, N.Y.: Doubleday, 1965.

Lomperis, Timothy. *The War Everyone Lost—and Won: America's Intervention in Viet Nam's Twin Struggles*. Baton Rouge: Louisiana State University Press, 1984.

McMaster, H. R. *Dereliction of Duty: Lyndon Johnson, Robert McNamara, the Joint Chiefs of Staff, and the Lies That Led to Vietnam*. New York: HarperCollins, 1997.

McNamara, Robert S. *In Retrospect: The Tragedy and Lessons of Vietnam*. New York: Times Books, 1995.

Nixon, Richard M. *The Real War*. New York: Warner, 1980.

——. *No More Vietnams*. New York: Arbor House, 1985.

Palmer, Bruce, Jr. *The Twenty-five-year War: America's Military Role in Vietnam*. Lexington: University of Kentucky Press, 1984.

Schlesinger, Arthur M., Jr. *The Bitter Heritage: Vietnam and American Democracy, 1941–1966*. Boston: Houghton Mifflin, 1966.

Sheehan, Neil. *A Bright Shining Lie: John Paul Vann and America in Vietnam*. New York: Random House, 1988.

Summers, Harry G., Jr. *On Strategy: A Critical Analysis of the Vietnam War*. Novato, Calif.: Presidio Press, 1982.

Westmoreland, William C. *A Soldier Reports*. Garden City, N.Y.: Doubleday, 1976.

The Women's Movement: Liberation for Whom?

Beth Bailey

In 1988, the wife of vice-presidential nominee Dan Quayle offered delegates to the Republican National Convention in Houston a resounding rejection of the women's liberation movement. "Most women," she claimed, "do not wish to be liberated from their essential natures as women." Looking back to her own experience in the 1960s, she reminded them, "Not everyone concluded that American society was so bad that it had to be radically remade by social revolution. Not everyone believed that the family was so oppressive that women could only thrive apart from it."[1]

On that point she is, of course, correct. If the Sixties were an era of radical protest and social change, they were also the seedbed of contemporary conservative movements. People struggled bitterly over the issues of the day, and women's liberation provoked as much controversy—though less public violence—among Americans as did the war in Vietnam or the civil rights movement. Marilyn Quayle's conservative dogma combines with more recent proclamations, such as the 1998 declaration by Southern Baptists (a denomination with 15.9 million members) that wives should "submit graciously" to their husbands, to demonstrate that conflicts over women's proper roles in the family and in American society did not end with the "Sixties."

But it was during the 1960s and early 1970s that most of the terms in which we continue to debate women's roles were set. Quayle sums them up admirably in her phrase "liberated from their essential natures as women." The critical debates over women's liberation have, since the 1960s, been framed around issues of *difference*. Do men and women have different "essential natures" that must be respected in social custom and law? Or are men and women essentially the same, divided more by the social construction of gender roles in society than by any fundamental facts of biology or psychology? Do the differences created by race, socioeconomic class, sexual orientation, or First World–versus–Third World/postcolonial status negate the utility of the category "woman," let alone the concept of woman's "essential nature"?

The most obvious divide here is between pro- and antifeminists, and a large number of contemporary Americans are unwilling to ally themselves fully with either camp. This split fits fairly neatly into a conservative versus liberal-to-progressive political framework, with the conservatives' position dependent on some notion of the "essential natures" of men and women and the centrality of what they call the "traditional" family. This is the conflict played out in the "culture wars" of the 1980s and beyond, the opposition that animates current struggles over public policy just as it framed the debates over the Equal Rights Amendment in the early 1970s. (A member of the U.S. Congress argued in the House debate over the ERA in 1971: "There is as much diversity between a man and a woman as there is between lightning and a lightning bug."[2])

The notions of difference and essential nature, however, have also been critical points of contention within the women's movement and among political liberals and progressives. Early "second wave" (1960s and 1970s) feminists struggled with such first principles and their implications. Many radical feminists based their beliefs on what they understood to be the essential—and opposite—natures of females and of males. Differences *among* women were equally difficult to resolve, and the women's liberation movement itself was ultimately rent by the problem of "difference."

While complex and important philosophical issues underlay all of these debates about women's liberation, the problem of difference was voiced most often, and most directly, in some version of the question: "Liberation for whom?" In the wrenching debates among 1960s/1970s white feminists, in the critical challenges posed by women of color and lesbians to the notion of a unified women's movement, and in the struggle for and defeat of the Equal Rights Amendment, that very basic question echoed.

On the question of liberation, writings about the women's movement fall into four major schools. First is that of the historians of the movement itself, who (while carefully conscious of the differences among women) embrace the notion of liberation and credit the women's movement with *Moving the Mountain* or making *The World Split Open* (titles of two of the major histories). Another category contains "backlash" books, which briefly recall the 1960s and 1970s to claim that during that era a reasonable feminism was perverted and ultimately served to betray, rather than liberate, women. Women of color, from a radically different stance, have questioned the relevance of a white feminist movement to their lives and struggles. And finally, more politically oriented works have looked not solely at the movement but also at the struggles over instruments of "liberation" such as the ERA and over women's roles in American society.

Historians of the women's liberation movement tend to agree on its general outlines. Most narratives describe two major strands of feminism emerging in the 1960s. Liberal feminism, centered in organizations such as NOW, worked through accepted political channels to seek equality for women in the existing system. Radical feminism—the women's *liberation* movement—emerged from the New Left and civil rights movements and, like other radical movements of the era, sought fundamental and revolutionary change in existing American society.

The standard popular narrative of the reemergence of the women's movement in the 1960s begins with Betty Friedan's *The Feminine Mystique*. In this tale—which contains more than a kernel of truth—women were stirred from the somnolence of the 1950s to recognize that they were trapped by the "feminine mystique," a set of constantly reinforced cultural myths that identified women's total fulfillment in their roles as wives and mothers. Historians have worked to complicate this story without dismissing it wholesale. Joanne Meyerowitz and the contributors to *Not June Cleaver* demonstrate that women's lives in the 1950s were not (as the title indicates) limited to such stereotypes. Leila Rupp and Verta Taylor describe the continued existence of a small women's movement after World War II in the aptly titled *Survival in the Doldrums*. Daniel Horowitz's meticulous research on Betty Friedan reveals that *The Feminine Mystique* had its roots not simply in Friedan's rising discontent with her own role as suburban housewife but also in her years of activism in labor unions and the antifascist left. He thus—sympathetically—argues for the radical roots of liberal feminism. And several histories of the movement do note that structural changes in American society (most important, the rising number of American women in the work force) help to explain the rise of liberal feminism in the 1960s.

Yet for many historians, themselves former participants in women's liberation groups, liberal feminism serves primarily as the prologue to the more compelling story of radical feminism. Critiques of liberal feminism made in the 1960s and 1970s, which continue to shape these histories, hold that liberal feminists simply demanded access to a racist society marred by many forms of inequity, while radicals sought to remake that society. Liberal feminists' focus on women's exclusion from the public sphere missed the point that their oppression in the "private" world of the family was as important as (and related to) their subordination in the public world. Historian Ruth Rosen titles her chapter on this portion of the women's movement "The Limits of Liberalism." In this vision, liberal feminism offered reforms that benefited women but certainly never approached the point of "liberating" anyone.

Most historians, building on Sara Evans's pathbreaking *Personal Politics*, tie radical feminism to other Sixties radical movements, rather than to its liberal sister or to the feminist movements of previous decades. Radical feminism, they argue, had its origins in (primarily white) women's experiences, first in the civil rights movement and then in the New Left. As women attempted to fight oppression in American society, they came to recognize their own oppression, both in that larger society and within the movement itself. Women realized that they were making the coffee and running the mimeograph machines while men made the decisions, that women "rose or fell [in an organization] depending on a man's sexual interest" and were jeered or even threatened when they attempted to speak out.[3] And women left the organizations in which they'd come to political consciousness and formed their own.

The groups that made up the "women's liberation movement" differed enormously from one another. All sought revolutionary change, and all accepted on some level the notion that "the personal is political." Yet they pursued vastly different tactics. Flora Davis, in *Moving the Mountain*, attributes those differences in part to the regional basis of groups and to the local situations they confronted. Alice Echols, in *Daring to Be Bad: Radical Feminism in America 1967–1975*, argues that the radical wing of the women's movement actually should be seen as two movements, radical feminism and cultural feminism, which have too often been conflated. "Most fundamentally," she argues, "radical feminism was a political movement dedicated to eliminating the race-class system, whereas cultural feminism was a countercultural movement aimed at reversing the cultural valuation of the male and the devaluation of the female." Radical feminists hoped to "render gender irrelevant," while cultural feminists "sought to celebrate femaleness." Thus, like liberal feminists, radical feminists tried to mobilize women "on the basis of their similarity to men," while cultural feminists organized around the notion of female difference from men.[4] Echols clearly favors the radical branch, arguing that in actions such as labeling the economic class struggle as "'male,' and thus irrelevant to women," cultural feminists turned away from the political struggle to transform the world.[5] According to Echols, they sought their own liberation through personal transformation rather than seeking liberation for all by transforming society.

Some critics have found Echols's schema too rigid, for many groups (as she herself notes) combined elements of cultural and radical feminism. Yet her work does help to explain why the women's liberation movement endured such wrenching struggles among its members, especially over the issue of difference. Begun in "sisterhood," with faith that they sought the liberation of all women, groups were torn apart as lesbians and working-class women demanded that the movement recognize the extent to which it was white, heterosexual, and middle class. Women of color often dismissed women's liberation as irrelevant to—or even contrary to—their own struggles on behalf of their "people." Flora Davis, in *Moving the Mountain*, points out that black women supported feminist goals earlier and in greater numbers than white women, but did not become active in the movement at least in part because they did not trust white women. She quotes feminist philosopher Elizabeth Spelman, who argues that white movement women tended to treat themselves as "some golden nugget of womanness," using the white middle-class heterosexual woman as the female norm.[6]

Recent works, such as Ruth Rosen's excellent *The World Split Open*, pay attention not only to the struggles over difference within the movement but also to the separate discussions of women of color. Conscious of their "double jeopardy" in gender and racial/ethnic terms, black women and Chicanas debated whether feminism could, in fact, offer them liberation. Many at the time decided, as Celestine Ware wrote in 1970, that "black feminism would be another attempt by the power structure to divide black men and women."[7] Begun as early as 1970, such discussions would continue over the following decades.

Works such as the enormously influential collection of writings, *This Bridge Called My Back: Writings by Radical Women of Color* (1981), and bell hooks's *Ain't I a Woman?: Black Women and Feminism* (1984) do not rewrite the history of the Sixties-era women's liberation movement, but in linking the issues of race and feminism they have had enormous impact on the ways historians of the women's movement and contemporary feminists alike view their projects. More recently, psychologist Aïda Hurtado, in *The Color of Privilege* (1996), surveyed the history of women's movements in the United States, attempting to explain why women of color historically have been unlikely to unite with a white feminist movement, even when many of its political and economic goals would benefit them. She concludes that "gender subordination, as imposed by white men, is experienced *differently* by white women and by women of Color," producing much of the disunity in women's movements from the nineteenth century through the end of the twentieth.[8]

Another set of writings has had less influence on historians but has greatly affected the public perception of feminism and the historical women's movement. Sometimes characterized as "backlash" works, books like Sylvia Hewitt's *A Lesser Life: The Myth of Women's Liberation in America* (1986) and Christina Hoff Sommers's *Who Stole Feminism?: How Women Have Be-*

trayed Women (1994) find little freedom in the legacy of "second wave" feminism. Hewitt described her own very frustrating experience trying to combine pregnancy and motherhood with her faculty position at Barnard College (a women's college that "had a reputation as a bastion of women's rights"). Caught, in her view, between the countercultural feminist model of earth mother and the "strident feminism of the seventies with its attempt to clone the male competitive model," Hewitt blames feminism for her plight. "The modern women's movement," she argues, "has not just been anti-men; it has also been profoundly anti-children and anti-motherhood." Hewitt does note that compared to Western European nations, the United States offers women a much weaker support system with which to mediate the dual roles of mother and worker, yet feminism, not government policies, bears the brunt of her criticism.[9]

Christina Hoff Sommers offers a polemic against contemporary "gender feminism," which she traces back to the Sixties era. According to her, gender feminism rejected the older liberal, or "equity," feminism that sought "equality and equal access for women." Instead, gender feminists viewed society through a "sex/gender prism," in which "even modern American women . . . are in thrall to a 'system of male dominance'."[10] The bulk of Sommers's work is an exposé of the extremes (mainly in academic circles) of this "New Feminism," which she characterizes as militantly gynocentric, self-preoccupied, resentful, and overly concerned with feminists' "own sense of hurt and their own feelings of embattlement and rage." Calling up the specter of government-sponsored gender-feminist "monitors" in every institution, she argues that gender feminists "speak in the name of women but do not represent them." The legacy of the women's liberation movement, in her view, is stifling and oppressive rather than liberating. She celebrates the older "classical equity feminism [that] is very much alive in the hearts of American women," and ends with a call for the large "mainstream" of women to rise up and reclaim "the pure and wholesome article first displayed at Seneca Falls," which is "American as apple pie."[11]

The question of Americans' support for feminism is highly contested, especially as public perceptions of its meaning and definition are at least as varied as the definitions explored above. Several works attempt to resolve that question in political terms. Social scientist Jane Mansbridge sought an explanation for *Why We Lost the ERA* (1986), offering explicit political lessons about promoting "the common good." Donald G. Mathews and Jane Sherron De Hart, in *Sex, Gender, and the Politics of the ERA* (1990), asked, "Why did women oppose a measure designed to benefit women?" and explored the perceived meaning of the ERA to those who believed that "sexual distinctiveness dictated rules and expectations so appropriately fitted to women that attempts to ignore it in the law were dangerous." Such an analysis, they argue, is less about why the ERA failed than about the place of the women's movement in America during the 1970s, and why, in 1980, Americans elected a president who campaigned against "feminism and the movement culture out of which it came."[12]

Sherrye Henry's *The Deep Divide: Why American Women Resist Equality* (1994) was born of her failed 1990 political campaign. She turned to focus groups to answer questions about why American women "fail to support candidates who would change the very system that crimps their lives and cripples the futures of their daughters." Concluding that the goal, after all, was to win (not just a campaign, but social change), she proposed a set of practical steps, one of which was jettisoning the term "feminist." "Words sometimes cannot shed their histories," she writes, comparing the term to "a good piece of furniture that has served a useful purpose but has gone out of style."[13]

While Henry's proposal that, in effect, the women's movement "shed [its] history" may be practical politics, Americans probably need to know more history, not less. And it is not so much the interorganizational struggles of the women's liberation movement that need to be recognized but its prehistory. Soccer moms (and dads) cheering on their daughters need to be reminded of a world before Title IX. Working people need to know that the want ads were, not so long ago, divided into "male" and "female" columns. College students need to know that in the 1950s, Harvard's Lamont Library was off limits to women—because they might distract male students. Americans need to be reminded of the profound changes that have taken place in our society, simply because the results have become so very *normal* that few remember when things were different.

Liberation for whom? In a society that continues to be divided by race and class and other categories of difference, the women's movement has not produced equal liberation for all. But both the liberal and the radical branches of the Sixties-era movement had profound impact on America, and for the better. Liberal feminism's successes in opening the public sphere to women are more quantifiable and more visible. Yet radical feminism's willingness to ask hard, disruptive, and revolutionary questions, to insist that "the personal is political," changed the lives of American women and men much more than most of us recognize. It was in conjunction that these movements produced, in whatever limited fashion, "liberation." With many excellent histories of "the movement," we now need to know more about how liberal and radical feminisms came together in the lives of American women—and men—to change the world.

NOTES

1. Tanya Melich, *The Republican War Against Women* (New York: Bantam, 1998), 318.

2. Flora Davis, *Moving the Mountain* (New York: Simon & Schuster, 1991), 130.

3. Ruth Rosen, *The World Split Open* (New York: Viking, 2000), 120, 130.

4. Alice Echols, *Daring to Be Bad* (Minneapolis: University of Minnesota Press, 1989), 6.

5. Ibid., 7.

6. Davis, *Moving the Mountain*, 359.

7. Rosen, *The World Split Open*, 279, cites Celestine Ware, *Woman Power: The Movement for Women's Liberation* (New York: Tower Publications, 1970).

8. Aïda Hurtado, *The Color of Privilege* (Ann Arbor: University of Michigan Press, 1996), viii. Italics hers.

9. Sylvia Hewitt, *A Lesser Life* (New York: Morrow, 1986), 185.

10. Christina Hoff Sommers, *Who Stole Feminism?* (New York: Simon and Schuster, 1994), 22–23.

11. Ibid., 24–25; 274–75.

12. Donald G. Mathews and Jane Sherron De Hart, *Sex, Gender, and the Politics of the ERA* (New York: Oxford University Press, 1990), xi, xii.

13. Sherrye Henry, *The Deep Divide* (New York: Macmillan, 1994), xxi, 408.

SOURCES

Berkeley, Kathleen C. *The Women's Liberation Movement in America.* Westport, Conn.: Greenwood, 1999.

Davis, Flora. *Moving the Mountain: The Women's Movement in America since 1960.* New York: Simon and Schuster, 1991.

Echols, Alice. *Daring to Be Bad: Radical Feminism in America 1967–1975.* Minneapolis: University of Minnesota Press, 1989.

Faludi, Susan. *Backlash: The Undeclared War Against American Women.* New York: Crown, 1991.

Giddings, Paula. *When and Where I Enter: The Impact of Black Women on Race and Sex in America.* New York: Morrow, 1984.

Henry, Sherrye. *The Deep Divide: Why American Women Resist Equality.* New York: Macmillan, 1994.

Hewlett, Sylvia Ann. *A Lesser Life*. New York: Morrow, 1986.

hooks, bell. *Ain't I A Woman?: Black Women and Feminism*. Boston: South End Press, 1982.

Horowitz, Daniel. *Betty Friedan and the Making of* The Feminine Mystique. Amherst: University of Massachusetts Press, 1998.

Hurtado, Aïda. *The Color of Privilege: Three Blasphemies on Race and Feminism*. Ann Arbor: University of Michigan Press, 1996.

Mathews, Donald G., and Jane Sherron De Hart. *Sex, Gender, and the Politics of the ERA: A State and the Nation*. New York: Oxford University Press, 1990.

Mansbridge, Jane J. *Why We Lost the ERA*. Chicago: University of Chicago Press, 1986.

Moraga, Cherríe, and Gloria Anzaldúa, eds. *This Bridge Called My Back: Writings by Radical Women of Color*. Watertown, Mass.: Persephone Press, 1981.

Meyerowitz, Joanne. *Not June Cleaver: Women and Gender in Postwar America, 1945–60*. Philadelphia: Temple University Press, 1994.

Rosen, Ruth. *The World Split Open: How the Modern Women's Movement Changed America*. New York: Viking, 2000.

Rupp, Leila, and Verta Taylor. *Survival in the Doldrums: The American Women's Rights Movement, 1945 to the 1960s*. New York: Oxford University Press, 1987.

The Sexual Revolution: Was It Revolutionary?

Beth Bailey

Was "the sexual revolution" really revolutionary? It's hard to argue otherwise.

In 1950, less than four percent of babies were born to unmarried women. The figure topped 30 percent in the 1990s, with approximately two-thirds of African-American births to single women.

In 1960, only 17,000 unmarried couples were living together "without benefit of matrimony," as it was described at the time. The number rose 900 percent by the end of the decade, and climbed steadily thereafter.

In 1963, a discussion on "The Sexual Revolution" was pulled from the schedule of a New York City TV station because the very topic was considered inappropriate for broadcast television. Meanwhile, married couples on TV sitcoms were consigned to twin beds; words like "pregnant" were frowned upon and no "off-color" language was allowed. In 1965, *The Sound of Music* won the Academy Award for best picture; in 1999 that accolade went to the R-rated film *American Beauty*.

In the 1960s, gay men and lesbians risked arrest, expulsion from school, and loss of employment if their sexual orientation was discovered. By the year 2000, many major corporations offered benefits to employees' same-sex domestic partners; most college campuses had active lesbian/gay/bisexual student organizations; and annual gay pride parades drew huge crowds of celebrants throughout the nation. (Gay men and women still were subject to dishonorable discharges from the military, and only one state recognized the unions—not marriages—of homosexual couples.)

Before the Supreme Court decision *Roe v. Wade* guaranteed a woman's constitutional right to abortion, women sought often-dangerous illegal abortions or attempted the process themselves, resorting to injections of lye, douching with bleach, or inserting coat hangers into their uteruses. In the early 1960s, Chicago's Cook County Hospital alone treated more than 5,000 women a year for abortion-related complications, some of which were fatal.[1]

In 1968, when a Barnard College student was discovered to be living off campus with her boyfriend, the incident became a national scandal. She was excoriated in newspapers throughout the United States, and Barnard received hundreds of calls and letters demanding her immediate expulsion for "immorality." Many of the writers used words like "alley cat" and "whore."

There have undoubtedly been fundamental changes in our society, and they are topics of great controversy and passionate debate in our public culture. The sexual revolution and its legacies have not receded into a nostalgic haze as have some other parts of "The Sixties." Public debates continue to rage over issues like abortion and homosexuality. Conservative Republican Dan Quayle attacked the fictional TV sitcom character Murphy Brown for glorifying unwed pregnancy and single motherhood in 1992, and "family values" has since become one of the most important political catchphrases of the day, with conservative, liberal, and progressive camps offering their own interpretations. Other critics go much further, attributing to the sexual revolution (sometimes in conjunction with the women's movement) the "collapse of the family," currently suffering from "unprecedented rates of illegitimacy, one-parent families, divorce, and abortion," and threatened by increased numbers of same-sex couples, which "separate the family from children, from the complementarity of the sexes, and from shame." According to this same critic, "freer sex has produced more rape," as, in a "liberated" culture, there is no reason for sexual consent to be withheld; it has also "worked to the advantage of men over women, the less aggressive sex." Finally, "the ideal of polymorphous perversity—that is, sex uninhibited by any notion of the shameful or of what is fitting—has received a rude shock from the emergence of AIDS." (The author continues, "Perhaps you should listen more carefully to the vague menaces of your mother, if she is sufficiently unenlightened, about what happens to people who do funny things for sex.")[2]

A great many Americans today support the changes encompassed under the umbrella term "sexual revolution," whether through direct advocacy of issues like abortion rights or simply as the beneficiaries, perhaps unwitting, of a cultural shift after which a woman's perceived "value" is no longer so directly related to her sexual "virtue." At the same time, the legacies of the sexual revolution are not stable and secure. Even in the liberal Clinton administration, Surgeon General Joycelyn Elders was forced to resign after she suggested that teaching students about masturbation in schools might be one strategy to promote sexual safety and slow the spread of the AIDS virus.

Public debates over the sexual revolution center on a fundamental question of judgment: bad or good? The specifics of the discussion are more or less nuanced, more or less sophisticated, but the key issue is whether or not the changes in our sexual culture have undermined or improved America. Historians are almost necessarily influenced: most are conscious that our histories may play a role in contemporary public policy debates. This awareness is an incentive to write with care, and with attention to the various possible audiences for and uses of our books. At the same time, historians' debates do not mirror the public contention over the sexual revolution. American historians of sexuality are an overwhelmingly liberal-to-progressive group on social issues (I can think of only one who writes about the United States who is avowedly conservative). Criticisms of the sexual revolution do exist in the scholarship, but they are likely to center on its limits, not its pernicious effects.

Oddly enough, historians have only recently begun to write about the sexual revolution of the 1960s and 1970s. Given the virtual mountain of books on the various social movements of the Sixties (especially civil rights), the number of works specifically about the sexual revolution is strikingly small. In fact, the majority of historical treatments (especially the earliest ones) are embedded in histories of movements for equality, social justice, or minority rights — those parts of the Sixties most widely accepted today, especially within academic cultures.

Estelle Freedman and John D'Emilio, in their pathbreaking work on the history of sexuality in America, *Intimate Matters* (1988), begin their discussion of the sexual revolution by describing the women's liberation protest at the 1968 Miss America Pageant in Atlantic City. While contestants were being judged on their poise, talent, and appearance in swimsuits inside the convention hall, a group of more than one hundred women protested outside, throwing bras, girdles, high-heeled shoes, and other objects of "enslavement" into a "Freedom Trashcan." Freedman and D'Emilio define the sexual revolution broadly (their chapter title is "Sexual Revolutions"), including *Playboy* and the "Cosmo girl" and singles bars and communes, but seem to find the heart of it in movements for social justice. "Sexuality emerged more clearly than ever as an issue of power and politics," they argue, noting that "women's liberation and gay liberation each presented a wide-ranging critique of deeply held assumptions about human sexual desire, its place in social life, and the hidden purposes it served. In particular, both movements analyzed the erotic as a vehicle for domination which, in complex ways, kept certain social groups in a subordinate place in society."[3]

Women's liberation and gay liberation, in fact, provide the framework for most early treatments of the sexual revolution and its prehistory. Historians of women and/or gender were particularly aware of the role of sex in their accounts of the emergence of the women's movement. Sara Evans's *Personal Politics: The Roots of Women's Liberation in the Civil Rights Movement and the New Left* (1979) identifies the complex role of sex in women's experiences of activism and liberation in the early 1960s. Elaine May, in *Homeward Bound*, locates a generation's activist spirit at least partly in the familial and sexual codes of the postwar American families in which its members grew up. Wini Brienes (*Young, White, and Miserable: Growing Up Female in the Fifties*) and Susan Douglas (*Where the Girls Are: Growing Up Female with the Mass Media*), in very different ways, find feminist visions an outgrowth of the cultural messages about sexuality that pervaded 1950s-era girlhood.

The gay liberation movement likewise provided both site and impetus for discussion of the sexual revolution. Like historians of women, scholars writing gay and lesbian histories sought to provide the validation of "a history of their own," seeking the voices and experiences of those who had been silenced. As Jonathan Katz wrote in the introduction to his 1976 documentary collection, *Gay American History*, "For long we were a people perceived out of time and out of place—socially unsituated, without a history. . . . Our existence as a long-oppressed, long-resistant social group was not explored. We remained an unknown people."[4] Much of this early work was devoted to demonstrating that gay life in America did not begin with the stand taken at the Stonewall Inn in 1969.

As historians started to write more directly about the sexual revolution, the question with which I began this essay—Was the sexual revolution really revolutionary?—was often the core around which they framed their work. Linda Grant (whose work encompassed both the British and American sexual revolutions) begins *Sexing the Millennium* (1994) on a poignant note. Describing her research to a whole series of women whose current lives would have been unimaginable a few decades earlier—before the sexual revolution—she was met with skepticism. Had there really been a sexual revolution? Grant was armed with the facts, with compelling descriptions of profound change. "And yet," she writes, "and yet . . . they had expected more."

The first two major histories of the sexual revolution build from that question of sufficiency. While it is blatantly obvious that much has changed, they ask, did those changes simply work to accommodate the existing power structure and ideological organization of sex? Was the sexual revolution "only [male] libertinage by another name"?[5] Was it "little more than a male fling and a setback for women," to whom the sexual revolution offered only "deepening objectification . . . as potential instruments of male pleasure"?[6]

Barbara Ehrenreich, Elizabeth Hess, and Gloria Jacobs, in an idiosyncratic and fairly breezy set of essays titled *Re-making Love: The Feminization of Sex* (1986), firmly reject that stance. *Playboy*, wife swapping—those represent the *men's* sexual revolution, a superficial set of changes that were, in fact, scarcely revolutionary. The *women's* sexual revolution, on the other hand, was revolutionary and liberating. Looking not to the avant garde of sexual experimentation or to sexual minority groups but to the everyday world of American mass culture, they argue that the winners of the revolution were not men but women, who entered a new era of sexual rights.

Linda Grant, in *Sexing the Millennium*, also begins with a dichotomy between male and female sexual revolutions, but moves to a less completely gender-based opposition. "The sexual revolution," she writes, "has its origins in the struggles of those who fought not to explore the crevices of their own desires, but to change the world." The former version appears as "the seediness of swinging and the disintegration of group marriages," the latter as a millenarian impulse, a desire to remake not only sex but society.[7]

Steven Seidman, in his 1991 *Romantic Longings*, rejects not only the idea of dual male and female/good and bad sexual revolutions but the very notion of revolution itself. He argues that America's sexual revolution was "more rhetoric than reality," as its main components—the "eroticization of female sexuality," the "rise of a homosexual identity and subculture," and "the sexualization of the public realm" all were part of a centurylong process of change, situated in a "cultural rebellion against Victorianism" in the early twentieth century, not in the rebellions of the Sixties. Seidman does find something truly revolutionary in the postwar era: a movement "to uncouple sex from love," or to reduce the importance of romance or love as the sole rationale for sexual expression, emphasizing notions of authentic selfhood, pleasure, and communication instead.[8] Seidman does not see this as the heart of the sexual revolution, for such understandings never fully challenged the dominance of the love-sex nexus. Instead, he sees it as an important countercultural stance, embraced by women as well as men, and most fully articulated in what he describes as the "community-building" role of casual sex in gay male social networks.

Recent works on the sexual revolution—what might be described as a "third wave" of scholarship—tend to manage the question of its nature not by positing dual movements (male/female; libertine/milleniarial) but by accepting the long-term, evolutionary nature of social-sexual change while still insisting on the importance of purposeful rebellions. The debate among these authors is not explicit but implicit. They look in different places for "the sexual revolution," and so find different revolutions.

At least superficially, the most similar books are James Peterson's popular survey, *A Century of Sex: Playboy's History of the Sexual Revolution, 1900–*

1999 (1999; commissioned by Hugh Hefner) and David Allyn's *Make Love, Not War: The Sexual Revolution: An Unfettered History* (2000). Both offer well-written narratives centering on the usual suspects—national figures like Hugh Hefner, Alfred Kinsey, and sex researchers Masters and Johnson, who undoubtedly helped to change the sexual culture of the United States. Each treats the sexual revolution as a set of struggles against repression, engaged in by people who (in Allyn's words) "devoted their lives to challenging society's views about sex."[9]

Allyn's definition of sexual revolution is much more woman-centered than Peterson's "Playboy's *History*," though that stance is somewhat complicated by the book jacket art: a close-up of a pair of "unfettered" female breasts, loosely confined in a halter on which is pinned a MAKE LOVE, NOT WAR button. Allyn locates the beginnings of the sexual revolution in the early 1960s because that is when "white middle-class Americans first really began to accept the idea of young women having pre-marital sex." He begins his first chapter: "When Helen Gurley Brown's *Sex and the Single Girl* hit bookstores in 1962, the sexual revolution was launched and there was no turning back."[10]

What Wild Ecstasy: The Rise and Fall of the Sexual Revolution (1997), by former *Penthouse Forum* editor John Heidenry, leaves behind the usual suspects to focus on sex's most ardent enthusiasts. Heidenry paints a disturbing (though not critical) portrait of the most extreme parts of America's sexual culture and, rather oddly, calls it the sexual revolution. He tells dark stories of *Deep Throat* "star" Linda Lovelace's physical and psychological abuse, including a description of her being "mounted" by a German Shepherd for a "dog movie"; describes sex communes like More House, devoted to oral sex and presided over by an obese forty-four-year-old man who had married a fifteen-year-old girl. This sexual revolution took place in Plato's Retreat and New York SM clubs like Hellfire; its heroes were people like Hellfire's Annie Sprinkle and Marco Vassi, a self-described "meta-sexual" who boasted that he'd had sex with 5,000 women and 10,000 men.

At the other end of the spectrum is my work, *Sex in the Heartland*, which portrays the sexual revolution in Lawrence, Kansas. While the movement would have looked much different without the "heroes" identified by Peterson, Allyn, and Heidenry, I argue, the acts of sexual revolutionaries do not in themselves constitute a revolution. It is when radical beliefs and practices are taken up (though perhaps less ardently embraced or strenuously practiced) by those who have *not* devoted their lives to subverting the norm that a true sexual revolution exists, rather than a set of sexual subcultures or bohemian lifestyles.

By looking to "ordinary" people in America's heartland, I show how wide-spread and fundamental the changes we call the sexual revolution really were. The movement I describe is mainstream, born of widely shared values and beliefs. It develops from major transformations in the structure of American society, such as the greater inclusiveness of the civil society that was created in part by federal interventions into local cultures in the years following World War II. It is made possible by people with absolutely no intention of fostering sexual freedom, such as policy makers who promoted birth control as a solution to the "population explosion" and college administrators who supported the end of parietal rules as a way to develop student "responsibility." Only after significant changes had already taken place in American culture was this nascent "revolution" engaged by purposeful revolutionaries.

Their revolution, however, was not a singular, unified movement. Even the committed sexual pioneers had radically divergent ideas about what they sought and how it might be achieved. In the 1960s and early 1970s, "living together" was quite different from "Free Love," which was not the same thing as "wife swapping," which was different from "The [SM] Scene," though all were, arguably, part of "the revolution." The rape fantasies that passed for "liberation" in some underground newspapers and newly "mainstream" pornography did not seem freeing to everyone who sought sexual liberation; many self-styled sexual revolutionaries were openly hostile to gay and lesbian struggles; many feminists confronted the role of sex—even "liberated" sex—in women's oppression, and movements for social justice splintered over what historian Ruth Rosen calls "the hidden injuries of sex." It is critically important to untangle the various strands of the sexual revolution, for a movement that encompasses both "The *Playboy* Philosophy" and "The Myth of the Vaginal Orgasm" is obviously not a coherent whole. At the same time, we must remember that most people did not experience these enormously diverse phenomena as separate and discrete. The world seemed in revolution because of the combined force of all these changes, not because of a single set of acts or beliefs.

Much of the recent writing on the sexual revolution has fallen prey to some of the problems that plagued early scholarship on the 1960s. The powerful temptation to look at the most extreme acts and actors leads to portraits of a sexual revolution that has little relevance to the lives of most Americans. And the urge to explain social change primarily by looking at the ideas and actions of leaders, great men and heroes of the cause (though the idea of Annie Sprinkle as a "great man" does give one pause), once again misses the point.

The sexual revolution in America was widespread and mainstream, and it was about more than just sex—it was also about concepts of rights and duties, citizenship, equality, who could belong to America's public culture and on what terms. In turn, the legacies of the sexual revolution are more than what sexual acts are legitimate, what sexual images can be seen by the American public. Instead, the sexual revolution fundamentally influenced our contemporary understandings of—and debates over—issues such as power, identity, gender, and diversity. Thus the revolutionary nature of the movement is not its extremism but its centrality to the mainstream of American life.

NOTES

1. Leslie J. Reagan, *When Abortion Was a Crime: Women, Medicine, and Law in the United States, 1867–1973* (Berkeley: University of California Press, 1997).

2. Harvey C. Mansfield, "The Legacy of the Late Sixties," in *Reassessing the Sixties: Debating the Political and Cultural Legacy*, edited by Stephen Macedo (New York: Norton, 1997), 24–25, 30.

3. John D'Emilio and Estelle Freedman, *Intimate Matters: A History of Sexuality in America* (New York: Harper and Row, 1988), 308.

4. Jonathan Katz, *Gay American History* (New York: Avon, 1976), 1.

5. Linda Grant, *Sexing the Millennium* (New York: Grove, 1994), 13.

6. Barbara Ehrenreich et al., *Re-Making Love* (New York: Doubleday, 1986), 1.

7. Grant, *Sexing the Millennium*, 26, 17.

8. Steven Seidman, *Romantic Longings* (New York: Routledge, 1991), 122–24.

9. David Allyn, *Make Love Not War* (Boston: Little, Brown, 2000), 7.

10. Ibid., 5, 10.

SOURCES

Allyn, David. *Make Love, Not War: The Sexual Revolution: An Unfettered History.* Boston: Little, Brown, 2000.

Bailey, Beth. *Sex in the Heartland.* Cambridge: Harvard University Press, 1999.

Breines, Wini. *Young, White, and Miserable: Growing Up Female in the Fifties.* Boston: Beacon, 1992.

D'Emilio, John, and Estelle Freedman. *Intimate Matters: A History of Sexuality in America.* New York: Harper and Row, 1988.

Douglas, Susan. *Where the Girls Are: Growing Up Female with the Mass Media.* New York: Times Books, 1994.

Ehrenreich, Barbara, Elizabeth Hess, and Gloria Jacobs. *Re-Making Love: The Feminization of Sex.* New York: Doubleday, 1986.

Evans, Sara. *Personal Politics: The Roots of Women's Liberation in the Civil Rights Movement and the New Left*. New York: Knopf, 1979.

Grant, Linda. *Sexing the Millennium: Women and the Sexual Revolution*. New York: Grove, 1994.

Heidenry, John. *What Wild Ecstasy: The Rise and Fall of the Sexual Revolution*. New York: Simon and Schuster, 1997.

Katz, Jonathan. *Gay American History: Lesbians and Gay Men in the U.S.A.* New York: Avon, 1976.

May, Elaine Tyler. *Homeward Bound: American Families in the Cold War Era*. New York: Basic, 1988.

Petersen, James. *A Century of Sex: Playboy's History of the Sexual Revolution*. New York: Grove, 1999.

Rosen, Ruth. *The World Split Open: How the Modern Women's Movement Changed America*. New York: Viking, 2000.

Seidman, Steven. *Romantic Longings: Love in America, 1830–1980*. New York: Routledge, 1991.

Debating the Counterculture: Ecstasy and Anxiety Over the Hip Alternative

Michael Wm. Doyle

"When the mode of the music changes, the walls of the city shake."

This epigram, attributed to Plato, was ubiquitous in the United States by the late 1960s. One encountered it frequently in the pages of the underground press, where it bestowed a hoary sanction on those who styled themselves "new barbarians" in laying siege to the citadels of culture and tradition. They used no battering rams or catapults — their weapons of choice were primarily instruments of culture in both the artistic and the anthropological sense, rather than those of politics, as that term was then conventionally understood. The apparatus of this cultural assault, as well as those who enlisted in the campaign, came to be known by the decade's end as the "counterculture."

The counterculture had its staunch defenders and its determined opponents. Nearly the only people without a polarized opinion about this social phenomenon were those who were unacquainted with it. Such a state of ignorance was difficult to sustain in the midst of the sensationalized news coverage that the "hippies" — as the denizens of the two major coastal bohemias, in San Francisco and New York, were called — generated in the news media, beginning in the mid-1960s and reaching its climax during the fabled "Summer of Love" in 1967.

The very word "hippies" connoted "junior-grade hipsters," a term purportedly coined by the Beats, their less numerous forerunners.[1] As late as the summer of 1963, the author of a *Newsweek* profile of Beat poet Gregory Corso observed that "nobody yet knows the name of the movement of the new decade except that it isn't Beat."[2]

Perhaps the earliest appearance in the popular press of the word "hippie" occurred in late 1964 in a *New York* magazine article which described and extolled "The New Bohemia" of Manhattan's Lower East Side. John Gruen, art critic for the *Herald Tribune*, noted the recent emergence of a community of "aggressively adventurous . . . artists, poets, dancers, musicians, actors and film makers," who could be clearly distinguished from earlier avant-garde figures—notably from the Beats, whose residence of choice was nearby in Greenwich Village.

What set these new bohemians apart was their dress ("representing the combined nostalgia for the rough-and-ready American frontier adventure, with 1930s international intrigue") and their long hair—unisex in style. Their "Whitmanian social awareness of 'the development of comradeship,'" Gruen explained, took the form of free-love communes, "violent dancing, cool talk, and a 'connection,' be it in the form of sex or dope." The East Village, he concluded, seemed poised to become a "focal point of serious dissension," albeit one, he presciently observed, beset by "a precariously balanced mixture of tensions."[3]

Less than a year later, on the other side of the continent, a San Francisco *Examiner* journalist contributed a four-part series on the birth of "a new bohemian quarter" in the Haight-Ashbury district. Here, lower rents and a less commercialized atmosphere than were found in North Beach had helped attract from that former Beat enclave "serious writers, painters and musicians, civil rights workers, crusaders for all kinds of causes, homosexuals, lesbians, marijuana users . . . and the outer fringe of the outer fringe—the 'hippies'."

The similarities between this "West Beach" neighborhood (the name never caught on) and the East Village were strikingly similar: a multiethnic blend of residents, coffee houses, and boutiques—even a chapter of the newly founded Sexual Freedom League. "Haight-Ashbury," the reporter noted, ". . . seems to be experiencing a renaissance that will make it a richer, better neighborhood in which to live."[4]

Both of these early accounts of the nascent counterculture provide upbeat, almost ethnographic descriptions of an incipient trend. The components of the later hype are all there—colorful characters, kinky sex, illegal drugs, "race-mixing"—offering just enough titillation to stimulate the audience's imaginings of what else might be found should one decide to go see it for oneself. The fact that these accounts were written primarily for a local readership suggests that by 1965 these neighborhoods were the site of a "scene" but not yet a scenario for a social movement.

That would soon change. Emissaries of the hip counterculture, notably including psychology professor Timothy Leary and novelist Ken Kesey, began proselytizing, each in his own way, for greater acceptance of psychedelic (literally, "mind-manifesting") drug use. Leary's devotion to that cause led him to forfeit his academic post at Harvard and found a "psychedelic research institute" (to all appearances, a hippie commune) in upstate New York. Kesey took a different route. Eschewing behavioral science as the only valid way of assessing the utility of psychotropic substances, he and a coterie of friends who styled themselves the Merry Pranksters set out on the open road in a converted and colorfully painted school bus to "drop acid" and "blow minds."

It wasn't long before the government stepped in and began criminalizing psychedelics. California, for example, enacted a law designating LSD a "controlled substance," set to take effect on October 6, 1966. In response, San Francisco's hip community organized the Love Pageant Rally on that date — not to protest the law, for to do so was rejected by some of their number as an overtly political act and thus in bad form for a new-wave cultural revolt. Instead, several hundred fancifully dressed people showed up in San Francisco's Golden Gate Park Panhandle to observe the occasion by getting high in public and grooving to live "acid rock" music.

A press release issued by the ad hoc group coordinating the event stated that the rally intended "to affirm our identity, community and innocence from influence of the fear of addiction of the general public as symbolized in this law."[5] The Pranksters attended with their bus "Furthur," although Kesey, who was then a fugitive from prosecution for a drug arrest, did not accompany them. A local newspaper reporter described the gathering as having been conducted "in the spirit of love," as the organizers had planned it. But then his glowing remarks leapt to the rather grandiose speculation that "if this movement ever catches on it could be the single most subversive influence on Western Civilization since Gutenberg."[6]

This journalist's approving comment resonated with other near chiliastic statements by representatives of the hip counterculture promoting their next major event, the Human Be-In. It was held on January 14, 1967, also in Golden Gate Park, and appears to have been the first such mass gathering to gain the attention of the national news media.

Organizers announced the event's significance with characteristic hyperbole: "Now in the evolving generation of America's young the humanization of the American man and woman can begin in joy and embrace without fear, dogma, suspicion, or dialectical righteousness. A new concert of human relations being developed within the youthful underground must emerge, become conscious, and be shared so that a revolution of form can be filled with a Renaissance of compassion, awareness, and love in the Revelation of the unity of all mankind. The Human Be-In is the joyful face-to-face beginning of the new epoch." "In unity," they proclaimed, "we shall shower the country with waves of ecstasy and purification."[7]

Some 20,000 free spirits and curiosity seekers responded to the pitch. Converging on the park's Polo Grounds, they were treated to speeches by such luminaries as Timothy Leary (making his first public appearance in the Bay area) and his associate in psychedelic experimentation, Richard Alpert; Beat poets Allen Ginsberg, Gary Snyder, Michael McClure, and Lenore Kandel; and Berkeley political activists Jerry Rubin and Jack Weinberg; interspersed with sets by rock bands including the Grateful Dead, Big Brother and the Holding Company, and the Jefferson Airplane.

Together, the Love Pageant Rally and the Human Be-In indicate that the counterculture was at least initially constructed with seductive, anticipatory rhetoric, as a kind of inchoate presence conjured up by wishful incantation. It was then embodied by the seduced, and elaborated in festive occasions designed to attract throngs of like-minded hedonists who willed themselves to believe that the experience of communal pleasure could somehow serve as the alternative to a repressed, repressive, unequal, and unjust society.

Not everyone agreed with the premises or the program. Curiously, the earliest and most thoroughgoing attacks on the counterculture emanated from the left. Veteran socialist Irving Howe, in a typological essay on "New Styles in 'Leftism'" (1965), assessed a range of radical responses evinced by his youthful contemporaries and found each of them wanting. "The small minority that does rebel tends to adopt a stance that seems to be political . . . ," Howe remarked, "but often turns out to be an effort to assert a personal style."

Howe rejected any endeavor that emphasized "how to live individually within this society, rather than how to change it collectively." The youthful radical, he charged, "tacitly accepts the 'givenness' of American society, has little hope or expectation of changing it, and thereby, in effect, settles for a mode of personal differentiation" by such affects as speech, clothing, and appearance. "If he cannot change [society], then at least he can outrage it." This approach was doomed to fail, he argued, because "the urban middle class can no longer be shocked"; on the contrary, "it positively yearns for and comes to depend upon the titillating assaults of its cultural enemies."[8]

Howe's criticism was amplified by Gershon Legman, a curmudgeon, folklorist, bibliographer, uncloseted homosexual, and champion of free speech, who issued his denunciatory manifesto *The Fake Revolt* two years later from the south of France. "The Gangsters of the New Freedom," he wrote, "have moved in on a very broad cultural front, and are already mopping up your kids with narcotic drugs and driveling pretenses of false revolt."

Legman's take-no-prisoners prose twitted the parents of these wayward youth: "You—you good Americans . . . are helpless to prevent your children from goofing out on marihuana and LSD, because you don't know how to give up drinking whiskey yourselves. . . ." His diatribe importantly took aim also at the creeping commodification of the counterculture, a strand of criticism that would find a full-scale analysis in sociologist Daniel Bell's *The Cultural Contradictions of Capitalism* (1976), and more recently in historian Tom Frank's *The Conquest of Cool: Business Culture, Counterculture, and the Rise of Hip Consumerism* (1997).

"The gangsterizing of the New Freedom is now moving on to become big business," Legman observed, ". . . with advertising, with publishing, . . . with broadcasting, television. . . . The Fake Revolt movement is, very simply, a trick of the money & power Organization and its dead-end culture, whereby all real révolté emotion and art are siphoned off into degenerate static and snowblitz, which *are no danger at all to the status quo*" [emphases in all quotations are rendered as in the originals]. It is, he concluded dismissively, "a revolt against nothing, and for nothing" which conveniently "replaces any revolt against the Atom Bomb and the profits system whose swan song it is."[9]

Legman's polemic was joined by other dissenting voices on the left that same year, 1967, when the hip counterculture reached its apogee in the Summer of Love. Warren Hinckle, the crusading editor of the monthly magazine *Ramparts*, in a much anthologized cover story entitled "A Social History of the Hippies," acknowledged "a clear vision of the ideal community" that the hippies were attempting, however erratically, to realize. It was, he wrote, a vision embodying "a radical political philosophy: communal life, drastic reduction of private property, rejection of violence, creativity before consumption, freedom before authority, de-emphasis of government and traditional forms of leadership."

Hinckle pointed out that in practice, however, a class of "merchant princes" (here he singled out Timothy Leary and rock promoter Bill Graham) had begun carving out potentially lucrative franchises in the "little psychedelic city-state" of the Haight-Ashbury. He also discerned a distinct "fascist trend . . . recognized by a totalitarian insistence on action and nihilism" in such figures as Ken Kesey and the Hell's Angels. (Kesey had introduced a Bay area chapter of the infamous motorcycle gang to LSD, thereby forging a precarious alliance. "We're in the same business," Hinckle reports Kesey as telling the Angels. "You break people's bones, I break people's heads.")

In the end Hinckle worried that "if more and more youngsters begin to share the hippie political posture of unrelenting quietism, the future of activist, serious politics is bound to be affected. The hippies have shown that it can be pleasant to drop out of the arduous task of attempting to steer a difficult, unrewarding society. But," he added ominously, "when that is done, you leave the driving to the Hell's Angels."[10] Two years hence, the violent debacle of an outdoor concert at Altamont, California, would provide fatal evidence that Hinckle's warning had gone unheeded.

Journalist Joan Didion spent part of that spring in the Haight doing a participant-observation piece for the *Saturday Evening Post*, publishing it a few months later (with a nod to Yeats's poem "The Second Coming") under the title "Slouching towards Bethlehem." The anomie and paranoia of the streets, where banal conversations were the rule, where adolescent runaways were preyed upon by scam artists and methedrine addicts, where mothers dispensed LSD and peyote to their five-year-olds, and finally the disconcerting weightlessness of the scene itself reflected and magnified her own admitted mental "instability."

"We were seeing the desperate attempt of a handful of pathetically unequipped children to create a community in a social vacuum," Didion wrote. "Once we had seen these children, we could no longer overlook the vacuum, no longer pretend that the society's atomization could be reversed." Her censorious tone injected a note of maternal concern, uttered from the other side of thirty. "This was not a traditional generational rebellion. At some point between 1945 and 1967 we had somehow neglected to tell these children the rules of the game we happened to be playing. Maybe we had stopped believing in the rules ourselves . . . ," Didion admitted ruefully. "They are less in rebellion against the society than ignorant of it, able only to feed back certain of its most publicized self-doubts, *Vietnam, Saran-Wrap, diet pills, the Bomb.*"[11]

Didion's lament was the flip side of the coin that had landed head's up in the mid-1960s. Where formerly at least some print journalists and hippie publicists had heralded the counterculture's arrival with millennial expectations, the press reports at the end of the Summer of Love overwhelmingly related how swarms of unworthy pilgrims had desecrated Psychedelphia and were now ushering in the apocalypse.

Didion's reading of the counterculture's origins and effects, like that of the left-leaning critics already cited, had much in common with that of commentators on the right. Philosopher Ayn Rand, for example, writing in her magazine *The Objectivist* (1970), acknowledged that "the hippies are right in one respect: the culture of today's Establishment is done for, it is rotted through and through—and rebelling against it is like rebelling against a dead horse. The hippies are wrong . . . ," she continued, "when they fancy themselves to be rebels. They are the distilled essence of the Establishment's culture, they are the embodiment of its soul, they are the personified ideal of generations of crypto-Dionysians now leaping out into the open."

Rand's repudiation of the dominant culture was at least as strident as the counterculture's, yet she had no intention of making common cause with this group of dissenters whom she despised utterly, and perhaps feared more than a little: "The hippies are a desperate herd looking for a master, to be taken over by anyone; anyone who would tell them how to live, without demanding the effort of thinking. Theirs is the mentality ready for a *Führer*."[12]

Ayn Rand's unsparing sentiments were echoed two years later in *Hippies, Drugs, and Promiscuity*, a featured selection of the Conservative Book Club authored by Suzanne Labin. Parisian-born and educated at the Sorbonne, Labin was forthright about the threat posed by the counterculture: "There is a certain softening already detectable in the fiber of American youth when it comes to will, initiative, patriotism, and love of science and success. . . . If it should continue to soak in the hippie-drug culture . . . then the nation will in the end decay. . . . And the whole West will follow America's decline."[13]

In this passage we have the elaboration of what might be called the domino theory of cultural decline: if the counterculture were allowed to topple traditional American culture, surely the rest of the developed world would succumb to this marauding menace and a new dark age would soon be upon us. The counterculture was now accorded the same demonic agency formerly reserved for characterizing Nazism and communism.

Significant attempts to rescue the counterculture from all the bad press it had garnered came more from its admirers than its participants. Among the most prominent were historian Theodore Roszak, in *The Making of a Counter Culture: Reflections on the Technocratic Society and Its Youthful Opposition* (1969), and legal scholar Charles A. Reich, with *The Greening of America* (1970).

Roszak's work, the more substantial of this best-selling pair, placed hippies and their fellow travelers within a broader oppositional framework and popularized the very name by which afterwards their movement has been collectively called. His work was among the first to provide a theoretical foundation for that movement. Roszak argued that the American "technocracy" (a managerial elite whose scientific worldview was hegemonic) had fostered a "myth of objectified consciousness" which produced and justified incessant warfare, unequal distribution of wealth, racial conflict, pollution, and overall an insidious coercion of citizens to abide by its rules. Against this formidable force he distinguished the "counter culture," a neo-Romantic movement peopled principally by those under thirty years of age. It was their active development of a subjective consciousness, as exhibited by their humanistic valorization of poetry, song, dance, shamanism, and communalism, that would ultimately redeem technological society.

While Roszak approved of the counterculture's embrace of mysticism and nonrational forms of artistic expression, he rejected its casual drug use as engendering a false consciousness. In the book's most soaring passage, Roszak adopted the first-person collective pronoun to identify "the primary project of our counter culture," which was "to proclaim a new heaven and a new earth so vast, so marvelous that the inordinate claims of technical expertise must of necessity withdraw in the presence of such splendor to a subordinate and marginal status in the lives of men."[14] This sweeping mandate strikes one as breathtakingly hubristic, even for a time that was rife with such declarations, harkening back to the ecstatic trope to represent the counterculture as a world-historical force.

What might be regarded as the first wave of Sixties counterculture historiography began in the 1980s with such works as Todd Gitlin's The Sixties: Years of Hope, Days of Rage (1987) and Jim Miller's Democracy Is in The Streets: From Port Huron to the Siege of Chicago (1987). Both books were authored by veteran New Left activists. Their insider knowledge and continuing commitment to political change brought the movement's history vividly to life. However, following earlier precedents among critics on the left, neither of them has anything very positive to say about the counterculture.

In fact, both Gitlin and Miller convey contempt for the period's cultural radicals. Miller collapses the counterculture into an all-encompassing new left movement, which permits him to disregard the distinction between the two modes of radicalism that other participants in these movements recognized and commented on at the time. For Gitlin the relationship between political and cultural radicals is much more clearly demarcated. The new left, he tells us, "had to confront a counterculture that was in many ways more attractive than radical politics. Should it outflank? Accommodate? Especially in California, the hip-political synthesis—along with violence—was the siren song of the late Sixties."[15]

The attraction, of course, emanated from that ubiquitous compound of sex, drugs, and rock 'n' roll. In Gitlin's view, when the politically committed allowed themselves to be seduced by hippie hedonism, the New Left movement succumbed to the allure of nihilism and self-destructed.

Miller and Gitlin owe an intellectual debt to Allen Matusow's The Unraveling of America (1984), which charts the denouement of postwar liberalism.

Prefacing a discussion of the intellectual foundations of the counterculture with the questionable assertion that "few hippies read much," Matusow nevertheless derives his interpretive framework from author Norman O. Brown, then a Wesleyan University classics scholar of Freudian persuasion. Brown's influential books, *Life Against Death* (1959) and *Love's Body* (1966), "forecast the hippie projects—Dionysian ecstasies, bodily and mystic," and helped launch a new Romantic era in which intuition and passion would triumph over reason and order.

In explaining what all this has to do with the decline of liberalism, however, Matusow falters. An inherently obstreperous counterculture adds color to the historian's narrative and allows him to convey some of the era's zaniness. But in trying to relate it to his larger theme, he makes the counterculture do double duty. It becomes both symptom ("hippies were only a spectacular exaggeration of tendencies transforming the larger society") and agent ("Dionysus had been absorbed into the dominant culture and domesticated, and in the process routed the Protestant ethic") of the breakdown in respect for authority and the other bourgeois values which undergirded the liberal consensus.[16]

A more recent entry in the field of Sixties studies is Terry H. Anderson's *The Movement and the Sixties* (1995). This is a comprehensive work which sympathetically explores the wide spectrum of social and political activism from the 1960 Greensboro sit-ins to the siege of Wounded Knee 13 years later. His periodization divides the era before and after the "riptide" year of 1968. Members of the "first wave" of the movement were preoccupied with civil rights, free speech and other campus-based issues, especially antiwar concerns. The "second wave" of activists who came of age after 1968, he argues, experienced the counterculture as a pervasive part of the political movement, along with new insurgencies among women, gays, and racial/ethnic groups such as Latinos and Native Americans.

Anderson attempts to synthesize the growing scholarship on the Sixties by showing how the calls for political empowerment which typified the first wave were united with the second wave's quest for liberation and focus on cultural rebellion. In assessing the legacy of those who participated in the counterculture, his judgment is balanced: "No doubt some of their values and behavior did contribute to social problems," he concedes, but their signal achievement is undeniable: they "significantly altered cold war culture. . . . The result is more personal freedom than at any time in the history of the Republic."[17]

Since the 1990s, public discourse over the counterculture's ultimate impact has often been subsumed under the term "culture wars," adopted from the title of a book by James Davison Hunter (1991).[18] Significantly, this rubric has produced a literature of declension among neoconservatives that, while continuing the critical stance first articulated in the 1960s by commentators from both ends of the political spectrum, also fits comfortably within the American jeremiad tradition.

Typifying this perspective is jurist Robert Bork, author of *Slouching toward Gomorrah* (1996), who in a recent speech asserted, "We are now two nations . . . two cultural nations. One embodies the counterculture of the 1960s, which is today the dominant culture. . . . The other nation, of those who ad-here to traditional norms and morality, is now a dissident culture."[19]

In a similar vein, Roger Kimball, managing editor of *The New Criterion*, in a ten-part series titled "Reflections on a Cultural Revolution" (1997–98), de-claimed that "the radical emancipationist demands of the sixties have . . . tri-umphed throughout society. They have insinuated themselves, disastrously, into the curricula of our schools and colleges; they have dramatically altered the texture of sexual relations and family life; they have played havoc with the authority of churches and repositories of moral wisdom; they have under-mined the claims of civic virtue and our national self-understanding; they have degraded the media and entertainment industry, and subverted muse-ums and other institutions entrusted with preserving and transmitting high culture. They have even, most poignantly, addled our hearts and innermost assumptions about what counts as the good life."[20]

The Sixties counterculture has triumphed utterly in this critique. Yet, iron-ically, only conservatives seem confident of such an all-embracing claim for its significance. For them it has come to stand for everything that has gone wrong in American society since the putative Golden Age of the 1950s. De-pending on the rhetorical construction, the counterculture is either the na-tion's scapegoat, which then must be ritually sacrificed, or else the cloven-hoofed Beast of prophecy whose reign must somehow be endured until the Second Coming.

The counterculture did not come out of nowhere. Its birth was midwifed by simultaneous booms in both the U.S. economy and population. In the final analysis it must be understood as an expression of the utopian premises that form the wellsprings of American civilization. The commitment to "life, lib-erty, and the pursuit of happiness" with which the new nation rationalized its independence to the world was deliberately left vague and ambiguous so as to maximize its universal appeal. Similarly the Constitution's dedication to realizing "a more perfect union" has at various times in our history been creative-ly reinterpreted so as to apply not just to states, but to states of mind and ways of living that seek to yoke heaven and earth in founding a New Jerusalem. Per-fectionism and realism are locked in a dialectical contest over the body politic of this nation as well as its soul.

The counterculture's quest for utopia was consonant, too, with the myth of American exceptionalism, a belief that posits the United States as both fundamentally different from and superior to other nations. It is character-ized by totalism, by novelty, and by openness to experimentation. It betrays a certain insouciance toward the strictures of tradition, which periodically swells into mass rebellion against legal authority. It exhibits a pronounced tendency to moralizing coupled paradoxically with the headlong pursuit of pleasure. Utopian projects all too often beget dystopian realities, as the record of the twentieth century attests. But those who deem themselves un-fettered by history are not conditioned to see past as prologue. Countercul-ture is inscribed in the American cultural pattern. If the witnesses to its most recent manifestation during the 1960s are credible, our civilization ebbs and flows on its waves.

NOTES

1. Charles Perry, *The Haight-Ashbury: A History* (New York: Random House / Rolling Stone, 1984), 5.

2. "Bye, Bye, Beatnik," *Newsweek*, 1 July 1963, p. 65.

3. John Gruen, "The New Bohemia," *New York, the Herald Tribune Magazine*, 29 Nov. 1964, pp. 8–9, 11–13, 17, 22, 24. Gruen later expanded his article into a book enti-tled *The New Bohemia: Art, Music, Drama, Sex, Film, Dance in New York's East Vil-lage* (New York: Grosset and Dunlap, 1966).

4. Michael Fallon, "A New Paradise for Beatniks," *San Francisco Examiner*, 5 Sept. 1965, sec. 1, p. 5.

5. [Allen Cohen], "A Prophecy of a Declaration of Independence," *San Francisco Oracle* 1:1 (20 Sept. 1966): 12.

6. "Love-Pageant-Rally Held to 'Celebrate' New LSD Law," *Sunday Ramparts* [San Francisco], 23 Oct. 1966, p. 6.

7. [Allen Cohen], "The Gathering of the Tribes," *San Francisco Oracle* 1:5 (Jan. 1967): 2.

8. Irving Howe, "New Styles in 'Leftism,'" *Dissent* 12(3) (Summer 1965): 295–323.

9. Gershon Legman, *The Fake Revolt* (New York: Breaking Point, 1967), 3, 5, 9; Daniel Bell, *The Cultural Contradictions of Capitalism* (New York: Basic, 1976); Tom

Frank, *The Conquest of Cool: Business Culture, Counterculture, and the Rise of Hip Consumerism* (Chicago: University of Chicago Press, 1997).

10. Warren Hinckle, "A Social History of the Hippies," *Ramparts* 5:9 (March 1967), 5-26 at 9, 19, 11, 17, 26.

11. Joan Didion, "Slouching towards Bethlehem," *Saturday Evening Post* 240, 23 Sept. 1967, pp. 25–31, reprinted in her book by the same title (New York: Farrar, Straus and Giroux / Noonday Press, 1990), 84–128. The quotations are from pp. 94 and 122–123 in the book.

12. Ayn Rand, "Apollo and Dionysis," *The Objectivist* (Dec. 1969–Jan. 1970), reprinted in her book *The New Left: The Anti-Industrial Revolution* (New York: Signet / New American Library, 1971), 57–81. The quotations are from pp. 77, 78 in the book.

13. Suzanne Labin, *Hippies, Drugs, and Promiscuity*, trans. Stephanie Winston (New Rochelle, N.Y.: Arlington House, 1972), 252–53.

14. Charles A. Reich, *The Greening of America* (New York: Bantam, 1970); Theodore Roszak, *The Making of a Counter Culture: Reflections on the Technocratic Society and Its Youthful Opposition* (Garden City, N.Y.: Anchor/Doubleday, 1969), 7–9, xii, 240.

15. Jim Miller, *"Democracy Is in the Streets": From Port Huron to the Siege of Chicago* (New York: Simon and Schuster, 1987); Todd Gitlin, *The Sixties: Years of Hope, Days of Rage* (New York: Bantam, 1987), 6.

16. Allen J. Matusow, *The Unraveling of America: A History of Liberalism in the 1960s* (New York: Harper and Row, 1984), 277, 279, 306, 307.

17. Terry H. Anderson, *The Movement and the Sixties: Protest in America from Greensboro to Wounded Knee* (New York: Oxford University Press, 1995), 421, 422.

18. James Davison Hunter, *Culture Wars: The Struggle to Define America* (New York: Basic, 1991).

19. Robert Bork, *Slouching toward Gomorrah: Modern Liberalism and America's Decline* (New York: Regan Books / HarperCollins, 1996); *idem*, "Conservatism and Culture," *The Intercollegiate Review, a Journal of Scholarship and Opinion* 34(2) (Spring 1999): 3–7, at 6.

20. Roger Kimball, "Reflections on a Cultural Revolution," a ten-part series in *The New Criterion* 16:1 (Sept. 1997) through 16:10 (June 1998). The quotation comes from his first article in the series: "Virtue Gone Mad," 4–11, at 4.

SOURCES

Anderson, Terry H. *The Movement and the Sixties: Protest in America from Greensboro to Wounded Knee*. New York: Oxford University Press, 1995.

Bork, Robert. "Conservatism and the Culture." *The Intercollegiate Review, a Journal of Scholarship and Opinion* 34:2 (Spring 1999).

——. *Slouching toward Gomorrah: Modern Liberalism and America's Decline.* New York: Regan Books / HarperCollins, 1996.

Bell, Daniel. *The Cultural Contradictions of Capitalism.* New York: Basic, 1976.

[Cohen, Allen]. "A Prophecy of a Declaration of Independence." *San Francisco Oracle* 1:1 (20 Sept. 1966).

——. "The Gathering of the Tribes." *San Francisco Oracle* 1:5 (Jan. 1967).

Didion, Joan. "Slouching towards Bethlehem." *Saturday Evening Post* 240 (23 Sept. 1967).

——. *Slouching towards Bethlehem.* 1968. Reprint, New York: Farrar, Straus and Giroux / Noonday Press, 1990

Fallon, Michael. "A New Paradise for Beatniks." *San Francisco Examiner* (5 Sept. 1965).

Frank, Tom. *The Conquest of Cool: Business Culture, Counterculture, and the Rise of Hip Consumerism.* Chicago: University of Chicago Press, 1997.

Gitlin, Todd. *The Sixties: Years of Hope, Days of Rage.* New York: Bantam, 1987.

Gruen, John. "The New Bohemia." *New York, the Herald Tribune Magazine* (29 Nov. 1964).

——. *The New Bohemia: Art, Music, Drama, Sex, Film, Dance in New York's East Village.* New York: Grosset and Dunlap, 1966.

Hinckle, Warren. "A Social History of the Hippies." *Ramparts* 5:9 (March 1967).

Howe, Irving. "New Styles in 'Leftism.'" *Dissent* 12:3 (Summer 1965).

Hunter, James Davison. *Culture Wars: The Struggle to Define America.* New York: Basic, 1991.

Kimball, Roger. "Virtue Gone Mad." *The New Criterion* 16:1 (Sept. 1997).

——. "Reflections on a Cultural Revolution," a ten-part series in *The New Criterion*, 16:1 (Sept. 1997) through 16:10 (June 1998).

Labin, Suzanne. *Hippies, Drugs, and Promiscuity.* Translated by Stephanie Winston. New Rochelle, N.Y.: Arlington House, 1972.

Legman, Gershon. *The Fake Revolt.* New York: Breaking Point, 1967.

"Love-Pageant-Rally Held to 'Celebrate' New LSD Law." *Sunday Ramparts* [San Francisco] (23 Oct. 1966).

Matusow, Allen J. *The Unraveling of America: A History of Liberalism in the 1960s.* New York: Harper and Row, 1984.

Miller, Jim. *"Democracy Is in The Streets": From Port Huron to the Siege of Chicago.* New York: Simon and Schuster, 1987.

Newsweek. "Bye, Bye, Beatnik." (1 July 1963).

Perry, Charles. *The Haight-Ashbury: A History.* New York: Random House / Rolling Stone, 1984.

Rand, Ayn. "Apollo and Dionysus," *The Objectivist* (Dec. 1969–Jan. 1970). Reprinted in her book *The New Left: The Anti-Industrial Revolution.* New York: Signet / New American Library, 1971.

Reich, Charles A. *The Greening of America*. New York: Bantam, 1970.
Roszak, Theodore. *The Making of a Counter Culture: Reflections on the Technocratic Society and Its Youthful Opposition*. Garden City, N.Y.: Anchor/Doubleday, 1969.
Williams, Rhys H., ed. *Cultural Wars in American Politics: Critical Reviews of a Popular Myth*. New York: Aldine de Gruyter, 1997.

Political Conservatism in the Sixties: Silent Majority or White Backlash?

Jeff Roche

There are several reasons why historians have tended to ignore or dismiss 1960s conservatives and their movement. Few within the academy sympathize with the political ideologies of Barry Goldwater or George Wallace or Richard Nixon. Moreover, many Sixties scholars who came of age during that era have tended to study the movements they themselves participated in or at least cheered from their carrels. Memory, as historian David Farber has pointed out, still has a powerful hold on historical interpretations of the decade. The civil rights movement and other rights revolutions, second-wave feminism, the New Left, and demonstrations against the war in Vietnam immediately leaped into scholars' and other Americans' consciousness. Consequently, the politics of protest dominated not only contemporary television newscasts and newspaper headlines but also most subsequent studies of the era.

Conservatism, on the other hand, emerged slowly in the Sixties. Discussions among friends, fellow students, co-workers, and neighbors at the barber shop, beauty parlor, lunch room, neighborhood association meetings, and union halls revealed like-minded people to one another. These primarily white Americans worried about the growth of federal welfare programs and affirmative action. They did not understand a Supreme Court that seemed more concerned with pushing school desegregation and upholding the rights of criminals than protecting hard-working, taxpaying Americans. A new generation of civil rights leaders, they observed, seemed dissatisfied with recent victories and demanded more than equality of opportunity—all that they themselves had asked. A rising feminism, a revolution in sexual attitudes, and the proliferation of pornography seemingly threatened the sanctity of the American family. Incredible increases in violent crime and drug use made them frightened in their own homes. And they looked with disdain at a generation of "spoiled" and unpatriotic college students protesting a war that few understood. By the late Sixties, these Americans were receptive to the messages of conservative politicians who promised a return to traditional morals and values.

When the door-to-door campaigners for Goldwater, Wallace, or Nixon came through their neighborhoods, they came to the door and listened. Later, they read the campaign literature the volunteers had given them. Some began to read William F. Buckley's newspaper columns. They attended political rallies. They began to speak out publicly about liberalism's impact on their neighborhoods or home towns. And in increasing numbers, they voted for conservative candidates. In the 1964 presidential election, conservative Republican Barry Goldwater ran against both the popular incumbent, Lyndon Johnson, and the memory of John F. Kennedy. Most media outlets portrayed Goldwater as an extremist with an itchy nuclear trigger finger. *Fact* magazine culled the "opinions" of hundreds of psychiatrists who overwhelmingly judged Goldwater mentally unfit to be president. He still won 27 million votes. Four years later, George Wallace, an unreconstructed segregationist running a rattletrap third-party campaign, won 13.5 percent of the popular vote. Richard Nixon, also running on a conservative platform, defeated both Wallace and liberal Hubert Humphrey.

How did this happen? How did conservatism, an ideology declared dead by most intellectuals just a decade earlier, suddenly come roaring back to life? How, in an era characterized by the seeming triumph of liberalism, did conservatives somehow manage to make their message palatable to a majority of Americans previously considered the bedrock of a Democratic/liberal coalition? Why did so many Americans come to reject the tenets of liberalism during the 1960s? For the last thirty years, scholars have sought to answer these questions.

To understand how historians and others have tried to explain the rise of conservatism, one must go back to a historiographic paradigm developed in the 1950s. The first social scientists to examine McCarthyism and the rise of what they described as the "radical right" believed that the United States had finally reached a political consensus. Most Americans and their politicians, they argued, accepted government's responsibility to ensure a healthy economy and to provide a limited safety net for those unfortunates who fell on hard times. Consensus scholars labeled the few Americans who were discontented with New Deal liberalism "pseudoconservatives," people clinging to nineteenth-century provinciality. Borrowing heavily from psychologist Theodor Adorno's theory of the authoritarian personality, sociologists Daniel Bell and Seymour Lipset, historian Richard Hofstadter, and others simply dismissed the followers of McCarthy (and later Goldwater and Wallace). People who believed that communists had infiltrated the federal government, they argued, were paranoids, temporarily anxious about their social and economic status, who blindly lashed out at elites. However, as the 1968, 1972, and 1980 presidential elections attest, the consensus interpretation of conservatism was not adequate to explain the revival of a popular conservative ideology.

As Alan Brinkley, Leonard J. Moore, and Michael Kazin have pointed out, a fundamental shift in the historiographic paradigm has only recently begun in earnest. In very basic terms, most postconsensus historians and political scientists examining the rise of conservative politics belong to one of two camps: those who study conservatism itself and those who attempt to explain the failure of liberalism. The latter has produced the dominant interpretation of Sixties conservative politics.

William Berman, in his study of modern conservatism, *America's Right Turn*, argues that most Americans supported an active federal government. They had a hard time, however, distinguishing between liberalism's economic programs and the social-cultural programs that focused on protecting individuals even in opposition to societal mores, and that seemed to promote radicalism and militancy, especially by minority groups. The legacy of the Vietnam War, the social upheavals of the Sixties, and, perhaps most important, the economic downturn in the early 1970s made liberalism suspect and conservatism attractive to many Americans. Conservatives were able to infuse a sense of small-town values into their more traditional anticommunist and antistatist philosophies and substitute distrust of big business for suspicion of big government.

Like Berman, scholars who argue that liberalism failed to maintain its hold on the American political tradition usually blame Democratic Party leadership and establishment elites for creating unpopular programs that engendered anger and frustration toward both the party and the federal government. Unlike Berman, most historians emphasize the role of race over economics. Beginning with the passage of the 1964 Civil Rights Act, the Democratic Party, by identifying itself with the civil rights movement, alienated enough segments of the New Deal coalition that conservative Republicans were able to create their own powerful coalition from voters disenchanted with Democratic liberalism. Race, the "backlash" scholars argue, played a significant role in this political realignment. By the late Sixties, white Southerners and working-class urban ethnics had grown weary of a decade of civil rights protests and leery of government attempts to redress discrimination in schools, neighborhoods, and the workplace. Moreover, these members of the New Deal coalition believed that their taxes went to pay for welfare programs primarily designed to help urban African Americans achieve more than simply an equality of opportunity. Conservatives within the Republican Party, therefore, were able to preach their message of limited government to a growing congregation who believed federal growth was directly linked to a civil rights agenda.

Perhaps the best example of the backlash school is Thomas Byrnes Edsall and Mary D. Edsall's *Chain Reaction: The Impact of Race, Rights, and Taxes on American Politics.* The Edsalls examine how and why white Southerners, and later white working-class Northerners, abandoned the Democratic Party over racial and economic issues. White southerners, according to the Edsalls, began to develop a viable two-party system as a reaction against the 1964 Civil Rights Act and the 1965 Voting Rights Act. Working-class whites in urban areas also turned their backs on the Democratic Party when the civil rights movement went north and targeted white neighborhoods for desegregation. The crucial moment came when rising tax burdens coincided with increases in welfare programs to alienate those who felt a significant portion of their paychecks was going to fund free money, free food, and free housing for African Americans. Conservative Republicans quickly stepped in and, using racial code words, won critical votes for their platform of limited government. The Democratic Party, rather than respond to constituents' shift in attitudes, enabled reforms within the party that took power from "mainstream" Democrats and gave it to a variety of "special-interest" groups, thus further weakening the ties between the party and segments of its New Deal coalition.

Other scholars of the backlash school come to similar conclusions. Jonathan Rieder's *Canarsie: The Jews and Italians of Brooklyn Against Liberalism* and Jim Sleeper's *The Closest of Strangers: Liberalism and the Politics of Race in New York* both blame the Democratic Party's promotion of a civil rights agenda and welfare programs for urban white ethnics' turn against liberalism. Sleeper reserves special comment for the increasing bellicosity of late-Sixties Black Power advocates. E. J. Dionne, a journalist, explores the impact of 1960s liberal and conservative ideology to explain why Americans hate politics. He argues that ideological polarization and backlash politics that began in the Sixties have left the American political landscape barren of original or productive ideas.

The backlash thesis, whether focusing on race, protest movements, or economics, depends, however, upon two critical assumptions: that race was not a crucial issue for white voters before the 1960s and that the breakup of the New Deal coalition was not an equitable price to pay to achieve social justice for African Americans. In a special issue of *The Nation* that appeared on December 9, 1991, Adolph Reed Jr., Julian Bond, Richard A. Cloward, Frances Fox Piven, and others level intense criticism at what they call the backlash orthodoxy. Reed and Bond especially decry the Edsalls' naiveté in assuming that race was not a factor in white attitudes toward politics before the 1960s and their unwillingness to consider the legitimacy of black demands in the late 1960s.

More recently, other historians have examined the impact of race among one segment of the New Deal coalition and found the backlash thesis wanting. Racial liberalism, "silent majority" scholars contend, was always a tenuous proposition and, in some cases, simply nonexistent at a local level. Thomas J. Sugrue insists in his study of postwar Detroit, *The Origins of the Urban Crisis*, that the ten years after World War II were the watershed era in race relations and engendered specific political attitudes of working-class white ethnics. Sugrue examines the efforts of white homeowners to prevent African Americans from moving into their neighborhoods and white workers to keep African Americans from all but the lowest paying jobs. He concludes that the politics of the 1960s were the culmination of twenty years of white resistance and the denouement of a trend toward popular conservatism. Arnold Hirsch agrees. In his study of residential segregation in the postwar Chicago neighborhood of Trumbull Park, he discovers that long before the tumultuous Sixties, Chicago's white ethnics had already demarcated the borders of black and white neighborhoods. In *Issue Evolution: Race and the Transformation of American Politics*, Edward G. Carmines and James A. Stimson explore the dynamics of race as an issue in American political culture. They argue that rather than suddenly appearing in the 1960s, race as a political issue evolved slowly from the 1940s.

Historians who have examined another significant segment of the New Deal coalition, white Southerners, have reached similar conclusions. They describe the ascendancy of racial politics in the North as the "southernization" of American politics. Dan T. Carter's important 1995 biography of George Wallace and his subsequent book, *From George Wallace to Newt Gingrich: Race and the Conservative Counterrevolution, 1963–1994*, both maintain that Wallace, well versed in massive resistance politics, manipulated racism and the media. His career foreshadowed the appearance of Southern racial politics on the national stage. Wallace realized after receiving thousands of supportive letters from all over the nation after his 1963 stand in the schoolhouse door at the University of Alabama that a large percentage of white Americans shared the racism of the South. As Carter demonstrates, Wallace's 1964, 1968, and 1972 presidential campaigns were designed to exploit racism as a campaign issue. The eruption of the civil rights movement and federal attempts to adjudicate or legislate racial justice in the North gave Wallace's message a strident salience for predisposed working-class white ethnics.

Carter attests that since the 1960s, conservative Republicans have dressed up Wallace's primarily racist message in code words like "busing," "property rights," "affirmative action," "welfare queens," and "law and order." Thus, they have been able to play the race card and receive support for their conservative agenda.

Few southern historians would deny that Wallace owed his popularity to the rise of massive resistance politics that followed the Supreme Court's 1954 *Brown v. Board of Education* decision. As Numan V. Bartley, Neil McMillen, Jeff Roche, and others have argued, the *Brown* decision unleashed the politics of race in the South to a degree unseen since the end of the nineteenth century. From 1954 through the 1960s, Southern politicians passed hundreds of laws designed to prevent any school desegregation regardless of the impact on local schools, communities, or economies. Massive resistance had two significant consequences for Southern politics. The first and most obvious was a resurgence of overtly racist politics on state and regional levels and a rising fervor over local control of schools, businesses, and community space that forced local Democratic politicians much farther right than the national party on civil rights. The second was the process, which I have described in *Restructured Resistance*, of the disintegration of a long-standing political alliance between Southern business elites and rural politicos. The destruction of the ruling coalition within the Democratic Party permitted businessmen to build a southern Republican Party based on an ideal of economic conservatism and working-class white southerners to support Republican social conservatism.

It is the convergence of social and economic conservatism within the Republican Party that dominates most historical interpretations of postwar conservatism. Unlike those who begin by witnessing the disintegration of the New Deal coalition, historians who study the conservative movement from outside a consensus framework have begun to question whether most Americans accepted liberalism as the natural culmination of the nation's political trajectory. Further, they challenge not only the notion of the permanency of the New Deal coalition but also the backlash paradigm by stressing the continuity of conservative political thought. Silent majority scholars face the daunting task of describing how the disparate threads of conservatism came together. By 1980, however, it was clear that libertarians, anticommunists, religious and social conservatives, business elites, white southerners, and many white working-class ethnics had joined to form a new coalition every bit as powerful and contentious as the New Deal coalition.

Scholars like Sidney Blumenthal and Jerome Himmelstein have been primarily concerned with the intellectual development of conservatism. They trace a straight line from opponents of the New Deal through Senator Joseph McCarthy's anticommunist crusade to Barry Goldwater's 1964 presidential campaign. What tied these different eras together was a renaissance in conservative thought in the immediate postwar years. In a time when most intellectuals had written off conservatism as an obsolete political ideology, books by Richard Weaver, Ayn Rand, Russell Kirk, and Friedrich von Hayek were quietly being passed, often hand to hand, among a growing number of politically minded intellectuals. Although very different in their arguments and core philosophies, these books denounced the modern welfare society and celebrated the order, morality, and individualism of their version of the past. It would be difficult to overestimate the importance of William F. Buckley's *National Review* in spurring the intellectual development of conservative thought. Editor Buckley and publisher William Rusher brought together many different, even contradictory, conservative thinkers to make the *National Review* the official mouthpiece for the burgeoning conservative movement.

Most historians agree that the crucial era for conservatism was the 1960s. Mary C. Brennan, John A. Andrew, Rebecca Klatch, Kurt Schuparra, and others have shown how ideological conservatives took control of the Republican Party between 1962 and 1972. Beginning shortly after Richard Nixon's 1960 defeat, conservatives working at the grassroots and precinct levels, including members of the John Birch Society and the Young Americans for Freedom, were determined to build an infrastructure and wrest control of the party from those they disdainfully described as the "Eastern Establishment." There was certainly a level of regional antagonism apparent within the party by 1964. As perhaps first and best explained by Kevin Phillips in his influential *The Emerging Republican Majority*, dissatisfied white Southerners and Westerners in the midst of incredible economic expansion could become the bases of support for a conservative Republican Party. Recently converted white Southerners had little patience for the liberal wing of the party that still supported civil rights advances. The overwhelming presence of the federal government in western states created a new breed of Western Republicans, well versed in the frontier myth of rugged individualism and hostile toward any expansion of federal power. As Robert A. Goldberg and Peter Iverson, two recent biographers of Goldwater, have pointed out, the Arizona senator personified the western conservative wing of the party and its doctrine of individualism. In 1964, despite numerous last-minute attempts by Eastern Republicans to deny Goldwater the nomination, conservatives, led by westerners, had taken over the party. Although Lyndon Johnson easily defeated the Arizona Republican, the infrastructure created to secure him the nomination remained in place.

The conservative wing of the party continued to gain adherents over the next decade and a half and by 1980 was in firm control of not only the Republican Party but also the presidency. If Barry Goldwater represented the western wing of the party, Reagan exemplified the culmination of Sixties conservatism; libertarians, anticommunists, white Southerners, white urban ethnics, and a growing force of religious conservatives flexing their political muscle for the first time rallied behind his campaign. That victory, however, was due to the conservatism of the 1960s. Those Americans, described by Richard Nixon as the silent majority—who had supported the war in Vietnam, grown weary of protest, feared that welfare programs threatened American self-reliance and individual initiative, been horrified over dramatic increases in crime and drug use, and did not understand long-haired advocates of free love and free speech—reconfigured the constituency of the Republican Party and breathed new life into conservative ideology. While some scholars may argue that these peoples' political attitudes formed in response to what they perceived as the excesses of the era, especially in the arena of civil rights, perhaps the more convincing argument comes from those who contend that this silent majority had always held particular if unarticulated beliefs about government, race relations, crime, and public behavior. The events of the 1960s forced these Americans to elucidate long-standing ideas. Consequently, the conservatism that emerged from the Sixties was both a continuation of a particular trend in American political thought and a response to the times.

SOURCES

Adorno, T. W., et al. *The Authoritarian Personality*. New York: Harper, 1950.

Andrew, John A. *The Other Side of the Sixties: Young Americans for Freedom and the Rise of Conservative Politics*. New Brunswick, N.J.: Rutgers University Press, 1997.

Bartley, Numan V. *The New South, 1945–1980*. Baton Rouge: Louisiana State University Press, 1994.

——. *The Rise of Massive Resistance: Race and Politics in the South During the 1950s*. Baton Rouge: Louisiana State University Press, 1999.

Bell, Daniel, ed. *The Radical Right: The New American Right Expanded and Updated*. Garden City, N.Y.: Doubleday, 1963.

David H. Bennett. *Party of Fear: From Nativist Movements to the New American Right in American History*. Chapel Hill: University of North Carolina Press, 1988.

Berman, William C. *America's Right Turn: From Nixon to Bush*. Baltimore: Johns Hopkins University Press, 1998.

Blumenthal, Sidney. *The Rise of the Counter-Establishment: From Conservative Ideology to Political Power*. New York: Times Books, 1986.

Brennan, Mary C. *Turning Right in the Sixties: The Conservative Capture of the GOP.* Chapel Hill: University of North Carolina Press, 1995.

Brinkley, Alan. *Voices of Protest: Huey Long, Father Coughlin, and the Great Depression.* New York: Knopf, 1982.

——. "The Problem of American Conservatism." *American Historical Review* 99 (April 1994): 409–429.

——. *Liberalism and Its Discontents.* Cambridge: Harvard University Press, 1998.

Carmines, Edward G. and James A. Stimson. *Issue Evolution: Race and the Transformation of American Politics.* Princeton, N.J.: Princeton University Press, 1989.

Carter, Dan T. *Politics of Rage: George Wallace, the Origins of the New Conservatism, and the Transformation of American Politics.* New York: Simon and Schuster, 1995.

——. *From George Wallace to Newt Gingrich: Race in the Conservative Counterrevolution, 1963–1994.* Baton Rouge: Louisiana State University Press, 1996.

Diamond, Sara Rose. *Roads to Dominion: Right-Wing Movements and Political Power in the United States.* New York: Guilford, 1995.

Dionne, E. J. *Why Americans Hate Politics.* New York: Touchstone, 1991.

Edsall, Thomas B. and Mary D. Edsall. *Chain Reaction: The Impact of Race, Rights, and Taxes on American Politics.* New York: Norton, 1991.

Farber, David. *The Age of Great Dreams: America in the 1960s.* New York: Hill and Wang, 1994.

——. "The Silent Majority and Talk About Revolution." In *The Sixties: From Memory to History,* ed. David Farber, 291–316. Chapel Hill: University of North Carolina Press, 1994.

——. "The 60s: Myth and Reality." *The Chronicle of Higher Education,* 7 Dec. 1994, B1–2.

Goldberg, Robert Alan. *Barry Goldwater.* New Haven: Yale University Press, 1995.

Hayek, Friedrich A. von (Friedrich August). *The Road to Serfdom.* Chicago: University of Chicago Press, 1944.

Himmelstein, Jerome. *To the Right: The Transformation of American Conservatism.* Berkeley: University of California Press, 1990.

Hirsch, Arnold R. "Massive Resistance in the Urban North: Trumbull Park, Chicago, 1953–1966." *Journal of American History* 82 (Sept. 1995): 522–50.

Hodgson, Godfrey. *The World Turned Right Side Up: A History of the Conservative Ascendancy in America.* Boston: Houghton Mifflin, 1996.

Hofstadter, Richard. *The Age of Reform: From Bryan to F.D.R.* New York: Vintage, 1955.

——. *The Paranoid Style in American Politics and Other Essays.* New York: Knopf, 1965.

Iverson, Peter. *Barry Goldwater: Native Arizonan.* Norman: University of Oklahoma Press, 1997.

Kazin, Michael. "The Grass-Roots Right: New Histories of U.S. Conservatism in the Twentieth Century." *American Historical Review* 97 (Feb. 1992): 136–155.

——. *The Populist Persuasion: An American History.* New York: Basic, 1995.

Kazin, Michael and Maurice Isserman. *America Divided: The Civil War of the 1960s.* New York: Oxford University Press, 2000.

Kirk, Russell. *The Conservative Mind: From Burke to Santayana.* Chicago: Regnery, 1953.

Klatch, Rebecca E. *Women of the New Right.* Philadelphia: Temple University Press, 1987.

——. *A Generation Divided: The New Left, the New Right, and the 1960s.* Berkeley: University of California Press, 1999.

Lipset, Seymour and Earl Raab. *The Politics of Unreason: Right-Wing Extremism in America, 1790–1970.* New York: Harper and Row, 1970.

McMillen, Neil R. *The Citizens' Councils: Organized Resistance to the Second Reconstruction.* Chicago: University of Illinois Press, 1971.

Moore, Leonard J. "Historical Interpretations of the 1920s Klan: The Traditional View and the Populist Revision." *Journal of Social History* 24 (Winter 1990): 341–357.

——. *Citizen Klansmen: The Ku Klux Klan in Indiana.* Chapel Hill: University of North Carolina Press, 1991.

The Nation. 253 (9 December 1991).

Phillips, Kevin P. *The Emerging Republican Majority.* New Rochelle, N.Y.: Arlington House, 1969.

Rand, Ayn. *The Fountainhead.* New York: Bobbs-Merrill, 1943.

——. *Atlas Shrugged.* New York: Random House, 1957.

Rieder, Jonathan. *Canarsie: The Jews and Italians of Brooklyn Against Liberalism.* Cambridge: Harvard University Press, 1985.

Roche, Jeff. *Restructured Resistance: The Sibley Commission and the Politics of Desegregation in Georgia.* Athens: University of Georgia Press, 1998.

Sleeper, Jim. *The Closest of Strangers: Liberalism and the Politics of Race in New York.* New York: Norton, 1990.

Schuparra, Kurt. *Triumph of the Right: The Rise of the California Conservative Movement, 1945–1966.* Armonk, N.Y.: M. E. Sharpe, 1998.

Sugrue, Thomas J. "Crabgrass-Roots Politics: Race, Rights, and the Reaction Against Liberalism in the Urban North, 1940–1964." *Journal of American History* 82 (Sept. 1992), 551–578.

——. *The Origins of the Urban Crisis: Race and Inequality in Postwar Detroit.* Princeton, N.J.: Princeton University Press, 1996.

Weaver, Richard M. *Ideas Have Consequences.* Chicago: University of Chicago Press, 1948.

The Sixties Legacy: "The Destructive Generation" or "Years of Hope"?

David Farber

In the United States Postal Service's millennial public balloting to choose stamps representing each decade of the last century, the "Super Bowl Kicks Off" (1967) easily out-polled Martin Luther King's "I Have a Dream" speech in the "How Do You Picture the 60s?" category. "Americans Demonstrate" finished near the bottom of the 30 listed choices. These days, images of the Sixties are not easily recalled in terms of antiwar protest, countercultural dissent, or a rights revolution. Americans seem to be including the Sixties within the newly recuperated happy-days-are-here-again, spectacle-driven, celebrity-inundated, free-market extravaganza that extends from the end of World War II through the go-go Clinton years.

Such images, both disturbing and inspiring, do not blend easily with the more ideological recollections of cultural-conservative revanchists, who regard "the Sixties" as the beginning of what they see as a battle for America's soul. After the Republican party won a majority in the House of Representatives in 1994, the staunchly conservative Texas congressman Dick Armey stated the issue as bluntly as possible: "To me all the problems began in the Sixties."[1]

At the same time, the trivialization of the Sixties into an era of mop-top singing groups and charismatic sports stars appalls those veterans of the social-change movement who envision themselves as having been the era's heroic protagonists. For many Sixties activists, it is hard to separate the cultural and political legacies of the era from their own, generally fond memories. Tom Hayden, one of the best known Sixties radicals, puts a gentle spin on the personal legacy: "Whatever the future holds, and as satisfactory as my life is today, I miss the Sixties and always will."[2]

Many participants of the Sixties era can remember exerting the power of collective political action in the name of moral good: ending racial segregation, protesting against a wrongful war, working to attain a more just society. In those memories, they see the advent of a more equitable, more humane nation—and a youth well spent.

Amid such a multiplicity of memories and political perspectives, the Sixties remain a contested era for scholars as well. They, too, continue to debate heatedly over the legacy of the Sixties. The most outstanding scholarly collection of essays on the subject is *Reassessing the Sixties* (1997), edited by Stephen Macedo. Although full of raging debate between Sixties-hating conservatives and a mélange of writers more sympathetic to the era, a thematic common ground does bring the two sides together—if only to provide a battlefield.

In the volume's introduction, Macedo stakes out that shared, thematic turf: " . . . [The Sixties'] controversies directly engaged fundamental American ideals of freedom and equality with a vigor and depth rarely matched before and not matched since. The question, all agree, is whether the changes associated with that notable decade represent a fuller realization of American ideals or their betrayal."[3]

Two of that volume's most conservative contributors, Harvey Mansfield and Jeremy Rabkin, make the case for betrayal. Like many of those who otherwise look back with horror at that tumultuous era, even these two firebrands level no charges against the early-1960s civil rights movement, which, in their estimation, was a peaceful call for integration and the enforcement of laws against racial discrimination. However, almost everything else about the era is, for them, fair game.

Mansfield condemns the Vietnam antiwar-movement activists, "who did their best to destroy" the bipartisan policy of cold-war communist containment and who succeeded in creating the "Vietnam Syndrome."[4] This "syndrome," Mansfield states, caused Americans to fear intervening militarily abroad, thus handcuffing American foreign policy from the early 1970s until 1991, when President George Bush successfully led the nation into the Persian Gulf War.

Two other conservative writers, Peter Collier and David Horowitz, in a different collection on the legacy of the Sixties, *Deconstructing the Left* (1991), add specifics to Mansfield's charges. Looking at American policy in Latin America in the 1980s, they argue that the antiwar movement "became a persuasion to do nothing about the expansionism of Marxist-Leninist regimes or about dominoes which might fall in our own hemisphere. . . ."[5] From this perspective, the primary legacy of the Sixties antiwar movement was the near failure of America's decades-long struggle against communism, which was only barely turned around by the successive presidencies of Ronald Reagan and George Bush.

By the late 1990s, as cold-war passions cooled, foreign policy of the 1960s diminished in interest to conservatives. While most critics of the Sixties maintained their position that the antiwar movement had been unpatriotic and wrongheaded, the decade's lingering "cultural rebellions" produced far greater outrage toward the end of the century, with the women's movement coming under particularly fierce fire. Critics accused feminists of fomenting sexual promiscuity (also sexual frigidity), destroying the traditional family, and seeking to overturn the timeless truths contained within the male and female social roles.

For many conservatives, especially religious conservatives, feminism remains the most subversive and dangerous legacy of the Sixties. Writing in the mid-1990s, Jeremy Rabkin asserted: "Only feminism still inspires the same spirit of shrill denunciation and nonnegotiable 'demands.' Only feminism still sets itself up for endless battle against 'oppressive social structures.'"[6]

Few, if any, active feminists of the 1990s fit this caricature, and one could easily argue that various small factions of radical environmentalists and racial/ethnic left- or right-wing activists better fit such a profile. Nonetheless, such a wholesale denunciation of feminism as the last, most fanatical "leftover" from the Sixties is indicative of the fury with which some conservatives view the cultural changes—especially the changing roles of women—forced on America, they would say, by Sixties-era activists.

In part, feminism, or the women's movement, works for conservative critics as a stand-in for harder-to-target cultural change, which they sometimes loosely denounce as "the Sixties counterculture." During the early 1990s, Vice President Dan Quayle, in a widely quoted speech, led the charge against his own "baby boom" generation: "When we were young, it was fashionable to declare war against traditional values. Indulgence and self-gratification seemed to have no consequences. Many of our generation glamorized casual sex and drug use, evaded responsibility, and trashed authority."[7]

As historian Paul Lyons writes in his insightful book, *New Left, New Right, and the Legacy of the Sixties* (1996), Quayle and other conservatives use the argument that the Sixties generation created a "poverty of values" that wracked American society in general but had particularly disastrous consequences for impoverished Americans.[8] In line with the old economic adage, "When the rich sneeze, the poor get pneumonia," the conservatives argue that middle-class countercultural flirtations with amoral hedonism broke down the fragile cultural and religious standards that kept less well-educated, less economically secure Americans from falling prey to destructive behavior. One of the most awful legacies of the Sixties, they say, was the cultural breakdown that caused the rise of a lawless, immoral underclass.

Adding to this charge, conservatives also argue that political liberals in the 1960s, who claimed to be waging a "war on poverty," actually made public policies which disastrously backfired, creating a class of Americans dependent on welfare. In such works as Charles Murray's *Losing Ground* (1980), the charge is made that well-meaning liberals, through profligate federal welfare programs, turned poor but self-sufficient Americans into government dependents. President Johnson's policies, in this view, became massive "hand-outs" which destroyed poor people's work ethic, rewarded mothers for out-of-wedlock babies, and weakened family and community bonds. To paraphrase President Ronald Reagan, in the 1960s government became not the solution but the problem. According to such conservative critics, the combined efforts of liberals and leftist radicals in the Sixties had sapped the will of the poor, degraded much of the middle class, and generally ripped apart the national fabric.

A few scholars, most of them one-time Sixties radicals, celebrate the decade of change with as much passion as many conservatives denounce it. The title of one of the first books to consider the Sixties legacy says it all: *The Sixties Without Apology* (1984). The most supportive of the decade's defenders argue that the legacy of the Sixties lies less in practical outcomes and more in the political possibilities that leftist activists opened up by example for future generations.

James Farrell, in *The Spirit of the Sixties* (1997), states: "One of the most important developments of the American 1960s was the understanding that the personal is political. Activists . . . taught Americans that everyday life was an arena of politics and that everyday choices had political implications."[9] He concludes: "The Sixties provide such a tradition for modern Americans, a tradition more important for questions than for answers, more important for assumptions than for conclusions, more important for ideas than for lasting institutions."[10]

In addition, while many conservatives bemoan the anti-traditionalist, liberationist experiments of the Sixties generation, many of the pro-Sixties writers take particular pride in this aspect of its legacy. In an April 18, 1999, piece titled "Seeing the 60's Through a 90's Corrective Lens," *New York Times* writer Stephen Holden wrote approvingly of the ". . . counterculture as a movement driven by passionate idealism and a reckless insistence on crashing through barriers. . . . The roots of that frenzied exploration still strikes me as an honest, if naive effort to improve the human condition by storming the barricades of consciousness."[11]

Wini Breines, in *Community and Organization in the New Left: The Great Refusal* (1982), also finds encouragement in the utopian aspects of the New Left movement. She argues that a key legacy of the New Left was its attempt to build a political community that united the public and private spheres of life. This attempt by New Leftists, she concludes, ". . . provided values by which to measure how we are forced to live, what we accept in the name of freedom, equality, democracy, or the 'free world'."[12]

The pro-Sixties writers turn the conservative critique on its head. Far from viewing "countercultural values" as dangerous, they argue that Sixties cultural rebels and political activists helped to reinvigorate American public and private life by asking people to be honest enough to examine their own individual moral and spiritual values, and to be brave enough to build a better society.

Most pro-Sixties writers accept the general claim that the rebels of that time helped to break apart a backward-looking, repressive set of cultural and political traditions. Some, however, offer a more measured, even ambivalent critique of that rebellion. Todd Gitlin, in *The Sixties: Years of Hope, Days of Rage* (rev. ed. 1993), his memoir and history of New Left activism, ponders four specific aspects of the Sixties legacy: "social equality (race, gender, sexuality); wide-open 'lifestyles' (sex, drugs, rock 'n' roll); the limitation of national violence and the care of the earth; and the spread of democratic activity."[13]

In the category of social equality, Gitlin points out the indisputable fact that because of Sixties-era activism, people of color, women, and gay men and lesbians have far greater legal and political rights at the end of the twentieth century. For Gitlin, on all counts, this change is an extraordinarily positive step toward creating a more just and equitable society. His regrets are not that civil rights activists, feminists, or gay and lesbian activists went too far but that too many Americans have resisted and continue to resist necessary changes.

The negative legacy, Gitlin argues, is that which is created by "[a] Republican politics of racial resentment. . . . conservatives whose idea of helping children is to send them to orphanages . . . who offer no remedy for the domestic violence of men but to throw more of them out of meaningful work."[14] He praises the social gains made by gays and lesbians while lamenting the fact that "to much of America, as to most of the rest of the world, homosexual love is a disease, a sin, or a crime. Nonetheless, the question of what is normal sexual life has been thrown open among much of the population, never to be slammed shut."[15]

Still, Gitlin worries about the degree to which the "wide-open lifestyles" associated with the counterculture have damaged Americans' cultural and moral integrity. Insightfully, he writes, "Every freedom comes wrapped in an anguish."[16] More than most former Sixties radicals, he remains concerned about the cultural legacies of the "sex, drugs and rock 'n' roll" mantra. Unlike conservatives, however, Gitlin attributes the cultural chaos of the post-Sixties era not to the radical activists but to far more powerful currents running through the twentieth century—what he calls "the main movement of modernity . . . 'the pursuit of happiness.'"[17]

It is America's consumer culture, built on marketplace demands and the insatiable search for new sensation and personal pleasure, that Gitlin believes bears major responsibility for our sexualized, amoral, often destructive social landscape. Nonetheless, he concedes that young people in the Sixties, helped by a legion of writers and cultural rebels, sped up and intensified this twentieth-century movement toward a "culture of excess."[18]

Regarding "the limitation of national violence," like the anti-Sixties writers, Gitlin recognizes a kind of "Vietnam Syndrome." However, he praises that legacy. A more militarily restrained America, he believes, is a better America, less likely to do harm abroad and more capable of open debate about foreign policy. While offering no simplistic answers to America's proper role in the world, he argues that a key legacy of the Sixties era is that, "whatever the rights and wrongs, there is unlikely to be a replay of Vietnam."[19]

Like most pro-Sixties writers, Gitlin concludes that the greatest legacy of the Sixties is a revitalized democratic citizenry. In principle, he celebrates a society in which "direct citizen action has become normal."[20] However, he also warns against "insurgent movements [that] choose tactics strictly for theatrical purposes . . . and fail to devise forms of action that appeal outside the immediate action."[21] Likewise he fears "self-righteous new orthodoxies" and rejects "'identity politics'—in which the principal purpose of organizing is to express a distinct social identity rather than achieve the collective good."[22] Gitlin respects the grassroots politics bequeathed to us by the Sixties but dares to hope that community-based politics can rise above narrow, sectarian motives and find common ground with others who are interested in a grand national purpose.

In my own work on the history of the Sixties era, I find myself falling into Todd Gitlin's camp. Thinking historically about the last third of the twentieth century, I argue that the Sixties legacy can be divided into two major areas. First, since that time, Americans have learned to work collectively, outside normal governmental channels, to challenge their own legal and cultural traditions as well as their "Establishment" leaders. Marginalized Americans have demanded equality and respect; citizens have rallied against their government's war policy; cultural rebels have acted out an alternative way of life.

From the perspective of a historian, this Sixties legacy is of a piece with Americans' enduring and often chaotic experiment in national, democratic self-creation. Like the late 18th-century revolutionary generation, the Jacksonians, the abolitionists and their pro-slavery foes, the populists and the progressives, the New Dealers, and hundreds, if not thousands of other historical groups and movements which attempted to make their historical era into a time of fruitful and positive national change, the Sixties generation of activists will take their place as standard-bearers in the American democratic tradition.

Secondly, "the Sixties," I believe, has become a kind of short-hand phrase for the immense economic and cultural changes that have transformed Americans from being a relatively isolated, provincial people—whose economy, culture, and politics were run for the most part by white Protestant men, almost all of whom believed with little critical perspective that their power and position was God-given—to a populace of global sophistication and responsibility. It is no accident that for many Americans, the Sixties began with the election, for the first time ever, of a Catholic to the presidency. That breakthrough, of course, was only the first, relatively small step of the many that followed.

For a great many Americans, the breakdown of the traditional elites' right to rule, as well as to determine moral standards—a process, of course, that had been ongoing for decades before the Sixties, but which had been rapidly escalating since the 1920s—threatened their status, their safety, and the security of their communities. Across the political spectrum, Americans have worried about the price their families and their society must pay for all the upheavals produced by the freedoms that a more affluent, more tolerant, more open American society provides. Since the political and cultural ruptures of the Sixties, a blow-up so long in the making, Americans have been struggling to find new means to ensure equality and justice, and to set new standards for safeguarding a moral society. One of the most compelling legacies of the Sixties era is the all-inclusive openmindedness of that great debate.

NOTES

1. Fred Barnes, "Revenge of the Squares," *New Republic* 212:11 (13 March 1995), 29.
2. Tom Hayden, *Reunion* (New York: Random House, 1988), 507.

3. Stephen Macedo, "Introduction," *Reassessing The Sixties*, ed. Stephen Macedo (New York: Norton, 1997), 16.

4. Harvey C. Mansfield, "The Legacy of the Late Sixties," *Reassessing the Sixties*, 27.

5. Peter Collier and David Horowitz, *Deconstructing the Left* (Studio City, Calif.: Second Thought Books, 1991), 17.

6. Jeremy Rabkin, "Feminism: Where the Spirit of the Sixties Lives on," *Reassessing the Sixties*, 46.

7. Paul Lyons, *New Left, New Right, and the Legacy of the Sixties* (Philadelphia: Temple University Press, 1996), 157.

8. Ibid, 157.

9. James Farrell, *The Spirit of the Sixties* (New York: Routledge, 1997), 5.

10. Ibid, 260.

11. Stephen Holden, "Seeing the 60's Through a 90's Corrective Lens," *New York Times*, 18 April 1999, E1.

12. Wini Breines, *The Great Refusal: Community and Organization in the New Left, 1962–1968* (New York: Praeger, 1982), 151-152.

13. Todd Gitlin, *The Sixties: Years of Hope, Days of Rage* (New York: Bantam, 1987), xv.

14. Ibid., xvi-xvii.

15. Ibid., xviii.

16. Ibid., xix.

17. Ibid.

18. Ibid.

19. Ibid., xx.

20. Ibid., xxi.

21. Ibid.

22. Ibid., xxii.

SOURCES

Breines, Wini. *Community and Organization in the New Left, 1962–1968*. New York: Praeger, 1982.

Farber, David. *The Age of Great Dreams: America in the 1960s*. New York: Hill and Wang, 1994.

Gitlin, Todd. *The Sixties: Years of Hope, Days of Rage*. New York: Bantam, 1987.

Hayden, Tom. *Reunion: a Memoir*. New York: Random House, 1988.

Horowitz, David and Peter Collier. *Deconstructing the Left*. Los Angeles: Second Thoughts Books, 1991.

Lyons, Paul. *New Left, New Right and the Legacy of the Sixties*. Philadelphia: Temple University Press, 1996.

Macedo, Stephen, ed. *Reassessing the Sixties*. New York: Norton, 1997.

Sayres, Sohnya, Anders Stephanson, Stanley Aronowitz, and Frederick Jameson, eds. *The 60s Without Apology*. Minneapolis: University of Minnesota Press, 1984.

PART III

The Sixties A to Z

abortion   The right to abortion was guaranteed by the Supreme Court's *Roe v. Wade* decision in January 1973. Though abortion was illegal in all 50 states during the 1960s (some allowed exemptions for pregnancies resulting from rape or incest or that threatened the health of the woman, and a few made abortion legal at the end of the decade), approximately one abortion took place for every four live births recorded. During the 1960s, many American women sought the repeal of antiabortion laws as a means to greater control over their own reproductive lives. According to a 1967 survey, 87 percent of American physicians supported the liberalization of abortion laws. Abortion also drew vehement opponents, most prominently the Roman Catholic Church. *See also* **NARAL**

Abzug, Bella Savitsky (1920–1998)   Abzug was elected to the U.S. House of Representatives from New York City's 19th District in 1970, following a distinguished career as a labor and civil rights lawyer. She helped found Women Strike for Peace (1961) and the National Women's Political Caucus (1961), which she also chaired. Known for her outspoken support for controversial causes, in Congress she was a strong advocate for women's rights and helped lead the movement against the war in Vietnam.

Agnew, Spiro T. (1918–1996)   When Richard Nixon named Spiro Agnew his running mate in the 1968 presidential race, few people had heard of this son of a Greek immigrant who had risen through Maryland politics to become the state's governor in 1966. Nixon selected Agnew to appeal to southern white voters, for the governor had gained national attention by publicly berating Baltimore's black leaders after riots erupted there in April 1968. Vice President Agnew served as Nixon's bulldog, first attacking Hubert Humphrey during the campaign and later lambasting young people, the press, and antiwar protesters. After the Nixon-Agnew reelection in 1972, Agnew came under investigation for taking illegal kickbacks from real estate developers (some actually made overdue payments to Agnew in the White House). Ironically, the 1973 Agnew investigation coincided with the Watergate investigation, bringing more unwanted attention to the Nixon administration. In October 1973, shortly after Agnew pleaded *nolo contendere* (no contest) to charges of income tax evasion, he resigned from office. He paid a $10,000 fine and received three years probation.

Alcatraz occupation   On November 9, 1969, a small group of Native American activists from the American Indian Movement occupied Alcatraz Island, the former site of Alcatraz prison, in San Francisco Bay. They claimed the island for native peoples and offered to buy it for $24 worth of glass beads and some red cloth. The number of occupiers rose to about 400 by the end of November. President Nixon ordered a "hands-off" policy but did not accede to any of the occupiers' demands for the establishment of Native American centers on Alcatraz. On June 11, 1971, the 15 activists who still remained on the island were removed, sparking a series of occupations of government facilities by other Indian activists throughout the United States. *See also* **Red Power**

Ali, Muhammed (b. 1942)   Heavyweight boxing champion Muhammed Ali (born Cassius Marcellus Clay Jr.) personified the changes in professional sports during the 1960s: he was a gifted athlete who understood the power of the media. Clay first gained national attention in the 1960 Olympic Games, where he won a gold medal. Entering professional boxing, Clay overwhelmed opponents with his hand speed and fluid style. After fewer than four years as a pro, Clay won the heavyweight title, making good on a pre-fight boast by knocking out Sonny Liston. The next day he announced his conversion to Islam and his new name: Muhammed Ali. In 1966, Ali refused to register for the draft. The World Boxing Association suspended his license and stripped him of his title. Although sentenced to five years in prison for violating the Selective Service Act, Ali won his release on appeal; the Supreme Court overturned his conviction in 1971, and he was reinstated as a professional boxer.

Altamont   The Rolling Stones, responding to complaints about exorbitant concert ticket prices, agreed to perform a free concert in San Francisco at the end of their 1969 tour. The Grateful Dead, Santana, Jefferson Airplane, and Crosby, Stills, Nash and Young also appeared. Poorly planned, the concert secured a venue, the Altamont Motor Speedway, fewer than twenty-four hours before the event. Three hundred thousand people showed up, many of them abandoning their cars on the highway and walking the last few miles to the racetrack. Concert "security" was provided by the Hell's Angels, many of them drunk or high on LSD. They proved particularly violent in beating fans back from the barely-elevated stage. When the Rolling Stones finally came on, Hell's Angels surrounded them with their motorcycles. In an example of particularly poor judgment, when tension between the crowd and the Hell's Angels peaked, the Rolling Stones broke into the song, "Sympathy for the Devil." The crowd surged and clashed with the Hell's Angels. An African-American man fleeing from the blows of the Angels pulled a gun, and they stabbed, beat, and kicked him to death. The concert film, *Gimme Shelter*, captured the event. For many, the tragedy of Altamont signaled an end to the promise of the Summer of Love and the Woodstock Nation.

Alvin Ailey American Dance Theater   Founded in 1958, the Alvin Ailey American Dance Theater became one of the most important venues for dance in the modern era. Ailey's choreography blends modern and jazz dance styles with ballet and African-American folk music to produce highly creative and original pieces. Alvin Ailey (1931–1989) created unprecedented opportunities for African-American dancers within ballet. His troupe also introduced African-American culture to the world of dance. Ailey's "Revelations," based on his religious upbringing, has become a staple in the modern dance repertoire.

American Indian Movement (AIM)   In 1968 Dennis Banks, George Mitchell, and Mary Jane Wilson founded the intertribal American Indian Movement in Minneapolis. Patterned after the Black Panthers, AIM monitored police actions against Native Americans in urban ghettos, where many had moved during the federal government's 1950s relocation efforts. AIM spread through the nation in 1969 and 1970. Among the movement's significant protests were the occupation of Alcatraz Island in San Francisco Bay (1969); a July 4, 1971 countercelebration atop Mount Rushmore; a Thanksgiving Day takeover of the Mayflower replica; and the November 1972 "Trail of Broken Treaties," in which hundreds of Native Americans marched to Washington, D.C., to air their grievances. In 1973, internal politics at the Pine Ridge reservation in South Dakota led to violence when tribal police loyal to an opposing faction prevented AIM spokespeople from leaving a press conference. AIM protesters barricaded themselves within a trading post at Wounded Knee (the site of an 1890 massacre of more than 150 Sioux by the U.S. Army). Federal agents responded with overwhelming force, and two Indians were killed in sporadic fighting during the three-month standoff. The American Indian Movement was the most radical organization for Indian activism in the 1960s. *See also* **Red Power**

arms race   When the USSR launched the first man-made satellite, Sputnik, into orbit in 1957, Americans were horrified; the Soviets had exploded a nuclear weapon long before U.S. scientists predicted that they would have that capacity, and now it seemed they were far ahead of the United States in rocketry. Concern about a "missile gap" led U.S. leaders to embark upon an extensive build-up of nuclear missiles. The USSR countered with an expansion of its nuclear arsenal. The arms race escalated and each nation continued to make more, more powerful weapons. Several groups organized in protest, including the National Committee for a Sane Nuclear Policy (SANE) and the Peacemakers. The Vietnam War drained attention from these groups by the mid-Sixties. In 1969, however, Richard Nixon began talks with the USSR to limit nuclear weapons. In 1972, he signed the Strategic Arms Limitation Treaty (SALT), which, for the first time, placed limits on the numbers of nuclear weapons each country was allowed.

back-to-the-land movement   For some Americans in the 1960s, protest took a different form than public activism. Weary from violent demonstrations in cities and on college campuses, back-to-the-land advocates broke away from mainstream culture to create rural utopian communities. BTLers believed that a "return" to nature would reunite them with their "true" selves, which had been lost in the political and social struggles of the age. Although communities varied widely in form and purpose, most were committed to challenging the consumerism, violence, greed, and exploitation they saw as central to the dominant culture. They created alternative systems for living, such as communal property ownership, collective child care and food production, and consensus decision making. With the rise of the environmental movement in the early 1970s, country communes became increasingly popular in small communities throughout the nation, such as Albion, California; Grants Pass, Oregon; and Brattleboro, Vermont. *See also* **communes**

Baez, Joan (b. 1941)   One of the leading folk singers of the 1960s, Baez was equally committed to social change movements. She released her first record in 1960 after appearing in the Newport Folk Festival. During the 1960s, she worked for the civil rights movement and was a prominent anti–Vietnam War protester. As an act of protest against the war, she recorded an album in Hanoi in 1972 while American planes bombed the city.

Baker, Ella (1903–1986)   An integral part of the civil rights movement for over half a century, Ella Baker first became active during the 1930s, while living in Harlem. In 1957, she helped Martin Luther King Jr. and Ralph D. Abernathy form the Southern Christian Leadership Conference (SCLS) and served as its executive director until 1960. That year she helped organize the Student Nonviolent Coordinating Committee (SNCC), urging the organization to remain independent of other civil rights groups. In 1964, Baker helped to organize Mississippi Freedom Summer voter registration drives.

Banks, Dennis (b. 1930)   An Anishinaabe from Leech Lake Indian Reservation in Minnesota, Banks was one of the leading voices of Native American activism in the 1960s. Along with George Mitchell and Mary Jane Wilson,

Banks formed the American Indian Movement (AIM), an intertribal organization originally intended to protect Native Americans in Minneapolis from police harassment. In addition to leading many of AIM's protests, Banks was involved in the 1973 Wounded Knee standoff with federal agents. Banks continues his activism, which now includes lecturing, teaching, and writing books; he also played key roles in the films *The Last of the Mohicans* and *Thunderheart* (both 1992).

Baraka, Amiri (b. 1934)   Baraka, who changed his name from LeRoi Jones in 1969, was one of the leading members of the Black Arts Movement (BAM) in the 1960s. He embraced agitprop theater, writing one-act, highly political plays that were intended to rouse strong emotions in their audiences. One of these, *The Dutchman*, won an Obie award as the best off-Broadway play of 1964. In the 1960s and early 1970s Jones/Baraka also published two books of theoretical essays on his revolutionary philosophy and explored BAM's concept of a black aesthetic in his poetry.

Bay of Pigs   This failed attempt by U.S.-backed Cuban exiles to overthrow Cuban leader Fidel Castro was one of the key events of the cold war. Castro took power in Cuba on January 1, 1959, overthrowing the corrupt Batista regime. He promised land and education reform and a nationwide housing program. However, Castro's plans involved redistributing the nation's wealth, including that substantial portion controlled by U.S. corporations. President Dwight D. Eisenhower broke off relations with Cuba and initiated a plan designed to oust the popular leader by training anti-Castro Cubans living in exile to retake the island. The "Bay of Pigs" invasion, carried out by President Kennedy in April 1961, proved a disaster for the anti-Castro army and for the prestige of the United States. The approximately 1,300 Cuban exiles carrying U.S.-furnished weapons who landed at the Bahía de Cochinos (Bay of Pigs) were quickly intercepted by Cuban forces, with 90 killed and the rest taken prisoner. Castro's popularity in Cuba increased, while the Kennedy administration was embarrassed by the fiasco. The tensions between Cuba and the United States, heightened by this invasion, would lead to the Cuban Missile Crisis. *See also* **Khrushchev, Nikita**

Beach Boys   They created the music of the Sixties' Southern California surfer culture and became one of the most successful bands of the decade. Brothers Brian, Carl, and Dennis Wilson, with their cousin Mike Love and a friend, Alan Jardine, formed the Beach Boys in 1961 while still in high school. They produced nine albums between 1963 and 1965 and reached the peak of their popularity in 1966. Hit songs included "Surfin' U.S.A." (1963); "Little Deuce Coupe" (1963); "California Girls" (1965); and "Good Vibrations" (1966).

Beatles   Perhaps no other band so strongly influenced and exemplified the course of popular music in the 1960s. The Beatles began in England as the Silver Beatles (an homage to Buddy Holly's Crickets) when John Lennon met Paul McCartney at a church picnic and suggested forming a band. George Harrison, a friend of McCartney's, later joined them. By 1961, the group (with shifting membership) had found some success as the house band for a popular Hamburg, Germany nightclub. But the Beatles' fortunes changed dramatically when they met manager Brian Epstein, who convinced EMI Records to sign the group on the condition that they take Ringo Starr on as their drummer. The Beatles' first hit in England was "Please, Please Me" (1963). In February 1964 the Beatles were seen by 53 million viewers when they made their first U.S. appearance on the *Ed Sullivan Show*. Beatlemania had arrived in America. Between 1964 and 1969, the Beatles had 30 songs on the top-ten pop music charts and moved from the simple style of their early songs to more innovative work, including "concept" albums such as *Sgt. Pepper's Lonely Hearts Club Band*, in which the songs were unified by a central theme. Immensely popular, the Beatles nonetheless provoked controversy about everything from their hair (considered long for 1964) to their use of psychedelic drugs to their embrace of Eastern religion. Despite the band's great success, the members' interests increasingly diverged, and John, Paul, George, and Ringo went their separate ways in the fall of 1969, though they kept the split from the public until the following spring. *See also* **Maharishi Mahesh Yogi**

Berrigan brothers   Daniel Berrigan (b. 1921) and his brother Philip (b. 1923), both Roman Catholic priests, engaged in radical protests against the Vietnam War and were the first members of the clergy in the United States to be sentenced to jail for political crimes.

Black Panther Party   Organized in Oakland, California in 1966 by Bobby Seale and Huey P. Newton, the Black Panthers constructed an ideology rooted in self-defense against racist aggression and police brutality. The media-savvy Panthers appeared in public dressed in berets and leather jackets, brandishing an impressive array of weaponry. They claimed that African Americans constituted an oppressed colony within a white oppressor country and demanded decent housing, education, exemption from military service, and full employment, stressing the need for black-controlled institutions. The Panther message of economic equality and social justice quickly spread among urban African Americans; the group's militancy attracted many who were disillusioned with the civil rights movement and its nonviolent tactics, while its violent rhetoric alienated others. The FBI targeted the Panthers, and two of its Chicago leaders were killed in a police raid in 1969. The group was a political force into the 1970s but lost support due to internal divisions, external pressures, and reports of corruption and illicit activities by Party leaders.

Black Power   As the civil rights movement fractured according to competing visions of social justice in the 1960s, the Black Power movement signaled a new racial consciousness among African Americans. Black Power meant different things to different people. Some emphasized the cultural heritage and African roots of American blacks; others sought self-determination and rejected the largely integration-oriented goals of the civil rights movement. Some advocates of Black Power, including the Black Panthers, embraced violence as part of their political ideology. Black Power appealed to many young African Americans who had become impatient with the slow progress of the movement and sought more direct means to black liberation.

Brown, H. Rap (Hubert Gerold; Jamil Abdullah al-Amin) (b. 1943)   Active in the civil rights movement from his college days in the early 1960s, Brown became president of SNCC (Student Nonviolent Coordinating Committee) in 1967 and embraced Black Power ideologies. One of the most radical of the new leaders, Brown once said that "violence is as American as apple pie," and in 1967 sparked riots by urging people attending a rally in Cambridge, Maryland, to "burn this town down." While president of SNCC, Brown purged several leaders, including Stokely Carmichael. Sought by the FBI on a variety of charges, Brown was arrested by the New York City police when he tried to rob a crap game. He served five years in the New York penal system. In prison Brown converted to Islam and took the name Jamil Abdullah al-Amin.

Brown, James (b. 1928)   "The Godfather of Soul," James Brown began his career as a gospel singer in the 1940s. He formed a soul group, James Brown and the Fabulous Flames, in the mid-1950s, and had 29 hit songs on the charts by 1964. During the 1960s, James Brown appeared at the top of both the R&B charts and the pop charts; major hits included "I Got You (I Feel Good)" in 1965. Brown frequently spoke about the importance of education and stressed the need for minority-owned businesses. After the assassination of Martin Luther King Jr. in 1968, he called for nonviolence in an attempt to calm the African-American community. His 1968 recording,

"Say It Loud (I'm Black and I'm Proud)" was a response to radical black leaders who attacked him as assimilationist for that position.

Brown Berets   Founded in East Los Angeles by David Sanchez in 1969, the Brown Berets were the vanguard of the Brown Power movement. This Mexican-American leftist organization protested police brutality and discrimination against Chicanos and questioned the larger percentage of Chicanos than whites serving in Vietnam. The Brown Berets allied with the Black Panthers and Students for a Democratic Society (SDS) on many of the issues of the 1960s.

Brown Power   Many young Mexican Americans in the 1960s rejected assimilation into the dominant U.S. culture and celebrated their Mexican heritage. Although various organizations supported Brown Power ideology, the Brown Berets perhaps best exemplified the movement. Brown Power advocates urged Mexican Americans to take pride in their Spanish and Indian roots and called on states and the federal government to support equal employment opportunities and bilingual and bicultural education, and to end discrimination against Chicanos.

Buckley, William F., Jr. (b. 1925)   William F. Buckley Jr. was perhaps the most influential conservative spokesperson in the 1960s. In his widely circulated syndicated newspaper column he offered a conservative interpretation of pressing political and social issues. More important for the development of a viable movement, he edited the monthly journal *National Review*, which brought together a variety of conservative thinkers and gave them a forum to express their ideas.

Carmichael, Stokely (1941–1998)   Born in Trinidad, Carmichael immigrated to the United States with his family when he was eleven and became active in the civil rights movement while a student at Howard University. He participated in the 1961 Freedom Rides and served as a voter registration coordinator in Mississippi during the summer of 1963. In May 1966 he was elected SNCC chairman and soon publicly split with Martin Luther King Jr. and other black leaders over his endorsement of Black Power. Carmichael served as prime minister of the Black Panther Party from 1968 into 1969, leaving because the party endorsed creating alliances with white activists. He adopted pan-Africanism, the belief that all people worldwide descended from Africa should unite. Carmichael established his permanent home in Guinea in 1969, and changed his name to Kwame Touré.

Carson, Rachel Louise (1907–1964)   Marine biologist Rachel Carson's 1962 book, *Silent Spring*, drew popular attention to the effects of chemical pesticides and helped to launch the modern environmental movement, which focused on the ecological impacts of human action. When it was published, Carson was already an accomplished popular author, having received a National Book Award for one of her previous works in 1952.

Cash, Johnny (b. 1932)   Johnny Cash rose to both country and rock and roll stardom in the late 1950s and early 1960s, outselling even the Beatles in 1969. Cash appealed to socially conscious fans through songs such as "The Ballad of Ira Hayes" and "What is Truth." Like the folk musicians of the 1930s, Cash addressed the issues Americans struggled with in difficult times.

Castro, Fidel (b. 1926)   Fidel Castro, leader of revolutionary forces that overthrew the Batista regime, which had seized control of the Cuban government in 1952, took power in Cuba in February 1959. Charismatic, youthful, and highly photogenic, Castro fervently supported revolutions by poor people around the world against the forces of capitalist development. Castro embraced communism and was financially and militarily supported by the USSR throughout the 1960s and until the collapse of the Soviet system in 1991.

Castro was hostile toward the United States in particular because the U.S. government had supported the corrupt and despotic Batista regime. Promising the Cuban people land and education reform and a nationwide housing program, Castro quickly nationalized many industries (including U.S.-owned oil refineries, sugar mills, and electric utility companies) and began redistributing wealth. The U.S. government responded with an economic embargo and then sponsored an attempt by anticommunist Cubans to overthrow Castro at the Bay of Pigs in April 1961. When the plan failed, the prestige of the United States suffered and Castro's popularity increased. The following year, Castro and U.S. President John F. Kennedy had a standoff over Soviet missiles placed on Cuban soil, well within striking range of the U.S. mainland. The world stood at the brink of nuclear war during the 1962 Cuban Missile Crisis until the Soviets backed down and President Kennedy promised never to invade Cuba. Throughout the Sixties, Castro remained popular not only in Cuba but also with many Latin Americans and with radical students in the United States. At the same time, he was hated by Cubans who had fled his communist dictatorship and resettled in America. Castro proved a thorn in the side of the United States by offering refuge to many American revolutionaries during the turbulence of the 1960s. Despite the Soviet collapse and American antagonism, Castro remained in power in Cuba into the twenty-first century.

Chávez, César Estrada (1927–1993)   Civil rights activist and labor union organizer César Chávez was born to migrant farm workers. After an eighth-grade education, he spent his youth working with his parents throughout California. Following military service in World War II and a decade with the migrant workers' Community Service Organization, Chávez became the first president of the National Farm Workers Association, which was chartered by the AFL-CIO in 1966 and later renamed the United Farm Workers. With the help of others, such as Dolores Huerta, Chávez turned the farm workers' plight into a mass movement for social justice. He came to national prominence when he organized a national boycott of California table grapes in 1968. Senator Robert Kennedy visited Chávez and the striking farm workers in California and publicly embraced their cause. The grape growers recognized the union and signed a labor contract in 1970. A stalwart champion of nonviolent social change, Chávez was a key figure in the Chicano movement.

Chicago, Judy (Judy Cohen) (b. 1939)   Judy Chicago played a critical role in the feminist art movement that emerged in the late 1960s. Her most famous works, *The Dinner Party* (1974–1979) and *The Birth Project* (1983), were executed later, but during the late 1960s and early 1970s she helped to create feminist art and spaces for women artists and their work. In 1970 she established a feminist art program at Fresno State University in California and the following year one at California Institute of the Arts. In 1972, working with artists Miriam Schapiro and Faith Wilding, she helped to create "Womanhouse," as they and their students renovated an old, dilapidated house into feminist "spaces," such as the "Nurturant Kitchen" and the "Menstruation Bathroom." She changed her name from Cohen to Chicago (the city of her birth) in 1970.

Chicago Democratic National Convention, 1968   The thirty-fifth Democratic Party national convention took place between August 26 and August 29, 1968 at the Chicago International Amphitheater. Vice President Hubert Humphrey won his party's presidential nomination on the first ballot. The convention was a milestone in Sixties-era turbulence.

Despite Humphrey's easy nomination, political conflict at the convention tore apart the Democratic Party. Inside the hall, delegates opposed to Humphrey and his pro–Vietnam War stance fought for a "peace plank" that would have committed the Democratic Party to supporting American withdrawal from Vietnam. Most of the delegates favoring the peace plank were supporters of the antiwar candidates, Minnesota Senator Eugene McCarthy and New York Senator Robert Kennedy, who had been assassinated on June 4, 1968. After a raucous floor debate, the peace plank was rejected by a vote of 1567 3/4 to 1041 1/4. Disconsolate antiwar Democrats, wearing black armbands, sang "We Shall Overcome" and then marched around the convention floor. Television audiences witnessed a bitterly divided Democratic Party.

On the streets of Chicago, viewers saw a far more brutal confrontation. Thousands of demonstrators had come to Chicago to protest the Vietnam War, racism, and the nomination of Hubert Humphrey, who was seen by most as a follower of President Lyndon Johnson's war policy. Some were supporters of the antiwar presidential candidates, others were nonviolent supporters of the National Mobilization to End the War in Vietnam, and a small minority were militant radicals, including some members of the Yippies and Students for a Democratic Society, who were looking for a confrontation with local authorities. Chicago Mayor Richard Daley, in an attempt to maintain law and order in his city, had refused to grant any of the protesters permits to camp out in city parks or to march peacefully to the convention hall. All during the convention week, police had violently attacked those who sought to stay in the parks after curfew or to demonstrate without legal permits. These police attacks climaxed on August 28, the day Hubert Humphrey won his party's nomination. About 15,000 protesters gathered for a peaceful rally. Afterward, they tried to march to the convention hall. Stopped by the police and Illinois National Guardsmen, thousands drifted into the nearby downtown streets. Most of these protesters were peaceful and law-abiding. A small minority yelled obscenities and threw objects at the police. A few police responded to the agitators and the general chaos by attacking, in a disorganized fashion, everyone in the area. They clubbed, sprayed Mace at, and beat hundreds of people, including convention delegates, peaceful protesters, news reporters, and bystanders. As people chanted, "the whole world is watching," television cameras broadcast the confrontation across the nation. Hubert Humphrey's presidential candidacy was substantially wounded by the violent and bitter images Americans took away from the 1968 Democratic Convention.

Chicago Indian Conference Almost 500 representatives from 90 tribes came together in Chicago in 1961 at a meeting sponsored by the National Conference of American Indians (NCAI). The group opposed the federal government policy of "termination," which had been endorsed by Congress in 1953. Termination policy sought to foster the assimilation of native peoples into mainstream U.S. society through various administrative and relocation efforts. At the point a tribe or band was judged to have reached a certain level of economic and social development, the federal government would terminate its relationship with that tribe, withdrawing all financial and legislative support and thus effectively terminating its tribal standing. The Chicago Indian Conference adopted a set of policy resolutions, including an emphasis on academic and economic development on reservation lands.

Chicago Seven   The Chicago Seven were the seven (originally eight) defendants on trial for conspiracy to incite a riot at the 1968 Democratic National Convention in Chicago. After protesters and police clashed for four nights during the convention, Chicago Mayor Richard J. Daley and new U.S. Attorney General John Mitchell were eager to prosecute those they saw as the instigators. Rennie Davis, David Dellinger, John Froines, Tom Hayden, Abbie Hoffman, Jerry Rubin, Bobby Seale, and Lee Weiner were indicted in spring 1969. (Seale's trial was severed from that of the other defendants after he repeatedly disrupted court proceedings and demanded his own attorney.) The five-month trial revealed the bitter divisions between the protesters and mainstream America. Most Americans, as public opinion polls demonstrated repeatedly, had no sympathy for the defendants and believed them guilty; they saw these men as dangerous radicals bent on disrupting American society. The jury convicted Davis, Dellinger, Hayden, Hoffman, and Rubin only on the charge of inciting a riot, not on conspiracy charges. The 7th Circuit Court of Appeals overturned the convictions in 1972 and the trial judge, Julius Hoffman, was reprimanded for his biased management of the original trial.

Chisholm, Shirley (b. 1924)   The first African-American woman to gain a seat in Congress, Shirley Chisholm, a Democrat, had served in the New York Assembly for four years before being elected to the U.S. House of Representatives in 1968. She was reelected seven times and served from 1969 to 1983. While in the House, Chisholm was a tireless advocate for political reform, women's rights, environmental justice, and protection of the rights of working families. She ran unsuccessfully for president in 1972.

Citizens' Councils   County-based Citizens' Councils organized throughout the South following the 1954 *Brown v. Board of Education* school desegregation decision. As a "white collar" alternative to the Ku Klux Klan and other violent racist groups, local Citizens' Councils worked to prevent the desegregation of southern schools through economic intimidation and political persuasion. Although the organization's influence had waned by the early 1960s, it remained a viable political force in Alabama and Mississippi.

Civil Rights Act of 1964   This federal legislation was first introduced to Congress by President John F. Kennedy and signed by President Lyndon B. Johnson. Often called the greatest liberal achievement of the Sixties era, this twenty-eight-page-long act made job discrimination and discrimination in all places of public accommodation on account of race, color, creed, national origin, or sex a federal crime. In addition, the act required the federal government to cut off all funding to any local government program that discriminated and strengthened the federal government's power to investigate and prosecute any acts of discrimination occurring anywhere in the United States.

Cleaver, Eldridge (1935–1998)   Cleaver was among the best known African-American political militants of the Sixties era. His turn to radical politics began in Folsom and San Quentin prisons (1957–1966), where he served time for rape. In prison Cleaver converted to Islam, and upon his release he moved to San Francisco, where Huey Newton and Bobby Seale, impressed with his writings, invited him to join the Black Panther Party and made him Minister of Information. In 1967, Cleaver published his best-selling memoir, *Soul on Ice*, a powerful statement of black radicalism. Fleeing the United States to avoid arrest for parole violation, he settled in Algeria in 1968; in 1971 he and Huey Newton expelled each other from the rapidly disintegrating Black Panther Party. Later in life, Cleaver converted to Mormonism, became a disciple of the Reverend Sun Myung Moon, was born again as a Christian, and even supported Ronald Reagan for president in 1984.

Clifford, Clark McAdams (1906–1998)   A trusted advisor to Presidents Truman, Kennedy, and Johnson, Clifford replaced Robert McNamara as Secretary of Defense in March 1968 and recommended changes in Vietnam War policy: stop the build-up of troops in the region, limit bombing to strategic sites in North Vietnam, and earnestly continue peace talks.

COINTELPRO   The FBI launched COINTELPRO (counter *intel*ligence *pro*gram) against several groups in the 1960s. COINTELPRO's goals were to gather information about the plans and programs of organizations from the radical left and right and to try to manipulate public perception of these groups. The program's tactics included spreading rumors to media outlets about certain group leaders, tapping phones and bugging offices, manufacturing correspondence to drive wedges between different factions within organizations, planting agents within organizations, and recruiting informers from within groups. *See also* **J. Edgar Hoover**

comix   The term describes alternative, underground comic books that originated in the 1960s. The form first appeared with Jaxson (Jack Jackson)'s
God Nose in 1963 but came into its own in 1967 with *Zap Comix*. These
underground comix featured bizarre characters, taboo subjects, and ob-
scene images and language, used to criticize or attack mainstream American society. *See also* **Robert Crumb**

communes   Many young people, turned off by American society, created
their own utopian communities. Living together and sharing both labor
and resources, people in communes rejected consumerism and capitalism
and forged small communities based on shared values. Most of these communities were rural and intended to become agriculturally self-sufficient.
Others, created in urban apartment buildings, sold crafts to sustain themselves. More than 10,000 communes were formed during the 1960s all over
the United States. *See also* **back-to-the-land movement**

Congress of Racial Equality (CORE)   Founded in Chicago in 1942 by
members of the Fellowship of Reconciliation, a pacifist organization, the
Congress of Racial Equality proposed using nonviolence to achieve social
change and racial justice. Founding members included James Farmer,
Bernice Fisher, Joseph Guinn, and Homer Jack. During its first two decades, CORE perfected the techniques of nonviolent protest against social
injustice primarily in northern campaigns. The organization cheered the
beginnings of a southern sit-in movement in 1960; the next year CORE appointed James Farmer director and organized the first "freedom rides" to
protest segregation on buses and in bus terminals in the South. CORE also
organized voter registration drives in the South and cosponsored the 1963
March on Washington. In 1966, reflecting the changes taking place in
other civil rights organizations, James Farmer was replaced by Floyd
McKissick, who advocated black control of the organization. By 1968,
when Roy Innis became director, CORE was advocating Black Power.

consciousness raising (CR)   Consciousness raising was a critical part of the
women's liberation movement in the late 1960s and early 1970s. Small
groups of women gathered to discuss their lives and experiences, realizing
that "the personal is political"—that the difficulties and problems they encountered in their personal lives were "common problems with social
causes and political solutions," in the words of feminist Jo Freeman. Ideal-
ly, the groups were to adopt some form of political or social action when
the consciousness-raising process was accomplished. CR was an adapta-
tion of techniques used in the New Left and SNCC, but it surpassed its
radical roots when the National Organization for Women adopted the

practice, *Ms.* magazine actively promoted it as feminist strategy, and middle-class white women throughout the nation took it up. *See also* **women's liberation; radical feminism**

Cosmo Cosmopolitan magazine was founded in 1886 and existed for almost a century as a general interest magazine. In the 1960s, editor Helen Gurley Brown transformed it into a slick magazine aimed at women who rejected strict sexual mores and believed that "nice girls *do.*" The "Cosmo girl" paralleled the male "Playboy," in that both were portrayed as sexually adventurous, materialistic, and willing to exploit the opposite sex.

Cronkite, Walter (b. 1916) America's most respected national newscaster during the 1960s, Cronkite anchored CBS's coverage of the 1956 and 1960 presidential nominating conventions, and then anchored the *CBS Evening News* from 1962 to 1986. After the Tet Offensive in 1968, Cronkite went to Vietnam and returned to proclaim on the evening news that the Vietnam War, which he to that point had supported, was unwinnable.

Crumb, Robert (b. 1932) Contributor to *Zap Comix* (1968) and creator of such characters as Mr. Natural and Shuman the Human, Robert Crumb was at the center of the early underground comix movement. His subjects were countercultural—sex, drugs, and hippie life—but his portrayals of them were cynical and unsparing.

Crusade for Justice Founded by Corky Gonzales in Denver in 1966, Crusade for Justice fought for the civil rights of Chicanos and created community-based programs meant to foster Chicano pride and preserve the cultural heritage and values of the community. This group also sponsored Chicano youth conferences in 1969. *See also* **Brown Power**

Cuban Missile Crisis This 1962 confrontation between the United States and the USSR over Soviet missile installations in Cuba brought the world to the brink of nuclear war. As the decade opened and relations between Cuba and the United States became more directly hostile, Nikita Khrushchev pondered the U.S. response to the installation of Soviet medium- and intermediate-range ballistic missiles in Cuba. He mistakenly assumed that President Kennedy would take no preventative measures. U.S. intelligence began monitoring Soviet-supported construction of missile silos in Cuba in the summer of 1962; on October 14, a U2 spy plane sighted the first ballistic missile on a Cuban launch pad, well within range of the U.S. mainland. On Monday, October 22, President Kennedy announced the presence of Soviet missiles in Cuba and placed a naval blockade around Cuba to prevent the arrival of more. For four days, the world waited to see what the USSR would do. Five Soviet vessels sent to Cuba to break the blockade turned back from their mission on the 24th; on October 28, Soviet Prime Minister Khrushchev agreed to remove the missiles in exchange for Kennedy's promise never to invade Cuba.

Daley, Richard Joseph (1915–1976)   The last of the big-city political bosses, Daley worked his way up through the local Chicago ward system, becoming mayor of the city in 1955. In his six consecutive terms as mayor (1955–1976), Daley worked closely with business and labor leaders. His absolute control of the city's politics enabled him to secure Illinois for Kennedy in the presidential election of 1960 and led the Democratic Party to choose his city as the site of its 1968 presidential nominating convention. Worried about possible disruption by antiwar protesters and others during the convention, Daley assembled a 25,000-man security force and ordered aggressive action against protesters. The ensuing police riots were seen on television across the nation. While many prominent Americans condemned Daley's handling of the situation, the majority supported the police and blamed demonstrators for the confrontations. *See also* **Chicago Democratic National Convention, 1968**

Davis, Angela (b. 1944)   The daughter of civil rights activists in Birmingham, Alabama, Davis became one of the leading Marxist spokespersons in the 1960s. Exposed at an early age to the tenets of Marxism-Leninism, Davis received her Ph.D. from the University of California, San Diego, under the direction of Herbert Marcuse. She joined SNCC and the Black Panthers in 1968 and the faculty of the University of California, Los Angeles philosophy department the following year. She was fired for her outspoken views and her declaration of solidarity with the Soledad Brothers, California prisoners who had killed a prison guard. Davis went underground when she was accused of helping the men escape from a courtroom. Tried in 1972, she was acquitted of charges of kidnapping, unlawful flight, murder, and conspiracy.

Dellinger, David (b. 1915)   A pacifist who spent three years in prison during World War II for refusing the draft, Dellinger was an early and vociferous opponent of the Vietnam War. In 1967, he and Rennie Davis founded the National Mobilization Committee to End the War in Vietnam (MOBE). The next year, joined by Tom Hayden, the group organized a protest around the Democratic National Convention in Chicago. Despite Dellinger's constant insistence on nonviolent tactics of protest, he was tried in federal court for conspiracy to incite a riot and for rioting following the outbreaks of violence in Chicago. His conviction for rioting was overturned in 1972. *See also* **Chicago Seven; Chicago Democratic National Convention, 1968**

Deloria, Vine, Jr. (b. 1933)   Standing Rock Sioux writer Vine Deloria Jr.'s first books, *Custer Died for Your Sins* (1969) and *God Is Red* (1973), were immensely influential in presenting Native American history and metaphysical concepts to the general public. Deloria argued that Indians should not seek to assimilate into mainstream U.S. culture but should instead study the traditional teachings of their peoples. During the 1960s, he served as executive director of the National Congress of American Indians (1964–1967) and worked with various Indian rights organizations. As a professor of political science, he continues to write on American Indian history, policy, and philosophy.

Didion, Joan (b. 1934)   Novelist, journalist, and screenwriter, Didion has had a career spanning several decades. During the 1960s she wrote essays on contemporary society and culture for several magazines; some of these were collected and published in 1968 as *Slouching Towards Bethlehem*. In this work, Didion offers a grim and despairing portrait of a society disintegrating, of the California counterculture as little more than children cast adrift, floundering in naive ignorance and abandoned by a society that had not even bothered to teach them the "rules."

Diggers   In the mid-1960s in the Haight-Ashbury district of San Francisco, this loosely affiliated group created a "Free City" that demonstrated the possibilities and limits of the Sixties-era counterculture. They set up a free housing network, a free communication system, free concerts, and a "free" store (for clothes and household goods), and held a regular food giveaway. The Diggers aimed to be "life actors" who scripted their own stories and turned everyday life into a theater of endless possibilities. Striving to be "edge-walkers," they combined their communitarian ethos with a "do-your-own-thing" spirit of adventure that included rampant use of narcotics (resulting in heroin addiction), thievery, and romanticization of the criminal underworld. By the late 1960s, Diggers had set up rural communes in Northern California and contributed to a growing ecological awareness.

Dohrn, Bernardine (b. 1942)   Born and raised in Chicago, after obtaining a B.A. and a law degree from the University of Chicago, Dohrn moved to New York to work for the National Lawyers Guild, organizing draft resistance. She participated in the 1968 strike at Columbia University and was subsequently elected interorganizational national secretary of Students for a Democratic Society (SDS). Allying herself with the Third World Marxist faction that had emerged in SDS, she was a leader in the move toward violence as the group emerged as the Weathermen in 1969, went underground, and began a campaign of terrorism against government facilities.

She was on the FBI's most wanted list in 1970 and lived underground for a decade before surrendering to federal authorities in 1980.

The Doors   One of the most important rock bands of the 1960s, the Doors were formed in Los Angeles in 1965. Lead singer Jim Morrison, keyboardist Ray Manzarek, guitarist Robby Krieger (who wrote the band's first hit, "Light My Fire"), and drummer John Densmore took their name from the title of Aldous Huxley's book, *The Doors of Perception*, thus drawing a connection to hallucinogenic drugs. The band's poetic lyrics and Manzarek's haunting keyboard melodies introduced a new, darker feel to rock and roll. Morrison's behavior during the band's live performances brought the group national notoriety; he feigned sexual acts and often tried to incite crowds to riot. After Morrison died of an apparent drug overdose in 1971, the group faded from public view.

Dylan, Bob (Robert Allen Zimmerman) (b. 1941)   Perhaps the most important pop musician of the Sixties, Dylan borrowed heavily from both country and folk music. After a short career playing in local rock bands and dabbling in folk music in and around Minneapolis, Dylan moved to Greenwich Village in 1960. Playing in coffeehouses like the famous Cafe Wha?, Dylan perfected his folk style. His first album, *Bob Dylan*, released in 1962, was a success. His second album, *The Freewheelin' Bob Dylan*, made him a star largely due to the popularity of the single, "Blowin' in the Wind." Dylan gained the admiration of many in the counterculture when he refused to appear on the *Ed Sullivan Show* because the producers of the program would not allow him to perform his song "Talkin' John Birch Society Blues." Many consider Dylan's *Highway 61 Revisited* the best album of the decade. Throughout his career, Dylan has experimented with rock and roll, country, and folk music, with varying degrees of commercial success.

Earth Day (April 22, 1970)   This nationwide demonstration, originally suggested by Senator Gaylord Nelson (WI), helped to raise public awareness about environmental issues. Congress adjourned for the day as the 12-hour demonstration at the Washington Monument attracted as many as 100,000 people. All across the country, speakers described the destruction of the environment by reckless industries. The event's 20 million participants (including 10 million schoolchildren) clearly demonstrated Americans' environmental concerns.

Easy Rider   Released in 1969, *Easy Rider* was the emblematic movie of the 1960s counterculture. This low-budget film, directed by Dennis Hopper and starring Peter Fonda, Dennis Hopper, Jack Nicholson, and Karen

Black, follows the three men as they ride through the United States on motorcycles, heading for Mardi Gras in New Orleans. The film concludes
with the casual murder of Hopper and Fonda by southern rednecks, but
the message is not so simple as the destruction of countercultural values by
bankrupt American society; the counterculture is also represented with
some ambivalence throughout the film.

Engel v. Vitale   This 1962 Supreme Court decision prohibited prayer in
public schools.

environmental movement   At the end of World War II, the dominant theme
in the American conservation movement was the efficient use and development of physical resources. Protecting water, trees, and soil from misuse
and waste remained a national priority. In the decades after the war, especially the 1960s, the goal of conservation was replaced with a new emphasis
on environmentalism, including concerns about air and water pollution,
overpopulation, and nuclear energy. Building support in local communities and grassroots organizations, environmental advocates of the 1960s
tried to redirect what they viewed as a dangerous escalation in population
and technological growth. By linking social values and environmental action, the environmental movement attempted to introduce concern for
natural stability and balance into modern America. Congress had enacted
the Wilderness Act of 1964, aimed at preserving some portion of the country "where earth and its community of life are untrammeled by man," and
the Wild and Scenic Rivers Act of 1968. Widespread popular concern
about the environment produced not only the first Earth Day in 1970 but
also important legislation, including the Clean Air Act (1970), the Clean
Water Act (1972), and the Endangered Species Act (1973). The National
Environmental Protection Act (1970) required an assessment of the environmental impact of all federally funded projects, and the Environmental
Protection Agency (1970) was created as a monitor.

Equal Rights Amendment   The term was used by proponents of women's
suffrage in the 1870s but was first proposed as a constitutional guarantee of
equal rights by feminist Alice Paul in 1923. Many feminists opposed the
idea of an equal rights amendment, supporting instead special protection
legislation that had been created during the Progressive era in the early
twentieth century. In 1967, Alice Paul gained the support of the National
Organization for Women, and the modern ERA movement began. Congress passed the amendment in 1972. It read: "Equality of Rights shall not
be denied or abridged by the United States or any state on account of sex."
Thirty of the necessary thirty-eight states ratified the amendment almost

immediately, but a powerful anti-ERA campaign raised questions about the legal and social consequences of such an amendment, and an antifeminist backlash grew in the 1970s. The amendment was not ratified by the (extended) deadline of June 30, 1982. Controversy over the ERA demonstrated the deep divisions in America over women's proper roles in society.

Esalen Institute   Founded near Big Sur, California, in 1962 by Richard Price and Michael Murphy, the Esalen Institute was an alternative education center. As part of the Human Potential Movement, which expanded greatly during the 1960s, the Esalen Institute offered exploration of various practices aimed at releasing the untapped potential of the human mind.

Fleming, Peggy (b. 1948)   Figure skater Peggy Fleming was the only American to win a gold medal at the 1968 winter Olympics. Her graceful, balletic style captivated Americans and drew public attention to the sport of figure skating.

Fonda, Jane (b. 1937)   In the 1960s, Jane Fonda, daughter of film actor Henry Fonda, was both a popular actress and a controversial political activist. Her acting career began in 1960 with debuts both on Broadway and in film. Fonda moved to France in the mid-1960s and married French film director Roger Vadim, who directed her in *Barbarella* (1968). In the late 1960s, Fonda rejected the "sex kitten" roles she had previously played for dramatic roles in films like *They Shoot Horses, Don't They?* (1969) and *Klute* (1971), for which she won an Academy Award. She also became increasingly involved in protest against the Vietnam War, even visiting the enemy capital of Hanoi in 1972, where she was photographed sitting on an antiaircraft gun singing antiwar songs. Her actions led some members of Congress to accuse her of treason, and earned her the nickname "Hanoi Jane." Fonda married activist and future California state legislator Tom Hayden in 1973 (they divorced in 1989), and remained active in politics, though of a less radical variety.

Franklin, Aretha (b. 1942)   "The Queen of Soul" began singing gospel as a child in her father's Detroit church and in her twenties became an acclaimed pop, rhythm and blues, and soul musician. She began her recording career with Columbia Records in 1960 but came to international attention after signing with Atlantic Records in 1966 and developing a powerful, emotional singing style. Her most famous 1960s hits included "Respect," "Baby I Love You," and "A Natural Woman (You Make Me Feel Like)."

Free Speech Movement   Early in the fall semester of 1964, University of California, Berkeley administrators refused to allow organizations to recruit civil rights workers for Mississippi on a stretch of Telegraph Avenue where political and other groups had traditionally distributed information. Many campus organizations ignored the ban, declaring it a violation of their right to free speech. When university officials summoned five students to a disciplinary hearing for breaking the new rule, hundreds showed up and demanded that they too be tried. On October 1, university officials ordered the arrest of a CORE worker who, along with members of a dozen other groups, had set up information tables outside the administration building. Students suddenly surrounded the police car that had come to execute the arrest and prevented it from leaving. The crowd eventually grew to almost 4,000. Speaker after speaker stood atop the police car, decrying the actions of the university officials. From this spontaneous protest the leaders of most politically active groups on campus—including both the Young Republicans and SNCC—created the Free Speech Movement (FSM). Protests continued through the fall semester as the FSM sought to guarantee students the right to voice their opinions and rejected all restrictions on speech. After a sit-in (in which 770 students were arrested) and a student strike, the movement won concessions that once again allowed political speech on Telegraph Avenue. The Free Speech Movement not only demonstrated to many college students their potential political power but also presaged many of the student movements over the course of the decade as students questioned their place within the university.

freedom rides   In June 1946 the U.S. Supreme Court deemed unconstitutional the southern practice of segregating interstate public transportation. The next year, an integrated group from the Congress of Racial Equality (CORE) and the Workers Defense League tested the decision by traveling by bus through the upper South. In 1955 the Interstate Commerce Commission ruled that the "separate but equal" seating on interstate public transportation violated the Interstate Commerce Act. James Farmer, the national director of CORE, planned the first freedom ride as a nonviolent test of the 1960 *Boynton v. Virginia* case, which set the precedent for the desegregation of railway and bus terminals. Thirteen people, including Farmer, left Washington, D.C. for Georgia, Alabama, and Mississippi on May 4, 1961. In Anniston, Alabama, one bus was destroyed, and the riders on the other bus were attacked and subjected to beatings, legal harassment, and arson. By November 1961 over a thousand participants had attempted similar freedom rides.

Freedom Summer   In 1964, the violence and hatred demonstrated by whites during the Freedom Summer voter registration drive in Mississippi created a turning point in the African-American civil rights movement and in the New Left. Many African Americans rejected nonviolence and embraced Black Power; many white volunteers began to question an American society that would allow such hatred to flourish. Freedom Summer came about when several civil rights organizations, including the SCLC, the NAACP, the SNCC, and CORE, came together in 1964 to expand voter registration in rural Mississippi. Seeking to bring one thousand young white volunteers to Mississippi, some leaders, including Robert Moses, argued that their presence would draw national attention to the struggle in Mississippi. Despite concerns that the white volunteers would displace the local African-American workers, other leaders eventually agreed to white participation. At Western College for Women in Ohio, volunteers were trained in the principles of nonviolence, voter registration techniques, and survival strategies. No one, however, was prepared for the level of violence they would experience. Three volunteers were murdered and their bodies hidden in a shallow grave outside Philadelphia, Mississippi. Angry whites burned churches, beat and jailed volunteers, and intimidated local African Americans. At the end of the summer, the Mississippi Freedom Democratic Party, which had been organized to offer African Americans an opportunity to vote outside the state's Democratic Party, unsuccessfully challenged the state's white delegates for official recognition at the Democratic National Convention.

Friedan, Betty Naomi (b. 1921)   With the publication of *The Feminine Mystique* in 1963, Friedan became a "founding mother" of mainstream American feminism. Her argument that idealized notions of women's roles as wives and mothers kept them from admitting and achieving their true potential struck a chord with many American women. In 1966, Friedan helped to found the National Organization for Women (NOW) and served as its first president. In 1971, with Bella Abzug and Gloria Steinem, she co-founded the National Women's Political Caucus. As more radical feminist groups emerged in the late 1960s, Friedan's feminist vision was challenged, but she remained an important leader in the women's movement, committed to the goal of gender equality and partnership between men and women.

Fulbright, J(ames) William (1905–1995)   A U.S. Senator (D-Ark.) from 1944 through 1974, Fulbright served as chairman of the Senate Foreign Relations Committee for fifteen years (1959–1974) and was an outspoken critic of U.S. involvement in Vietnam. He also sponsored the Fulbright Act of 1946 (amended by the Fulbright-Hays Act in 1961), which created opportunities for the exchange of scholars, students, and teachers between the United States and other nations.

Fuller, Richard Buckminster (1895–1983) An eccentric and brilliant inventor with a career spanning decades, Fuller is best known for his invention of the geodesic dome. This architectural innovation, a sphere composed of interlocking triangular shapes, was innovative from both engineering and aesthetic standpoints and earned its inventor a fortune. A geodesic dome designed by Fuller was used for the United States Pavilion in the 1967 Montreal World's Fair. Fuller's belief that the purpose of technology was to make human life more efficient, or "dymaxion," along with his unorthodox image, created a following among portions of America's diverse counterculture.

gay liberation movement The events at the Stonewall Inn in Greenwich Village in June 1969 symbolize the beginnings of the gay liberation movement. Even before Stonewall, gay men and lesbians had created vibrant, if vulnerable, communities, and there were long-standing, if often secret, "homophile" organizations devoted to ending discrimination against homosexuals. However, the gay liberation movement was fundamentally a creation of the 1960s, influenced not only by the changes in sexual behavior and opinion that contemporaries called "the sexual revolution" but also by the struggles and victories of the civil rights and Black Power movements and the tactics of protest in the 1960s. Following Stonewall, gay liberation groups were founded throughout the nation, often with names such as "Gay Liberation Front," which signaled their allegiance to broader movements for social change. Unlike the homophile movement, which sought assimilation, the gay liberation movement proclaimed "gay power" and sought the transformation of society. By 1973 almost 800 openly gay organizations existed in the United States.

Gay Liberation Front (GLF) Formed in New York following the events at the Stonewall Inn in June 1969, the Gay Liberation Front was the most prominent of the gay liberation groups that emerged to fight the oppression of homosexuals in the United States. The GLF organized the first Gay Pride Week to mark the first anniversary of Stonewall; approximately 10,000 gay men and lesbians celebrated gay pride by marching in the New York City parade.

Gideon* v. *Wainwright This 1963 Supreme Court decision held that the states were responsible for providing lawyers to indigent defendants in any U.S. criminal case.

Ginsberg, Irwin Allen (1926–1997) Poet, activist, and leading countercultural figure of the 1960s, Allen Ginsberg gained fame as the founding father of the Beat generation of the 1950s. His poem, "Howl" (1956), was the anthem of the Beats, revealing a subculture built around drug experimentation, sexual freedom, and a search for the authentic. Ginsberg claimed that homosexuality was a sign of positive nonconformity rather than of deviance, and explored both Jewish and Buddhist spirituality. He participated in Ken Kesey's Acid Tests, led the crowd in chants at the 1967 San Francisco Be-In, and was present at the Chicago antiwar protests in 1968. Ginsberg was not a reformer but a countercultural revolutionary whose influence spanned four decades.

Giovanni, Nikki (b. 1943)   Born Yolande Cornelia Giovanni, Nikki Giovanni emerged as one of the key members of the Black Arts Movement (BAM) in the late 1960s, along with LeRoi Jones (later Amiri Baraka) and Sonia Sanchez. BAM advocated revolution, and Giovanni embraced the role of political agitator, using shocking language and anger to reach her audiences. During the 1960s she published two very successful books of poetry, and in 1971 she recorded an award-winning album on which she read her poetry to the accompaniment of a Harlem gospel choir. As her politics later became less militant, Giovanni was rejected by the Black Arts Movement.

Glenn, John Herschel (b. 1921)   A former fighter pilot who served in both World War II and the Korean War, John Glenn joined the space program at its inception. Although he was the oldest of the original Mercury astronauts, Glenn was the first to orbit the Earth in February 1962. He retired from the space program two years later and was elected to the U.S. Senate from Ohio in 1974. He served three terms in the Senate, and became the oldest person to travel in space when he completed a space shuttle mission in 1998.

Goldwater, Barry (1909–1998)   Known as "Mr. Conservative" in political circles, Goldwater was the Republican standard-bearer in the 1964 presidential election. Shortly after the defeat of Richard Nixon in 1960, an enthusiastic cadre of conservatives resolved to wrest control of the Republican Party away from those they considered the liberal "Eastern establishment." Their ideal candidate was the tough-talking senator from Arizona. Goldwater's blend of laissez-faire economic principles, militant anticommunism, and frontier rhetoric appealed to that growing conservative faction within the Republican Party. Goldwater suffered an ignominious defeat at the hands of Lyndon Johnson in the election. However, the infrastructure of grassroots Republican Party volunteers, precinct captains, and supporters put together to nominate Goldwater in 1964 proved invaluable in building a conservative political movement and changing the nature of American politics. *See also* **Young Americans for Freedom**

Gonzáles, Rodolfo "Corky" (b. 1928)   Chicano movement activist and poet Corky Gonzáles grew up in a migrant worker family, graduating from high school in Denver in the mid-1940s. After close to a decade spent as a boxer, Gonzáles became involved in politics, working for the Kennedy campaign in 1960 and focusing his efforts on Chicano youths. In 1966 he founded the Crusade for Justice, an organization that promoted Mexican-American pride and sought to end discrimination against Chicanos. Gonzáles is probably best known as the author of "Yo Soy Joaquín" (1969), a poem that inspired Chicano pride and activism in the 1960s and 1970s. He also helped to formulate "El Plan Espiritual de Aztlán," a statement of Mexican-American political and cultural nationalism, which was adopted by more than 1,000 representatives of Chicano organizations at the National Chicano Liberation Youth Conference Gonzáles sponsored in Denver in 1969.

The Graduate   Released in 1967 with a soundtrack by Simon and Garfunkel, *The Graduate* was one of the landmark youth films of the 1960s, widely praised for its portrayal of youthful idealism challenging the cynicism of the older generation. *The Graduate* was directed by Mike Nichols and starred Dustin Hoffman in his first major film role.

Graham, Bill (1931–1991)   Rock music promoter and impresario Bill Graham helped to shape the 1960s counterculture and to define American popular music for three decades. Born to a Jewish family in Germany, Wolfgang Grajonca (his original name) arrived in New York in 1941, having been sent away by his mother to protect him from the Nazis. In 1965, associated with the new San Francisco Mime Troupe, Graham began organizing fund-raising benefits. Their success led him to stage his own concerts, first at the Fillmore Auditorium near the Haight-Ashbury district in San Francisco and then, from 1967, at the Fillmore East in New York City. He worked with all the major rock groups of the era and continued to promote rock concerts until his death in 1991.

Graham, Billy (William Franklin Graham) (b. 1918)   Perhaps the most prominent evangelical Protestant minister in American history, Graham was ordained in the Southern Baptist Convention in 1939. By 1949 he had become a full-time evangelist, and in the following decades he would conduct a series of evangelical crusades, preaching to millions of people around the world. During the 1960s, Graham was closely associated with President Richard Nixon. Following the Watergate scandal, feeling betrayed, he withdrew from the political world; he never closely aligned himself with the New Religious Right that emerged in the 1980s.

The Great Society   After taking office in 1963, Lyndon B. Johnson sought to extend the legacy of John F. Kennedy and take advantage of a cooperative Congress. He created a program he called "The Great Society," stating in 1964, "We have the opportunity to move not only toward the rich society and the powerful society, but toward the Great Society that demands an end to poverty and racial injustice, to which we are totally committed in our time." This sweeping legislative agenda, involving more than 400 separate pieces of legislation, was designed to combat ignorance, poverty, and racism in America. Toward this end, Great Society programs implemented during the 1960s included civil rights legislation, public housing initiatives, urban renewal projects, federally subsidized health care, job programs, education reform, programs for inner-city youth, work training, public television, and support for the arts. By 1967, the rapid expansion of the federal bureaucracy under the Great Society provided its enemies fodder for criticism and popular support waned, just as the Johnson administration was also losing national support for its Vietnam War policies. While Great Society programs helped to alleviate poverty, especially among the elderly, and moved the nation closer to goals of racial justice, it did not fulfill Johnson's vision. Scholars, politicians, and other critics disagree to this day about what factors limited the success of this ambitious effort.

Green Berets   The U.S. Army Special Forces, or "Green Berets," were organized in 1952. President Kennedy enlarged the Special Forces from 2,500 to 10,000 members and expanded its mission from guerrilla warfare to include counterinsurgency tactics, including psychological operations and political subversion. In Vietnam, most members organized Civilian Irregular Defense Groups among Montagnard tribesmen in remote areas of Vietnam's Central Highlands. Others helped to train South Vietnamese special forces or worked in intelligence operations. In 1968, actor John Wayne produced, directed, and starred in a pro–Vietnam War film, *The Green Berets*.

Greer, Germaine (b. 1939)   Australian feminist theorist Germaine Greer's book, *The Female Eunuch*, had a powerful impact on the women's liberation movement in the United States. Greer, who in the late 1960s was a lecturer at the University of Warwick and heavily involved in England's countercultural movements, offered a revolutionary critique of the nuclear family and argued that "female sexuality has been masked and deformed" by sexist society. *The Female Eunuch*, published in 1970 in Great Britain and in 1971 in the United States, became an international best-seller and made Greer one of the most prominent feminists of the era.

Gregory, Dick (b. 1932)   Active in the civil rights movement from an early age (he led a march protesting school segregation while still in high school), Gregory provided much-appreciated humor in the civil rights struggle. While leading a sit-in at a lunch counter in 1961, Gregory was told, "We don't serve Negroes." Gregory quipped, "No problem, I don't eat Negroes." Gregory participated in many of the important civil rights campaigns of the decade and later protested the war in Vietnam.

Griswold v. Connecticut   In 1965 the U.S. Supreme Court ruled, 7–2, that a Connecticut law prohibiting the sale of contraceptives was unconstitutional.

Guthrie, Arlo (b. 1947)   An important figure in the folk music scene of the late 1960s, Guthrie is the son of folk singer and social activist Woody Guthrie. Arlo Guthrie was most famous for his eighteen-minute song, "Alice's Restaurant" (1967), which became an antiwar folk classic. Guthrie continued his social activism after the end of the Sixties era.

Haggard, Merle (b. 1937)   One of the top figures in country music in the 1960s, Haggard was best known for the song, "Okie from Muskogee" (1969). This celebration of patriotism and small-town values, set in contrast to the world of long-haired hippies and draft card burners, found a large audience among those whose ways of life were challenged by the upheavals of the era.

Haight-Ashbury   This San Francisco neighborhood was the epicenter of the counterculture in the 1960s. By the mid-1960s, about 15,000 young people interested in creating an alternative urban community had been drawn to the neighborhood by its cheap rents and to San Francisco in general by the city's bohemian tradition and relatively permissive atmosphere. By 1966, Haight-Ashbury became known as a psychedelic drug center and the home of "hippies" who were dedicated to turning their LSD visions into everyday reality. "Head" shops opened; a psychedelic newspaper, *The Oracle*, was regularly published; and the Diggers, a loosely connected group of free-form artists and rebels, contributed to a lively street scene. On January 14, 1967, this new community celebrated its existence with "The Gathering of the Tribes for a Human Be-In." In 1967, Haight-Ashbury attracted upwards of 75,000 young people, many of them lured by mass media hype that promoted a "Summer of Love." By 1969, most of the original members of the Haight-Ashbury alternative community had left the neighborhood, driven out by thousands of runaway teenagers, emotionally disturbed people, and criminals drawn by the neighborhood's reputation as a center for promiscuous sex and wide-open drug use.

Hair   A Broadway show about the counterculture, *Hair* was billed as "a tribal love-rock musical." Written by James Rado and Gerome Ragni, with
music by Galt MacDermot, it opened at the Biltmore Theater in New York
on April 29, 1969. Several songs from *Hair*, including "The Age of Aquarius" and "Hair," were recorded by cover artists and reached the top ten on
the pop charts. A film version, starring Treat Williams and John Savage,
was released in 1979.

Hamer, Fannie Lou (1917–1977)   Hamer was the youngest of twenty children born to sharecroppers in Mississippi. As a young adult, she worked on
farms owned by white men. After she was sterilized by doctors without her
consent during an operation, Hamer dedicated the rest of her life to
achieving civil rights for African Americans in Mississippi. She helped to
organize the Mississippi Freedom Democratic Party in 1963 to challenge
the all-white state Democratic Party's stranglehold on state politics. In
1964, Hamer and the Freedom Party delegation attended the Democratic
Party's national convention and tried to unseat the white delegates. In her
testimony before the credentials committee (which was charged with de-
ciding which delegation would represent Mississippi), Hamer described
how, following her arrest for attempting to organize black voters, state highway patrol officers had ordered other black prisoners to beat her with black-
jacks. Her nationally televised testimony was one of the most emotionally
powerful moments of the African-American struggle for civil rights.

A Hard Day's Night   Filmed and released at the height of Beatlemania, *A
Hard Day's Night* introduced the world to the personalities and humor of
John, Paul, George, and Ringo. The film, which depicts a day with the
band as they prepare for a television appearance, is usually considered the
first "rockumentary." It has influenced the production of rock movies and
videos ever since. *See also* **Beatles**

Hare Krishna   The International Society for Krishna Consciousness was
founded in New York in 1965 by A. C. Bhaktivedanta, a chemist and Sanskrit scholar from Calcutta. Bhaktivedanta, called Swami Prabhupada by
his followers, spread the teaching of the Hindu deity Krishna. His followers
shaved their heads, wore saffron robes, and devoted themselves to a life of
proselytizing. The group, with its now-familiar chant of "Hare Krishna,"
spread rapidly through the United States and the world.

Harris, LaDonna (b. 1931)   Throughout the 1960s, Harris worked for the
welfare of native peoples and for world peace. A Comanche from Oklahoma, she entered the national political scene in 1960 as the wife of Oklahoma's senator, Fred Harris (D). In 1970 she founded Americans for Indian

Opportunity, an organization that assisted tribal groups in achieving their economic, political, and social goals.

Hayden, Tom (Thomas Emmet Hayden) (b. 1939) A cofounder of Students for a Democratic Society (SDS), Hayden became a social activist while a student at the University of Michigan. He joined the civil rights organization SNCC in 1960 and spent time in the South helping with African-American voter registration campaigns. In 1962, Hayden drafted the manifesto that became SDS's Port Huron Statement and served as the key statement of New Left policy and beliefs in the 1960s. He was also a dedicated leader of the anti–Vietnam War movement, helping to organize protests at the 1968 Democratic National Convention. He was later tried for those activities as one of the Chicago Seven. Following his experiences in Chicago, Hayden attempted to foster revolution, working with groups such as the Black Panther Party and the Weathermen. By the mid-1970s, he had repudiated revolution and committed himself to working for social change within the democratic system. Hayden was married to Jane Fonda from 1973 to 1989.

Hefner, Hugh (b. 1926) The most famous "playboy" in the world, Hugh Hefner came up with the idea for *Playboy* magazine while working in the subscription department of *Esquire*. Hefner, who divorced his wife in 1959, six years after launching his magazine, created an empire including *Playboy* magazine, the Playboy Press, Playboy Clubs, and a whole series of Playboy products, ranging from keychains to cruises. He built the Playboy Mansion, a 100-room residence on North State Parkway in Chicago, with a plaque on the front door that read: *Si Non Oscillas, Noli Tintinnare* (If you don't swing, don't ring). Hefner claimed to have had sex with more than 2,000 women, and used his magazine to promote his own "Playboy philosophy." Hefner's daughter, Christie, took over Playboy Enterprises in 1988.

Hell's Angels Formed after World War II, the Hell's Angels were the most famous of the motorcycle clubs that rode the California highways. They were, in effect, a counterculture, working sporadically, obsessed with motorcycles (almost without exception Harley Davidson 74s), and wearing their own uniform of sleeveless denim jackets, greasy Levi's, long hair, and beards; but their association with California's hippie and antiwar counterculture in the 1960s exposed the limits of understanding between those who would reject conformity. The Hell's Angels dropped acid with Ken Kesey and his Merry Pranksters, but they also "stomped" antiwar demonstrators at rallies. *See also* **Altamont; Tom Wolfe**

Hendrix, Jimi (James Marshall Hendrix) (1942–1970)   Guitar virtuoso Jimi Hendrix's musical style has been copied by rock and roll guitarists for thirty years. Largely influenced by blues guitarists, Hendrix played with the Isley Brothers, Sam Cooke, Little Richard, James Brown, and Ike and Tina Turner before going solo while living in England. He gained fame first in Europe, and The Jimi Hendrix Experience debuted on American shores at the Monterey Pop Festival in 1967. *Billboard* and *Rolling Stone* proclaimed Hendrix "Artist of the Year" in 1968. His performance at Woodstock in 1969 brilliantly displayed his showmanship and his gift for using distortion and feedback to create a unique guitar sound. He died of a drug overdose in 1970.

Ho Chi Minh (Nguyen That Thanh, Nguyen Ai Quoc) (1890–1969)   The son of an impoverished rural scholar in Vietnam, Ho Chi Minh grew up to lead his country's revolution against France, and North Vietnam's war against South Vietnam and its ally the United States. From 1919, when he presented a petition at the Versailles Peace Conference, until his death in 1969, Ho Chi Minh would dedicate his life to the cause of a free, united, and communist Vietnam. He and his armies defeated the French in 1954 and then withstood near-constant bombing from the United States in the latter half of the 1960s, until peace was finally declared in 1973. Ho, however, would not live to see his dream fulfilled. He died during peace negotiations in 1969. The name Ho Chi Minh, which he adopted at the age of 52, means "he who enlightens."

Hoffa, Jimmy (James Riddle Hoffa) (1913–?1975)   International president of the Teamsters Union, Jimmy Hoffa symbolized the power of organized labor and the corruption associated with unions during the Sixties era. As president of the Teamsters from 1957 through 1971, he negotiated several favorable collective bargaining arrangements and organized 90 percent of long-haul truckers, increasing the union's membership to more than 2 million. However, Hoffa and the Teamsters were under investigation by the federal government throughout this era for suspected links with organized crime. Hoffa's troubles with the federal government, especially with Attorney General Robert Kennedy, led to a jury tampering conviction in 1967. Richard Nixon later commuted Hoffa's sentence with the understanding that he would not resume union activities. In July 1975, Hoffa disappeared en route to a meeting with reputed Mafia figures in Michigan. He has not been seen since; he was declared legally dead in 1983.

Hoffman, Abbie (1936–1989)   Among the best known political radicals of the Sixties and cofounder of Yippie!, Abbie Hoffman was born in Worcester, Massachusetts to middle-class Jewish parents. In the early 1960s he became active in the civil rights movement. By the mid-1960s, Hoffman was experimenting with drugs and had become an enthusiastic community organizer in the New York City counterculture. Still a dedicated antiwar and racial justice activist, Hoffman blended his political work with his counter-cultural ethos in a series of famous pranks that included burning money at the New York Stock Exchange, organizing a Be-In at Grand Central Station, and marching through New York City declaring, "the War is over!"

Hoffman, with Rubin and other allies, created Yippie! in 1968 to bring unpoliticized young people to Chicago during the Democratic National Convention. Hoffman hoped to stage a "Festival of Life," complete with rock bands, during the convention week as an alternative to what he called "the convention of death." Chicago's Mayor Richard J. Daley refused to give the Yippies any permits for their festival. Instead, police attacked young people who refused to leave the festival's site, Lincoln Park, after the city curfew. After Nixon took office in 1969, Hoffman and seven other radical activists were charged with conspiracy to incite a riot for their Chicago protest activities. After a lengthy trial and appeals process, the Chicago Seven (one of the activists was tried separately) were found not guilty of the major charges against them. The trial made Hoffman a nationally known figure.

In 1974, rather than face drug charges, Hoffman went underground, assumed a new identity, and became an environmental activist in upstate New York. In 1980, he turned himself in and served almost a year in jail. Suffering from severe and chronic bipolar disorder, Hoffman committed suicide in 1989.

Hoover, J(ohn) Edgar (1895–1972)   The controversial head of the Federal Bureau of Investigation (FBI), Hoover charged antiwar activists and civil rights protesters with being subversives led by communists. Hoover was appointed head of the Bureau of Investigation of the Justice Department in 1924, and when that division became the FBI in 1935 he became its director. During his long reign he amassed immense power by using the FBI to collect information on tens of thousands of Americans, including congressional representatives, senators, and even presidents. A fierce anticommunist, Hoover believed that protesters in the 1960s were threats to the security of the United States. He was convinced, inaccurately, that Martin Luther King Jr. was controlled by Soviet communist agents and so informed Presidents Kennedy and Johnson, as well as leading members of the mass media. Hoover used the FBI to hound Dr. King until his death in

1968. Hoover oversaw a major operation, COINTELPRO, that aimed to destroy major antiwar, student, and racial justice organizations. By the late 1960s, critics accused Hoover of turning the FBI against American citizens exercising their constitutionally protected rights. Despite such charges, Hoover remained as director of the FBI until he died in 1972.

Huerta, Dolores (b. 1930)   A leading labor and political organizer in the 1960s, Huerta cofounded the United Farm Workers Union in 1962. Along with César Chávez, she led strikes in California, helped coordinate the national boycott against table grapes, and successfully negotiated labor contracts for the farm workers. By the late 1960s, Huerta was a nationally recognized leader of the Chicano movement and a spokesperson for Chicana rights. In 1972, Huerta co-chaired the California state delegation to the Democratic National Convention. Huerta has continued to work as a labor organizer and political activist.

Humphrey, Hubert Horatio (1911–1978)   Hubert Humphrey served as vice president under Lyndon Johnson and was the Democratic Party's presidential candidate in 1968. First elected to the U.S. Senate in 1948, Humphrey was a key figure in the cold war liberal wing of the Democratic Party, introducing bills to outlaw the Communist Party, advocating nuclear disarmament, and promoting civil rights for African Americans. Johnson chose Humphrey for his running mate in 1964, but Humphrey's opposition to Johnson's Vietnam policy in early 1965 angered the president; Humphrey only returned to Johnson's graces when he became an outspoken supporter of the war. When Johnson decided not to run in 1968, Humphrey became the early front-runner for the Democratic nomination. After the disastrous Democratic National Convention in Chicago, Humphrey trailed Republican candidate Richard Nixon by 28 percentage points. He continued to support the Johnson war policy until late September. After he staked out his own position to end the war, Humphrey's campaign gained momentum. He lost the election by only 500,000 votes but was crushed in the Electoral College.

The Huntley-Brinkley Report   The NBC nightly news show, with Chet Huntley and David Brinkley, originated when the two men were teamed to cover the Democratic and Republican national conventions in 1956. *The Huntley-Brinkley Report* lasted fourteen seasons, until Huntley retired in 1970, and was the top-rated news program on television through most of the 1960s.

Immigration Act of 1965   Immigration policy established in 1924 created quotas based on "national origins," favoring the nations of northern and western Europe. Though intervening legislation somewhat altered the im-migration profile, the Immigration Act of 1965 was the first comprehensive move to alter the restrictionist intent of earlier laws. In keeping with other legislation aimed at ending racial discrimination, the act replaced national origins quotas with hemispheric "ceilings," established high priority for professionals and skilled technical workers, and emphasized family reunifi-cation. The 1965 Immigration Act changed the demographics of the Amer-ican population enormously by allowing, even encouraging, immigration from Asia and the Americas.

in loco parentis   Colleges and universities acted "in the place of parents" to regulate the lives of their students. In practice, *in loco parentis* mainly translated into curfews and "hours" for women students; men were not subject to such regulations. Only the Vietnam War evoked more student protests in the 1960s. Administrators gradually rejected *in loco parentis*, in part because of student protests but also because many believed that such policies inhibited the development of students' sense of responsibility for their own actions. Others worried that the doctrine made colleges and uni-versities legally liable for anything that happened to students under their care.

Jackson, Jesse (Louis) (b. 1941)   Though Jesse Jackson's greatest political prominence came in later decades, he was a key member of the civil rights movement of the 1960s. He worked with Martin Luther King Jr. and the Southern Christian Leadership Council (SCLC), and in the mid-1960s was appointed head of the Chicago Operation Breadbasket (an effort to in-volve the business community in creating job opportunities for blacks) and then of the national Operation Breadbasket. Jackson remained associated with SCLC after King's assassination, but in 1971 he left that organization to found Operation PUSH (People United to Save Humanity).

Jackson State   Five days after National Guardsmen opened fire on an anti-war protest at Kent State University, police shot into a women's dormitory at Jackson State University, killing two students and wounding twelve oth-ers. The shootings on May 14, 1970 were related to racial tensions in Jack-son, Mississippi rather than to antiwar protests. The deaths of students at predominately black Jackson State attracted far less media attention and outrage than did the shootings at Kent State, which many African Ameri-cans saw as evidence of the nation's continuing racism.

Jesus freaks   Membership in the 1960s counterculture often involved some form of spiritual quest. Some "freaks" embraced Christianity, looking back from the established churches of the twentieth century to their image of early Christianity as a countercultural movement itself. The Jesus freaks were never an organized movement, but people using the name began about fifty underground newspapers and established campus groups, communes, and coffeehouses throughout the nation. Most Jesus freaks were religiously fundamentalist but not socially conservative.

John Birch Society   Founded in 1958 by candy manufacturer Robert Welch, the ultraconservative John Birch Society (JBS) gained a large membership in the early 1960s. The JBS was virulently anticommunist and prone to espousing conspiracy theories about high-ranking members of government (including President Eisenhower). Extremely powerful in Southern California, the JBS helped influence the conservative wing of the Republican Party in the 1960s.

Johnson, Lyndon Baines (1908–1973)   The thirty-sixth president of the United States took office on November 22, 1963 after the assassination of John F. Kennedy. During his five years as president, Johnson fought a War on Poverty at home and the Vietnam War abroad. He was vilified by many for his failed strategy in Vietnam; his record at home was mixed. His successful championing of civil rights legislation produced his greatest historical achievement.

Johnson was born in Gillespie County, Texas, where his parents had a cotton farm. The farm failed and the family moved to the small town of Johnson City, where Johnson grew up. He attended nearby Southwest Texas State Teachers College. Johnson's humble origins stayed with him all his life and made him both suspicious and awed of people who came from more cosmopolitan and sophisticated backgrounds.

After working briefly as the principal at a school for Mexican-American children and then as a teacher, in 1931 Johnson got his first political job working for a Texas congressman in Washington, D.C. Johnson was a man of prodigious energy and ambition, and he soon became a well-recognized figure on Capitol Hill. A sign of his growing success was his marriage in 1934 to the charming and talented Claudia Alta ("Lady Bird") Taylor, the daughter of a prosperous Texas family. The following year Franklin D. Roosevelt appointed Johnson director of the Texas National Youth Administration. When a congressional seat opened up in Texas in 1937, Johnson successfully ran for it as an ardent New Deal liberal. Based on his experiences growing up during hard times in the Texas hill country, his work with racially oppressed Mexican-American children, and his intense admiration for President Roosevelt, Johnson became a lifelong believer in the moral necessity of using the power of the federal government to help the downtrodden and to keep the economic playing field level for common people.

After five terms as a congressman and a failed Senate bid, in 1948 LBJ was elected to the U.S. Senate. After a race marred by corruption on both sides, Johnson won by just eighty-seven votes, earning him the nickname, "Landslide Lyndon." In the Senate, Johnson's forceful personality and political savvy made him a leader. He perfected what became known as the "Johnson Treatment." Armed with a detailed knowledge of every senator's home state needs and personal ambitions, Johnson used flattery, threats, and promises to create majority support for an array of important legislation, including the 1957 Civil Rights Act.

In 1960, LBJ was Senate majority leader with an eye on the White House. Unable to gain support for his presidential bid, he accepted Kennedy's offer of the vice presidency. He campaigned hard for the ticket and helped Kennedy win vital states in the South and West. Despite Johnson's election success, Kennedy offered his vice president little to do, and Johnson bitterly languished in office. After Kennedy's assassination in November 1963, Johnson appeared before the nation in a televised address: "Today, in this moment of new resolve, I would say to all my fellow Americans, let us continue." The change in presidential leadership was startling; Johnson was as crude a man as Kennedy had been polished. The tall Texan, who favored cowboy hats and boots, spoke with a twang and feared that the American people (and especially the East Coast mass media pundits) would never respect him as they had the Harvard-educated scion of great wealth, the martyred John F. Kennedy. The Kennedy shadow would be a constant companion to Johnson throughout his presidency.

In his own bid for presidential greatness, Johnson aimed to end racial injustice and to wage a War on Poverty. In the midst of a record-setting economic expansion, LBJ believed that Americans had the duty to expand opportunity and to provide a decent standard of living for every citizen. The president used all his persuasive powers, honed during his Senate days, to craft a bipartisan congressional coalition that passed the Civil Rights Act of 1964 and the Voting Rights Act of 1965. No president before or since has done more to extend equal opportunity and equal rights to all Americans regardless of their race, ethnicity, national origins, or gender.

The political fallout of Johnson's commitment to the civil rights cause was immediate. Arizona Senator Barry Goldwater, the 1964 Republican presidential challenger to Johnson, voted against the 1964 Civil Rights Act and spoke in favor of individuals' and states' rights to discriminate against racial minorities. While Johnson crushed Goldwater overall, the conservative Republican won a vast majority of white votes in the deep South; it was the first time in history that a Republican had won in the deep South, and it marked the turn of the once all-Democratic South toward the Republican camp.

Johnson divided his elected term in office between his cherished Great Society legislative program and the ever-deepening crisis in Vietnam. The Great Society was Johnson's version of his beloved Franklin D. Roosevelt's New Deal. Johnson believed he could end poverty in America by ending employment discrimination, providing educational and job training opportunities for all who needed them, and providing direct aid to those deemed in need, such as the elderly and mothers and their dependent children. Some of these programs, mostly those targeted at the elderly such as Medicare, have become bipartisan successes. But most of the programs aimed at the nonelderly poor were controversial to begin with and have remained so ever since.

Vietnam destroyed the Johnson presidency and turned Lyndon Johnson into an old man before his time. Before his presidency, Johnson had spent little time thinking about America's international role. As a senator, he had embraced the cold war and anticommunism, like almost every other liberal in Congress. His ingenuity and interests, however, remained fixed on domestic policy and political infighting. When he became president, his first international priority was demonstrating to other world leaders, especially his Kremlin opponents, that he would be a strong leader with whom they had best not trifle. As problems heated up in Vietnam in 1964, Johnson felt it essential to maintain his own credibility by showing the world, as well as his Republican opposition at home, that he would not let the United States "lose" another country (like China in 1949 and Cuba in 1959) to the forces of international communism.

Nothing in Johnson's background or experiences had prepared him to understand the resolve of those Vietnamese who were fighting to unify their nation after the defeat of French colonialism back in 1954. The advisors he had inherited from the Kennedy administration did nothing to help him rethink the situation in Vietnam. As Johnson chose to commit American ground troops in Vietnam in early 1965, his experiences as a master political negotiator made him think that by applying enough pressure, he could convince North Vietnamese leader Ho Chi Minh to work out an acceptable deal.

With each incremental escalation of American involvement in the war,

Johnson lost one constituency after another. Martin Luther King Jr. publicly broke with LBJ over the war in early 1967. Student protestors and an ever-expanding antiwar movement blamed him personally for the war, chanting "Hey, hey, LBJ, how many kids did you kill today?" In 1967, many liberals in the Democratic Party broke with Johnson; first Minnesota Senator Eugene McCarthy and then New York Senator Robert Kennedy challenged him for the 1968 Democratic presidential nomination.

Johnson was heartbroken. In his mind, African Americans had betrayed him and his civil rights efforts by rioting in dozens of cities and then turning publicly against his war policy. Students, so many of whom had been helped by Johnson's Great Society higher education programs, had become his most outspoken critics. Even his own political party was turning on him. Ravaged by myriad health problems, including heart disease, Johnson shocked the nation on March 31, 1968 by announcing during a nationally televised speech that he would not run for reelection. He promised instead to use all his energies to negotiate a successful end to the Vietnam War.

Between his announcement and the November presidential victory of Republican Richard Nixon over Johnson's hand-picked successor, Vice President Hubert Humphrey, Johnson oversaw more tragedy, some legislative victories, and a continuing stalemate in Vietnam. The assassination of Martin Luther King Jr. in April unleashed a firestorm of violent uprisings in inner-city, African-American neighborhoods. Johnson could do little to stop the riots, but he did push through the pathbreaking 1968 Open Housing Act that ended housing discrimination. His Vietnam negotiations went nowhere.

Johnson left the White House a broken man. He spent the few remaining years of his life on his ranch in Texas. He died of a heart attack on January 22, 1973.

Joplin, Janis (1943–1970)   Janis Joplin was an acclaimed white female blues singer and a powerful symbol of women's rejection of traditional roles in the 1960s. After leaving home (Port Arthur, Texas) at seventeen to seek a musical career, she became involved in the 1960s San Francisco music scene. As the lead singer of Big Brother and the Holding Company, Joplin became famous following their performance at the 1967 Monterey International Pop Music Festival. Striking out as a solo performer in 1968, Joplin recorded five albums before her death of a drug overdose in 1970.

Kennedy, John F. (1917–1963)   The thirty-fifth president served in office just over a thousand days, yet his foreign and domestic policies shaped the entire Sixties era. His personal style, leadership abilities, and tragic death made him a legend.

The second son (of nine children) of Joseph Patrick and Rose Fitzgerald Kennedy, John Fitzgerald Kennedy was born into a wealthy and politically powerful family. His father had served in the Franklin Roosevelt administration and his mother's family was active in local Boston politics. World War II postponed Kennedy's entry into the political arena but made him a national hero. The commander of a PT boat that was rammed by a Japanese destroyer in the Solomon Islands, Kennedy towed one of the ten surviving crew members three miles to land by clenching the strap of the injured man's life jacket in his teeth as he swam.

In 1946 Kennedy, only twenty-nine years old, returned to Massachusetts and won a seat in the U.S. House of Representatives. In Congress, Kennedy proved a fierce opponent of communism both abroad and in the United States. In 1952, continuing his whirlwind political advancement, Kennedy was elected to the Senate. He then began to position himself as a national political figure. While recovering from back surgery, Kennedy wrote *Profiles in Courage*, which won a Pulitzer Prize. Kennedy's efforts in the presidential campaign of Adlai Stevenson in 1956 (Kennedy also gave the nominating speech at the convention) won him much support among Democrats.

In 1960, Kennedy went after the Democratic Party presidential nomination. Many Democrats questioned whether a Roman Catholic could win the presidency. Furthermore, many white southerners were uncomfortable with Kennedy's positions on civil rights. Kennedy quieted many of his critics with a primary win in mostly Protestant West Virginia and by continually outlining his devotion to the separation of church and state. He won the support of many white southerners when he chose Texas Senator Lyndon B. Johnson as his running mate.

Kennedy ran against Republican Richard M. Nixon, the incumbent vice president under Dwight D. Eisenhower. The election was one of the closest contests in U.S. history. Out of 69 million votes, Kennedy won by a little more than one percent. Thanks to victories in large states, however, Kennedy won the electoral college 303 to 219.

Several factors that would become increasingly important in American politics contributed to his victory. Kennedy's mastery of television performance helped him immensely; most viewers agreed that his confident appearance offered a stark contrast to Nixon's haggard look and nervous demeanor in the candidates' four nationally televised debates. Urban African

Americans, who were impressed with Kennedy's efforts to secure the release of Martin Luther King Jr. from a Georgia prison the week before the election, provided the margin of victory in several states. And finally, Kennedy's campaign program, the New Frontier, which promised new economic and domestic programs combined with efforts to combat Soviet expansion, appealed to Americans suffering through an economic slump and fearful of Soviet advances.

In his inaugural address, Kennedy's calls for self-sacrifice and patriotism seemed to express Americans' best hope for the future. Within a few short months, Kennedy, his wife Jacqueline, and their children, Caroline and John, brought vigor and glamour to the White House. The Kennedys hosted elegant parties and invited renowned artists, scientists, authors, and thinkers to join them. Kennedy filled his cabinet and administration with energetic scholars, businessmen, and others described as the "best and the brightest."

During his presidency, Kennedy pursued his vision of a free, democratic world. Preferring an activist foreign policy and determined to stop the advance of communism, Kennedy worked hard to build up conventional as well as nuclear forces. Shortly after his inauguration, Kennedy put his activist foreign policy to the test by going ahead with a planned invasion of Cuba. However, the Bay of Pigs was a disaster both militarily and politically for the fledgling Kennedy presidency.

The botched Cuban invasion did temper Kennedy's foreign policy. He reached out to other Latin American countries through the Alliance for Progress, which ushered in a new era in U.S.–Latin American relations. He also searched for diplomatic solutions in preference to committing U.S. troops around the world. In August 1961, when Khrushchev ordered a wall built to separate East and West Berlin, Kennedy sent in troops to protect West Berlin but never challenged the building of the wall. Perhaps his most original approach to foreign policy was the Peace Corps, which sent young, college-educated Americans around the world in efforts to assist people in Third World countries.

Kennedy's tempered approach to foreign policy received its greatest test in October 1962, in the Cuban Missile Crisis. Speaking to a television audience on October 22, Kennedy revealed the existence of Soviet nuclear missiles in Cuba and demanded their removal. He warned Khrushchev (as he had in an earlier private communiqué) not to try to circumvent a U.S. naval blockade of Cuba. After four days, Khrushchev agreed to remove the missiles.

Though there is some debate about what course Kennedy would have followed had he lived, his actions in Vietnam set the nation on a path to war. He increased the number of American military "advisors" in Vietnam from 1,000 to over 16,000 and built up the presence of special forces, dubbed the Green Berets. Kennedy did not prevent a coup or the assassination of South Vietnamese leader Ngo Dinh Diem in fall 1963 and left his successor Johnson with an extremely unstable situation in Southeast Asia.

At home, Kennedy confronted two primary challenges: trying to push through his own New Frontier domestic agenda and responding to the escalation of the civil rights movement. Kennedy had limited success in the former. He secured a modest increase in the minimum wage, increased federal spending in economically depressed Appalachia, secured equal pay for women in some professions, and ended sex discrimination in federal hiring. He failed, however, to create a health insurance program, substantially increase urban renewal, or provide federal aid to education.

Kennedy's actions on civil rights were primarily reactive, not proactive. Though hesitant to support the civil rights movement early in his presidency, Kennedy did take a monumental step on June 11, 1963. On national television he embraced the civil rights struggle and asked Americans to join him in supporting national legislation that would end racial segregation in all public accommodations.

In November, President Kennedy's civil rights bill was bottled up in committee when he made a trip to Dallas, hoping to mend political fences in Texas. On November 22, as Kennedy's motorcade wound through downtown Dallas, the president was assassinated. Although the Kennedy assassination fueled speculation about a possible conspiracy, the Warren Commission, appointed by Johnson to investigate the crime, concluded that Lee Harvey Oswald had acted alone.

The nation reacted to news of Kennedy's death with an outpouring of grief and shock. Normal television programming was suspended for almost four days as the networks covered the tragedy, from initial news of the shooting through the funeral procession. Most Americans who were alive at the time can remember exactly where they were when they heard that Kennedy had been shot, and in the nation's collective memory that moment stands, however paradoxically, for our loss of innocence.

Kennedy, Robert F. (1925–1968)   Bobby Kennedy, the younger brother of John F. Kennedy, first came to national attention in 1953 when he resigned his position as an attorney for the Senate Internal Security Subcommittee over Joseph McCarthy's tactics. After managing his brother's 1960 presidential campaign, Kennedy was named to the post of Attorney General. In that role, Kennedy focused on enforcing civil rights law and trying to curtail organized crime. He won a New York Senate seat in 1964 and entered the 1968 presidential race as an antiwar candidate. A passionate and charismatic champion of both the civil rights movement and white working-class Americans, Bobby Kennedy had a powerful following. Moments after concluding a victory speech following the California Democratic presidential primary, Robert F. Kennedy was assassinated. The assassin, Sirhan Sirhan, was a Jerusalem-born Jordanian angered by Kennedy's pro-Israel stance.

Kennedy assassination   On November 22, 1963, President John F. Kennedy was shot and killed as his motorcade made its way through the streets of Dallas. Governor of Texas John P. Connally was wounded. That afternoon, police arrested Lee Harvey Oswald, a self-proclaimed Marxist who had lived for a time in the USSR, and later that evening police charged him with Kennedy's murder. Two days later, as police transferred Oswald from one jail to another, Dallas nightclub owner Jack Ruby shot him in full view of Americans watching the live television transmission. Lyndon B. Johnson appointed a federal commission, led by Chief Justice Earl Warren, to investigate Kennedy's assassination. The Warren Commission, after a ten-month investigation, concluded that Oswald had acted alone. However, competing conspiracy theories continue to surround Kennedy's death.

Kennedy's assassination—the first in a decade of violent deaths of American leaders—shocked the nation. Television stations abandoned regularly scheduled programming for several days, offering constant coverage of the nation's mourning. The sudden loss of this young and vibrant president contributed to the continuing mystique of the Kennedy administration, dubbed "Camelot," which somewhat oddly, given its cold war politics, came to symbolize America's lost innocence.

Kent State   On May 4, 1970, National Guardsmen opened fire on Kent State University students protesting President Nixon's expansion of the Vietnam War into the neighboring nation of Cambodia. Four were killed, nine more wounded. Students throughout the nation were outraged, and more than four hundred colleges and universities throughout the nation were temporarily closed following the shootings. Vice President Agnew blamed the students, saying that the deaths were "predictable" given the "traitors and thieves and perverts in our midst." *See also* **Jackson State**

Kesey, Ken (b. 1935)   Author of the influential novel *One Flew Over the Cuckoo's Nest* (1962), Kesey was a key figure in the 1960s counterculture and drug culture. In 1964, along with a band of "Merry Pranksters," he began a journey from San Francisco to New York in a psychedelic-painted school bus. Having first tried LSD as a subject in an experimental program at a veteran's hospital in 1959, Kesey believed that the drug could create a new cosmic consciousness in its users. With the Merry Pranksters, he staged "Acid Tests," events in which people dropped acid in a total environment created through psychedelic music and light shows.

Khrushchev, Nikita Sergeyevich (1894–1971) The son of a miner in the Ukraine, this former pipe fitter rose to become the premier of the USSR and a prime architect of the Soviet Union's cold war policies. In 1961, he ordered the construction of the Berlin Wall. In 1962, he attempted to place nuclear weapons on Cuban soil and brought the world to the brink of nuclear war. After he agreed to withdraw the missiles, he and U.S. President John F. Kennedy began discussing limiting the build-up of nuclear weapons. Khrushchev was forced by hard-liners in the USSR to retire in 1964. *See also* **Cuban Missile Crisis**

King, Billie Jean (Moffitt) (b. 1943) Tennis player Billie Jean King brought recognition to women athletes in the 1960s and actively promoted equal opportunities for women in sports throughout her career. By 1965, she was the top-ranked woman player in the United States; she had won virtually every major event in the sport within five years, including Wimbledon and the U.S. Open. Her most famous match was in 1973 against Bobby Riggs, a retired men's champion, who bragged that he could defeat any top woman player. Billed as the "Battle of the Sexes," the two-hour-and-five-minute match attracted fifty million TV viewers. King won.

King, Martin Luther, Jr. (1929–1968) Dr. Martin Luther King Jr., the spiritual and political leader of the African-American civil rights movement, was born in Atlanta in 1929. His father, Martin Luther King Sr., was the minister of the Ebenezer Baptist Church and a leader in the African-American community. King studied at Morehouse College, where he came under the influence of Dr. Benjamin Mays, an outspoken advocate of social justice. King went on to Crozer Theological Seminary and later received a Ph.D. in theology from Boston University. In Boston, he met his future bride, Coretta Scott, a music student from Alabama.

After receiving his Ph.D., King moved to Montgomery, Alabama and served as a pastor for the Dexter Avenue Baptist Church. Shortly after his arrival, African Americans chose King to lead a boycott of city buses in protest against segregated seating. The Montgomery Bus Boycott lasted over a year. King's leadership, oratorical skills, and insistence on nonviolence brought him to national prominence. When the Supreme Court ordered the buses desegregated, King celebrated the victory by helping to create a new civil rights organization, the Southern Christian Leadership Conference (SCLC). He believed the SCLC could expand the successes of nonviolent protest across the South. The choice of the words "Southern" and "Christian" reveal two important aspects of King's philosophy toward civil rights. Southern African Americans should lead the fight for social justice and they should anchor their movement within Christian doctrine.

For the first few years after forming the SCLC, King worked to raise money for the organization. He traveled extensively in the United States, giving speeches and sermons. King cultivated relationships with influential northern civil rights leaders, white pastors, and other advocates of social justice. He also traveled to India and studied Gandhi's philosophy of nonviolent protest. As leader of the SCLC, King determined that employing the tactic of nonviolent confrontation to protest injustice in the South would thrust civil rights into the national consciousness.

The sit-in campaign initiated by black college students across the South in spring 1960 energized nonviolent protest. King encouraged the college students when they formed the Student Nonviolent Coordinating Committee (SNCC); he sat in at a prominent Atlanta eating establishment in October 1960 and was arrested. Atlanta police transferred King to another county to face parole violation charges stemming from an earlier traffic ticket. When the judge ordered King to the state prison, Robert F. Kennedy worked to secure his release. John F. Kennedy, in the week before the presidential election, placed a highly publicized phone call to Coretta Scott King to express his sympathy. These efforts on King's behalf may well have helped Kennedy gain a significant majority among African-American voters and thus win the election.

King's first major victory through nonviolent protest occurred in Birmingham, Alabama. The local sheriff, Eugene "Bull" Conner, was known for encouraging violence toward black protesters, and King knew that a confrontation in Birmingham would create national publicity for the civil rights cause. Conner did not disappoint. He ordered his men to turn fire hoses and loose attack dogs on defenseless protesters, including children. Conner arrested King. While incarcerated, King penned his "Letter from a Birmingham Jail." This widely read document offered the best expression of King's moral justification for the civil rights movement. The events in Birmingham focused national attention on the movement by offering clear distinctions between the noble nonviolence of black protesters and the violent injustice of southern society. Local white leaders brokered an end to the confrontation and granted concessions for African Americans.

King followed the successful Birmingham movement by helping to organize the 1963 March on Washington. In front of a crowd of over 200,000 on the Washington Mall and millions of television viewers, King delivered one of the most important speeches in American history. His "I Have a Dream" speech, an eloquent and powerful appeal for social justice, helped define the goals of the civil rights movement for countless Americans. The next year, the Nobel Prize Committee awarded King the Nobel Peace Prize for his efforts on behalf of African Americans.

Even as King assumed the mantle as head of the civil rights movement, detractors of his nonviolent ideology emerged. Malcolm X challenged both King's nonviolence and the movement's goal of integration into white America. Furthermore, some key SNCC members had come to believe that nonviolence was no longer practical after the incredible violence turned on the participants in the Freedom Summer. These SNCC workers had also begun to promote a long-term strategy of working within the black community and resented King's publicity-driven protest marches. Ironically, these divisions appeared when the civil rights movement was close to achieving a major goal. The civil rights legislation taken up by Congress in the Sixties included the 1964 Civil Rights Act, which prohibited segregation in public accommodations and forbade educators and employers from discrimination on the basis of race.

King and the SCLC next turned their attention to achieving basic political rights for southern African Americans. The Selma Movement perhaps marked the last and greatest victory for King's nonviolent protest method. He used the overwhelming violence and racism of local whites to create a national groundswell of support for the movement and for voting rights.

Having made remarkable strides toward achieving civil rights for southern African Americans in ten short years, King began to focus on national issues, particularly economic equality for African Americans and an end to the Vietnam War. Waiting until after the Voting Rights Bill was signed into law, he expressed his opposition to U.S. involvement in Southeast Asia. He opposed the war on moral grounds, arguing that it reflected white America's racism toward all nonwhite peoples and that the cost of this war took money away from other programs that aided the inner cities. King moved his headquarters to Chicago and began to address the *de facto* segregation and economic inequalities in northern ghettos.

In April 1968, King visited Memphis, Tennessee to lend his support to a strike by black sanitation workers. Working with others to plan a march on City Hall, King was assassinated by James Earl Ray as he stood on the balcony of his motel. Riots broke out in cities across the nation, despite pleas for calm from President Johnson and prominent black leaders. Eighteen years later, Congress declared King's birthday a national holiday.

Kissinger, Henry Alfred (b. 1923) The former director of the Defense Studies Program at Harvard University and an expert on U.S. foreign policy, German-born Henry Kissinger was tapped by Richard Nixon to head the National Security Council in 1969 and served in that position until 1975. He sought better relations with the USSR, leading to the 1969 Strategic Arms Limitation Talks (SALT). Kissinger also helped engineer the expansion of the Vietnam War through the bombing of Cambodia. In 1973, he helped to negotiate a cease-fire agreement with the North Vietnamese and the withdrawal of U.S. troops from Vietnam. He was awarded the Nobel Peace Prize for his efforts. He served as Secretary of State from 1973 until 1977.

Ku Klux Klan (KKK) Originally founded as a terrorist organization to combat black equality during the immediate post–Civil War years, the Ku Klux Klan underwent several transformations during the next century. Several different, and often extremely violent, factions and independent chapters emerged in the 1950s and 1960s in response to African-American civil rights victories. Klan members are believed to have been responsible for hundreds of acts of intimidation, including dozens of bombings of black homes and churches, especially in Alabama.

Leary, Timothy (1922–1996) Best known for advising American youths to "turn on, tune in, and drop out," Leary encouraged the use of psychedelic drugs as a means to expand consciousness. Unauthorized experimentation with psychedelics led to his dismissal from the psychology faculty at Harvard University in 1963, after which Leary founded two communities dedicated to research on the uses of LSD.

Liddy, G. Gordon (b. 1930) The head of the "plumbers" (Richard Nixon's secret group to plug leaks from the White House), Liddy organized the Watergate burglary. Richard Nixon brought Liddy, a former FBI agent, to the White House to work under Chief of Staff H. R. Haldeman and spy on political enemies. In his first assignment, Liddy organized the break-in of a psychiatrist's office, seeking potentially scandalous information about one of the patients, Daniel Ellsberg. This former State Department employee had leaked the top-secret Pentagon Papers, which documented government lies about U.S. Vietnam policy, to the press. Liddy was convicted for the Watergate break-in and for violating the civil rights of Dr. Lewis J. Fielding (Ellsberg's psychiatrist). Liddy served five years in prison before Jimmy Carter reduced his sentence. He was paroled in 1977.

Loving v. Virginia In 1967 the U.S. Supreme Court ruled that laws forbidding interracial marriages were unconstitutional. In 1965, nineteen states had had such a law on the books.

LSD Lysergic acid diethylamide was the quintessential drug of the 1960s counterculture, embraced by visionaries who sought new planes of consciousness and by the tens of thousands of young people who simply sought adventure. LSD was invented by accident in 1943; a Swiss chemist working for the giant corporation Sandoz Pharmaceuticals was experimenting with medication for migraine headaches and instead created a powerful hallucinogen. LSD was legal in the United States until 1966; it was used by psychiatrists in private practice and by the CIA during the 1950s before advocates like Timothy Leary and Ken Kesey began to spread the word among the population at large during the 1960s. *See also* **Augustus Owsley Stanley III; Haight-Ashbury**

McCarthy, Eugene (b. 1916) As a peace candidate in 1968, McCarthy attempted to win the Democratic Party nomination for president. Beginning in 1967, the relatively unknown U.S. Senator from Minnesota challenged Lyndon Johnson and the Vietnam War, and his attempt to unseat a powerful incumbent from his own party captured the attention of many Americans tired of the war in Southeast Asia. Thousands of college students flocked to his campaign, including those who shaved and cut their hair or traded blue jeans for skirts to go "clean for Gene." After fighting Johnson to a near-draw in the New Hampshire primary, the McCarthy forces confronted a significant obstacle when Robert F. Kennedy announced his candidacy. After Johnson withdrew from the race on March 31, 1968, and Bobby Kennedy was assassinated on June 6, McCarthy and Vice President Hubert Humphrey fought a spirited contest for the nomination. Humphrey won. McCarthy, first elected to the Senate in 1958, continued to represent Minnesota there until 1971.

McGovern, George Stanley (b. 1922) The 1972 Democratic Party candidate for president, George McGovern campaigned to end the war in Vietnam. An early and outspoken opponent of the war, the senator from South Dakota defeated a host of heavily favored rivals for the 1972 nomination. After the 1968 Democratic Party Convention debacle, McGovern had been chairman of the committee that reformed his party's presidential nominating process. His reforms ended party boss control and made delegate selection more democratic. The McGovern reforms also mandated that each state delegation include women and members of minority groups. After winning the Democratic nomination, McGovern ran against Nixon's war policy, stating that he would cut defense spending and promising to strengthen government social programs. He lost to Richard Nixon by an overwhelming margin. McGovern continued to represent South Dakota in the Senate until defeated by a Republican candidate in 1980.

McLuhan, (Herbert) Marshall (1911–1980) McLuhan's theories of media and communications profoundly influenced the social thought of the 1960s. His most famous phrase, "the medium is the message," encapsulated his idea that the medium (oral, printed word, electronic) through which a society communicated information determined the character of the society and, to some extent, the psyche of its people. McLuhan was embraced by cultural critics for his criticism of industrial civilization and his idea that electronic media might re-create superior "tribal" forms in a new "global community." McLuhan, a Canadian, taught at the University of Toronto from 1946 to 1980.

McNamara, Robert Strange (b. 1916) As U.S. Secretary of Defense from 1961 to 1968, Robert McNamara helped guide American military policy for a crucial period of the cold war and much of the Vietnam War. McNamara had been a professor at the Harvard Business School; then during World War II he had helped devise the air war on Germany based on sophisticated quantitative analyses; after the war, using a systems analysis approach, he turned the nearly bankrupt Ford Motor Company into a highly profitable corporate giant. An immensely talented man, McNamara was dubbed by journalist David Halberstam as one of America's "best and the brightest," but ironically, McNamara sunk the United States into the Vietnam quagmire. He supported the escalation of the war in Vietnam until 1967, when he realized the quantitative, systems analysis approach he had used so successfully in his prior careers did not work in Vietnam. In 1968, he advised President Johnson to seek peace. He resigned that year and became the head of the World Bank. The dark shadow cast by his failed Vietnam policy ever after shrouded his life.

Maharishi Mahesh Yogi (b. 1918?) One of the most prominent gurus, or teachers, of meditation practice, Maharishi Mahesh Yogi began teaching transcendental meditation (TM) in the United States in 1960. Seeking to draw practitioners, he hired public relations experts, appeared on talk shows, and courted celebrities. In 1967, the Beatles announced that they were giving up psychedelic drugs for meditation and went to study with him in India. Other famous followers included Mia Farrow, Buckminster Fuller, Joe Namath, and Marshall McLuhan.

Mailer, Norman (b. 1923) Norman Mailer's first published novel, *The Naked and the Dead* (1946), established him as a leading writer of his generation. Throughout the post–World War II years, Mailer wrote brilliant novels, short stories, essays, and works of nonfiction that condemned American society for its materialism, conformity, racism, and moral hypocrisy. During the 1960s, Mailer wrote what he called nonfiction novels, most famously *Armies of the Night* (1968). Mailer used novelistic techniques like character development, plot, and internal monologues in book-length reports on the antiwar march on the Pentagon in 1967 and the presidential nominating conventions of 1968. A great self-promoter as well as a great writer, Mailer was a national celebrity in the Sixties, famous for his public opposition to the Vietnam War, his drunken brawling, and his outspoken opposition to the women's movement.

Manson, Charles (b. 1934) On successive nights in August 1969, Charles Manson, a sociopath and lifelong criminal, ordered followers he called his "family" to brutally murder and mutilate two different groups of strangers. They left behind bloody "clues": the word "PIG" scrawled in blood along a wall; "WAR" carved in one victim's stomach. On the surface, the "family" looked like many other groups of young people that gathered in California in the late 1960s: they dressed like hippies, did drugs, enjoyed sex, and reveled in their freedom. However, many in this group, including several young women, worshiped Charles Manson and were willing to kill for him. The mainstream media attributed the Manson murders to "hippie culture," intensifying establishment suspicion of the counterculture. And some sophisticated members of the counterculture worried that Manson's "family" showed how vulnerable a culture of freedom might be to strong-willed men bent on doing evil.

March on Washington (August 28, 1963) The March on Washington for Jobs and Freedom was organized by civil rights leaders seeking to win national support for John F. Kennedy's civil rights legislation. The less-often quoted statement of goals in the march's title signaled the shifting focus of the civil rights movement toward economic issues. Roy Wilkins of the NAACP, Whitney Young of the National Urban League, James Farmer of CORE, John Lewis of SNCC, and Martin Luther King Jr. of SCLC led the march, including more than 300,000 people of all classes and races. Covered live by two of the national television networks, civil rights leaders spoke to the nation about their struggle. Martin Luther King's "I Have a Dream" speech dramatized the power of the movement and has ever since been hailed as one of the great speeches in American history; the march was the largest civil rights demonstration in American history.

Marshall, Thurgood (1908–1993)   Perhaps the best known African-American attorney of his generation and the first African American to serve on the Supreme Court, Marshall headed the NAACP efforts to end segregation during the 1950s and 1960s. He successfully argued twenty-nine cases (including *Brown v. Board of Education*) before the Supreme Court as head of the NAACP legal team. He was appointed to the U.S. Second Court of Appeals by President Kennedy in 1961 and served as Solicitor General under President Johnson from 1965 to 1967, when Johnson appointed him to the Supreme Court, then headed by Earl Warren. Marshall was an important liberal voice on the court until poor health forced his retirement in 1991.

Masters and Johnson   William H(owell) Masters (b. 1915), a gynecologist, and Virginia Eshelman Johnson (b. 1925), a psychologist, collaborated in studies of human sexuality, devising laboratory methods for measuring sexual response and pioneering in the field of sex therapy. They coauthored three works, *Human Sexual Response* (1966), *Human Sexual Inadequacy* (1970), and *Homosexuality in Perspective* (1979), all of which challenged conventional notions about sexuality. The pair married in 1971 and divorced in 1991.

Max, Peter (b. 1937)   A psychedelic, pop culture artist whose posters sold millions in the late 1960s, Peter Max helped to develop a countercultural visual style. Max lived in China and Israel after fleeing his native Germany with his family upon the outbreak of World War II; he moved to the United States in 1953 and subsequently studied art and Eastern religions.

Means, Russell (b. 1939)   An early leader in the American Indian Movement (AIM), Russell Means participated in both the "Trail of Broken Treaties" and the takeover of the Bureau of Indian Affairs building in Washington, D.C. He was also a key organizer in AIM's standoff against federal marshals and FBI agents at Wounded Knee, South Dakota in 1973. He resigned from AIM during the 1980s and now records music and acts in films.

Meany, William George (1894–1980)   A militant anticommunist, as president of the AFL-CIO from 1955 through 1979, George Meany led the organization away from its radical roots and pushed it to play a greater role in mainstream politics. Like many cold war liberals, Meany supported civil rights for African Americans, Johnson's Great Society, and the Vietnam War. However, many felt that by the end of the 1960s he had lost touch with his followers because of his unyielding views on many issues.

military-industrial complex   In his 1961 presidential farewell address, Dwight D. Eisenhower warned of the new "conjunction of an immense military establishment and a large arms industry," a "military-industrial complex" that held the "potential for the disastrous rise of misplaced power." Antiwar groups and social activists in the 1960s saw this relationship as a critical flaw in American democracy and tried to expose the interconnectedness of the military and American corporations. *See also* **Students for a Democratic Society; New Left**

Millet, Kate (b. 1934)   Kate Millet's Columbia University doctoral dissertation, published by Doubleday in 1970, six months after she received her degree, propelled her to national prominence in the women's liberation movement. *Sexual Politics*, which sold 80,000 copies in its first year, offered both a feminist reading of authors including Henry Miller and Norman Mailer and a theoretical analysis of the construction of gender in patriarchal society. Media attention to Millet, often despite her express wishes not to be treated as "the" spokesperson for women's liberation, created tensions within the movement over her role. Her public confirmation that she was a lesbian in 1970 led to criticism not only in the mainstream press but also from some in the women's movement who saw no place for lesbians and lesbianism. Since 1970, Millet has continued to work as a visual artist and writer.

Miranda v. Arizona   This 5–4 Supreme Court decision is the origin of "Miranda rights." The justices held that anyone taken into custody must be warned by police of his or her right to have a lawyer (provided by the court if the accused cannot afford one) and to remain silent, even during police questioning.

Mississippi Freedom Democratic Party   Organized in 1963 as part of a voter registration campaign in Mississippi, the Mississippi Freedom Democratic Party (MFDP) exposed the political injustice in the South to a nationwide audience during the 1964 Democratic National Convention. The MFDP challenged the validity of the all-white Mississippi delegation, claiming it did not represent Mississippi. The credentials committee held hearings on the MFDP motion and heard from several of its members. The most damning testimony came from Fannie Lou Hamer, who described the vicious beatings she received when she tried to register blacks to vote. A horrified Lyndon B. Johnson first called an immediate press conference to interrupt televised testimony and then brokered a compromise unacceptable to members of the MFDP. Despite Johnson's back-room dealings and a near-constant stream of national civil rights leaders urging a settlement, most MFDP members refused to compromise. The events in Atlantic City that summer drove many civil rights activists to seek social justice outside the established political arena.

Morgan, Robin (b. 1941)   A radical feminist writer and activist, Morgan developed her politics in the New Left antiwar and civil rights movements of the mid-1960s. In 1968 she helped to create the New York Radical Feminists and to organize the widely publicized feminist protest at the 1968 Miss America Pageant. Becoming increasingly frustrated with sexism that existed within the movement as well as outside it, Morgan participated in the feminist takeover of the New York underground paper, *Rat*, and wrote the immensely influential article, "Good-bye to All That," a condemnation of the male-led New Left and its sexist practices, for the first women's issue. Morgan also criticized the mainstream and moderate feminism of organizations like NOW. In 1970 she edited the collection, *Sisterhood Is Powerful*, and she continued her work as a writer, poet, and social activist over the following decades.

Moses, Robert Paris (b. 1935)   Bob Moses, the inspirational leader of SNCC's early voter registration efforts in Mississippi, was born in New York City in 1935. He worked as a high school teacher before moving to Atlanta to work with the SCLC in 1960. While in Atlanta, Moses was impressed with SNCC's efforts in Mississippi; at the suggestion of Ella Baker, he joined them. Despite threats on his life by local whites, the soft-spoken Moses helped register thousands of black Mississippians to vote. In 1963 he directed the voter registration efforts and mock elections of the Council of Federated Organizations (COFO), as well as Freedom Summer in 1964. During that year's Democratic National Convention, Moses led the Mississippi Freedom Democratic Party's (MFDP) challenge of the white delegation from Mississippi. Angered by the MFDP's reception among civil rights leaders and in the Democratic Party, Moses left SNCC and abandoned an integrationist philosophy. He left the country and taught school in Africa. He returned to the United States in 1977 and started a math program for inner-city children.

Motown Record Company (Tamla Motown Record Company)   Founded by Berry Gordy Jr. in 1959, Motown became the largest black-owned business in the United States. Named for its location in Detroit, the Motor City, Motown discovered and promoted some of the most important musical acts of the 1960s, including Marvin Gaye, Smokey Robinson, the Supremes, the Temptations, and Stevie Wonder. Many of Motown's hits were "crossovers," a contemporary term for a recording that "crossed over" from its expected category of *Billboard* music chart (for example, rhythm and blues) to another (say, pop). In fact, "crossover" was often used to signal that a black artist appealed to white audiences as well as to black. Gordy moved Motown from Detroit to Los Angeles in 1971 and sold it to a consortium led by MCA Records in 1988.

Ms.   Since the 1940s, secretaries had used this form of address for women whose marital status was unknown, but it was not in common usage. With the rise of the women's movement in the late 1960s and early 1970s, many women who did not wish to be defined by their relationship to a man replaced "Miss" or "Mrs." with "Ms."

Ms.   *Ms.* was the longest running and most successful feminist magazine of the twentieth century. Gloria Steinem and several other feminists founded *Ms.* in 1972; by 1973 it had over 200,000 subscribers. Intended to encourage women to fight for gender equality, *Ms.* provided an important forum for discussion of feminist issues such as reproductive freedom, child care, equality in employment, the elimination of sexual exploitation, and the passage of the Equal Rights Amendment.

My Lai Massacre   On March 16, 1968, U.S. soldiers entered the village of My Lai, in the Quang Ngai Province of South Vietnam, expecting to find a National Liberation Front stronghold. Instead, they found only women, children, and elderly people. The infantry platoon, under the command of Lieutenant William Calley, murdered five hundred civilians that day, including babies. They raped and sodomized women and mutilated corpses. The villagers never fired a shot at the soldiers, and none of the dead appeared to be Vietcong. The U.S. Army kept the details of the attack out of the press and even described it as a major victory over an NLF stronghold. News of the massacre, however, seeped out when Ronald Ridenhour, a member of another unit, heard about it in March 1969 and contacted his congressman and Secretary of Defense Melvin Laird. In spring 1970 *Life* magazine published color photographs taken during the massacre, and public outrage spread. An Army court found only one man, Lt. William Calley, guilty. Protests erupted from those who believed that Calley was only a symptom of the larger disease of the war and from those who felt he was only a scapegoat being used by the Army brass. Calley served just three years in house arrest. Nevertheless, the My Lai Massacre exposed the brutality of the Vietnam War even to its supporters.

Nader, Ralph (b. 1934)   Consumer-protection activist and attorney Ralph Nader published *Unsafe at Any Speed*, an exposé of the American automobile industry, in 1965. His work led to the 1966 National Traffic and Motor Vehicle Safety Act, and launched his high-profile career as an investigator of corporate practices and health hazards ranging from meat packing (1967) to environmental pollution.

Namath, Joe (b. 1943)   In 1965, after a stellar collegiate football career at the University of Alabama, Namath joined the New York Jets. An immediate standout quarterback, he led the American Football League in passing during the 1966 season. In 1969, Namath led the Jets to defeat the Baltimore Colts in Super Bowl III. Namath's brash pregame prediction that the Jets would defeat the heavily favored Colts, along with his off-the-field lifestyle (which earned him the nickname "Broadway Joe"), signaled the arrival of a new type of athlete in professional sports.

National Abortion Rights Action League (NARAL)   Formed in 1969 as the National Association for the Repeal of Abortion Laws, after the Supreme Court decision *Roe* v. *Wade* overturned state laws prohibiting abortion in 1973 the organization took on a new name and new mission: to "keep abortion safe, legal, and accessible for all women."

National Association for the Advancement of Colored People (NAACP)   Founded in 1909 to combat lynching and other violence and discrimination targeting African Americans, the NAACP was the primary civil rights organization for African Americans for the next fifty years. The NAACP fought discrimination in voting laws, housing restrictions, and segregation in education and public facilities. Through its Legal Defense and Education division, the NAACP used the federal courts to strike down discriminatory laws. Its greatest victory came in the Supreme Court's 1954 *Brown* v. *Board of Education* decision, which declared segregation in the public schools unconstitutional. Throughout the 1960s, although groups like the SCLC and the SNCC challenged its dominance as the nation's primary civil rights organization, the NAACP continued to push for legislation and court rulings to ensure social justice for African Americans.

National Endowment for the Humanities   The National Endowment for the Humanities was created in 1965 with the support of President Lyndon B. Johnson. It provides government funding for grants and fellowships for scholars to research, publish, and produce works in the humanities.

National Farm Workers Association (NFWA)   Organized by César Chávez, the National Farm Workers Association successfully organized migrant farm laborers, most of whom were Mexican Americans, in the United

States. This union was chartered by the American Federation of Labor and Congress of Industrial Organizations (AFL-CIO) in 1966. The NFWA borrowed tactics from the civil rights movement and sought not only economic security but also social equality for its members. The organization created a co-op to distribute gasoline, health care, groceries, and banking services to members. Its drive for a national boycott of California table grapes in 1968 captured the attention of many Americans and led to successful negotiation of worker contracts.

National Indian Youth Council   Founded by ten university students—a Paiute, a Mohawk, a Ute, a Ponca, a Shoshone-Bannock, a Potawatomi, a Tuscarora, two Navajos, and a Crow—in Gallup, New Mexico on August 10, 1960, this group helped to launch a new Native American movement. Citing their responsibilities as the "younger generation," the members of the Youth Council opposed the policy of "termination," under which the federal government worked toward ending all relationships with tribes, including all treaties, services, and trusteeship of tribal lands (which would pass into private hands), thus ending tribes' sovereignty within the United States. Instead, they sought a greater degree of self-determination for native peoples. The NIYC grew steadily during the 1960s and fostered "red nationalism" and pride in Indian heritages. *See also* **Red Power**

National Liberation Front (NLF)   Formed in Vietnam in 1960, the National Liberation Front was a nationalist, communist-led organization dedicated to overthrowing the government of South Vietnam and reunifying the nation, which had been divided into North and South in 1954 at the end of an eight-year war between the French and the Viet Minh. The NLF, which was based in the South and was closely allied with the government of the Democratic Republic of Vietnam (North Vietnam), believed that the South Vietnamese government was illegitimate and corrupt. They had wide support in rural areas of South Vietnam, in part because the first president of South Vietnam, Ngo Dinh Diem, had rescinded a popular land reform plan implemented by the communists and forced peasants from their lands. The NLF fought against South Vietnam's Army of the Republic of Vietnam (ARVN) and their U.S. allies, infiltrated the government and military of South Vietnam, and were represented in the peace talks that took place between 1968 and 1973.

National Organization for Women (NOW)   NOW was founded in 1966 by a group of twenty-eight women who had attended a Washington, D.C., conference on the status of women. The organization's first president was author Betty Friedan, whose 1963 book, *The Feminine Mystique*, had helped to provide the impetus for a new women's movement in the 1960s. Modeled on civil rights organizations, NOW stated its objective as "to bring women into full participation in the mainstream of American society now, assuming all the privileges and responsibilities thereof in truly equal partnership with men." NOW was a pragmatic organization that performed traditional political lobbying functions, working for the enforcement of legislation against sex discrimination and, after 1967, for the passage of a federal Equal Rights Amendment (ERA). Much of NOW's influence was through local chapters, which adopted the feminist practice of consciousness raising, in which small groups of women met to explore the relationship between their personal lives and larger political and social structures. From its beginnings, NOW recognized women's work both within and outside the home. More radical women's groups in the late 1960s and early 1970s criticized NOW for trying to win women's equality within the existing society instead of seeking full-scale revolution and for its social conservatism (for example, NOW did not recognize "the oppression of lesbians as a legitimate concern of feminism" until 1971). Despite controversies within American feminism during the 1960s, NOW has been an effective advocate for women's rights for more than three decades. At the end of the twentieth century, NOW was the largest feminist organization in the United States, with chapters in every state and the District of Columbia.

The New Frontier Presidential nominee John F. Kennedy offered the American public a "New Frontier" in 1960. The term described both his domestic legislative agenda (civil rights for African Americans, urban renewal, social welfare, and public education) and his foreign policy initiatives, including the Peace Corps and the Alliance for Progress, which provided manpower and money to "modernize" Latin American nations. The New Frontier reflected the sense of optimism that accompanied much of the Kennedy presidency.

New Left The term described a loosely organized political movement primarily among young people on college campuses, many of whom had been inspired by the civil rights movement. The New Left was new in comparison with the Old Left, which had embraced a Soviet-style communism in which the state assumed control over many aspects of life. In contrast, the New Left not only rejected state power but also proposed to replace the system of representative democracy, in which elected representatives made decisions about policy and programs, with a direct or participatory democracy, in which all Americans made decisions about issues affecting their lives. They believed that only in this fashion could the nation address fundamental problems such as racism and economic inequality. New Left advocates also opposed the war in Vietnam and the U.S. military-industrial complex. Though no single group represented the New Left, Students for a Democratic Society was perhaps the largest and most visible organization in the movement.

New York Times v. *Sullivan* In 1964 the U.S. Supreme Court ruled that a public official cannot recover damages for criticism of his public performance in that office without proving deliberate malice. This ruling in favor of the *New York Times* strengthened the doctrine of freedom of the press.

Newton, Huey P. (1942–1989) After a troubled youth in Oakland, California, Newton met Bobby Seale and in 1966 formed the Black Panthers. Rejecting the nonviolent resistance practiced by southern civil rights protesters, the charismatic Newton urged his followers to arm themselves. In October 1967, following an altercation during a traffic stop in which a police officer was shot and killed, Newton was charged with first-degree murder. During his trial, the Black Panther Party, which believed that Newton had been targeted by police attempting to destroy the Black Panthers, launched a "Free Huey Newton" campaign that garnered national attention and increased membership. Newton was convicted of voluntary manslaughter, but the California Supreme Court later overturned his conviction. Upon his release, Newton shifted Panther focus to free health clinics, breakfasts for children, and voter registration. Attempting to avoid prosecution on a number of criminal charges, Newton fled to Cuba in 1973. He returned to the United States in 1977 and received a Ph.D from the University of California in 1980. Newton was killed by a drug dealer in August 1989.

1968 Olympics In the 1968 Olympic Games in Mexico City, U.S. gold medalist Tommie Smith and bronze medalist John Carlos bowed their heads during the playing of "The Star-Spangled Banner" and raised black-gloved left fists in the Black Power salute. Their symbolic protest against continued racial injustice in the United States drew international attention, and the U.S. Olympic Committee, under pressure from the International Olympic Committee, suspended the two from the team for advocating a political cause.

Nixon, Richard Milhous (1913–1994) The only two-term president of the 1960s and 1970s, Nixon successfully articulated the changing political attitudes of those Americans he once called "the silent majority."

The second son of a small-town grocer, Richard Nixon was born in Yor-ba Linda, California in 1913 and spent his youth in nearby Whitier. He at-tended law school at Duke University on a scholarship and graduated third in his class. After failing to get a job at a large eastern law firm, Nixon moved back to Whitier and practiced law. He also met, courted, and mar-ried Pat Ryan. The couple moved to Washington, D.C., during World War II and Nixon took a job with the Office of Price Administration, which, he later claimed, created a long-standing distaste for government bureaucra-cy. After only seven months, he joined the navy and spent the remainder of the war as a supply officer in the South Pacific.

In 1946, Nixon ran for Congress as a Republican in Southern California and defeated five-term Democratic incumbent Jerry Voorhis. During the campaign, Nixon engaged in "red-baiting," accusing his opponent of hav-ing the support of communists. When Nixon was appointed to the House Un-American Activities Committee, he continued his anticommunist cru-sade. He authored a bill that would force members of the Communist Par-ty to register with the federal government and he accused Alger Hiss, a high-ranking State Department official, of being a Soviet spy. Hiss denied the charges but was later convicted of perjury. Nixon's anticommunist cru-sade brought him national praise from many conservatives and scorn from many liberals who saw his zealotry as a cynical manipulation of the Ameri-can people.

In 1950, Nixon ran for the U.S. Senate in California. He defeated his opponent, Helen Douglas, with anticommunist innuendo similar to that he had used four years earlier. Douglas responded to Nixon's harsh tactics with the nickname that would dog him the rest of his life—"Tricky Dick."

In 1952, Dwight D. Eisenhower, taking the advice of top Republican of-ficials, chose Nixon as his vice-presidential running mate. When an $18,000 Nixon campaign slush fund was revealed, Nixon went on national television, disclosed his finances, and promised that he would keep at least one campaign donation—a dog, Checkers, that was a gift to his children. Although pundits labeled the "Checkers" speech maudlin and sentimental pabulum, Americans responded favorably to Nixon's directness.

As vice president, Nixon visited over fifty countries including Vietnam, Ghana, and most of Latin America. In 1959, in Moscow to open an Ameri-can exhibit, he demonstrated, as he and Nikita Khrushchev walked through a model, modern American kitchen, the advantages of the capi-talist West. The "kitchen debate," widely broadcast in America, exhibited Nixon's quick intelligence and ability to react under pressure. He emerged after 1958 as his party's leading candidate for the presidency in 1960. However, he lost the election to John F. Kennedy in one of the closest presidential contests in American history. Nixon ran a poor campaign, squandering an early lead in most polls by allowing Kennedy to take the initiative, underestimating the power of television, and not making clearer his own record on civil rights or foreign policy.

Nixon retired from public life but soon emerged to challenge Edmund "Pat" Brown in the 1962 California gubernatorial campaign. For the second time in two years, Nixon lost. In a press conference after the election, he mocked the press, whom he believed were against him, by telling them they would no longer have "Nixon to kick around anymore."

Nixon took a job with a prestigious law firm in New York and became a party stalwart, speaking on behalf of candidates across the nation. After Barry Goldwater's ignominious defeat at the hands of Lyndon Johnson in 1964, Nixon worked to bridge the divide between the conservative and moderate wings of his party. He also traveled extensively abroad and renewed friendships with world leaders he had met while vice president.

By 1968, Nixon was poised for another run for the White House. He held off challengers from within his party to become again the Republican nominee for president. He chose Maryland governor Spiro T. Agnew as his running mate. Nixon was deliberately vague about domestic policy but worked to position himself as a centrist. His two opponents made this possible. Humphrey's platform sought to extend Great Society programs that many traditional Democratic voters had come to believe were too expensive. On Nixon's right, George Wallace, a segregationist governor from Alabama, sought to nationalize racist politics. Lastly, Nixon promised war-weary Americans that he had a "secret" plan to end the war in Vietnam. Nixon won a close contest by 500,000 votes over Humphrey.

Despite a Democratic majority in both the House and the Senate, the new president set out a rigorous agenda that reflected the concerns of his "silent majority." Appealing to traditional economic conservatives, Nixon sought to cut the bureaucracy in the federal government. To appease "white backlash" voters in the North, his administration tried to prevent using busing to achieve racial integration. The Nixon administration responded to higher crime rates and increases in rioting and protests by rigorously prosecuting those they considered troublemakers. To appeal to religious conservatives, including many Catholics who voted Republican for the first time in 1968, Nixon supported prayer in schools and opposed legalizing abortion.

In other ways, Nixon supported many of the movements begun in the 1960s. Working with George Schultz, he approved a federal affirmative action plan for minorities in construction work. Nixon also worked to protect the environment, creating the Environmental Protection Agency. And he proposed sweeping welfare reform that would have guaranteed a minimum income for Americans but was defeated in the Senate.

Nixon's primary interest was in foreign policy. He inherited an unpopular and perhaps unwinnable war in Vietnam. In his 1968 campaign Nixon had promised a secret way to achieve "peace with honor." His plan, "Vietnamization," turned combat over to the South Vietnamese. He began recalling troops less than a year after the election. Peace talks with the North Vietnamese continued both in the open and secretly. Nixon's plan enabled him to quell temporarily the mounting opposition to the war while he intensified bombing campaigns and expanded U.S. attacks into nearby Cambodia and Laos. When U.S. troops entered Cambodia in early May 1970, protests erupted.

By 1971, a large majority of Americans just wanted the Vietnam War over. In March 1971, Lieutenant William Calley, accused of murdering innocents in the My Lai Massacre, was found guilty by a military court. Two months later, the *New York Times* published the "Pentagon Papers," which described in detail how the Kennedy and Johnson administrations had misled the American people about U.S. involvement in Vietnam. Nixon attempted to prevent the publication of the documents but was overruled by the U.S. Supreme Court.

In anticipation of a peace treaty and in response to an offensive against South Vietnam in 1972, Nixon stepped up bombing raids to include the north. Henry Kissinger worked diligently and secretly through summer and fall 1972 to negotiate a peace in Southeast Asia by the November elections. Kissinger announced on October 31 that "peace" was near. After winning the 1972 election, Nixon began bombing North Vietnam again and dropped 36,000 tons of bombs on Hanoi during the last two weeks of December. A peace treaty was signed two weeks later, and the United States pulled out of Vietnam.

Nixon proved successful on other diplomatic fronts. Throughout his first term, he made gestures toward the People's Republic of China; the two countries even exchanged visits by table tennis teams. "Ping-Pong" diplomacy led to Nixon's ten-day visit to China in February 1972. He also achieved détente with the USSR. A summit meeting between Nixon and Soviet leader Leonid Brezhnev in May 1972 led to the Strategic Arms Limitation Treaty (SALT), which limited future arms build-up. The two leaders also made trade agreements, and the Soviets began purchasing U.S. wheat.

Nixon's foreign policy successes and a very possible end to the Vietnam War on the horizon made him a formidable incumbent in the 1972 presidential race. He defeated the Democratic candidate, George McGovern, who was labeled by Nixon's campaign team as the candidate of "Amnesty," (for Vietnam draft dodgers), "Abortion," and "Acid." Nixon's victory was one of the largest in American history.

Nixon's celebration and mandate were short-lived, however. Angered over the publication of the Pentagon Papers and obsessed with winning the 1972 election, Nixon had created a "dirty tricks" squad. Members of this group were caught breaking into the Democratic Headquarters at the Watergate Hotel in June 1972. The investigative efforts of Carl Bernstein and Bob Woodward, two *Washington Post* reporters, revealed Nixon's involvement in what was known as the Watergate scandal. A Senate investigation discovered dozens of different illegal activities, from break-ins to wire taps to solicitation of campaign funds, all linked to Nixon. Moreover, the Senate committee hearings revealed that the president himself attempted to cover up these activities. When the U.S. House of Representatives moved toward impeaching him, Nixon resigned on August 9, 1974.

Gerald Ford, who had replaced Spiro T. Agnew when he resigned over a different scandal the year before, pardoned Nixon for any crimes he might have committed as president a month later. Nixon remained active in public life; he wrote several books aimed at restoring his fallen reputation, consulted with presidents on foreign affairs, and continued to meet with world leaders. He died in April 1994, still despised by many for the ignominy he had brought to the presidency.

Oswald, Lee Harvey (1939–1963)   The accused assassin of President John F. Kennedy, Oswald was killed before standing trial. After a brief stint in the Marine Corps in the 1950s, Oswald had defected to the USSR, where he was denied citizenship. He returned to the United States and in November 1963 took a job at the Texas School Book Depository, the building from which the shots were fired that killed President Kennedy and wounded Texas Governor John Connelly as their motorcade passed by on November 22. Dallas police soon thereafter arrested Oswald for killing a police officer who had pulled him over for questioning about the Kennedy assassination. Two days later, as police were transferring him from city jail to county jail, Dallas nightclub owner Jack Ruby shot and killed Oswald before live television cameras. The 1964 Warren Report concluded that Oswald acted alone in assassinating the president, but rumors of conspiracy persist to this day. *See also* **Kennedy assassination**

Peace Corps   The Peace Corps program, which sent American volunteers to provide assistance to the "developing" countries of Asia, Africa, and Latin America, was created by John F. Kennedy in 1961, only six weeks after taking office. Kennedy, who was a strong cold war opponent of the USSR, believed that such a program would help to improve relations between the United States and poorer nations, thus promoting world peace and helping to stem the spread of communism. Five hundred volunteers were placed in nine countries by the end of 1961. By 1966, at its peak, the Peace Corps had about sixteen thousand volunteers, most of whom were recent college graduates, working in fifty-nine countries. During the 1960s, about half of the volunteers served their two-year term as teachers; others worked in community development, agricultural development, or medical training programs in rural hospitals. During the 1970s, the Peace Corps declined, partly due to public suspicion of United States involvement in the affairs of other nations; in the 1990s the Corps saw a resurgence, with volunteers more likely to include older Americans with specific technical skills.

Peltier, Leonard (b. 1944)   From North Dakota, Peltier became a leader of the American Indian Movement (AIM), which he joined in 1970. He participated in the "Trail of Broken Treaties" caravan that traveled to Washington, D.C., in 1972, and, with approximately four hundred others, occupied the Bureau of Indian Affairs building when officials refused to meet with them. In 1975, Peltier was involved in a violent confrontation at the Pine Ridge Reservation in South Dakota between AIM members and a coalition of federal officials and corrupt Sioux officials. Two FBI agents and one AIM member were killed. Peltier was charged with murder and, following a trial marked by controversial judicial rulings, was sentenced in 1977 to two life terms, served consecutively.

Pentagon Papers   Published by the *New York Times* in 1971, the Pentagon Papers exposed the history of the United States' long involvement in the Vietnam War. Daniel Ellsberg, a former policy analyst, gave a *Times* reporter the results of a secret study of U.S. policy in Southeast Asia since the 1940s. The Pentagon Papers revealed the duplicity behind the build-up of ground forces and long-range U.S. policy. Convinced that the report would undermine his administration, Richard Nixon tried to prevent its publication. In a landmark decision, the Supreme Court determined that stopping publication violated the First Amendment. The newspaper's publishing of the material contained in the Pentagon Papers led to increased protests against the war in Vietnam.

The Pill   Oral contraceptives, often called simply "the Pill," have often been credited with bringing about the sexual revolution. This tiny tablet, approved for contraceptive use in the United States in 1960, did indeed change the experience of heterosexual intercourse. It was 99+ percent effective in preventing pregnancy, did not interfere with the sexual act in any way, and did not require either the cooperation or the knowledge of the woman's partner. By 1969, almost 8.5 million American women were "on the Pill"; their numbers had grown by almost one million a year throughout the decade.

However, this new reproductive technology did not, in and of itself, bring about changes in sexual behavior. Birth control was illegal in parts of the United States until 1966 the Supreme Court decision *Griswold* v. *Connecticut* in 1966, and birth control could be legally denied to unmarried women and men until 1972 (*Eisenstadt* v. *Baird*). Few doctors were willing, at first, to prescribe the Pill to single women, so cultural change and technological advancement went hand in hand to make a sexual revolution possible. With increased publicity about the side effects and possible dangers of oral contraceptives, by the end of the decade many women questioned the safety of the Pill, pointing to what they saw as a male-controlled medical establishment that promoted it without regard for women's health.

Playboy **magazine**   A product of the 1950s, *Playboy* magazine symbolized one aspect of the 1960s sexual revolution. Featuring a bachelor lifestyle, which included not only a luxurious apartment but also plenty of no-strings-attached sex with willing and beautiful women, *Playboy* expanded into a virtual empire during the Sixties. The Playboy Clubs, offering entertainment for men and staffed by young women in skimpy costumes with bunny ears and tails, were launched in Chicago in 1960 and quickly spread throughout the nation. By 1967, 450,000 men were members of 16 Playboy clubs, and the circulation of *Playboy* magazine was four million. While *Playboy* represented the opposite of what many sought from a "sexual revolution," it contributed to a freer sexual atmosphere in the United States. In some ways it was a victim of its own success: subscriptions to *Playboy* peaked in 1973 at close to 7 million and then dropped as competition from more sexually explicit male-oriented magazines—for which *Playboy* had paved the way—challenged its dominance. *See also* **Hugh Hefner**

Port Huron Statement   In June 1962, members of Students for a Democratic Society (SDS) gathered at a retreat in Port Huron, Michigan, to discuss the philosophy of the new organization and consider a seventy-five-page manifesto written earlier by Tom Hayden. The revised manifesto, issued as the "Port Huron Statement," called a new generation of college students to action. This fundamental document of the New Left expressed a new vision of American life based on concepts of participatory democracy.

President's Commission on the Status of Women   Formed by President Kennedy in December 1961, the Commission on the Status of Women investigated "prejudices and outmoded customs [that] act as barriers to the full realization of women's basic rights." The group was originally chaired by Eleanor Roosevelt. Upon her death in 1962, Esther Peterson (Assistant Secretary of Labor and director of the Women's Bureau, who had proposed the commission to Kennedy) took over. The commission did not endorse the Equal Rights Amendment, at least partly because Peterson and other members believed strongly in the importance of labor legislation that protected women and children, but it did propose far-reaching reforms. In part due to the commission's efforts, President Kennedy signed the Equal Pay Act (mandating equal wages for equal work in the private sector) and ordered federal agencies to hire and manage their employees on a gender-blind basis.

Presley, Elvis Aron (1938–1977)   Known as the King of Rock and Roll, Elvis Presley was rock's first superstar. His records dominated the charts in the 1950s; he had eighteen number-one singles, beginning with "Heartbreak Hotel" in 1955. During the 1960s, Elvis starred in dozens of movies and continued to top the charts with romantic ballads. His 1969 "comeback" television special introduced Elvis to a new generation of fans. He died of a drug overdose in 1977.

Quant, Mary (b. 1934)   British fashion designer Mary Quant was the "mother of the miniskirt." From the Chelsea boutique she ran with her husband, Alexander Plunket Greene, she had been outfitting hip British youth for ten years before the miniskirt's popularity propelled her to international fame in 1965. (Some credit couture designer Courrèges with creating the miniskirt; Quant says it originated on the streets before either of them picked it up.) Her bright, youthful clothes are synonymous with 1960s fashion.

radical feminism   A political movement that grew in response to male domination within the overlapping radical movements of the 1960s, including the antiwar movement, student uprisings, the New Left, and movements for racial/ethnic empowerment, radical feminism held that women were members of an oppressed sex class held subordinate by systems of male domination. Distinguishing themselves from socialist feminists, radical feminists maintained that gender inequality, rather than socioeconomic class, was the root cause of women's oppression. Unlike their liberal feminist counterparts, radical feminists rejected equality with men as their ultimate objective. Instead, they called for revolution in which women would seize power by rejecting normative conceptions of family, marriage, love, and heterosexuality.

Reagan, Ronald Wilson (b. 1911)   Before he was elected president in 1980, Ronald Reagan served as governor of California from 1967 to 1975 and was a presidential candidate in both 1968 and 1976. He first achieved fame as a Hollywood actor in the 1940s and 1950s, making more than fifty films, and was elected president of the Screen Actors Guild six times. During the House Un-American Activities Committee's investigation of Hollywood, Reagan took a strong anticommunist stand and testified before the committee about the communist influence in the film industry. In the 1964 presidential election, Reagan's televised speech on behalf of conservative Republican Barry Goldwater brought him national attention. Two years later, amid mounting disturbances on college campuses and in the nation's ghettos, California conservatives convinced Reagan to run for governor of the state. He promised to put protesters in their place, and in 1968 sent three thousand armed National Guardsmen in full battle gear to clear "People's Park" in Berkeley, saying flatly, "If it takes a bloodbath, let's get it over with. No more appeasement." Reagan's election as president in 1980 would mark the culmination of 1960s conservatism.

Red Power   Influenced by the Black Power movement, Native American activists who sought political and cultural sovereignty and social and economic equality in the 1960s adopted the slogan "Red Power." The term also served as an expression of pan-Indian unity exemplified by organizations such as the National Indian Youth Council and the American Indian Movement.

Redstockings   This militant radical feminist group was committed to both direct action and consciousness raising. The Redstockings were founded in New York by Ellen Willis and Shulamith Firestone in 1969. Early actions included theatrical "speak outs" on abortion. Although the Redstockings rejected the Marxist view that gender inequality would disappear with the eradication of capitalism, they adhered to a general Marxist ideology. The group defined their interests as identical to "that of the poorest, most brutally exploited woman." All women, they argued, should renounce their privileges and unite to defeat the dual forces of capitalism and patriarchy.

Rockefeller, Nelson (1908–1979)   The son of John D. Rockefeller Jr., Nelson Rockefeller served four terms as governor of New York and then two years as vice president of the United States under Gerald Ford. During the 1960s, Rockefeller was the leader of the liberal wing of the Republican Party; in 1964 he challenged Barry Goldwater for the Republican nomination. In 1971, with "law and order" the unofficial slogan of the Republican Party, Governor Rockefeller ordered state police and prison guards to end a bloody prison riot at Attica, New York's maximum-security facility. With guns blazing, the police and guards killed forty-three people, including ten hostages, in retaking the facility. Gerald Ford nominated Rockefeller for vice president when he took office in August 1974.

Roe v. Wade   The 1973 Supreme Court decision guaranteeing a woman's right to abortion in the first trimester and limiting the grounds for state intervention thereafter was in response to a 1969 class-action suit brought in Texas by Norma McCorvey (under the pseudonym "Jane Roe") against Texas district attorney Henry Wade. The court ruled that the "right of privacy" expressed in the Fourteenth and Ninth Amendments was "broad enough to encompass a woman's decision to terminate her pregnancy." *See also* **NARAL**

Rolling Stone   What would become the most successful popular music magazine in the world began small, selling only 6,000 copies of its first press run of 40,000 in 1967. *Rolling Stone* was created by Jann Wenner in San Francisco as a source of information about the contemporary music scene (the magazine moved its editorial offices to New York in 1977). It drew heavily on the New Journalism of the era, publishing work by journalists and critics such as Hunter S. Thompson.

The Rolling Stones   Formed in 1962 by Mick Jagger, Keith Richards, Brian Jones, Bill Wyman, and Charlie Watts, this British band was one of the most popular rock and roll groups of the 1960s. Their early music drew heavily from American blues and early rock and roll, and they were among the first rock bands to explore explicitly sexual topics and dark themes in their music. The high-energy stage performances for which they were known turned to tragedy during a free concert at Altamont Race Track near San Francisco in 1969, when a young man was stabbed to death by the Hell's Angels hired to provide security for the show. Among their many hits in the 1960s were such rock and roll classics as "Time Is on My Side," "Satisfaction," "Get off of My Cloud," and "Sympathy for the Devil."

Rostow, Walt Whitman (b. 1916)   A strong proponent of military intervention in Vietnam, as chair of the State Department Policy Planning Council (1961–1966) and then as special assistant to President Johnson (1966–1969), Rostow helped to shape U.S. war policy. Rostow, an economist, was a Rhodes scholar, served in the Office of Strategic Services during World War II, and held a position as professor of economic history at MIT from 1950–1960. In 1969, following the election of Richard Nixon, Rostow took a professorial position at the University of Texas.

Rubin, Jerry (1938–1994)   Jerry Rubin was one of the best publicized political voices of his generation. After graduating from the University of Cincinnati in 1961, Rubin worked as a reporter and studied in Israel before beginning work on a Ph.D. in sociology at Berkeley in 1964. Rubin was active in the Free Speech Movement and led teach-ins to protest the war in Vietnam. An integral part of the Bay Area protest movement, Rubin appeared before the House Un-American Activities Committee dressed as a soldier from the American Revolution; he ran for mayor of Berkeley and continued to protest the Vietnam War. Rubin met Abbie Hoffman in 1967 at a Washington, D.C. antiwar protest, and that December the two men founded Yippie!. Rubin and Hoffman attempted to use street theater and media manipulation to create a political consciousness among America's youths; Yippie! sought to blend countercultural freedom with New Left politics. After clashes between protestors and police disrupted the 1968 Chicago Democratic National Convention, Rubin was tried as one of the Chicago Seven. He became a stockbroker the same year that Ronald Reagan was elected president. In 1994, he died after being hit by a car while crossing a Denver street.

Rusk, Dean (1909–1994)   Rusk served as Secretary of State from 1961 until 1969, first under President Kennedy and then in the Johnson administration. Following military service in World War II, Rusk entered the Department of State in 1946 and, as Assistant Secretary of State for Far Eastern Affairs, played a major role in crafting U.S. policy toward Korea. A strong anticommunist, Rusk supported U.S. intervention in Vietnam and the war policies of President Johnson.

SANE (Committee for a Sane Nuclear Policy)   The Committee for a Sane Nuclear Policy, more commonly known as SANE, was founded in 1957 in response to a build-up of the U.S. nuclear arsenal. The organization sponsored protests in the late 1950s and early 1960s and opened chapters on college campuses around the country. The rise of protest movements against the Vietnam War, however, drew membership and support away from the organization.

Savio, Mario (1942–1994)   The leader of Berkeley's Free Speech Movement in 1964, Mario Savio first worked in the civil rights movement. After attending Queens College in New York City, Savio transferred to Berkeley in 1963 and spent the following summer in Mississippi as an SNCC worker. When university officials began to curb political speech on campus, Savio helped organize the United Front to protest. He continued to lead protests against administration policies regarding political speech on campus. His impassioned plea for justice combined with anger over administrative bureaucracy produced intense interest among Berkeley students. He helped them gain an agreement from the administration that it would not abridge students' First Amendment right to free speech. Savio remained an activist involved in educational reform efforts throughout his life.

Selma Movement   A major civil rights protest led by Martin Luther King Jr. in 1965, the Selma Movement aimed to bring the lack of voting rights for African Americans in Alabama to the attention of the nation. The movement climaxed when several hundred African Americans attempted to march from Selma to the state capital, Montgomery, on March 7, 1965. When they reached the Edmund Pettus Bridge, Alabama state troopers attacked them with billy clubs, tear gas, and lengths of hose wrapped in barbed wire. That evening the television networks interrupted programming to show the violent scenes from what became known as "Bloody Sunday." The nation was outraged. As a result of this public outcry, Lyndon Johnson was able to push through the Voting Rights Act of 1965, guaranteeing African Americans the right to vote throughout the United States.

Sharon Statement   The conservative parallel to the Port Huron Statement, the Sharon Statement was crafted by the Young Americans for Freedom (YAF) at their organizing conference at the family estate of William F. Buckley in Sharon, Connecticut, in September 1960. Delegates endorsed a short ideological credo that began: "In this time of moral and political crisis, it is the responsibility of the youth of America to affirm certain eternal truths." It embraced strong anticommunism, the primacy of the free market, and an extremely limited governmental role in both economy and society.

silent majority   The phrase "silent majority" entered the political lexicon in November 1969. In response to increasing protest over the Vietnam War, President Nixon declared that "the great silent majority" of Americans supported his efforts in Southeast Asia. Professional pundits picked up the phrase and used it to describe those Americans who were growing weary of

the civil rights movement, Vietnam War demonstrators, women's liberation, and other protest movements of the era.

Southern Christian Leadership Conference (SCLC) The SCLC was
founded in 1957 following the success of the Montgomery bus boycott. Its
leadership was primarily drawn from African-American ministers; Dr. Martin Luther King Jr. led the organization until his death in 1968. The primary goals of the SCLC were to eliminate segregation in public accommodations, increase black voter registration, and bring national attention
to the plight of black southerners. The SCLC dedicated itself to the principles of nonviolence and helped to lead many of the most significant
protests of the era, including the Birmingham, Alabama protests and the
March on Washington, both in 1963, and the Selma-to-Montgomery
March in 1965. After 1965, SCLC turned its attention north and established a headquarters in Chicago from which to focus on housing issues
and economic discrimination. After King was assassinated in 1968, Ralph
Abernathy assumed leadership of the organization, overseeing the Poor
People's Campaign and March in 1968, broadening the organization's
goals for social justice, and forging alliances with labor organizations.

space program Responding to advances by the Soviets in the field of rocket
science, Congress created the National Aeronautics and Space Administration (NASA), a civilian agency, in 1958. Its first mission, the Mercury Project, was to send an American into space. Mercury began with great fanfare
by recruiting pilots from the military to become America's first astronauts.
In the beginning, the United States trailed the USSR in the "space race,"
launching its first manned spacecraft on May 5, 1961, just twenty-three days
after Soviet cosmonaut Yury Gagarin had become the first human being in
space. John Glenn became the first American to orbit the Earth in February 1962. The Mercury Program was considered an incredible success by
almost everyone, and the president and NASA began preparations to send
a man to the Moon by the end of the decade. The experimental Gemini
Program marked the transition phase between launching men into outer
space and sending them on a mission to the Moon. John F. Kennedy began
the Apollo Program in 1961 with the sole purpose of sending astronauts to
the Moon and returning them to Earth. The program succeeded, and Neil
Armstrong became the first human to walk on the surface of the Moon on
July 20, 1969. Over the next three years, ten other Apollo astronauts walked
(or golfed) on the Moon's surface.

Spock, Benjamin McLane (b. 1903) *Baby and Child Care*, published by
pediatrician and child psychiatrist Benjamin Spock in 1946, sold more

than 24 million copies in the following 25 years and shaped the child-rearing practices of millions of American parents. Spock's work broke sharply with the rigid parenting advice that predominated in the years before World War II. Instead of advising parents to impose a feeding schedule on babies, he advocated feeding on demand and other more child-centered and "permissive" approaches. In the 1960s, conservative critics blamed Spock for creating a generation of spoiled youths; Vice President Spiro Agnew charged that hippies and war protesters had been "raised on a book by Dr. Spock and a paralyzing permissive philosophy pervades every policy they espouse." With the rise of the feminist movement, others criticized Spock for ignoring the role of fathers, using only the pronoun "he" to discuss children, and suggesting that a full-time homemaker mother was necessary for a child's well-being. Spock himself was a highly visible opponent of the war in Vietnam and of nuclear weapons. In 1972, he ran for the presidency of the United States as the candidate of the People's Party.

Stanley, Augustus Owsley III, or Owsley (b. 1935) A counterculture legend in his own time, Owsley produced the LSD that fueled the development of Haight-Ashbury as a counterculture mecca. LSD was legal in 1965 when Owsley began to manufacture it on a large scale; supposedly he sold almost 10 million aspirin-size tablets for $2 each and gave a great deal of the drug away. LSD did not remain legal for long, and Owsley's lab was raided by federal agents in December 1967.

Steinem, Gloria Marie (b. 1934) Author, editor, and feminist activist, Gloria Steinem discovered her love of politics and journalism as a student at Smith College in the 1950s. After leaving Smith, she worked as a freelance writer; her first success was a story titled "I Was a Playboy Bunny," about her experiences working—undercover—in a Manhattan Playboy Club. In 1968 she became a contributing editor and political columnist for *New York* magazine and began writing on the emerging women's movement. In 1971, Steinem helped to found the National Women's Political Caucus; in 1972 she became the founding editor of *Ms.* magazine, which represented the mainstream, liberal wing of the women's liberation movement.

Stonewall The confrontation at the Stonewall Inn in New York's Greenwich Village on June 27, 1969, is often hailed as the symbolic beginning of the gay liberation movement. Police intending to raid this gay bar, based on a New York State liquor authority ruling that a bar could allow no more than three homosexual patrons at any given time, met unexpected resistance. After a struggle that left four police officers injured, gay men and women filled the streets on subsequent nights, chanting "gay power." A newly formed Gay Liberation Front (GLF) began to work publicly against discrimination and on the first anniversary of Stonewall organized a Gay Pride Week that drew more than ten thousand people to march in support of gay rights.

Student Nonviolent Coordinating Committee (SNCC)   The vanguard civil rights organization of the 1960s, SNCC had its roots in the sit-in movement that began in Greensboro, North Carolina on February 1, 1960, when four black students from North Carolina A & T College began a sit-in at a whites-only lunch counter. In the following weeks, students throughout the South initiated sit-ins to protest segregated facilities. Determined to create a lasting organization for their movement, three hundred students from fifty-eight colleges met at Shaw University on April 15 and formed the Student Nonviolent Coordinating Committee. Chicago journalist James Foreman became SNCC's first executive secretary in 1961. Instrumental in organizing and leading the Albany Movement, Freedom Summer, the Mississippi Freedom Democratic Party, and voter registration drives throughout the South, SNCC remained at the vanguard of the civil rights movement. Its often tenuous relationship with other civil rights organizations grew more serious during 1965's Selma-to-Montgomery March, when SNCC staffers grew frustrated at the seeming timidity of Martin Luther King Jr. and the SCLC. In 1966, under the leadership of chairman Stokely Carmichael, the SNCC shifted away from the traditional civil rights platform. On the "James Meredith March Against Fear," Carmichael and others questioned the sanctity of nonviolence, even as they championed Black Power. H. Rap Brown replaced Carmichael as chairman the next year and continued to proclaim militancy. Increased attention and infiltration from the police and FBI took a serious toll on the SNCC until the organization's membership dwindled to a handful of full-time workers.

Students for a Democratic Society (SDS)   A radical organization based on college campuses throughout the United States, Students for a Democratic Society questioned basic tenets of postwar American society. SDS protested the Vietnam War, opposed the growing technocracy of American life and government, supported the civil rights movement, and called for a more participatory democracy in the United States. Individual SDS chapters on college campuses formed a loose national coalition but were free to address local problems and issues. SDS was originally a student "chapter" of the League of Industrial Democracy, an "Old Left" labor union ally, and in its early days was led by two students at the University of Michigan, Al

Haber and Tom Hayden. The Port Huron Statement, issued by SDS in 1962 and written largely by Hayden, criticized the left for accepting the status quo and the right for embracing extremism, and called upon the current generation to develop a new sense of individualism and participatory democracy. The leadership of a "New Left," the original members believed, would come not from the traditional source, labor unions, but from college students and a new generation of youths.

In 1964, SDS initiated the Economic Research and Action Project in urban ghettos to help the nation's poor. From 1965, national SDS focused on the escalation of the war in Vietnam, staging a peace rally in Washington, D.C. in April 1965 that drew 25,000 people and was the largest antiwar demonstration to date. As the war dragged on, SDS chapters moved toward more confrontational tactics: they sponsored draft card burnings, targeted induction centers and arms manufacturers for protests, and rallied outside the Pentagon. In spring 1968, the Columbia University SDS chapter took over several buildings on campus to protest what they saw as a racist expansion of the university into the surrounding poor, black neighborhoods. Later that year the protests at the Democratic National Convention brought SDS national membership to over 100,000. By the next year, however, internal divisions had severely weakened the effectiveness of the national organization, and violent factions, such as the Weathermen, had splintered off from the group.

Summer of Love   In the spring and summer of 1967, thousands of America's youths made a "pilgrimage" to San Francisco. Invited by Haight-Ashbury's Council for a Summer of Love and drawn by media coverage so intensive that people joked about bead-wearing *Life* magazine reporters interviewing bead-wearing *Look* magazine reporters, more than 75,000 young people flooded into the district. They came for "free love," drugs, and a chance to help build a new community of young people. Unlike those who had been creating an alternative community in the Haight for the past three years, many if not most of the newcomers were poorly equipped for the task at hand. Hip businesses flourished, but rape, disease, exploitation, violence, and bad drug experiences skyrocketed. At the end of the summer the Diggers, the group most committed to creating a counterculture in the Haight, proclaimed the "death of Hippie," but the numbers of young people calling themselves hippies and seeking a countercultural lifestyle continued to grow.

Supremes   Diana Ross, Mary Wilson, and Florence Ballard (replaced in 1968 by Cindy Birdsong) formed the Motown girl group, the Supremes, which hit the top of the pop charts repeatedly between 1964 and 1969 with songs like "Stop! In the Name of Love," "Baby Love," and "Love Child." This phenomenon—music by black performers reaching the national (presumably "white") charts, was called "crossing over." Berry Gordy, head of Motown, had the Supremes and members of all Motown's other "girl groups" attend charm school for coaching in grooming and manners so that they would appear "respectable." Diana Ross left the Supremes in 1969 for a successful solo career, which included acting roles.

Tet Offensive   On the last day of January 1968 (the Vietnamese holiday of Tet, the lunar new year), forces from the National Liberation Front in South Vietnam, supported by the North Vietnamese Army, attacked major cities throughout South Vietnam. The attack was a complete surprise; the combatant nations were under a flag of truce in honor of the holiday. Eighty-five thousand NLF troops descended upon every major city in South Vietnam. They attacked the U.S. embassy in Saigon. From a military standpoint the offensive failed; American and South Vietnamese forces retook the cities in just a few days. The attack, however, had a profound impact on U.S. public opinion. Americans had been reassured for months that the war was in its final stages; the Tet Offensive revealed the falseness of such claims and the potential for a long, bloody conflict. When CBS news anchor Walter Cronkite, who had previously supported the administration's efforts in Southeast Asia, reported from Vietnam that the war was mired in a stalemate, public opinion turned further against President Johnson's policies.

Thompson, Hunter S. (b. 1939)   Hunter Thompson invented "gonzo journalism," political reporting that featured a subjective, participatory style and blended imagination with factual information. Thompson's first book was an account of his year spent riding with the Hell's Angels. He next wrote an astute, if largely fabricated, account of the 1972 election, *Fear and Loathing on the Campaign Trail, '72*. That same year he published *Fear and Loathing in Las Vegas: A Savage Journey to the Heart of the American Dream*, a searing critique of white middle-class values as seen through the lens of the drug counterculture.

Tijerina, Reies (b. 1926)   Born in Texas, one of eight children of migrant farm workers, Reies Tijerina grew up to fight for the land rights of Hispanic New Mexicans, or Nuevo Mexicanos. A former Assembly of God preacher, Tijerina moved to Rio Arriba County in northern New Mexico after fleeing criminal charges in Arizona, where he had established a religious commune. In 1962, he established the Alianza Federal de Mercedes

(Federal Alliance of Land Grants). Many local *hispano* residents were angry at those they believed had stolen their lands—Anglo farmers, and most particularly the federal government, which had begun to tighten regulations governing the use of U.S. Forest Service lands. Tijerina and his organization sought the return of land they declared belonged to *hispano* villagers according to the 1848 Treaty of Guadalupe Hidalgo. Emulating the Black Power movement, he and his followers sought attention and support for their claims by staging several protests, including a 1966 takeover of Kit Carson National Forest. Violence marred this movement the following year when the Alianza, attempting to free eight members jailed for unlawful assembly, shot a state policeman and a deputy sheriff. Tijerina was acquitted on charges stemming from the courthouse violence but was convicted on federal charges for earlier incidents. As part of his parole he agreed no longer to participate in Alianza Federal.

Title IX   Part of the Educational Amendments Act of 1972, this federal law requires that both sexes have equal opportunity in all educational programs that receive federal funds, including athletics. Before Title IX was implemented, colleges and universities frequently allocated as little as one percent of their athletic budgets to women's sports. In high schools during the 1970–71 school year, fewer than 300,000 girls participated in sports, compared to more than 3.5 million boys. By 1978, more than two million high school girls were involved in sports programs. There was strong initial opposition from those who saw Title IX as taking resources away from men's sports; some of that opposition persists today. However, increased access and funding have made an enormous difference in the quality of women's sports and in the options available to young women.

Trail of Broken Treaties   American Indian Movement activist Robert Burnette organized Indians from throughout the United States to march on Washington just before the 1972 presidential election in order to draw attention to Native American issues. Those coming from the southwest followed the Cherokee Trail of Tears (1838), and the Sioux passed the site of the Wounded Knee massacre (1890). When federal officials refused to meet with AIM leaders, between six and eight hundred marchers took over the Bureau of Indian Affairs building. Once inside, AIM members made public files that demonstrated the corruption of the agency. The group issued a set of demands, including improvement of economic conditions for Indians and the repeal of termination policies. A negotiated settlement was reached after a week, with the government promising to review the activists' demands.

transcendental meditation   Introduced to the United States by the Maharishi Mahesh Yogi in 1960, transcendental meditation acquired more
than six hundred thousand practitioners by its peak in 1975. Students were
each given a personal mantra, a Sanskrit word, which was to be repeated
throughout twice-daily, twenty-minute meditation periods. During the
1960s, TM was closely associated with youth culture, especially when the
Beatles briefly followed the Maharishi. When they became quickly—and
publicly—disillusioned, TM declined in popularity. It reemerged in the
1970s, though it was no longer so closely associated with youth or countercultural spirituality.

Twiggy (b. 1949)   The most famous fashion model of the 1960s, Twiggy had
a very thin, childlike body and large, expressive eyes. Born and raised in a
working-class suburb of London, Twiggy (whose birth name was Leslie
Hornby) dropped out of school at the age of fifteen. Her boyfriend, twenty-
five-year-old hairdresser Nigel Davies (who changed his own name to
Justin de Villeneuve), became her manager, promoting her as the embodiment of "mod" fashion. Twiggy arrived in the United States in 1967. She
was photographed by Richard Avedon and appeared in leading magazines
and in a television special on her career.

Underground Press Syndicate   This was an extremely loose organization of
underground newspapers formed in 1967, which allowed member papers
to reprint each other's material and shared information through a newsletter, the *Free Ranger Intertribal News Service*. Differing agendas created tensions within the organization, and more politically oriented members
quickly broke away to form the Liberation News Service, which itself
would break apart within a year.

Vatican Council, Second (Vatican II)   Called by Pope John XXIII in 1959,
the council was intended to signal the Roman Catholic Church's openness
to engage in dialogue with the modern world. More than 2,500 bishops
and others eligible to attend participated in 178 meetings, which took place
between 1962 and 1965. The bishops issued pastoral statements on many
topics, including the role of the Church in the modern world, religious liberty and relations with non-Catholics, marriage and the family, and the
celebration of Mass. The reforms begun by the Second Vatican Council
were far-reaching and, though controversial, have had a major impact on
the practice of Roman Catholicism in the United States and the world.

Vietnam Veterans Against the War (VVAW)   One of the most influential
and controversial antiwar groups, the VVAW was created by six Vietnam
War veterans in 1967 and had thousands of members by the end of the de-

cade. At the VVAW "Winter Soldier Investigation" in early 1971, 116 veterans testified about atrocities committed by U.S. troops in a "war gone berserk." In April of that year, more than 1,000 members, including many permanently disabled by injuries from the war, participated in the 200,000-strong march on Washington, D.C. and held a memorial service at the Tomb of the Unknown Soldier. President Nixon obtained a court order preventing them from laying wreaths on the graves of the dead at Arlington Cemetery, but they violated the order. Three days later, on April 23, almost 2,000 veterans threw medals awarded to them for service in Vietnam over police barricades onto the steps of the Capitol in protest against the continuing war.

Wallace, George Corley (1919–1998) The Alabama governor and perennial presidential candidate brought southern racist politics to a national audience during the 1960s. After losing in his bid for the Alabama governorship in 1958 to an outspoken segregationist candidate, Wallace, a state judge, vowed never to lose another election by being considered a racial moderate. In his 1962 campaign for governor, when massive resistance politics had faded in most Southern states, Wallace made the preservation of segregation his primary platform. In his inauguration speech he promised "segregation forever." A few months later, in a carefully choreographed performance, he temporarily blocked the admission of two African-American students to the University of Alabama. His display brought him national attention, and he entered a few presidential primaries in 1964. Buoyed by his success, Wallace entered the presidential race as an independent candidate in 1968 and, running on a segregationist platform with a healthy dose of antibureaucratic rhetoric, garnered over 13 percent of the vote. He won reelection as Alabama's governor in 1970. (His wife Lurleen, acting as Wallace's stand-in, had won in 1966.) While campaigning for the Democratic nomination in 1972, and after winning several primaries, Wallace was shot by Arthur Bremer. His legs paralyzed, Wallace withdrew from the race. He later apologized for his segregationist stances and rhetoric and was reelected governor of Alabama in 1974 and 1982.

War on Poverty Part of Lyndon B. Johnson's Great Society, the War on Poverty was a series of legislative proposals designed to eradicate poverty in the United States. In his first State of the Union address, Johnson pledged to the nation that his administration "today, here and now, declares unconditional war on poverty in America." The programs included education reform, employment and job training, housing projects, food stamps, welfare, and urban renewal.

Warhol, Andy (1928–1987)   Warhol was the key figure in the 1960s pop art movement, making experimental films and creating paintings based on popular culture images and icons such as Campbell soup cans, Brillo pads, and film star Marilyn Monroe. Working from his New York studio, which he called "The Factory," Warhol made art that was, like the surrounding society, mass produced. Warhol's most frequently quoted line was, "In the future, everyone will be world-famous for fifteen minutes."

Warren, Earl (1891–1974)   Perhaps the most influential Chief Justice of the United States Supreme Court in the twentieth century, Earl Warren helped to change the social fabric of America. President Eisenhower appointed Warren, a former Governor of California and 1948 Republican Party vice-presidential candidate, Chief Justice in 1953. The next year, Warren wrote the majority opinion in the single most important case in the history of the civil rights movement. His opinion in *Brown v. Board of Education* that separate schools for black and white children were "inherently unequal" changed the course of race relations in America forever. The Warren Court continued to break down *de jure* discrimination (or discrimination by law, not just by practice) throughout the 1960s. Under Warren the Supreme Court took a more activist approach to other social problems. It worked to protect the rights of those accused of crimes as well as to defend the rights of individuals against the majority. In 1963, Lyndon Johnson appointed Warren to head a commission investigating the assassination of John F. Kennedy. The Warren Commission determined that Lee Harvey Oswald acted alone. Warren resigned from the Supreme Court in 1969 and died five years later.

Warren Court (1953–1969)   The Supreme Court under Chief Justice Earl Warren fundamentally changed American jurisprudence. As the Court moved toward an interpretation of the Constitution that protected individual rights, it became an agent of social and political change. The first landmark decision by the court was *Brown v. Board of Education of Topeka, Kansas* (1954), which ruled the southern practice of school segregation unconstitutional. In addition to civil rights, the court established generally liberal rulings on religious freedom, censorship, and the rights of those accused of crimes.

Watts riots   Coming shortly after the passage of the 1965 Voting Rights Act, the riots among African Americans in the primarily black Watts area of Los Angeles confused many Americans. On August 11, 1965, after a white police officer arrested a black motorist on suspicion of driving under the influence of alcohol, a crowd gathered and began shouting at the officer. Police reinforcements were met with thrown rocks and bottles. People moved into the streets, setting fires, looting, and attacking white drivers. Eventually there were more than 15,000 police and National Guardsmen sent into Watts. For five days, the neighborhood seethed. Thirty-four people were killed, more than 1,000 were injured, and 4,000 were arrested; property damage was estimated at $35–$40 million. A special commission convened to study the causes of the riots pointed to anger over economic conditions where the black unemployment rate was 30 percent despite the booming economy of the time. Up to that point the civil rights movement had focused primarily on the political rights of black southerners; Watts and other urban uprisings demonstrated that race was not just a "southern problem." The violence in the streets of Watts was also used to justify a "white backlash" against the civil rights claims of African Americans.

Weathermen, or Weather Underground   Organized to foment violent revolution and overthrow the U.S. government, the Weathermen was one of the small groups that emerged from Students for a Democratic Society as it disintegrated in 1969. Led by Mark Rudd, Bernardine Dohrn, and James Mellen, the group never numbered more than a few hundred people. They took their name from a line in a Bob Dylan song: "You don't need a weatherman to know which way the wind blows," changing it from "Weathermen" to "Weather Underground" in December 1969 when core members of the group went underground as a terrorist organization.

Before going underground, the group had tried to recruit members through tactics such as invading high school and college classrooms, tying up teachers and professors, and giving revolutionary speeches. In early October 1969, they launched a "direct action" in Chicago, attacking police and vandalizing property in what the media called the "Days of Rage"; they also brought violence to the Moratorium, an anti–Vietnam War march in Washington, D.C. Once underground, the group continued violent tactics, eventually claiming responsibility for twenty bombings. Three Weathermen were killed on March, 6, 1970 when they accidentally detonated a bomb they were building in a New York townhouse. The Weathermen received publicity well in excess of their numbers but came no closer to their revolutionary goals. Instead, their violence alienated most Americans and was used by opponents to discredit the left.

Westmoreland, William Childs (b. 1914)   Commander of U.S. troops in Vietnam from 1964 through 1968, Westmoreland strongly advocated the expansion of the American role in Vietnam from advisory capacity in 1964 to full combat operations in 1965. He implemented a strategy of attrition in which the enemy body count was treated as the key measure of success. After the Tet Offensive, when General Westmoreland called for still more American troops, President Johnson brought him back to Washington, where he served as U.S. Army Chief of Staff. He retired from the military in 1972.

Whole Earth Catalog   First published in 1968 by Stewart Brand, the *Whole Earth Catalog* was the "how-to" book of the counterculture, devoted to helping the individual "to conduct his own education, find his own inspiration, shape his own environment, and share his adventure with whoever is interested." The *Whole Earth Catalog* offered everything from windmills to wood-burning stoves to earth shoes for sale, but also included advice on living outside the mainstream. It sold more than two million copies between 1968 and 1970, and won the National Book Award in 1971.

Wolfe, Tom (b. 1931)   As a journalist, Tom Wolfe provided some of the most perceptive portrayals of 1960s culture in his nonfiction accounts of the era. Writing in the New Journalism style, which combined objective reporting with subjective interpretation, Wolfe helped to define the incredible changes wrought during the decade. Between 1965 and 1970 Wolfe published *The Kandy-Kolored Tangerine-Flake Streamline Baby, The Pump House Gang, The Electric Kool-Aid Acid Test,* and *Radical Chic and Mau-Mauing the Flak Catchers.*

women's liberation movement   The women's movement of the 1960s and 1970s included widely divergent groups embracing various and sometimes antithetical beliefs ranging from the liberal politics of NOW (the National Organization for Women) to separatist organizations' belief that men and women were fundamentally different from each other. This entire range of organizations and ideologies, as well as many individual women who simply questioned their lot in life, was too often lumped together, especially by critics who attempted to ridicule "women's libbers." The women's liberation movement, however, was most specifically a set of women's groups that emerged from the New Left and civil rights movements. Radical women seeking to end oppression in society began to draw analogies between the status of other oppressed groups and their own condition. In increasing numbers they rebelled at their subordination even within groups devoted to social change, as male members too often took the leadership roles and expected women to make the coffee, do the typing, and be sexually available. In general, women's liberation groups did not seek equality with men within the existing social and economic system, but meant to bring about larger revolutionary changes in society. *See also* **radical feminism; consciousness raising**

Woodstock   Originally advertised as "three days of peace and music," Woodstock became the cultural touchstone for a generation. Trying to cash in on the wave of rock festivals that became popular in the late 1960s, Woodstock's promoters envisioned an event that would draw about 100,000 young people to hear performers including Jimi Hendrix, Joan Baez, Jefferson Airplane, Arlo Guthrie, and the Grateful Dead. Instead, 500,000 people poured into 600 acres outside Bethel, New York, to become part of "Woodstock Nation." Amazingly, even with chronic food shortages, few bathrooms, inadequate medical facilities, no security, and heavy rain, the festival was relatively peaceful and convinced many participants and observers of the potential for creating alternative communities.

Woodward and Bernstein   Reporters for the *Washington Post* Bob Woodward and Carl Bernstein helped to expose the Watergate break-in and subsequent cover-up. Assigned to cover the break-in at the Democratic National Headquarters at the Watergate, the two reporters eventually traced the burglary to White House officials. Their investigation also revealed other illegal activities organized by high-ranking members of Richard Nixon's staff. Their reportage eventually led to a congressional investigation into the actions of Richard Nixon and caused his subsequent resignation. Woodward and Bernstein's coverage of Watergate earned the *Post* a Pulitzer Prize for public service.

Wounded Knee   On February 27, 1973, a group of approximately 200 Sioux, led by members of AIM (American Indian Movement), occupied the town of Wounded Knee, South Dakota, site of the 1890 massacre of more than 150 Sioux men, women, and children by the U.S. Army. Originally prompted by an internal struggle between traditionalists and the elected head of the Pine Ridge Reservation Tribal Council, whom they charged with corruption and with using violence to enforce his power, the confrontation turned into a 71-day siege that involved almost 2,000 Indians and 300 FBI agents and federal marshals. Though two people were killed and 12 wounded, the siege was ended by a negotiated settlement. The occupation attracted much media attention and increased knowledge of and sympathy for the Native American movement for civil rights and self-determination.

X, Malcolm (Malcolm Little; El Hajj Malik El-Shabazz) (1925–1965)   Considered by many to be the originator of the Black Power ideology, Mal-

colm X was a fiery speaker who chastised white Americans as he demanded justice for African Americans. As a child, Malcolm Little experienced
intense racism: his family was chased from Omaha, Nebraska by the Ku
Klux Klan and his father was murdered by whites who threw him under
the wheels of a streetcar in Lansing, Michigan. As a young man, while in
prison for attempted burglary, Little studied religion, philosophy, history,
and law; converted to the Islamic faith; and changed his name from the
"slave name" Little to "X," which stood for the African family name he did
not know.

Upon his parole, Malcolm X joined the Nation of Islam (sometimes
known as Black Muslims) and quickly became its chief spokesperson. Arguing for black nationalism and a separatist culture, he ridiculed Martin
Luther King Jr. and other black leaders for their integrationist goals and de-
pendence on "white devils." Following the assassination of John F.
Kennedy, disobeying a direct order from Nation of Islam leader Elijah
Muhammed not to comment, Malcolm X claimed that the assassination
represented "the chickens coming home to roost." Elijah Muhammed was
furious, and Malcolm X was gradually driven out of the Nation of Islam. In
April 1964, following a pilgrimage to Mecca, he softened his antiwhite
rhetoric, adopted the name El Hajj Malik El-Shabazz, and founded the
Organization for Afro-American Unity to promote cooperation between
the races. On February 21, 1965, Malcolm X was killed while speaking at
the Audubon Ballroom in Manhattan. Three members of the Nation of Islam were convicted of his murder.

Yippie!   Formed in December 1967 by Abbie Hoffman, Anita Hoffman, Jerry Rubin, Nancy Kurshan, and Paul Krassner, Yippie! was a convergence
of street theater, political participation, protest, and the counterculture
that gained national attention during events of 1968, especially the Democratic National Convention. The Yippies began extending invitations
through underground newspapers to all "rebels, youth spirits, rock min-
strels, truth seekers, peacock freaks, poets, barricade jumpers, dancers,
lovers, [and] artisans" to join them in their Festival of Life in Chicago. The
festival, Yippies believed, would offer a stark contrast to the Democrats'
"Convention of Death." That spring the Yippies held several events to pub-
licize their plans. Thousands attended a poorly organized "Yip-in" at
Grand Central Station that was broken up by police swinging billy clubs. It
was but a taste of what the Yippies could expect in Chicago. Mayor Daley
refused to issue permits for any Yippie! activities and warned he would not
allow protests. The Yippies responded to these threats by issuing outra-

geous threats of their own, including dancing naked in the streets, seducing the wives and daughters of the conventioneers, and dumping LSD in the city water supply. In Chicago, the Yippies introduced their own candidate for president, Pigasus, a huge pig. When the convention began, the Yippies and other protesters were ill-prepared for the violence wrought by the Chicago police. Every night during the convention, police teargassed and fought with the young people who were gathered in Lincoln Park. After the convention, Rubin and Hoffman, along with six others (the Chicago Eight, then the Chicago Seven) who had been arrested, were charged with conspiracy to incite a riot.

Young Americans for Freedom While the radical youth politics of the 1960s are most commonly linked with the left, youths also played a critical role in shaping the politics of the right. The Young Americans for Freedom was formed in 1960 by a group of college-age conservatives at the family estate of William F. Buckley in Sharon, Connecticut. Their "Sharon Statement" expressed a profoundly conservative political ideology. The group sought to develop new conservative leadership and, through grassroots organizing, gain control of the Republican Party and shift it toward the political right. The YAF campaigned vigorously for Barry Goldwater in 1964 and helped lay a foundation for modern conservative politics.

Young Lords A group of young Puerto Ricans in Chicago formed the Young Lords to combat police harassment. In the late 1960s, the Young Lords spread quickly to other urban areas and expanded their mission to include political participation and community solidarity. The group started breakfast programs, improved sanitation in Puerto Rican neighborhoods, published newspapers, and set up health clinics. Their efforts led to an increased sense of pride in Puerto Rican identity and Puerto Rican nationalism.

ZPG The organization Zero Population Growth was founded in 1968 to raise public awareness of the relation between environmental degradation and uncontrolled population growth. Using slogans such as "The pill in time saves nine" and "This line is too long. Join ZPG," the ZPG sought to slow population growth rates and to ensure Americans the means and right to control reproduction. By 1972, ZPG reported 35,000 members in local chapters.

PART IV

Short Topical Essays

Cities and Suburbs

Amy Scott

From 1945 to 1960, demographic movement, economic change, and federal government policy restructured urban America. Three trends during the postwar years are critically important to understanding the state of America's cities on the eve of the Sixties: the Second Great Migration of African Americans from the rural South to urban industrial centers in the North and West; the creation of a suburban car culture; and sustained economic and population growth in Sunbelt cities. The efforts of local and national leaders to deal with the repercussions of these societal transitions laid the groundwork for the urban crisis of the 1960s.

The massive migration of African Americans from the South to northern and western cities began in the 1930s as southern agriculture was mechanized and fewer farm laborers were needed. Migration increased drastically during World War II, as the labor shortage in war plants and factories created new opportunities for black workers. By 1960, nearly half of the African-American population lived in regions other than the South, compared to 23 percent in 1941.

Following the war, federal government policies and postwar affluence created the nation's growing suburbs. To counter a housing shortage, the federal government revolutionized the housing development industry by offering low-interest Veteran's Administration and Federal Housing Administration loans and mortgage agreements. With guaranteed payment from Uncle Sam, enterprising developers such as William Levitt secured large parcels of land on the urban fringe and threw up prefabricated tract houses at the astonishing rate of one home every 16 minutes. In 1949, families could purchase one of Levitt's four models for $90 down and $58 per month for 25 years. Aside from its affordability, the detached, single-family house outside the city appealed to many Americans who, following decades of economic depression and war, sought a better life for their growing families. Suburban living offered many possibilities and advantages to young families in the baby boom era, and those who could defected *en masse*, creating new communities but also turning their backs on urban culture and cities, which were increasingly poor and black.

Improved pathways leading to, through, and out of cities made the massive migration of mainstream American life to suburbia possible. The most striking transformation on the urban landscape stemmed from the federal government's decision to build an interstate highway system. Congress authorized 37,000 miles of highway in 1947 and passed the National Interstate and Defense Highway Act in 1956, authorizing another 42,500 miles of roads. Freeways fostered a car culture that blew cities apart on an unprecedented geographical scale, transformed what remained at the center, and sped white flight to the suburbs; in 1965, Americans owned 75 million cars, compared to 25 million in 1945. Traditionally, downtown, a collection of commercial, employment, retail, and civic spaces where citizens lived, worked, shopped, and played, had been the organizing hub of American cities and the heart of American urbanism. But with the construction of interstate highways and generous federal subsidization of suburban housing, wealth and power conglomerated in suburbs and downtowns were no longer central to urban life. Central city revenues shrunk as retailers, manufacturers, and service-oriented businesses followed consumers to the "crabgrass frontier," where cheap land abounded and ample parking catered to the car culture.

For black Americans, suburban living was rarely an option. A wall of exclusivity, fortified with racially based restrictive covenants, discriminatory lending practices, and unspoken agreements between developers and homeowners, barred blacks from suburbia. Between 1946 and 1959, homes owned by blacks accounted for less than 2 percent of those financed through federal mortgage insurance. By 1960, America was predominately suburban, but only 5 percent of blacks lived in suburbs.

Black migration to central cities and white flight to the suburbs created an urban geography of socioeconomic and racial segregation; homogenous, white, middle-class suburbs ringed decaying central cities peopled by minorities and characterized by poverty and unemployment. Census data reveal the scale of this racial transition in postwar American cities: from 1950 to 1960, a net total of 4.5 million nonwhites migrated to America's 12 largest cities, while a net total of 3.6 million whites moved to the suburbs. During this decade, New York City's white population decreased by 7 percent and its African-American population rose 46 percent. Racial transitioning in Chicago was even more defined: the white population declined 13 percent, while the number of blacks rose 65 percent.

As suburbanization intensified, older municipal governments inherited decaying infrastructures and impoverished populations; shrinking tax bases caused by urban disinvestment made financing for municipal operations scarce and funds for social services nonexistent. The Taft-Ellender-Wagner Housing Act of 1949, which established Urban Renewal, represented the federal government's initial solution to white flight and central city poverty and physical decay. The act appropriated funds for 810,000 public housing units. But when the real estate lobby, development interests, and conservative congressmen rejected public housing as socialistic, Congress placed responsibility for redevelopment in the hands of local officials and private interests. Through condemnation and eminent domain, municipal governments acquired "blighted" sections of the city with Urban Renewal funds. After they had relocated the poor and cleared the land, developers constructed middle-class housing, luxury apartments, convention centers, and interdispersal loops around downtown. Less than half of the federally proposed housing was built, and by the mid-Sixties, nationwide Urban Renewal programs had demolished 400,000 buildings and displaced over 1.4 million people.

Ironically, the American West, a region celebrated for its wide-open spaces and rustic qualities, epitomized the promise and peril of postwar urbanization. Mobilization for World War II and federal defense spending for the cold war, Korean War, and Vietnam War created sustained economic growth in the Sunbelt—a super-region of cities stretching from Florida to California and including Miami, Atlanta, Tampa Bay, Orlando, Dallas, Houston, Denver, Oklahoma City, Albuquerque, Phoenix, Las Vegas, San Jose, San Diego, Orange County, and Los Angeles. From 1950 to 1960, 75 percent of the nation's 30 fastest-growing urban areas were in the West, and during the Sixties the figure was 50 percent. By 1970, the West was the most urbanized region of the country.

Government-supported defense research and development carried out by American industry and universities drove economic growth in the cold war West; the synergy among business, government, and research universities— the military-industrial complex—catalyzed a booming high-tech, information-based economy. By the 1960s, federal government defense spending had underwritten the development of the West's most lucrative industries, and all of them—electronics, aerospace, communications, and computers—were centered in cities. Silicon Valley, a high-technology industrial sector in Santa Clara County, California, represented the transforming power that the West's new economy had on its urban landscape.

The genesis of the military-industrial complex in the West was no accident; it was the baby of a business-government growth coalition after World War II.

Boosters won defense installations and lured companies to their cities by touting their region's climate and recreational opportunities, promising low tax rates and land giveaways, and extending city utilities to industrial parks in the suburbs. They aggressively used Urban Renewal funds to clear land for sports facilities, central office buildings, airports, and convention centers.

Phoenix, Arizona provides the best example of postwar Sunbelt boosterism. One observer reported that, "industrial scouts are met at the plane, entertained, offered free land, tax deals, and an electorate willing to approve millions in business-backed bond issues." This strategy proved successful: almost 300 manufacturing firms opened shop in the Valley of the Sun from 1948 to 1960, and Phoenix's population mushroomed from 106,818 to 439,170 during the Fifties. Phoenix boosters attracted enough high-tech companies to promote their city as the "Silicon Oasis."

The Colorado Front Range corridor that stretches from Fort Collins in northern Colorado through the sprawling Denver-Boulder-Longmont triangle and south to Pueblo is another example of transforming economic and population growth in the Sunbelt. In the 1950s, Denver's government cooperated with local business interests to build an airport, transmountain water diversion tunnels, and a revitalized downtown. Their promotional efforts yielded a scientific-research-military complex concentrated along the mountain base from Colorado Springs to Fort Collins. By 1963, the Denver-Boulder area—"Silicon Mountain"—ranked tenth among metropolitan areas in federal research and development funds received. Firms relocating to Colorado included Martin Marietta Aerospace Corporation, Hewlett Packard, Ampex, Kodak, Honeywell, Sunstrand, Ball Brothers Research, Beech Aircraft, and IBM.

The booming economy, rapid growth, and middle-class demand for homes in the suburbs coalesced in Western cities as an extreme pattern of dispersal, decentralization, and sprawl. In Southern California, which developed as an automobile metropolis, development devoured open space; by 1970, freeways, streets, parking lots, and driveways covered a third of Los Angeles's surface area. In response to radically unplanned growth, westerners pioneered new cityscapes and leisure landscapes, including Disneyland, Stanford Industrial Park, Sun City Retirement Community in Arizona, and the Las Vegas strip.

But attempts at rationalizing sprawl did not alleviate westerners' anxiety as developers bulldozed the Southern California citrus empire, paved the region's pristine landscape, and rolled toward the desert. By the mid-Sixties, progressive residents questioned the synonymy of growth with progress and for the first time, weighed the social and ecological costs of development. Middle-class suburbanites forged a new brand of lifestyle politics and opposed breakneck development, loss of open space, and automobile pollution. In some cities, such as Boulder, Colorado, citizens waged aggressive no-growth campaigns. Fear of California-style sprawl roused nativist ire in several Western states and was displayed on inhospitable bumper stickers: CALIFORNIANS GO HOME, AND TAKE A TEXAN WITH YOU and DON'T CALIFORNICATE COLORADO. In the early Seventies, Oregon Governor Tom McCall invited Californians to visit but pleaded, "For God's sake, don't move here." Other suburbanites, who worried less about protecting the environment than about maintaining their property values, organized homeowners associations to fight busing, protest public housing, and exclude "undesirables." These decade-long campaigns emphasizing the spatial aspect of urban politics culminated in 1978 when California's "suburban radicals" led a tax revolt that pioneered the privatization of American civic space.

The expanding cities of the West reveled in their newfound position as the country's pacesetters. In 1962 California topped New York in population, and by 1965 it boasted a state economy that ranked "sixth among the nations of the world." When asked if California contributed regionally to the national culture, Western novelist and historian Wallace Stegner replied, "Contribute regionally to the national culture? We are the national culture, at its most energetic end."

But the Watts riot in August 1965 made clear that no region, not even "Lotusland," would escape the violence and destruction exploding from pockets of deprivation secluded amid suburban affluence. African Americans in northern and western cities fully expected racial equality, economic opportunity, and all the rights of American citizenship denied them by legal segregation in the South. Although they escaped the dehumanizing conditions of *de jure* segregation, they endured *de facto* discrimination—enforced by custom—in employment, housing, and education. The trend of decentralization in manufacturing and the shift of industry to the suburbs worsened the plight of urban blacks as stable jobs and opportunities for economic mobility moved beyond their reach. Proximity to the American dream with little chance of obtaining it led to relative deprivation and resentment. Rioting erupted in Watts—a south central Los Angeles neighborhood with 30 percent unemployment and 60 percent of its residents on welfare—after police arrested a black man for driving while intoxicated. Six days of burning and looting ended with 34 dead, 1,032 injured, and $40 million of property damage. The Watts riot drove home the bitter reality of social, racial, and economic polarization in 1960s urban America. Low-income residents were confined to crime-infested slums with few public services, no jobs, and substandard schools, while upper- and middle-class suburbanites remained comfortably insulated on the urban fringe, surrounded by brand-new shopping malls, quality schools, and a booming job market.

As industry and the middle class fled to the suburbs and rioting rocked central cities, debate about the social responsibility of government was magnified at the local level. Faced with a shrinking tax base, little funding for capital improvements, deteriorating schools, and no strategy to counter economic stagnation, many municipal governments willingly accepted federal government assistance. In 1960, 44 federal programs for cities paid out $3.9 billion; by 1969, 500 programs existed and annual appropriations ballooned to $14 billion. Between 1964 and 1968, a succession of Great Society programs redefined the federal government's relationship to cities and the urban poor; they included Community Action (1964), Urban Mass Transportation (1964), the Housing and Urban Development Act (1965), Model Cities (1966), and the Open Housing Act (1968). The most significant Great Society initiatives originated in the belief that political disempowerment caused poverty. Under the Economic Opportunity Act of 1964, national liberals created the Community Action Program to force open local political structures and empower the poor, awarding categorical grants to agencies independent of city governments and requiring "maximum feasible participation" of the poor.

Community Action spanned the time period during which many African Americans, frustrated by the limits of legislation, rejected the nonviolent, integrationist approach of the civil rights movement and adopted Black Power rhetoric and an ideology of separatism to achieve political and economic strength. Black urban America, replete with racial segregation, police harassment, inadequate housing, and high unemployment, provided a volatile milieu for an incendiary brand of black nationalism.

As in earlier days of the civil rights movement—for instance, the Montgomery bus boycott and the Woolworth's lunch counter sit-ins in Greensboro, North Carolina—cities provided Black Power advocates with the means for collective action. In several cities, the poor and minorities challenged officials for control of Community Action boards, and some programs became forums for bashing local government and bases for radical opposition to local political leadership. In response, mayors lambasted Community Action as "federally sponsored radicalism" deliberately designed to spark "class warfare." By 1965, a contingent of Democratic mayors led by Mayor Daley of Chicago met with Vice President Hubert Humphrey to protest the program. They claimed that in addition to fomenting radicalism among the inner-city poor, Community Action's inflexible categorical grants neither provided comprehensive solutions to urban problems nor accommodated local needs. Mayors wanted federal money, but with fewer strings attached.

The tensions inherent in federal government programs, whose rigid controls pitted national goals for racial and economic justice against local government power structures, urban poor, and minorities who clamored for community resources, threatened to tumble an already shaky liberal consensus. Big-city mayors and the urban poor, both constituencies of the Democratic Party, vied for control of federal monies. Fearing more violent uprisings in black ghettos, President Johnson appointed a task force to devise a solution to the escalating urban crisis.

Their answer was Model Cities. This innovative program, administered by the newly created Department of Housing and Urban Development (1965), combined physical rehabilitation and social programs to rebuild economies, transportation and health care systems, schools, housing, and recreational facilities in depressed "target areas." To avoid the controversies of Community Action, the program maintained a strong element of citizen participation in planning and implementation, but primary responsibility rested with mayors. By channeling funds through mayors' offices, the federal government avoided the appearance of national dictation of local policy, but in truth, more than 40 pages of federal guidelines structured the program. Through Model Cities, liberals imposed national urban policy under the guise of local control.

Congress narrowly passed the Demonstration Cities Act, and Johnson signed it into law on November 3, 1966. The ambitious goals of Model Cities—to eradicate poverty and revitalize slums in 66 cities—were not matched by an ambitious appropriation from Congress, drawing only $12 million for first-year planning and $575 million to implement plans over a 5-year period. Furthermore, Model Cities was too little and too late to stop urban unrest and insistence on community control from inner-city poor and minorities. In September 1966, East Harlem residents demanded control of their neighborhood schools: "Let us pick the principal, let us set the standards and make sure they are met." The National Welfare Rights Organization held marches in Los Angeles, Boston, New York City, Chicago, and San Francisco, rallying the poor to demand more money and humane treatment. New York City set up a "war room" to deal with the disturbances by welfare recipients and at one sit-in handed out $135,000 to pacify protesters.

The image of the city as a place of confrontation, violence, and lawlessness took on greater significance during the summer of 1967; from January to September, 164 disturbances and eight major riots occurred. Black Power leader H. Rap Brown's fiery rhetoric ominously predicted the mass destruction that swept Detroit in the worst rioting in American history: "Black folks built America, and if America don't come around, we're going to burn America down." In July 1967, nine days of rioting in Detroit resulted in 43 deaths, 7,200 arrests, 683 buildings destroyed, and $50 million worth of property damage. The smoke still lingered over Detroit's "Charcoal Allies" when LBJ appointed the National Advisory Commission on Civil Disorders (Kerner Commission) on July 29, 1967 to investigate urban rioting and recommend a new direction for federal policy. The commission's March 1968 report cited racism as the cause of rioting and warned that with continued inequality, the rebellion of the inner-city poor would escalate: "Our nation is moving toward two societies, one black, one white—separate and unequal." On this advice, Congress passed the Open Housing Act of 1968, banning discrimination in public or private housing; in part, liberal policy makers intended the legislation to free blacks from inner-city ghettos so that they could follow jobs to suburbia. But middle-class Americans, Nixon's "great silent majority," increasingly resented "ghetto-gilding" federal programs that they believed favored rioters and threatened to open suburbia to poor blacks.

Nixon tapped this vein of middle-class disapproval to win the White House in 1968, and he institutionalized a turn to the right with his "New Federalism." Sensing that the Great Society's mandate had expired, he proclaimed that his administration planned to pursue social justice not by "pouring billions of federal dollars into programs that have failed, but by enlisting the greatest engine of progress ever developed in the history of man—American private enterprise."

Great Society place-based urban programs, such as Community Action and Model Cities, had allowed an interplay of national policy with local initiative. They provided communities the opportunity to fit federal programs to local needs, yet maintained national standards that encouraged institutional reform and racial and economic justice by requiring a partial redistribution of political power to the poor. Nixon's New Federalism, implemented through General Revenue Sharing block grants, rejected the vision of liberals as undesirable and impossible to achieve. His program held that local control could only be effective in the absence of national goals and guidelines.

Despite his conservative rhetoric, Nixon's administration did not immediately abandon cities; in fact, federal appropriations to cities nearly doubled during his presidency, rising from $14 billion in 1969 to $26.8 billion in 1974. But through the State and Local Fiscal Assistance Act (1972), his effort to reform welfare with the Family Assistance Plan (1971–1972), and his Housing and Community Development Act (1974), Nixon separated social welfare policy from urban policy for purposes of federal funding and reversed Great Society liberals' efforts to empower urban poor and minorities. By awarding the block grants with no target-area requirements or guidelines for spending, Nixon returned political authority to local elected officials.

Under Revenue Sharing, it hardly mattered that leaders of poor and minority communities had gained political experience through the Community Action and Model Cities programs. When Nixon gave them a choice, municipal governments ignored the social and economic problems of the poor and minorities. Cities used the bulk of federal funds for capital improvements and tax reduction and stabilization, and as alternatives to issuing bonds. Expenditures for health and social services averaged 5.7 percent to 7.5 percent of total Revenue Sharing funds.

The poor and minorities, who still had not achieved representation in local governments, were hit hard by the loss of federal pressure on local officials. Nixon's New Federalism ended the progress of a national coalition for social change and represented the turning away of the majority of Americans from the poverty and destitution in inner cities.

SOURCES

Abbott, Carl. *The Metropolitan Frontier: Cities in the Modern American West.* Tucson: University of Arizona Press, 1993.

———. *The New Urban America: Growth and Politics in Sunbelt Cities.* Chapel Hill: University of North Carolina Press, 1981.

Chudacoff, Howard P. and Judith E. Smith. *The Evolution of Urban Society.* 3rd ed. Englewood Cliffs, N.J.: Prentice Hall, 1988.

Findlay, John. *Magic Lands: Western Cityscapes and American Culture After 1940.* Berkeley: University of California Press, 1992.

Fox, Kenneth. *Metropolitan America: Urban Life and Urban Policy in the United States.* New York: MacMillan, 1985.

Gale, Dennis E. *Understanding Urban Unrest from Reverend King to Rodney King.* Thousand Oaks, Calif.: Sage Publications, 1996.

Galster, George C. and Edward W. Hill, eds. *The Metropolis in Black & White.* New Brunswick, N.J.: Center for Urban Policy Research, 1992.

Katz, Michael B. *In the Shadow of the Poorhouse: A Social History of Welfare in America*. New York: Basic, 1996.

Malone, Michael P. and Richard W. Etulain. *The American West: A Twentieth-Century History*. Lincoln: University of Nebraska Press, 1989.

Teaford, Jon C. *The Twentieth-Century American City*. 2nd ed. Baltimore: Johns Hopkins University Press, 1986.

Environmentalism

Jeff Sanders

"The earth's a big blue marble when you see it from up there."

Every episode of a popular PBS children's show from the early 1970s began
with this song and the famous photograph of planet Earth floating alone in
the darkness of space. At the close of a divisive decade, this ubiquitous image,
made possible by President Kennedy's Apollo space program, appeared on
signs and magazine covers, on flags at rallies, and on posters in elementary
schools.

Viewed from a distance, the image of Earth evoked a sense of calm. The
big blue marble offered symbolic hope for reconciliation as well as for restrained and rational thinking; it reminded Americans of what was at stake in
the imminent threats of massive chemical pollution and nuclear apocalypse.
Like most popular symbols, the blue orb's simplicity masked conflict and contradiction. Nevertheless, by the early 1970s, people with diverse concerns
about such problems as ecological degradation, wilderness preservation, consumer protection, and resistance to control by "the establishment," had somehow managed to cohere around this unifying icon and the uplifting new banner of environmentalism.

Of course, forests, birds, and charismatic megafauna like moose and deer
had long been the concern of conservation-minded groups in the United
States. The Sierra Club, established in 1892 by the prototypical California
poet, naturalist, and back-to-the-land advocate John Muir, strengthened its
campaign to protect the scenic wilderness throughout the the 1960s. David
Brower, the group's controversial director during this critical decade, used the
club's publishing arm and lobbying efforts to promote environmental preservation, and worked to transform the Sierra Club from a more conservative
conservationist movement of concerned hikers into an activist and reform-
oriented lobbying organization.

Wilderness-preservation groups like the Sierra Club and the Wilderness
Society had slowly chipped away at the older "mixed use" policy governing

the Forest Service, the Bureau of Land Management, and the Bureau of Reclamation throughout the late 1950s. Their efforts culminated with the passage of the Wilderness Act (1964). Under Brower's leadership in the early 1960s, a new nature ethos began to triumph over the old in the battle to prevent the Bureau of Reclamation from building two dams on the Colorado River in the Grand Canyon National Park. The Sierra Club helped to organize grassroots groups nationally, created full-page ads and letter-writing campaigns, and successfully marshaled an unprecedented public outcry against the dams. Congress dropped the project by the end of the decade.

Sierra Club coffee-table books and calendars of sublime Ansel Adams landscape photographs also aroused public concern about threatened rivers and forests, and made the wilderness "out there" relevant to a generation of baby boomers and their parents. Brower's picture books and calendars helped define nature as a quality-of-life-issue. For an affluent postwar populace, nature had become not merely a resource to harness for progress but a pristine place for spiritual seclusion and meditative reflection.

Rachel Carson's *Silent Spring* startled an American public comfortable with the Sierra Club's placid images and cautionary tales. With *Silent Spring*, appearing first as a series in the *New Yorker* in 1962 and later as a best-selling book, Carson radically redefined the popular discussion of nature and preservation. Instead of dealing with heroic confrontations between dams and unspoiled wilderness, Carson's was a more complex story about ecology—"the intricate web of life whose interwoven strands lead from microbes to man." With accessible and evocative descriptions of ecological processes, Carson launched a devastating critique of the thriving postwar chemical industry and the harmful and indiscriminate use of inorganic chemical pesticides like DDT. *Silent Spring* revealed the biological wilderness that existed within everyday life.

Carson's rhetoric resonated with the swelling audience of youth grown suspicious of big science and of their parents' world. Many of those who had read her book or saw her CBS special on television had come of age in an era of "duck and cover" atomic-air-raid drills and mutant "creatures from the black lagoon." They were primed for Carson's more insidious picture of contamination. As Carson traced the course of mutating chemicals through the environment—from blanket spraying of forests and rivers, to fish and birds, to human livers—she compared the process to the ubiquitous poisoning of radioactive fallout. Pressured by groups such as the Committee for Nuclear Information, Congress passed the Partial Nuclear Test-Ban Treaty and an amended Clean Air Act in 1963—both early examples of the sort of legislation that by the 1970s would come to characterize the new reform movement.

Silent Spring appeared at a promising moment in 1960s politics. Carson's emphasis on interrelated human and environmental worlds also contained an implicit critique of corporate power, corrupted government, the war economy, and mindless consumption; she even revealed ecological dangers lurking in the suburban front lawn. Carson's description of chemically tainted foods also encouraged grassroots consumer activism. Called hysterical by her many male critics, she presented an early feminist challenge to male expertise and authority. By showing the permeable boundaries between people and nature—between suburban safety and industrial pollution—Carson coupled nature conservation with a broader cultural critique and by the beginning of the next decade had helped to inspire new forms of activism.

By 1965 the idea of ecology had already seeped into the American consciousness, but environmentalism would remain an amorphous and often contradictory set of concerns and strategies throughout the decade. Personal politics of liberation and individual rights bumped up against more mainstream liberal ideas of control and regulation. The "straight"-sounding reformist ideas of people working within "the establishment" would coexist with the counterculture's distrust of mainstream authority. Lady Bird Johnson's flower-planting beautification program and the New Left student activists' radical critique of the liberal establishment represented two ends of a wide spectrum of potential environmental activism and thought at mid-decade. Such contrasts were inherent in the movement, but they would also determine the possibilities for the movement's mainstream success.

Out of this swirl of kindred and contradictory ideas and approaches came the first reformers. These mostly young, white middle-class professionals, inspired by the civil rights movement and President Johnson's Great Society, fanned out across the American landscape to practice the expert-driven politics of regulation, preservation, and protection.

The new reformers joined and strengthened existing environmental groups like the Sierra Club (whose membership increased by leaps and bounds from 1964 onward) and created new ones such as the Chesapeake Bay Foundation (1966), the Population Crisis Committee (1965), and the Environmental Defense Fund (1967). Like their Progressive-era counterparts, these lobbying groups and concerned citizens often used their status as professionals to address a broad set of interrelated environmental and human concerns. Hopeful lawyers, academics, and publicists still had faith in working from the inside—with science and new technologies, and within the legislative process—to effect change and wrest control of government agencies from corporate corruption and official mismanagement.

Reformers saw the government apparatus and rational application of science and technology as a means by which to protect both the human and natural world. These "best and brightest" thinkers followed one thread of Carson's call to action, elaborating on themes of more rational, informed control. Activist intellectuals like Barry Commoner, Paul Ehrlich, Garrett Hardin (all biology professors), and Ralph Nader, a consumer advocate and lawyer who set the tone for grassroots lobbying, emboldened this growing liberal reform movement. Commoner's *Science and Survival* (1963) pushed for a more prudent, less secretive, and morally informed use of science. Ehrlich's *The Population Bomb* (1968), along with Hardin's essay "The Tragedy of the Commons," argued that controls were necessary to limit overpopulation and overuse of common lands. They would further professionalize the movement, and they would pave the way for the major legislative protections of the 1960s and 1970s.

Professional lobbyists, lawyers and concerned grassroots organizations found a receptive climate in Washington during the early years of the Johnson administration. Natural beauty and outdoor recreation formed an important piece of LBJ's vision of the Great Society. In his annual speech in 1964, the same year he signed the Wilderness Act, Johnson stressed the importance of natural and scenic places. In addition to outdoor recreation and the more aesthetic flower- planting beautification programs that Lady Bird Johnson championed, Johnson supported legislation that would limit air, water, and solid-waste pollution. In 1966 he created the Council on Recreation and Natural Beauty, which produced a report recommending increased government intervention in the preservation and management of nature.

On Johnson's watch Congress passed traditional preservation-related legislation such as the National Wildlife Refuge System (1966), the National Wild and Scenic Rivers Act (1968), and the National Trails Act (1968). But with increasing public pressure and awareness of environmental problems, Congress also passed the Water Quality Act (1965), the Solid Waste Disposal Act (1965), and the Clean Air Act (1965). And finally, in 1968, after a decade-long battle with the Bureau of Reclamation, the Sierra Club helped to defeat the Grand Canyon dams bill with the support of a Congress and administration sensitized to wilderness preservation and environmental concerns. By the late 1960s, LBJ's activist stance on environmental issues would dissipate as Vietnam drew his attention away from the domestic agenda. Nixon would later use environmentalism to draw public attention away from the failures in Vietnam.

Reformers and the administration drew support from an increasingly mobilized, middle-class, television-informed public. Every night, by the late

1960s, television brought the Vietnam War into American households, but it also brought images of environmental degradation. If threats to the environment seemed vague at the beginning of the decade, by the late 1960s they became undeniably concrete. Visions of Dow Chemical Corporation–produced incendiaries like napalm and defoliants like Agent Orange, inflicted upon a verdant third-world landscape and people by a technologically advanced, industrial war machine confirmed, for increasing numbers, the relevance of linking environmental and social critiques.

A series of hideous environmental disasters during the late 1960s horrified a broader segment of the American public. In March 1967, a ship named the *Torrey Canyon* spilled 117,000 tons of crude oil into the English Channel. In February 1969, an oil rig off the coast of Santa Barbara, California, spilled millions of gallons of crude oil that washed up on the beaches of appalled and normally privileged and comfortable homeowners. The same year in Ohio, the severely polluted Cuyahoga River actually caught fire, and Lake Erie was declared endangered by chemical and sewage pollution.

War in Vietnam and pollution at home rallied widespread public support for a plethora of environmental protections. In the last months of 1968 and the first half of 1969, more than 130 environment-related bills were introduced before Congress. Americans began to question the costs of progress and the destruction brought by prosperity. Though rarely making direct connections between their own affluence and environmental degradation, the public supported legislation like the National Environmental Policy Act, a prelude to the establishment of the Environmentalism Protection Agency in 1969.

While "square" bureaucrats and a growing stock of environmental lawyers created legislation to protect the environment, a broad swath of protest groups and a growing counterculture began to incorporate the idea of "ecology" into their revolt. Many in the New Left were suspicious, however, of this renewed interest in nature. Groups like the Students for a Democratic Society had formed partly in response to cold-war ecological concerns regarding nuclear fallout and weapons testing. But as their focus evolved into a broader critique of a racist and repressive culture, concern for nature alone, in isolation from these other problems, appeared to many such radicals a diversion at best and escapist at worst.

Nevertheless, toward the end of the decade, the idea of ecology had infused the rhetoric of diverse movements and protests. The activists involved in these movements intertwined ecology with the politics of identity and class, sometimes using both to unite diverse groups. From these kinds of origins, members of the United Farm Workers of California saw the obvious links in their everyday lives between racism, their marginal status as migrant workers, and the environment. Ecology was never a detached notion; workers' exposure to harmful pesticides in the course of a day's work was central to their political and economic struggle.

Native American activists in the 1960s and early 1970s sought to re-learn tribal wisdom about the land and environment. In a series of land seizures and occupations in 1969, protesters used existing associations of Indian identity and relationship to the earth both to help justify reclaiming land and to bring public attention to Native American poverty in urban areas and on rural reservations.

The struggle for People's Park in Berkeley (1968) was not attached to specific ethnic politics or identity, but was an example of political cross-fertilization made possible by a focus on ecology and attention to a particular place. The protest over People's Park, a parking-lot property "liberated" from the University of California and made into an oasis of personal freedom by the Berkeley Community, was somehow able to bring counterculturalists, radicals, and middle-class neighbors together at a time when the movement was fragmenting. Saving the park, a symbol of nature in the city, created momentary consensus. Each of these efforts highlighted the potential of ecology, or "green" politics, to bring interrelated social and environmental problems into focus.

While some groups found in ecology a practical politics, others turned to nature as an escape from the ills of American society. Idealized nature and antimodernism had been strong features of environmentalism since the Progressive era, and it is not surprising that some members of the counterculture would look to nature in their attempts to create a more authentic and transformed consciousness.

In his best-selling book *The Greening of America* (1970), Charles A. Reich attempted to describe this new countercultural consciousness, a "coming American revolution" offering "a new and enduring wholeness and beauty — a renewed relationship of man to himself, to other men, to society, to nature, and to the land." Inspired by the blend of nature and Eastern religion in the works of poet Gary Snyder and others, many young people set about to change themselves as a means of changing society. Nature became the site for locating a natural self, a mirror of authenticity that city-worn protesters and counterculturalists held up to themselves. Personal liberation and being green became synonymous.

The counterculture's personalized green politics could be antimodern, utopian and escapist. Despite its alternative, "freak" exterior, the green counterculture shared a lot with the antiprogressive, romantic origins of groups like the Sierra Club—whose bearded founder wrote beautifully of nature, and could not stand San Francisco–style civilization. Like Muir, many counterculturalists dropped out of the grid-dominated, polluted cities, "going up the country" to set up rural communal living experiments outside such idyllic locations as Taos, New Mexico and Eugene, Oregon, and on "The Farm" in Tennessee.

Not all communards headed for utopian rural experiments, and many rural communes remained politically engaged. But the choice to search for authentic alternatives within a more natural setting had similarities to "white flight" from urban America by the 1970s. In search of green vistas and relief from the complexities of urban life, young people, reared in utopian suburbs like Levittown, searched for the next ideal place.

With the help of television, news magazines, and popular books like Reich's, environmentalism began to saturate mainstream consciousness. By the 1970s Americans sat in living rooms full of ferns and spider plants, watched Marlon Perkins subdue endangered beasts on Mutual of Omaha's *Wild Kingdom*, and read about Earth Day in *Time* and *Newsweek*. Population control, pollution, and endangered species were more and more the concern of middle-class Americans, and Earth Day marked the crescendo ending a decade of environmentalist activism and legislation.

Wisconsin senator Gaylord Nelson proposed the idea for the massive Earth Day environmental teach-in and celebration during a speech at the University of Washington in 1969. Such teach-ins were already a regular feature of the political arena, but for environmentalism, it was an intentional separation of Earth Day from the radical street politics of the late 1960s. Earth Day would be more like a secular religious celebration.

One of the largest mass demonstrations of the era, taking place on April 22 in several major cities across the country, Earth Day convinced politicians (including then president Richard Nixon) of the political value of the new environmentalism. The result was a flurry of organization of regulatory structures such as the Environmental Protection Agency and the Occupational Safety and Health Act. From the counterculture to the "silent majority," broadening concern for environmental issues offered a new consensus infused with the spirit of problem-solving. Richard Nixon and a growing constituency began to tackle environmental problems with new regulations, quick-fix clean-ups, and technological solutions. Media coverage tended to avoid race and poverty issues and any critique of the urban industrial order related to the environment, making environmentalism a more palatable mainstream movement.

The popular environmental crusade seemed to transcend race riots, assassinations, and generational conflict. Pressured by an increasingly mobilized public and powerful reform lobby, including the Public Interest Research Groups (1970), the League of Conservation Voters (1970), and the Natural Resource Defense Council (1970), politicians during the early 1970s enacted a wide range of legislation that sought effective limits on corporate pollution and wise management of natural resources.

By 1972, ten years after Carson's warning about chemicals in *Silent Spring*, Congress finally outlawed DDT. Long before Earth Day, environmentalists had fought grassroots campaigns over specific public spaces, and their protection from pollution, as part of a diverse movement. The ubiquitous big blue marble icon represented a powerful confluence of radical and mainstream currents by decade's end.

SOURCES

Gottlieb, Robert. *Forcing the Spring: The Transformation of the American Environmental Movement*. Washington, D.C.: Island Press, 1993.

Hays, Samuel P. *Beauty, Health, and Permanence: Environmental Politics in the United States, 1955–1985*. Cambridge: Cambridge University Press, 1987.

Killingsworth, M. Jimmie, and Jacqueline S. Palmer. *Ecospeak: Rhetoric and Environmental Politics in America*. Carbondale: Southern Illinois University Press, 1992.

Lutts, Ralph H. "Chemical Fallout: Rachel Carson's Silent Spring, Radioactive Fallout and the Environmental Movement." *Environmental Review* 9(3) (1985): 210-25.

Pulido, Laura. *Environmentalism and Economic Justice: Two Chicano Struggles in the Southwest*. Tucson: University of Arizona Press, 1996.

Rothman, Hal K. *The Greening of a Nation?: Environmentalism in the United States Since 1945*. Fort Worth, Texas: Harcourt Brace, 1998.

Sale, Kirkpatrick. *The Green Revolution: The American Environmental Movement 1962–1992*. New York: Hill and Wang, 1993.

Scheffer, Victor B. *The Shaping of Environmentalism in America*. Seattle: University of Washington Press, 1991.

Schrepfer, Susan R. *The Fight to Save the Redwoods: A History of Environmental Reform, 1917–1978*. Madison: University of Wisconsin Press, 1983.

Law and Justice

Rusty L. Monhollon

In a democratic society, according to the political philosopher John Rawls in his classic *Theory of Justice*, concepts of justice are based on the belief that all citizens should be free and equal. Justice, therefore, is the moral basis for a democratic society. Neither justice nor the law is static; each must evolve to meet society's changing needs. However, when citizens in a democracy embrace divergent ideals of freedom and equality and thus of justice, struggles frequently occur in the nation's legal and political systems over those ideals, over the state's proper role in protecting and enforcing them, and over the appropriate means to distribute responsibilities and benefits among the nation's citizens.

This was especially true in the United States in the 1960s, as altered conceptions of justice and methods for promoting them emerged from the post–World War II movements for social justice and equality. By the 1960s, decisions by U.S. courts and actions of the federal government increasingly were grounded in three important principles: the rights of all individuals to equal protection under the law; a national standard of justice, supplanting deference to local traditions and customs, and applied equally to all people; and a public, rather than private, instrument for establishing justice—an activist judiciary and the vigorous administration of public policy. These principles reflected a vision of distributive justice in which the government assumed responsibility for actively protecting citizens' individual rights and economic opportunities, rather than simply not interfering with their enjoyment of those rights and opportunities. The principles also reflected a society in transition, in which the nationalizing forces of economic growth, demographic change, and the mass media challenged local and traditional sources of authority and legitimacy.

Americans struggling for freedom and equality after 1945 demanded that the federal government ensure the equal protection of the law to all citizens, particularly those who previously had suffered clear discrimination and inequality, and the government responded. Congress, though often with narrow margins of support and much public acrimony, changed the meaning of justice in America during the 1960s through such critical legislation as the Civil Rights Act of 1964. Lyndon Johnson's Great Society also sought to address the national issues of poverty and racial discrimination. While all three branches of government helped to facilitate the change, the judiciary was at the forefront. Between the 1954 *Brown* v. *Board of Education of Topeka* decision and Chief Justice Earl Warren's retirement in 1969, the Supreme Court transformed American federalism by replacing local power and standards with national standards of civil rights and liberties, criminal procedure, education, employment, and public accommodations.

As some legal scholars have argued, the Warren Court has had no equal in American history in expanding civil liberties and political freedom and setting the boundaries of police power; one might add that no other court has been so controversial. Under Warren's direction, the court's overriding concerns were equality and fairness, and it affirmed the government's responsibility to protect those virtues. As the Chief Justice himself noted, the court took action because the political process, through legislative and executive branch inaction, had failed to enforce the civil rights of all Americans. The Warren Court came under fire in the 1950s and 1960s and thereafter from both those who felt that judicial activism was a dangerous course and the large number of Americans who opposed specific decisions ranging from integrating public schools to outlawing prayer in public schools.

CIVIL RIGHTS

Boldly egalitarian, the Civil Rights Act of 1964 was intended to end racial discrimination and segregation in the workplace and in places of public accommodation. Later that year, the court gave its approval to the law, ruling in *Heart of Atlanta Motel* v. *United States* that Congress could exercise its power to regulate interstate commerce to remedy "moral wrongs" such as racial discrimination. The court later expanded its definition of "public accommodations" to small, local businesses such as barber shops, taverns, and skating rinks.

Although African Americans were seen as the primary beneficiaries of the law, its language was broad and far-reaching, prohibiting not only discrimination based on race and color but also that based on religion, sex, and national origins. The act reached far beyond the African-American civil rights movement, laying the groundwork for the more complete inclusion of women, Hispanics, Native Americans, and other minority groups into American civil life. Indeed, the Civil Rights Act's full effects would not be felt until the 1970s and beyond, when it gave momentum to the movement for greater gender equality in the United States. While the act did not bring about immediate change, it set in motion a number of administrative and judicial mechanisms to work against future discrimination and, when combined with the Supreme Court's imposition of national standards in interpreting the law, was revolutionary.

Other measures were equally significant. In 1962 Congress approved, and in 1964 the states ratified, the Twenty-fourth Amendment, which prohibited the poll tax (long a symbol of localism and states' rights) and helped enfranchise many African Americans. Similarly, the Voting Rights Act of 1965 abolished literacy tests and other devices intended to prevent blacks from voting, empowered the attorney general to oversee voter registration in areas where less than half of the minority residents were registered to vote, and required that the Justice Department approve electoral changes in recalcitrant counties. The act was generally successful in spurring massive voter participation in the South. In Mississippi, for example, the percentage of registered black voters increased eightfold between 1964 and 1968.

The Supreme Court's 1962 decision in *Baker* v. *Carr* (which Warren called the "most vital" of his tenure) and its 1964 ruling in the Reapportionment Cases (of which *Reynolds* v. *Sims* was the lead case) established the principle of "one person, one vote" by declaring that population was the only basis for representation in Congress. The decisions provided for the reapportionment of congressional districts, reducing the power of sparsely populated rural districts and increasing the strength of urban districts, which were generally more liberal and in much of the nation had a greater percentage of minority residents.

CIVIL LIBERTIES

Perhaps nowhere was judicial activism more controversial, during the 1960s and beyond, than in rulings involving the separation of church and state and the rights of the accused. In *Engel* v. *Vitale* (1962) and *School District of Abington Township* v. *Schempp* (1963) the court ruled that mandatory school prayer and Bible reading violated the First Amendment's establishment clause. The decisions elicited the greatest outpouring of protest in the court's history. The debate, including repeated calls for a constitutional amendment to protect school prayer, has continued uninterrupted to the present day.

Likewise, the court's opinions regarding criminal procedure evoked a passionate response. In *Gideon* v. *Wainwright* (1963), the Warren Court declared that indigent defendants could not be ensured a fair trial without the assistance of proper counsel, which must be provided by the state if necessary. In *Escobedo* v. *Illinois* (1964), the court ruled that the police must permit the accused to consult with their attorneys during interrogation, which invalidated many confessions, both voluntary and coerced. In *Miranda* v. *Arizona* (1966), the court required the police to inform all arrested suspects of the Fifth Amendment's protection against self-incrimination and advise them of the right to free legal counsel. While critics argued the decisions would hamper law enforcement, civil libertarians applauded the rulings as an appropriate expansion and federal protection of individual freedoms.

The *Gideon*, *Escobedo*, and *Miranda* decisions changed the basic criminal procedure in the United States by creating a national standard, applying the Bill of Rights as a limitation on state laws and extending the Fourteenth Amendment's due process guarantee to include self-incrimination. The common thread here, as in other matters before the Warren Court, was attention to the equal protection of the individual before the law, even when it superseded majority opinion or community standards.

EDUCATION

President Lyndon Johnson made greater access to education a cornerstone of his Great Society, and, as part of the Economic Opportunity Act of 1964, created Headstart (implemented in 1965) to provide preschool preparation to disadvantaged children. The Elementary and Secondary Education Act (1965), the nation's single largest education aid program ever, attempted to ameliorate the effects of poverty by providing federal funds to needy school districts (typically funded by local taxes, and thus dependent on the economic status of the districts). The Department of Health, Education and Welfare threatened to pull the federal funding from school districts that continued to spend less on the education of minority children than on predominately white schools.

Increasingly in the 1960s, the federal government took affirmative action to assist people harmed by past discriminatory employment and educational practices. Such governmental efforts have been an important, if controversial, legacy of the 1960s. In that era, the judiciary often, though not always, upheld such intervention. In *U.S.* v. *Jefferson County Board of Education* (1966), the Fifth Circuit Court approved the government's school desegregation guidelines. In *Green* v. *County School Board of New Kent County* (1968), the Supreme Court concluded that "freedom of choice" was unlikely to desegregate schools and ordered the process of desegregation to begin in earnest. The ruling redirected *Brown's* emphasis to schools' "racial composition" rather than on providing equal educational opportunities.

The decisions were controversial but affirmed the government's responsibility to actively promote equal treatment for all rather than simply removing barriers to equality, such as obviously discriminatory laws. Other rulings also sanctioned an affirmative approach. In *Alexander* v. *Holmes* (1969), the court approved busing as a means to maintain racial balance in school districts, and two years later, in *Swann* v. *Charlotte-Mecklenburg Board of Education*, the justices upheld a North Carolina school desegregation plan that included the crosstown busing of children in order to achieve racial balance. By the late 1970s, however, a reconfigured court had pulled back from its support of affirmative action, most notably in *Regents of the University of California* v. *Bakke* (1978). There the court ruled that a separate policy for minorities with a specified number of openings unavailable to white students violated the equal protection clause.

GENDER EQUALITY

Like criminal procedure and school prayer decisions, governmental activism was highly contested in the emotionally charged matters of gender equality and the right to privacy. In 1972, Congress passed the Equal Rights Amendment, which prohibited gender discrimination in all aspects of American public life, and sent it to the states for ratification. Supporters believed it was necessary to ensure equality between men and women, particularly in the workplace.

Opponents came from different camps. Some feared that such an amendment would undermine special protections women received under the law, especially in the workplace. Others feared it would destroy the traditional roles of men and women and harm America's families. Thirty-five states ratified the ERA (several of which later rescinded or attempted to rescind their ratification), but the measure fell three states short. While the amendment was unsuccessful, the debate over the ERA highlighted, for both supporters and opponents, ways in which the activism of the 1960s had changed the nation and the extent to which Americans disagreed on such fundamental questions about justice and how to attain it.

PRIVACY

The dissension evident over the ERA, however, paled in comparison to that over matters of privacy and reproductive rights. Privacy, Justice Hugo Black once noted, is a "broad, abstract and ambiguous concept," and setting its boundaries is difficult at best. The Supreme Court established the right of privacy as a constitutional principle in *Griswold* v. *Connecticut* (1965). In overturning the convictions of two people found guilty of violating an 1879 Connecticut law prohibiting the distribution of contraceptives, the court held that the law infringed upon married individuals' right to privacy. Several of the concurring justices based their decisions on the notion of "implied rights": those that, in theory, are implied by the First, Third, Fourth, Fifth, and Ninth Amendments.

In *Eisenstadt* v. *Baird* (1972), the court declared that banning the distribution of contraceptives to unmarried individuals was equally impermissible because it violated the Fourteenth Amendment's equal protection clause. Writing for the majority, William Brennan argued, "if the right of privacy means anything, it is the right of the individual, married or single, to be free from unwarranted governmental intrusion into matters so fundamentally affecting a person as the decision whether to bear or beget a child."

That sentiment prevailed in *Roe* v. *Wade* (1972) and *Doe* v. *Bolton* (1973), which protected abortion rights by invalidating criminal penalties for performing abortions. The court ruled that while the states had some valid interest in regulating abortions, a woman had the constitutionally protected right to choose to abort her pregnancy, especially in the first trimester, when that right was nearly unrestricted. In the third trimester, the states' interest in protecting the potential life of the unborn fetus was so great as to justify restrictions; even then, the states must permit an abortion to save a woman's life. These decisions generated massive opposition among portions of the American public.

CONCLUSION

During the Sixties era, the federal government acted decisively to create national standards of justice that greatly expanded legal protections for racial and ethnic minorities and for women. An activist Supreme Court guaranteed constitutional rights for criminal suspects and limited local communities' ability to mandate certain religious and moral practices, such as school-sponsored prayer. In almost every case, these new national standards were fiercely contested. Even as civil rights groups and civil liberties activists celebrated the legal reforms, a powerful conservative movement developed to oppose many aspects. Some of the new national standards, such as racial and gender equality in the workplace and before the law, have now become widely accepted. Other legal reforms, such as a woman's right to choose to have an abortion and the outlawing of school-sponsored prayer, continue to cause major political conflict. As in the 1960s, Americans continue to debate the limits of individual liberty, community rights, the rights of minorities, and the use of public versus private power to make the United States a just society.

SOURCES

Chalmers, David. *And the Crooked Places Made Straight: The Struggle for Social Change in the 1960s*. 2nd ed. Baltimore: Johns Hopkins University Press, 1996.

Graham, Hugh Davis. *The Civil Rights Era: Origins and Development of a National Policy, 1960–1965*. New York: Oxford University Press, 1990.

Horowitz, Morton J. *The Warren Court and the Pursuit of Justice*. New York: Hill and Wang, 1998.

Irons, Peter. *A People's History of the Supreme Court*. New York: Viking, 1999.

Rawls, John A. *A Theory of Justice*. Rev. ed. Cambridge, Mass.: Belknap Press of Harvard University Press, 1999.

Schwartz, Bernard. *Main Currents in American Legal Thought*. Durham, N.C.: Carolina Academic Press, 1993.

Popular Music
Durwood Ball

Sixties popular music was a sonic bridge from the proscriptions of the cold war to personal transformation, spiritual ecstasy, and social freedom. Baby boomers invoked the secular trinity—sex, drugs, and rock and roll—to distinguish their counterculture from their parents' "repressive" world. The soundtrack to upheaval, Sixties pop embraced cultural pluralism and sought to heal racial, social, and political divisions. Despite these ideals, the music industry still saw the baby boomers, whites especially, as a cash cow and categorized pop music by race and audience. Sixties pop included jazz, country, gospel, and other genres, but rock and roll—rockabilly, rhythm and blues, folk rock, acid rock, funk, soul, and others—boasted greater historical agency and musically defined the decade.

Emerging in the mid-1950s, rock and roll blended black rhythm and blues (R & B) and white country. This "hopped-up" hybrid, immortalized by rockabilly singer Elvis Presley, celebrated teenage rebellion, commodified adolescent subculture, and captivated American youths discontented with cold war cultural homogenization. Unlike mainstream pop, this music seemed raw, primitive, authentic to the ever-growing population of adolescents, especially middle-class whites. The number of high school teenagers increased from 5.6 million in 1946 to 11.8 million in 1960. Postwar affluence gave this cohort more money and leisure than any previous adolescent generation.

During the cold war fog, rock and roll rebellion rattled American cultural watchdogs and tastemakers. The licentious beat, suggestive lyrics, and lewd performances, they declared, undermined the authority of church, family, and state. By decade's end, the alarmists had suppressed rock labels, disk jockeys, and performers. Their backlash was also an assault on African Americans, whom they accused of poisoning white youth with "primitive" "jungle" rhythms and who were skillfully battling American segregation.

The record industry's response, the factory system, was to manufacture unprovocative American pop idols. Music producers tamed the beat, purified the lyrics, and whitened the artists. The clean-teen pop industry created stars

such as Fabian, Connie Francis, and the Shirelles and restricted pop's transformative powers merely to influencing the winning or losing of boyfriends or
girlfriends. Defying the conservative assault, gritty rock and roll and R & B
still thrived in regional enclaves such as Southern California, Chicago, Memphis, and New Orleans, and across the Atlantic in England. Inspired by Dr.
Martin Luther King Jr.'s integrationist dream, African American entrepreneur
Berry Gordy of Motown Records began packaging R & B to cross the color
line to white listeners.

To cultivate a nationwide audience, ambitious musicians became more
American than the right-wing reactionaries. Capturing the spotlight around
1960, the folk movement tapped the rich veins of traditional American music,
particularly protest forms best represented by Woody Guthrie. Folk musicians
such as Pete Seeger and Joan Baez took inspiration from the Old Left and allied themselves with civil rights, free speech, and peace. Their audience was
liberal and urban, but their music was traditional and rural. At events like the
Newport Folk Festival, the lineups were integrated, and acoustic blues legends such as Lightnin' Hopkins played to some of their first white audiences.
A direct assault on cold war madness, industrial destruction, and American
segregation, the folk movement politically awakened large numbers of middle-class, college-aged whites, many of whom joined Sixties civil rights
marches in the Deep South.

The biggest figure to emerge from Sixties folk was Robert Zimmerman,
better known as Bob Dylan. He was originally a rocker in Duluth, Minnesota,
but, with the idiom seemingly dead, he entered the folk scene of Greenwich
Village, New York, consciously positioned himself as Guthrie's heir, and soon
dominated the movement. Like Presley, Chuck Berry, and other rock greats,
Dylan had absorbed a vast suite of American folk and pop music, and on *Freewheelin' Bob Dylan*, his poetic gift produced landmark protest anthems such
as "Masters of War," "A Hard Rain's a-Gonna Fall," and the much-covered
"Blowin' in the Wind."

However, folk's dominance was short-lived. In early 1964, the Beatles, a
four-piece British band, blew American pop music wide open. Their first appearance on *The Ed Sullivan Show* was watched by 73 million viewers, and
their four concerts triggered unprecedented popular hysteria, especially
among adolescent women. Their wit, charm, and vulnerable masculinity coincided with the early stirrings of the sexual revolution, and their optimism
complemented the promise of the Civil Rights Act and the Great Society.

The Beatles' musical tastes ranged from thrashing rockabilly and grinding
R & B to loping country and pop ballads. Their polish, popularity, and ac-

ceptance cleared a cultural beachhead in America for other more "menacing" British Invasion bands such as the Rolling Stones, the Yardbirds, and The Who, and helped legitimize some factory artists. The Beatles' mastery of wide-ranging musical idioms and their rapid lyrical development made them favorites also of parents and critics. Their powerful rock and roll synthesis and huge following unified the diverse Sixties pop music community.

The Beatles' worldwide adulation lured the fame-hungry Bob Dylan back to electric rock and roll in *Bringin' It All Back Home* (1965) and *Highway 61 Revisited* (1965). Having exhausted traditional folk forms, Dylan demolished the standard two-and-a-half-minute pop-song format and its love won–love lost content. The musicianship was often ragged but always spirited and thunderous, and Dylan's richly poetic lyrics set the standard for pop introspection and commentary, compelling the Beatles, Rolling Stones, and other groups to compose serious, personal songs. Folk audiences accused Dylan of selling out, but, combined with his *Blonde on Blonde* (1966), Dylan's first two electric albums lit the fuse to the folk rock explosion that spawned the Byrds, the Turtles, Buffalo Springfield, and other bands.

In the mid-Sixties, electricity, poetry, sex, and rhythm mixed with another combustible element, drugs, to create psychedelia. Baby boomer parents worshipped doctors and high medicine and avidly ingested antidepressants and other medications to achieve altered states of mental and physical health. Likewise, baby boomers' drug experimentation aimed for transport to a new personal and world consciousness that would eliminate human barriers— class, race, ideology—dividing their parents' world. By 1965, a suite of drugs coursed through the rock community. Dylan and marijuana influenced the Beatles' *Rubber Soul* (1965), a folk rock record of soft edges and personal introspection. Attracting a male following, The Who, the Mod heroes, thrashed through early singles such as "Anyway, Anyhow, Anywhere" and "My Generation" with amphetamine-fed punk fury.

The drug most identified with the new baby boomer counterculture was the psychoactive LSD. Also known as acid, it swept away cultural and psychic rubbish and melted the human ego. By 1966 San Francisco was the counterculture's ground zero. In Haight-Ashbury, baby boomers tried to cultivate a cooperative, egalitarian "hippie" community that would transcend history. The rock concert or festival was their tribal ritual, where free-form improvisation reigned in fashion, make-up, human relations, and music and where free LSD, legal until late 1966, was available—often in a spiked punch known as the Kool-Aid Acid Test. Incorporating acid experiences into their music, bands such as the Grateful Dead, Jefferson Airplane, and Big Brother and the

Holding Company vastly expanded the sonic structures and lyrical visions of rock and roll. The poetry of songs like "Somebody to Love" (1967) and "White Rabbit" (1967) by Grace Slick and Jefferson Airplane, respectively, helped codify the acid trip and counterculture psychedelia for American youths.

Acid rock borrowed sounds, scales, chords, and rhythms from around the world to distort space and time. The Byrds' "Eight Miles High" adapted Indian ragas and modal jazz to dislodge the rhythmic anchor and erase the four cardinal directions. In England, the Beatles were introduced to acid in 1965; they recorded *Revolver* a year later. Their variable tape speeds, tape loops, backward guitar and voice lines, and other experiments transformed basic rock and roll chords, beats, and voices into a tableau of acid-soaked sound, rhythm, and poetry. Especially disorienting was "Tomorrow Never Knows," an early trance-rock number. Ringo Starr's bass drum figure, a human heartbeat, kicked time in reverse, while John Lennon's filtered vocals, chants inspired by the Tibetan *Book of the Dead*, seemed piped in from creation.

Released in summer 1967, the ultimate psychedelic pop culture statement was the Beatles' *Sgt. Pepper's Lonely Hearts Club Band*. On vinyl, the Beatles recast themselves as a traditional British concert hall band and took their listeners through a counterculture song cycle featuring acid rivers, Indian sitars, Scottish farm animals, carnival acrobatics, adolescent runaways, leaking roofs, and a British meter maid. At the end, they explored "A Day in the Life," which climaxed with an orchestral chromatic three-octave crescendo punctuated with a crashing E-major chord and fade-out. Although it has not aged well, *Sgt. Pepper's* was well-crafted, self-conscious pop art laced with wit, charm, buoyancy, camp, and youthful idealism, and it captured the Summer of Love like no other rock album. Bands from the Rolling Stones to the Beach Boys scrambled to record their own versions of *Sgt. Pepper's*.

The Beatles' works, especially *Sgt. Pepper's*, forced musicians and critics to consider rock music as serious pop art. In the early Sixties, pop artists had rejected the distinction between high and low culture, denied emotion in artistic creation, and disavowed the transformative power of art. As the decade progressed, pop musicians, rock and roll artists particularly, also challenged the gap between high and low; rock and roll was emotionally charged performance, and musicians and their listeners repeatedly declared that this music transformed their lives and could alter human history. On June 25, 1967, telecasted via satellite to five continents, the Beatles' performance of "All You Need Is Love" on the BBC's *Our World* demonstrated the counterculture's profound faith in the healing power of Sixties rock.

Pop music unity, however, was only Beatle deep, and countercurrents were eroding Pepperland's cultural cohesion. Student and African-American riots, the intensification of the Vietnam War, and the assassinations of Martin Luther King and Robert Kennedy sobered up some love-drunk baby boomers and radicalized many rock musicians. Detroit's MC5, a white band, helped create the White Panther Party to provoke a revolution, but the Rolling Stones and the Beatles reacted ambivalently with "Street Fightin' Man" and "Revolution," respectively, in 1968. The pop song was a powerful mass-media weapon, but most rockers—part artist, part entertainer, part escapist—struggled to reconcile politics and music.

In Pepperland the rock band was a tiny community, but instrumental virtuosos such as Eric Clapton and Jimi Hendrix created the electric-guitar god, the rock and roll superman. On stage, their power trios, Cream and The Experience, respectively, indulged in long, loud workouts of heavy rock and blues. During 1966, Clapton's blues prowess inspired his fans to scrawl CLAPTON IS GOD around London. In Hendrix's magical hands, the guitar became a sonic wand producing never before heard sounds, distortions, and explosions. His machine-gun riffs, cosmic lyrics, and psychedelic eye made *Are You Experienced?* a Summer of Love classic. He and Clapton established the guitar king as a rock and roll icon.

Another turn away from Pepperland led into rural and historic America. Bob Dylan's *John Wesley Hardin* (1968) offered stark arrangements of country and folk, and lyrics of rural Americana and biblical foreboding. Working closely with Dylan, The Band followed suit with *Music from Big Pink* (1968) and *The Band* (1969), richly imagined vignettes of American myth, history, and people. The Grateful Dead, Creedence Clearwater Revival, the Byrds, and other bands also explored the sounds, harmonies, rhythms, and themes of American country and folk music. Complex expositions on American land, myth, and history, these albums held up better than *Sgt. Pepper's* and psychedelia, which too often dissipated into inside jokes, unresolved melodies, and self-indulgent sound collages.

The sonic bridge of rock and roll also crossed the chasm to hard social realities. By 1968, psychedelia was beginning to implode. In San Francisco's Haight-Ashbury, New York's East Village, and other hippie havens, a grim, desperate drug culture of addiction, violence, and poverty was displacing the middle-class acid dream. The previous year in New York City, The Velvet Underground released *The Velvet Underground and Nico* (1967), which explored the chilling byproducts of addiction, prostitution, and the underworld. Between 1968 and 1972, breaking free of the Beatles' long shadow, the Rolling Stones recorded a quartet of fierce, dark albums—*Beggar's Banquet, Let It*

Bleed, Sticky Fingers, and *Exile on Main Street*—that returned to their blues and country roots and shed Sixties innocence for Seventies narcissism, despair, and cynicism.

Aside from Hendrix's rock, psychedelia was generally a white phenomenon, and African Americans worked in three parallel grooves. In Detroit, Motown achieved Gordy's dream. His artists—Smokey Robinson and the Miracles, the Supremes, the Temptations, and others—sold millions of records to enthusiastic black and white audiences, but African-American upheaval and King's assassination frayed and consumed his vision with bullets and fire. Not even the Motown promise could convince young black musicians to conceal their anger for the sake of selling records to white kids. Feeling monetarily shut out, older R & B musicians often grumbled that the explosion of rock and roll—a black sound, in their opinion—had rewarded them with few dollars but had made millionaires of white musicians.

Some African-American performers, such as Aretha Franklin, Otis Redding, Sam Cooke, and James Brown, poured their anger into soul, R & B charged with black pride. In the wake of African-American rioting in 1967, Black Power politicized performers; soul became the secular gospel of African American community, and their records exploded onto the charts. In an ironic twist, whites crossed the color line to buy soul records for a window into black culture.

At decade's end, electric blues became hugely popular with white audiences. The combination of African-American unrest and Clapton's and Hendrix's fame pushed electric or urban blues into the rock and roll spotlight. White blues musicians—Steve Miller, Edgar Winters, the Allman Brothers, Canned Heat—promoted their African-American heroes—B. B. King, Albert King, John Lee Hooker, Muddy Waters, James Cotton, and other blues legends. The electric blues explosion introduced black blues to white adolescents and college kids too young to have seen Delta bluesmen in the folk movement during the early Sixties.

The Beatles' breakup in 1970 accentuated the end of the Sixties and pop-music unity. *The Beatles,* or *White Album* (1968), bared their fragmentation. Lennon returned to primitive rock, while McCartney expanded his forays into pop from flappers' jazz to shrieking rock. Their next effort, *Get Back,* was a full-fledged return to rock and roll roots but went awry in personal feuds. Pulling together for a final album, they produced *Abbey Road,* a pop masterpiece, and dissolved afterward. The decade lost its biggest symbol.

In his first post-Beatles solo album, Lennon sang, "The dream is over." His *Plastic Ono Band* (1970), angry antipop, foresaw Sixties disenchantment.

Trading his Beatle identity for rockabilly attitude, Lennon disavowed the decade's icons—Beatles included—and ideologies. Like their boomer fans, the Beatles had advocated expansive pop concepts, but an angry Lennon, reembracing rock primitivism, stripped down to a guitar, piano, bass, and drums. His howling confessions, such as "Mother," "Well, Well, Well" and "I Found Out," anticipated punk rock rage, and his acoustic ballads, such as "Working-Class Hero" and "Look at Me," looked toward Seventies singer-songwriter introspection.

Lennon, Dylan, and rock and roll survived the Sixties, but other musicians and ideals did not. After the last counterculture hurrah at Woodstock in August 1969, Hell's Angels murdered an African-American fan at Altamont, an outdoor Rolling Stones concert in December of that year. At the same time, President Richard Nixon escalated the Vietnam War, and at Kent State University, National Guardsmen shot down student protesters in spring 1970. In two years, Sixties optimism seemed to expire. Their mission apparently completed—and possibly failed—Janis Joplin, Jimi Hendrix, Jim Morrison, and Al Wilson suffered drug-related deaths in 1970.

Pop music went on, but, having lost its communal vision, the genre became ethereal, self-indulgent, and personal. Having dislodged Hollywood soundtracks with *Sgt. Pepper's Lonely Hearts Club Band* in 1967, rock and soul now dominated the top of the pop charts in the United States and became a huge cultural and economic leviathan. Glam rock, heavy metal, country rock, funk, disco, and other forms flooded the Seventies airwaves. The ideals and vision of performers in these genres seemed to share little with Sixties pop. The new music appealed more to individual pleasures than to collective dreams and hopes. However, each generation of teenagers still adopts a form of popular music—whether punk, new wave, rap, or grunge—as a critical piece of its collective identity, and rock and roll still serves as a sonic bridge to freedom, real and imagined.

SOURCES

Archer, Michael. *Art Since 1960*. World of Art series. London: Thames and Hudson, 1997.

Davies, Hunter. *The Beatles*. New York: McGraw-Hill, 1984.

Friedlander, Paul. *Rock and Roll: A Social History*. Boulder, Colo.: Westview, 1996.

Greil, Marcus. *Mystery Train*. New York: Dutton, 1975.

Guralnick, Peter. *Lost Highway: Journeys and Arrivals of American Musicians*. Boston: Godine, 1979.

Norman, Philip. *Shout! The Beatles in Their Generation*. New York: Simon and Schuster, 1981.

Palmer, Robert. *Rock & Roll: An Unruly History*. New York: Harmony, 1995.

Reyes, David and Tom Waldman. *Land of a Thousand Dances: Chicano Rock 'n' Roll from Southern California*. Albuquerque: University of New Mexico Press, 1998.

Szatmary, David P. *Rockin' in Time: A Social History of Rock and Roll*. 3rd ed. New York: Shirmer, 1996.

Ward, Ed, Geoffrey Stokes, and Ken Tucker. *Rock of Ages: The* Rolling Stone *History of Rock & Roll*. Introduction by Jann S. Wenner. New York: Rolling Stone Press and Summit Books, 1986.

Religion

Beth Bailey

Religion in the America of the Sixties, like so much else, was chaotic and fluid, animated by conflict and by new levels of commitment and possibility. It was a time of reformation and revival, as fundamental political realignments created new patterns in American life and religiously based activism changed American society in critically important ways.

Religion affected most Americans in the 1960s not through the details of complex theological debate but through its very public role in American life. Many of the movements for social justice were, at least partially, grounded in religion or spirituality, and established churches became increasingly involved in the social and political issues of the day. Social activism expressed the heart of the American religious experience in the 1960s.

Related to the embrace of social activism was a pronounced desire for "relevance." During the 1950s, by most measurements, Americans had become a more religious people. Church attendance and membership had risen steadily; in 1960 Americans spent $1 billion to build houses of worship, 40 times the total since 1945. It was during the 1950s that America placed the motto "In God We Trust" on coins and inserted the phrase "one nation, under God" into the Pledge of Allegiance. Yet theologians and secular critics alike bemoaned the banality and sterility of current religious belief and practice, and many viewed the recasting of American religious life in the 1960s as a reaction to the insufficiencies of spiritual life in the 1950s.

The desire for relevance, however, took many forms, some antithetical to one another. Those who found in religious belief the necessity to work for a better world, whether in the struggle for African-American civil rights, opposition to the war in Vietnam, or espousal of yet another cause, often found themselves on opposite sides, politically and culturally, from those who sought relevance in a "born again" commitment to a living God. The desire for relevance was manifest in the results of the Roman Catholic Church's Second Vatican Council ("Vatican II"), as well as in the metaphysics of those who embraced traditional Eastern religions, followed gurus, or consulted astrology or the *I Ching*. They took different paths in the pursuit of different goals, but all rejected the sort of religion that asked of its followers only an hour on Sunday (or Saturday) out of the week.

Along with the proliferation of alternative religions and spiritual practices, the 1960s also witnessed a rise in religious tolerance. Most of that kind of change occurred within the established religions. Among Protestants, Jews, and Catholics, interfaith initiatives proliferated, especially with the Second Vatican Council advocating increased dialogue with Protestant denominations.

Other measures of increased tolerance were also important. In 1968 (as measured by a Gallup Poll), the number of Americans who disapproved of marriage between Jews and non-Jews had fallen to 21 percent, and only 22 percent disapproved of marriage between Catholics and Protestants. (For comparison, 72 percent disapproved of marriage between whites and non-whites.)[1] Some historians have argued that these numbers reflect religious tolerance less than they signal that religion was losing importance or being increasingly dismissed as a simple matter of "personal belief," not significant enough to determine the choice of a spouse.

Yet such attitudes did reflect a diminished institutional discrimination against religious minorities. (Before this era, Catholics and Jews were often barred from private clubs and faced quota systems in colleges and universities, while many suburbs stayed not only white but Protestant, through the use of restrictive codes and covenants.) And while "alternative" and Eastern religions never challenged the primacy of mainstream Protestant, Roman Catholic, and Jewish faith, there was increasing openness in the American religious landscape for different modes of worship, which sometimes served as an inspiration even for mainstream churches. "Folk services" or "rock services" turned up in suburban churches all over the country. More adventurous and/or ecumenical churches offered workshops on yoga or meditation, and integrated philosophical concepts of Eastern religions or Native American spiritual beliefs into their Sunday school curricula.

Finally, as Michael Kazin and Maurice Isserman argue in *America Divided: The Civil War of the 1960s*, it was during this time that the religious foundation for contemporary "culture wars" was laid. In this decade, differences among denominations of Christians and Jews became less important than the divide between theological liberals and conservatives.[2] The liberals and progressives, drawn primarily (among whites) from the better educated and more affluent classes, supported the activist role of the church/synagogue in promoting equality among the races and between the sexes. The conservatives initially rejected a public and politically activist role for religion (that would change by the late 1970s), embraced fundamentalist religious doctrines, and often believed that the sort of change sought by liberals would destroy their nation and their church.

In the 1960s, the majority of Americans who thought about it assumed that the conflict between Christian fundamentalists (those who believe in the literal truth of the Bible) and religious modernists had been long settled, as seen in the defeat of the anti-evolution forces in the 1920s Scopes Trial in Tennessee. But they were wrong. As fundamentalism drew hundreds of thousands of new believers in the 1960s, few outside that movement understood its religious, social, and political significance for the succeeding decades.

THE ACTIVIST CHURCH AND ITS OPPONENTS

The post–World War II African-American civil rights movement was, from its beginnings in the 1950s, anchored in the church, which had traditionally been the strongest institutional base for African-American communities in the South. The black citizens of Montgomery, Alabama, met in the Dexter Street Baptist Church to hear the Reverend Martin Luther King Jr. call them to a boycott of the city's segregated bus system. Amid a chorus of Amens, King preached the moral necessity of nonviolent protest.

The animating vision of the early civil rights movement was grounded in notions of Christian love and couched in biblical language. As King told the men and women gathered in Montgomery in late 1955, "If you will protest courageously and yet with dignity and Christian love, when the history books are written in future generations, the historians will have to pause and say, 'There lived a great people—a black people—who injected new meaning and dignity into the veins of civilization.'"[3] Throughout the long and dangerous struggle for civil rights, participants found material and spiritual support in their churches.

In the 1960s, as some young black men and women became frustrated with the slow course of change and alienated from the goal of integration into white society, many of them expressed their disappointment and anger at least partially in religious terms. Episcopal theologian Nathan Wright called for black people to turn away from the "honkified version of the faith" that Christianity had become.[4] Rejecting not only white society but also the "slave religion" of Christianity, some, like Malcolm X, turned to the Nation of Islam, sometimes called "Black Muslims." (Following his hajj, or pilgrimage to Mecca, Malcolm X converted to orthodox Islam.)

The Nation of Islam was not a branch of the orthodox Islamic religion, but instead was based on the teachings of a Detroit peddler named Wallace C. Fard, who had disappeared during the 1930s. Fard wove together his readings of Islamic texts with his own prophetic visions. The black race, he claimed, was "sixty-six trillion" years old, and had ruled the earth until 6,000 years ago, when an evil scientist had created an evil white race. Whites would eventually be destroyed, he promised, and blacks would be saved from the coming apocalypse by spaceships descending from the sky.

Fard's teachings had been popularized in the 1950s and 1960s by Elijah Muhammad, but he and most who embraced them were drawn not by such creation stories so much as by the powerful teachings of black pride and the spiritual and physical discipline—drawn from orthodox Islam—that the religion offered: Black Muslims did not drink alcohol, or smoke, or use drugs. The Nation of Islam never rivaled the mainstream Protestant religions among African Americans, but it was a significant presence during the 1960s. In subsequent decades, increasing numbers of African Americans turned to the teachings of orthodox Islam as well.

Native American movements for social justice were, perhaps more than any others, rooted in spirituality. Rejecting notions of an established church, or "religion" as a category separate from the rest of life, many Native American activists sought a return to the old ways. As Sioux activist Ernie Peters explained, "You can't do anything without thanking the Creator for it, and when you are done you give thanks again. You own nothing. You don't even possess your body; it belongs to mother earth. All you possess is your spirit. . . . Spirituality is what [our movement] is all about."[5]

Such beliefs were put forward not only in works like Vine Deloria's *God is Red*, but also in the Taos Pueblo's successful struggle to reclaim its sacred Blue Lake from the jurisdiction of the federal government. The lake had been incorporated into the Carson National Forest in 1906; but in 1970, Congress recognized that the lake was sacred to Native peoples and relinquished federal claims to it.

The public struggles of some of America's citizens for full equality forced many of the nation's established churches to confront difficult decisions about their proper roles. Many did turn to greater activism; the civil rights movement found great support in some white or predominantly white churches and synagogues, such as New York City's Riverside Church. Many members of the clergy addressed their congregations on the moral issues of the day. The National Clergy and Laity Concerned about Vietnam (NCLCAV) was prominent in antiwar protests; Roman Catholic nuns marched against the war; Jesuit priest Daniel Berrigan was indicted for burning hundreds of draft files in a Selective Service office in Maryland.

While some actions were based in individual conscience, they found institutional support. The National Council of Churches, an umbrella organization of Protestant churches formed in 1950, funded the civil rights movement in the South and discussed the virtues of draft resistance. The Second Vatican Council not only created more participatory forms of worship for Catholics by accepting the Mass conducted in the language of the participants, rather than in Latin, but called for "the followers of Christ" to treat the "joys and hopes, the griefs and the anxieties of the men of this age, especially those who are poor or in any way afflicted" as their own.[6]

A group of radical Protestant theologians called for churches to dispense with the mystical aspects of their faith, proposing (in a phrase calculated to create controversy) "the death of God." Instead of faith, they argued, Christians should emphasize moral principles and the struggle for social justice. God, thus, was "dead," but Jesus lived as an example to Christians. (A review of one of the key books laying out this theological argument was titled, "There Is No God and Jesus Is His Son.")[7]

Many Americans were horrified by the activist church. Some, quite simply, did not believe in the causes for which they were exhorted to fight. A majority of Americans supported the government's policy toward the war in Vietnam; in 1968, 72 percent of southern Presbyterians supported waging war with "all strength needed for victory."[8] Many, especially southern whites and white ethnics in the north, did not embrace the civil rights struggle as their own. Individual churches and entire denominations were torn apart by arguments over the issues of the day.

But the arguments went deeper yet. Americans were struggling over the nature of religion, over the proper roles of churches and synagogues, clergy and laypeople. Many sought in religion a refuge from the tumultuousness of their world. They wanted the sense of timelessness embodied in traditional rituals, not guitar music and civil rights anthems. Many believed strongly that the bedrock of the church must be spiritual faith, not worldly activism. Evangelical preacher Jerry Falwell told his flock at the Thomas Road Baptist Church on March 21, 1965, as the civil rights marchers in Selma regrouped from a violent attack and tried again to march to Montgomery: "Believing in the Bible as I do, I would find it impossible to stop preaching the pure saving gospel of Jesus Christ, and begin doing anything else—including fighting Communism, or participating in Civil Rights reforms. Preachers are not called to be politicians but to be soul winners."[9] With so much else dividing them during this era, Americans also split over the meaning and proper role of religion in their lives and in the public life of their nation.

SPIRITUAL SEEKING

While many Americans found that their religious beliefs propelled them to social activism, others rejected that path for a different form of spirituality. Conservative, evangelical Christianity grew dramatically from the mid-1960s. Eastern and "New Age" religions attracted relatively small but influential followings. Many young Jews revived traditional religious observations and created communities for themselves. The southern Pentecostalist "speaking in tongues," the Zen Buddhist "sitting" in California, and the Jewish women in New York developing a nonsexist religious community had almost nothing in common—except that all were dissatisfied with the traditional, mainstream practices of American religions and were seeking something more, albeit in radically different ways.

In the ten years following 1965, all of America's mainstream liberal Protestant churches lost members: Episcopalian membership shrank by 17 percent; the United Presbyterians and the Church of Christ each dropped 12 percent; the United Methodist Church lost 10 percent of its members. In contrast, the conservative Southern Baptists grew by 18 percent. Protestant denominations that offered a more intense spirituality focused on salvation from sin through belief in Jesus Christ rather than on social activism, and that were fundamentalist (i.e., stressing a literal interpretation of the Bible), expanded greatly during this era. Evangelical preachers such as Pat Robertson and Jerry Falwell reached out to worshipers over the airwaves, the more successful building "televangelism" empires.

Meanwhile, some Mexican-American Roman Catholics turned to the *cursillo* movement, a "little course" in faith, and throughout the nation Catholics joined a "charismatic" revival akin to the Protestant movement in its turn toward a "personal relationship" with God.

Even the counterculture had its Christian movement. "Jesus freaks" professed Jesus as the greatest high, "witnessing" to others about their salvation from drugs or impersonal sex or a meaningless life through the power of Jesus Christ. The Campus Crusade for Christ, founded in the early 1950s, adopted the tools of the counterculture in its drive to save souls. The Reverend Chuck Smith, in Orange County, California, baptized hippies in his swimming pool. Evangelical organizations aimed at young people included the Christian World Liberation Front and the Jesus Christ Light and Power Company. The popular rock opera *Jesus Christ Superstar* brought the counterculture Jesus to the nation and the world.

Jews also participated in the spiritual revivals of the 1960s. Historian of comparative religion Martin Marty suggests that it was the Six Days War fought by Israel against its Arab neighbors that awakened a spiritual renewal among American Jews, especially young adults, by encouraging them to seek the Jewish roots of their identity.[10] By 1970, approximately 400 colleges and universities were offering courses in Jewish Studies, and 40 Jewish student newspapers were published. Families who had been both secularized and as-similated began to observe the Jewish Sabbath, lighting candles on Friday evening. Some young people created communities of believers called *havu-rah* ("fellowship" in Hebrew), which offered an intense spirituality and the sort of sexual equality still unimaginable in most synagogues. Many of these young people retained their commitments to the New Left or the ideals of the counterculture.

Much smaller numbers of Americans left behind the Judeo-Christian tra-dition altogether. (Even in the San Francisco Bay area, with the greatest con-centration of alternative spiritual practices, probably fewer than ten percent of the population turned to other forms of religious experience.) Some of them embarked upon the disciplined practice of non-Western religions. Others tried out—or creatively combined—various "alternative" religions or "New Age" practices. Through the mass media, Americans became familiar with a succession of gurus or teachers and their celebrity disciples, as the Beatles fol-lowed the Maharishi Mahesh Yogi to India, and "EST" founder Werner Er-hard was profiled in popular magazines.

Major religious or spiritual movements that drew American converts in the 1960s included Zen Buddhism, the Krishna Consciousness Movement ("*Hare Krishna*"), and Transcendental Meditation ("TM"), as well as many other manifestations of the "human potential movement" and various mysti-cal practices, including astrology, witchcraft, and versions of Native American spiritual practices that most likely had become unrecognizable to those who had originated them. Some of these movements were short-lived, soon rele-gated to the wreckage of those turbulent times. Others continue to flourish, and to enrich the religious landscape of the United States.

The legacy of the religious movements of the 1960s is complex, continuing to evolve in a multiplicity of directions. Religious practice in America as transformed in the Sixties was enriched by a new level of engagement among the nation's people, and by the emergence of new or newly recovered spiritual experiences. But at the same time that Americans became more tolerant of the religious differences among themselves, religion played a central role in the polarization of the American public—one that did not necessarily end in a resolution of difficult issues raised in the Sixties but which continues to this day.

NOTES

1. Gallup Poll, 1968, p. 2168.

2. Maurice Isserman and Michael Kazin, *America Divided: The Civil War of the 1960s* (New York: Oxford University Press, 2000), 259.

3. Harvard Sitkoff, *The Struggle for Black Equality, 1954–1980* (New York: Hill and Wang, 1981), 50.

4. Gayraud S. Wilmore, *Black Religion and Black Radicalism*, 3rd edition (Maryknoll, N.Y.: Orbis, 1998), 218.

5. Martin E. Marty, *Pilgrims in Their Own Land: 500 Years of Religion in America* (Boston: Little, Brown, 1984), 439.

6. Isserman and Kazin, *America Divided*, 248.

7. Robert W. Ellwood, *The Sixties Spiritual Awakening: American Religion Moving from Modern to Postmodern* (New Brunswick, N.J.: Rutgers University Press, 1994), 137.

8. James Reichley, *Religion in American Public Life* (Washington, D.C.: Brookings Institute, 1985), 252.

9. J. Gordon Melton, Phillip Charles Lucas, and Jon R. Stone, *Prime-Time Religion: An Encyclopedia of Religious Broadcasting* (Phoenix: Oryx Press, 1997), 94.

10. Marty, *Pilgrims in Their Own Land*, 462.

SOURCES

Balmer, Randall. *Blessed Assurance: A History of Evangelicalism in America*. Boston: Beacon Press, 1999.

Ellwood, Robert S. *The Sixties Spiritual Awakening: American Religion Moving from Modern to Postmodern*. New Brunswick, N.J.: Rutgers University Press, 1994.

Isserman, Maurice, and Michael Kazin. *America Divided: The Civil War of the 1960s*. New York: Oxford University Press, 2000.

Lippy, Charles H. "Religion." In *Encyclopedia of American Social History*, edited by Mary Kupiec Cayton et al. New York: Scribner's, 1993.

Marty, Martin. *Pilgrims in Their Own Land: 500 Years of Religion in America*. Boston: Little, Brown, 1984.

Melton, J. Gordon, Phillip Charles Lucas, and Jon R. Stone. *Prime-Time Religion: An Encyclopedia of Religious Broadcasting*. Phoenix: Oryx Press, 1997.

Reichley, James. *Religion in American Public Life*. Washington, D.C.: The Brookings Institute, 1985.

Tweed, Thomas and Stephen Prothero. *Asian Religions in America: A Documentary History*. New York: Oxford University Press, 1999.

Wilmore, Gayraud S. *Black Religion and Black Radicalism*. 3rd edition. Maryknoll, N.Y.: Orbis, 1998.

Wuthnow, Robert. *After Heaven: Spirituality in America Since the 1950s*. Berkeley: University of California Press, 1998.

York, Michael. *The Emerging Network: A Sociology of the New Age and Neo-Pagan Movements*. Lanham, Md.: Rowman and Littlefield, 1995.

The End of Enthusiasm:
Science and Technology

Timothy Moy

Quarks. Quasars. Lasers. Apollo. Heart transplants. Computers. Nylon. Color
TV. Pampers. The Pill. LSD. Napalm. DDT. Thalidomide. Mutual Assured
Destruction. *Star Trek. Dr. Strangelove.* The Sixties had them all.

For most of the twentieth century, Americans had enjoyed an enthusiastic
and profitable relationship with science and technology. Much of the nation's
economic and military ascendancy during the American Century was largely
due to its technical prowess. And while positive attitudes about science and its
products had wavered during the Depression and after Hiroshima, the prosperity of the 1950s had helped make science and high technology seem as
wholesome and American as apple pie.

During the 1960s, America's romance with scientific progress and technology came to an end. Though the fruits of science continued to dazzle, popular anxiety over the political and social impacts of technology eventually coalesced into a broad-based critique of the value of such enterprises.

THE HEYDAY OF GEE WHIZ

Scientific and technical developments during the 1960s continued to feed
Americans' fascination with the wonders of modernity. The first successful
heart transplants, the increasing effectiveness and availability of childhood
vaccinations, and the promise of new therapies for diabetes, arthritis, kidney
disease, and even cancer permitted a soaring (and ultimately unfounded) optimism that medical technology stood on the edge of eliminating disease.

The United States' competition with the USSR in space appeared to make
real the Buck Rogers fantasies of decades past. The space race had begun in
the late 1950s with the first successful launches of artificial satellites. On a
purely technical level, this was probably the most important consequence of
the space program during the 1960s, as the growing network of communica-

tion satellites became the infrastructure for an explosion in communication systems; NASA launched *Telstar I* for Bell Telephone in 1962, and by the end of the decade satellites were routinely employed for telephone and television communications, weather forecasting, and military surveillance. But on a political and cultural level, the human space flight program was what truly fired public imagination for much of the decade. The Mercury and Gemini programs, which sent the first American astronauts into Earth orbit, made national heroes of Alan Shepard and John Glenn. For many Americans, the heart and soul of the space program were these flights in which young American space warriors rode columns of fire to engage their cosmonaut adversaries in cold war combat among the stars. The public romance became real political capital for NASA in 1961 with Kennedy's pledge for a manned Moon shot before the decade was out. The ensuing Apollo Program, which enjoyed nearly limitless political enthusiasm and a $20 billion budget, climaxed in the summer of 1969; Americans alive at the time still recall Neil Armstrong's first step onto the lunar surface as a bright and proud moment in an otherwise turbulent period.

Technical developments back on the ground continued to delight the public as well. Consumer electronics like color television and home audio systems created a market base in the entertainment industry that in later decades would include VCRs, cable television, and personal computers. These were largely enabled by the development of the integrated circuit microchip—a single flake of silicon that could replace hundreds of thousands (and later millions) of individual transistors—which was developed in the 1960s but not commercially viable until the very end of the decade. At the same time, Teflon, nylon, and vinyl were literally transforming the stuff of American society. It is difficult to exaggerate the impact (social and environmental) of home air conditioners and disposable diapers.

Americans were captivated even by developments in the arcane world of abstract sciences that had little prospect of affecting daily life. As newspapers and magazines increased their coverage of science news during the Sixties, Americans read about, even if they did not entirely understand, the discovery of quarks (subatomic particles more basic than protons and electrons), pulsars (stars that broadcast radio signals so regular that they were initially mistaken for extraterrestrial communication signals), and quasars (extremely distant and powerful astronomical objects that travel at near the speed of light and shine as brightly as a thousand galaxies combined). Even these less-than-applicable discoveries of science maintained a "gee whiz" appeal.

GROWING ANXIETY

But despite the continuing allure of scientific and technological marvels, there was a growing tension over their social, cultural, and political meaning. In some ways, the seemingly boundless promise of new technologies led to bitter disenchantment when they failed to deliver. It became rapidly apparent, for example, that the ability to send men to the Moon might not (in contrast to the glowing forecasts of the New Frontiersmen) yield much in the way of solutions to poverty or urban decay, or even the ability to keep the electricity flowing in New York City.

Americans' changing attitudes about science and technology, as about so many developments in the Sixties, were exacerbated by the widening war in Vietnam. In what had become a stereotypical response to the crisis, military planners turned to technological solutions. The most advanced technology in the arsenal—short of nuclear weapons—went to war in Vietnam: chemical defoliants, the latest bomber and fighter aircraft, and a complex combination of motion sensors, command and control systems, and combat forces known as the Electronic Battlefield. The failure of these technological systems to bring victory ultimately called into question not only specific military actions but also faith in science and technology in general. In addition, on many university campuses, student protest often centered on the university's ties to the war in the form of research and development contracts with the Department of Defense; napalm may have been produced by Dow, but it had been developed in the chemistry department at Harvard.

During the Sixties, this tension over the social costs and benefits of science and technology evolved into full-blown critique. Some of the criticism was relatively narrow. Many Americans sympathized with Federal Communications Commission Chairman Newton Minnow's lament in 1961 that television had failed to live up to its educational and cultural promise and had instead devolved into an "idiot box," whose programming had become "a vast wasteland" of game shows, formulaic comedies, violence, and commercials. The dehumanizing effects of computer automation likewise became a popular theme in movies like *2001: A Space Odyssey* and the earlier Tracy and Hepburn comedy *Desk Set*.

Among intellectual elites, the anxiety broadened to include an indictment of technology-based society as politically degenerate. Among American intellecutals the writings of critics like Jacques Ellul, Herbert Marcuse, Lewis Mumford, and Theodore Roszak became popular as a basis for the counterculture critique of technocracy. Mumford, for example, had been enthusiastic in the 1930s about the technological promise of an increasingly just and humane civilization. But during the 1960s, his anxiety over the growing militarization of technical pursuits evolved into a wholesale critique of science and technology as dehumanizing tools of the corporate and military "megamachine."

THE TENSION OF *SILENT SPRING*

America's love-hate relationship with science and technology during the Sixties was evident in one of the most influential works of popular science in the postwar period: Rachel Carson's *Silent Spring*. Carson was a writer and scientist (she received a master's degree in zoology from Johns Hopkins University in 1932) who had written radio scripts and publications for the U.S. Fish and Wildlife Service and had also published popular books and articles on marine biology since before World War II. After the war, her concern over the increasing use of chemical pesticides turned her writings more and more often to ecological matters. Published in 1962, *Silent Spring* (serialized in *The New Yorker* that same year) documented what Carson regarded as the indiscriminate and profligate use of chemical pesticides (especially the insecticide DDT, which she identified as carcinogenic) and their devastating effects on wildlife and public health.

The book and articles were an instant sensation; *Silent Spring* became a best-seller in the United States and Great Britain, and was eventually translated into thirty languages. The book's political impact was as intense. Despite widespread criticism and ridicule from the chemical industry, Carson's tales of toxic horror quickly influenced policy in Washington. Carson testified on pesticide regulation before congressional committees; several members of Congress read large excerpts of *Silent Spring* into the *Congressional Record*; and her views shaped a pesticide report issued by the Kennedy administration's Science Advisory Committee in 1963.

Carson died of cancer in 1964, but *Silent Spring* provided a focus for what had been a disjointed environmental movement in the United States for the rest of the 1960s. The book directly stimulated legislation that regulated the use of pesticides (and virtually eliminated the widespread use of DDT); it also provided a political boost for protection of federal wilderness areas in the Wilderness Act of 1964. The book's long shadow reached beyond the 1960s and at least indirectly contributed to the passage of the Environmental Protection Act in 1970 and the Endangered Species Act in 1973, and to the annual celebration of Earth Day since 1970.

But often lost in thumbnail sketches of *Silent Spring* was the book's ironic tension over the relationship between science and ecological well-being. While many readers remembered vividly Carson's criticisms of chemical corporations and federal agencies for unnecessarily drenching open areas with toxic and carcinogenic chemicals, many overlooked her proposed alternative: biological engineering. Instead of chemical pesticides, Carson suggested, pest control should be accomplished by turning life against itself. Her favorite approaches: massive releases of chemically sterilized males to interrupt the reproduction cycles of insect species and the use of specially designed pathogens (viruses, bacteria, fungi, or parasites) to decimate insect populations. Clearly, Carson's principal criticism was not of modern science running roughshod over pristine nature; rather, she was concerned that Americans had become too enamored of the wrong science—chemistry—rather than a more effective and elegant science—biology. *Silent Spring* was a critique only of the careless use of some science; it was a ringing reaffirmation of the power and beneficence of science as a whole.

PARADIGM SHIFT

A trend in thinking about technology that emerged in the later 1960s mirrored Carson's tension over the fruits of science. The growing concern that large, industrial, technological systems were destroying local cultures, economies, political relationships, and ecosystems took shape as an interest in "appropriate technology"—smaller, simpler, greener, cheaper technologies that at least appeared less tied to the interests of corporate capitalism. The best-known manifestation of the appropriate technology vision was the enormously popular *Whole Earth Catalog*. Inspired by the critics of the megamachine but still optimistic about the ability of technology to empower, Stewart Brand first published the catalog in 1968; this encyclopedia of high-quality, simple, nonpolluting devices—ergonomic tools, windmills, water pumps, spinning wheels, and solar cookers—quickly became a national best-seller and a kind of handbook for communal and countercultural living. The catalog's extensive text on the importance of returning to a lifestyle that was simpler and more harmonious, yet still empowered by humane technologies, earned it a National Book Award; the award jurors described the catalog as a "space age Walden." Although it would reach its widest audience in the 1970s (with the writings of

R. Buckminster Fuller and E. F. Schumacher), the appropriate technology movement had its roots firmly in the 1960s.

A much quieter but more radical analysis of science in the modern world also had its roots in the Sixties but its greatest impact in the Seventies. Thomas Kuhn's *The Structure of Scientific Revolutions*, published in 1962, was in one sense an academic analysis of the history and philosophy of science in the Western world but was also a widespread and popular indictment of the traditional understanding of science as a form of natural truth. Kuhn argued that large changes in scientific understanding were not gradual and rational accumulations of knowledge but rather discontinuous, radical, and often non-rational "paradigm shifts"—fundamental redefinitions of scientific terms allowing new accounts of natural phenomena that might seem more universal but were in no meaningful sense more truthful descriptions of what actually occurs in nature.

Initially, interest in Kuhn's book remained confined to the community of academic historians and philosophers of science. For much of the 1960s, the debate on *Structure* swirled around whether Kuhn's vision constituted a kind of relativistic anarchy (Kuhn insisted it did not). But by the later 1960s, the book was appearing on reading lists for many college courses, especially in the social sciences. By the 1970s it had become an academic best-seller; *Structure* was translated into sixteen languages and sold over one million copies. The term "paradigm shift" became a vernacular synonym for radical intellectual change, and not only in academia; eventually, even bumper stickers carried the antiestablishment battle cry: SUBVERT THE DOMINANT PARADIGM!.

The Kuhnian account of scientific change dovetailed well with the intellectual climate of the Sixties. While it never really supported radical relativism (as many of its critics and supporters contended), it certainly provided further ammunition for the counterculture critique of technocracy by highlighting the value-laden character of scientific statements. That fundamental doubt about the truth-value of science, which spread much more widely than Kuhn's book itself, cut to the heart of the popular perception of science's role in society.

CONCLUSION

As with so many trends in the 1960s, developments in science and technology, and Americans' relationship with them, were marked by a tension and anxiety that would persist for the remainder of the century. While Americans would continue to embrace the power and comforts of high technology, they would also regard science and its products with a skepticism—and even fear—that would have seemed un-American in the first half of the twentieth century.

SOURCES

Carson, Rachel. *Silent Spring*. Boston: Houghton Mifflin, 1962.

Cowan, Ruth Schwartz. *A Social History of American Technology*. New York: Oxford University Press, 1997.

Hughes, Thomas P. *American Genesis*. New York: Penguin, 1989.

Kuhn, Thomas S. *The Structure of Scientific Revolutions*. Chicago: University of Chicago Press, 1962.

Lear, Linda. *Rachel Carson: Witness for Nature*. New York: Holt, 1997.

Mumford, Lewis. *The Pentagon of Power*. New York: Harcourt Brace, 1970.

Wolfe, Tom. *The Right Stuff*. New York: Farrar, Straus and Giroux, 1979.

Sports
David Key

Sports in the 1960s might be remembered for any number of dramatic on-field images televised into the national consciousness. From Bill Mazeroski's World Series–winning home run in 1960 to the Miracle Mets in 1969; from the Green Bay Packers' dominance of the early Super Bowls to the upstart Jets' victory—even the Super Bowl itself; from the great duels between Wilt Chamberlain and Bill Russell indoors to the battles between Arnold Palmer and Jack Nicklaus out of doors, the 1960s and early 1970s offered fans classic and memorable competition. Yet such athletic feats are not characteristic of only one era, and are not the reason the Sixties are so significant to the history of sports. Rather, it was the off-field events that became truly significant, changing athletic environments, broadening participation, and heightening the organization of individual sports. In the process, whether through the lens of a television camera or through the newsletter of a local jogging club, a new sort of sports hero arose.

ALTERING SPORTS ENVIRONMENTS

In 1965 the Houston Astrodome, hailed as "the eighth wonder of the world" by financier and promoter Roy Hofheinz, opened its doors and ushered in a new era of sports. The Astrodome's clear Lucite ceiling was soon painted over so that Houston's baseball players (formerly the Colt .45s but renamed the Astros) could see fly balls without squinting through the glare. The natural grass died quickly after that and artificial grass (AstroTurf) became the substitute. In other cities, such as Cincinnati, Pittsburgh, and St. Louis, multipurpose, AstroTurfed stadiums soon followed, while domed stadiums were planned to decorate the skylines of places as diverse as New Orleans and Pontiac. American cities had long featured sports arenas, but the multipurpose or "cookie-cutter" stadiums became a symbol of athletics in the 1960s. They were often funded through business and government cooperation, and became centers of competition not only for athletes performing inside them but also for cities competing against one another for sports franchises. Even political candidates used various stadium-building or -renovating plans as planks in their platforms.

The number of cities hosting "major league" athletic teams increased as franchises followed the population, dispersing throughout the Sunbelt, into the Pacific Northwest, and even up to Canada. Major League Baseball (MLB) continued expansive trends begun in the 1950s, placing new teams in a variety of cities including San Diego, Minneapolis, Houston, and Montreal while also reestablishing teams in New York City and Washington, D.C. In all, ten new baseball franchises began in the 1960s and 1970s. Two other major sports leagues, the National Football League (NFL) and the National Basketball Association (NBA), also expanded, but through different means. The NFL merged with the American Football League in 1966. A year later, the American Basketball Association was formed, but it was destined for merger in the 1970s. Houston is just one example of a city transformed into a "major league" metropolis, gaining baseball, football, and basketball teams.

Professional teams were not the only way sports expanded. As more individuals participated in athletics (or simply sought to get "fit"), cities and towns throughout America realized that sports were good for citizens and business and changed their environments to accommodate them. Jogging trails were set aside or constructed, and the number of marathons increased from 38 in 1968 to 135 nationwide by 1974. In some cities, such as Boulder, Colorado, the cement tops of sewage plants were transformed into tennis courts. Closer to home the environment was changed as the phrase "rec room" made its way into the suburban lexicon. Expansion into "crabgrass frontiers" also changed inner-city areas, forcing such institutions as the YMCA to alter their philosophies in order to reverse declining membership.

BROADENING THE SPECTRUM OF PARTICIPATION

As sports changed environments, people were changing sports. The most notable cases were athletes in previously underrepresented groups, particularly African Americans and women. *Sports Illustrated* exposés were important in notifying America of problems facing these athletes, but of greater importance was the activism of the athletes, sometimes augmented by the actions of government.

Fittingly, the Astrodome was the site of some of the best-remembered athletic events of the Sixties involving athletes competing against discrimination. There, in February 1966, Muhammad Ali (born Cassius Clay) fought World Boxing Association heavyweight champion Ernie Terrell in an event that serves as a parable for African-American athletes during the decade. Terrell, who refused to recognize Ali's Black Muslim name, was soundly defeated. During the fight, Ali repeatedly taunted Terrell with shouts of "What's my name?" and "Uncle Tom!" Yet through the physical and verbal abuse, Terrell, bleeding and bruised, kept his feet and kept moving toward Ali. After the bout, Ali had to admit, "he a brave man." Other black athletes of the era, such as the Harlem Globetrotters, were criticized for perpetuating traditional stereotypes, but both politically outspoken African Americans and those with a less overt racial agenda made lasting headway toward equality with their white counterparts. The difficulties facing black athletes received widespread attention in a series of Sports Illustrated articles in 1967. But just as essential to success were the grace of Army Lt. Arthur Ashe, who led American amateurs to tennis's Davis Cup in 1968; the persistence of Cardinals first baseman Bill White, who prompted MLB to fight segregation in Florida's Spring Training towns; and the ironic wit of Celtics center Bill Russell, who once refused to speak at a banquet for less money than white teammate Bob Cousey had been offered because it would be disrespectful to Cousey.

In some cases, black athletes sacrificed bright futures to end discrimination and improve the lives of all athletes. An example was in the 1968 Olympics, when Tommie Smith and John Carlos stood upon the victors' podium, bowed their heads, and raised the closed-fisted Black Power salute during "The Star-Spangled Banner." The act increased international awareness of the plight of America's blacks but also brought a U.S. Olympic Committee (USOC) ban on the two men's future participation. In another instance, center fielder Curt Flood challenged MLB's reserve clause—which allowed teams to swap players according to whim—for the benefit of all players. Flood, who lost his case in the U.S. Supreme Court and was ostracized by MLB afterward, privately acknowledged the civil rights movement as a compelling influence. Although Flood failed, MLB, which was being surpassed in popularity by the NFL and could little afford adverse publicity, began relaxing its rules, and subsequent actions by players ushered in the era of free agency.

Not all black athletes' careers ended when they fought discrimination. Throughout the 1973 season, Henry Aaron had been approaching Babe Ruth's venerable career home run record. With every home run, he received more hate mail, some of which included death threats. Aaron, who played in Atlanta, remarkably maintained his composure, although he did not break the record in 1973. Mercifully, early in the 1974 season, Al Downing, a black

Los Angeles pitcher who wore the same jersey number as Aaron, grooved a waist-high fastball over the plate, and Aaron sent a shot over the left-field wall. While Fulton County Stadium's spectators cheered and millions of viewers watched on television, Aaron circled the bases, escorted at one point by two white fans who, presumably, did not care what his skin color was. Like Hank Aaron, many black athletes in this era won the admiration of white sports fans who wanted only for their team to win. Equality was not yet complete, but on-field leaders like Bill White and Henry Aaron would also lead blacks into executive positions in sports, although they have remained underrepresented at that level.

For women, the challenge was greater. Primarily limited to Olympic competition, females lacked professional team sports, television coverage, fame, and earning potential during the 1960s. During the early 1970s, however, the situation began to change. Again, the Astrodome was the site of a significant event, this time the 1973 "battle of the sexes," a tennis exhibition pitting one of the best women professionals, Billie Jean King, against former Wimbledon champion Bobby Riggs. Proclaiming himself "king of the male chauvinist pigs," Riggs had already defeated Margaret Court. But King was prepared for Riggs's "psyche job," and before a crowd of more than 30,000 in the Astrodome and some 50 million more watching on television, defeated the 55-year-old Riggs in straight sets. Although King championed the feminist cause in the match, she also saw the event as a victory for tennis, proving the sport could attract and excite large television audiences. Her efforts against Riggs and her excellence throughout 1973, including Wimbledon's singles, doubles, and mixed doubles championships, helped make King *Sports Illustrated*'s first female Sportsman of the Year.

As symbolically important as "the battle of the sexes" was Little League Baseball's inclusion of females. The change in rules came slowly, and females did not step into the batter's box until 1975. Leading the challenge was Maria Pepe, a Hoboken, New Jersey youth who, in 1972, tried out for and made the roster of the Young Democrats, a local team. Little League promptly revoked that team's charter. "In the good old days," commented James Michener in 1976, "that would have taken care of Miss Pepe, but those days are gone." Indeed, the American Civil Liberties Union, backed by considerable popular support and the New Jersey courts, made sure of the demise of "the good old days," and Little League reluctantly accepted the change. The dramatic stands taken by King and Pepe made clear to Americans that women wanted to participate in sports and that they were capable athletes even when competing against males.

It was an act of Congress in 1972, however, that mandated change. Title IX of the Educational Amendments Act, commonly referred to only as Title IX, stipulated that in every situation where federal funding was involved (which included civic and educational systems), equal monies must be allocated to men's and women's sports. Feminists immediately saw Title IX as a victory in the battle for equal wages, since female coaches would be more fairly compensated. Yet Title IX has had a much greater significance for athletes, enabling the transition from amateur individuals to (eventually) professional teams for women. The beginnings were dramatic. Enforcement of Title IX was virtually impossible until 1975, when the Department of Health, Education and Welfare declared that educational institutions must comply with the act by the summer of 1978. Gallup polls showed that this decree was wildly popular among students of both sexes. Female athletes began to select colleges based upon their compliance with Title IX. During the 1970s, the number of high school female athletes increased 431 percent, and the number of high schools offering sports for girls also increased. Basketball, for instance, was added to 12,761 schools by the end of the decade. Colleges and universities followed the trend, doubling the number of women's competitive sports available. Before Title IX, the average college allocated less than one percent of its budget to women's sports. By the end of the 1970s, this figure had increased to an average of 16.4 percent.

Seen from even another angle, Title IX was also a brilliant stroke of cold war policy that required no additional funds from the government but that ensured future victories on the battlegrounds of international athletics. Thus the 1999 victory of American women over China in soccer's World Cup is part of the Nixon administration legacy. In all, the significance of the era for women's sports, and consequently for sports fans, cannot be overstated.

ORGANIZING INDIVIDUAL SPORTS

Team sports underwent enormous changes during the Sixties, but the era was also important to the history of individual athletics. Established sports, such as marathon running, bicycling, and surfing, gained immense popularity. New sports arrived on the scene as well. Probably the most popular of these, Frisbee, did not truly exist until 1959, when it became a registered trademark of the Wham-O toy company. Initially, competition centered on a game called Guts, but in 1969 the first Ultimate game was played in New Jersey. In 1970 the University of Oregon offered the first college course in Frisbee, and in 1971 Sacramento State College offered a similar course, and for academic credit. By that time, Frisbee associations, complete with publications, had arisen, the largest being the International Frisbee Association in 1967.

It might seem odd to refer to Frisbee as an individual sport, given the early development of teams, leagues, and associations, but similar developments typified individual sports throughout the era. Jogging, for instance, may be classified as an individual sport, but thousands running in the New York City Marathon, an event requiring a large organizational apparatus and the cooperation of business and government, indicates that sport had entered an era of organized individuals. Even surfing, which simultaneously developed popular and countercultural followings during the 1960s, moved toward rigid codes at the competitive level in order to attract both fans and sponsors. Cycling too became better understood as a team sport. While the typical American cyclist road a Schwinn Varsity on a sidewalk, Americans were becoming increasingly involved in European professional racing, although rarely with great success. Yet the top American female, Audrey McElmury, won the World Championship in 1969. Perhaps of even greater significance to American cycling, McElmury began to train and coach in Boulder, Colorado, a move that helped make that city the center of U.S. bicycling and in the process brought Colorado corporate sponsorship from Red Zinger Tea and established the best-known of U.S. road racing events. Considering the enormous growth of cycling in the 1960s (3.7 million bicycles were bought in 1960, compared with 8.5 million in 1971), the sport needed such a center. The rising popularity of bicycling resulted in USOC development funds and, in time, a national velodrome in Boulder—yet another case of an individual sport becoming organized.

CREATING NEW HEROES

The enormous increase in sports participants in the era fostered a large and knowledgeable sport fan base. The combination of participants and spectators—a goodly part of the population—made sports a big business, a trend clearly understood by Roy Hofheinz, who placed restaurants throughout his Astrodome and made over a million dollars in 1965 by giving dollar-a-person tours of the new stadium. In another case, the Nike empire followed close upon the heels of Bill Bowerman's 1971 idea for the waffle-soled jogging shoe, greatly increasing endorsement dollars for athletes in the process. Less likely businesses also used sports personalities for profit—Miller introduced Lite Beer in 1973 and immediately linked it to sports and fitness.

But the most important business involved in sports was clearly network television. Professional and collegiate football, professional wrestling, golf, auto racing, tennis, baseball, basketball, and other sports all profited from developments in broadcasting technology. Certainly, the inherent quality of the sport and some memorable events were essential to success. But while, for instance, the Nicklaus/Palmer battles made for good golf, telephoto lenses, Technicolor, and "color" commentary made for good television, enlisting millions instead of hundreds in Arnie's Army. Thus TV producers, such as Roone Arledge, hold important places in sports history.

The dramatic role television played in the sports world was partly based upon the Sports Antitrust Broadcast Act, passed by Congress in the early 1960s. This act allowed professional sports leagues to sell "packages" to television networks. Professional football, in particular, was quick to see the benefits of televising games. The NFL sold a $4.6 million package to CBS in 1961 and more than trebled the amount of the contract in 1964. During that period, viewer ratings increased by 50 percent. The merger of the AFL and the NFL decreased competition for TV dollars among football franchises, and the benefits were immediately realized; the first year of Monday night football was sold to ABC for $8 million. Perhaps more important for football was the response of fans. Gallup polls showed that baseball was America's favorite spectator sport in 1960, with football a distant second. A 1972 poll, however, showed football as the clear front runner.

Major League Baseball responded by revamping the game to allow for more offense. A lowered pitcher's mound and the new designated hitter did increase run production, but it remained for a new generation of team owners in the 1970s, particularly cable baron Ted Turner, to reposition MLB in the TV market. Viewership increased in large local markets, where teams were able to take advantage of free agency and assure their audience of expensive star players. Teams in smaller markets, however, found themselves unable to compete with either the TV ratings or the free-agent purchasing power of franchises in New York and California. Problems arising from increasing discrepancies in wealth continue to divide team owners.

While some owners lamented changes in the game, baseball players greatly benefited from free agency and television dollars. In 1965, the average salary of a MLB player was $19,000, but that increased to more than $52,000 in 1976, and then to more than $500,000 by 1989. Other major league sports players saw similar monetary benefits. Such changes brought with them greater scrutiny and criticism, as players bargained for enormous salaries during the "malaise" of the 1970s.

Obviously, there could be a downside to a sports world dominated by TV, corporate sponsors, and highly paid athletes. In an early assessment, sports historian Richard Crepeau argued that the 1960s brought a decline in sports heroes and the beginning of sports personalities, citing the examples of Muhammad "The Greatest" Ali and "Broadway" Joe Namath. To some extent this argument remains valid, for increased media coverage has, if nothing else, proven that athletes sometimes have bad habits. On the other hand, not every athlete is a professional. Given the origin of the marathon and how completing it made one messenger a hero of legend, by that standard there must be tens of thousands of heroes throughout this country. Certainly Maria Pepe, who insisted on playing Little League, and Bill White, who hastened desegregation in the South, deserve to be remembered among them.

Sports spread throughout the United States during the 1960s and early 1970s. They included ever more diverse populations and regions, became better organized, and altered environments. They fostered more and newer types of heroes who, in some ways, became as important to the present as any other group of people in the era. Some monuments from the decade, such as the Astrodome, have been torn down or altered. Sports environments continue to change, as the latest trend in stadiums is away from the "cookie cutter" variety and toward an ideal of the pre-1960s playing fields. The legacy of the 1960s and early 1970s, however, cannot be so easily dismissed.

SOURCES

Chalip, Laurence, et al., eds. *National Sports Policies*. Westport, Conn.: Greenwood, 1996.

Collins, Bud and Zander Hollander, eds. *Bud Collins' Modern Encyclopedia of Tennis*. Detroit: Gale, 1994.

Davies, Richard O. *America's Obsession: Sports and Society Since 1945*. New York: Harcourt Brace College Publishers, 1994.

Hickok, Ralph. *The Encyclopedia of North American Sports History*. New York: Facts on File, 1992.

Johnson, Stancil E. D. *Frisbee*. New York: Workman, 1975.

Klatell, David A., and Norman Marcus. *Sports for Sale: Television, Money, and the Fans*. New York: Oxford University Press, 1988.

Michener, James A. *Sports in America*. New York: Random House, 1976.

Miller, Marvin. *A Whole Different Ball Game: The Inside Story of Baseball's New Deal*. New York: Carol, 1991.

Nye, Peter. *Hearts of Lions: The History of American Bicycle Racing*. New York: Norton, 1988.

Roberts, Randy, and James Olson. *Winning is the Only Thing: Sports in America Since 1945*. Baltimore: Johns Hopkins University Press, 1989.

Twombly, Wells. *200 Years of Sport in America: A Pageant of a Nation at Play*. New York: McGraw-Hill, 1976.

Will, George F. *Men at Work: The Craft of Baseball*. New York: Macmillan, 1990.

Art: Expanding Conceptions, Sites, and Audiences

Suzaan Boettger

The expansive sense of possibility that swept across America in the early 1960s fundamentally altered ideas about art and its relation to its consumers. As in so many other arenas in that period, but unlike any other phase of American art before or since, the decade produced an intense proliferation of new forms. And the innovations appeared with a rapidity that even in retrospect seems dizzying: in 1959, semiplanned group interactions with temporary sculptural installations called "Happenings"; in 1962, cartoon figuration and the monumentalization of grocery store merchandise in Pop Art; in 1965, the vertiginous geometric patterns of Op Art; in 1966, the overbearing austerity of Minimalism's unadorned blocks; in 1968, Postminimalism's reactive pliability and dispersal, one aspect of which was the large-scale earthen environments called "earthworks"; and across these years, an increasing emphasis on the conceptual element of art. Many of those movements have had a lasting impact on the look of art. Yet even more significant, these challenges to traditional formats altered assumptions about what "art" is, its proper relation to viewer/participants, the places where it may be sited, and who pays for it.

These bold experiments manifested on the visual culture front the expansive confidence of John F. Kennedy's identification of America as a pioneer of the "new frontier of the 1960s." That confidence galvanized younger artists' vigorous rejection of the avant-garde form of the 1940s and 1950s, Abstract Expressionism, which by the early 1960s had become official. Through exhibitions of large canvases by Willem de Kooning, Jackson Pollock, Barnett Newman, Mark Rothko, Clyfford Still, and others, organized by New York's Museum of Modern Art to circulate in Europe during 1958 and 1959 under the auspices of the United States Information Agency, contemporary American painting had reached a greater audience than ever before. In contrast to the gritty art being produced in those war-torn countries, these dramatic abstractions presented images of America's freedom of individual expression and robust culture. But for the New York art world, AbEx's fields of deep color and dynamic swaths and drips of paint had become not a mark of hard-won introspection but a clichéd sign of that, a convention.

Thus, when Roy Lichtenstein, Claes Oldenburg, James Rosenquist, and Andy Warhol glorified the bright packaging of common commodities, inane comic strips, and mythic movie stars, they rejected abstract painting and its evocation of interiority and spirituality. Instead, these "pop" artists (that is, imagists of "pop"ular culture), with producers of Photorealist painting, gave a fine-art face to America's satisfactions with prosperity. Not incidentally, these easily identifiable, emotionally unambiguous images appealed to beginner, newly rich collectors of newly fashionable *American* contemporary art.

Yet simultaneously, another fun form prominent in the first half of the Sixties implicitly rejected commodification: "Happenings." Announcing in the October 1958 *Art News* an alternative "Legacy of Jackson Pollock," Allan Kaprow stated, "Pollock left us at the point where we must become preoccupied with and even dazzled by the space and objects of our everyday life. . . . Not satisfied with the *suggestion*, through paint of our other senses, we shall utilize the specific substances of sight, sound, movement, people, odors, touch." Kaprow, as well as Jim Dine, Red Grooms, and Robert Whitman, orchestrated events that mixed installations of painting and sculpture with lightly scripted group acts that allowed for chance and spontaneous participation. First performing in front of an audience in a gallery, they soon accommodated their draw of large crowds by moving to downtown outdoor sites.

The artistic medium where that sense of broad experimentation so endemic to the Sixties was particularly displayed was sculpture. In the hierarchy of artistic media, sculpture has traditionally been ranked, as Charles Baudelaire noted in his review of the Ecole des Beaux Arts' 1846 Salon, as "nothing else but a *complementary* art . . . a humble associate of painting and architecture." In the 1960s that custom was turned on its head. In the spring of 1966, New York's Jewish Museum highlighted the new abstract, pared-down steel or wood constructions by linking work by forty-two sculptors under the exhibition title "Primary Structures." Styles ranged from the dynamic equilibrium of David Smith's jumbled *Cubi* arrangements to the huge cantilevered thrusts of Robert Grosvenor to Carl Andre's long, floor-bound line of plain, unattached bricks. Ronald Bladen and architect/artist Tony Smith were prominent in this genre, as were the sculptor/critics Donald Judd and Robert Morris. Works by the younger generation showed no evidence of the hand of the artist, and in fact were often industrially fabricated. The very austerity of these forms led them to be termed "Minimal Art," but that emphasized only the most obvious aspect, their look. More radical was these reductive works' promotion of a shift in the observer's attention from a discrete object to its interaction with the configuration of its site, as well as to the viewer's own relative size and position. In effect, the viewer became more of an active participant in generating the experience of the work, which was beyond the perceptual, a more holistic experience of object, space, and environment.

Within the social milieu of sit-ins, civil rights protests, and the antiwar movement, these blunt, "environmental"-scale sculptures could also be taken as oppositional. "It's really anti-collector, anti-museum art," declared curator Kynaston McShine regarding "Primary Structures" (*New York Times*, April 24, 1966). "In it there's implied social criticism. Most of it is designed for indoor use but who could house works of this scale? It may in fact provoke hostility in the viewer." Actually, after the customary initial bewilderment, private and public collections extended the Sixties' enthusiasm for the new and the outrageous to these mammoth constructions, finding new places to "house" them in atriums, plazas, courtyards, and gardens. This effort was aided by two federal programs initiated in the mid-1960s to commission architecturally scaled work. The General Services Administration's "Fine Arts in New Buildings Program," begun in 1963 in response to a report requested by President John F. Kennedy on federal architecture, commissioned the creation of large tapestries, mosaics, murals, and sculpture. (The government suspended the program in 1966 due to "the economic pressures of the Vietnam War" and reactivated it in 1973 as the GSA Art-in-Architecture Program.) The National Endowment for the Arts, founded in 1965, established the Art in Public Places Program early in 1967 to award matching funds to nonprofit organizations for the purchase and installation of works of art in publicly accessible spaces.

In the same *New York Times* interview, McShine also addressed artists' new professionalism and their intention to rethink their medium. He saw the young sculptors of the Sixties as "hip, sophisticated, articulate. Most are university-bred. They've read philosophy, have a keen sense of history, and know that they're supposed to be reading too. Their art doesn't answer questions, it asks them. Mostly, questions how to go about making sculpture." Around this time this reflexive attitude soon flipped over into Conceptual Art, which diminished the material properties of art and bolstered the other part of the equation, the idea. For Joseph Kosuth, creating art became intellectual research: his own works were photostats of dictionary definitions, documentary photographs, and "information rooms" (books splayed on exhibition tables). Lawrence Weiner affixed earnestly indecipherable propositions directly on a wall in a line or so of type; John Baldessari withdrew the aesthetic component by posting a certificate that he had cremated his earlier paintings, displaying the repeatedly handwritten line, "I will not make any more boring art," or using stock photography scenes with anonymous figures, their faces obscured by colored disks. Serving as purgatives for a commercialized culture, these puritanical investigations aimed to thwart viewers' desires for sensory pleasure, emotional engagement, and portable collectibles.

Conceptual Art's increasing prominence toward the end of the decade corresponded to the broadening influence of the anti–Vietnam War movement, which led many to dispute the authority of governmental, academic, and corporate institutions. Yet it was only with the founding of the Art Workers Coalition in early 1969 that power structures in the art world itself began to be recognized. The AWC sponsored group protests of museum trustees' links between culture and politics and the initial omission of black artists from the Museum of Modern Art's Martin Luther King Jr. memorial exhibition. Gender bias in exhibition rosters was rarely addressed before the formation in 1969 of the Women Artists in Revolution (WAR) and in 1970, the AWC Ad Hoc Women Artists Committee. In the 1970s, the feminist art movement became an influential presence. Nationalistic chauvinism was typical of postwar American artists both eager to be "free from weight of European culture" (as the artist and intellectual Barnett Newman had urged in "The Sublime is Now" in 1948) and avid for recognition in Europe's capitals of modernism. Also, New York's dominance of the American art world was simply taken for granted. San Francisco, Los Angeles, and Chicago possessed substantial communities of artists, each displaying a regional sensibility distinct from one another and from Manhattan's. But only in New York City was there the critical mass of museums, galleries, collectors, publications and critics sufficient to catapult local artists to international attention and economic security. A rare example of geographical inclusiveness was evinced in the massive survey exhibition "American Sculpture of the Sixties" in the spring of 1967, but this was clearly prompted by its "outsider" point of origin: the Los Angeles County Museum of Art. The West Coast perspective encompassed not only New Yorkers' exhibits in "Primary Structures" but also California work such as Edward Kienholz's pungent tableaux, Bruce Connor's funk assemblages, and John McCracken's luminous fiberglass planarity. Expansive also in media, the show included the ceramic expressionism of Peter Voulkos and the pristine, perverse wood laminations by Chicagoan H. C. Westermann.

If the spectacle of a jumble of Warhol's gigantic boxes of Brillo cleaning pads typified art in the early Sixties, by the end of the decade the sculptural material engulfing the art world was dirt. From 1966, Eva Hesse's pendulous sculptures of loosely arranged rope, netting, and/or rubber tubing presented transitional work. As the force of gravity emphasized natural processes of hanging or sagging, Hesse's piece and those by Morris, Richard Sierra, Barry LeVa, and others refused the formal rigidity of Minimalism and came to be called Process Art or Postminimalism. In 1968, Robert Smithson brought intricate bins of rocks indoors, and Walter De Maria and Morris aggressively displayed piles of dirt. Carl Andre, Michael Heizer, and Dennis Oppenheim had recently made work outdoors in wilderness or countryside terrains. Smithson's grand *Spiral Jetty* (1970), a landfill 15 feet wide by 1,500 feet long extending from the north shore of Utah's Great Salt Lake, is often cited as an icon of Sixties idealism. Locating this work distant from any art community, using Caterpillar trucks for the primitive technique of mound making, and shaping it as a mystical mandala situated in water of an eerie red color (caused by microbacteria, red algae, and brine shrimp in saline water) that one was supposed to experience by walking toward its center "point of beginning" exemplifies visionary creativity.

Society's increased concern for the natural environment prompted attention to the Earthworkers, but such massive rearrangements of land actually dramatized the period's ambivalence, not only about the status of culture but also about proper behavior in nature. These artists' putative refusal of commercialization depended upon the patronage of collectors and dealers who themselves benefited from the purchase and sale of the artists' ongoing gallery-scale work. Earth art can be taken as the most extreme instance of a 1960s motivation to counter dominant high culture. This dialectical stance unites it with the preceding avant garde's oppositions to the "Academy," except that earlier artists sought to supplant established styles with their own approaches to fine art. Pop Art circumvented such internecine conflicts, embraced the increasing domination of the marketplace, and produced legible images appealing to wits and nitwits alike. It is to the influence of Pop Art and its parallel 1960s democratizing forms of fashion, design, music, and social mores that we can attribute the ensuing erosion of high/low cultural distinctions.

SOURCES

Banes, Sally. *Greenwich Village 1963: Avant-Garde Performance and the Effervescent Body.* Durham, N.C.: Duke University Press, 1993.

Battcock, Gregory, ed. *Minimal Art.* Introduction by Anne M. Wagner. 1968. Reprint, Berkeley: University of California Press, 1995.

Boettger, Suzaan. *Earthworks: Art and the Landscape of the Late Sixties.* Berkeley: University of California Press, 2001.

Crow, Thomas. *The Rise of the Sixties: American and European Art in the Era of Dissent.* New York: Perspectives / Harry N. Abrams, 1996.

Lippard, Lucy. *Six Years: The Dematerialization of the Art Object from 1966 to 1972.* 1973. Reprint, Berkeley: University of California Press, 1997.

Livingstone, Marco, ed. *Pop Art*. London: Royal Academy of Arts and Weidenfield and Nicolson, 1991.

Sandler, Irving. *American Art of the 1960s*. New York: Harper and Row, 1988.

The Studio Museum in Harlem. *Tradition and Conflict: Images of a Turbulent Decade, 1963–1973*. New York: The Studio Museum in Harlem, 1985.

Wetenhall, John. "Camelot's Legacy to Public Art: Aesthetic Ideology in the New Frontier." In *Critical Issues in Public Art*, edited by Harrie Senie and Sally Webster. New York: HarperCollins, 1992, 142–157.

PART V

Special Sections

Portrait of a Nation

POPULATION

	World Population	U.S. Population	U.S. as percentage of World Population
1930	2 billion	123,077,000	6.15%
1960	3 billion	180,700,000	6.0%
1970	3.63 billion	204,900,000	5.6%
2000	6.08 billion	275,142,741	4.5%

Geographic Center of U.S. Population

Number of People per Square Mile of Land

	U.S. Total	Northeast	North Central	South	West
1950	42.6	241.2	58.8	53.7	11.5
1960	50.6	273.4	68.6	62.8	16.0
1970	57.5	300.4	75.2	71.9	19.9

U.S. total population density per square mile in 1998: 76.4

Median Age

1940	29.0
1950	30.2
1960	29.5
1970	28.1
1999	35.5

Median Age at First Marriage

	1940	1950	1960	1970	1996
Bride	21.5	20.3	20.3	20.8	24.8
Groom	24.3	22.8	22.8	23.2	27.1

Percentage of women, age 25–29, who had never been married

1970	11
1996	38

Percentage of men, age 25–29, who had never been married

1970	19
1996	52

Marriage and Divorce Rates

	Marriage	Divorce
1950	166.4	10.3
1960	148.0	9.2
1970	140.2	14.9
1996	81.5	19.5

Marriage rate per 1,000 unmarried women, age 15–44
Divorce rate per 1,000 married women, age 15–44

Percentage of adults, age 18 and older, who were married
1970	72
1996	60

Number of cohabiting couples
1960	17,000
1970	143,000

Percentage of adults, age 18 and older, who were divorced
1970	3
1996	10

State with highest divorce rate per 1,000 population in 1970: Oklahoma, 6.6%*

State with lowest divorce rate per 1,000 population in 1970: New York, New Jersey, and North Dakota, tied at 1.5%

* *Information for six states, including Nevada, not included.*

Number of Births per 1,000 Women, Age 15–44

	Total	White	African American and Other Non-White
1940	79.9	77.1	102.4
1950	106.2	102.3	137.3
1960	118.0	113.2	153.6
1965	96.6	91.4	133.9
1966	91.3	86.4	125.9
1967	87.6	83.1	119.8
1968	85.7	81.5	114.9

Birth rate to 15–19-year-old women
1960	89.1%
1968	66.1%

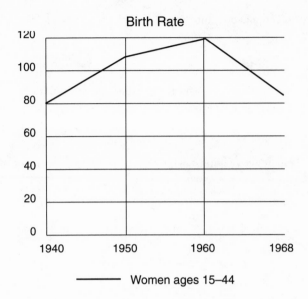

Birth Rate

——— Women ages 15–44

Births for unmarried women
(as percentage of all births)

Year	Percentage
1950	3.9%
1960	5.3%
1965	7.7%
1970	10.7%
1975	14.2%
1993	31.0%

Average size of family

Year	Size
1960	3.67
1970	3.62
1998	3.18

Favorite Baby Names
1900: John and Mary
1998: Michael and Kaitlyn

	1960		1970
Boy	*Girl*	*Boy*	*Girl*
David	Mary	Michael	Jennifer
Michael	Susan	David	Lisa
John	Maria	John	Kimberly
James	Karen	James	Michelle
Robert	Lisa	Robert	Angela
Mark	Linda	Christopher	Maria
William	Donna	William	Amy
Richard	Patricia	Mark	Melissa
Thomas	Debra	Richard	Mary
Steven	Deborah	Brian	Tracy

As compiled by the Social Security Administration.

Names that appear on both 1970 and 1998 list: Michael and Christopher.

Attitudes Toward Sex

Percentage of men (25 years and under, with at least one year of college) who want to marry a virgin, according to the 1948 Kinsey Report: 50.7%
Percentage of college men who want to marry a virgin, according to a 1970 Gallup Poll: 24

Percentage of Americans in 1969 who said it was wrong for a man and woman to have sex relations before marriage: 68
Percentage of women students at the University of Kansas in 1964 who said it was "morally or ethically right" for a couple who were not engaged to have sex relations: 2
Percentage of teenagers in 1966 (according to *Look* magazine, September. 20, 1966) who believed it was okay for a couple to "live together" if they were in love: 45

Percentage of Americans in 1968 who believed that life today "in terms of morals" was getting better: 8; was getting worse: 78

Total amount spent on contraceptives in the United States in 1960: $200 million

Amount of that total spent on condoms: $150 million

Cost of birth control pills, per month, when they were introduced for contraceptive use in 1960: $11 ($61.12 in 1999 dollars, or approximately $3 each pill)

Number of American women "on the Pill" in 1969: 8.5 million

Percentage of American women who disapproved of the Pill being prescribed to unmarried college students in 1965, according to Gallup Poll: 77

Year that the General Assembly of the Southern Presbyterian Church declared that it was not sinful to have marital relations without procreative intent: 1960

Year that Supreme Court ruled that unmarried persons could not be denied birth control: 1972

SOURCES FOR "POPULATION" SECTION

Associated Women Students Survey. Archives, University of Kansas.

Gallup, George H. *The Gallup Poll: Public Opinion 1935–1971.* Vol. 3. New York: Random House, 1972.

Information Please Entertainment Almanac. http://www.infoplease.lycos.com

Kinsey, Alfred C. *Sexual Behavior in the Human Male.* Philadelphia: W. B. Saunders, 1948.

U.S. Bureau of the Census. *Historical Statistics of the United States, Colonial Times to 1970, Bicentennial Edition.* Washington, D.C., 1975.

U.S. Bureau of the Census. *Statistical Abstract of the United States: 1999.* Washington, D.C., 1999.

U.S. Bureau of the Census. *Statistical Abstract of the United States: 1973.* Washington, D.C., 1973.

RACE AND ETHNICITY

U.S. Population, by Race

1960

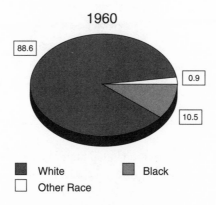

88.6

0.9

10.5

■ White   ■ Black
□ Other Race

1999

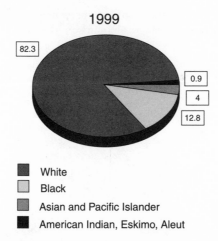

82.3

0.9

4

12.8

■ White
□ Black
■ Asian and Pacific Islander
■ American Indian, Eskimo, Aleut

Statistics on Hispanic origin were not collected in 1960; approximately 11.5% of Americans were of Hispanic origin in 1999. Hispanics in the above charts may belong to any racial category.

Ethnic Origins of Americans

	1940	1960	1970
White/European American	89.8%	88.6%	87.6%
Black/African American	9.8%	10.5%	11.1%
Indian/Native American	0.2%	0.29%	0.3%
Japanese	0.096%	0.25%	0.29%
Chinese	0.058%	0.13%	0.21%
Filipino	0.034%	0.09%	0.16%
Other	0.03%	0.12%	0.35%

"Other" includes Asian Indians, Hawaiians, Aleuts, Koreans, Polynesians, Eskimos, Indonesians, and all others not specified. Racial and ethnic categories are partially conflated in these statistics.

Rate of immigration to the United States (per 1,000 population)

1901–1910	10.4
1941–1950	0.7
1961–1970	1.7

"Foreign Stock" Americans as a percentage of population
("foreign stock" refers to those who are foreign-born or who have at least one foreign-born parent)

1900	48
1960	18
1970	15.5

Source of immigration to the United States, 1961–70

Europe	33.8%
Americas	51.7%
Asia	12.8%

Percentage of Japanese-Americans in the United States who lived outside Hawaii and California in 1970: 28

Puerto Ricans as percentage of New York City population in 1969: 11

Number of Chinese Americans living in Atlanta in 1970: 589

Percentage of Americans who claimed English as their first language in 1970: 79

Percentage who claimed Spanish as their first language: 4

Percentage who claimed Yiddish: 0.8

Attitudes Toward Race

1962   The Crayola Crayon company renames its "Flesh" crayon "Peach."
1965   The *Amos 'n' Andy* TV show is withdrawn from syndication in the United States.
1967   The New York *Amsterdam News*, the most influential African-American newspaper in the United States, announced that the term "Negro" would no longer be used in its pages.

States with law against interracial marriages in 1965: Alabama, Arkansas, Delaware, Florida, Georgia, Maryland, Mississippi, Missouri, Oklahoma, Louisiana, Kentucky, North Carolina, South Carolina, Tennessee, Texas, Virginia, West Virginia, Wyoming.
Percentage of Americans who approved of marriage between a "white and nonwhite" in 1968: 20
  between Catholic and Protestant: 63
  between Jews and non-Jews: 59
Percentage of all Americans in 1961 who said they approved of the Supreme Court ruling against racial segregation in public schools: 62
Percentage of white southerners who approved: 24

Percentage of all white Americans in 1966 who said they would not move if "colored people" came to live next door: 66
Percentage who said they would not move if "colored people moved in great numbers" to their neighborhood: 30

SOURCES FOR "RACE AND ETHNICITY" SECTION

Bernardo, Stephanie. *The Ethnic Almanac*. Garden City, N.Y.: Doubleday and Company, 1981.
Carnes, Mark C., ed. *American History*. New York: Macmillan Library Reference, 1996.
Gallup, George H. *The Gallup Poll: Public Opinion 1935–1971*. Vol. 3. New York: Random House, 1972.
Hirschfelder, Arlene and Martha Kreipe de Montano. *The Native American Almanac*. New York: Prentice Hall General Reference, 1993.
Information Please Entertainment Almanac. http://www.infoplease.lycos.com
Trager, James. *The People's Chronology: A Year-by-Year Record of Human Events from Prehistory to the Present*. New York: Henry Holt and Company, 1992 and 1994.

U.S. Bureau of the Census. *Historical Statistics of the United States, Colonial Times to 1970, Bicentennial Edition.* Washington, D.C., 1975.

U.S. Bureau of the Census. *Statistical Abstract of the United States: 1999.* Washington, D.C., 1999.

U.S. Bureau of the Census. *Statistical Abstract of the United States: 1973.* Washington, D.C., 1973.

1970 Reader's Digest Almanac and Yearbook. Pleasantville, N.Y.: The Reader's Digest Association, 1970.

HEALTH

Life Expectancy for a Child Born In:

	Male	*Female*
1940	60.8	68.2
1950	65.6	71.1
1960	66.6	73.1
1970	67.1	74.6
1996	73.9	79.1

Average number of visits per year to a physician
1971: 4.3 for men; 5.5 for women
1996: 4.9 for men; 6.9 for women

Measles cases reported in 1962: 400,000
Measles cases reported in 1968, as a result of the Endus vaccine: 22,231

Civilian cases of gonorrhea
| 1960 | 258,933 |
| 1970 | 600,072 |

Decrease in rate of diseases among Native Americans, 1955–1971
Tuberculosis	80%
Syphilis	75%
Dysentery	90%

Death Rates
per 1000 population of specified group

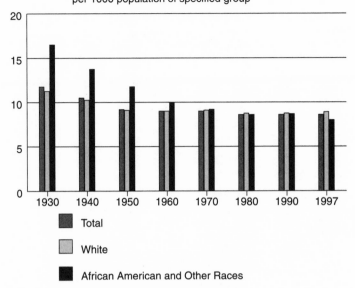

■ Total

▨ White

■ African American and Other Races

National health expenditures as a percentage of the Gross National
Product (GNP)

1950	4.6
1960	5.2
1965	5.9
1970	7.1
1971	7.5

Average Hospital Expense per Patient per Day

	Current Dollars	*1999 Dollars*
1950	$7.98	$54.24
1960	$6.46	$91.45
1970	$53.95	$238.31
1997	$1,033.00	$1,067.37

Pounds of tranquilizers sold in the United States in 1969: 1,204 thousand

Admissions to mental hospitals
(number per 1,000 people)

1950	2.0
1960	2.3
1970	3.3

Percent of Americans who had safety belts in their cars in 1962: 12%

Calories available per person per day

1960	3,140
1970	3,300

Pounds of beef eaten each year by an average American

1960	85.1
1970	113.7
1997	63.8

Pounds of butter eaten each year by an average American

1960	7.5
1970	5.3
1997	4.2

Pounds of fresh vegetables eaten each year by an average American,

1960	105.9
1970	99.5
1997	185.6

Gallons of beer drunk each year by the average adult

1960	24.02
1970	28.55
1997	33.9

Sugar as a percentage of Lucky Charms, a new breakfast cereal introduced in 1964: 50.4

Percentage of U.S. population with fluoridated water

1950	1.0%
1960	22.9%
1970	41.1%

Cigarettes

1958
Joseph Cullman III, head of Philip Morris: "The health scare is receding—the worst is over."

1960
Rise in unit sales of cigarettes, 1950–1960: 30%

1961
U.S. cigarette companies spend $115 million on television advertising.

1962
Philip Morris launches the Marlboro Country advertising campaign: "From the canyons of New York to the canyons of Colorado . . . a man's world of flavor in this cigarette."

JFK, asked in May 1962 what his administration was going to do to address concerns about smoking and health: "That matter is sensitive enough and the stock market is in sufficient difficulty without my giving you an answer which is not based on complete information, which I don't have."

Percentage of Americans who believe smoking causes lung cancer, according to a Gallup survey: 38

1964
The Surgeon General's 150,000-word report linking cigarette smoking to lung cancer and other diseases was released to 200 members of the press in the State Department auditorium on Saturday, January 11, 1964. Saturday was chosen to minimize the effect on the stock market.

Approximate number of Americans who smoke cigarettes: 70 million

Percentage of Americans 21 and older who smoke cigarettes: 42.5

Stockholders in tobacco companies: 300,000

Percentage of U.S. congressional districts in which tobacco was grown: 12

Percent of North Carolina's income from farm commodities that came from tobacco: 47%

Howard Cullman, president of the Tobacco Merchants Association, in response to the Surgeon General's Report: "We don't accept the idea that there are harmful agents in tobacco."

Years since President Johnson had quit smoking: 9 (He quit in 1955, following a major heart attack.)

Low-tar cigarettes were introduced but did not become popular until the 1970s.

1965
Congress orders caution label placed on cigarette packages.

Percentage of Americans who believe cancer is the worst ailment that can happen to them: 62

1966
Congress votes to send 600 million cigarettes to flood victims in India.

1967
American Tobacco launches new cigarette, aimed at women, with the slogan: Cigarettes are like girls. The best ones are rich and thin.

American Tobacco at 1967 annual meeting: "No clinical or biological evidence has been produced which demonstrates how cigarettes relate to cancer or any other disease in human beings."

Federal Trade Commission releases first tar-and-nicotine report.

1968
Percentage of Americans who believe that cigarettes cause lung cancer, according to a Gallup survey: 71

Introduction of Virginia Slims (100mm long, 23mm circumference when most ultra-long brands were 25mm). Aimed at women, it offered the long-lasting slogan "You've come a long way, baby."

The FTC estimates that every American home with a television is exposed to 800 cigarette commercials each year.

Filter tips dominate the cigarette market.

1969
Forty percent of American adults in a Gallup Poll said they'd smoked in the past week.

Ralph Nader asks the FAA to ban smoking on airplanes; Pan American Airlines creates first nonsmoking section.

1970
Percentage of Americans 21 and older who smoke cigarettes: 36.3

1971

Cigarette commercials are banned from television, beginning at midnight, January 1. Philip Morris ran a 90-second Marlboro commercial, scheduled to end precisely at midnight.

1972

New Surgeon General's report on the hazards of second-hand cigarette smoke.

Number of cigarettes sold	
1964	524 billion (215 packs/adult)
1967	572.6 billion (210 packs/adult)
1968	571.1 billion (205 packs/adult)
1971	547.2 billion

SOURCES FOR "HEALTH" SECTION

Gallup, George H. *The Gallup Poll: Public Opinion 1935–1971.* Vol. 3. New York: Random House, 1972.

Hirschfelder, Arlene and Martha Kreipe de Montano. *The Native American Almanac.* New York: Prentice Hall General Reference, 1993.

Kluger, Richard. *Ashes to Ashes.* New York: A. A. Knopf, 1996.

Tate, Cassandra. *Cigarette Wars.* New York: Oxford University Press, 1999.

"Tobacco Timeline." http://www.tomacco.com.

Trager, James. *The People's Chronology: A Year-by-Year Record of Human Events from Prehistory to the Present.* New York: Henry Holt and Company, 1992 and 1994.

U.S. Bureau of the Census. *Historical Statistics of the United States, Colonial Times to 1970, Bicentennial Edition.* Washington, D.C., 1975.

U.S. Bureau of the Census. *Statistical Abstract of the United States: 1999.* Washington, D.C., 1999.

U.S. Bureau of the Census. *Statistical Abstract of the United States: 1973.* Washington, D.C., 1973.

EDUCATION

Years of School Completed (Median) by Persons 25 Years and Older

	1960	1970
All	10.6	12.2
White men	10.7	12.2
White women	11.2	12.2
Black men	7.7	9.6
Black women	8.6	10.2
Urban Native American men	NA	11.2
Rural Native American men	NA	8.7

Years of school completed (median) by African Americans who were age 25–29 in 1970: 12.2

Percentage of Americans 25 years and older who had not
graduated high school

1940	75.5
1970	44.8

Completed Four Years of High School
For persons 25 years and older.

	Total	White	Black	Hispanic
1960	41.1%	43.2%	20.1%	NA
1965	49.0%	51.3%	27.2%	NA
1970	52.3%	54.5%	31.4%	32.1%
1998	82.8%	83.7%	76.0%	55.5%

Percentage of all Hispanics 25 and older who had completed 4 years of high
school or more in 1970: 32.1
Percentage of people of Mexican origin: 24.2

Percentage of African Americans 25 years and older who had
five years or less schooling

1940	42
1970	15

State with highest percentage of high school graduates in 1970: Utah (67%)
State with lowest percentage of high school graduates in 1970: South Carolina (38%)

Percentage of Americans age 14 or older who were illiterate in 1960: 2.2

Percentage of African Americans who were illiterate
1960	7.5
1970	3.6

Percentage of black students attending integrated schools
in the 17 southern states
1960	6.4
1970	84.3

Parochial school enrollment
1964	5.6 million (all-time high figure)
1974	3.5 million

Pupil–teacher ratio in elementary schools
1960	29.4 students per teacher
1970	24.6 students per teacher
1996	18.4 students per teacher

Money spent on education (public and private) as a percentage of GNP
1930	3.1
1960	5.1
1970	7.5

Percentage of all public high-school students enrolled in a
foreign-language course
1970	28.4
1994	40.6

Percent of public high-school students studying Spanish
1970	13.6
1994	27.2

Higher Education

Completed Four Years of College

	Total	White	Black	Hispanic
1960	7.7%	8.1%	3.1%	NA
1965	9.4%	9.9%	4.7%	NA
1970	10.7%	11.3%	4.4%	4.5%
1998	24.4%	25.0%	14.7%	11.0%

Of persons 25 years and older; "White" refers to whites who were 25 and older.

Recent High-School Graduates Attending College

	Total	Male	Female
1960	45.1%	54.0%	37.9%
1970	51.8%	55.2%	48.5%
1997	67.0%	63.5%	70.3%

Number of colleges and universities
(institutions of higher education)

1930	1,409
1960	2,008
1970	2,525
1995	3,706

Enrollment in institutions of higher education

1930	1,101,000
1960	3,216,000
1970	7,136,000
1995	14,261,800

Average verbal SAT score

1967	543
1990	500

Average math SAT score

1967	516
1990	501

(On each SAT section, minimum score 200, maximum score 800)

Average composite ACT score

1970	19.9
1998	21.0

(Minimum ACT score 1; maximum score 36)

African Americans as percentage of those taking ACT

1970	4
1998	11

Percentage of college freshmen who had an "A" average in high school

1970	16
1998	33

Percentage of college freshmen who applied to 3 or more colleges

1970	15
1998	37

Percentage of female college freshmen in 1970 who wanted to earn an advanced degree: 41

Percentage of college freshmen in 1970 who agreed that "the activities of married women are best confined to home and family": 48

Number of doctorates earned

1940	3,000
1960	10,000
1970	30,000

Professional Degrees Awarded

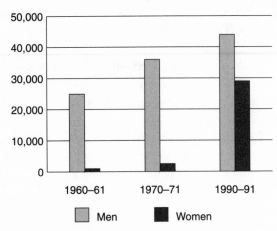

Percentage of female college faculty in 1969 who were married: 47

Percentage of male college faculty who were married: 87

Percentage of college faculty in 1969 who were under 40 years old: 49.7

Percentage of 60,028 faculty members surveyed by Carnegie Commission in 1969 who identified themselves as radical: 5.1

who identified themselves as conservative: 27.7

who identified themselves as liberal: 41.5

CAMPUS UNREST

The "Five Major Student Gripes" of 1967, by Order of Frequency

1. Not enough student participation in administration
2. Hours for women in dormitories
3. Housing regulations
4. Dissatisfaction with food in dormitories
5. War in Vietnam

Based on a poll of the 41 largest (enrollment) universities conducted by the University of Missouri; 25 universities responded.

Percentage of Americans in 1969 who said college students who break laws while participating in a demonstration should be expelled: 82

Percentage of college students in 1969 who believed that students should have a greater say in the running of colleges: 81

Percentage of the general public: 25

Percentage of Americans in 1969 who said there was a "major difference in the point of view of young people and older people today": 73

Percentage of faculty in Carnegie Commission survey who said that radical student activists were a threat to academic freedom: 83

Percentage of science, engineering, and agriculture faculty who disapproved of student activism: 72

Percentage of English faculty who supported an immediate withdrawal or deescalation of the Vietnam War: 73

Percentage of engineering faculty who supported a military escalation of the war: 64

SOURCES FOR "EDUCATION" SECTION

Andersen, Charles J., compiler. *Fact Book on Higher Education*, 1997 edition. Phoenix, Ariz.: Oryx Press, 1998.

Heineman, Kenneth J. *Campus Wars*. New York: New York University Press, 1993.

Hirschfelder, Arlene and Martha Kreipe de Montano, *The Native American Almanac*. New York: Prentice Hall General Reference, 1993.

Taeuber, Cynthia M. *Statistical Handbook of Women in America*. 2nd edition. Phoenix, Ariz.: Oryx Press, 1996.

U.S. Bureau of the Census. *Historical Statistics of the United States, Colonial Times to 1970, Bicentennial Edition*. Washington, D.C., 1975.

U.S. Bureau of the Census. *Statistical Abstract of the United States: 1999*. Washington, D.C., 1999.

U.S. Bureau of the Census. *Statistical Abstract of the United States: 1973* (94th edition). Washington, D.C., 1973.

"Student Protest" files. Archives, University of Kansas.

1970 Reader's Digest Almanac and Yearbook. Pleasantville, N.Y.: The Reader's Digest Association, 1970.

CRIME

Victims of Crime in 1965
(per 100,000 population of specific group)

	Total	Rape	Robbery	Aggravated Assault	Burglary
African American	2,592	82	204	347	1,306
White	1,860	22	58	186	822

Average annual increase in the total crime rate, 1960–1970: 9%

Crimes Committed

1963	1993
1 murder/hour	1 murder/28 minutes
1 forcible rape/32 minutes	1 forcible rape/6 minutes
1 auto theft/minute	1 auto theft/29 seconds

Homicide rate
(per 100,000 population age 16 and older)

1930	12.4
1940	8.6
1950	7.3
1960	7.0
1970	11.0
1996	7.9

State with highest crime rate
(per 100,000 inhabitants)

1963	Nevada
1993	Washington, DC

State with lowest crime rate
(per 100,000 inhabitants)

1963	Mississippi
1993	West Virginia

Percentage of those arrested for murder who were under 18 of age

1963	7.8
1993	16.2

Total number of inmates in federal and state prisons

1950	166,123
1960	212,953
1970	196,429
1997	1,197,590

Rate of imprisonment
(per 100,000 population)

1950	110.3
1970	96.7
1960	118.6
1997	445.0

Percent of Americans answering a 1965 Gallup Poll who believed there was police brutality in their area: 9%

Arrests for drug offenses

1960	31,486
1970	272,465

Percentage of those arrested for drug offenses who were under 18 years of age

1960	5
1970	20

Number of handguns produced in the United States

1960	475,000
1969	2,840,000

What do you think is the cause of "lack of respect for law and the increase of crime in the United States today"? (Gallup Poll, October 14, 1964)

Parents, home life to blame	41%
Need for tougher law enforcement	18%
Defiance, lack of respect on part of teenagers	9%
Young people are spoiled, have too much	6%
Moral deterioration of society	6%

Which is more to blame for crime and lawlessness—the individual or society? (Gallup Poll, December 3, 1970)

Society	58%
Individual	35%
No opinion	7%

SOURCES FOR "CRIME" SECTION

Durham, Jennifer L. *Crime in America: A Reference Handbook*. Santa Barbara, Calif.: ABC–CLIO, 1996

Gallup, George H. *The Gallup Poll: Public Opinion 1935–1971*. Vol. 3. New York: Random House, 1972.

U.S. Bureau of the Census. *Historical Statistics of the United States, Colonial Times to 1970, Bicentennial Edition*. Washington, D.C., 1975.

U.S. Bureau of the Census. *Statistical Abstract of the United States: 1999*. Washington, D.C., 1999.

U.S. Bureau of the Census. *Statistical Abstract of the United States: 1973*. Washington, D.C., 1973.

TRAVEL AND RECREATION

(See also Arts and Entertainment, Sports)

Percentage of Americans who had "been up in an airplane" (according to a Gallup Poll) in 1961: 48

Airline passengers
1950	19 million
1960	62 million
1970	169 million
1997	575 million

Successful hijacking attempts on U.S. registered aircraft
1960	0
1969	33

Total number of passports issued
1950	300,000
1960	853,000
1970	2,219,000

Number of American travelers whose first destination was Africa
1960	8,000
1969	20,000

Number of American travelers whose first destination was Europe
1960	670,000
1969	1,460,000

Number of U.S. mass transit rides
1945	23 billion
1967	8 billion

Percentage of world's automobiles that were in use in the United States, 1963: 66

United States population as percentage of world population, 1963: 6

Average speed per hour on rural interstate highways
1970	63.8 mph
1993	60.8 mph

Percentage of vehicles exceeding 65 mph
1970	44
1980	7
1993	24

Number of citations written for speeding on interstate highways (annually)
1970	200,000
1993	6,433,000

Amount spent on recreation by Americans
1950	$11 million
1960	$18 million
1970	$40 million

Percentage of Americans 12 years old and over in 1972 who
went camping in a developed camp ground:	11
camped in a wilderness area:	5
went sailing:	3
went horseback riding:	5
went bicycling:	10
went fishing:	24
played tennis:	5
played golf:	5
went driving for pleasure:	34
went picnicking:	47

Number of golf courses in the United States
1960	6,385
1970	10,188

Number of bowling lanes (tenpin) in the United States
1960	107,908
1970	141,492

Number of movie theaters in the United States

1960	16,000
1970	14,000

Number of major symphony orchestras in the United States

1960	25
1970	28

Attendance at concerts by major symphony orchestras

1955	5 million
1970	9 million

Total number of persons who fished and/or hunted

1960	30 million
1970	36 million

SOURCES FOR "TRANSPORTATION AND RECREATION" SECTION

Gallup, George H. *The Gallup Poll: Public Opinion 1935–1971*. Vol. 3. New York: Random House, 1972.

Trager, James. *The People's Chronology: A Year-by-Year Record of Human Events from Prehistory to the Present*. New York: Henry Holt and Company, 1992 and 1994.

U.S. Bureau of the Census. *Historical Statistics of the United States, Colonial Times to 1970, Bicentennial Edition*. Washington, D.C., 1975.

U.S. Bureau of the Census. *Statistical Abstract of the United States: 1999*. Washington, D.C., 1999.

U.S. Bureau of the Census. *Statistical Abstract of the United States: 1973*. Washington, D.C., 1973.

1970 Reader's Digest Almanac and Yearbook. Pleasantville, N.Y.: Reader's Digest Association, 1970.

Economy and Labor

Dow Jones Industrial Average

Year	High	Low
1960	685	566
1961	734	610
1962	767	723
1963	767	646
1964	891	776
1965	969	867
1966	1,000	744
1967	943	786
1968	985	825
1969	952	769
1970	842	669

Dow Jones Industrial Average closes above 1,000 for the first time: November 14, 1972

Average volume on New York stock exchange
1960	3 million shares
1970	11.6 million shares

Gross National Product
(in billions of dollars)

Year	GNP	in 1998 $
1940	$99.7	$1,144.93
1950	$284.8	$1,905.22
1960	$503.7	$2,754.49
1965	$684.9	$3,521.6
1970	$976.4	$4,245.03
1998	$8,490.5	$8,490.5

Government spending as a percentage of GNP

1960	27
1970	32

Prime Rate

1940	0.6%
1950	1.5%
1960	3.9%
1970	7.7%

Employment, 1930
(Non-Agricultural)

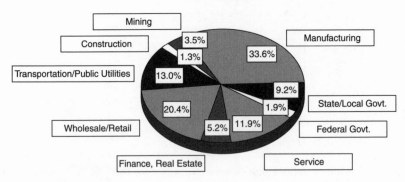

Employment, 1968
(Non-Agricultural)

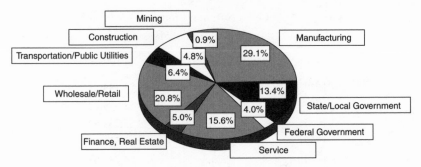

Manufacturing as percentage of employment in 1998: 13.4
Percentage increase in federal government employment, 1930 to 1968: 500
Percentage increase in average salaries of engineers, 1961–1972: 59.5

Number of lawyers in the United States in 1960: 252,385
  Proportion of male-to-female lawyers: 38 : 1
Number of lawyers in the United States in 1970: 324,818
  Proportion of male to female lawyers: 35 : 1

Daily wages (median) for farm workers in 1970: $9.30
  for white farm workers: $9.70
  for African American and nonwhite farm workers: $8.00
  for migratory farm workers (age 20 and older): $13.10

Percentage of American work force on farms

1940	18
1973	5

Number of people for whom the average farm worker produced food

1963	31
1973	50

Increase in productivity of average farm worker, 1960–1970: 7.7% per year

Tenant farms as percentage of "minority race" farms

1959	52
1969	20

Farms

	Number	Land in Farms (in millions of acres)	Average Acreage
1940	6,102,000	1,065	175
1959	3,711,000	1,124	303
1969	2,730,000	1,110	390
1998	2,192,000	954	435

Number of farmers who received government subsidies of $20,000 or more in
  1967: 10,000
Number who received subsidies of $1 million or more: 5

Hourly wage (average) in manufacturing

1960	$2.26 (in 1998 dollars: $12.36)
1970	$3.36 (in 1998 dollars: $14.61)
1998	$8.19

States with lowest average hourly wage in manufacturing in 1970: Mississippi ($2.43); North Carolina ($2.46)

States with highest average hourly wage in manufacturing in 1970: Alaska ($4.66); Michigan ($4.15); Washington ($4.06)

Federal Minimum Wage Rates

Year	Current Dollars	Constant (1996) Dollars
1956	$1.00	$5.77
1960	$1.00	$5.30
1961	$1.15	$6.03
1962	$1.15	$5.97
1963	$1.25	$6.41
1964	$1.25	$6.33
1965	$1.25	$6.23
1966	$1.25	$6.05
1967	$1.40	$6.58
1968	$1.60	$7.21
1969	$1.60	$6.84
1970	$1.60	$6.47
1980	$3.10	$5.90
1989	$3.35	$4.24
1997	$5.15	$5.03

Labor Union Membership
(as percentage of non-agricultural workforce)

1945	35.5
1955	33.2
1960	31.4
1965	28.4
1970	27.4
1998	13.9

Work Stoppages

	Number	Workers involved	As percent of total employed	Average duration
1930	637	183,000	.8%	22.3 days
1946	4,985	4,600,000	14.5%	24.2 days
1960	3,333	1,320,000	2.4%	23.4 days
1961	3,367	1,450,000	3.2%	23.7 days
1962	3,614	1,230,000	2.2%	24.6 days
1963	3,362	941,000	1.1%	23.0 days
1964	3,655	1,640,000	2.7%	22.9 days
1965	3,963	1,550,000	2.5%	25 days
1966	4,405	1,960,000	3.0%	22.2 days
1967	4,595	2,870,000	4.3%	22.8 days
1968	5,045	2,649,000	3.8%	24.5 days
1969	5,700	2,481,000	3.5%	22.5 days
1970	5,716	3,305,000	4.7%	25 days

Unemployment Rates

Year	Total	White	Non-White	Men	Women
1950	5.3%	4.9%	9.0%	5.1%	5.7%
1960	5.5%	4.9%	10.2%	5.4%	5.9%
1961	6.7%	6.0%	12.4%	6.4%	7.2%
1962	5.5%	4.9%	10.9%	5.2%	6.2%
1963	5.7%	5.0%	10.8%	5.2%	6.5%
1964	5.2%	4.6%	9.6%	4.6%	6.2%
1965	4.5%	4.1%	8.1%	4.0%	5.5%
1966	3.8%	3.3%	7.3%	3.2%	4.8%
1967	3.8%	3.4%	7.4%	3.1%	5.2%
1968	3.6%	3.2%	6.7%	2.9%	4.8%
1969	3.5%	3.1%	6.4%	2.8%	4.7%
1970	4.9%	4.5%	8.2%	4.4%	5.9%

Percentage of single women (16 and over) in the labor force in 1960: 58.6
Percentage of single men in the labor force in 1960: 69.8

Percentage of married women (husband present) with children under age six
who were employed

1948	10.8
1955	16.2
1960	18.6
1965	23.3
1970	30.3
1998	63.7

Percentage of all women (16 and older) in the labor force

1960	34.8
1970	42.6

Percent of white families (with both husband and wife present) in which the
husband was the only earner

1959	47
1970	34

Percentage of Americans in 1969 who said they disapproved of a married woman earning money if her husband could support her: 40

Work Time Required to Buy Goods and Services in 1968

Product	Time	Cost
Automobile (new 4-dr, 8-cyl)	26 2/5 weeks	$3,200.00
Beer (6–12 oz)	24 minutes	$1.22
Butter (1 lb)	16 minutes	$0.83
Cigarettes (pack of 20)	7 minutes	$0.37
Eggs (1 dozen large, grade A)	7 minutes	$0.37
Electricity (250 kw hours)	2 hours, 28 minutes	$7.48
Gasoline (1 gal., premium)	8 minutes	$0.38
Ground Beef (1 lb)	11 minutes	$0.57
Motion Picture Admission (adult)	32 minutes	$1.61
Radio, table model	5 hours, 59 minutes	$18.21
Television set (18")	46 hours, 33 minutes	$141.49
Washing Machine (electric)	72 hours, 1 minute	$218.94

Services

Hospital, semiprivate room (per day)	13 hours, 30 minutes	$41.04
Domestic service (housework, 8-hour day)	4 hours, 1 minute	$12.23
Permanent Wave	4 hours, 33 minutes	$13.82
Bus Fare	5 minutes	$0.27
Time of 8-hour workday required to pay taxes in 1968:	2 hrs, 26 minutes	

Based on worker in manufacturing average wage, including overtime, of $3.04/hour and average price of goods and services; from Bureau of Labor Statistics.

Low Income Population
(as percentage of total population; threshold is $3,601
for a nonfarm family in 1970)

	1959	1965	1970	1997
Total	22.4%	17.3%	12.6%	13.3%
White	18.1%	13.3%	9.9%	11.0%
African American and Other Non-White	56.2%	47.1%	32.0%	26.5%*
Hispanic	NA	NA	25.6%	27.1%
Appalachian	25.6%	NA	15.4%	NA
Asian/Pacific Islander	NA	NA	NA	14.0%

*1997 figure is African American only; Hispanics may be of any race, and are included in racial categories (i.e.: "White" includes Hispanics).

Median Family Income

in constant 1971 dollars

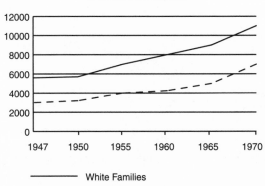

——————— White Families

– – – – African American and Other Non-White Families

States with a "low income level" population of 35% or more in 1959: Alabama (42.5%); Arkansas (48.3%); Georgia (39.0%); Kentucky (38.3%); Louisiana (39.5%); Mississippi (54.5%); North Carolina (40.6%); South Carolina (45.4%); Tennessee (39.3%)

Number of those states outside the South: 0

States with a "low income population" of 35% or more in 1969: Mississippi (35.4%)

Percentage of Americans in 1964 who said people were poor primarily because of "lack of effort": 30

Percentage who said "circumstances" were to blame: 31

Percentage who blamed both circumstances and lack of effort: 34

Government Social Welfare Expenditures
(and comparison with National Defense Spending)

	Social Welfare (as % of total federal outlays)	Social Welfare Spending (federal, state, and local; in billions of dollars)	Social Welfare (as % of GDP)	National Defense (as % of total federal outlays)
1950	26.2%	$23.5	8.2%*	30.4%
1960	28.1%	$52.3	10.3%	49.8%
1965	32.6%	$77.1	11.5%	41.9%
1968	35.1%	$113.6	13.4%	45.0%
1970	40.0%	$145.6	14.8%	40.8%
1972	47.2%	$190.3	16.6%	33.8%
1990	51.1%	$1,045.4	19.1%	NA

*1950 figure represents percentage of GNP

Credit Cards

1966

California's Bank of America creates BankAmerica Service Corp. to license other banks to issue BankAmericard.

The MasterCharge credit card is first issued.

Two million Americans have BankAmericards. They are accepted by 64,000 merchants.

1967
5.7 million MasterCharge card holders charge $312 million in purchases.

1968
4 million Americans have BankAmericards. They are accepted by 316,000 merchants.

1976
40 million MasterCharge cardholders charge $13.5 billion in purchases.

SOURCES FOR "ECONOMY AND LABOR" SECTION

Gordon, Lois and Alan Gordon. *American Chronicle: Six Decades in American Life 1920–1980.* New York: Atheneum, 1987.

Stanley, Harold W. and Richard G. Niemi. *Vital Statistics on American Politics.* Congressional Quarterly Press, 1997.

Taeuber, Cynthia M. *Statistical Handbook of Women in America.* 2nd edition. Phoenix, Ariz: Oryx Press, 1996.

Trager, James. *The People's Chronology: A Year-by-Year Record of Human Events from Prehistory to the Present.* New York: Henry Holt and Company, 1992 and 1994.

U.S. Bureau of the Census. *Historical Statistics of the United States, Colonial Times to 1970, Bicentennial Edition.* Washington, D.C., 1975.

U.S. Bureau of the Census. *Statistical Abstract of the United States: 1999.* Washington, D.C., 1999.

U.S. Bureau of the Census. *Statistical Abstract of the United States: 1973.* Washington, D.C., 1973.

1970 Reader's Digest Almanac and Yearbook. Pleasantville, N.Y.: The Reader's Digest Association, 1970.

National Politics and Elections

Participation in Presidential Elections (percentage of voting age population)		Voter Registration in Southern States (11) (percentage of voting age population)		
1932	52.4%	1960	white	61.1%
1940	58.9%		black	29.1%
1952	61.6%	1971	white	65.0%
1960	62.8%		black	58.0%
1964	61.8%			
1968	60.9%			
1972	55.7%			
1996	48.9%			

Percentage Increase in African-American Voter registration, 1960–1966, Following Voting Rights Act of 1965

Alabama	278.8
Mississippi	695.4
Georgia	66.7

States with no African-American elected officials in 1973: Hawaii, Idaho, Montana, North Dakota, South Dakota, Utah

Region with the greatest number of African-American elected officials in 1973: South (1,381)

Number of African-American elected officials in the Northeast: 444

If your party nominated a qualified woman for president, would you vote for her? (Gallup Poll, November 1963)

Men	Women
Yes 58%	Yes 51%
No 37%	No 45%
No opinion 5%	No opinion 4%

Number of delegates to the Democratic Presidential Nomination Convention

1960	1,521
1972	3,016

Number of delegates to the Republican Presidential Nomination Convention

1960	1,331
1972	1,348

Congress

Year	Congress	House	Senate
1961	87th	D 263, R 174	D 65, R 35
1963	88th	D 258, R 177	D 67, R 33
1965	89th	D 295, R 140	D 68, R 32
1967	90th	D 247, R 187	D 64, R 36
1969	91st	D 243, R 192	D 57, R 43
1971	92nd	D 254, R 180	D 54, R 44, Other 2
1973	93rd	D 239, R 192*	D 56, R 42, Other 2

* House had three vacancies at the beginning of the term.

Number of Female Members of Congress

	Senate	House
1961	2	15
1967	1	10
1969	1	10
1971	1	12
1973	0	14

PRESIDENTIAL ELECTIONS

1960 Election

The Candidates

Democratic Ticket	*Republican Ticket*
John F. Kennedy	Richard M. Nixon
Lyndon B. Johnson	Henry Cabot Lodge, Jr.

THE NOMINATION

THE DEMOCRATS

Major candidates for the presidential nomination, with percentage of primary vote

John F. Kennedy, Massachusetts	32.5
Edmund G. Brown, California	23.8
George H. McLain, California	11.4
Hubert H. Humphrey, Minnesota	10.4
George A. Smathers, Florida	5.7

Democratic Presidential Nominating Convention, Los Angeles, July 1960

Keynote speaker: Frank Church, Idaho

Kennedy was nominated on the first ballot.
He selected Lyndon Johnson as his running mate.

John F. Kennedy, accepting the Democratic presidential nomination at the Los Angeles Coliseum, July 1960:

"I stand tonight facing west on what was once the last frontier. From the lands that stretch 3,300 miles behind me, the pioneers of old gave up their safety, their comfort, and sometimes their lives to build a new world here in the West. . . . Today some would say that those struggles are all over, that all the horizons have been explored, that all the battles have been won, that there is no longer an American frontier. But the problems are not all solved and the battles are not all won, and we stand today on the edge of a new frontier—the frontier of the 1960s—a frontier of unknown opportunities and perils—a frontier of unfulfilled hopes and threats. . . . it would be easier to shrink back from that frontier, to look to the safe mediocrity of the past. . . . But I believe the times demand invention, innovation, imagination, decision. I am asking each of you to be new pioneers on that new frontier."

THE REPUBLICANS

Major candidates for presidential nomination and percentage of primary vote

Richard M. Nixon, California	89.9
Nelson Rockefeller, New York	0.6

Presidential Nominating Convention, Chicago, July 25–28, 1960

Keynote speaker: Walter H. Judd, Minnesota

Richard Nixon was nominated on the first ballot.
He chose Henry Cabot Lodge as his running mate.

Nixon's key opponent for the nomination, Nelson Rockefeller, introduced
    Nixon to the convention. Nixon delivered his acceptance speech following
    three days without sleep due to struggles over the Republican Party plat-
    form.

**Richard M. Nixon, accepting the Republican Party nomination for presi-
dent:**

"What we must do is wage the battles for peace and freedom with the same
. . . dedication with which we wage battles in war. . . . The only answer to a
strategy of victory for the Communist world is a strategy of victory for the free
world. Let the victory we seek . . . be the victory of freedom over tyranny, of
plenty over hunger, of health over disease, in every country of the world. . . .
When Mr. Khrushchev says our grandchildren will live under Communism,
let us say his grandchildren will live in freedom."

THE CAMPAIGN

COSTS

Amount spent on television political broadcasts during general election (by party, not by presidential campaign)

Republicans $5,431,000
Democrats $4,415,000

JFK and his family spent $150,000 on Kennedy's primary campaign and bought a $385,000 airplane that the family leased to his campaign.

Joseph P. Kennedy, JFK's father:

"With all the money I spent, I could have elected my chauffeur."
—*quoted in Nigel Hamilton,* JFK: Reckless Youth

USE OF TELEVISION AND OTHER MEDIA

The first televised debate between the two candidates gave Kennedy's campaign a big boost. Nixon had been recently hospitalized and was very thin. He had banged his knee badly exiting the car that brought him to the TV studio, reinjuring it, and stood slouched to one side during the debate because it hurt. He had a tendency to sweat heavily under the hot TV lights, and he had himself made up with a product called Lazy-Shave, which did little to hide his heavy beard and instead made him look ill. In contrast, Kennedy appeared relaxed and confident. Those who watched the debate on TV felt that Kennedy won; those who listed on the radio gave the edge to Nixon. The Kennedy campaign used segments of the debate in a five-minute paid advertisement, including a scene where Nixon seemed to be shaking his head in agreement with Kennedy's point.

KENNEDY CAMPAIGN

Kennedy, speaking to the Greater Houston Ministerial Association, a gathering of Protestant ministers, attempted to defuse the issue of his religion. The campaign made one- and five-minute television ads from this speech, as well as a half-hour program. The ads were shown in heavily Protestant areas; the full program in areas with a large percentage of Roman Catholic voters.

Because I am a Catholic, and no Catholic has ever been elected president, it is apparently necessary for me to state once again—not what kind of church I believe in, for that should be important only to me, but what kind of America I believe in. I believe in an America where the separation of Church and State is absolute, where no Catholic prelate would tell the president (should he be a Catholic) how to act and no Protestant minister would tell his parishioners for whom to vote.

NIXON CAMPAIGN

"[Nixon's] story is living proof to the world that America is the land of opportunity for those of humble origin."
—*from a 32-page supplement included in Sunday papers on November 6*

CAMPAIGN SLOGANS

Nixon and Lodge

THEY UNDERSTAND WHAT PEACE DEMANDS
EXPERIENCE COUNTS

Year that Nixon was first elected to Congress: 1946
Year that Kennedy was first elected to Congress: 1946

Kennedy's age: 43
Nixon's age: 47

Kennedy and Johnson

KENNEDY: LEADERSHIP FOR THE '60S

Bumper Sticker: BE THANKFUL ONLY ONE CAN WIN

THE ELECTION

Popular Vote

Kennedy   49.7% (34.2 million votes)
Nixon   49.5% (34.1 million votes)

Electoral College

Kennedy	303
Nixon	219
Byrd	15

Other Parties

Prohibition Party	46,203 votes
National States' Rights Party	44,977 votes
Socialist Workers Party	40,165 votes
Conservative Party of New Jersey	8,708 votes
Conservative Party of Virginia	4,204 votes
Tax Cut Party	1,767 votes
Constitution Party	1,401 votes
Independent Afro-American Unity Party	1,485 votes

1964 Election

The Candidates

Democratic Ticket	*Republican Ticket*
Lyndon Baines Johnson	Barry Goldwater
Hubert H. Humphrey	William E. Miller

THE NOMINATION

THE REPUBLICANS

Major candidates for presidential nomination, with percentage of primary vote

Barry Goldwater, Arizona	38.2
Nelson Rockefeller, New York	22.0
James A. Rhodes, Ohio	10.4
Henry Cabot Lodge, Ambassador to Vietnam	6.5
John W. Byrnes, Wisconsin	5.0
William Scranton, Pennsylvania	4.1

Nominated on first ballot: Barry Goldwater

Goldwater selected New York congressman and chairman of the Republican

National Committee, William Miller, as his running mate. Skeptics chanted: "Here's a riddle, it's a killer. Who the hell is William Miller?"

Republican Presidential Nominating Convention, San Francisco, July 13–16, 1964

Keynote Speaker: Mark O. Hatfield, Oregon

Barry Goldwater, accepting the Republican nomination for president, July 16, 1964:

"Our people have followed false prophets. We must, and we shall, return to proven ways — not because they are old, but because they are true. . . .

"I would remind you that extremism in the defense of liberty is no vice. And let me remind you also that moderation in the pursuit of justice is no virtue."

THE DEMOCRATS

Democratic Presidential Nominating Convention, Atlantic City, August 24–27

Keynote speaker: John O. Pastore, Rhode Island
LBJ was unopposed for the Democratic Presidential Nomination at the convention and was selected by acclamation. He selected Humbert H. Humphrey, Senator from Minnesota, as his running mate.

Lyndon Baines Johnson accepting the Democratic nomination for president, August 27, 1964:

"The Founding Fathers dreamed America before it was. The pioneers dreamt of great cities on the wilderness that they had crossed. Our tomorrow is on its way. It can be a shape of darkness or it can be a thing of beauty. The choice is ours."

THE CAMPAIGN

COSTS

Total spent on television political broadcasts during general election (by party, not only for presidential candidate's campaign)

Republicans $9,431,000
Democrats $7,715,000

Johnson and Humphrey

ALL THE WAY WITH LBJ

VOTE FOR PRESIDENT JOHNSON ON NOVEMBER 3, THE STAKES ARE TOO HIGH
FOR YOU TO STAY HOME.

Goldwater and Miller

A CHOICE NOT AN ECHO

$AuH_2O = 1964$

IN YOUR HEART YOU KNOW HE'S RIGHT

In response to Goldwater's slogan, LBJ supporters punned:

IN YOUR HEART YOU KNOW HE'S RIGHT . . . FAR RIGHT

IN YOUR HEART YOU KNOW HE MIGHT [USE NUCLEAR WEAPONS]

IN YOUR HEAD YOU KNOW HE'S WRONG

IN YOUR GUTS YOU KNOW HE'S NUTS

Johnson Campaign

The Daisy ad, created by Tony Schwartz for Doyle Dane Bernbach.

A little girl stands in a meadow, pulling petals from a daisy as she counts: 1, 2, 3, 4, 5, 7, 6, 6, 8, 9. As she reaches nine, a NASA mission control-type voice begins a countdown: 10, 9, 8, ... When he reaches zero, the camera dissolves from a close-up of the child's eye to a mushroom cloud. Voiceover, LBJ: "These are the stakes. To make a world in which all of God's children can live, or to go into the dark. We must either love each other or we must die."

The Democrats aired this ad once on a single network, but it created such controversy that all three networks played in on their news programs, thus giving it extensive—and free—distribution. The Goldwater campaign filed a complaint with the Fair Campaign Practices Committee, but the Democrats pulled the ad after a single use.

Goldwater Campaign

A half-hour film, *Choice*, sponsored by Mothers for a Moral America, a "front group" set up by the Goldwater Campaign to sponsor controversial material.

The film focused on America's "moral decline" and offered viewers a "choice" between degenerate youth doing the twist and schoolchildren reciting the Pledge of Allegiance, between books like *Call Me Nympho* and the *Declaration of Independence*, and between African Americans rioting and committing acts of violence and those contentedly picking cotton.

The film was distributed to local groups and a five-minute segment aired on television in California. It was scheduled to air nationally on NBC at 2 P.M. October 22 (the timeslot was chosen to reach an audience of housewives). The official advertising agency of the Republican National Committee announced publicly that it had no association with the film and Goldwater had it pulled from the network schedule the day it was to air; the following day he explained that it was "racist."

THE ELECTION

Popular Vote

Johnson	61.1% (43.1 million votes)
Goldwater	38.5% (27.2 million votes)

Electoral College

Johnson	486
Goldwater	52

Other Parties

Prohibition	23,267 votes
National States' Rights	6,953 votes
Constitution Party	5,060 votes

1968 Election

The Candidates

Democratic Ticket	*Republican Ticket*	*Independent Ticket*
Hubert H. Humphrey	Richard M. Nixon	George Wallace
Edmund Muskie	Spiro Agnew	Curtis LeMay

THE NOMINATION

THE REPUBLICANS

Republican Presidential Nominating Convention, Miami Beach, August 5–9, 1968

Keynote Speaker: Daniel J. Evans, Washington

Major candidates for the presidential nomination, with percentage of primary votes

Ronald Reagan, California	37.9
Richard M. Nixon, California (former vice president)	37.5
James A. Rhodes, Ohio	13.7
Nelson Rockefeller, New York	3.7

Nominated on the first ballot: Richard M. Nixon
Nixon selected Maryland Governor Spiro Agnew as his running mate.

Spiro Agnew, placing Nixon's name in nomination:

"When a nation is in crisis and history speaks firmly to that nation, it needs a man to match the time. You don't create such a man—you don't discover such a man—you recognize such a man."

Richard Nixon, accepting the Republican party nomination for president, July 1968:

"Let us begin by committing ourselves to the truth—to see it as it is, and tell it like it is—to find the truth, to speak the truth, and to live the truth.

"As we look at America, we see cities enveloped in smoke and flame. We hear sirens in the night. We see Americans dying on distant battlefields abroad. We see Americans hating each other, fighting each other, killing each other at home. And as we see and hear these things, millions of Americans cry out in anguish: did we come all this way for this? Did American boys die in Normandy and Korea and Valley Forge for this? Listen to the answers to those questions. It is another voice, it is a quiet voice in the tumult of the shouting. It is the voice of the great majority of Americans, the forgotten Americans, the nonshouters, the nondemonstrators. The answer of course is no."

Major candidates for the presidential nomination, with percentage of primary vote

Eugene McCarthy, Minnesota	38.7
Robert F. Kennedy, Massachusetts	30.6
Lyndon Johnson (President)	5.1
Hubert H. Humphrey, Minnesota	2.2

President Lyndon Johnson, removing himself from consideration March 31, 1968, in televised address to the nation:

"There is division in the American house now. . . . And holding the trust that is mine, as president of all the people, I cannot disregard the peril to the . . . prospect for peace. . . . I do not believe that I should devote an hour or a day of my time to any personal partisan course. . . . Accordingly, I shall not seek, and I will not accept, the nomination of my party for another term as your president."

Robert Kennedy, senator from Massachusetts

Declared his candidacy on March 16, 1968
Assassinated June 5, 1968, following his victory in the California primary

Eugene McCarthy, senator from Minnesota, declaring his candidacy November 30, 1967:

"There is growing evidence of a deepening moral crisis in America—discontent, frustration, and a disposition to take extra legal . . . actions to manifest protest. I am hopeful that this challenge . . . may alleviate . . . this sense of political helplessness and restore to many people a belief in the processes of American . . . government."

Vice President Hubert H. Humphrey, declaring his candidacy, April 27, 1968:

"Here we are, the way politics ought to be in America, the politics of happiness, the politics of purpose, the politics of joy."

Presidential nominating convention: Chicago, August 26–29, 1968

Keynote Speaker: Daniel K. Inouye, Hawai'i

Outside the convention hall police beat protestors, who had come to oppose "the Convention of Death," as well as reporters and bystanders. Television broadcasts juxtaposed scenes of violence outside the hall with the nomination of Hubert Humphrey.

Hubert Humphrey was nominated on the first ballot.
He chose Edmund Muskie, senator from Maine, as his running mate.

Hubert Humphrey's acceptance speech:

"Put aside recrimination and disunion. Turn away from violence and hatred."

Major Platform Fight

A minority report on the Vietnam War called for the end of bombing of North Vietnam, stopping offensive search-and-destroy missions by U.S. troops, negotiated withdrawal of American troops, and the establishment of a coalition government in South Vietnam. It was defeated, 1,567 (3/4) to 1,041 (1/4).

THE CAMPAIGN

COSTS

Amount spent on television political broadcasts during general election (by party, not only for presidential candidate's campaign)

Republicans $15,183,000
Democrats $10,424,000
Third parties $ 1,480,000

NOTABLE TELEVISION ADS

HUMPHREY CAMPAIGN

"President Agnew?" theme:
"Spiro Agnew for Vice President" appears on the screen as a man laughs so hard he begins to choke. More words appear: "This would be funny if it weren't so serious."

Anti-Wallace ad:
E. G. Marshall, in front of a large picture of Wallace, says: "When I see this man, I think of feelings of my own, which I don't like but I have anyway.

They're called prejudices. . . . I think we have to recognize the fact that we have these feelings and that we have the right to conceal them or express them. . . . Wallace is devoted now to his single strongest prejudice. He would take that prejudice and make it into national law."

NIXON CAMPAIGN

The commercial begins with a still shot of the Chicago Democratic Convention, and then intercuts photos of Humphrey with scenes of rioting, of a poor family in Appalachia, of wounded U.S. servicemen in Vietnam. "There's a Hot Time in the Old Town Tonight" plays, becoming increasingly dissonant. Finally, a voice states: "This time vote like your whole world depended on it. Nixon."

This ad aired on October 28th during the very popular *Rowan and Martin's Laugh-In*. Some viewers thought it was part of the show. Democrats filed a complaint, and the network asked Nixon's advertising agency to review the ad. It ran once more, and then was pulled by the Nixon campaign.

CAMPAIGN SLOGANS

NIXON AND AGNEW

VOTE LIKE YOUR WHOLE WORLD DEPENDED ON IT

NIXON'S THE ONE *(An apocryphal story claims that Democrats planted very pregnant women carrying signs reading "Nixon's the One" in audiences to which Nixon spoke.)*

HUMPHREY AND MUSKIE

HUMPHREY–MUSKIE: THERE IS NO ALTERNATIVE

TRUST HUMPHREY

THE ELECTION

Popular Vote

Nixon	43.4% (31.8 million votes)
Humphrey	42.7% (31.3 million votes)
Wallace	13.5 % (9.9 million votes)

Nixon won with approximately 2.5 million fewer votes than he had received in 1960, when he lost to JFK.

Electoral College

Nixon	301
Humphrey	191
Wallace	46

States that voted for Wallace

Alabama, Georgia, Louisiana, Mississippi, Arkansas, and 1 of North Carolina's 13 electoral college votes.

Other Parties

Freedom and Peace (Dick Gregory)	47,133
Socialist Workers (Fred Halstead)	41,388
Peace and Freedom (Eldridge Cleaver)	36,563
Eugene McCarthy	25,552
Prohibition (E. Harold Munn)	15,123
People's Constitution (Ventura Chavez)	1,519
Communist (Charlene Mitchell)	1,075

1972 *Election*

The Candidates

Democratic Ticket	*Republican Ticket*
George McGovern	Richard M. Nixon
Sargent Shriver*	Spiro Agnew**

McGovern originally selected Thomas Eagleton; see page 379.

**Spiro Agnew stood for reelection with Nixon in 1972 but resigned from the vice presidency in scandal and was replaced by Gerald Ford, who would in turn replace Nixon as president when he resigned on August 9, 1974, in the wake of the Watergate scandal.*

THE NOMINATION

THE REPUBLICANS

Major candidates for presidential nomination, with percentage of primary vote

Richard Nixon, President of the United States	86.9
John Ashbrook, Ohio	5.0
Pete McCloskey, California	2.1

Republican Presidential Nominating Convention, Miami Beach, August 21–23

Keynote Speakers: Richard G. Lugar, Indiana, and Anne Armstrong, Texas

Nixon was nominated on the first ballot.
He named his vice president, Spiro Agnew, as his running mate for a second term.

Nixon, accepting the Republican nomination for president, asked Americans to "join our new majority."

THE DEMOCRATS

Major candidates for the presidential nomination and percentage of primary vote:

Hubert Humphrey, former vice president and 1968 nominee	25.8
George McGovern, South Dakota	25.3
George Wallace, Alabama*	23.5
Edmund Muskie, Maine	11.5
Eugene McCarthy, Minnesota	3.5
Henry (Scoop) Jackson, Washington	3.2
Shirley Chisolm, New York	2.7

Shot and paralyzed during an assassination attempt, May 15, 1972; withdrew.

Democratic Presidential Nominating Convention, Miami Beach, July 10–13, 1972

Keynote Speaker: Reubin Askew, Florida

McGovern was nominated on the first ballot.
McGovern selected Thomas F. Eagleton, senator from Missouri, as his running mate, but he withdrew from the ticket on July 31, following reports that he had had electric shock and other psychiatric treatment. Sargent Shriver, director of the Peace Corps, replaced him on the ticket.

McGovern, accepting the Democratic nomination for president (at 3 A.M., Eastern Time):

"Come home, America. . . ."
    "I make these pledges above all others—the doors of government will be opened, and that brutal war will be closed."

Major Platform Fights

A women's rights plank supporting abortion rights was defeated, 1,572.8 to 1,101.37.

A minority report that proposed a government-guaranteed annual income of $6,500 for a family of four was defeated, 1,852.86 to 999.34.

THE CAMPAIGN

COSTS

Amount spent on television political broadcasts during general election (by party, not only for presidential candidate's campaign)

Republicans	$11,619,000
Democrats	$11,433,000

> The Federal Election Campaign Act of 1972 limited the amount each candidate could spend on broadcast advertising (after the primaries) to $8.4 million. Personal expenditures were limited to $50,000.

NOTABLE TELEVISION ADS

NIXON CAMPAIGN

A construction worker in hard hat sits down to eat his brown-bag lunch. Voice-over:

> Senator George McGovern recently submitted a welfare bill to the congress. According to an analysis by the Senate Finance Committee, the McGovern bill would make 47 percent of the people in the United States eligible for welfare — 47 percent. . . . And who's going to pay for this? Well, if you're not the one out of two people on welfare, you do.

The man, astonished, stares at the camera.

Weather-vane ad:

A political placard bearing McGovern's picture spins in the wind — like a weather vane — as the voiceover recounts changes in his positions on a variety of issues.

MCGOVERN CAMPAIGN

An advertisement created to link Nixon with the Vietnam War was vetoed by McGovern and his top advisors:

Henry Kissenger's voice is heard over footage of a Vietnamese woman running down the road, clutching her napalmed dead baby: "We have restricted our bombing, in effect, to the battle area, in order to show our good will." Then a child's voice asks: "Does a president know that planes bomb children?"

CAMPAIGN SLOGANS

NIXON AND AGNEW

PRESIDENT NIXON. NOW MORE THAN EVER.

MCGOVERN AND SHRIVER

MCGOVERN. DEMOCRAT. FOR THE PEOPLE.

In the primaries, McGovern's major slogan was "Right from the Start," a reference to his longstanding opposition to the Vietnam War. After he replaced Eagleton with Shriver as his running mate, the McGovern campaign decided that this slogan no longer worked.

THE ELECTION

Popular Vote

Nixon	60.7% (47.1 million votes)
McGovern	37.5% (29.2 million votes)
John G. Schmitz	1.4% (1 million votes)

Electoral College

Nixon	520
McGovern	17

Number of southern states that voted Democratic: 0
Only state to vote for McGovern: Massachusetts
Bumper sticker seen during Watergate scandal: DON'T BLAME ME. I'M FROM MASSACHUSETTS.

Other Parties

Socialist Labor (Louis Fisher)	53,814 votes
Socialist Workers (Linda Jenness)	52,799 votes
Communist (Gus Hall)	25,595 votes
Prohibition (E. Harold Munn)	13,505 votes
Libertarian (John Hospers)	3,673 votes

SOURCES FOR "NATIONAL POLITICS AND ELECTIONS" SECTION

Ambrose, Stephen. *Nixon*. New York: Simon and Schuster, 1987.

Congressional Quarterly. *Presidential Elections, 1789–1996*. Washington, D.C.: Congressional Quarterly, Inc., 1997.

Divine, Robert A., et al. *America Past and Present*. 2nd edition. Glenview, Ill.: Scott, Foresman and Company, 1987.

Information Please Entertainment Almanac. http://www.infoplease.lycos.com

Jamieson, Kathleen Hall. *Packaging the Presidency*. New York: Oxford, 1996.

Nixon, Richard. *The Memoirs of Richard Nixon*. New York: Grosset and Dunlap, 1978.

U.S. Bureau of the Census. *Statistical Abstract of the United States: 1973*. Washington, D.C., 1973.

The Vietnam War

Land mass of the United States: 3,787, 319 sq. miles

Land mass of North and South Vietnam, combined: 127, 246 sq. miles

Population of United States, 1970: 204,879,000
Population of North Vietnam: 21,154,000
Population of South Vietnam: 17,333,388

Gross National Product of the United States in 1965: $684.9 billion
Gross National Product of South Vietnam: $2.4 billion (144.5 billion piasters)
Gross National Product of North Vietnam: $1.42 billion (5.03 billion dong viet)

Nations other than the United States and North and South Vietnam in combat roles: South Korea, Philippines, Thailand, Australia, New Zealand

Average age of U.S. servicemen in Vietnam War: 19
Average age of U.S. servicemen in World War II: 26

Status of Selective Service Draftees

Examined for Military Service

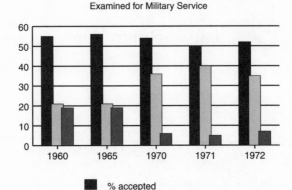

- ■ % accepted
- □ % disqualified–medical
- ■ % disqualified–mental

Number of American men who came of draft age during Vietnam era: 26.8 million

Number of American men inducted by the selective service: 2.2 million

Number of American men who volunteered for military service: 8.7 million

Number of draft-eligible American men who legally did not serve: 16 million

State with highest rate of selective-service draftees accepted, 1960–1972: Nebraska (69.2%)

State with lowest rate: South Carolina (39.6%)

Estimated number of draft offenders during Vietnam War: 570,000

Number of Americans indicted for draft law violations, 1965–1975: 22,000

Number of Americans convicted on these charges: 8,756

Number of women in the armed forces during the Vietnam era: 265,000

Number of women service personnel who served in Vietnam: 11,500

Draftees as percentage of combat deaths: 33

Volunteers as percentage of combat deaths: 67

Percentage of marines killed in Vietnam who were teenagers: 40

Percentage of 18–26-year-old registrants deferred from military service in 1969: 32

Total number of eligible men deferred or exempted from service: 8,769,000

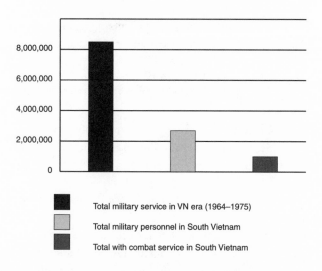

Combat in South Vietnam as Proportion Total Military Service

Total military service in VN era (1964–1975)

Total military personnel in South Vietnam

Total with combat service in South Vietnam

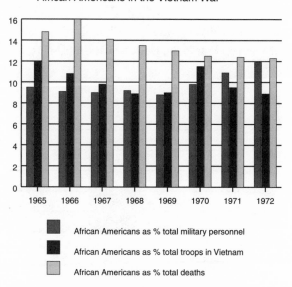

African Americans in the Vietnam War

African Americans as % total military personnel

African Americans as % total troops in Vietnam

African Americans as % total deaths

Percentage of those who received student deferment: 4 (371,000)
Percentage of those deferred as conscientious objectors: 1.9 (171,700)

Number of Harvard University's 1,200-member 1970 graduating class who served in Vietnam: 2

WAGING WAR

Number of American tenured professors specializing in Vietnam in 1970: 0
Number of Americans studying the Vietnamese language: 30

Tonnage of bombs dropped in Vietnam War: 7 million
Tonnage of bombs dropped in World War II: 2 million

Total defoliation of land in Vietnam, in acres, from 1962 to 1970: 5,182,307
Gallons of herbicide used in Operation Ranch Hand in 1967: 4.8 million
Gallons of Agent Orange used in Vietnam: 11,220,000

Other major herbicides used in Vietnam: Agents Purple, Pink, Green, Blue, and White
Diseases that the Department of Defense officially recognized in 1992 as caused by dioxin, a chemical component of Agent Orange: Hodgkins' Disease, Non-Hodgkins lymphoma, soft tissue carcinoma, birth defects, chloracne.

U.S. aid to South Vietnam, 1955–1961: $1.65 billion
Direct costs of Vietnam War to the United States, 1964–1975: $140 billion

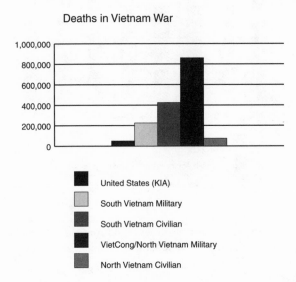

Deaths in Vietnam War

Total U.S. combat deaths in Vietnam War: 45,941
Total U.S. noncombat deaths: 10,420

Number of deaths registered as suicide among U.S. troops: 379
Number of murders among U.S. troops: 190
Number of deaths from illness: 929

Number of documented cases of officers and NCOs killed or wounded by
their own men (fragged): 1,017
Number of those who died: 83

Percentage of combat deaths that occurred during first three months of the
one-year tour of duty: 40
Percentage that occurred during the last three months: 6

Average length of time from combat wound to hospital treatment

Vietnam War	2.8 hours
Korean War	6.3 hours
World War II	10.5 hours

Troop strength in Vietnam

1961	3,164	1968	536,100
1962	11,326	1969	475,200
1963	16,263	1970	334,600
1964	23,310	1971	156,800
1965	184,300	1972	24,200
1966	385,300	1973	50
1967	485,600	1974	50

Total U.S. air sorties flown in South Vietnam, 1966–1973 (both fixed-wing and
helicopter): 38,227,069
Total U.S. aircraft losses, 1962–1973: 8,588

Names given by U.S. prisoners of war to the eleven POW camps in North
Vietnam: Hanoi Hilton, Briarpatch, Faith, Hope, Skidrow, D-1, the Zoo,
Rockpile, Plantation, Alcatraz, Dogpatch

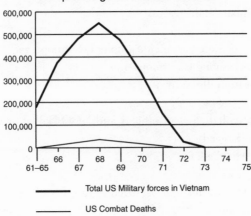

Troop Strength & Combat Deaths

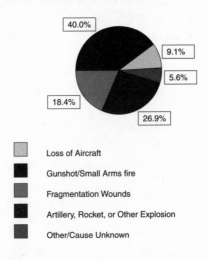

Causes of U.S. Combat Deaths

U.S. military VD rate in Vietnam, 1972: 700 cases per 1,000 servicemen

Number arrested by military police, per week, in Vietnam for possession of
    marijuana in 1969: 1,000
Estimated number of American heroin users in South Vietnam in 1971: 81,300
Estimated number of heroin users in the United States in 1971: 68,000
Cost per day of heroin for addict in Chicago in 1969: $150
Cost per day in Saigon: $2

Department of Defense estimated percentage of U.S. servicemen using the
following drugs in March, 1971:

Marijuana	58.5
Amphetamines	16.4
Barbiturates	15.46
LSD	9.54
Opium	19.59
Heroin	22.68

U.S. Army desertion rate

1966	14.7 per 1,000
1971	73.5 per 1,000

Highest army desertion rate for Korean War (1953): 22.3 per 1,000
Number of men who deserted *after* finishing their tours of duty in Vietnam:
20,000

Total "man-years" of military service lost to desertion and AWOL incidents
during Vietnam era: 1 million
Approximate "man-years" spent by U.S. troops in Vietnam: 2 million

---

President Dwight D. Eisenhower:
"The loss of South Vietnam would set in motion a crumbling process that
could, as it progressed, have consequences for us and for freedom."
    —1959

President John F. Kennedy:

"The United States is determined to help Vietnam preserve its independence,
protect its people against Communist assassins, and build a better life through
economic growth."
    —1961

President Lyndon B. Johnson:

"We are not about to send American boys nine or ten thousand miles away
from home to do what Asian boys ought to be doing for themselves."
    —televised speech, October 21, 1964
"We did not choose to be the guardians of the gate, but there is no one else."
    —on continued intervention in Vietnam, July 28, 1964

Unknown:

"It became necessary to destroy the town to save it."
        —unidentified major's comment on bombing of Bentre, South Vietnam, *New York Times*, February 8, 1968

Henry A. Kissinger (national security advisor):

"We lost sight of one of the cardinal maxims of guerrilla war: the guerrilla wins if he does not lose. The conventional army loses if it does not win."
        —*Foreign Affairs*, January 1969
"Peace is at hand."
        —statement made just before the 1972 presidential election

---

MEDIA

Number of U.S. journalists accredited by the military command in Saigon in
        January 1968: 179
Number of *New York Times* reporters stationed in Saigon in 1964: 1
        In 1965: 3
        In 1968: 4

Amount each of the three major networks spent each year beginning in 1967
        to cover the war in Vietnam: $1 million

Date it was first possible to relay film by satellite from Tokyo to New York:
        February 1967
Cost of five-minute transmission from Tokyo to New York: $5,000
Days before film of most events reached U.S. television audiences: 2
Weight of cameras carried by network crews: 27 pounds

Percentage of network news stories broadcast between 1965 and 1970 that
        showed heavy fighting, with images of dead or wounded: 3
Approximate percentage of casualties shown on television news that were
        civilian: 16
Estimated percentage of actual casualties that were civilian: 28–45

Shows CBS aired when it broke off coverage of Senate Foreign Relations
        Committee hearings disputing Johnson's Vietnam policy in 1966: reruns of
        I Love Lucy, *The Real McCoys*, and *The Andy Griffith Show*.

Walter Cronkite (CBS News anchor):

"To say that we are closer to victory today is to believe, in the face of the evidence, the optimists who have been wrong in the past. To suggest we are on the edge of defeat is to yield to unreasonable pessimism. To say that we are mired in stalemate seems the only realistic, yet unsatisfactory, conclusion. On the off chance that military and political analysts are right, in the next few months we must test the enemy's intentions, in case this is indeed his last gasp before negotiations. But it is increasingly clear to this reporter that the only rational way out then will be to negotiate, not as victors, but as an honorable people who lived up to their pledge to defend democracy, and did the best they could. This is Walter Cronkite. Good night."
—*CBS Evening News*, February 27, 1968, following Tet Offensive

President Lyndon B. Johnson, in response:

"If I have lost Walter Cronkite, I have lost Mr. Average Citizen."
—February 1968

Frank McGee (*NBC Evening News* reporter)

"We must decide whether it is futile to destroy Vietnam in an effort to save it."
—March 1968

John Wayne, explaining his goals in making *The Green Berets*:

"[To] tell the story of our fighting men in Vietnam with reason, emotion, characterization, and action. We want to do it in a manner that will inspire a patriotic attitude on the part of fellow Americans—a feeling which we have always had in this country in the past during stress and trouble."
—1966

Renata Adler, in *New York Times* film review of *The Green Berets*:

"*The Green Berets* is a film so unspeakable, so stupid, so rotten and false . . . that it passes through being fun, through being funny, through being camp, through everything and becomes an invitation to grieve, not for our soldiers in Vietnam or for Vietnam (the film could not be more false or do a greater disservice to either of them) but for what has happened to the fantasy-making apparatus."
—1966

THE WAR AT HOME

In relation to the Vietnam War, percentage of male college students describing themselves in May 1967 as "hawks": 56
Those describing themselves as "doves": 30%
Those as having "no opinion": 14%

Weeks "The Ballad of the Green Berets" stayed at number one on the charts in 1966: 5
Weeks that the Beach Boys' "Good Vibrations" was at number one in 1966: 1

Pentagon's official designation for Jane Fonda in 1962: "Miss Army Recruiting"
Her unofficial designation after visiting North Vietnam in 1972: "Hanoi Jane"

Percentage of Americans who believed the United States had made a mistake in sending troops to fight in Vietnam in 1966: 35
Percentage who believed it in 1971: 61

Percentage of black Americans in 1971 who believed the United States had made a mistake in sending troops to fight in Vietnam: 83
Percentage of white Americans who believed it: 67

Number of people who protested against the war in a march in Washington DC on November 15, 1969: 500,000

Number of college and university campuses with major antiwar protests in the first six months of 1969: 232
Percentage of those protests that became violent: 24
Number of students arrested: 3,652

Number of Vietnamese killed in My Lai massacre on March 16, 1968: 500
Counts of premeditated murder with which a military tribunal charged Lt. William Calley : 22
Number of other defendants brought to trial: 0
Number of years of his sentence (life in prison at hard labor) Lt. Calley served: 0
Years spent under house arrest: 3

Paul Potter:

"I do not believe that the President or Mr. Rusk or Mr. McNamara or even McGeorge Bundy are particularly evil men. If asked to throw napalm on the back of a ten-year-old child, they would shrink in horror—but their decisions have led to mutilation and death of thousands and thousands of people.

What kind of system is it that allows good men to make those kinds of decisions? What kind of system is it that justifies the United States or any country seizing the destinies of the Vietnamese people and using them callously for its own purpose? . . . We must name that system. We must name it, describe it, analyze it, understand it, and change it."
— "We Must Name the System," Washington DC, April 17, 1965

J. William Fulbright:

"There are in fact two wars going on. One is the war of power politics, which our soldiers are fighting in the jungles of southeast Asia. The other is a war for America's soul, which is being fought in the streets of Newark and Detroit and in the halls of Congress, in churches and protest meetings and on college campuses, and in the hearts and minds of silent Americans from Maine to Hawaii. I believe that the two wars have something to do with each other, not in the direct, tangibly causal way that bureaucrats require as proof of a connection between two things, but in a subtler, moral, and qualitative way that is no less real for being intangible."
— "A Sick Society," 1st session, 90th Congress, Congressional Record, 1967

LBJ's nickname for Senator Fulbright: "Halfbright"

Martin Luther King Jr.:

"I could never again raise my voice against the violence of the oppressed in the ghetto without having first spoken out clearly to the greatest purveyor of violence in the world today—my own government. We are at a moment when our lives must be placed on the line if our nation is to survive its own folly. . . . I oppose the war in Vietnam because I love America. I speak out against it not in anger but with anxiety and sorrow in my heart. . . . This war is a blasphemy against all that America stands for."
— Riverside Church, April 1967

Vietnam War Protest Chants:

Ho Ho Ho Chi Minh
Viet Cong are gonna win!

Hey, hey, LBJ
How many kids did you kill today?

Bumper Sticker, Vietnam Era:

AMERICA, LOVE IT OR LEAVE IT

LEGACIES OF THE WAR

Number of Medals of Honor awarded for service in the Vietnam War: 239
Number of those that were awarded posthumously: 150

Number of Vietnam veterans classified as totally disabled (service-related) in 1997: 73,000
Number of U.S. veterans who survived the war as quadriplegics or multiple amputees: 74,000
Percentage of men incarcerated in San Francisco jails in 1973 who had served in Vietnam: 35

Number of U.S. service personnel officially unaccounted for at end of Vietnam War: 2,273
At the end of Korean War: 8,000
At the end of World War II: 80,000

Number of people who contributed funds to build the Vietnam War Memorial in Washington, DC: 650,000
Number of names inscribed on the Vietnam Memorial in Washington, DC: 58,175

Total population of Saigon in 1975: 4 million
Estimated number of Vietnamese heroin addicts in Saigon in 1975: 150,000
Estimated number of prostitutes and "bar girls" in Saigon in 1972: 500,000
Estimated number of orphans living on the street in Saigon in 1972: 800,000
(Note: these categories overlap)

Communist nations in Southeast Asia in 1960: North Vietnam
Communist nations in Southeast Asia in 1980: Vietnam, Laos, Cambodia

Date that President Bill Clinton extended diplomatic recognition to Vietnam:
July 11, 1995

SOURCES FOR "THE VIETNAM WAR" SECTION

Baughman, James L. *The Republic of Mass Culture*. Baltimore: Johns Hopkins University Press, 1992.

Clodfelter, Michael. *Vietnam in Military Statistics: A History of the Indochina Wars, 1772–1991*. Jefferson, N.C.: McFarland and Company, 1995.

Clymer, Kenton J, ed. *The Vietnam War: Its History, Literature, and Music*. El Paso: Texas Western Press, 1998.

The Europa Year Book: A World Survey. London: Europa Publications Limited, 1971, 1972, 1974.

Farber, David. *The Age of Great Dreams: America in the 1960s*. New York: Hill and Wang, 1994.

Hallin, Daniel C. *The Uncensored War: The Media and Vietnam*. Berkeley: University of California Press, 1986.

Kutler, Stanley I., ed. *Encyclopedia of the Vietnam War*. New York: Charles Scribner's Sons, 1996.

Levy, Peter B., ed. *America in the Sixties: Right, Left, and Center: A Documentary History*. Westport, Conn.: Praeger, 1998.

Moss, George Donelson. *Vietnam: An American Ordeal*. 2nd ed. Englewood Cliffs, NJ: Prentice Hall, 1994.

Olson, James S. and Randy Roberts. *Where the Domino Fell: America and Vietnam, 1945–1995*. 2nd ed. New York: St. Martin's Press, 1996.

Pach, Chester. "And That's The Way It Was: The Vietnam War on the Network Nightly News." In David Farber, ed., *The Sixties: From Memory to History*. Chapel Hill: University of North Carolina Press, 1994.

Summers, Harry G., Jr. *Historical Atlas of the Vietnam War*. Boston: Houghton Mifflin, 1995.

———. *Vietnam War Almanac*. New York: Facts on File Publications, 1985.

Tucker, Spencer C., ed. *Encyclopedia of the Vietnam War: A Political, Social, and Military History*. Santa Barbara, CA: ABC–CLIO, 1998.

United Nations. *Statistical Yearbook for Asia and the Far East: 1968*. New York: United Nations, 1968.

U.S. Army. http://www.army.mil

U.S. Bureau of the Census. *Statistical Abstract of the United States: 1973*. Washington, D.C., 1973.

Entertainment, Popular Arts, and Publications

TELEVISION

Percentage of American households with a television set
1960	88
1970	96

Percentage of American households with a telephone
1960	78
1970	92

Color TV ownership
1961	1.2
1970	9.2

City with highest rate of color TV ownership in 1967: Lubbock, Texas (35%)

Percentage of homes with color TV in New York City in 1967: 17

Number of networks
1960	3
1970	3

Sets tuned to network programming in late 1960s: 90%

American homes with TV sets capable of receiving UHF signals
1961	7%
1970	73%

Average number of hours of TV viewing per day, by household

| 1963 | 5.85 |
| 1970 | 6.5 |

Most popular magazine in the United States during the 1960s: *TV Guide*

What was Censored in the Sixties

SMOTHERS BROTHERS' COMEDY HOUR
(Began February 5, 1967, scheduled opposite the top-rated show, *Bonanza*)

The line "Ronald Reagan is a known heterosexual" (reason: too many viewers might not know what the word meant).

Folk singer Pete Seeger's guest appearance on the *Smothers Brothers*. Seeger, who was blacklisted during the McCarthy era, had never before appeared on network primetime television. His performance of "Waist Deep in the Big Muddy" (containing the line, "and the big fool says to push on") was killed by CBS censors because of its political analogy to the Vietnam War and President Johnson. Following public outcry, CBS rescheduled Seeger and allowed him to perform this song.

Allowed: Goldie O'Keefe's regular segments, "Share a little tea with Goldie," a parody of the afternoon shows aimed at housewives. "Hi—and glad of it," Goldie began.

Time magazine on the Smothers Brothers, June 1967:

"The boys have the jug-eared look of Nebraska citybillies, or malt-shop cowboys. Even when they are mildly suggestive, they seem as harmless as two choirboys sneaking a smoke behind the organ."

Tom Smothers:

"We're so college-looking and clean-cut. The American Legion likes us and so does the left wing."

Duet sung in opening segment, September 1968:

"The weekly grind is stretching out before us
The bleeping censors lurking in the wings
CBS would like to give us notice

And some of you don't like the things we say
But we're still here
We're still here
You may not think we're funny
But we're still here"

Tommy Smothers, after CBS canceled *The Smothers Brothers* on April 3, 1969, explaining that they had not sent in an acceptable broadcast tape in time for the CBS "Program Practices" department and CBS affiliated stations to review it:

"I didn't realize I was important until they made me shut up."
　　　—*Time*, March 30, 1970

ROWAN AND MARTIN'S LAUGH-IN
Censored: "You don't have to be happy to be gay."
Censored: "It's not how long you make it, it's how often."
Accepted: "Luther Burbank dug pansies" (reason: Luther Burbank was actually a botanist).

The first time Goldie Hawn said "Look that up in your Funk and Wagnalls," the censor objected. The line was changed to "Look that up in your Funk and Wagnall's Dictionary." The network was still nervous, and inserted the words "FUNK AND WAGNALLS" at the bottom of the screen as Hawn said the line.

"Sock it to me," *Laugh-In*'s most famous phrase, had been banned from radio in the years before television took it up. In rhythm and blues, "sock it to me" had clear sexual connotations; in *Laugh-In*'s universe, it signaled that Judy Carne was about to get drenched with a bucket of water or hit on the head with a huge hammer.

On Color TV:

"Often, as Huntley and Brinkley report, the audience just gets Chet tinted correctly (healthy suntan, hazel-brown eyes) when the producer cuts to David, who comes in as a lurid lavender. By the time Brinkley is attuned (pale pink skin, blue eyes) there is a switch to a remote Frank McGee looking sickly green at Cape Kennedy."
　　　—"The Hue of All Flesh," *Time*, March 4, 1966

On Color on TV

A network vice president, quoted in *Newsweek*, April 3, 1967, on the lack of shows featuring African Americans:

"An audience, using drama as escape, can fantasize best with a universal character in a white, Anglo-Saxon, middle-class town in the Midwest. . . . You've got to ask yourself if this is discrimination."

Number of significant African-American characters appearing in the 84 shows on network primetime during one week in March 1967, according to *Newsweek*: 9

Newsweek, September 30, 1968:

"If there is a new look to the tube this season, color it black. Thirty Negro actors will be filling continuing roles on weekly series, and dozens more will be doing one-shots and commercials. Now it becomes a question of whether they appear as recognizable blacks acting within a recognizable black context or as just attractive ebony furniture."

Julia, the first situation comedy starring an African American, began airing on NBC's primetime lineup in 1968. The series featured Diahann Carroll as Julia Baker, the widowed mother of a six-year-old boy (her husband, an Air Force captain, had been shot down and killed in Vietnam). She worked as a registered nurse in an aerospace industrial clinic and lived in a racially integrated (though seemingly otherwise all white) building.

Number of national sponsors for *Nat King Cole* NBC found after trying for one year in 1956: 0
Number of national sponsors for NBC's *Julia* in 1968: 3 (General Foods, Mattel, and Monley and James Laboratories [pharmaceutical company])
Number of stations carrying *Julia* in Fall 1968: 150–200, including Atlanta, Houston, Richmond, and Jackson, Mississippi

Hal Kanter, writer-producer-director of *Julia*:

"We're going to tell the truth. We're going to show it like it is.
    "*Julia* shows the humorous aspects of discrimination . . . properly handled . . . without rancor, without inflammation, and withal telling their attempts to enjoy the American dream."

Diahann Carroll:

"I'd like a couple of million of them [white Americans] to watch and say, 'Hey, so that's what they do when they go home at night.'"

Robert Lewis Shayon, television critic, in *Saturday Review*, May 1968:

"[*Julia*] is a far, far cry from the bitter realities of Negro life in the urban ghetto, the pit of America's explosion potential."

Ebony, November 1968:

"As a slice of Black America, *Julia* does not explode on the TV screen with the impact of a ghetto riot. It is not that kind of show. Since the networks have had a rash of shows dealing with the nation's racial problems, the light-hearted *Julia* provides welcome relief, if, indeed, relief is even acceptable in these troubled times."

From *Julia*:

Julia and her son, Corey, have recently moved into the building. Corey is playing with his new friend, who is white. They see Corey's mother.
    Friend: "You know what? Your mother's colored."
    Corey: "Sure. So am I."
    Friend: "You are?"

The two boys are playing when a white neighbor walks by.
    Friend: "Hi."
    Neighbor: "Who's your friend?"
    Friend: "This is my friend Corey. He's colored."
    Neighbor: "Yes. Well, I guess it runs in his family."

On Rural Shows:

Number of CBS sitcoms in mid-1960s with rural setting or characters: 5 of 14

Andy Griffith Show (1960–68)
Beverly Hillbillies (1962–71)
Green Acres (1965–71)
Petticoat Junction (1963–70)
Gomer Pyle, USMC (1964–70)

Percentage of these shows appearing in yearly top ten Nielsen rankings: 100

Number of years *The Andy Griffith Show* was in the top ten Nielsen rankings, 1960–1970: 8

Average number of letters received by Granny on *The Beverly Hillbillies* each week in 1963: 1,000

Newsweek, July 14, 1969:

"A few TV critics have suggested that [these] popular shows answer a peculiar hunger of Americans for Ozark humor. They argue that many newly affluent Americans, bewildered by the technological '60s, see themselves as bumbling hillbillies lost in suburbia."

Top Ten TV Shows
(by Nielsen ratings)

1960	1961	1962	1963	1964
Gunsmoke	Wagon Train	The Beverly Hillbillies	The Beverly Hillbillies	Bonanza
Wagon Train	Bonanza	Candid Camera	Bonanza	Bewitched
Have Gun, Will Travel	Gunsmoke	The Red Skelton Show	Dick Van Dyke Show	Gomer Pyle, USMC
Andy Griffith Show	Hazel	Bonanza	Petticoat Junction	Andy Griffith Show
The Real McCoys	Perry Mason	The Lucy Show	Andy Griffith Show	The Fugitive
Rawhide	The Red Skelton Show	Andy Griffith Show	The Lucy Show	The Red Skelton Show
Candid Camera	Andy Griffith Show	Ben Casey	Candid Camera	Dick Van Dyke Show
The Untouchables	Danny Thomas Show	Danny Thomas Show	The Ed Sullivan Show	The Lucy Show
The Price Is Right	Dr. Kildare	Dick Van Dyke Show	Danny Thomas Show	Peyton Place II
The Jack Benny Show	Candid Camera	Gunsmoke	My Favorite Martian	Combat

1965	1966	1967	1968	1969	1970
Bonanza	Bonanza	The Andy Griffith Show	Rowan and Martin's Laugh-In	Rowan and Martin's Laugh-In	Marcus Welby, M.D.
Gomer Pyle, USMC	The Red Skelton Hour	The Lucy Show	Gomer Pyle, USMC	Gunsmoke	The Flip Wilson Show
The Lucy Show	The Andy Griffith Show	Gomer Pyle, USMC	Bonanza	Bonanza	Here's Lucy
The Red Skelton Hour	The Lucy Show	Gunsmoke	Mayberry RFD	Mayberry RFD	Ironside
Batman	The Jackie Gleason Show	Family Affair	Family Affair	Family Affair	Gunsmoke
The Andy Griffith Show	Green Acres	Bonanza	Gunsmoke	Here's Lucy	ABC Movie of the Week
Bewitched	Daktari	The Red Skelton Hour	Julia	The Red Skelton Hour	Hawaii Five-O
The Beverly Hillbillies	Bewitched	The Dean Martin Show	The Dean Martin Show	Marcus Welby, M.D.	Medical Center
Hogan's Heroes	The Beverly Hillbillies	The Jackie Gleason Show	Here's Lucy	Walt Disney's Wonderful World of Color	Bonanza
Green Acres	Gomer Pyle, USMC	Saturday Night at the Movies	The Beverly Hillbillies	The Doris Day Show	The F.B.I.

1971	1972
All in the Family	All in the Family
The Flip Wilson Show	Sanford and Son
Marcus Welby, M.D.	Hawaii Five-O
Gunsmoke	Maude
ABC Movie of the Week	Bridget Loves Bernie
Sanford and Son	Sunday Mystery Movie
Mannix	The Mary Tyler Moore Show
Funny Face	Gunsmoke
Adam-12	Wonderful World of Disney
The Mary Tyler Moore Show	Ironside

MOVIES

Average price of a movie ticket

1960	$0.69 (in 1999 dollars: $3.83)
1970	$1.552 (in 1999 dollars: $6.86)

Percentage of U.S. recreational spending that went to movie tickets

1943	25.7
1960	5.2
1970	2.86

Number of films released (U.S.–produced only)

1943	397
1960	154
1970	186

Academy Awards

Year	Academy Award for Best Picture	Top Moneymaking Film
1960	The Apartment	Ben-Hur
1961	West Side Story	The Guns of Navarone
1962	Lawrence of Arabia	Spartacus
1963	Tom Jones	Cleopatra
1964	My Fair Lady	The Carpetbaggers
1965	The Sound of Music	Mary Poppins
1966	A Man for All Seasons	Thunderball
1967	In the Heat of the Night	The Dirty Dozen
1968	Oliver!	The Graduate
1969	Midnight Cowboy	The Love Bug
1970	Patton	Airport

Note: "Moneymaking" ranks are based on rental income (money paid by theater to distributor), not box office receipts, and includes only domestic (U.S.) rentals during the calendar year indicated. Some films considered for the Academy Awards are released late in the year and their moneymaking rankings are calculated during the following year. None, however, achieved first place.

POPULAR MUSIC

Percentage of cars in United States with radio

1960	68.1
1970	92.5

Number of commercial FM stations

1960	688
1970	2,184

Percentage of households with AM/FM or FM only radios

1960	10
1970	50

Top 25 Hits of the Decade
(based on weeks spent as #1 on the Billboard "Hot 100" Chart)

1.	"Hey Jude"	The Beatles	1968
2.	"The Theme from *A Summer Place*"	Percy Faith	1960
3.	"Tossin' and Turnin'"	Bobby Lewis	1961
4.	"I Want to Hold Your Hand"	The Beatles	1964
5.	"I'm a Believer"	The Monkees	1966
6.	"I Heard It Through the Grapevine"	Marvin Gaye	1968
7.	"Aquarius/Let the Sunshine In"	The 5th Dimension	1969
8.	"Are You Lonesome Tonight?"	Elvis Presley	1960
9.	"In the Year 2525"	Zager and Evans	1969
10.	"It's Now or Never"	Elvis Presley	1960
11.	"I Can't Stop Loving You"	Ray Charles	1962
12.	"Love Is Blue"	Paul Mauriat	1968
13.	"Big Girls Don't Cry"	The Four Seasons	1962
14.	"Big Bad John"	Jimmy Dean	1961
15.	"Sugar Shack"	Jimmy Gilmer and the Fireballs	1963
16.	"Honey"	Bobby Goldsboro	1968
17.	"To Sir with Love"	Lulu	1967
18.	"Cathy's Clown"	The Everly Brothers	1960
19.	"People Got to Be Free"	The Rascals	1968
20.	"Get Back"	The Beatles with Billy Preston	1969
21.	"The Ballad of the Green Berets"	Sgt. Barry Sadler	1966
22.	"Sherry"	The Four Seasons	1962
23.	"Can't Buy Me Love"	The Beatles	1964
24.	"Sugar, Sugar"	The Archies	1969
25.	"(Sittin' on) The Dock of the Bay"	Otis Redding	1968

Billboard Number 1 Hit (based on weeks as #1 on the Billboard "Hot 100" Chart)	Grammy Record of the Year
1960 Percy Faith, "Theme from *A Summer Place*"	
1961 Bobby Lewis, "Tossin' and Turnin'"	Henry Mancini, "Moon River"
1962 Ray Charles, "I Can't Stop Loving You"	Tony Bennett, "I Left My Heart in San Francisco"
1963 Jimmy Gilmer and the Fireballs, "Sugar Shack"	Henry Mancini, "Days of Wine and Roses"
1964 The Beatles, "I Want to Hold Your Hand"	Stan Getz and Astrud Gilberto, "The Girl from Ipanema"
1965 The Rolling Stones, "(I Can't Get No) Satisfaction"	Herb Alpert and the Tijuana Brass, "A Taste of Honey"
1966 The Monkees, "I'm a Believer"	Frank Sinatra, "Strangers in the Night"
1967 Lulu, "To Sir With Love"	The 5th Dimension, "Up, Up and Away"
1968 The Beatles, "Hey Jude"	Simon and Garfunkel, "Mrs. Robinson"
1969 The 5th Dimension, "Aquarius/Let the Sunshine In"	The 5th Dimension, "Aquarius/ Let the Sunshine In"
1970 Simon and Garfunkel, "Bridge Over Troubled Water"	Simon and Garfunkel, "Bridge Over Troubled Water"

THE BEATLES

John Lennon:

"Christianity will go. It will vanish and shrink. I needn't argue about that: I'm right, and I will be proved right. We're more popular than Jesus Christ now; I don't know which will go first—rock 'n' roll or Christianity. Jesus was all right, but his disciples were thick and ordinary. It's them twisting it that ruins it for me."

—in *Datebook*, a U.S. teen magazine, August 1966, quoted in *Newsweek*, August 22, 1966

Grand Wizard, Ku Klux Klan, in response:

"Get out there, you teenagers, and cut off your Beatle-style long hair. Join those at the bonfires and throw your locks into the fire! Burn, burn, burn everything that is Beatle!"

American teenager, quoted in *Newsweek:*

"My friends and I don't agree with what John said . . . but we've loved the Beatles for three years and just can't stop now."
  —*Newsweek*, August 22, 1966

Lennon at Chicago press conference:

"I do believe Christianity is shrinking . . . that doesn't mean that I have un-Christian thoughts. I could have said TV, cinema, or big cars were more popular than Jesus. Sometimes we forget we are Beatles and say things we'd say to a friend across a bar. I am sorry I opened my mouth."
  —*Newsweek*, August 22, 1966

Women in Rock

Grace Slick, Jefferson Airplane:

"It's weird to be a girl in a male band. In a group you have to get used to functioning as a guy does. It definitely makes you more masculine—either that or you go crazy. You can't hold five guys up with your manicure."

Linda Ronstadt, Linda and the Stone Poneys:

"Girl singers, man, they always get the bad end of the stick. Everyone gangs up on them. She always gets credited with the least amount of brains, and she always gets delegated all the squaw labor. The men form a kinship. There's always competition between the sexes."

Janis Joplin, Big Brother and the Holding Company:

"The tenor of the band is different now. The guys are starting to sing and there is something to build around: me."
  —all quotes from "The Queen Bees," *Newsweek*, January 15, 1968

"The Mamas and the Papas are two beards, a beauty, and a Big Bertha."
  —Joplin quoted in *Time*, October 28, 1966

On Janis Joplin:

"Janis Joplin sang the blues, a black man's music, even though she was white, because she was born with ready-made grief inside her. . . . She sound-

ed her barbaric yawp into a mike plugged into the world. She never hesitated to sacrifice the beautiful tone for the raw power of emotion, for the animal sounds that accompanied the animal sensual grace of her passionate body."
—from *Newsweek* obituary for Joplin, October 19, 1970

On James Brown:

"For one frenetic hour, Brown commanded the stage like a one-man riot. Stocky as a fireplug, hair teased into a luxuriant pompadour, he danced, preached, mugged, strutted, and sang with a mounting intensity carefully calculated to inflame. . . . [As the self-proclaimed] biggest Negro cat in show business right now . . . he is attended by two hairdressers who give him a daily coiffure, sleeps in a round bed, owns a fire-engine-red Sting Ray and a brace of Cadillacs."
—*Time*, April 1, 1966

Number of pairs of shoes James Brown owned in 1966, according to *Time* magazine: 80
Number of pairs of boots Nancy Sinatra bought following her hit, "These Boots Are Made for Walking": 250

BOOKS

Is there any recently published book that you would especially like to read?
(Gallup Poll, February 1963)

Yes	16%
No	84%

Paperback book sales in 1960: $300 million

Fiction

Best-Selling Hardcover	*Pulitzer Prize, Fiction*
1960 Allen Drury, *Advise and Consent*	Allen Drury, *Advise and Consent*
1961 Irving Stone, *The Agony and the Ecstasy*	Harper Lee, *To Kill a Mockingbird*
1962 Katherine Anne Porter, *Ship of Fools*	Edwin O'Connor, *The Edge of Sadness*
1963 Morris L. West, *The Shoes of the Fisherman*	William Faulkner, *The Reivers*

1964	John Le Carre, *The Spy Who Came in From the Cold*	No award
1965	James A, Michener, *The Source*	Shirley Ann Grau, *The Keepers of the House*
1966	Jacqueline Susann, *Valley of the Dolls*	Katherine Anne Porter, *The Collected Stories of Katherine Anne Porter*
1967	Elia Kazan, *The Arrangement*	Bernard Malamud, *The Fixer*
1968	Arthur Hailey, *Airport*	William Styron, *The Confessions of Nat Turner*
1969	Philip Roth, *Portnoy's Complaint*	N. Scott Momaday, *House Made of Dawn*
1970	Erich Segal, *Love Story*	Jean Stafford, *Collected Stories*
1971	Arthur Hailey, *Wheels*	No award
1972	Richard Bach, *Jonathon Livingston Seagull*	Wallace Stegner, *Angle of Repose*

Non-Fiction

	Best-Selling Hardcover	Pulitzer Prize, General Non-Fiction
1960	D. C. Jarvis, *Folk Medicine*	————
1961	*The New English Bible: The New Testament*	————
1962	Dr. Herman Taller, *Calories Don't Count*	Theodore H. White, *The Making of the President*
1963	Charles M. Shultz, *Happiness Is a Warm Puppy*	Barbara W. Tuchman, *The Guns of August*
1964	American Heritage and United Press International, *Four Days*	Richard Hofstadter, *Anti-Intellectualism in American Life*
1965	Dan Greenburg, *How to Be a Jewish Mother*	Howard Mumford Jones, *O Strange New World*
1966	Norman F. Dacey, *How to Avoid Probate*	Edwin Way Teale, *Wandering Through Time*
1967	William Manchester, *The Death of a President*	David Brion Davis, *The Problem of Slavery in Western Culture*
1968	*Better Homes and Gardens New Cook Book*	Will and Ariel Durant, *Rousseau and Revolution*

1969   *American Heritage Dictionary of the English Language*

Rene Jules Dubos, *So Human and Animal*; Norman Mailer, *The Armies of the Night*

1970   David Reuben, M.D., *Everything You Wanted to Know About Sex but Were Afraid to Ask*

Erik H. Erikson, *Gandhi's Truth*

1971   "M," *The Sensuous Man*

John Toland, *The Rising Sun*

1972   Kenneth Taylor, *The Living Bible*

Barbara W. Tuchman, *Stilwell and the American Experience in China, 1911–1945*

Hugo Prize, Science Fiction

1960   Robert A. Heinlein, *Starship Troopers*
1961   Walter M. Miller, *A Canticle for Leibowitz*
1962   Robert A. Heinlein, *Stranger in a Strange Land*
1963   Philip K. Dick, *The Man in the High Castle*
1964   Clifford D. Simak, *Way Station*
1965   Fritz Leiber, *The Wanderer*
1966   Roger Zelazny, . . . *And Call Me Conrad*; Frank Herbert, *Dune*
1967   Robert A. Heinlein, *The Moon is a Harsh Mistress*
1968   Roger Zelazny, *Lord of Light*
1969   John Brunner, *Stand on Zanzibar*
1970   Ursula K. Le Guin, *The Left Hand of Darkness*
1971   Larry Niven, *Ringworld*
1972   Philip Jose Farmer, *To Your Scattered Bodies Go*

Caldecott Medal, Children's Book

1960   Marie Hall Ets, *Aurora Labastida, Nine Days to Christmas*
1961   Ruth Robbins, *Baboushka and the Three Kings*
1962   Marcia Brown, *Once a Mouse*
1963   Ezra Jack Keats, *Snowy Day*
1964   Maurice Sendak, *Where the Wild Things Are*
1965   Beatrice Schenk De Regniers, *May I Bring a Friend?*
1966   Sorche Leodhas, Nonny Hogrogian, *Always Room for One More*
1967   Evaline Ness, *Sam, Bangs, and Moonshine*
1968   Barbara Emberley, *Drummer Hoff*
1969   Arthur Ransome, *The Fool of the World and the Flying Ship*
1970   William Steig, *Sylvester and the Magic Pebble*

1971   Gail E. Haley, A *Story, a Story: An African Tale*
1972   Nonny Hogrogian, *One Fine Day*

Poetry

Poetry Consultant to the Library of Congress:

The position of Poet Laureate was created by Congress in 1985, but from 1937 to 1985 the Poetry Consultant to the Library of Congress was considered the de facto Poet Laureate.

Richard Eberhart	1959–61
Louis Untermeyer	1961–63
Howard Nemerov	1963–64
Reed Whittemore	1964–65
Stephen Spender	1965–66
James Dickey	1966–68
William Jay Smith	1968–70
William Stafford	1970–71
Josephine Jacobson	1971–73

NEWS MEDIA

Number of magazines that failed in the 1960s (1962–72): 160
Number of magazines that were started in that period: 753

Amount that *Life* magazine paid for the color footage of JFK's assassination taken by a bystander (the Zapruder film): $150,000
Cost of *Life* subscription in 1971: 12 cents an issue
Cost to publish it: 41 cents an issue

Increase in circulation of *Time* magazine, 1961–1970: 62%

Percentage of daily newspapers owned by newspaper groups	
1960	31.8
1970	50.3

Number of nonwhite reporters at *Los Angeles Times* before 1965 Watts uprising: 0

Total number of column-inches *Los Angeles Times* devoted to LA black community, 1943–1965: 120

Number of daily newspapers published in New York

1960	7
1967	3

SOURCES FOR "ENTERTAINMENT, POPULAR ARTS, AND PUBLICATIONS" SECTION

Baughman, James L. *The Republic of Mass Culture*. Baltimore: Johns Hopkins University Press, 1992.

Information Please Entertainment Almanac. http://www.infoplease.lycos.com

Movie Site. http://www.moviesite.net

Newcombe, Horace, et al., eds. *Encyclopedia of Television*. Chicago: Fitzroy Dearborn, 1997.

Rood, Karen L. *American Culture After World War II*. Detroit: Gale Research, 1994.

Steinberg, Cobbett S. *Film Facts*. New York: Facts on File, 1980.

——. *TV Facts*. New York: Facts on File, 1985.

Stern, Jane, and Michael Stern. *Encyclopedia of Pop Culture*. New York: HarperPerrenial, 1992.

Ultimate TV. http://www.ultimatetv.com

Whitburn, Joel. *Joel Whitburn's Top Pop Singles 1955–1996*. 8th ed. Menomonee, Wisc.: Record Research Inc., 1997.

Issues of *Time, Newsweek, New Yorker*.

Fashion

FASHION AND FAD TIMELINE (FOR WOMEN)

1960
Jackie Kennedy look: pillbox hat, clean necklines, suits with short jackets, large (and few) buttons and three-quarter length sleeves

1961
Bell bottoms and crop tops with bare midriff
Gingham capri pants (lined) with Capezio thong sandals
Tight knit stretch pants with stirrups and flats

1962
Mary Quant mod look: knee-length jumpers; dark eye makeup with heavy eyeliner and white or very pale pink lipstick—"the look of the precocious child"

1963
Shift dresses
Vidal Sassoon introduces geometric, asymmetric, and bob haircuts

1964
Rudy Gernreich's topless bathing suit, the "monokini," was a high-waisted, black knit brief with suspenders. More than 3,000 were sold in Europe.
Trouser suits introduced in Paris collections

1965
Miniskirts dominate U.S. fashion
Go-go boots (white, mid-calf)
Over-the-knee boots to go with miniskirts
Culotte dresses

1966
Pantsuits: lean look, with snug, longer jackets, often double-breasted. Pantsuits were not acceptable dress for many schools, restaurants, and offices. Tent and baby doll dresses

1967
Paper dresses: they creased easily and were highly flammable
Capes

1969
Midi skirts

1971
Hot pants
Granny dresses

Percentage of Americans who said they would object to a daughter of theirs wearing a miniskirt 1967: 70

Percentage of Americans in 1966 who believed it was "in bad taste" for women to wear shorts in public: 60

Percentage of Americans in 1965 who believed that schools should ban the "Beatle haircut" on boys: 80

Pairs of pantyhose produced	
1968	200 million
1969	624 million

Polyester fabric as a percentage of the U.S. textile market	
1960	11
1970	41

The Paper Dress

Scott Paper Company offered paper dresses as a promotional gimmick in March 1966. The company was introducing its new line of napkins, paper towels, and toilet paper, which was called "Colorful Explosions." By August more than half a million Americans had sent in the product coupon with $1.25 postage and received a paper dress in return. Other companies joined in, as did fashion designers and boutiques. Soon there were 60 manufacturers with total sales estimated between $50 and $100 million dollars. Most dresses sold for under $3.

Paper dresses weren't exactly made of paper. Different companies offered different "fabrics" (Scott's was its own patented "Dura-Weve"), but all were some version of nonwoven tissue somewhat similar to light-weight felt. Most were made of cellulose strengthened with rayon mesh.

Paper dresses' greatest drawback—or advantage, depending on your perspective—was that they couldn't be washed or drycleaned. That was in large part because they were extremely flammable, and were treated with a fire retardant that couldn't withstand laundering.

SOURCES FOR "FASHION" SECTION

The 1960s Ladies' Style Site. http://www.geocities.com/SoHo/4473

Melinkoff, Ellen. *What We Wore*. New York: Quill, 1984.

Palmer, Alexandra. "Paper Clothes: Not Just a Fad." In Patricia A. Cunningham and Susan Voso Lab, eds., *Dress and Popular Culture*. Bowling Green, OH: Bowling Green State University Popular Press, 1991.

Trager, James. *The People's Chronology: A Year-by-Year Record of Human Events from Prehistory to the Present*. New York: Henry Holt, 1992 and 1994.

Sports and Olympics

SPORTS

Associated Press Athlete of the Year

MALE		FEMALE	
1960	Rafer Johnson, Decathlon	1960	Wilma Rudolph, Track
1961	Roger Maris, Baseball	1961	Wilma Rudolph, Track
1962	Maury Wills, Baseball	1962	Dawn Fraser, Swimming
1963	Sandy Koufax, Baseball	1963	Mickey Wright, Golf
1964	Don Schollander, Swimming	1964	Mickey Wright, Golf
1965	Sandy Koufax, Baseball	1965	Kathy Whitworth, Golf
1966	Frank Robinson, Baseball	1966	Kathy Whitworth, Golf
1967	Carl Yastrzemski, Baseball	1967	Billie Jean King, Tennis
1968	Denny McLain, Baseball	1968	Peggy Fleming, Skating
1969	Tom Seaver, Baseball	1969	Debby Meyer, Swimming
1970	George Blanda, Football	1970	Chi Cheng, Track
1971	Lee Trevino, Golf	1971	Evonne Goolagong, Tennis
1972	Mark Spitz, Swimming	1972	Olga Korbut, Gymnastics

Average Salary of Professional Athletes

	1967	1975
Baseball	$19,000	$46,000
Basketball	$20,000	$107,000
Football	$25,000	$42,000

Baseball

World Series

Year	Winner	Series	Loser
1960	Pittsburgh Pirates	4–3 (WLLWWLW)	NY Yankees
1961	NY Yankees	4–1 (WLWWW)	Cincinnati Reds
1962	NY Yankees	4–3 (WLWLWLW)	SF Giants
1963	LA Dodgers	4–0	NY Yankees
1964	St. Louis Cardinals	4–3 (WLLWWLW)	NY Yankees
1965	LA Dodgers	4–3 (LLWWWLW)	Minnesota Twins
1966	Baltimore Orioles	4–0	LA Dodgers
1967	St. Louis Cardinals	4–3 (WLWWLLW)	Boston Red Sox
1968	Detroit Tigers	4–3 (LWLLWWW)	St. Louis Cardinals
1969	NY Mets	4–1 (LWWWW)	Baltimore Orioles
1970	Baltimore Orioles	4–1 (WWWLW)	Cincinnati Reds

WORLD SERIES MOST VALUABLE PLAYER
(presented by *Sport* magazine, 1955–88)

1960	Bobby Richardson, NY, 2B
1961	Whitey Ford, NY, P
1962	Ralph Terry, NY, P
1963	Sandy Koufax, LA, P
1964	Bob Gibson, St. Louis, P
1965	Sandy Koufax, LA, P
1966	Frank Robinson, Baltimore, OF
1967	Bob Gibson, St. Louis, P
1968	Mickey Lolich, Detroit, P
1969	Donn Clendenon, NY, 1B
1970	Brooks Robinson, Baltimore, 3B

FRANCHISE EXPANSIONS AND CHANGES DURING THE 1960S

1961	Los Angeles Angels join American League
	Washington Senators join American League
1962	Houston Colt .45s join National League
	New York Mets join National League
1969	Montreal Expos join National League
	San Diego Padres join National League

Kansas City Royals join American League
Seattle Pilots join American League

CITY AND NAME CHANGES

NATIONAL LEAGUE
Dodgers, from Brooklyn to Los Angeles, 1958
Giants, from New York to San Francisco, 1958
Colt .45s (Houston), renamed Astros, 1965
Braves, from Milwaukee to Atlanta, 1966

AMERICAN LEAGUE
Senators, from Washington to Bloomington, MN, and renamed Minnesota
   Twins, 1961
Angels, Los Angeles Angels renamed California Angels, 1965; from Los Ange-
   les to Anaheim, 1966
Athletics, from Kansas City to Oakland, 1968

IMPACT OF TELEVISION

Year that Major League Baseball owners repealed their ban against their
games being broadcast in minor-league territories: 1951

Number of minor league clubs
1949	51
1970	20

Attendance at minor league games
1949	24 million
1969	10 million

Average length of baseball game in early 20th century: 1 1/2 hour
Average length of baseball game by mid-1960s: over 2 1/2 hours
TV Guide's description of Major League Baseball: "Delay, Dally, and Stall"
Year that Major League Baseball Rules Committee enlarged the strike zone,
   possibly attempting to speed up the game for television: 1963
Drop in the number of major league runs, 1962–63: 1,681
Drop in number of home runs, 1962–63: 297
Drop in batting averages, 1962–63: 12 points

Basketball

NBA Championship

Year	Winner	Series	Loser
1960	Boston Celtics	4–3 (WLWLWLW)	St. Louis Hawks
1961	Boston Celtics	4–1 (WWLWW)	St. Louis Hawks
1962	Boston Celtics	4–3 (WLLWLWW)	LA Lakers
1963	Boston Celtics	4–2 (WWLWLW)	LA Lakers
1964	Boston Celtics	4–1 (WWLWW)	SF Warriors
1965	Boston Celtics	4–1 (WWLWW)	LA Lakers
1966	Boston Celtics	4–3 (LWWWLLW)	LA Lakers
1967	Philadelphia '76ers	4–2 (WWLWLW)	SF Warriors
1968	Boston Celtics	4–2 (WLWLWW)	LA Lakers
1969	Boston Celtics	4–3 (LLWWLWW)	LA Lakers
1970	New York Knicks	4–3 (WLWLWLW)	LA Lakers

Most Valuable Player and Scoring Averages
(selected by NBA players between 1956 and 1980)

1960	Wilt Chamberlain, Philadelphia, C	37.6
1961	Bill Russell, Boston, C	16.9
1962	Bill Russell, Boston, C	18.9
1963	Bill Russell, Boston, C	16.8
1964	Oscar Robertson, Cincinnati, G	31.4
1965	Bill Russell, Boston, C	14.1
1966	Wilt Chamberlain, Philadelphia, C	33.5
1967	Wilt Chamberlain, Philadelphia, C	24.1
1968	Wilt Chamberlain, Philadelphia, C	24.3
1969	Wes Unseld, Baltimore, C	13.8
1970	Willis Reed, New York, C	1.7

FRANCHISE ORIGINS AND CHANGES DURING THE 1960S
(ABA = American Basketball Association; NBA teams are not labeled)

NEW WESTERN CONFERENCE TEAMS
Denver Nuggets, 1967 (ABA)
Phoenix Suns, 1968
Portland Trail Blazers, 1970
Seattle Super Sonics, 1967
San Diego Rockets, 1967
Dallas Spurs, 1967 (ABA)
Buffalo Braves, 1970

MAJOR FRANCHISE MOVES
Philadelphia Warriors to San
    Francisco, 1962
Minneapolis Lakers to Los
    Angeles, 1960

NEW EASTERN CONFERENCE TEAMS
Chicago Bulls, 1966
Cleveland Cavaliers, 1970
Indiana Pacers, 1967 (ABA)
Milwaukee Bucks, 1968
New Jersey Nets, 1967 (ABA)
Chicago Packers, 1961; renamed
    Zephyrs, 1962

MAJOR FRANCHISE MOVES
St. Louis Hawks to Atlanta,
    1968
Syracuse Nationals to
    Philadelphia ('76ers), 1963
Chicago Zephyrs to Baltimore
    (Bullets), 1963

Number of NBA teams
1960   8
1970   14

American Basketball Association began play in 1967 with 11 teams; it merged four teams with the NBA following the 1975–76 season.

College Basketball

NCAA Championship

	Champion	*Runner-up*
1960	Ohio State	California
1961	Cincinnati	Ohio State
1962	Cincinnati	Ohio State
1963	Loyola, IL	Cincinnati
1964	UCLA	Duke
1965	UCLA	Michigan

1966	Texas Western	Kentucky
1967	UCLA	Dayton
1968	UCLA	North Carolina
1969	UCLA	Purdue
1970	UCLA	Jacksonville

Football

NFL–NFC Championship

Year	Winner	Loser	Score
1960	Philadelphia Eagles	Green Bay Packers	17–13
1961	Green Bay Packers	New York Jets	37–0
1962	Green Bay Packers	New York Jets	16–7
1963	Chicago Bears	New York Jets	14–10
1964	Cleveland Browns	Baltimore Colts	27–0
1965	Green Bay Packers	Cleveland Browns	23–12
1966	Green Bay Packers	Dallas Cowboys	34–27
1967	Green Bay Packers	Dallas Cowboys	21–17
1968	Baltimore Colts	Cleveland Browns	34–0
1969	Minnesota Vikings	Cleveland Browns	27–7
1970	Dallas Cowboys	San Francisco 49ers	17–10

Note: NFL Champions through 1969, when NFL and AFL merged following 1969 season; 1970 is NFC championship.

AFL–AFC Championships

Year	Winner	Loser	Score
1960	Houston Oilers	LA Chargers	24–16
1961	Houston Oilers	SD Chargers	10–3
1962	Dallas Cowboys	Houston Oilers	20–17*
1963	San Diego Chargers	Boston Patriots	51–10
1964	Buffalo Bills	San Diego Chargers	20–7
1965	Buffalo Bills	San Diego Chargers	23–0
1966	Kansas City Chiefs	Buffalo Bills	31–7
1967	Oakland Raiders	Houston Oilers	40–7
1968	NY Jets	Oakland Raiders	27–23
1969	Kansas City Chiefs	Oakland Raiders	17–7
1970	Baltimore Colts	Oakland Raiders	27–17

* Sudden death overtime. 1970 is AFC Championship, following NFL–AFL merger in 1969.

Super Bowl

	Win	Lose	Score	Place	Date
I	Green Bay Packers	Kansas City Chiefs	35–10	Los Angeles	Jan. 15, 1967
II	Green Bay Packers	Oakland Raiders	33–14	Miami	Jan. 14, 1968
III	NY Jets	Baltimore Colts	16–7	Miami	Jan. 12, 1969
IV	Kansas City Chiefs	Minnesota Vikings	23–7	New Orleans	Jan. 11, 1970
V	Baltimore Colts	Dallas Cowboys	16–13	Miami	Jan. 17, 1971

SUPER BOWL MOST VALUABLE PLAYER

(Pete Rozelle Award for Super Bowl MVP; presented by *Sport* magazine)

I	Bart Starr, Green Bay, QB
II	Bart Starr, Green Bay, QB
III	Joe Namath, NY Jets, QB
IV	Len Dawson, Kansas City, QB
V	Chuck Howley, Dallas, LB

FRANCHISE ORIGINS AND CHANGES DURING THE 1960S

NEW FRANCHISES	*MAJOR FRANCHISE MOVES*
NFL	
1960　Dallas Cowboys	Chicago Cardinals to St. Louis, 1960
1961　Minnesota Vikings	
1966　Atlanta Falcons	
1967　New Orleans Saints	
AFL	
1960　Buffalo Bills	LA Chargers to San Diego, 1961
1960　Denver Broncos	New York Titans renamed Jets, 1963
1960　Kansas City Chiefs	Dallas Texans to Kansas City (Chiefs),
1960　New England Patriots	1963
1960　New York Titans	
1960　Oakland Raiders	
1960　Los Angeles Chargers	
1960　Tennessee Oilers	
1966　Miami Dolphins	
1968　Cincinnati Bengals	

The American Football League (AFL) was created in 1959 and began play in 1960 with eight teams. The AFL and NFL agreed to a merger in 1966, leading to the first Super Bowl in January 1967. (The Super Bowl was originally called the AFL–NFL World Championship Game.) In 1970 the AFL's ten teams— New England Patriots, Buffalo Bills, Cincinnati Bengals, Denver Broncos, Houston Oilers, Kansas City Chiefs, Miami Dolphins, New York Jets, Oakland Raiders, and San Diego Chargers—joined the National Football Conference (NFC) as the NFL and AFL merged. This merger created a 26-team league, made up of two conferences with three divisions each.

IMPACT OF TELEVISION

Year Monday Night Football began: 1970

Average audience for televised games
1967   11 million
1977   20 million

Year that instant replay was first used in broadcast of football games: 1963

Amount that AFL signed Joe Namath for (3 years) in 1965: $420,000
Percentage rise in ticket sales during Namath's first year with the NY Jets: 100
Percentage of NFL players making less than $15,000 a season in 1968: 20

Vince Lombardi, coach, Green Bay Packers:

"Everywhere you look there is a call for freedom, independence . . . [but] we must learn again to respect authority, because to disavow it is contrary to our individual natures."
   —quoted in "The Toughest Man in Pro Football," *Esquire*, January 1968

Golf

The Masters

Year	Winner	Score	Runner-up
1960	Arnold Palmer	282	Ken Venturi (283)
1961	Gary Player	280	Arnold Palmer and Charles R. Coe (281)
1962	Arnold Palmer*	280	Dow Finsterwald and Gary Player (280)
1963	Jack Nicklaus	286	Tony Lema (287)
1964	Arnold Palmer	276	Jack Nicklaus and Dave Marr (282)

1965	Jack Nicklaus	271	Arnold Palmer and Gary Player (280)
1966	Jack Nicklaus*	288	Gay Brewer Jr. and Tommy Jacobs (288)
1967	Gay Brewer, Jr.	280	Bobby Nichols (281)
1968	Bob Goalby	277	Roberto DeVicenzo (278)
1969	George Archer	281	Billy Casper, George Knudson, and Tom Weiskopf (289)
1970	Billy Casper*	279	Gene Littler (279)

* Playoffs, 18 holes. 1962: Palmer (68), Player (71), Finsterwald (77); 1966: Nicklaus (70), Jacobs (72), Brewer (78); 1970: Casper (69), Littler (74)

U.S. Women's Open

1960	Betsy Rawls
1961	Mickey Wright
1962	Murle Lindstrom
1963	Mary Mills
1964	Mickey Wright
1965	Carol Mann
1966	Sandra Souzich
1967	Catherine Lacoste
1968	Susie M. Berning
1969	Donna Caponi
1970	JoAnne Carner

Tennis

U.S. Open

Men

Year	Winner	Loser
1960	Neale Fraser	R. Laver
1961	Roy Emerson	R. Laver
1962	Rod Laver	R. Emerson
1963	Rafael Osuna	F. Froeling
1964	Roy Emerson	F. Stolle
1965	Manuel Santana	C. Drysdale
1966	Fred Stolle	J. Newcombe
1967	John Newcombe	C. Graebner
1968	Arthur Ashe (amateur)	B. Lutz

1968	Arthur Ashe (open)	T. Okker
1969	Stan Smith (amateur)	B. Lutz
1969	Rod Laver (open)	T. Roche
1970	Ren Rosewall	T. Roche

In 1968 and 1969, both Amateur and Open Championships were held.

Women

Year	Winner	Loser
1960	Darlene Hard	M. Bueno
1961	Darlene Hard	A. Haydon
1962	Margaret Smith	D. Hard
1963	Maria Bueno	M. Smith
1964	Maria Bueno	C. Graebner
1965	Margaret Smith	B.J. Moffitt
1966	Maria Bueno	N. Richey
1967	Billie Jean King	A. Jones
1968	Margaret Court (amateur)	M. Bueno
1968	Virginia Wade (open)	B. J. King
1969	Margaret Court (amateur)	V. Wade
1969	Margaret Court (open)	N. Richey
1970	Margaret Court	R. Casals

In 1968 and 1969, both Amateur and Open Championships were held.

Boxing

Heavyweight Titleholders

Ingemar Johansson	1959–60
Floyd Patterson	1960–62
Sonny Liston	1962–64
Muhammad Ali (Cassius Clay)	1964–70

Note: Muhammad Ali was stripped of his world championship title in 1967, when he refused to be drafted into the U.S. military.

Ring Magazine "Fight of the Year"

Year	Winner	Loser	Result
1960	Floyd Patterson	Ingemar Johansson	KO (5)
1961	Joe Brown	Dave Charnley	W (15)
1962	Joey Giardello	Henry Hank	W (10)
1963	Cassius Clay	Doug Jones	W (10)
1964	Cassius Clay	Sonny Liston	KO (7)
1965	Floyd Patterson	George Chuvalo	W (12)
1966	Jose Torres	Eddie Cotton	W (15)
1967	Nino Benvenuti	Emile Griffith	W (15)
1968	Dick Tiger	Frank DePaula	W (10)
1969	Joe Frazier	Jerry Quarry	KO (7)
1970	Carlos Monzon	Nino Benvenuti	KO (12)

Hockey

Stanley Cup Champions

Year	Winner	Series	Loser
1960	Montreal Canadiens	4–0	Toronto Maple Leafs
1961	Chicago	4–2 (WLWLWW)	Detroit Red Wings
1962	Toronto Maple Leafs	4–2 (WWLLWW)	Chicago Black Hawks
1963	Toronto Maple Leafs	4–1 (WWLWW)	Detroit Red Wings
1964	Toronto Maple Leafs	4–3 (WLLWLWW)	Detroit Red Wings
1965	Montreal Canadiens	4–3 (WWLLWLW)	Chicago Black Hawks
1966	Montreal Canadiens	4–2 (LLWWWW)	Detroit Red Wings
1967	Toronto Maple Leafs	4–2 (LWWLWW)	Montreal Canadiens
1968	Montreal Canadiens	4–0	St. Louis Blues
1969	Montreal Canadiens	4–0	St. Louis Blues
1970	Boston Bruins	4–0	St. Louis Blues

Auto Racing

Indianapolis 500

Year	Winner	Car	MPH
1960	Jim Rathmann	Ken–Paul Special	138.767
1961	A.J. Foyt	Bower Seal Fast Special	139.130

1962	Roger Ward	Leader Card 500 Roadster	140.293
1963	Parnell Jones	Agajanian–Willard Special	143.137
1964	A.J. Foyt	Sheraton–Thompson Special	147.350
1965	Jim Clark	Lotus Ford	150.686
1966	Graham Hill	American Red Ball Special	144.317
1967	A.J. Foyt	Sheraton–Thompson Special	151.207
1968	Bobby Unser	Rislone Special	152.882
1969	Mario Andretti	STP Oil Treatment Special	156.867
1970	Al Unser	Johnny Lightning Special	155.749

Horse Racing

Kentucky Derby

Year	Horse	Time	Jockey
1960	Venetian Way	2:02 2/5	Bill Hartack
1961	Carry Back	2:04	John Sellers
1962	Decidedly	2:00 2/5	Bill Hartack
1963	Chateaugay	2:01 4/5	Braulio Baeza
1964	Northern Dancer	2:00	Bill Hartack
1965	Lucky Debonair	2:01 1/5	Bill Shoemaker
1966	Kauai King	2:02	Don Brumfield
1967	Proud Clarion	2:00 3/5	Bobby Ussery
1968	Forward Pass	—*	Ismael Valenzuela
1969	Majestic Prince	2:01 4/5	Bill Hartack
1970	Dust Commander	2:03 2/5	Mike Manganello

*Winner disqualified.

OLYMPICS

		WINTER	SUMMER
1960	XVII Olympiad	Squaw Valley, Calif., USA	Rome, Italy
1964	XVIII Olympiad	Innsbruck, Austria	Tokyo, Japan
1968	XIX Olympiad	Grenoble, France	Mexico City, Mexico
1972	XX Olympiad	Sapporo, Japan	Munich, Germany

Rights fees paid for television coverage

1956 (summer):	TV stations refused to pay fee
1960 (summer):	$394,000, CBS
1972 (summer):	$7.5 million, ABC
1996 (summer):	$456 million, NBC

Hours of televised coverage

1960 (summer):	20
1972 (summer):	63

Rome, 1960

August 25–September 10
Number of nations participating: 83
Number of athletes competing: 5,348

Total Medals Won by Leading Nations

	Gold	Silver	Bronze
Soviet Union	43	29	31
United States	34	21	16
Italy	13	10	13
West Germany	10	10	6
Australia	8	8	6
Turkey	7	2	0
Hungary	6	8	7
Japan	4	7	7
Poland	4	6	11
East Germany*	3	9	7

*See "Political Issues"; athletes identified by nation of origin here.

POLITICAL ISSUES

Both East and West Germany wished to compete, and both had formed Olympic Committees, though the East German committee only had provisional status with the International Olympic Committee (IOC). The two nations had competed in the 1956 Games in Melbourne with a single team, and the IOC negotiated a similar solution: East and West Germany competed as a single team, with one flag and one national anthem.

The People's Republic of China (PRC), though not a member of the IOC, insisted that Nationalist China (Taiwan) could not compete under the designation "China." Nonaligned nations and those in the Eastern Bloc supported the PRC. The IOC declared that a nation might call itself whatever it wished internally, but that in the Olympic Games its designation must be consistent with the territory it actually ruled/occupied. Thus Nationalist China could compete only as "Taiwan (Formosa)." The PRC, angry that Taiwan was allowed to compete at all, did not attend the Rome Games. This ruling set a precedent that allowed for divided nations, such as East and West Germany and North and South Korea, to compete as separate teams.

South Africa's apartheid policies led to strong opposition.

FIRSTS

The Olympic Games returned to Rome, the final site of the ancient Olympic Games, which were suspended in 3 A.D. by Theodosius I.

Television rights were sold to both the United States' CBS and to Eurovision, making the Olympic Games potentially profitable and much more widely seen.

ATHLETES

Ethiopia's Abebe Bikila, the first black African to win an Olympic gold medal, ran the marathon barefoot, triumphing in the nation that had invaded his country in 1935.

United States' Cassius Clay, age 18, won the light-heavyweight division in boxing.

U.S. sprinter Wilma Rudolph, who was one of 19 children in her family and was not able to walk without braces until she was eleven years old, won three gold medals.

Tokyo, 1964

October 10–24
Number of nations participating: 93
Number of athletes competing: 5,140

Total Medals Won by Leading Nations

	Gold	Silver	Bronze
United States	36	26	28
Soviet Union	30	31	35
Japan	16	5	8
Italy	10	10	7
Hungary	10	7	5
West Germany	7	14	14
Poland	7	6	10
Australia	6	2	10
Czechoslovakia	5	6	3
Great Britain	4	12	2

POLITICAL ISSUES

The IOC had suspended Indonesia over its resistance to admitting teams from Israel and Taiwan to the Fourth Asian Games in Jakarta in 1962. Indonesia, in reaction, organized the Games of the New Emergency Forces (GANEFO), and the IOC declared that any nation participating in GANEFO would be barred from the Tokyo Olympics. Thus Indonesia and North Korea were not allowed to participate in the 1964 Olympics.

South Africa was banned from the Tokyo Games because of its apartheid policies and refusal to allow black athletes to participate on South Africa's Olympic teams.

FIRSTS

Japan hosted the Games for the first time. Tokyo had been selected as the site of the 1940 Games, but when the nation went to full-scale war with China in 1937 Tokyo withdrew as host city.

In Lima, Peru, 328 people were killed in a riot following a pre-Olympic soccer qualifying match between Peru and Argentina.

ATHLETES

Japan's women's volleyball team were local favorites, and their victory over the Soviet Union's team drew an 80% audience share on Japanese television.

Ethiopia's Abebe Bikila became the first athlete to win the Olympic marathon twice.

Ukrainian gymnast Larysa Latynina won six medals, bringing her career total to eighteen.

Mexico City, 1968

October 12–27
Number of nations participating: 112
Number of athletes competing: 5,531

Total Number of Medals Won by Leading Nations

	Gold	Silver	Bronze
Unites States	45	28	34
Soviet Union	29	32	30
Japan	11	7	7
Hungary	10	10	12
East Germany	9	9	7
France	7	3	5
Czechoslovakia	7	2	4
West Germany	5	11	10
Australia	5	7	5
Great Britain	5	5	3

POLITICAL ISSUES

After South Africa was banned from competition in the 1964 Games, it pledged to moderate its selection process so that black athletes might compete. Less than a year before the 1968 Games, the IOC lifted its ban against South Africa, which still officially practiced apartheid. African nations began a boycott and secured support from Eastern Europe, Islamic nations, and the West Indies, as well as a threat from the Soviet Union to participate in the boycott. The IOC could not negotiate a compromise, and withdrew its invitation from South Africa and also from Rhodesia, which, though it had created integrated teams, had racial policies offensive to the African states.

As student movements gathered strength around the world, university students in Mexico also mounted demonstrations and called for a general strike. The student movement of July–October, 1968, was met with force, most particularly on October 2, ten days before the Olympic opening ceremonies, when troops fired upon a demonstration at the Plaza of the Three Cultures, or Tlatelolco, killing up to 500 people and wounding as many as one thousand. Many protestors subsequently were arrested and tortured. Critics argued that the government responded so harshly in part because it feared the student protests would disrupt the Olympics and ruin Mexico's bid for international recognition. The IOC dismissed this event as "an internal affair."

U.S. athletes Tommie Smith and John Carlos, accepting medals for their victories in the 200-meter sprint, bowed their heads and gave Black Power salutes with black-gloved hands during the playing of the American national anthem. Each man appeared without shoes, wearing only high black socks to symbolize African-American poverty. They had considered boycotting the games to protest U.S. racial discrimination and had helped to organize the Olympic Project for Human Rights (OPHR). They were suspended from the U.S. team but drew international attention to U.S. racial discrimination. Several other black U.S. athletes symbolically expressed their solidarity with Smith and Carlos, but George Foreman instead waved a small American flag after winning a gold medal in boxing.

FIRSTS

Mexico City, with an altitude of 7,400 feet, was the highest site for a Summer Olympics thus far. Oxygen resuscitation took place sixteen times during rowing events, but 252 athletes surpassed previous Olympic records as the thin air helped athletes in race events of 1,500 meters or less and contributed to U.S. long jumper Bob Beamon's jump that broke the world's record by almost two feet.

The first woman to carry the Olympic torch into the stadium and light the Olympic flame was Norma Enriqueta Basilio, a 20-year-old hurdler.

A synthetic track, called "Tartan," developed by the 3M company, was used for track and field events.

Sweden's Hans-Gunnar Liljenvall, modern pentathlon, was the first Olympic athlete disqualified for using prohibited drugs: he had drunk alcohol to steady his nerves before the shooting portion of his event.

ABC scheduled 44 hours of TV coverage, almost three times as many as had aired in 1964. Using the sorts of techniques developed in the network's popular ABC's *Wide World of Sports*, ABC offered personal profiles of the athletes and compelling graphics to create a more dramatic television experience.

ATHLETES

U.S. high jumper Dick Fosbury won the gold, set a record, and established a new standard technique, "the Fosbury Flop," by going over the bar backward.

Gymnast Vera Čáslavská of Czechoslovakia was the most popular competitor; she won three gold medals and then got married in a Mexican church surrounded by thousands of fans.

Munich, 1972

August 26–September 10
Number of nations participating: 122
Number of athletes competing: 7,147

Total Number of Medals Won by Leading Nations

	Gold	Silver	Bronze
Soviet Union	50	27	22
United States	33	31	30
East Germany	20	23	23
West Germany	13	11	16
Japan	13	8	8
Australia	8	7	2
Poland	7	5	9
Hungary	6	13	16
Bulgaria	6	10	5
Italy	5	3	10

POLITICAL ISSUES

In 1970 the IOC officially expelled South Africa from the Olympic Games because of its apartheid policies.

On September 5 eight Palestinian terrorists, members of the group "Black September," scaled the fence surrounding the Olympic Village and broke into the dormitory section where the Israeli national team was sleeping. They killed two members of the team and took nine hostage (one escaped through a window), issuing demands for the release of 200 Arabs held in Israeli prisons and helicopters to transport them, with hostages, out of West Germany. All the hostages, one police officer, and five of the terrorists died during a failed rescue attempt. Games were suspended for 34 hours, and a memorial service was held in the Olympic stadium.

ATHLETES

USSR gymnast Olga Korbut became the star of the 1972 Olympics.

U.S. swimmer Mark Spitz won seven gold medals.

Frank Shorter was the first American in 64 years to win a gold medal for the marathon.

SOURCES FOR "SPORTS AND OLYMPICS" SECTION

ESPN Information Sports Almanac. New York: Hyperion Books, 1999.

Findling, John E. and Kimberly D. Pelle, eds. *Historical Dictionary of the Modern Olympic Movement.* Westport, Conn.: Greenwood Press, 1996.

Hickok Sports. http://www.hickoksports.com

Information Please Entertainment Almanac. http://infoplease.lycos.com.

Newcombe, Horace, et al., eds. *Encyclopedia of Television.* Chicago: Fitzroy Dearborn, 1997.

Rader, Benjamin G. *American Sports.* Englewood Cliffs, N.J.: Prentice-Hall, Inc., 1990.

PART VI

Chronology

BRIEF CHRONOLOGY

1960   National Liberation Front (NLF) established in Vietnam.
        Cuba seizes U.S. assets.
        African-American students begin a sit-in movement at a lunch
            counter in Greensboro, North Carolina; the movement
            spreads throughout the South.
        Student Non-Violent Coordinating Committee (SNCC)
            founded.
        Students for a Democratic Society (SDS) founded.
        Young Americans for Freedom (YAF) founded; issue their
            "Sharon Statement."
        Nixon-Kennedy debate watched by largest TV audience ever–
            75 million.
        Democrats John F. Kennedy and his running mate Lyndon
            Baines Johnson win presidential election; Kennedy is the
            first Roman Catholic elected U.S. president.
        First communication satellite (*Echo I*) and first weather satel-
            lite (*Tiros I*) are launched.
        New York Circuit Court of Appeals rules that *Lady Chatter-
            ley's Lover* is not obscene.
        Camelot opens on Broadway with Robert Goulet, Julie An-
            drews, and Richard Burton.
        Hit songs include "Itsy Bitsy Teenie Weenie Yellow Polka Dot
            Bikini."
        Pepsi begins its "For those who think young" campaign.
        "The Pill" approved for contraceptive use by the Food and
            Drug Administration.

1961   Berlin Wall is erected, signaling the heightening of cold-war
            tensions.
        Bay of Pigs invasion of Cuba fails.
        Peace Corps founded.
        Yuri Gagarin (USSR) becomes first human in space (orbiting
            for 1 hour, 49 minutes); second Soviet manned flight stays
            aloft 25 hours.
        Alan Shepard becomes the first American in space; suborbital
            flight of the Freedom 7 lasts 15 minutes.
        President Kennedy urges Americans to set a goal of landing a
            man on the Moon before the end of the decade.

Freedom Riders challenge segregation of interstate travel facilities in the South; Interstate Commerce Commission (ICC) bans segregation in all interstate facilities.

JFK appoints a Commission on the Status of Women.

Harper Lee's *To Kill a Mockingbird* and Joseph Heller's *Catch-22* are published. Henry Miller's previously banned *Tropic of Cancer* is published in the United States and reaches the best-seller list.

Movies: *Splendor in the Grass* and *Raisin in the Sun*.

Timothy Leary and Richard Alpert are fired from Harvard University for using undergraduates in their research on hallucenogenic drugs.

Ray Kroc buys out the McDonald brothers for $14 million and founds the McDonald's chain with 200 restaurants.

The Supremes sign with Motown and release their first records.

1962   Cuban Missile Crisis.

MACV (U.S. Military Assistance Command, Vietnam) is established, beginning buildup of U.S. personnel. Kennedy authorizes U.S. military advisors to return fire if attacked.

Astronaut John Glenn orbits the Earth three times.

Kennedy sends in federal troops when rioting breaks out as African-American student James Meredith attempts to attend the University of Mississippi; Governor Ross Barnett personally bars his way, violating a federal appellate court order.

Jacqueline Kennedy's televised tour of the White House is watched by more than 46 million Americans.

The Port Huron Statement is issued by SDS.

Supreme Court rules against prayer in public schools (*Engel* v. *Vitale*).

Telstar communications satellite makes possible transatlantic TV broadcasts of up to 20 minutes.

Rachel Carson warns of environmental pollution in *Silent Spring*.

Second Vatican Council opens.

Helen Gurley Brown in *Sex and the Single Girl* says "nice girls do."

Dr. No, the first James Bond film, premieres.

1963 The United States and Soviet Union agree to nuclear-test ban, covering atmosphere and water; Minuteman ICBM declared combat-ready.

Hot line is established between Washington and Moscow

Ngo Dinh Diem, President of South Vietnam, is ousted from power and assassinated.

March on Washington for Jobs and Freedom draws 250,000 civil-rights marchers; Martin Luther King delivers "I Have a Dream" speech

Birmingham police chief Bull Connor turns fire hoses and attack dogs on civil-rights marchers, including children.

Martin Luther King writes "Letter from Birmingham Jail."

Four girls are killed in the bombing of an African-American church in Birmingham, Alabama.

Betty Friedan in *The Feminine Mystique* describes "the problem with no name," helping to launch a new women's movement.

The Beatles' first hit record in the United States: "I Want to Hold Your Hand."

Charles Schultz's *Happiness Is a Warm Puppy* makes the best-seller list.

Hit songs include "Puff (the Magic Dragon)," "Blowin' in the Wind," and "The Times They Are A-Changin'."

President Kennedy assassinated; Lyndon Johnson sworn in as president, November 22.

1964 U.S. destroyer Maddox is allegedly attacked by North Vietnamese in the Gulf of Tonkin (August 2); Congress passes Gulf of Tonkin resolution (August 7), giving President Johnson the authority to wage war in Vietnam.

LBJ defeats Republican candidate Barry Goldwater in November presidential election.

Congress passes the Civil Rights Act of 1964.

Food Stamp program begins.

Freedom Summer; three volunteers and 12 others are murdered.

Free-speech movement begins at University of California, Berkeley.

U.S. Surgeon General's Report links cigarette smoking to lung cancer and other diseases.

Kitty Genovese is attacked and murdered in Brooklyn while her neighbors watch from their windows; no one calls the police until after she has been beaten to death.

First liver and lung transplants are performed.

Movies include: *Dr. Strangelove*; *My Fair Lady*; *Mary Poppins*; *The Pink Panther*.

Go-go girls dancing on raised platforms are a fad; topless go-go girls appear in San Francisco; Rudy Gernreich introduces the topless bathing suit; the bra-less look becomes popular.

Beatles tour the United States and are met by 10,000 fans at JFK airport in New York.

1965 First U.S. combat troops (U.S. Third Marine regiment) arrive in Vietnam.

First teach-in is held at the University of Michigan; others follow, with more than 100,000 attending teach-ins on more than 100 campuses.

SDS sponsors the first national demonstration, in Washington, D.C., against the Vietnam War; antiwar protests take place in 40 cities.

Civil-rights demonstrators attempting to march from Selma to Montgomery, Alabama, are attacked; 3,200 demonstrators later complete the 54-mile "Freedom March."

Congress passes the Voting Rights Act.

Cesar Chavez and the United Farm Workers launch a national consumer strike against California table-grape growers.

Malcolm X is assassinated by members of the Nation of Islam.

First major urban riot takes place in the Watts section of Los Angeles; 34 people die.

Immigration Act abolishes the quota system based on national origins.

Supreme Court strikes down law prohibiting access to birth control (*Griswold* v. *Connecticut*).

Medicare bill is passed.

NBC evening news expands to 30 minutes; prime-time shows are in color.

Gemini space missions make progress toward lunar landing; astronaut Edward White walks in space.

Ralph Nader publishes *Unsafe at Any Speed*.

Major power failure in the Northeast affects 30 million people in the United States and Canada.

Supreme Court eliminates film censorship on state and local levels.

The Grateful Dead begin performing in San Francisco.

1966 Senate Foreign Relations Committee holds televised hearings on the Vietnam War.

Blanket student deferments from the draft are abolished.

The first "rare and endangered species" list is issued by the U.S. Department of the Interior.

Supreme Court guarantees the rights of those accused of crimes in the *Miranda* decision.

NOW (National Organization for Women) is formed.

NOW petitions the Equal Employment Opportunity Commission (EEOC) to end the segregation of employment ads by gender.

The Association to Repeal Abortion Laws is founded in California.

The Black Power movement emerges; the Black Panther Party is formed.

Star Trek premieres on television, along with *Batman, The Smothers Brothers Comedy Hour, Mission: Impossible, The Monkees, The Hollywood Squares,* and *The Dating Game.*

Best-selling books include Jacqueline Susann's *Valley of the Dolls* and Masters and Johnson's *Human Sexual Response.*

A ratings code is instituted by movie studios.

Time magazine names "Twenty-five and Under" as its "Man of the Year."

1967 March on the Pentagon by antiwar protesters.

Astronauts Roger Chaffee, Virgil Grisson, and Edward White are killed in a fire during a test launch of Apollo.

"Summer of Love" takes place in San Francisco.

Riots break out in Newark and Detroit ghettos.

Thurgood Marshall becomes first African-American Supreme Court Justice.

The Public Broadcasting Act, funding public television, is passed.

Movie premieres include: *The Graduate, Guess Who's Coming to Dinner, Bonnie and Clyde,* and *In the Heat of the Night.*

First heart transplant is performed by Dr. Christiaan Barnard in Capetown, South Africa.

1968   Tet Offensive begins in South Vietnam; Walter Cronkite tells the nation on the CBS Evening News that the war is unwinnable.

My Lai massacre takes place.

Paris peace talks begin between United States and North Vietnamese government.

Martin Luther King Jr. is assassinated in Memphis; riots in 125 cities follow.

President Johnson announces his decision not to run for reelection

Robert Kennedy is assassinated in Los Angeles after winning the California Democratic primary.

New books include Eldridge Cleaver's *Soul on Ice* and Tom Wolfe's *The Electric Kool-Aid Acid Test*.

Yale College begins admitting women.

Hair premieres off-off-Broadway.

Volkswagens make up 57 percent of U.S. automobile imports.

Protesters at the Miss America Pageant throw bras, girdles, and high heels into a "freedom trashcan."

"Consciousness-raising" begins in women's liberation groups.

Democratic National Convention in Chicago nominates Hubert Humphrey, while police clash with antiwar demonstrators.

Republican Richard Nixon is elected president on a "law and order" platform; he defeats Hubert Humphrey by a narrow margin.

1969   "Vietnamization" of the war; U.S. troops decrease in number.

Ho Chi Minh dies.

My Lai massacre becomes public knowledge.

Vietnam Moratorium Day.

Gay liberation movement begins following conflict between police and gay patrons of the Stonewall Inn, a bar in New York City's Greenwich Village.

First La Raza conference is held in Denver.

SDS breaks apart; a small violent faction, the Weathermen, emerges.

Astronaut Neil Armstrong is the first human to walk on the Moon (July 20).

Testimony that mothers' milk contains four times the amount of DDT permitted in cows' milk is presented to Congressional committee.

Woodstock and Altamont rock festivals.

Charles Manson and his "family" perform cult murder of Sharon Tate Polanski and others.

Sesame Street premieres.

Movies include: *I am Curious (Yellow)*; *Bob and Carol and Ted and Alice*, and *Easy Rider*, *Oh! Calcutta*, the first nude musical, opens.

1970 United States invades Cambodia.

Four students are killed by National Guardsmen at Kent State University at a protest against the U.S. invasion of Cambodia.

Two students are killed at Jackson State University by National Guardsmen.

Liberalized abortion laws are passed by New York, Alaska, and Hawaii.

Congress repeals the Gulf of Tonkin Resolution.

California adopts the first "no fault" divorce law.

The first Earth Day (April 22) symbolizes the emerging environmental movement.

Environmental Protection Agency is created by Congress.

Hit songs include "Do the Funky Chicken" and "We've Only Just Begun."

Beatles disband.

Everything You Always Wanted to Know About Sex but Were Afraid to Ask makes the best-seller list.

1971 *The Pentagon Papers*, classified documents that detail U.S. involvement in Vietnam since the end of World War II, are published by the *New York Times*.

Twenty-sixth Amendment lowers U.S. voting age from 21 to 18.

The National Press Club begins to admit women as full members.

Winter Soldier Investigation.

U.S. imports top exports for the first time since 1888.

1972 President Nixon visits Beijing; establishes diplomatic relations with China.

Watergate break-in and arrests.

Richard Nixon reelected president, defeating Democratic candidate George McGovern in a landslide.

Final U.S. combat troops leave Vietnam.

Okinawa is returned to Japan after 27 years of U.S. occupation following World War II.

Alabama governor George Wallace is shot while campaigning for the Democratic presidential nomination.

Bill authorizing the development of the space shuttle is signed by Nixon.

Ms. magazine begins publication.

Life magazine ends publication after 36 years.

Equal Rights Amendment passes House and Senate; goes to states for ratification

Phyllis Schlafly forms "Stop ERA."

Supreme Court rules that laws prohibiting dispensing contraceptives to unmarried persons are unconstitutional.

1973   Worldwide energy crisis, exacerbated by Arab nations' oil embargo; economic recession begins in the United States

Peace agreement signed in Paris by the United States, South Vietnam, North Vietnam, and the National Liberation Front.

War Powers Resolution passed over presidential veto.

American Indian Movement (AIM) members occupy Wounded Knee, South Dakota.

Supreme Court guarantees abortion rights (*Roe* v. *Wade*).

U.S. Tennis Association begins awarding equal prize money to women and men.

1974   Facing impeachment following the Watergate hearings, Richard Nixon resigns the presidency on August 9; Vice President Gerald Ford becomes president.

President Ford offers clemency to military deserters and draft resisters.

Little League baseball is opened to girls.

1975   Communist forces capture Saigon on April 29-30 and begin reunification of North and South Vietnam; all U.S. personnel and some South Vietnamese are evacuated in Operation Frequent Wind.

The Vietnam War ends.

"INTRODUCED IN" LIST

1959	Barbie doll
	Lycra
1960	Felt-tip pen
	AstroTurf
	Lasers (Light Amplification caused by Simulated Emission of Radiation)
1961	Electric toothbrush
	IBM Selectric typewriter with moving "golf ball" for type
1962	Polaroid color film
	Tab and Diet Rite colas
	Tab-opening aluminum cans for soft drinks replace removable-tab cans
	Regularly scheduled color television broadcasting (ABC has 3.5 hours a week)
1963	5-digit zip codes
	Weight Watchers
	Trimline phone
	Kodak Instamatic camera
1964	Pop Tarts
	Ford Mustang
	Movies on airplanes
	Freeze-dried coffee
	G.I. Joe action figure
1965	Miniskirt
	Sony home videotape recorder
1966	Stereo cassette decks
	Lyrics on record albums
1967	Microwave for home use ($495; $2,471 in 1999 dollars)
	Corporation for Public Broadcasting
1968	911 emergency number (in New York City only)
	Jacuzzi whirlpool bath ($700 "Roman Bath" model at the Orange County, California, county fair)
1969	ATMs in banks (Chemical Bank, New York City)
	Concorde airplane first flight
1970	No-fault divorce law (California)
	Quadraphonic sound

	Safety tops on drugs and poisons
1971	Soft contact lenses (FDA approval); cost $300 ($1,251 in 1999 dollars)
1972	Federal Express founded (Memphis); Nike founded
1973	UPC (Universal Product Codes)

PART VII

Annotated Bibliography

General Works
Social-Change Movements
  African-American Movements
    Civil Rights Movement
    Black Nationalism
    Memoirs and Personal Accounts
  Urban Unrest
  Antiwar Movement
  Chicano/as
  Conservative Movements
  Environmental Movement
  Gay Liberation Movement
  Native American Movements
  The New Left
  Women's Movement
Culture and Society
  The Counterculture
  Gender and Sexuality
  Immigration/Ethnicity
  Science, Technology, and Culture
  Education
  Religion
  Consumerism/Advertising
  Arts, Media, Entertainment
    Arts, Theater, Dance, Literature
    Film and Television
    Popular Music
Politics and Government
  Liberalism
  Political Leaders and Presidential Administrations
    Barry Goldwater
    Lyndon B. Johnson
    John F. Kennedy
    Richard M. Nixon
    Watergate
    George Wallace
  Social Policy and Programs: The New Frontier and the Great Society
  The Warren Court
The Economy

GENERAL WORKS

Blum, John. *Years of Discord: American Politics and Society, 1961–1974.* New York: Norton, 1991. A readable narrative centered on liberal politics.

Brick, Howard. *Age of Contradiction: American Thought and Culture in the 1960s.* New York: Twayne, 1998.

Cavallo, Dominick. *A Fiction of the Past: The Sixties in American History.* New York: St. Martin's, 1999. Overview, focused on radical youth culture.

Collier, Peter, and David Horowitz. *Destructive Generation: Second Thoughts About the Sixties.* New York: Summit, 1989. Former Sixties activists turned right. Especially critical of the New Left.

Farber, David. *Age of Great Dreams.* New York: Hill and Wang, 1994. Well-written, relatively brief narrative, offering broad overview of Vietnam War, political and cultural changes.

Farber, David, ed. *The Sixties: From History to Memory.* Chapel Hill: University of North Carolina Press, 1994. Scholarly essays by some of the leading historians of the Sixties era.

Isserman, Maurice, and Michael Kazin, *America Divided: The Civil War of the 1960s.* New York: Oxford University Press, 2000. A sympathetic overview of leftist politics and cultural change.

Kaiser, Charles. *1968 in America: Music, Politics, Chaos, Counterculture, and the Shaping of a Generation.* New York: Weidenfeld and Nicolson, 1988. An impressionistic account.

Jones, Landon. *Great Expectations: America and the Baby Boom Generation.* New York: Coward, McCann, and Geoghegan, 1980.

Lyons, Paul. *New Left, New Right, and the Legacy of the Sixties.* Philadelphia: Temple University Press, 1996.

Margolis, Jon. *The Last Innocent Year: America in 1964: The Beginning of the "Sixties."* New York: Morrow, 1999. A snapshot of America in 1964.

Marwick, Arthur. *The Sixties: Social and Cultural Transformation in Britain, France,*

Italy, and the United States, 1958–1974. New York: Oxford University Press, 1998. Huge (928 pages) and excellent international comparative perspective.

McQuaid, Kim. *The Anxious Years: America in the Vietnam-Watergate Era.* New York: Basic, 1989.

Morris, Charles. *A Time of Passion: America, 1960–1980.* New York: Harper and Row, 1984. A pragmatic look at the Sixties and its aftermath.

Patterson, James T. *Grand Expectations: The United States, 1945–1974.* New York: Oxford University Press, 1996. The best account of the larger historical period.

Steigerwald, David. *The Sixties and the End of Modern America.* New York: St. Martin's, 1995. A critical look at the Sixties.

SOCIAL-CHANGE MOVEMENTS

Anderson, Terry. *The Movement and the Sixties: Protest in America from Greensboro to Wounded Knee.* New York: Oxford University Press, 1995. An engaging and encyclopedic account of social-change movements.

Breines, Wini, and Alexander Bloom. *"Takin' it to the Streets": A Sixties Reader.* Oxford University Press, 1995. Collection of primary documents, focusing on social-change movements.

Chalmers, David. *And the Crooked Places Made Straight.* Baltimore: Johns Hopkins University Press, 1991. Very well-written, relatively brief overview of social-change movements.

Morgan, Edward P. *The 60s Experience: Hard Lessons About Modern America.* Philadelphia: Temple University Press, 1991.

Obst, David. *Too Good To Be Forgotten: Changing America in the 60s and 70s.* New York: Wiley, 1998. A personal history of the era by a journalist and antiwar activist.

Tischler, Barbara L., ed. *Sights on the Sixties.* New Brunswick, N.J.: Rutgers University Press, 1992.

African-American Movements

CIVIL RIGHTS MOVEMENT

Belknap, Michael R. *Federal Law and Southern Order: Racial Violence and Constitutional Conflict in the Post-Brown South.* Athens: University of Georgia Press, 1987. An analysis of white Southern opposition to the civil rights movement.

Bloom, Jack. *Class, Race, and the Civil Rights Movement: The Political Economy of Southern Racism.* Bloomington: Indiana University Press, 1987.

Branch, Taylor. *Parting the Waters: America in the King Years, 1954–1963.* New York: Simon and Schuster, 1988. Beautifully written account of the early movement, focused on King.

——. *Pillar of Fire: America in the King Years, 1963–65*. New York: Simon and Schuster, 1998. Continues the narrative begun in *Parting the Waters*.

Brauer, Carl. *John F. Kennedy and the Second Reconstruction*. New York: Columbia University Press, 1977.

Burner, Eric. *And Gently He Shall Lead Them: Robert Parris Moses and Civil Rights in Mississippi*. New York: New York University Press, 1994.

Burns, Stewart, ed. *Daybreak of Freedom: The Montgomery Bus Boycott*. Chapel Hill: University of North Carolina Press, 1997. Documentary history.

Carson, Clayborne. *In Struggle: SNCC and the Black Awakening of the 1960s*. Cambridge: Harvard University Press, 1981.

Chafe, William. *Civilities and Civil Rights: Greensboro, North Carolina and the Black Struggle for Freedom*. New York: Oxford University Press, 1980.

Cone, James H. *Martin and Malcolm and America: A Dream or a Nightmare?* Maryknoll, N.Y.: Orbis Books, 1991. Argues that King and Malcolm X had complementary, not opposite, visions.

Crawford, Vicki L., Jacqueline Anne Rouse, and Barbara Woods, eds. *Women in the Civil Rights Movement: Trailblazers and Torchbearers, 1941–1965*. Brooklyn: Carlson Publishing, 1990. Papers from 1988 conference on contributions of African-American women to the civil rights movement.

Dittmer, John. *Local People: The Struggle for Civil Rights in Mississippi*. Urbana: University of Illinois Press, 1994. Detailed study of civil rights struggle in Mississippi from World War II through the Sixties.

Eskew, Glenn T. *But for Birmingham: The Local and National Movements in the Civil Rights Struggle*. Chapel Hill: University of North Carolina Press, 1997. Focuses on the 1950s to early 1960s.

Fairclough, Adam. *To Redeem the Soul of America: The Southern Christian Leadership Conference and Martin Luther King, Jr*. Athens: University of Georgia Press, 1987. An organizational history.

——. *Race and Democracy: The Civil Rights Struggle in Louisiana, 1915–1972*. Athens: University of Georgia Press, 1995. British historian places Sixties-era activism in context of long struggle that preceded it.

Formisano, Ronald P. *Boston Against Busing: Race, Class, and Ethnicity in the 1960s and 1970s*. Chapel Hill: University of North Carolina Press, 1991.

Gaillard, Frye. *The Dream Long Deferred*. Chapel Hill: University of North Carolina Press, 1988. The story of school desegregation and busing in Charlotte, North Carolina.

Garrow, David. *The FBI and Martin Luther King, Jr.: From "Solo" to Memphis*. New York: Norton, 1981. Account of FBI's surveillance of King and its attempts to destroy him.

——. *Bearing the Cross: Martin Luther King, Jr., and the Southern Christian Leadership Conference*. New York: Morrow, 1986. Beautifully written study of King's public and private life and his sense of mission, based, in part, on more than 700 interviews and King's extensive FBI files.

Goldfield, David. *Black, White, and Southern: Race Relations and Southern Culture, 1940 to the Present.* Baton Rouge: Louisiana State University Press, 1990.

Graham, Hugh Davis. *The Civil Rights Era: Origins and Development of National Policy, 1960–1972.* New York: Oxford University Press, 1990.

Grant, Joanne. *Ella Baker: Freedom Bound.* New York: Wiley, 1998. Definitive biography of major civil rights activist, with forward by Julian Bond.

Lawson, Steven. *Black Ballots: Voting Rights in the South, 1944–1969.* New York: Columbia University Press, 1976. Rev. ed., Lanham, Md.: Lexington Books, 1999.

——. *In Pursuit of Power: Southern Blacks and Electoral Politics, 1965–1982.* New York: Columbia University Press, 1985.

Marable, Manning. *Race, Reform, and Rebellion: The Second Reconstruction in Black America, 1945–1990.* Jackson: University Press of Mississippi, 1991.

McAdam, Doug. *Freedom Summer.* New York: Oxford, 1988. Superb history of 1964 Freedom Summer, primarily focused on experiences of white volunteers.

Meier, August and Elliot Rudwick. *CORE: A Study in the Civil Rights Movement, 1942–1968.* New York: Oxford University Press, 1973. An early organizational history.

Mills, Kay. *This Little Light of Mine: The Life of Fannie Lou Hamer.* New York: Plume, 1993. Popular biography.

Morris, Aldon. *The Origins of the Civil Rights Movement: Black Communities Organizing for Change.* New York: Free Press, 1984.

O'Reilly, Kenneth. *"Racial Matters": The FBI's Secret File on Black America, 1960–1972.* New York: Free Press, 1989.

Parker, Frank M. *Black Votes Count: Political Empowerment in Mississippi After 1965.* Chapel Hill: University of North Carolina Press, 1990. Struggle for voting rights and efforts of Mississippi political establishment to avoid implementing the 1965 Voting Rights Act.

Payne, Charles M. *I've Got the Light of Freedom: The Organizing Tradition and the Mississippi Freedom Struggle.* Berkeley: University of California Press, 1995. The early civil rights movement at the grassroots level.

Robnett, Belinda. *How Long? How Long? African-American Women in the Struggle for Civil Rights.* New York: Oxford University Press, 1997.

Sitkoff, Harvard. *The Struggle for Black Equality, 1954–1992.* New York: Hill and Wang, 1993. A major overview.

Stern, Mark. *Calculating Visions: Kennedy, Johnson, and Civil Rights.* New Brunswick, N.J.: Rutgers University Press, 1992. Analyzes roles of moral vision and political calculation in Kennedy's and Johnson's approaches to civil rights.

Weisbrot, Robert. *Freedom Bound: A History of America's Civil Rights Movement.* New York: Norton, 1990. Vivid and balanced single-volume overview.

Whalen, Charles, and Barbara Whalen. *The Longest Debate: A Legislative History of the 1964 Civil Rights Act.* New York: New American Library, 1985.

BLACK NATIONALISM

Bush, Rod. *We Are Not What We Seem: Black Nationalism and Class Struggle in the American Century.* New York: New York University Press, 1999. Reassessment of Black Power movement, with particular emphasis on the role of the urban poor.

Button, James W. *Black Violence: Political Impact of the 1960s Riots.* Princeton, N.J.: Princeton University Press, 1978.

Carson, Clayborne. *Malcolm X: The FBI File.* New York: Carroll and Graf, 1991.

Haines, Herbert. *Black Radicals and the Civil Rights Mainstream, 1954–1970.* Knoxville: University of Tennessee Press, 1988. A general study of the Black Power movement.

Pearson, Hugh. *Shadow of the Panther: Huey Newton and the Price of Black Power in America.* Reading, MA: Addison-Wesley, 1994. A negative portrayal by an African-American journalist.

Perkins, Margo. *Autobiography as Activism: Three Black Women of the Sixties.* Jackson: University Press of Mississippi, 2000. Analysis of the autobiographies of Elaine Brown, Angela Davis, and Assata Shakur.

Tyson, Timothy B. *Radio Free Dixie: Robert F. Williams and the Roots of Black Power.* Chapel Hill: University of North Carolina Press, 1999. Williams practiced armed self-defense against the Klan in North Carolina in the 1950s, fled to Cuba in the Sixties and from there broadcast his "Radio Free Dixie" program to the United States.

Van Deburg, William. *New Day in Babylon: The Black Power Movement and American Culture, 1965–1975.* Chicago: University of Chicago Press, 1992. Analysis of Black Power as a cultural movement.

Ture, Kwame (Stokely Carmichael), and Charles V. Hamilton. *Black Power: The Politics of Liberation in America.* New York: Random House, 1967. Rev. ed., New York: Vintage, 1992. A classic account of the Black Power movement by two of its leaders.

MEMOIRS AND PERSONAL ACCOUNTS

Brown, Elaine. *A Taste of Power: A Black Woman's Story.* New York: Pantheon, 1992. Brown's memoir; including rise to leadership in the Black Panther Party.

Cleaver, Eldridge. *Soul on Ice.* New York: McGraw-Hill, 1968. Very influential prison memoirs of man who became Black Panther.

Curry, Constance, et al. *Deep in Our Hearts: Nine White Women in the Freedom Movement.* Athens: University of Georgia Press, 2000. First-person accounts; discusses what motivated each of these young white women to join civil rights struggle.

Davis, Angela. *Angela Davis: An Autobiography.* New York: Random House, 1974. Reprint, New York: International Press, 1988.

Honigsberg, Peter Jan. *Crossing Border Street: A Civil Rights Memoir.* Berkeley: University of California Press, 2000. Law-student volunteer in Louisiana, working with the Deacons for Defense and Justice.

King, Martin L., Jr. *Strength to Love.* New York: Harper and Row, 1963. Memoir.

King, Mary. *Freedom Song: A Personal Story of the 1960s Civil Rights Movement.* New York: Morrow, 1987.

Lewis, John, and Michael D'Orso. *Walking with the Wind: A Memoir of the Movement.* New York: Simon and Schuster, 1998.

Moody, Anne. *Coming of Age in Mississippi.* New York: Dial, 1968. Powerful memoir of a civil rights activist written during the 1960s.

Parsons, Sara Mitchell. *From Southern Wrongs to Civil Rights: The Memoir of a White Civil Rights Activist.* Tuscaloosa: University of Alabama Press, 2000.

Raines, Howell, ed. *My Soul Is Rested: Movement Days in the Deep South Remembered.* New York: Putnam, 1977. A collection of memoirs by civil rights activists.

Robinson, Jo Ann Gibson. Edited, with a foreword, by David J. Garrow. *The Montgomery Bus Boycott and the Women Who Started It: The Memoir of Jo Ann Gibson Robinson.* Knoxville: University of Tennessee Press, 1987.

Seale, Bobby; foreword by James Baldwin. *A Lonely Rage: The Autobiography of Bobby Seale.* New York: Times Books, 1978.

Shakur, Assata. *Assata: An Autobiography.* Westport, Conn.: L. Hill, 1987.

X, Malcolm, and Alex Haley. *The Autobiography of Malcolm X.* New York: Ballantine, 1965. A classic; still powerful.

Urban Unrest

Belknap, Michael R. *Administrative History of the Civil Rights Division of the Department of Justice During the Johnson Administration.* New York: Garland, 1991.

Conot, Robert. *Rivers of Blood, Years of Darkness: The Unforgettable Classic Account of the Watts Riot.* New York: Morrow, 1967.

Fine, Sidney. *Violence in the Model City: The Cavanaugh Administration, Race Relations and the Detroit Riot of 1967.* Ann Arbor: University of Michigan Press, 1989.

Horne, Gerald. *Fire This Time: The Watts Uprising and the Meaning of the 1960s.* Charlottesville: University Press of Virginia, 1995. Detailed account from archival research; argues that repression of the Left in Los Angeles created space for the rise of black nationalism that exploded in Watts uprising.

Jacobs, Ronald N. *Race, Media, and the Crisis of Civil Society: From the Watts Riots to Rodney King.* New York: Cambridge University Press, 2000.

Kerner, Otto. *Kerner Report: The 1968 Report of the National Advisory Commission on Civil Disorders.* New York: Pantheon, 1968; rev. ed., 1988.

Antiwar Movement

Berman, William C. J. *William Fulbright and the Vietnam War: The Dissent of a Political Realist.* Kent, Ohio: Kent State University Press, 1988. The story of the Arkansas senator and establishment opposition to the war.

DeBenedetti, Charles, and Charles Chatfield. *An American Ordeal: The Antiwar Movement of the Vietnam Era.* Syracuse, N.Y.: Syracuse University Press, 1990. An encyclopedic account of the antiwar movement.

Clinton, James W. *The Loyal Opposition: Americans in North Vietnam, 1965–1972.* Niwot: University Press of Colorado, 1995. Interviews with U.S. opponents of the Vietnam War who traveled to North Vietnam during the war.

Dickerson, James. *North to Canada: Men and Women Against the Vietnam War.* Westport, Conn.: Praeger, 1999. Journalist's account of the lives of draft resisters who fled to Canada and stayed there permanently.

Ehrhart, W. D. *Passing Time: Memoir of a Vietnam Veteran Against the War.* Jefferson, N.C.: McFarland, 1989.

Farber, David. *Chicago '68.* Chicago: University of Chicago Press, 1988. The 1968 Democratic National Convention, told from the perspectives of the Yippies, the New Left, and Chicago's political establishment.

Garfinkle, Adam. *Telltale Hearts: The Origins and Impact of the Vietnam Antiwar Movement.* New York: St. Martin's, 1995. Argues that the antiwar movement did not shorten the war, but inadvertently helped to prolong it.

Gottlieb, Sherry Gershon. *Hell No, We Won't Go: Resisting the Draft During the Vietnam War.* New York: Viking, 1991. Based on interviews with draft resisters.

Halstead, Fred. *Out Now!: A Participant's Account of the Movement in the United States Against the Vietnam War.* New York: Pathfinder Press, 1991.

Heineman, Kenneth J. *Campus Wars: The Peace Movement at American State Universities in the Vietnam Era.* New York: New York University Press, 1993. Case studies of the antiwar movement at non-elite universities.

Hershberger, Mary. *Traveling to Vietnam: American Peace Activists and the War.* Syracuse, N.Y.: Syracuse University Press, 1998. Study of U.S. travelers to North Vietnam during the war and U.S. government policies toward such travel.

Hunt, Andrew. *The Turning Point: A History of Vietnam Veterans Against the War.* New York: New York University Press, 1999. Excellent account of VVAW.

Levy, David W. *The Debate Over Vietnam.* Baltimore: Johns Hopkins University Press, 1991. Analyzes the broad social categories and beliefs that shaped the bitter debate.

Jeffreys-Jones, Rhodri. *Peace Now! American Society and the Ending of the Vietnam War.* New Haven: Yale University Press, 1999. Study of development of antiwar activism among four segments of the population (women, students, African Americans, and labor) and the impact each had on government policy.

Robbins, Mary Susannah. *Against the Vietnam War: Writings by Activists.* Syracuse,

N.Y.: Syracuse University Press, 1999. Twenty-five essays, some from the time, some more recent.

Small, Melvin. *Johnson, Nixon, and the Doves*. New Brunswick, N.J.: Rutgers University Press, 1988. Reveals modest influence of antiwar movement on Nixon and Johnson presidential administrations.

——. *Covering Dissent: The Media and the Anti-Vietnam War Movement*. New Brunswick, N.J.: Rutgers University Press, 1995.

Small, Melvin, and William D. Hoover. *Give Peace a Chance: Exploring the Vietnam Antiwar Movement; Essays from the Charles DeBenedetti Memorial Conference*. Syracuse, N.Y.: Syracuse University Press, 1992.

Stacewicz, Richard. *Winter Soldiers: An Oral History of the Vietnam Veterans Against the War*. New York: Twayne, 1997.

Swerdlow, Amy. *Women Strike for Peace: Traditional Motherhood and Radical Politics in the 1960s*. Chicago: University of Chicago Press, 1993.

Tollefson, James W. *The Strength Not to Fight: An Oral History of Conscientious Objectors of the Vietnam War*. Boston: Little, Brown, 1993.

Wells, Tom. *The War Within: America's Battle Over Vietnam*. Berkeley: University of California Press, 1994. Argues that the antiwar movement had a powerful influence in ending the war; analyzes struggles within the antiwar movement as well as struggles over the war itself.

Zaroulis, Nancy and Gerald Sullivan. *Who Spoke Up: An American Protest Against the War in Vietnam*. Garden City, N.Y.: Doubleday, 1984.

Chicano/as

Acuna, Rudolfo. *Occupied America: A History of Chicanos*. 4th ed. New York: Longman, 2000. A radical perspective on Chicano history.

Browning, Rufus T., Dale R. Marshall, and David H. Tabb. *Protest is Not Enough: The Struggle of Blacks and Hispanics for Equality in Urban Politics*. Berkeley: University of California Press, 1984. Based on study of ten Northern California cities.

Broyles-Gonzales, Yolanda. *El Teatro Campesino: Theater in the Chicano Movement*. Austin: University of Texas Press, 1994.

Garcia, F. Chris. *La Causa Política: A Chicano Politics Reader*. Notre Dame, IN: University of Notre Dame Press, 1975.

Garcia, Ignacio M. *Chicanismo: The Forging of a Militant Ethos Among Mexican-Americans*. Tucson: University of Arizona Press, 1997.

Gómez-Quiñones, Juan. *Chicano Politics: Reality and Promise, 1940-1990*. Albuquerque: University of New Mexico Press, 1990. The Calvin P. Horn lectures in Western history and culture.

Griswold del Castillo, Richard, and Richard A. Garcia. *César Chávez: A Triumph of Spirit*. Norman: University of Oklahoma Press, 1995.

Hammerback, John C., Richard J. Jensen, and Jose Angel Gutiérrez. *A War of Words: Chicano Protest in the 1960s and 1970s.* Westport, Conn.: Greenwood Press, 1985. Rhetorical analysis of leading Chicano activists.

Jenkins, Craig J. *The Politics of Insurgency: The Farm Workers Movement in the 1960s.* New York: Columbia University Press, 1985.

Levy, Jacques E. *César Chávez: Autobiography of La Causa.* New York: Norton, 1975. A collection of memoirs of Chávez and UFW activists.

Meister, Dick, and Anne Loftis. *A Long Time Coming: The Struggle to Unionize America's Farm Workers.* New York: Macmillan, 1977.

Mirande, Alfredo, and Evangelina Enriquez. *La Chicana: The Mexican-American Woman.* Chicago: University of Chicago Press, 1979.

Muñoz, Carlos, Jr. *Youth, Identity, Power: The Chicano Movement.* London: Verso, 1989; rev. ed., 2000. Major study of the origins and development of the Chicano movement.

Nabokov, Peter. *Tijerina and the Courthouse Raid.* Albuquerque: University of New Mexico Press, 1969. Journalistic account of New Mexico land-grant movement.

Conservative Movements

Andrew, John A., III. *The Other Side of the Sixties: Young Americans for Freedom and the Rise of Conservative Politics.* New Brunswick, N.J.: Rutgers University Press, 1997. Institutional history of key conservative student group.

Brennan, Mary C. *Turning Right in the Sixties: The Conservative Capture of the GOP.* Chapel Hill: University of North Carolina Press, 1995. History of the origins of modern conservatism; various groups on the conservative fringe of the Republican party consolidate control of the party in the 1960s.

Crawford, Alan. *Thunder on the Right: The "New Right" and the Politics of Resentment.* New York: Pantheon, 1980.

Himmelstein, Jerome. *To the Right: The Transformation of American Conservatism.* Berkeley: University of California Press, 1990. Focused on the 1970s and 1980s; traces New Right back to the Old Right of the 1950s.

Klatch, Rebecca E. *Generation Divided: The New Left, the New Right, and the 1960s.* Berkeley: University of California Press, 1999. Astute interpretation of traditional and libertarian young right-wing men and women in the 1960s.

Phillips, Kevin. *The Emerging Republican Majority.* New Rochelle, N.Y.: Arlington House, 1969. A contemporary assessment of the growing conservative movement by a Republican political analyst.

——. *Post-Conservative America: People, Politics, and Ideology in a Time of Crisis.* New York: Random House, 1982.

Rieder, Jonathan. *Canarsie: The Jews and Italians of Brooklyn Against Liberalism.* Cambridge: Harvard University Press, 1985. Explores white "backlash."

Schneider, Gregory L. *Cadres for Conservatism: Young Americans for Freedom and the*

Rise of the Contemporary Right. New York: New York University Press, 1999. Young Americans for Freedom in the 1960s, and its continuing legacy for American political life.

Unger, Irwin, and Debi Unger. *Turning Point: 1968*. New York: Scribners, 1988.

Environmental Movement

Carson, Rachel. *Silent Spring*. New York: Houghton Mifflin, 1962. A classic of the environmental movement.

Ehrlich, Paul R. *The Population Bomb*. New York: Ballantine, 1968. Very influential Sixties text.

Gottlieb, Robert. *Forcing the Spring: The Transformation of the American Environmental Movement*. Washington, D.C.: Island Press, 1993. Environmentalism from the 1890s to the present, with a chapter on the 1960s.

Hays, Samuel. *Beauty, Health, and Permanence: Environmental Politics in the United States, 1955–1985*. New York: Cambridge University Press, 1987.

Kline, Benjamin. *First Along the River: A Brief History of the U.S. Environmental Movement*. San Francisco: Acada Books, 2000. Overview, colonial era to the present.

Lacey, Michael, ed. *Government and Environmental Politics: Essays on Historical Developments since World War II*. Baltimore: Johns Hopkins University Press, 1991. Eight scholarly essays examining development of post–World War II environmental movement and governmental response.

Lear, Linda. *Rachel Carson: Witness for Nature*. New York: Holt, 1997. Biography.

McCormick, John. *Reclaiming Paradise: The Global Environmental Movement*. Bloomington: University of Indiana Press, 1989.

Rothman, Hal. *The Greening of a Nation? Environmentalism in the United States Since 1945*. New York: Harcourt, 1997. Evolution of environmentalism.

——. *Saving the Planet: The American Response to the Environment in the Twentieth Century*. New York: Ivan R. Dee, 2000. Traces influences on and changes in Americans' cultural attitudes toward the environment.

Sale, Kirpatrick. *The Green Revolution: The American Environmental Movement, 1962–1992*. New York: Hill and Wang, 1993. A very short, useful history of the environmental movement.

Slater, Philip. *Earthwalk*. Garden City, N.Y.: Anchor, 1974.

Gay Liberation Movement

Adam, Barry. *The Rise of a Gay and Lesbian Movement*. Boston: Twayne, 1987. Rev. ed, Macmillan Library Reference, 1995. Broad, transnational overview reaching back to medieval times, updated to include the 1980s; comparative historical sociology.

Bull, Chris, ed. *Witness to Revolution: The Advocate Reports on Gay and Lesbian Politics, 1967–1998.* Los Angeles: Alyson; Turnaround, 1999. Collection of articles from the gay newspaper of record, *The Advocate,* including many from the Sixties era.

Clendinen, Dudley, and Adam Nagourney. *Out For Good: The Struggle to Build a Gay Rights Movement in America.* New York: Simon and Schuster, 1999. Detailed narrative of gay and lesbian rights movement, 1969–1992, by *New York Times* reporters; uses extensive interviews with activists in and opponents of the movement.

Cruikshank, Margaret. *The Gay and Lesbian Liberation Movement.* New York: Routledge, 1992.

D'Emilio, John. *Sexual Politics, Sexual Communities: The Making of a Homosexual Minority in the United States, 1940–1970.* Chicago: University of Chicago Press, 1983. The standard account of the pre-Stonewall "homophile" movement.

——. *Making Trouble: Essays on Gay History, Politics, and the University.* New York: Routledge, 1992. Essays by prominent historian.

Duberman, Martin. *Stonewall.* New York: Dutton, 1993. Narrative woven around the lives of six activists.

Humphreys, Laud. *Out of the Closets: The Sociology of Homosexual Liberation.* Englewood Cliffs, N.J.: Prentice-Hall, 1972. Important work from early gay liberation era.

Jay, Karla. *Tales of the Lavender Menace: A Memoir of Liberation.* New York: Basic, 1999. Tales of the radical women's movement and gay liberation; an engaging memoir.

Marcus, Eric. *Making History: The Struggle for Gay and Lesbian Equal Rights, 1945–1990.* New York: HarperCollins, 1992.

Marotta, Toby. *The Politics of Homosexuality.* Boston: Houghton Mifflin, 1981.

Rutledge, Leigh W. *The Gay Decades, from Stonewall to the Present: The People and Events that Shaped Gay Lives.* New York: Plume, 1992.

Teal, Donn. *The Gay Militants.* New York: St. Martin's, 1995. First-person account, originally published in 1971.

Wittman, Carl. *A Gay Manifesto.* Boston: New England Free Press, 1970.

Native American Movements

Blue Cloud, Peter. *Alcatraz Is Not an Island.* Berkeley, Calif.: Wingbow Press (distributed by Book People), 1972. Reprint, Mohawk Nation, Rooseveltown, N.Y.: Akwesasne Notes, 1980. Includes a 60-minute, recorded interview with Peter Blue Cloud; originally broadcast on the recorded interview with Peter Blue Cloud; originally broadcast on the radio program *You Are on Indian Land.*

Burnette, Robert, and John Koster. *The Road to Wounded Knee.* New York: Bantam, 1974.

Cornell, Stephen. *The Return of the Native: American Indian Political Resurgence.* New York: Oxford University Press, 1988.

Deloria, Vine, Jr. *Custer Died for Your Sins: An Indian Manifesto.* New York: Macmillan, 1969.

——. *We Talk, You Listen: New Tribes, New Turf.* New York: Dell, 1970.

——. *Behind the Trail of Broken Treaties: An Indian Declaration of Independence.* 1974; reprint, Austin: University of Texas Press, 1985.

——, ed. *American Indian Policy in the Twentieth Century.* Norman: University of Oklahoma Press, 1985.

Deloria, Vine, Jr., and Clifford M. Lytle. *American Indians, American Justice.* Austin: University of Texas Press, 1983.

——. *The Nations Within: The Past and Future of American Indian Sovereignty.* New York: Pantheon, 1984.

Dewing, Rolland. *Wounded Knee: The Meaning and Significance of the Second Incident.* New York: Irvington, 1985.

Fixico, Donald. *Termination and Relocation.* Albuquerque: University of New Mexico Press, 1986. A study of federal government Indian policy from 1945 to 1970.

Forbes, Jack D. *Native Americans and Nixon: Presidential Politics and Minority Self-Determination, 1969–1972.* Los Angeles: American Indian Studies Center (UCLA), 1981.

Hertzberg, Hazel W. *The Search for an American Indian Identity: Modern Pan-Indian Movements.* Syracuse, N.Y.: Syracuse University Press, 1971.

Josephy, Alvin, Jr., Joane Nagel, and Troy Johnson, eds. *Red Power: The American Indians' Fight for Freedom.* 2nd ed. Lincoln: University of Nebraska Press, 1999.

Mathiessen, Peter. *In the Spirit of Crazy Horse.* New York: Viking, 1983. Focuses on 1975 shoot-out at Pine Ridge; sympathetic portrait of traditionalist Native Americans.

Means, Russell, with Marvin J. Wolf. *Where White Men Fear to Tread: The Autobiography of Russell Means.* New York: St. Martin's, 1995. Controversial "as-told-to" autobiography of controversial activist.

McNickle, D'Arcy. *Native American Tribalism: Indian Survivals and Renewals.* New York: Oxford University Press, 1973.

Parmon, Donald L. *Indians and the American West in the Twentieth Century.* Bloomington: Indiana University Press, 1994. Good overview with a chapter on "Self Determination and Red Power."

Sayer, John William. *Ghost Dancing the Law: The Wounded Knee Trials.* Cambridge: Harvard University Press, 1997.

Smith, Paul Chaat, and Robert Allen Warrior. *Like a Hurricane: The Indian Movement from Alcatraz to Wounded Knee.* New York: New Press, 1996. Lively narrative focuses on three actions—the takeovers of Alcatraz, the national Bureau of Indian Affairs, and Wounded Knee—and offers a thoughtful evaluation of the successes and failures of the movement.

Szasz, Margaret Connell. *Education and the American Indian: The Road to Self-Determination, 1928–1973*. Albuquerque: University of New Mexico Press, 1974.

The New Left

Bates, Tom. *Rads: The 1970 Bombing of the Army Math Research Center at the University of Wisconsin and Its Aftermath*. New York: HarperCollins, 1992. Analyzes violent antiwar protest.

Bokina, John, and Timothy J. Lukes, eds. *Marcuse: From the New Left to the Next Left*. Lawrence: University Press of Kansas, 1994. Discusses Herbert Marcuse's influence on the New Left.

Brienes, Wini. *Community and Organization in the New Left, 1962–1968: The Great Refusal*. New Brunswick, N.J.: Rutgers University Press, 1989. New Left's community organization projects.

Buhle, Mari Jo, Paul Buhle, and Harvey J. Kaye, eds. *The American Radical*. New York: Routledge, 1994. Informative essays on Leftist leaders.

Darnovsky, Marcy, Barbara Epstein, and Richard Flacks, eds. *Cultural Politics and Social Movements*. Philadelphia: Temple University Press, 1995. Collection of essays based in social-movement theory; approximately one-third of the book is on Sixties movements.

Dellinger, David. *More Power than We Know: The People's Movement Toward Democracy*. Garden City, N.Y.: Doubleday, 1975. Dellinger's personal account of the New Left movement.

——. *From Yale to Jail: The Life Story of a Moral Dissenter*. New York: Pantheon, 1993. Dellinger's autobiography.

Diggins, John. *The Rise and Fall of the American Left*. New York: Norton, 1992.

Gitlin, Todd. *"The Whole World Is Watching": Mass Media in the Making and Unmaking of the New Left*. Berkeley: University of California Press, 1980.

——. *The Sixties: Years of Hope, Days of Rage*. New York: Bantam, 1993. A thoughtful combination of autobiography and history.

Hayden, Tom. *Reunion*. New York: Random House, 1988. A moving memoir by an important student leader and New Leftist in the 1960s.

Isserman, Maurice. *If I Had a Hammer: The Death of the Old Left and the Birth of the New Left*. New York: Basic, 1987. Traces the influence of the Old Left and liberal reform movements on the New Left.

Jacobs, Harold, ed. *Weatherman*. Berkeley: Ramparts Press, 1970. A collection of documents on violence and student protest.

Jezer, Marty. *Abbie Hoffman: American Rebel*. New Brunswick, N.J.: Rutgers University Press, 1992. Biography of Yippie activist who blended counterculture and New Left politics.

Katsiaficas, George N. *The Imagination of the New Left: A Global Analysis of 1968.* Boston: South End Press, 1987.

Levy, Peter B. *The New Left and Labor in the 1960s.* Urbana: University of Illinois Press, 1993. Examines the influence of organized labor on the New Left.

Miller, James. *"Democracy is in the Streets": From Port Huron to the Siege of Chicago.* New York: Simon and Schuster, 1987. The best account of the New Left and its political ideology.

Rorabaugh, W. J. *Berkeley at War: The 1960s.* New York: Oxford University Press, 1989. History of the Berkeley scene.

Rossinow, Doug. *The Politics of Authenticity: Liberalism, Christianity, and the New Left in America.* New York: Columbia University Press, 1998. A cultural, political, and social history of the New Left in Austin, Texas.

Rothman, Stanley and S. Robert Lichter. *Roots of Radicalism: Jews, Christians and the New Left.* New York: Oxford University Press, 1982. Attempts to provide a character sketch of "the radical" and examines the role of Jews in the New Left.

Sale, Kirkpatrick. *SDS.* New York: Random House, 1973. An early history of Students for a Democratic Society.

Stephens, Julie. *Anti-disciplinary Protest: Sixties Radicalism and Postmodernism.* New York: Cambridge University Press, 1998.

Stern, Susan. *With the Weathermen: The Personal Journal of a Revolutionary Woman.* New York: Doubleday, 1975. Memoir of experiences in one of the most radical organizations of the Sixties.

Women's Movement

Brownmiller, Susan. *In Our Time: Memoir of a Revolution.* New York: Dial 1999.

Chafe, William. *The Paradox of Change: American Women in the 20th Century.* New York: Oxford University Press, 1991. One of the best surveys of women's history in twentieth-century America.

Cohen, Marcia. *The Sisterhood: The True Story of the Women Who Changed the World.* New York: Simon and Schuster, 1988.

Davis, Flora. *Moving the Mountain: The Women's Movement in America Since 1960.* New York: Simon and Schuster, 1991; rev. ed. 1999. A grassroots history.

Duplessis, Rachel Blau, and Ann Snitow, eds. *The Feminist Memoir Project: Voices from Women's Liberation.* New York: Three Rivers Press, 1998. Memoirs of 32 women who were at the vanguard of the women's liberation movement.

Echols, Alice. *Daring to Be Bad: Radical Feminism in America, 1967–1975.* Minneapolis: University of Minnesota Press, 1989. Best history of radical feminism in the 1960s and early 1970s.

Evans, Sara. *Personal Politics: The Roots of Women's Liberation in the Civil Rights Movement and the New Left.* 1979; reprint, New York: Vintage, 1980. A moving history, emphasizing the religious roots and intertwined origins of the various movements.

Firestone, Shulamith. *The Dialectic of Sex: The Case for Feminist Revolution*. New York: Morrow, 1970. Important contemporary work.

Freeman, Jo. *The Politics of Women's Liberation: A Case Study of an Emerging Social Movement and Its Relation to the Policy Process*. New York: McKay, 1975.

Friedan, Betty. *The Feminine Mystique*. New York: Norton, 1963. Friedan's description of "the problem with no name" influenced many women in the early 1960s.

Greer, Gremaine. *The Female Eunuch*. New York: McGraw-Hill, 1972. Revolutionary critique of the nuclear family and the deformation of women's sexuality; key movement text.

Harrison, Cynthia. *On Account of Sex: The Politics of Women's Issues, 1945–1968*. Berkeley: University of California Press, 1988. Examines period before the Sixties revival of feminism.

Hartmann, Susan. *From Margin to Mainstream: American Women and Politics Since 1960*. Philadelphia: Temple University Press, 1989. Overview of women's struggle to move into political system; argues that women's politicization has reshaped American politics.

Heilbrun, Carolyn G. *The Education of a Woman: The Life of Gloria Steinem*. New York: Dial, 1995.

Horowitz, Daniel. *Betty Friedan and the Making of The Feminine Mystique: The American Left, the Cold War, and Modern Feminism*. Amherst: University of Massachusetts Press, 1998. Resituates Friedan's feminism in an older progressive tradition.

Koedt, Ann, Ellen Levine, and Anita Rapone, eds. *Radical Feminism*. New York: Quadrangle Books, 1973. Classic collection.

Linden-Ward, Blanche, and Carol Hurd Green. *Changing the Future: American Women in the 1960s*. New York: Twayne, 1993. A good general overview.

Matthews, Donald, and Jane Sherron De Hart. *Sex, Gender, and the Politics of the ERA: A State and the Nation*. New York: Oxford University Press, 1990. Case study of North Carolina.

Millet, Kate. *Sexual Politics*. Garden City, N.Y.: Doubleday, 1970. Important contemporary work.

Morgan, Robin. *Saturday's Child: A Memoir*. New York: Norton, 2000.

Morgan, Robin, ed. *Sisterhood is Powerful*. New York: Random House, 1970. Classic anthology of women's liberation documents.

Rosen, Ruth. *The World Split Open: How the Modern Women's Movement Changed America*. New York: Viking, 2000. Powerful story of second-wave feminism by an historian who is also a participant.

Rupp, Leila J., and Verta Taylor. *Survival in the Doldrums: The American Women's Rights Movement, 1945 to the 1960s*. New York: Oxford University Press, 1987.

CULTURE AND SOCIETY

The Counterculture

Belasco, Warren J. *Appetite for Change: How the Counterculture Took on the Food Industry, 1966–1988.* New York: Pantheon, 1989. Traces the heightened interest in health foods to the counterculture.

Brand, Stewart, ed. *The Whole Earth Catalog.* New York: Random House, 1971.

Buliosi, Vincent and Curt Gentry. *Helter Skelter: The True Story of the Manson Murders.* New York: Norton, 1974.

Cain, Chelsea, and Moon Unit Zappa, eds. *Wild Child: Girlhoods in the Counterculture.* Seattle: Seal Press, 1999. Memoirs from "daughters of the hippie generation."

Case, John, and Rosemary C. R. Taylor, eds. *Co-ops, Communes, and Collectives: Experiments in Social Change in the 1960s and 1970s.* New York: Pantheon, 1979.

Coyote, Peter. *Sleeping Where I Fall: A Chronicle.* Washington, D.C.: Counterpoint, 1999. The best memoir to come out of the counterculture.

Cox, Craig. *Storefront Revolution: Food Co-ops and the Counterculture.* New Brunswick, N.J.: Rutgers University Press, 1994. A look at the food co-op movement in Minneapolis and St. Paul, Minnesota.

Dickstein, Morris. *Gates of Eden: American Culture in the Sixties.* 1977; reprint, New York: Penguin, 1989. An early history of the counterculture.

Didion, Joan. *Slouching Towards Bethlehem.* New York: Dell, 1968. Powerful essays.

——. *The White Album.* New York: Simon and Schuster, 1979.

Fike, Rupert, ed. *Voices from the Farm: Adventures in Community Living.* Summertown, Tenn.: Book Publishing Company, 1998. Stories from long-lived rural Tennessee commune, "The Farm."

Grogan, Emmett. *Ringolevio: A Life Played for Keeps.* London: Heinemann, 1972. Counterculture memoir of Digger Emmet Grogan.

Keith, Michael C. *Voices in the Purple Haze: Underground Radio and the Sixties.* Westport, Conn.: Praeger, 1997. History of the underground radio movement, based on insights of 30 of its early participants.

Kesey, Ken. *The Further Inquiry.* New York: Viking, 1990. Kesey revisits his Sixties experiences.

Klinkowitz, Jerome. *The American 1960s: Imaginative Acts in a Decade of Change.* Ames: Iowa State University Press, 1980. Examines counterculture literature.

Laffan, Barry. *Communal Organization and Social Transition: A Case Study from the Counterculture of the Sixties and Seventies.* New York: P. Lang, 1997. Ethnography of Jackson Meadows commune.

Lee, Martin A. and Bruce Shlain. *Acid Dreams: The CIA, LSD, and the Sixties Rebellion.* New York: Grove, 1985. An account of the psychedelic movement and Sixties drug culture.

Miller, Timothy. *The Hippies and American Values.* Knoxville: University of Tennessee Press, 1991. Analyzes hippie movement for its ethical values; focuses on drugs, sex, music, and community.

——. *The 60s Communes: Hippies and Beyond.* Syracuse, N.Y.: Syracuse University Press, 1999. Based partly on interviews conducted for the 1960s Communes Project; emphasizes the diversity of these communities. Includes directory of communes.

Monkerud, Don, Malcolm Terence, and Susan Keese, eds. *Free Land, Free Love: Tales of a Wilderness Commune.* Aptos, Calif.: Black Bear Mining and Publishing Company, 2000. Anthology of memoirs from Northern California commune Black Bear Ranch, founded in 1968.

Ohle, David, et al. *Cows are Freaky When They Look at You: An Oral History of the Kaw Valley Hemp Pickers.* Topeka, KS: Watermark Press, 1991. Fascinating tales of counterculture in Lawrence, Kansas.

Peck, Abe. *Uncovering the Sixties: The Life and Times of the Underground Press.* New York: Pantheon, 1985. The pathbreaking study.

Perry, Charles. *The Haight-Ashbury: A History.* New York: Random House, 1984. Day-to-day history.

Perry, Paul, Ken Babbs, Michael Schwartz, and Neil Ortenberg. *On the Bus: The Complete Guide to the Legendary Trip of Ken Kesey and the Merry Pranksters and the Birth of the Counterculture.* New York: Thunder's Mouth Press, 1990. A narrative of Kesey's 1964 cross-country bus trip.

Powe-Temperley, Kitty. *The 60s: Mods and Hippies.* Milwaukee: Gareth Stevens Audio, 2000. Sixties fashion.

Puterbaugh, Parke, et al., eds. *I Want to Take You Higher: The Psychedelic Era. 1965–1969.* San Francisco: Chronicle, 1997. Companion volume to the exhibit, at the Rock and Roll Hall of Fame and Museum, for the thirtieth anniversary of the Summer of Love.

Reich, Charles. *The Greening of America.* New York: Random House, 1970. Environmentalism and the counterculture; contemporary work.

Roszak, Theodore. *The Making of a Counter-Culture: Reflections on the Technocratic Society and Its Youthful Opposition.* New York: Garden City, N.Y.: Anchor, 1969. Reprint, Berkeley: University of California Press, 1995. The first account of the 1960s counterculture; a celebration.

Selvin, Joel. *Summer of Love: The Inside Story of LSD, Rock and Roll, Free Love and High Times in the Wild West.* New York: Dutton, 1994. Detailed and well-researched history by pop-music critic from the *San Francisco Chronicle.*

Stevens, Jay. *Storming Heaven: LSD and the American Dream.* New York: Atlantic Monthly Press, 1987. Very readable and well-researched account of the psychedelic movement and the drug culture.

Stone, Skip. *Hippies from A to Z: Their Sex, Drugs, Music, and Impact from the Sixties to the Present.* Hip, Inc. (http://hipplanet.com/books/atozinfo.htm), 1999. Popular reference book by Web master of "Hippyland" (www.hippy.com); includes glossary.

Thompson, Hunter S. *Fear and Loathing in Las Vegas: A Savage Journey to the Heart of the American Dream.* New York: Random House, 1971. Thompson's memoir and social commentary on the Sixties.

Tipton, Steven M. *Getting Saved from the Sixties: Moral Meaning in Conversion and Cultural Change.* Berkeley: University of California Press, 1982. Discusses the "turn by the young to nontraditional forms of religion."

Whitmer, Peter O. *Aquarius Revisited: Seven Who Created the Sixties Counterculture That Changed America.* New York: Macmillan, 1987. Examines the influence of intellectuals on the counterculture.

Wolfe, Tom. *The Electric Kool-Aid Acid Test.* New York: Bantam, 1968.

Yinger, Milton. *Countercultures: The Promise and the Peril of a World Turned Upside Down.* New York: Free Press, 1982. A sociological assessment.

Gender and Sexuality

Allyn, David. *Make Love, Not War: The Sexual Revolution, An Unfettered History.* Boston: Little, Brown, 2000. Overview.

Bailey, Beth. *Sex in the Heartland.* Cambridge: Harvard University Press, 1999. The "mainsteam" sexual revolution in Lawrence, Kansas.

Brown, Helen Gurley. *Sex and the Single Girl.* New York: Pocket, 1962. "Nice girls do."

Douglas, Susan J. *Where the Girls Are: Growing Up Female with the Mass Media.* New York: Random House, 1994.

Ehrenreich, Barbara, et al. *Re-making Love: The Feminization of Sex.* New York: Doubleday, 1986. Women's sexual revolution.

Escoffier, Jeffrey. *American Homo: Community and Perversity.* Berkeley: University of California Press, 1998. Collection of essays; first section is on the Sixties era.

Faderman, Lillian. *Odd Girls and Twilight Lovers: A History of Lesbian Life in Twentieth Century America.* New York: Columbia University Press, 1991. Key historical overview.

Garrow, David J. *Liberty and Sexuality: The Right to Privacy and the Making of Roe v. Wade.* New York: Macmillan, 1994. Careful, densely researched analysis of the origins of *Roe v. Wade*.

Grant, Linda. *Sexing the Millennium: Women and the Sexual Revolution.* New York: Grove, 1994. Anecdotal.

Heidnry, John. *What Wild Ecstasy: The Rise and Fall of the Sexual Revolution.* New York: Simon and Schuster, 1997. Sexual revolution portrayed as its most extreme elements: SM clubs, hardcore pornography.

Kaplan, Laura. *The Story of Jane: The Legendary Underground Feminist Abortion Service*. New York: Pantheon, 1995. "Collective memoir" of the women who formed Chicago's "Jane" between 1969 and 1973.

Kennedy, Elizabeth Lapovsky, and Madeline D. Davis (contributor). *Boots of Leather, Slippers of Gold: The History of a Lesbian Community*. New York: Routledge, 1993. Lives of lesbians in Buffalo, New York, 1930s through 1960s, based on oral histories.

Modell, John. *Into One's Own: From Youth to Adulthood in the United States, 1920–1975*. Berkeley: University of California Press, 1989. Good information on courtship, sexuality.

Moran, Jeffrey P. *Teaching Sex: The Shaping of Adolescence in the Twentieth Century*. Cambridge: Harvard University Press, 2000. Includes 1960s struggles over sex education.

Reagan, Leslie J. *When Abortion Was a Crime: Women, Medicine, and Law in the United States, 1867–1973*. Berkeley: University of California Press, 1997. Excellent analysis; focus on earlier period.

Seidman, Steven. *Romantic Longings: Love in America, 1983–1980*. New York: Routledge, 1991. Best on gay community-building in the post-Stonewall era.

Sinfield, Alan. *Out on Stage: Lesbian and Gay Theatre in the Twentieth Century*. New Haven: Yale University Press, 1999. Analysis focuses on gender and sexuality in lesbian and gay British and American theater; contains a chapter on the Sixties.

Solinger, Rickie. *Wake Up Little Susie: Single Pregnancy and Race before Roe v. Wade*. New York: Routledge, 1992.

——, ed. *Abortion Wars: A Half Century of Struggle, 1950–2000*. Berkeley: University of California Press, 1998. Anthology of essays; first section focuses on pre-*Roe* era.

Stein, Marc. *City of Sisterly and Brotherly Loves: Lesbian and Gay Philadelphia, 1945–1972*. Chicago: University of Chicago Press, 2000.

Umansky, Lauri. *Motherhood Reconceived: Feminism and the Legacy of the Sixties*. New York: New York University Press, 1996.

Watkins, Elizabeth Siegal. *On the Pill*. Baltimore: Johns Hopkins University Press, 1998. A social history of oral contraceptives.

Immigration/Ethnicity

Novak, Michael. *The Rise of the Unmeltable Ethnics: Politics and Culture in American Life*. 2nd ed. New Brunswick, N.J.: Transaction, 1996.

Reimers, David. *Still the Golden Door: The Third World Comes to America*. New York: Columbia University Press, 1985. An analysis of post-1945 immigration.

Ueda, Reed. *Postwar Immigrant America: A Social History*. New York: St. Martin's (Bedford Books), 1994. A good overview and reference.

Science, Technology, and Culture

Collins, Martin J., and the Division of Space History, National Air and Space Museum, the Smithsonian Institution. *Space Race: The U.S.–U.S.S.R. Competition to Reach the Moon.* San Francisco: Pomegranate Communications, 1999.

Cowan, Ruth Schwartz. *A Social History of American Technology.* New York: Oxford University Press, 1996. Overview, with chapters on communication and biotechnology.

Heppenheimer, T. A. *Countdown: A History of Space Flight.* New York: Wiley, 1997. Acclaimed history of U.S. and Soviet space programs, with strong technological explanations.

Hughes, Thomas Parke. *American Genesis: A History of the American Genius for Invention.* New York: Penguin, 1990. Includes a section on counterculture anxiety about technocracy.

Judson, Horace Freeland. *The Eighth Day of Creation: Makers of the Revolution in Biology.* Plainview, N.Y.: CSHL Press, 1996. On molecular biology.

Kleidman, Robert. *Organizing for Peace: Neutrality, the Test Ban, and the Freeze.* Syracuse, N.Y.: Syracuse University Press, 1993.

McCurdy, Howard E. *Inside NASA: High Technology and Organizational Change in the American Space Program.* Baltimore: Johns Hopkins University Press, 1994.

McDougall, Walter. *The Heavens and the Earth: A Political History of the Space Age.* New York: Basic, 1985.

Noble, David F. *Forces of Production: A Social History of Industrial Automation.* New York: Knopf, 1984.

Titus, M. Costandina. *Bombs in the Backyard: Atomic Testing and American Politics.* Reno: University of Nevada Press, 1986.

Walsh, Patrick J. *Echoes Among the Stars: A Short History of the U.S. Space Program.* Armonk, N.Y.: M. E. Sharpe, 1999. Emphasis on the politics of the space race.

Weart, Spencer R. *Nuclear Fear: A History of Images.* Cambridge: Harvard University Press, 1988.

Winkler, Allan. *Life Under a Cloud: American Anxiety about the Atom.* Urbana: University of Illinois Press, 1999.

Wolfe, Tom. *The Right Stuff.* London: Bantam, 1981. An account of the early years of the space program.

York, Herbert F. *Making Weapons, Talking Peace: A Physicist's Odyssey from Hiroshima to Geneva.* New York: Basic, 1987.

Education

Fass, Paula. *Outside In: Minorities and the Transformation of American Education.* New York: Oxford University Press, 1989.

Kimball, Roger. *Tenured Radicals: How Politics Has Corrupted Our Higher Education*. New York: Harper and Row, 1990.

Lowen, Rebecca S. *Creating the Cold War University: The Transformation of Stanford*. Berkeley: University of California Press, 1997.

Knight, Douglas. *Street of Dreams*. Durham, N.C.: Duke University Press, 1989. Memoir.

Ravitch, Diane. *The Troubled Crusade: American Education, 1945–1980*. New York: Basic, 1983.

Religion

Ellwood, Robert S. *The Sixties Spiritual Awakening: American Religion Moving from Modern to Postmodern*. New Brunswick, N.J.: Rutgers University Press, 1994. Broad-based study of religious and spiritual facets of American life in the Sixties.

Gilbert, James B. *Redeeming Culture: American Religion in an Age of Science, 1925–1962*. Chicago: University of Chicago Press, 1997. From the Scopes Trial through the 1962 "Space Age" Seattle World's Fair.

Hall, Mitchell. *Because of Their Faith*. New York: Columbia University Press, 1991. History of CALV, antiwar religious group.

Hudnut-Beumler, James. *Looking for God in the Suburbs: The Religion of the American Dream and its Critics, 1945–1965*. New Brunswick, N.J.: Rutgers University Press, 1994. Seeks in social critics such as David Riesman a link between the complacent church of the 1950s and the radical church of the 1960s.

Miller, Timothy, and Harold Coward, eds. *America's Alternative Religions*. Albany: State University of New York Press, 1995. History and impact of most significant alternative religions in the United States.

Wuthnow, Robert. *After Heaven: Spirituality in American since the 1950s*. Berkeley: University of California Press, 1998. Analysis of changing meaning of religion and spirituality in the United States.

Consumerism/Advertising

Fox, Richard, and T. J. Jackson Lears, eds. *The Culture of Consumption: Critical Essays in American History, 1880–1980*. New York: Pantheon, 1983.

Frank, Thomas. *The Conquest of Cool: Business Culture, Counterculture, and the Rise of Hip Consumerism*. Chicago: University of Chicago Press, 1997.

Lears, T. J. Jackson. *Fables of Abundance: A Cultural History of American Advertising*. New York: Basic, 1994.

Arts, Media, Entertainment

ART, THEATER, DANCE, LITERATURE

Archer, Michael. *Art Snce 1960*. World of Art series. London: Thames and Hudson, 1997.

Banes, Sally. *Greenwich Village 1963: Avant-Garde Performance and the Effervescent Body*. Durham, N.C.: Duke University Press, 1993.

Bercovitch, Sacvan, ed. *The Cambridge History of American Literature: Prose Writing, 1940–1990*. Vol. 7. New York: Cambridge University Press, 1999.

Brustein, Robert. *Revolution as Theatre: Notes on the New Radical Style*. New York: Liveright, 1971.

Busch, Julia M. *A Decade of Sculpture: The Sixties*. Philadelphia: Art Alliance Press, 1974.

Elderfield, John, ed. *American Art of the 1960s*. New York: Museum of Modern Art, 1991.

Goldberg, RoseLee. *Performance: Live Art 1909 to the Present*. New York: Harry N. Abrams, 1979.

Newhouse, Thomas. *The Beat Generation and the Popular Novel in the United States, 1945–1970*. Jefferson, N.C.: McFarland, 2000.

Phillips, Lisa. *The American Century: Art and Culture, 1950–2000*. New York: Norton, 1999. The catalog for the Whitney Museum of American Art exhibit.

Phillips, Lisa, et al. *Beat Culture and the New America, 1950–1965*. New York: Whitney Museum of American Art, 1995.

Phillips, Rod. *"Forest Beatnicks" and "Urban Thoreaus": Gary Snyder, Jack Kerouac, Lew Welch, and Michael McClure*. New York: Peter Lang, 2000.

Sandford, Mariellen R., ed. *Happenings and Other Acts*. New York: Routledge, 1995.

Vanden Heuvel, Michael. *Performing Drama/Dramatizing Performance*. Ann Arbor: University of Michigan Press, 1991.

Williams, Mance. *Black Theatre in the 1960s and 1970s: A Historical-Critical Analysis of the Movement*. Westport, Conn.: Greenwood Press, 1985.

Wood, Paul, et al. *Modernism in Dispute: Art Since the Forties*. New Haven: Yale University Press, 1993.

Woodhouse, Reed. *Unlimited Embrace: A Canon of Gay Fiction, 1945–1995*. Amherst: University of Massachusetts Press, 1998.

FILM AND TELEVISION

Baughman, James. *Television's Guardians: The FCC and the Politics of Programming, 1958–1967*. Knoxville: University of Tennessee Press, 1985.

——. *The Republic of Mass Culture: Journalism, Filmmaking, and Broadcasting in*

America Since 1941. 2d ed. Baltimore: Johns Hopkins University Press, 1997. Excellent overview.

Bernardi, Daniel. *Star Trek and History: Race-ing toward a White Future.* New Brunswick, N.J.: Rutgers University Press, 1998. Cultural-studies analysis of *Star Trek's* construction of "race."

Brauer, Ralph. *The Horse, the Gun, and the Piece of Property: Changing Images of the TV Western.* Bowling Green, Ohio: Bowling Green University Popular Press, 1975.

Czitrom, Daniel. *Media and the American Mind: From Morse to McLuhan.* Chapel Hill: University of North Carolina Press, 1982.

Curtin, Michael. *Redeeming the Wasteland: Television Documentary and Cold War Politics.* New Brunswick, N.J.: Rutgers University Press, 1995. Flourishing of network documentaries, 1960–1964, as piece of New Frontier.

Luke, Carmen. *Constructing the Child Viewer: A History of the American Discourse on Television and Children, 1950–1980.* New York: Praeger, 1990.

Mordden, Ethan. *Medium Cool: The Movies of the 1960s.* New York: Knopf, 1990.

Sayre, Nora. *Running Time: Films of the Cold War.* New York: Dial, 1982.

Smith, Patricia Juliana, ed. *The Queer Sixties.* New York: Routledge, 1999. Essays offering queer readings of Sixties icons and events.

Smith, Ronald L. *Sweethearts of 60s TV.* New York: St. Martin's, 1989. Popular work.

Spigel, Lynn, and Michael Curtin. *The Revolution Wasn't Televised: Sixties Television and Social Conflict.* New York: Routledge, 1997. Very good anthology, covering broad range of Sixties programming.

Spigel, Lynn, and Denise Mann. *Private Screenings: Television and the Female Consumer.* Minneapolis: University of Minnesota Press, 1992. Includes Sixties era.

Staiger, Janet. *Blockbuster TV: Must-See Sitcoms in the Network Era.* New York: New York University Press, 2000. Analyzes construction of mass audiences through case studies of four popular shows, including *The Beverly Hillbillies* and *All in the Family.*

Suarez, Juan Antonio. *Bike Boys, Drag Queens, and Superstars: Avant-Garde, Mass Culture and Gay Identities in the 1960s Underground Cinema.* Bloomington: Indiana University Press, 1996. Cultural studies approach.

POPULAR MUSIC

Davies, Hunter. *The Beatles.* New York: McGraw-Hill, 1984.

Denisoff, R. Serge, and Richard A. Peterson, eds. *The Sounds of Social Change: Studies in Popular Culture.* Chicago: Rand McNally, 1972. Essays on the relationship between music and social change in the Sixties.

Dunson, Josh. *Freedom in the Air: Song Movements of the Sixties.* 1965; reprint, Westport, Conn.: Greenwood, 1980. Freedom songs from the civil rights movement and northern folksong movement.

Early, Gerald. *One Nation Under a Groove: Motown and American Culture.* Hopewell, N.J.: Ecco Press, 1995.

Echols, Alice. *Scars of Sweet Paradise*. New York: Metropolitan Books, 1999. Biography of Janis Joplin.

Friedlander, Paul. *Rock and Roll: A Social History*. Boulder, Colo.: Westview, 1996.

Jackson, John A. *American Bandstand: Dick Clark and the Making of a Rock 'n' Roll Empire*. New York: Oxford University Press, 1997.

London, Herbert. *Closing the Circle: A Cultural History of the Rock Revolution*. Chicago: Nelson-Hall, 1985. An analysis of rock music and Sixties rebellion.

Marcus, Greil. *Mystery Train: Images of America in Rock'n'Roll Music*. New York: Dutton, 1990.

Orman, John. *The Politics of Rock Music*. Chicago: Nelson-Hall, 1985.

Palmer, Robert. *Rock and Roll: An Unruly History*. New York: Harmony, 1995.

Shank, Barry. *Dissonant Identities: The Rock 'n' Roll Scene in Austin, Texas*. Hanover, NH: Wesleyan University Press / University Press of New England, 1994. Includes the Sixties era.

Smith, Suzanne E. *Dancing in the Street: Motown and the Cultural Politics of Detroit*. Cambridge: Harvard University Press, 1999. Uses Motown (the music and the company) to analyze changes in African-American ideologies; social history.

Szatmary, David P. *Rockin' in Time: A Social History of Rock and Roll*. 3d ed. New York: Shirmer Books, 1996. Overview of the influence of rock and roll on U.S. society and culture.

Ward, Ed, Geoffrey Stokes, and Ken Tucker. *Rock of Ages: The Rolling Stone History of Rock and Roll*. New York: Rolling Stone Press and Summit Books, 1986.

Weiner, Jonathan. *Come Together: John Lennon in His Times*. 1984; reprint, Urbana: University of Illinois Press, 1991.

POLITICS AND GOVERNMENT

Liberalism

Alonzo Hamby. *Liberalism and Its Challengers: From FDR to Bush*. 2d ed. New York: Oxford University Press, 1992. A collection of essays on important political figures.

Chafe, William. *Never Stop Running: Allard Lowenstein and the Struggle to Save American Liberalism*. New York: Basic, 1993. Biography of civil rights and antiwar activist.

Edsall, Thomas, with Mary D. Edsall. *Chain Reaction*. New York: Norton, 1991. A history of the demise of liberalism.

Fraser, Steve, and Gary Gerstle, eds. *The Rise and Fall of the New Deal Order, 1930–1980*. Princeton, N.J.: Princeton University Press, 1989.

Graham, Hugh Davis. *Civil Rights and the Presidency: Race and Gender in American Politics, 1960–1972*. New York: Oxford University Press, 1992. A scholarly account of liberalism's greatest triumph.

Matusow, Allen. *The Unraveling of America: A History of Liberalism in the 1960s*. New York: Harper and Row, 1984. Overview of liberalism and its discontents, best on national politics.

Schulman, Bruce. *Lyndon Johnson and American Liberalism*. New York: St. Martin's, 1995. A brief biography with documents; very accessible.

Political Leaders and Presidential Administrations

BARRY GOLDWATER

Goldberg, Robert Alan. *Barry Goldwater*. New Haven: Yale University Press, 1995.

Goldwater, Barry. *The Conscience of a Conservative*. New York: McFadden-Bartell, 1961. A strong defense of conservative principles by 1964 Republican presidential candidate.

Iverson, Peter. *Barry Goldwater: Native Arizonan*. Norman: University of Oklahoma Press, 1997.

McDowell, Edwin. *Barry Goldwater: Portrait of an Arizonan*. Chicago: H. Regnery, 1964.

LYNDON B. JOHNSON

Beschloss, Michael R., ed. *Taking Charge: The Johnson White House Tapes, 1963–1964*. New York: Simon and Schuster, 1997. Johnson's secretly recorded tapes, very well-edited and annotated.

Califano, Joseph. *The Triumph and Tragedy of Lyndon Johnson: The White House Years*. New York: Simon and Schuster, 1991. A former advisor's analysis of the Johnson presidency.

Caro, Robert. *The Years of Lyndon Johnson: The Path to Power*. New York: Knopf, 1982. An extremely critical historical narrative of Johnson's life ending with his controversial election to the Senate in 1948.

——. *The Years of Lyndon Johnson: Means of Ascent*. New York: Knopf, 1990. A critical history of Johnson's career in the Senate and his presidency.

Conkin, Paul. *Big Daddy from the Pedernales: Lyndon Baines Johnson*. Boston: Twayne, 1986.

Dallek, Robert. *Lone Star Rising: Lyndon Johnson and His Times, 1908–1960*. New York: Oxford University Press, 1991. Portrays Johnson's life and political career up to his vice presidency.

——. *Flawed Giant: Lyndon Johnson and His Times, 1961–1973*. New York: Oxford University Press, 1998. An excellent biography of Johnson from his vice presidency to his death.

Johnson, Lyndon B. *The Vantage Point*. New York: Holt, Rinehart, and Winston, 1971. Johnson's account of his presidency.

Kearns, Doris. *Lyndon Johnson and the American Dream*. New York: Harper and Row, 1976. By former Johnson aide and political commentator.

Shesol, Jeff. *Mutual Contempt: Lyndon Johnson, Robert Kennedy, and the Feud That Defined a Decade*. New York: Norton, 1997.

Unger, Irwin, and Debi Unger. *LBJ: A Life*. New York: Wiley, 1999.

JOHN F. KENNEDY

Burner, David. *John F. Kennedy and a New Generation*. Boston: Little, Brown, 1988. A pithy biography of Kennedy.

Giglio, James. *The Presidency of John F. Kennedy*. Lawrence: University Press of Kansas, 1991. A solid account of Kennedy's presidency.

Mahoney, Richard D. *Sons and Brothers: The Days of Jack and Bobby Kennedy*. New York: Arcade Publishers, 1999.

May, Ernest R., and Philip D. Zelikow, eds. *The Kennedy Tapes: Inside the White House during the Cuban Missile Crisis*. Cambridge: Harvard University Press (Belknap Press), 1997. Transcriptions of Kennedy's secret tapes, with analysis.

Naftali, Timothy, et al., eds. *The Presidential Recordings: John F. Kennedy:* Vols. 1–3, *The Great Crises*. New York: Norton, 2001. Complete transcripts, fully annotated, of secret recordings. Comes with three multi-media CD-ROMs, containing full audio recordings and more.

Parmet, Herbert. *JFK: The Presidency of John F. Kennedy*. New York: Dial, 1983. Well-written account of Kennedy's presidency.

Posner, Gerald. *Case Closed: Lee Harvey Oswald and the Assassination of JFK*. New York: Random House, 1993. Well-researched, scholarly argument that refutes the major conspiracy theories on the assassination of John Kennedy.

Reeves, Richard. *President Kennedy: Profile of Power*. New York: Simon and Schuster, 1993.

Reeves, Thomas. *A Question of Character: A Life of John F. Kennedy*. New York: Free Press, 1991. A negative assessment of Kennedy's presidency.

Schlesinger, Arthur, Jr. *A Thousand Days: John F. Kennedy in the White House*. Boston: Houghton Mifflin, 1965. A widely read, celebratory history of the Kennedy presidency by one of his advisors.

Sorenson, Theodore. *Kennedy*. New York: Bantam, 1966. A positive, contemporary account of Kennedy's presidency by a close advisor.

RICHARD M. NIXON

Ambrose, Stephen. *Nixon: The Education of a Politician, 1913–1962*. New York: Simon and Schuster, 1987.

——. *Nixon: The Triumph of a Politician, 1962-1972*. New York: Simon and Schuster, 1989.

——. *Nixon: Ruin and Recovery, 1973–1990*. New York: Simon and Schuster, 1992.

Ehrlichman, John. *Witness to Power: The Nixon Years*. New York: Simon and Schuster, 1982. An account of Nixon's presidency and Watergate his personal aide.

Genovese, Michael A. *The Nixon Presidency: Power and Politics in Turbulent Times*. New York: Greenwood, 1990.

Hoff, Joan. *Nixon Reconsidered*. New York: Basic, 1994. A revisionist account of Nixon's presidency.

Kissinger, Henry. *The White House Years*. Boston: Little, Brown, 1979. The memoirs and commentary of Nixon's Secretary of State.

——. *Years of Upheaval*. Boston: Little, Brown, 1982. A second volume of Kissinger's memoirs and analysis.

Kutler, Stanley, ed. *Abuse of Power: The New Nixon Tapes*. New York: Free Press, 1997. Annotated transcripts of second set of released Nixon White House tapes.

Nixon, Richard M. *RN: The Memoirs of Richard Nixon*. New York: Grosset and Dunlap, 1978.

Parmet, Herbert. *Richard Nixon and His America*. Boston: Little, Brown, 1990.

Safire, William. *Before the Fall*. Garden City, N.Y.: Doubleday, 1975.

Strober, Gerald S., and Deborah H. Strober. *Nixon, an Oral History of His Presidency*. New York: HarperCollins, 1994.

Wills, Garry. *Nixon Agonistes: The Crisis of the Self-Made Man*. Boston: Houghton Mifflin, 1970.

WATERGATE

Bernstein, Carl, and Bob Woodward. *All the President's Men*. New York: Simon and Schuster, 1974. By the *Washington Post* journalists who broke the Watergate burglary story.

——. *The Final Days*. New York: Simon and Schuster, 1976.

Dean, John. *Blind Ambition*. New York: Simon and Schuster, 1976. An account of Watergate by Nixon's White House counsel.

Haldeman, H. R. *The Ends of Power*. New York: Times Books, 1978. The story of Watergate from Nixon's personal aide.

Kutler, Stanley. *The Wars of Watergate: The Last Crisis of Richard Nixon*. New York: Knopf, 1990. Very critical account.

Schudson, Michael. *Watergate in American Memory: How We Remember, Forget, and Reconstruct the Past*. New York: Basic, 1992.

White, Theodore H. *Breach of Faith: The Fall of Richard Nixon*. New York: Dell, 1975.

GEORGE WALLACE

Carter, Dan. *The Politics of Rage: George Wallace, the Origins of the New Conservatism, and the Transformation of American Politics*. New York: Simon and Schuster, 1995. Powerful account of Governor George Wallace and race politics.

Frady, Marshall. *Wallace*. New York: World, 1968.

Lesher, Stephan. *George Wallace: American Populist*. Reading, MA: Addison-Wesley, 1994.

Social Policy and Programs: The New Frontier and the Great Society

Andrew, John A., III. *Lyndon Johnson and the Great Society.* Chicago: Ivan R. Dee, 1998. A summary of major Great Society programs; little analysis.

Berkowitz, Edward. *America's Welfare State: From Roosevelt to Reagan.* Baltimore: Johns Hopkins University Press, 1991. Both social history and history of policy making.

Bernstein, Irving. *Promises Kept: John F. Kennedy's New Frontier.* New York: Oxford University Press, 1990. A positive account of Kennedy's programs.

——. *Guns or Butter: The Presidency of Lyndon Johnson.* New York: Oxford University Press, 1996. Excellent analysis.

Cloward, Richard, and Frances Fox Piven. *The Politics of Turmoil: Essays on Poverty, Race, and the Urban Crisis.* New York: Pantheon, 1972. Leftist critique of the War on Poverty by two well-known sociologists.

Divine, Robert, ed. *Exploring the Johnson Years.* Austin: University of Texas Press, 1981. A collection of essays exploring Johnson's domestic and foreign policies.

——. *The Johnson Years: Vietnam, the Environment and Science.* Vol. 2. Lawrence: University Press of Kansas, 1987. Collection of scholarly essays.

Fox, Kenneth. *Metropolitan America: Urban Life and Urban Policy in the United States, 1940–1980.* London: Macmillan, 1985. A good overview.

Friedan, Bernard J., and Marshall Kaplan. *The Politics of Neglect: Urban Aid from Model Cities to Revenue Sharing.* Cambridge: Massachusetts Institute of Technology Press, 1975. A leftist analysis of federal government social programs.

Gale, Dennis E. *Understanding Urban Unrest: From Reverend King to Rodney King.* Thousand Oaks, Calif.: Sage, 1996. An analysis of federal urban policy, especially Model Cities, and Sixties riots.

Gans, Herbert J. *The War Against the Poor: The Underclass and Antipoverty Policy.* New York: Basic, 1995.

Gillette, Michael. *Launching the War on Poverty: An Oral History.* New York: Twayne, 1996. Based on the Lyndon B. Johnson Presidential Library's oral history collections. Very useful.

Graham, Hugh Davis. *The Uncertain Triumph: Federal Education Policy in the Kennedy and Johnson Years.* Chapel Hill: University of North Carolina Press, 1984.

Harrington, Michael. *The Other America: Poverty in the United States.* New York: Macmillan, 1963. Important contemporary work that directed the attention of national leaders to America's poverty problem.

Jeffrey, Julie Roy. *Education for Children of the Poor: A Study of the Origins and Implementation of the Elementary and Secondary Education Act of 1965.* Columbus: Ohio State University Press, 1978.

Jenks, Christopher. *Rethinking Social Policy: Race, Poverty, and the Underclass.* Cambridge: Harvard University Press, 1992.

Kaplan, Marshall, and Peggy Cucity, eds. *The Great Society and Its Legacy: Twenty Years of U.S. Social Policy*. Durham, N.C.: Duke University Press, 1986. A collection of essays; favorable assessment.

Katz, Michael, ed. *The Undeserving Poor*. New York: Pantheon, 1989.

——. *The "Underclass" Debate: Views from History*. Princeton, N.J.: Princeton University Press, 1993.

Kauffman, James L. *Selling Outer Space: Kennedy, the Media, and Funding for Project Apollo, 1961–1963*. Tuscaloosa: University of Alabama Press, 1994.

Levitan, Sar. *The Great Society's Poor Law: A New Approach to Poverty*. Baltimore: Johns Hopkins University Press, 1969. Key text from the time.

Levitan, Sar, and Robert Taggart. *The Promise of Greatness*. Cambridge: Harvard University Press, 1976.

Marris, Peter, and Martin Rein. *Dilemmas of Social Reform: Poverty and Community Action in the United States*. 2d ed. Chicago: Aldine, 1973.

Massey, Douglas S., and Nancy A. Denton. *American Apartheid: Segregation and the Making of the Underclass*. Cambridge: Harvard University Press, 1993.

Moynihan, Daniel Patrick. *Maximum Feasible Misunderstanding: Community Action in the War on Poverty*. New York: Free Press, 1969. Moynihan claims that OEO bureaucrats used Community Action to radically politicize the inner-city poor.

Murray, Charles. *Losing Ground: American Social Policy, 1950–1980*. New York: Basic, 1984. A conservative attack on liberal welfare programs that sparked substantial debate.

Patterson, James. *America's Struggle Against Poverty, 1900–1994*. Cambridge: Harvard University Press, 1995. The best short history of poverty in twentieth-century America; covers federal social policy of the Sixties.

Piven, Frances Fox, and Richard Cloward. *Regulating the Poor: The Functions of Public Welfare*. New York: Vintage, 1972. A leftist interpretation of government welfare programs by sociologists.

Schwarz, John. *America's Hidden Success: A Reassessment of Twenty Years of Public Policy*. New York: Norton, 1983. A positive assessment of Great Society programs.

Sundquist, James, ed. *On Fighting Poverty: Perspectives from Experience*. New York: Basic, 1969.

Unger, Irwin. *The Best of Intentions: The Triumph and Failure of the Great Society under Kennedy, Johnson and Nixon*. New York: Brandywine Press, 1995.

Weir, Margaret, Ann Orloff, and Theda Skocpol, eds. *The Politics of Social Policy in the United States*. Princeton, N.J.: Princeton University Press, 1988.

Zigler, Edward, and Susan Muenchow. *Head Start: The Inside Story of America's Most Successful Educational Experiment*. New York: Basic, 1992. A participant's favorable history and analysis of the program.

The Warren Court

Biskupic, Joan and Elder Witt. *Guide to the U.S. Supreme Court*. 3d ed. Washington, D.C.: Congressional Quarterly, 1997. A useful reference source to Supreme Court cases.

Cray, Ed. *Chief Justice: A Biography of Earl Warren*. New York: Simon and Schuster, 1997.

Horowitz, Morton J. *The Warren Court and the Pursuit of Justice: A Critical Issue*. New York: Hill and Wang, 1998. Positive assessment of Warren Court; a basic overview.

Kalman, Laura. *Abe Fortas: A Biography*. New Haven: Yale University Press, 1990.

———. *The Strange Career of Legal Liberalism*. New Haven: Yale University Press, 1996. An excellent intellectual history.

Powe, L. A. Scot. *The Warren Court and American Politics*. Cambridge: Harvard University Press, 2000. Examines the Warren Court in the context of Kennedy-Johnson liberalism; argues that the Court helped to impose liberal-elite values on Americans (rural, Southern, Roman Catholic) outside that tradition.

Schwartz, Bernard. *Super Chief*. New York: New York University Press, 1983. A good account of the Warren Court by a respected legal scholar.

———, ed. *The Warren Court: A Retrospective*. New York: Oxford University Press, 1996. Twenty-five essays; based on conference at University of Tulsa College of Law.

Tussman, Joseph, ed. *The Supreme Court on Racial Discrimination*. New York: Oxford University Press, 1963. Contains Court decisions dealing with race.

Tushnett, Mark. *Making Constitutional Law: Thurgood Marshall and the Supreme Court, 1961–1991*. New York: Oxford University Press, 1997.

Tushnet, Mark, ed. *The Warren Court in Historical and Political Perspective*. Charlottesville: University Press of Virginia, 1994. Nine essays, covering legal, biographical, and historical perspectives.

Weddington, Sarah R. *A Question of Choice*. New York: Putnam, 1991. An account of *Roe v. Wade* from the attorney who represented Norma McCorvey (Roe).

Wilkinson, J. Harvie, III. *From Brown to Bakke: The Supreme Court and School Integration, 1954–1978*. New York: Oxford University Press, 1979.

Williams, Juan. *Thurgood Marshall: American Revolutionary*. New York: Crown, 1998. Biography.

THE ECONOMY

Collins, Robert M. *The Business Response to Keynes, 1929–1964*. New York: Columbia University Press, 1981.

———. *More: The Politics of Economic Growth in Postwar America*. New York: Oxford University Press, 2000. Analyzes postwar "growth regimes."

Galbraith, John Kenneth. *The Affluent Society*. Boston: Houghton Mifflin, 1958. Influential contemporary analysis of the economy.

——. *The New Industrial State*. Boston: Houghton Mifflin, 1967.

Karier, Thomas Mark. *Great Experiments in American Economic Policy: From Kennedy to Reagan*. Westport, Conn.: Praeger, 1997. Compares economic experiments of the 1980s with the Keynesianism of the 1960s.

Kolko, Gabriel. *Wealth and Power in America: An Analysis of Social Class and Income Distribution*. New York: Praeger, 1962. A contemporary study of the economy.

Matusow, Allen J. *Nixon's Economy: Booms, Busts, Dollars, and Votes*. Lawrence: University Press of Kansas, 1998. Clearly written analysis of Nixon's inconsistent economic policies in relation to his political struggles and domestic and foreign-policy goals.

INTERNATIONAL RELATIONS

Ambrose, Stephen, and Douglas G. Brinkley. *Rise to Globalism: American Foreign Policy Since 1938*. 8th ed. New York: Penguin, 1997. An analytical survey of post–World War II foreign policy including U.S.–Soviet relations, Vietnam, and the Middle East.

Bailey, Samuel. *The United States and the Development of South America, 1945–1975*. New York: New Viewpoints, 1976.

Beschloss, Michael. *The Crisis Years: Kennedy and Khrushchev, 1960–1963*. New York: Edward Burlingame, 1991.

Brands, H. W., ed. *The Foreign Policies of Lyndon Johnson: Beyond Vietnam*. College Station: Texas A and M University Press, 1999. Collection of essays by major diplomatic historians, covering Europe, the Middle East, the Americas, and Asia.

Cohen, Warren I., and Nancy Bernkopf Tucker, eds. *Lyndon Johnson Confronts the World: American Foreign Policy, 1963–1968*. New York: Cambridge University Press, 1994. Middle East to the Congo, Asia to Latin America.

Freedman, Lawrence. *Kennedy's Wars: Berlin, Cuba, Laos, and Vietnam*. New York: Oxford University Press, 2000.

Fursenko, Aleksandr and Timothy Naftali. *"One Hell of a Gamble": Khrushchev, Castro, and Kennedy, 1958-1964*. New York: Norton, 1997. The best book on Soviet-Cuban-American relations and the Cuban Missile Crisis; extensive use of Soviet archival documents.

Garthoff, Raymond. *Détente and Confrontation: American-Soviet Relations from Nixon to Reagan*. Washington, D.C.: Brookings Institution, 1985; rev. ed., 1994. Revised edition uses newly declassified Russian sources; analyzes both U.S. and Soviet policy.

Hoffman, Elizabeth Cobbs. *All You Need is Love: The Peace Corps and the Spirit of the*

1960s. Cambridge: Harvard University Press, 1998. Excellent account, encompassing both geopolitics and the experiences of volunteers.

Kennedy, Robert F. *Thirteen Days: A Memoir of the Cuban Missile Crisis*. New York: Norton, 1969.

Kern, Montague, et al. *The Kennedy Crises: The Press, the Presidency, and Foreign Policy*. Chapel Hill: University of North Carolina Press, 1983.

Klinghoffer, Judith Apter. *Vietnam, Jews, and the Middle East: Unintended Consequences*. New York: St. Martin's, 1999. Argues that the USSR instigated the Six Day War as a "second front" to weaken the United States in Vietnam.

Kolko, Gabriel. *Confronting the Third World, 1945–1980*. New York: Pantheon, 1988. A critical analysis of U.S. foreign policy.

Kunz, Diane, ed. *The Diplomacy of the Crucial Decade*. New York: Columbia University Press, 1994. Collection of essays; contributors argue that U.S. foreign policy of the 1960s must be understood in context of the fight against communism.

LaFeber, Walter. *America, Russia, and the Cold War, 1945–1990*. 8th ed. New York: McGraw-Hill, 1997. One of the best overviews of the cold war.

Litwak, Robert. *Détente and the Nixon Doctrine: American Foreign Policy and the Pursuit of Stability, 1969–1976*. New York: Cambridge University Press, 1984.

Nathan, James A., ed. *The Cuban Missile Crisis Revisited*. New York: St. Martin's, 1992. Collection of nine essays, drawing on materials from U.S., Soviet, and Cuban governments.

Paterson, Thomas G. *On Every Front: The Making and Unmaking of the Cold War*. New York: Norton, 1979; rev. ed., 1992. A good overview.

———. *Contesting Castro: The United States and the Triumph of the Cuban Revolution*. New York: Oxford University Press, 1994. How Castro came to power; focuses on U.S. role and perceptions.

———, ed. *Kennedy's Quest for Victory: American Foreign Policy, 1961–1963*. New York: Oxford University Press, 1989.

Rice, Gerald T. *The Bold Experiment: JFK's Peace Corp*. Notre Dame, Ind.: University of Notre Dame Press, 1986.

Seaborg, Glenn T. *Kennedy and the Test-Ban*. Berkeley: University of California Press, 1983.

Shapley, Deborah. *Promises and Power: The Life and Times of Robert McNamara*. Boston: Little, Brown, 1993. A good biography of the Kennedy and Johnson administrations' secretary of defense.

Shawcross, William. *Sideshow: Kissinger, Nixon, and the Destruction of Cambodia*. New York: Simon and Schuster, 1979. America's role in creating Cambodian war.

Schulzinger, Robert D. *Henry Kissinger: Doctor of Diplomacy*. New York: Columbia University Press, 1989. Balanced account of Kissinger's role, 1969–1976.

Szulc, Tad. *The Illusion of Peace: Foreign Policy in the Nixon Years*. New York: Viking, 1978. An overview.

Terriff, Terry. *The Nixon Administration and the Making of U.S. Nuclear Strategy*.

Ithaca, N.Y.: Cornell University Press, 1995. Analyzes shift in nuclear targeting policy.

Thornton, Richard C. *The Nixon-Kissinger Years: Reshaping America's Foreign Policy.* New York: Paragon House, 1989.

Weldes, Jutta. *Constructing National Interests: The United States and the Cuban Missile Crisis.* Minneapolis: University of Minnesota Press, 1999. Cultural studies approach.

Zeiler, Thomas W. *Dean Rusk: Defending the American Mission Abroad.* Wilmington, Del.: Scholarly Resources, 2000. A biography of the secretary of state during the Kennedy and Johnson administrations that encapsulates the major themes of U.S. foreign policy during the Sixties.

THE VIETNAM WAR

Anderson, David L. *Trapped By Success: The Eisenhower Administration and Vietnam, 1953–1961.* New York: Columbia University Press, 1991.

——, ed. *Shadow on the White House: Presidents and the Vietnam War, 1945–1975.* Lawrence: University Press of Kansas, 1993. Collection of essays by prominent diplomatic historians.

Baritz, Loren. *Backfire: A History of How American Culture Led Us into Vietnam and Made Us Fight the Way We Did.* New York: Morrow, 1985. National myths and illusions, including faith in technology and in U.S. moral supremacy, shaped U.S. role in the Vietnam War and its legacy.

Barrett, David M. *Uncertain Warriors: Lyndon Johnson and His Vietnam Advisors.* Lawrence: University Press of Kansas, 1993. Challenges common wisdom that LBJ refused to seek appropriate advice; careful study of decision-making process and his relations with war advisors.

Berman, Larry. *Planning a Tragedy: The Americanization of the War in Vietnam.* New York: Norton, 1982.

——. *Lyndon Johnson's War: The Road to Stalemate in Vietnam.* New York: Norton, 1989. A critical commentary on Johnson's execution of the war.

Blair, Anne E. *Lodge in Vietnam: A Patriot Abroad.* New Haven: Yale University Press, 1995. Henry Cabot Lodge's ambassadorship to South Vietnam, 1963–64; combined biography and diplomatic history.

Chanoff, David. *Vietnam: A Portrait of Its People at War.* New York: I.B. Tauris, 1996. Valuable work; accounts of the war from the people of North and South Vietnam.

Clifford, Clark. *Counsel to the President: A Memoir.* New York: Random House, 1991. Clifford, Johnson's second secretary of defense, recounts his effort to convince LBJ to de-escalate the war.

Clodfelter, Michael. *Vietnam in Military Statistics: A History of the Indochina Wars, 1772–1991.* Jefferson, N.C.: McFarland, 1995. Comprehensive statistical portrait.

DeGroot, Gerald J. *A Noble Cause? America and the Vietnam War.* London: Longman, 1999. An attempt by a British historian to synthesize scholarship on the Vietnam War. Includes useful footnotes, and bibliography; the introduction is a good historiographical essay.

FitzGerald, Frances. *The Fire in the Lake: The Vietnamese and the Americans in Vietnam.* Boston: Little, Brown, 1972. Pulitzer-winning classic; analyzes war in terms of differences between U.S. and Vietnamese cultures.

Gardner, Lloyd C. *Approaching Vietnam: From World War II Through Dienbienphu, 1941–1954.* New York: Norton, 1988. Background to Sixties-era U.S. involvement.

Herring, George. *America's Longest War: The United States and Vietnam, 1950–1975.* New York: Wiley, 1979. 2d ed., New York: Knopf, 1986. 3d ed., New York: McGraw-Hill, 1996. Very good overview.

———. *LBJ and Vietnam: A Different Kind of War.* Austin: University of Texas Press, 1994. Analysis of LBJ's management of the war.

Hess, Gary R. *Vietnam and the United States: Origins and Legacy of War.* Boston: Twayne, 1991. Overview; with bibliographic essay.

Hunt, Michael. *Lyndon Johnson's War: America's Cold War Crusade in Vietnam.* New York: Hill and Wang, 1996. Based on both U.S. and Vietnamese archival sources; a critique of American arrogance.

Kaiser, David E. *American Tragedy: Kennedy, Johnson, and the Origins of the Vietnam War.* Cambridge: Harvard University Press, 2000. Argues Eisenhower administration's culpability for U.S. role in Vietnam, Kennedy's caution.

Karnow, Stanley. *Vietnam: A History.* New York: Viking, 1991. Basis for the PBS documentary series.

Kimball, Jeffrey P. *Nixon's Vietnam War.* Lawrence: University Press of Kansas, 1998. Rejects "peace with honor" as a myth constructed by Nixon and his administration.

Kolko, Gabriel. *Anatomy of a War: Vietnam, the United States, and the Modern Historical Experience.* New York: Pantheon, 1985.

Lind, Michael. *Vietnam, The Necessary War: A Reinterpretation of America's Most Disastrous Military Conflict.* New York: Free Press, 1999. U.S. involvement in Vietnam was not only unavoidable, but necessary. Controversial work, sympathetic to cold-war policy makers.

Logevall, Fredrik. *Choosing War: The Last Chance for Peace and the Escalation of War in Vietnam.* Berkeley: University of California Press, 1999. Argues that U.S. leaders repeatedly chose to escalate involvement in Vietnam; the Vietnam War was not unavoidable.

Lomperis, Timothy. *From People's War to People's Rule: Insurgency, Intervention, and the Lessons of Vietnam.* Chapel Hill: University of North Carolina Press, 1996. Lessons of Vietnam can be drawn through comparison to other Third World wars.

McNamara, Robert. *In Retrospect: The Tradgedy and Lessons of Vietnam.* New York: Times Books, 1995. An apologetic account of American policy in Vietnam by the secretary of defense during the Kennedy and Johnson administrations.

Moise, Edwin. *Tonkin Gulf and the Escalation of the Vietnam War.* Chapel Hill: University of North Carolina Press, 1996. Very detailed study.

Olson, James S. *Dictionary of the Vietnam War.* Westport, Conn.: Greenwood, 1988. A good reference book.

——. *The Vietnam War: Handbook of the Literature and Research.* Westport, Conn.: Greenwood, 1993. Bibliographical essays.

Olson, James S., and Randy Roberts. *Where the Domino Fell: America and Vietnam, 1945 to 1990.* New York: St. Martin's, 1991. Good overview.

The Pentagon Papers: The Defense Department History of United States Decisionmaking on Vietnam. The Senator Gravel Edition. 5 vols. Boston: Beacon, 1971–1972. A classic collection of documents on American involvement in Vietnam.

Rotter, Andrew J. *The Path to Vietnam: Origins of the American Commitment to Southeast Asia.* Ithaca: Cornell University Press, 1987.

Schafer, D. Michael. *Deadly Paradigms: The Failure of U.S. Counterinsurgency Policy.* Princeton, N.J.: Princeton University Press, 1987.

Schulzinger, Robert. *A Time for War: The United States and Vietnam, 1941–1975.* New York: Oxford University Press, 1997. Excellent narrative and analysis.

Sheehan, Neil. *A Bright Shining Lie: John Paul Vann and America in Vietnam.* New York: Random House, 1989. The Pulitzer Prize–winning story of American involvement in Vietnam, focusing on the career of John Paul Vann.

Shultz, Richard H. *The Secret War Against Hanoi: Kennedy's and Johnson's Use of Spies, Saboteurs, and Covert Warriors in North Vietnam.* New York: HarperCollins, 1999. Description and analysis of covert operations by the Pentagon's Special Operations Group (SOG).

Smith, Ralph B. *An International History of the Vietnam War: The Kennedy Strategy.* New York: St. Martin's, 1986.

Thies, Wallace J. *When Governments Collide: Coercion and Diplomacy in the Vietnam Conflict, 1964-1968.* Berkeley: University of California Press, 1980. An analysis of the peace process.

VanDeMark, Brian. *Into the Quagmire: Lyndon Johnson and the Escalation of the Vietnam War.* New York: Oxford University Press, 1991. Virtually a day-by-day account of escalation over a nine-month period.

Woods, Randall Bennett. J. *William Fulbright, Vietnam, and the Search for a Cold War Foreign Policy.* New York: Cambridge University Press, 1998. Abridgement of Woods's biography of Fulbright, focusing on his role as opponent of the Vietnam War.

Young, Marilyn. *The Vietnam Wars, 1945–1990.* New York: HarperPerennial, 1991. Very critical account of American involvement in Vietnam.

Vietnam and American Society

Anderegg, Michael, ed. *Inventing Vietnam: The War in Film and Television*. Philadelphia: Temple University Press, 1991. Anthology of essays on representations of Vietnam War.

Auster, Albert and Leonard Quart. *How the War Was Remembered: Hollywood and Vietnam*. New York: Praeger, 1988. Creates typology of films; analyzes the portrayals of the war from *China Gate* to *Hamburger Hill*.

Bates, Milton J. *The Wars We Took to Vietnam: Cultural Conflict and Storytelling*. Berkeley: University of California Press, 1996. The other conflicts (race, class, sex, generation) Americans brought to the war, and how they helped to shape U.S. war stories; literary and historical analysis.

Beattie, Keith. *The Scar that Binds: American Culture and the Vietnam War*. New York: New York University Press, 1998. Readings of fiction and film of the Vietnam era for ideological strategies.

Devine, Jeremy M., and Thomas Schatz. *Vietnam at 24 Frames a Second: A Critical and Thematic Analysis of Over 400 Films about the Vietnam War*. Jefferson, N.C.: McFarland, 1995. Chronological, encyclopedic volume.

Gustainis, Justin. *American Rhetoric and the Vietnam War*. Westport, Conn.: Praeger, 1993. Analyzes the rhetoric of both opponents and supporters of the war, including presidential rhetoric and popular culture representations.

Dittmar, Linda, and Gene Michaud, eds. *From Hanoi to Hollywood: The Vietnam War in American Film*. New Brunswick, N.J.: Rutgers University Press, 1990. Nineteen scholarly essays, most addressing the social context in which the films were produced.

Gruhzit-Hoyt, Olga. *A Time Remembered: American Women in the Vietnam War*. Novato, Calif.: Presidio, 1999. Biography-based work on women in nurse corps, Army Special Services, Red Cross, USAID, and Women's Army Corps.

Hass, Kristin Ann. *Carried to the Wall: American Memory and the Vietnam Veterans Memorial*. Berkeley: University of California Press, 1998.

Jefford, Susan. *The Remasculinization of America: Gender and the Vietnam War*. Bloomington: Indiana University Press, 1989. Insightful analysis of representations of Vietnam War; gender, rather than race or class, is critical factor.

Lembcke, Jerry. *The Spitting Image: Myth, Memory, and the Legacy of Vietnam*. New York: New York University Press, 1998. Antiwar protesters spitting at returning veteran is a myth; Lembcke makes that case and discusses the several uses of the myth.

Malo, Jean-Jacques and Tony Williams. *Vietnam War Films: Over 600 Feature, Made-for-TV, Pilot and Short Movies, 1939–1992*. Jefferson, N.C.: McFarland, 1994. Comprehensive, international filmography.

Mariscal, George, ed. *Aztlan and Vietnam: Chicano and Chicana Experiences of the*

War. Berkeley: University of California Press, 1999. Anthology of short stories, speeches, literature; portrays experience of soldiers and of Chicano/as at home.

Martin, Andrew. *Receptions of War: Vietnam in American Culture.* Norman: University of Oklahoma Press, 1993. Critical essays and a chronology of war films.

Muse, Eben J. *The Land of Nam: The Vietnam War in American Film.* Lanham, Md.: Scarecrow Press, 1995. Critical essays, filmography, and bibliography.

O'Nan, Stewart, ed. *The Vietnam Reader: The Definitive Collection of American Fiction and Nonfiction on the War.* New York: Anchor, 1998. Wide-ranging and thoughtfully constructed anthology.

Palmer, Laura Kay. *Shrapnel in the Heart: Letters and Remembrance from the Vietnam Veterans Memorial.* New York: Random House, 1988.

Rabe, David. *The Vietnam Plays.* New York: Grove Press, 1993.

Shafer, D. Michael, ed. *The Legacy: The Vietnam War in the American Imagination.* Boston: Beacon, 1990. Scholars from various disciplines assess impact of Vietnam War on American life.

Tomes, Robert R. *Apocalypse Then: American Intellectuals and the Vietnam War, 1954–1975.* New York: New York University Press, 1998. Intellectual history of the collapse of the liberal consensus.

The Soldiers' Experience

Appy, Christian. *Working-Class War: American Combat Soldiers in Vietnam.* Chapel Hill: University of North Carolina Press, 1993. The experiences and attitudes of those who fought, in sociocultural context; argues that class was most important factor determining who fought the war.

Baker, Mark. *Nam: The Vietnam War in the Words of the Men and Women Who Fought There.* New York: Morrow, 1981.

Bergerud, Eric M. *Red Thunder, Tropic Lightning: The World of a Combat Division in Vietnam.* Boulder, Colo.: Westview, 1993. Powerful account of war through the eyes of the 25th Infantry Division (in which Oliver Stone served and which inspired the film *Platoon*), created from interviews and divisional records.

Camp, Norman M., Robert H. Stretch, and William C. Marshall. *Stress, Strain, and Vietnam: An Annotated Bibliography of Two Decades of Psychiatric and Social Sciences Literature Reflecting the Effect of the War on the American Soldier.* Westport, Conn.: Greenwood, 1988. Consists of 851 citations (including summaries) to psychiatric and social science literature, 1965–1987.

Caputo, Philip. *A Rumor of War.* New York: Holt, Rinehart and Winston, 1977. A powerful memoir by an American marine.

Edelman, Bernard, ed. *Dear America: Letters Home from Vietnam.* New York: Norton, 1985. Letters written by more than 100 men and women, organized to follow a tour of duty. Accompanies HBO special with same title.

Fawcett, Bill, ed. *Hunters and Shooters: An Oral History of the U.S. Navy SEALs in Vietnam*. New York: Morrow, 1995. Stories of fifteen former SEALs.

Herr, Michael. *Dispatches*. New York: Knopf, 1977. Powerful, impressionistic memoir by war correspondent; a classic.

Howes, Craig. *Voices of the Vietnam POWs: Witnesses to Their Fight*. New York: Oxford University Press, 1993. Personal narratives of captivity and analysis of their accounts.

Jenson-Stevenson, Monika. *Spite House: The Last Secret of the War in Vietnam*. New York: Norton, 1997. The story of Marine Private Robert Garwood, a POW in Vietnam from 1965 to 1979, who was then tried for collaborating with the enemy; author argues that he was targeted for assassination by the United States.

Kovic, Ron. *Born on the Fourth of July*. New York: McGraw-Hill, 1976. Kovic's riveting memoir, on which the film was based.

Lehrack, Otto J. *No Shining Armor: The Marines at War in Vietnam, An Oral History*. Lawrence: University Press of Kansas, 1992.

Lifton, Robert Jay. *Home from the War: Vietnam Veterans: Neither Victims nor Executioners*. 1973; reprint, New York: Basic, 1985.

Maurer, Harry. *Strange Ground: Americans in Vietnam, 1945–1975, An Oral History*. New York: Holt, 1989.

Ninh, Bao. *The Sorrow of War: A Novel of North Vietnam*. New York: Pantheon, 1995. A novel/memoir by a North Vietnamese veteran.

Page, Caroline. *U.S. Official Propaganda During the Vietnam War, 1965–1973: The Limits of Persuasion*. New York: Leicester University Press, 1996. Offers European perspectives.

Ramirez, Juan. *A Patriot After All: The Story of a Chicano Veteran*. Albuquerque: University of New Mexico Press, 1999.

Santoli, Al. *Everything We Had: An Oral History of the Vietnam War by Thirty-Three American Soldiers Who Fought It*. New York: Random House, 1981.

Smith, Winnie. *American Daughter Gone to War: On the Front Lines with an Army Nurse in Vietnam*. New York: Pocket, 1994.

TeCube, Leroy. *Year in Nam: A Native American Soldier's Story*. Lincoln: University of Nebraska Press, 1999. Jicarilla Apache soldier's 1968–1969 tour in Vietnam.

Terry, Wallace, ed. *Bloods: An Oral History of the Vietnam War by Black Veterans*. New York: Random House, 1984. National best-seller.

Veith, George J. *Code Name Bright-Light: The Untold Story of U.S. POW Rescue Efforts during the Vietnam War*. New York: Free Press, 1998. Historical analysis of the efforts made to rescue American POWs during the war and reasons for their failures.

Walker, Keith. *A Piece of My Heart: The Stories of Twenty-Six American Women Who Served in Vietnam*. Novato, Calif.: Presidio Press, 1997.

Wittman, Sandra M. *Writing About Vietnam: A Bibliography of the Literature of the*

Vietnam Conflict. Boston: G. K. Hall, 1989. A guide to the wartime memoirs of American soldiers, antiwar activists, and supporters of the war.

The Media

Arnett, Peter. *Live from the Battlefield: From Vietnam to Baghdad.* New York: Touchstone, 1994. Memoir.

Elwood-Akers, Virginia. *Women War Correspondents in Vietnam, 1961–1975.* Metuchen, N.J.: Scarecrow Press, 1988.

Hallin, Daniel. *The "Uncensored War": The Media and Vietnam.* New York: Oxford University Press, 1986. Analyzes coverage by network news and in the *New York Times*.

Hammond, William M. *Public Affairs: The Military and the Media, 1962–1968.* Washington, D.C.: U.S. Government Printing Office, 1990.

——. *Reporting Vietnam: The Media and Military at War.* Lawrence: University Press of Kansas, 1998. Official attempts to manage the media; very well researched.

Moeller, Susan D. *Shooting the War: Photography and the American Experience of Combat.* New York: Basic, 1989. Analyzes war photography in five major wars of the twentieth century.

Prochnau, William W. *Once upon a Distant War: David Halberstam, Neil Sheehau, Peter Arnett—Young War Correspondents and Their Early Vietnam Battles.* New York: Times Books, 1995.

Reporting Vietnam: American Journalism, 1959–1975. New York: Library of America, 1998. Excellent collection of contemporary journalism.

Turner, Kathleen J. *Lyndon Johnson's Dual War: Vietnam and the Press.* Chicago: University of Chicago Press, 1985.

Wyatt, Clarence R. *Paper Soldiers: The American Press and the Vietnam War.* New York: Norton, 1993. Rejects the then common wisdom that the press undermined the U.S. war effort through hostile reporting.

SELECTED SIXTIES WEBSITES

The Sixties Project. http://lists.village.virginia.edu/sixties
Very useful site both for scholars and browsers. Offers filmographies; collections of primary documents, including posters and buttons; course syllabi, a personal narrative project, and online issues of *Vietnam Generation.*

Sixties Net. http://www.sixties.net
Links to other sites (not always current); popular, celebratory, and participatory site.

The Diggers. http://www.diggers.org

Baby Boomer HeadQuarters. http://www.bbhq.com
Popular site, with trivia, music info, a general timeline. Includes the 1970s.

Other Sixties Web-based (Re)Sources

Sixties-L discussion list. For subscription information: http://lists.village.virginia.edu/
sixties
Sixties Net Internet Radio. Access through http://www.sixties.net
Sixties World Timeline. History Channel. http://www.historychannel.com
Vietnam Generation: A Journal of Recent History and Contemporary Issues. Founded
in 1988 by Kali Tal; no new issues since 1996. Back issues available online at http://
lists.village.virginia.edu/sixties (select "Scholars")
Vietnam on Film and Television: Documentaries in the Library of Congress. Compiled
by Victoria Johnson, 1989. Includes the Embassy of South Vietnam Collection.
Available online at http://lists.village.virginia.edu/sixties

Sound and Video Clips; Photographs

Webcorp Historic Audio Archives; includes Nixon audio archives and "Voices of the
Civil Rights Era." http://www.webcorp.com/sounds
History Channel. Large collection of speeches. http://www.historychannel.com/
speeches/index.html
NASA: extensive information about the Space Program. http://www.ksc.nasa.gov/
history
National Archives and Records Administration. http://www.nara.gov

TV, Film, and Music

Alternative Entertainment Network. Highlight is the censored material from *The
Smothers Brothers* TV show. http://www.aentv.com
The Greatest Films. Comprehensive reference site. http://www.filmsite.org
Rock and Roll Hall of Fame and Museum. Website offers profiles of 2000 inductees.
http://www.rockhall.com
UCLA Film and Television Archives. Includes 220,000 films and television programs
and 27 million feet of newsreel footage. For information: http://www.cinema.
ucla.edu
Yahoo! Geocities. Offers links to fan pages (some very elaborate and informative) for
Sixties TV and film. http://geocities.yahoo.com; select "Hollywood."

Index